ECONOMETRIC MODELS AND ECONOMIC FORECASTS

FOURTH EDITION

Robert S. Pindyck
Massachusetts Institute of Technology

Daniel L. Rubinfeld
University of California at Berkeley

Irwin
McGraw-Hill

Boston, Massachusetts   Burr Ridge, Illinois   Dubuque, Iowa   Madison, Wisconsin
New York, New York   San Francisco, California   St. Louis, Missouri

Irwin/McGraw-Hill

A Division of The **McGraw·Hill** Companies

ECONOMETRIC MODELS AND ECONOMIC FORECASTS

Copyright © 1998, 1991, 1981, 1976 by The McGraw-Hill Companies, Inc. All rights reserved. Printed in the United States of America. Except as permitted under the United States Copyright Act of 1976, no part of this publication may be reproduced or distributed in any form or by any means, or stored in a data base or retrieval system, without the prior written permission of the publisher.

This book is printed on acid-free paper.
5 6 7 8 9 0 DOC DOC 0 9 8 7 6 5 4 3 2 1

P/N 050208-0
Part of ISBN 0-07-913292-8

Publisher: Gary Burke
Sponsoring editor: Lucille H. Sutton
Project manager: Ira C. Roberts
Production supervisors: Leroy A. Young and Scott M. Hamilton
Design manager: Charles A. Carson
Compositor: Ruttle, Shaw & Wetherill, Inc.
Typeface: 10/12 Times Roman
Printer: R. R. Donnelley & Sons Company

Library of Congress Cataloging-in-Publication Data

Pindyck, Robert S.
    Econometric models and economic forecasts / Robert S. Pindyck, Daniel L. Rubinfeld. — 4th ed.
        p.   cm.
    Includes index.
    ISBN 0-07-050208-0
    1. Economic forecasting—Econometric models. 2. Econometrics. I. Rubinfeld, Daniel L. II. Title.
HB3730.P54 1997
330'.01'5195—dc21   97-10357
                                                     CIP

http://www.mhhe.com

ABOUT THE AUTHORS

ROBERT S. PINDYCK is Mitsubishi Bank Professor of Applied Economics in the Sloan School of Management at the Massachusetts Institute of Technology. Professor Pindyck joined the faculty at M.I.T. after receiving a Ph.D. there in 1971. He has also been a Visiting Professor of Economics at Tel Aviv University and is a Research Associate of the National Bureau of Economic Research. He is coauthor, with Daniel Rubinfeld, of *Microeconomics,* currently in its fourth edition.

DANIEL L. RUBINFELD is Robert L. Bridges Professor of Law and Professor of Economics at the University of California, Berkeley. Professor Rubinfeld received a Ph.D. in 1972 from M.I.T. He has taught at Suffolk University, Wellesley College, and the University of Michigan. He has been a fellow of the National Bureau of Economic Research, The Center for Advanced Study in the Behavioral Sciences and The Guggenheim Foundation, and is currently coeditor of the *International Review of Law and Economics.*

to our wives,
Nurit and Gail

מוקדש לנשותינו –
נורית וגייל

CONTENTS

EXAMPLES

PREFACE

New developments in econometrics, as well as comments and suggestions from a large number of users of the first three editions, have led us to make extensive changes in the fourth edition of this book. We have added a number of new topics and new examples and have updated many of the older examples. In addition, we have restructured the book, which is now organized in four rather than three parts.

In terms of content, Part One of the book now covers material that gives the student a basic understanding of the multiple regression model. Chapter 2, on elementary statistics, has been revised and expanded. It now includes new material on descriptive statistics as well as new examples.

Part Two now covers material on single-equation regression models. Chapter 10, which contains an in-depth treatment of nonlinear and maximum-likelihood estimation, is new. The addition of this chapter reflects the growing importance of these topics in recent years. Chapter 10 also contains a new section on the estimation and use of ARCH and GARCH models, which have found many applications in finance and macroeconomics. Other major changes in Part Two include new material on tests for heteroscedasticity in Chapter 6 and the section on the use of panel data in Chapter 9.

Part Three of the book concentrates on multi-equation models. In addition to new and updated examples, we have revised much of the exposition and have included a respecified and reestimated small macroeconomic model (constructed by Michael Donahue of Colby College) in Appendix 14.1.

Part Four includes a revised and updated discussion of time-series analysis. Chapter 18 combines two chapters from the third edition, the first on estimation and the second on forecasting with time-series models.

As in the previous edition, the data for many of the examples have been included either in the text or in the *Instructor's Manual*. In this edition, the data are also provided in a separate data diskette which comes with the book. The *Instructor's Manual* also contains answers to all the end-of-chapter questions. All the empirical questions relate to data sets that are given in the text and in the *Instructor's Manual* and are also included in the diskette so that instructors can make direct use of the assignments in their classes.

In developing this book through the fourth edition, we have benefited greatly from the comments and criticisms of our colleagues and students as well as from suggestions given to us by a wide variety of individuals. We thank Steven Dietrich and Annette Hall, who helped plan and edit the first edition; Bonnie Lieberman and Susan Norton, who helped with the second edition; and Scott Stratford, who inspired our work on the third edition. Lucille Sutton and her associates at McGraw-Hill have been of great assistance in the preparation of this fourth edition.

We cannot possibly thank everyone who provided help with this new edition, but we want to give special thanks to Sergio Schmukler, who helped us rework and update many of the examples; to Michael Donahue, who developed the new macroeconomic model that appears in the appendix to Chapter 14; and to Jeanette Sayre and Lynn Steele, who provided valuable editorial and administrative support. We also want to thank our colleagues Ernst Berndt, Bronwyn Hall, Paul Ruud, and Thomas Stoker for providing numerous helpful comments and suggestions.

We also want to thank the reviewers who offered their guidance during the planning and development of the fourth edition: Walter Park, The American University; Houson Stokes, University of Illinois—Chicago; William Parke, University of North Carolina, Chapel Hill; Walter Mayer, University of Mississippi; Mukhtar M. Al:, University of Kentucky; Tom Taylor, Wright State University; Carl Moody, College of William and Mary; David Selover, Wesleyan University; Steven Hansen, Western Washington University. Further, we should mention some of the people who have corresponded with us, suggesting many changes and improvements in the book. They include Imad Al-Akhdar, Center Bank of Jordan; Walter Bell, Princeton University; Christiaan Heij and Marius Ooms, Erasmus University, Rotterdam; Hiroyuki Kawakatsu, University of California, Irvine, California; Huston McCulloch, Ohio State University; Jeffrey Perloff, University of California, Berkeley; Robert Rycroft, Mary Washington College; Sergio Schmukler, Berkeley, California; and Kenneth White, University of British Columbia.

We would also like to extend thanks to Data Resources Incorporated, a subsidiary of McGraw-Hill, Inc., for making its Citibase database available for use in many of our examples; to David Lilien and Quantitative Micro Software of Irvine, California, for providing us with the use of the EVIEWS software program; and to Bronwyn Hall and TSP International for its comparable offer of its PC-TSP program.

The *Instructor's Manual* is updated from the third edition. Two software guides are available: the EVIEWS manual by Hiroyuki Kawakatsu and the TSP manual by Sergio Schmukler. These software guides, as well as the *Instructor's Manual,* can be obtained directly from McGraw-Hill.

Robert S. Pindyck
Daniel L. Rubinfeld

INTRODUCTION

"Persons pretending to forecast the future shall be considered disorderly under subdivision 3, section 901 of the criminal code and liable to a fine of $250 and/or six months in prison."

Section 889, New York State Code of Criminal Procedure

This book is an introduction to the science and art of building and using models. Contrary to the criminal laws of New York, which are directed toward those who pretend to forecast with crystal balls, we believe that these models can be a very useful forecasting tool. The science of model building consists of a set of quantitative tools which are used to construct and then test mathematical representations of the real world. The development and use of these tools are subsumed under the subject heading of econometrics. The art of model building is, unfortunately, harder to describe in words, since it consists mostly of intuitive judgments that are made during the modeling process. Since there are no clear-cut rules for making these judgments, the art of model building can be difficult to master. Nonetheless, one of the purposes of this book is to convey the nature of that art. This will be done in part by examples and discussions of technique but also by encouraging readers to build models of their own.

The book focuses on models of processes that occur in business, economics, and the social sciences in general. These may include models of aggregate economic activity, the sales of an individual firm, or a political process. As one might expect, many types of models can and often have been used for both policy analysis and forecasting. This book does not attempt to cover the spectrum of model types and modeling methodologies; instead, it concentrates on models that can be expressed in equation form, relating variables quantitatively. Data are then used to estimate the parameters of the equation or equations, and theoretical relationships are tested statistically. This still leaves a rather wide range of models from which to choose. On one end of this range one might determine the effect of alternative monetary policies on the behavior of the U.S. economy by constructing a large multi-equation econometric model of the economy and then simulating it using different monetary policies. The resulting model would be rather complicated and would presume to explain a complex structure in the real world. On the other end of the range one might wish to forecast the sales volume of a firm and, believing that those sales follow a strong cyclical pattern, use a time-series model to extrapolate from the past behavior of sales.

This range of models is the subject matter of this book. Our objective is to give the reader some understanding of the science and art of determining what type of model to build, building the model which is most appropriate, testing the model statistically, and then applying the model to practical problems in forecasting and analysis.

1   WHY MODELS?

Many of us often either use or produce forecasts of one sort or another. Few of us recognize, however, that some kind of logical structure, or model, is implicit in every forecast. Consider, for example, a stockbroker who tells you that the Dow Jones Industrial Average will rise next year. The stockbroker may have made this forecast because the Dow Jones average has been rising during the past few years and the broker feels that whatever it was that made it rise in the past will continue to make it rise in the future. Alternatively, the feeling that the Dow Jones will rise next year may result from a belief that this variable is linked to a set of economic and political variables through a complex set of relationships. The broker may believe, for example, that the Dow Jones average is related in a certain way to the gross national product and to interest rates, so that given certain other beliefs about the most probable future behavior of those variables, a rise in the Dow Jones average would appear likely.

If we have to find a word to describe the method by which our stockbroker made this forecast, we would probably say that it was intuitive, although the chain of reasoning differed substantially in the two cases cited above. Yet in each case some *implicit* form of model building was involved. A stockbroker who has based the optimistic forecast for the Dow Jones average on past increases has in effect constructed a *time-series model* that extrapolates past trends into the future. If, instead, the forecast was based on a knowledge of economics, a model would still be implicitly involved; it would be composed of the relationships that were loosely conceived in the stockbroker's mind as a result of past experience.

Thus, even an intuitive forecaster constructs some type of model, perhaps without being aware of doing so. Of course, it is reasonable to ask why one might want to work with an *explicit* model to produce forecasts. Would it be worth the trouble, for example, for our stockbroker to read this book in order to construct an explicit model, estimate it, and test it statistically? Our response is that there are several advantages to working with models explicitly. Model building forces the individual to think clearly about, and account for, all the important interrelationships involved in a problem. The reliance on intuition can be dangerous at times because of the possibility that important relationships will be ignored or improperly used. In addition, it is important that individual relationships be validated in some way. Unfortunately, this usually is not done when intuitive forecasts are made. In the process of building a model, however, a person must validate not only the model as a whole but also the individual relationships that make up the model.

In making a forecast, it is also important to provide a measure of how accurate one can expect the forecast to be. The use of intuitive methods usually precludes any quantitative measure of confidence in the resulting forecast. The statistical analysis of the individual relationships that make up a model, and of the model as a whole, makes it possible to attach a measure of confidence to the model's forecasts.

Once a model has been constructed and fitted to data, a sensitivity analysis can be used to study many of its properties. In particular, the effects of small changes in individual variables in the model can be evaluated. For example, in the case of a model that describes and predicts interest rates, one could measure the effect on a particular interest rate of a change in the rate of inflation. This type of sensitivity study can be performed only if the model is an explicit one.

2   TYPES OF MODELS

In this book we examine three general classes of models that can be constructed for purposes of forecasting or policy analysis. Each involves a different degree of model complexity and presumes a different level of comprehension about the processes one is trying to model.

Time-Series Models   In this class of models we presume to know nothing about the causality that affects the variable we are trying to forecast. Instead, we examine the past behavior of a time series in order to infer something about its future behavior. The method used to produce a forecast may involve the use of a simple deterministic model such as a linear extrapolation or the use of a complex stochastic model for adaptive forecasting.

One example of the use of time-series analysis would be the simple extrapolation of a past trend in predicting population growth. Another example would be the development of a complex linear stochastic model for passenger loads on an airline. Time-series models have been used to forecast the demand for airline capacity, seasonal telephone demand, the movement of short-term interest rates, and other economic variables. Time-series models are particularly useful when little is known about the underlying process one is trying to forecast. The limited structure in time-series models makes them reliable only in the short run, but they are nonetheless rather useful.

Single-Equation Regression Models   In this class of models the variable under study is explained by a single function (linear or nonlinear) of a number of explanatory variables. The equation will often be time-dependent (i.e., the time index will appear explicitly in the model), so that one can predict the response over time of the variable under study to changes in one or more of the explanatory variables.

An example of a single-equation regression model would be an equation that relates a particular interest rate, such as the 3-month Treasury bill rate, to a set of explanatory variables such as the money supply, the rate of inflation, and the rate of change in the gross national product.

Multi-Equation Models In this class of models the variable to be studied may be a function of several explanatory variables, which now are related to each other as well as to the variable under study through a set of equations. The construction of a multi-equation model begins with the specification of a set of individual relationships, each of which is fitted to available data. Simulation is the process of solving those equations simultaneously over some range in time.

An example of a multi-equation model would be a complete model of the U.S. textile industry that contains equations explaining variables such as textile demand, textile output, employment of production workers in the textile industry, investment in the industry, and textile prices. These variables would be related to each other and to other variables (such as total national income, the Consumer Price Index, and interest rates) through a set of linear or nonlinear equations. Given assumptions about the future behavior of national income, interest rates, etc., one could simulate this model into the future and obtain a forecast for each of the model's variables. A model such as this can be used to analyze the impact on an industry of changes in external economic variables.

Multi-equation models presume to explain a great deal about the structure of the actual process being studied. Not only are individual relationships specified, the model also accounts for the interaction of all these interrelationships. Thus, a five-equation model actually contains more information than the sum of five individual regression equations. The model not only explains the five individual relationships but also describes the dynamic structure implied by the simultaneous operation of those relationships.

The choice of the type of model to develop involves trade-offs between time, energy, costs, and desired forecast precision. The construction of a multi-equation simulation model may require large expenditures of time and money. The gains from this effort may include a better understanding of the relationships and structure involved as well as the ability to make a better forecast. However, in some cases these gains may be small enough to be outweighed by the heavy costs involved. Because the multi-equation model necessitates a good deal of knowledge about the process being studied, the construction of such models may be extremely difficult.

The decision to build a time-series model usually occurs when little or nothing is known about the determinants of the variable being studied, when a large number of data points are available, and when the model is to be used largely for short-term forecasting. Given some information about the processes involved, however, it may be reasonable for a forecaster to construct both types of models and compare their relative performance.

3   WHAT THE BOOK CONTAINS

The book is divided into four parts, each concentrating on a different class of models. The most fundamental class, discussed in Parts One and Two of the book, is the single-equation regression model. The econometric methods developed and used to construct single-equation regression models will, with modification, find application in the construction of multi-equation models and time-series models.

Chapters 1 and 2 begin Part One with an introduction to the basic concepts of regression analysis and a review of elementary statistics. The regression model then is developed in detail, beginning with a two-variable model in Chapter 3 and proceeding to the multiple regression model in Chapter 4.

Chapter 5 begins Part Two, by continuing Chapter 4's development of statistical tests and procedures that can be used to evaluate a regression model. The estimation techniques used in simple regression analysis require that certain assumptions be made about both the data and the model. At times these assumptions break down. Chapters 6 and 7 begin a discussion of what can be done in some of these cases. Chapter 6 deals with heteroscedasticity and serial correlation and includes statistical tests for these problems as well as estimation methods that account for them. Chapter 7 deals with measurement error and errors caused by misspecification. It concentrates on the development of the instrumental variable estimation technique and regression diagnostics.

Chapter 8 discusses the use of a single-equation regression model for forecasting purposes. The chapter discusses not only the methods by which a forecast is produced but also measures that describe the reliability of a forecast, such as confidence intervals and the error of forecast.

The last three chapters in Part Two consider extensions of the regression model. These chapters are somewhat more advanced in nature and can be skipped by beginning students. Chapter 9 deals with the problems of missing observations, distributed lag models, the use of panel data, and causality tests. Chapter 10 discusses nonlinear and maximum-likelihood estimation, including ARCH and GARCH models. Chapter 11 deals with models in which the variable to be explained is qualitative in nature. These include linear probability, probit, logit, and censored regression models.

The foundation of econometrics in Parts One and Two is essential for the development of multi-equation models in Part Three of the book. Part Three begins with a chapter on estimation techniques particular to simultaneous-equation models. This includes problems of model identification as well as techniques such as two-stage and three-stage least squares. Chapters 13 and 14 discuss the methodology of constructing and using multi-equation models. Chapter 13 is an introduction to simulation models and includes a discussion of the simulation process, methods of evaluating simulation models, alternative methods of estimating simulation models, and general approaches to model construction. Chapter 14 is more technical in nature and discusses methods of analyzing the dynamic behavior of simulation models, including questions of model stability, dynamic multipliers, and methods of tuning and adjusting simulation models. Chapter 14 concludes with a discussion of sensitivity analysis and stochastic simulation. A small macro model of the U.S. economy is constructed and used for simple policy analysis in the appendix to the chapter.

Part Four of this book is devoted to time-series models, which can be viewed as a special class of single-equation regression models. Thus, the econometric tools developed in Parts One and Two will find extensive application in Part Four. Part Four begins with Chapters 15 and 16, which discuss basic smoothing and extrapolation techniques and introduce the basic properties of random time series as well as the notion of a time-series model. Chapter 16 also discusses the properties of stationary and nonstationary time series, the autocorrelation function, unit root tests, and the concept of co-integrated time series.

Chapters 17 and 18 develop the methods by which time-series models are specified, estimated, and used for forecasting. Chapter 17 covers linear time-series models in detail, including moving average models, autoregressive models, mixed models, and finally models of nonstationary time series. Chapter 18 develops regression methods that can be used to estimate a time-series model as well as methods of diagnostic checking that can be used to ascertain how well the estimated model "fits" the data. Chapter 18 also deals with the computation of the minimum mean-square-error forecast, forecast error, and forecast confidence intervals.

The last chapter of Part Four is devoted entirely to examples of the construction and use of time-series models. After we review the modeling process, we construct models of several economic variables and use them to produce short-term forecasts. Finally, we demonstrate how models can be constructed that combine time-series with regression analysis.

4   USE OF MATHEMATICAL TOOLS

This book is written on a rather elementary level, and can be understood by readers with a limited knowledge of calculus and no knowledge of matrix algebra. Mathematical derivations and proofs are generally reserved for appendixes or suppressed entirely. In Parts One and Two of the book, the development of the regression model in matrix form is included in the appendixes. Thus, most if not all of the book should be accessible to advanced undergraduate students as well as graduate students.

It is desirable that the reader of this book have some background in statistics. Although Chapter 2 contains a brief review of probability and statistics, a student with *no* background in statistics may find parts of the book somewhat difficult. Typically, this book would be used in an applied econometrics or business-forecasting course which a student would take after completing an introductory course in statistics.

5 ALTERNATIVE USES OF THE BOOK

The book is intended to have a wide spectrum of uses. Curriculum uses include an undergraduate or introductory graduate course in econometrics and an undergraduate or graduate course in business forecasting. In addition, this book can be of considerable value as a reference book for people doing statistical analyses of economic and business data or for a social scientist or business analyst interested in the application of dynamic simulation models to forecasting or policy analysis.

Coverage in an introductory econometrics or business forecasting course must, of course, depend to some extent on the background of the students and the goals of the instructor. Emphasis on the use of econometric techniques for the purpose of forecasting would provide for one focus, but alternatives are available. We list several alternative uses of the book below but stress that the variety of material leaves a good deal of discretion to the instructor.

1. Undergraduate econometrics (one semester)
    a. *Standard*
        Part One: Chapters 1 to 4
        Part Two: Chapters 5 to 7; portions of Chapters 8 to 11 optional
    b. *Simulation emphasis*
        Part One: Chapters 1 to 4
        Part Two: Chapters 5, 6, 8
        Part Three: Chapters 12 to 14
        Both courses would omit all matrix appendixes.
2. First-year graduate econometrics
    a. *One semester*
        Part One: Chapters 1 to 4
        Part Two: Chapters 5, 6, 8; Chapters 9 to 11 optional
        Part Three: Chapters 12 to 14
        Portions of the above and the appendixes may be optional.
    b. *Two semesters*
        Part One: Chapters 1 to 4
        Part Two: Chapters 5 to 11
        Part Three: Chapters 12 to 14
        Part Four: Chapters 15 to 17; portions of Chapters 17 to 19 optional
        Emphasis on either simulation and/or time-series analysis would depend upon the interest of the instructor.
3. Business forecasting (graduate or advanced undergraduate)
    a. *One semester*
        Part Two: Chapter 8 plus review of Chapters 1 to 7
        Part Three: Chapters 13, 14
        Part Four: Chapters 15 to 19 (selected portions)

b. *Two semesters*
Part One: Chapters 1 to 4
Part Two: Chapters 5 to 8
Part Three: Chapters 12 to 14
Part Four: Chapters 15 to 19
4. Quantitative methods for policy analysis
   a. *Undergraduate, one semester*
   Part One: Chapters 1 to 4
   Part Two: Chapters 5 to 8
   Part Three: Chapters 13, 14
   b. *Graduate, one semester*
   Part One: Chapters 1 to 4
   Part Two: Chapters 5 to 8
   Part Three: Chapters 12 to 14
   c. *Graduate, two semesters*
   Part One: Chapters 1 to 4
   Part Two: Chapters 5 to 8; Chapters 9 to 11 optional
   Part Three: Chapters 12 to 14
   Part Four: Chapters 15 to 19

The book also can be used for courses in quantitative social science modeling (as taught in departments of sociology or political science). Such a course using this book as a text would probably cover most of Parts One through Three.

6   WHAT DISTINGUISHES THIS BOOK FROM OTHERS?

Most textbooks on econometrics develop the single-equation regression model as a self-contained and isolated entity. The reader often infers that statistical regression models are somehow distinct and independent from other aspects of modeling, such as the analysis of a model's dynamic structure and the use of time-series analysis to forecast one or more exogenous variables in the model. This is certainly not the case. In developing a multi-equation model, for example, one must be knowledgeable not only about regression methods but also about how a model's dynamic behavior results from the interaction of its individual equations.

We believe that this wide breadth of coverage is desirable. The simulation and time-series techniques that make up Parts Three and Four of this book usually are presented only at an advanced level. We feel that a strength of this book is that the coverage is broad and includes these advanced techniques but is presented on a level that can be understood and appreciated by a beginning student.

THE BASICS OF
REGRESSION ANALYSIS

Part One of this book deals with the most basic concepts of econometric modeling. The focus is on single-equation regression models, which are simple in form but quite powerful in terms of the variety of their possible business and economic applications. In these models, the variable under study is taken to be a linear function of several explanatory variables. Single-equation regression models are important, not only because they can be used to test hypotheses and to forecast, but also because they form the groundwork for the analysis of simultaneous-equation models and time-series models.

In Chapter 1 elementary curve-fitting concepts and the notion of least squares are developed. Chapter 2 contains an extensive review of the basic statistical ideas necessary for the analysis that follows. The two-variable model is used in Chapter 3 as a means of focusing on the statistical properties that are needed for regression parameter estimates. Emphasis is placed on hypothesis testing and measuring goodness of fit. Chapter 4 extends the regression model to the multiple-variable case. The presence of more than one explanatory variable in the regression model leads to additional econometric problems including multicollinearity that affect the interpretation of regression coefficients. Additional regression statistics which help with these problems are discussed.

CHAPTER 1

INTRODUCTION TO THE REGRESSION MODEL

In this chapter we begin our discussion of econometrics with the two-variable linear regression model. In the first section curve fitting is discussed, using an example based on students' grade-point averages. The least-squares criterion for curve fitting is presented and compared with several alternative curve-fitting schemes. In the second section we derive the least-squares estimation procedure. The chapter concludes with three elementary applications of the least-squares regression technique.

1.1 CURVE FITTING

Data resulting from the measurement of variables may come from any number of sources and in a variety of forms. Data which describe the movement of a variable over time are called *time-series* data and may be daily, weekly, monthly, quarterly, or annual. Data which describe the activities of individual persons, firms, or other units at a given point in time are called *cross-section* data. A marketing study dealing with family expenditures at a given time is likely to utilize cross-section data. Cross-section data also might be used to examine a group of business accounting statements for the purpose of studying patterns of behavior among individual firms in an industry. *Pooled data,* which combine time-series and cross-section data, may be used to study the behavior of a group of firms over time.

Suppose we are interested in the relationship between two variables, X and Y. To describe this relationship statistically we need a set of observations for each variable and a hypothesis that sets forth the explicit mathematical form

TABLE 1.1
GRADE-POINT AVERAGE AND FAMILY INCOME

Y (grade-point average)	X (income of parents in $1,000)
4.0	21.0
3.0	15.0
3.5	15.0
2.0	9.0
3.0	12.0
3.5	18.0
2.5	6.0
2.5	12.0

of the relationship. The set of observations is called a *sample.*[1] We will be concerned primarily with the case in which the relationship between X and Y is assumed to be linear, i.e., described by a straight line. Given linearity, our objective is to specify a rule by which the "best" straight line relating X to Y can be determined.

For example, suppose we wish to test the hypothesis that the grade-point average of a student can be explained by the income of that student's parents. Eight sample points were obtained (hypothetically) and are described in Table 1.1 and plotted as a scatter diagram in Fig. 1.1. Many straight lines can be chosen to fit the points. One could connect the points from the lowest X value to the highest X value (line l_1), or one could draw a line by eye which appears to fit the full scatter of points (line l_2). A better procedure might be to choose a line so that the sum of the vertical distances (positive and negative) from the points on the graph to the line is zero. (These distances, known as *deviations*, are shown in Fig. 1.2.) This criterion would assure that deviations which are equal in magnitude and equal in sign are given equal importance. Unfortunately, this procedure has the undesirable property that deviations which are equal in size but opposite in sign cancel out. As a result, one could find a line (or more than one, for that matter) which had a zero sum of deviations but which fit the data quite poorly.

We could improve on this method if we minimized the absolute value of the deviations of the sample points from the fitted line. Implicit here is the judgment that the importance of the deviation is proportional to its magnitude. While the minimization of the sum of absolute deviations is appealing, it suffers from several disadvantages. First, the procedure is computationally difficult. Second, it is reasonable that large deviations should be treated with relatively greater attention than small deviations. For example, a prediction involving a 2-unit error would probably be considered worse than a prediction involving two errors of 1 unit each.

---

[1] The sample data are observations which have been chosen from an underlying *population* which represents the true relationship under study.

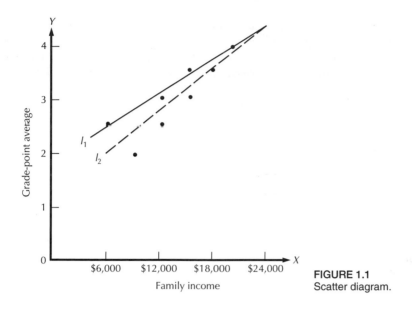

FIGURE 1.1
Scatter diagram.

A procedure exists which is computationally simple and penalizes large errors relatively more than it penalizes small errors. This is the method of *least squares*. The least-squares criterion is as follows: *The "line of best fit" is said to be that which minimizes the sum of the squared deviations of the points of the graph from the points of the straight line (with distances measured vertically).* We will see in the next two chapters that least squares is also convenient in that it permits statistical testing.

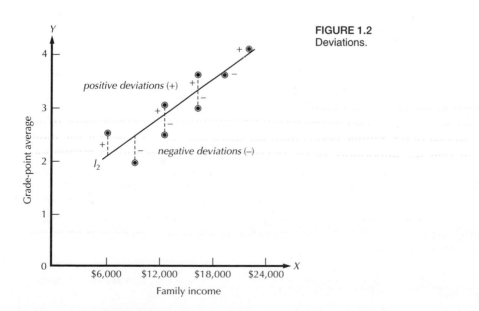

FIGURE 1.2
Deviations.

We will rely heavily on the least-squares procedure in this book, but other estimation techniques are feasible and occasionally desirable. We can see how least squares relates to some of these alternative techniques by looking at Fig. 1.3*a* and *b*. Figure 1.3*a* graphs the deviation of a data point from the straight line on the horizontal axis and the "loss" associated with that deviation on the vertical axis. With least squares, the loss associated with each individual deviation is that deviation squared. With least-absolute-value estimation, the loss is the absolute value of the deviation. The *loss functions* associated with both least squares and least absolute values are symmetric with respect to the sign of the deviation, but the least-squares loss function penalizes large deviations more than the least-absolute-value loss function does.

One problem with least squares occurs when there are one or more large deviations. Assume that a reporting error was made with respect to the grade-point average of the first student, with a grade of 1.0 being reported rather than the correct figure of 4.0. If line l_2 in Fig. 1.1 were considered as a possible least-squares line, the deviation associated with the first data point would be very large and the deviation squared would be even larger. The best-fitting least-squares line will change substantially, with the slope getting flatter. The large penalty associated with least squares has forced the estimation procedure to put great emphasis on the relationship between the straight line and the first data point. The result is that the slope (and intercept) of the least-squares line is very sensitive to data points which lie far from the true regression line. We

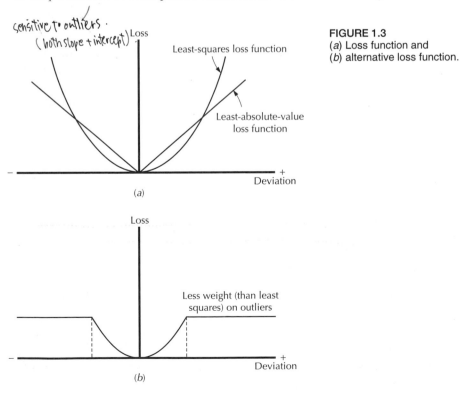

Sensitive to outliers .
(both slope + intercept)

(*a*)

(*b*)

FIGURE 1.3
(*a*) Loss function and
(*b*) alternative loss function.

call data points which are more than an arbitrary distance from the regression line *outliers*. Of course, outliers may represent important information about the relationship between several variables. Thus, one should never throw out an outlier without further analysis. Indeed, a careful examination of outliers may help us find mistakes, in which case a correction can be made.

What can be done about the sensitivity of least squares to outliers? The simplest solution is to recalculate the least-squares line with the outlier removed. By reporting both the original and the new least-squares slopes and intercepts, we can determine the sensitivity of our results to the presence of outliers. Because the decision about what makes an outlier is arbitrary, a better procedure would place relatively less weight on large deviations. One example of such a procedure is given in Fig 1.3*b*, showing a loss function which is less sensitive than least squares or least absolute value to outliers.

1.2   DERIVATION OF LEAST SQUARES

The purpose of constructing statistical relationships usually is to predict or explain the effects on one variable resulting from changes in one or more predictor or explanatory variables. For the scatter of points in Fig. 1.1, we can write the linear equation $Y = a + bX$, where Y, the left-hand variable, is called the *dependent variable* and X, the right-hand variable, is called the *independent variable*. Because we are trying to explain or predict movements in Y, it is natural to choose as our objective the minimization of the vertical sum of the squared deviations from the fitted line.[2]

To obtain the least-squares formula for calculating values of a and b, we must use some basic mathematical tools. For those uncertain about the properties of *summation operators*, we suggest a brief review of Appendix 1.1, and for those unsure about the use of partial derivatives, we stress that it is not important that one understand all the details.

The least-squares criterion can be restated formally as follows:

$$\text{Minimize} \sum_{i=1}^{N} (Y_i - \hat{Y_i})^2 \tag{1.1}$$

where $\hat{Y_i} = a + bX_i$ represents the equation for a straight line with intercept a and slope b. In this notation Y_i is the actual value of Y for observation i and corresponds to the value of X for that observation, while N is the number of

---

[2] In general, our decision to write an equation in the form $Y = a + bX$ rather than the reverse form $X = A + BY$ implies that a judgment has been made that movements in the variable Y are "caused" by movements in the variable X and not vice versa. Thus, in the grade-point-average example we have assumed implicitly that grade-point average is determined by family income. If we revised our view of causality to one which states that family income is determined by grade-point average, we would write the equation $X = A + BY$ and our curve-fitting criterion would be adjusted accordingly. This is important because the two equations generate two different regression lines.

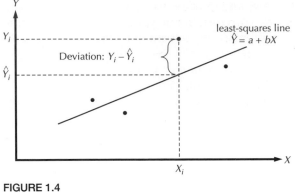

FIGURE 1.4
Fitted values.

observations. $\hat{Y}_i$, called the *fitted* or *predicted value* of Y_i, is the value of Y on the straight line associated with observation X_i. This can be clearly seen in Fig. 1.4, where the deviation is calculated by subtracting the fitted value of Y_i from the actual value. Thus, for each observation on X, there is a corresponding deviation of the fitted value from the actual value of Y. The sum of squares of these deviations is what we wish to minimize; it will allow us (in Chapter 3) to calculate a measure of how well the straight line fits the data.

The problem is to choose values for a and b which minimize the expression in Eq. (1.1). This can be done by using elementary calculus or algebra. To keep our discussion direct and to the point, we have put the details of the calculus derivation in Appendix 1.1.[3] As shown there, the least-squares solutions for the slope and intercept are

$$b = \frac{N \sum X_i Y_i - \sum X_i \sum Y_i}{N \sum X_i^2 - (\sum X_i)^2} \tag{1.2}$$

$$a = \frac{\sum Y_i}{N} - b \frac{\sum X_i}{N} = \overline{Y} - b\overline{X} \tag{1.3}$$

where $\overline{Y}$ and $\overline{X}$ are the sample means of Y and X, respectively.

Now consider how the formulas in Eqs. (1.2) and (1.3) simplify in the special case when X and Y both have sample means of 0. First, rewriting Eq. (1.3), we notice that

$$a = \overline{Y} - b\overline{X} = 0 \tag{1.4}$$

---

[3] We encourage the reader to follow the derivation to become more familiar with our notation and our use of summation operators.

Thus, when the sample means of X and Y are 0, the intercept of the fitted regression line will be 0. To obtain the corresponding slope estimate in this special case, we divide both the numerator and the denominator of Eq. (1.2) by N^2:

$$b = \frac{\Sigma X_i Y_i / N - (\Sigma X_i / N)(\Sigma Y_i / N)}{\Sigma X_i^2 / N - (\Sigma X_i / N)^2}$$

Substituting $\overline{X}$ and $\overline{Y}$ gives

$$b = \frac{\Sigma X_i Y_i / N - \overline{X}\,\overline{Y}}{\Sigma X_i^2 / N - \overline{X}^2}$$

But $\overline{X} = \overline{Y} = 0$ by assumption. Therefore,

$$b = \frac{\Sigma X_i Y_i / N}{\Sigma X_i^2 / N} = \frac{\Sigma X_i Y_i}{\Sigma X_i^2} \tag{1.5}$$

The fact that Eq. (1.5) is less complicated than Eq. (1.2) suggests that it will simplify matters and increase our understanding if we write the least-squares estimates in terms of variables that are expressed as deviations from their respective sample means whether or not those means are zero. To do so, we transform the data to *deviations form* by expressing each observation on X and Y in terms of deviations from their respective means:

$$x_i = X_i - \overline{X} \qquad y_i = Y_i - \overline{Y}$$

With this definition, the least-squares slope estimate can be obtained (in the general case) directly from Eq. (1.5), since variables x and y have zero mean.[4] In effect we have centered the data by moving the origin of the graph relating X and Y to the sample mean. In this case the lowercase variables are "centered" versions of the uppercase variables.

The least-squares slope estimate is

$$b = \frac{\Sigma x_i y_i}{\Sigma x_i^2} \tag{1.6}$$

The centering process which transforms the variables into deviations form is depicted in Fig. 1.5. The regression line is graphed using the original observations in Fig. 1.5*a*, while the deviations form is used in Fig. 1.5*b*. Note that the estimated slopes of both regression lines are identical. This is obvious from Eq.

---

[4] E.g., $\bar{x} = \dfrac{\Sigma x_i}{N} = \dfrac{\Sigma(X_i - \overline{X})}{N} = \dfrac{\Sigma X_i}{N} - \overline{X} = \overline{X} - \overline{X} = 0$

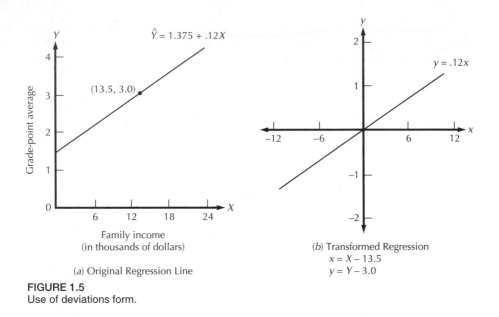

FIGURE 1.5
Use of deviations form.

(1.6), since only variables in deviations form enter the calculation. However, the intercept of the regression line in Fig. 1.5b is identically equal to 0. This follows from Eq. (1.4) and the fact that $\bar{x}$ and $\bar{y}$ are equal to 0. Thus, if we choose to work with data in deviations form, we move the origin of the regression line to the sample mean but do not alter the slope. Note also that the line in Fig. 1.5b passes through the origin. This is equivalent to the fact that the line in Fig. 1.5a passes through the point of means $(\bar{X}, \bar{Y})$.

Example 1.1 Grade-Point Average   In the grade-point-average example described in the text, the least-squares procedure allows us to obtain an intercept of 1.375 and a slope of .12, yielding the line $\hat{Y} = 1.375 + .12X$.[5] The details of the calculations appear in Table 1.2. (The regression line l_2 and the original data points are shown in Fig. 1.2.) For any given family income X, the regression line allows us to predict a value for the grade-point average Y. For example, a family income of \$12,000 would lead to a predicted grade-point average of $\hat{Y} = 1.375 + .12(12) \doteq 2.815$. While the predicted grade-point average will not necessarily give an accurate estimate every time, it will provide a good approximation. For example, we might notice that the two students in the original sample (see Table 1.1) with parents who have

---

[5] Throughout Part One we place a "hat" above the dependent variable to denote the fitted value. We will relax this rule in other portions of the text to simplify the presentation.

TABLE 1.2
GRADE-POINT-AVERAGE EXAMPLE (CALCULATIONS)
$\bar{X} = 13.5 \qquad \bar{Y} = 3.0$

(1) $x_i = X_i - \bar{X}$	(2) $y_i = Y_i - \bar{Y}$	(3) $x_i y_i$	(4) x_i^2
7.5	1.0	7.5	56.25
1.5	.0	.0	2.25
1.5	.5	.75	2.25
−4.5	−1.0	4.5	20.25
−1.5	.0	.0	2.25
4.5	.5	2.25	20.25
−7.5	− .5	3.75	56.25
−1.5	− .5	.75	2.25
$\Sigma x_i = 0$	$\Sigma y_i = 0$	$\Sigma x_i y_i = 19.50$	$\Sigma x_i^2 = 162.00$

$$b = \frac{\Sigma x_i y_i}{\Sigma x_i^2} = .120 \qquad a = \bar{Y} - b\bar{X} = 1.375 \qquad \hat{Y} = 1.375 + .12$$

incomes of $12,000 had grade-point averages of 3.0 and 2.5. The predicted grade-point average happens to lie between the two actual data points.

The slope tells us that a $1,000 change in family income will lead to an expected change of .12 in grade-point average. The positive value for the slope is consistent with the hypothesis that students with relatively high grade-point averages come from families with relatively high incomes. The intercept of 1.375 tells us that if family income were projected at $0, the best prediction for grade-point average would be 1.375. Since none of the families in our sample had an income near zero, we do not place much confidence in this result.

We shall examine the two-variable linear regression model in much greater detail in Chapter 3, but a final comment is appropriate here. In the model $Y = a + bX$, the slope b is an estimate of dY/dX, the ratio of a change in Y to a change in X. This allows us to interpret the regression slope quite naturally. The interpretation of the intercept, however, depends on whether sufficient observations near $X = 0$ are available to yield statistically meaningful results. If this is the case, we can interpret the intercept as an estimate of Y when $X = 0$. However, if sufficient observations are not available, the intercept is simply the height of the least-squares line.

Example 1.2 The Litigation Explosion How rapidly has the number of cases filed in courts in the United States grown over time, and how steady has this growth been? A recent study of trends in civil rights suits provides some useful information.[6] Using quarterly time-series data for the period beginning in the second quarter of 1977 and running through the third quarter of 1988, a regression equation was estimated that related the number of suits filed per quarter, Y, to a time trend variable, T, which is defined to be equal to 1 in the second quarter of 1977 and to increase by 1 in each quarter thereafter. The estimated equation is

$$\hat{Y} = 13.00 + 51.03T$$

The regression slope coefficient tells us that there was indeed an explosion, with the number of cases filed increasing by slightly over 51 in each quarter. Of course, a regression equation is not essential for one to calculate this rate of litigation growth. We will see in Chapter 3 that an important advantage of the regression approach is that it allows us to determine the statistical significance of the estimate of the growth rate.

Litigation growth was not constant throughout the time period of study. The study found that litigation is sensitive to the business cycle; the higher the unemployment rate, U, the more likely it is that civil rights suits will be filed. The estimated regression equation is

$$\hat{Y} = -144.38 + 168.91U$$

This equation tells us that for every 1 percent increase in the unemployment rate, nearly 170 additional cases were filed.

Example 1.3 Stock Prices of Public Utility Companies   As part of a larger corporate finance study, it is hypothesized that the price-earnings ratios for public utilities are influenced by their debt-equity ratios. This is reasonable, since one would expect a higher debt-equity ratio to lead to a more variable earning pattern for a company and one would expect this added risk to lead to a lower stock price and thus a lower price-earnings ratio. The model can be expressed formally as

$$Y = a + bX$$

where Y = the price-earnings ratio of the company (the price of a share of common stock divided by earnings per share)
  X = its debt-equity ratio (long-term debt divided by debt plus equity)

---

[6] See P. Siegelman and J. J. Donohue III, "The Selection of Employment Discrimination Disputes for Litigation: Using Business Cycle Effects to Test the Priest-Klein Hypothesis," *Journal of Legal Studies,* vol. 24, pp. 427–462, June 1995. These reported results are a simplification of the substantially more complete study described in the article.

We expect b to have a negative value but have no *a priori* expectation regarding the value of the intercept. Observations were obtained for variables Y and X for a cross section of public utilities (at a fixed point in time). The linear regression result is

$$\hat{Y} = 10.2 - 4.07X$$

The coefficient of -4.07 appears to confirm the stated hypothesis. However, to know in more detail how confident we are about the hypothesis, we need to use some of the statistical tests discussed in Chapter 2.

APPENDIX 1.1 The Use of Summation Operators

Because many elementary propositions in econometrics involve the use of sums of numbers, it will be useful to review (or become acquainted with) summation signs. Throughout the book the capital Greek letter sigma, Σ, represents the summation of the values of each of the observations for a variable. For example, let X represent the variable "family income." Then, using subscript notation,

$$X_1, X_2, \ldots, X_N$$

represents the values taken by each of the N observations of family income. Then total family income $(X_1 + X_2 + \cdots + X_N)$ can be represented as

$$\sum_{i=1}^{N} X_i = X_1 + X_2 + \cdots + X_N \tag{A1.1}$$

The following summation operator rules are useful.

Rule 1   The summation of a constant k times a variable is equal to the constant times the summation of that variable.

$$\sum_{i=1}^{N} kX_i = k \sum_{i=1}^{N} X_i \tag{A1.2}$$

Rule 2   The summation of the sum of observations on two variables is equal to the sum of their summations.

$$\sum_{i=1}^{N} (X_i + Y_i) = \sum_{i=1}^{N} X_i + \sum_{i=1}^{N} Y_i \tag{A1.3}$$

Rule 3   The summation of a constant over N observations equals the product of the constant and N.

$$\sum_{i=1}^{N} k = kN \tag{A1.4}$$

Using these three rules, we can obtain some useful results concerning means, variances, and covariances of random variables. Since these concepts are discussed more completely in Chapter 2, we will restrict ourselves here to a discussion of algebraic (rather than statistical) properties. First, we define the mean or average of N observations on variable X to be

$$\overline{X} = \frac{1}{N} \sum_{i=1}^{N} X_i \tag{A1.5}$$

Using this definition, we can prove Rule 4.

Rule 4   The summation of the deviations of observations on X about its mean is zero.

$$\sum_{i=1}^{N} (X_i - \overline{X}) = 0 \tag{A1.6}$$

(See footnote 4 for proof.) In the text we will have frequent opportunities to use the deviations form. Using lowercase letters to represent deviations form, that is, $x_i = X_i - \overline{X}$, Rule 4 becomes

$$\sum_{i=1}^{N} x_i = 0 \tag{A1.7}$$

Now we define the variance of X to be

$$\text{Var}(X) = \frac{1}{N} \sum_{i=1}^{N} (X_i - \overline{X})^2 \tag{A1.8}$$

and the covariance of X and Y to be

$$\text{Cov}(X, Y) = \frac{1}{N} \sum_{i=1}^{N} (X_i - \overline{X})(Y_i - \overline{Y}) \tag{A1.9}$$

Using these definitions and our earlier results, we can prove the last two summation rules.

Rule 5   The covariance between X and Y is equal to the mean of the products of observations on X and Y minus the product of their means:

$$\frac{1}{N}\sum_{i=1}^{N}(X_i - \bar{X})(Y_i - \bar{Y}) = \frac{1}{N}\sum_{i=1}^{N}X_iY_i - \bar{X}\,\bar{Y} \tag{A1.10}$$

PROOF

$$\frac{1}{N}\sum_{i=1}^{N}(X_i - \bar{X})(Y_i - \bar{Y}) = \frac{1}{N}\sum_{i=1}^{N}X_iY_i - \frac{1}{N}\sum_{i=1}^{N}\bar{X}Y_i$$

$$- \frac{1}{N}\sum_{i=1}^{N}X_i\bar{Y} + \frac{1}{N}\sum_{i=1}^{N}\bar{X}\,\bar{Y}$$

and using Rule 1, we get

$$\text{Cov}(X, Y) = \frac{1}{N}\sum_{i=1}^{N}X_iY_i - \frac{1}{N}\bar{X}\sum_{i=1}^{N}Y_i - \frac{1}{N}\bar{Y}\sum_{i=1}^{N}X_i + \frac{1}{N}\sum_{i=1}^{N}\bar{X}\,\bar{Y}$$

Now, recalling the definition of the mean of X and the mean of Y, we have

$$\text{Cov}(X, Y) = \frac{1}{N}\sum_{i=1}^{N}X_iY_i - \bar{X}\,\bar{Y} - \bar{Y}\bar{X} + \frac{1}{N}\sum_{i=1}^{N}\bar{X}\,\bar{Y}$$

$$= \frac{1}{N}\sum_{i=1}^{N}X_iY_i - 2\,\bar{X}\,\bar{Y} + \bar{X}\,\bar{Y} \qquad \text{since } \sum_{i=1}^{N}\bar{X}\,\bar{Y} = N\bar{X}\,\bar{Y} \text{ by Rule 3}$$

$$= \frac{1}{N}\sum_{i=1}^{N}X_iY_i - \bar{X}\,\bar{Y}$$

Rule 6 follows easily from Rule 5, since it applies to the case in which X and X again are the two variables.

Rule 6   The variance of X is equal to the mean of the squares of observations on X minus its mean squared.

$$\frac{1}{N}\sum_{i=1}^{N}(X_i - \bar{X})^2 = \frac{1}{N}\sum_{i=1}^{N}X_i^2 - \bar{X}^2 \tag{A1.11}$$

Note, incidentally, that when X and Y happen to have zero means (as occurs when they are measured as deviations about their means), the definitions of covariance and variance become (we have omitted the range of the index here)

$$\text{Cov}(x, y) = \frac{1}{N}\sum x_iy_i \qquad \text{and} \qquad \text{Var}(x) = \frac{1}{N}\sum x_i^2$$

In certain situations it will be necessary to use summations which apply to two random variables, called *double summations*. Specifically, let X_{ij} be a random variable which takes on N values for each outcome of i and j. There will, of course, be N^2 total outcomes. Now we define the double summation of these N^2 outcomes as

$$\sum_{i=1}^{N} \sum_{j=1}^{N} X_{ij} = \sum_{i=1}^{N} (X_{i1} + X_{i2} + \cdots + X_{iN})$$

$$= (X_{11} + X_{12} + \cdots + X_{1N}) + (X_{21} + X_{22} + \cdots + X_{2N})$$

$$+ \cdots + (X_{N1} + X_{N2} + \cdots + X_{NN})$$

The following two double-summation rules will be useful.

Rule 7

$$\sum_{i=1}^{N} \sum_{j=1}^{N} X_i Y_j = \left(\sum_{i=1}^{N} X_i \right) \left(\sum_{j=1}^{N} Y_j \right) \tag{A1.12}$$

Note that the double summation in Rule 7 is very different from the single summation $\sum_{i=1}^{N} X_i Y_i$, which contains N (rather than N^2) terms.

Rule 8

$$\sum_{i=1}^{N} \sum_{j=1}^{N} (X_{ij} + Y_{ij}) = \sum_{i=1}^{N} \sum_{j=1}^{N} X_{ij} + \sum_{i=1}^{N} \sum_{j=1}^{N} Y_{ij} \tag{A1.13}$$

APPENDIX 1.2 Derivation of Least-Squares Parameter Estimates

As stated in the text, our goal is to minimize $\sum(Y_i - \hat{Y}_i)^2$, where $\hat{Y}_i = a + bX_i$ is the fitted value of Y_i corresponding to a particular observation X_i.

We minimize the expression by taking the partial derivatives with respect to a and b, setting each equal to 0, and solving the resulting pair of simultaneous equations:[7]

$$\frac{\partial}{\partial a} \sum (Y_i - a - bX_i)^2 = -2\sum(Y_i - a - bX_i) \tag{A1.14}$$

$$\frac{\partial}{\partial b} \sum (Y_i - a - bX_i)^2 = -2\sum X_i(Y_i - a - bX_i) \tag{A1.15}$$

---

[7] An index does not appear in the summation signs, but the index is assumed to range over all observations $1, 2, \ldots, N$.

Equating these derivatives to zero and dividing by -2, we get

$$\Sigma(Y_i - a - bX_i) = 0 \tag{A1.16}$$

$$\Sigma X_i(Y_i - a - bX_i) = 0 \tag{A1.17}$$

Finally, by rewriting Eqs. (A1.16) and (A1.17) we obtain a pair of simultaneous equations (known as the *normal equations*):

$$\Sigma Y_i = aN + b\Sigma X_i \tag{A1.18}$$

$$\Sigma X_i Y_i = a\Sigma X_i + b\Sigma X_i^2 \tag{A1.19}$$

Now we can solve for a and b simultaneously by multiplying Eq. (A1.18) by ΣX_i and multiplying Eq. (A1.19) by N:

$$\Sigma X_i \Sigma Y_i = aN \Sigma X_i + b(\Sigma X_i)^2 \tag{A1.20}$$

$$N \Sigma X_i Y_i = aN \Sigma X_i + bN \Sigma X_i^2 \tag{A1.21}$$

Subtracting Eq. (A1.20) from Eq. (A1.21), we get

$$N \Sigma X_i Y_i - \Sigma X_i \Sigma Y_i = b[N \Sigma X_i^2 - (\Sigma X_i)^2] \tag{A1.22}$$

from which it follows that

$$b = \frac{N \Sigma X_i Y_i - \Sigma X_i \Sigma Y_i}{N \Sigma X_i^2 - (\Sigma X_i)^2} \tag{A1.23}$$

Given b, we may calculate a from Eq. (A1.18):

$$a = \frac{\Sigma Y_i}{N} - b\frac{\Sigma X_i}{N} \tag{A1.24}$$

EXERCISES

1.1 Assume that you are in charge of the central monetary authority in a mythical country. You are given the following historical data on the quantity of money and national income (both in millions of dollars):

Year	Quantity of money	National income	Year	Quantity of money	National income
1987	2.0	5.0	1992	4.0	7.7
1988	2.5	5.5	1993	4.2	8.4
1989	3.2	6.0	1994	4.6	9.0
1990	3.6	7.0	1995	4.8	9.7
1991	3.3	7.2	1996	5.0	10.0

(*a*) Plot these points on a scatter diagram. Then estimate the regression of national income *Y* on the quantity of money *X* and plot the line on the scatter diagram.

(*b*) How do you interpret the intercept and slope of the regression line?

(*c*) If you had sole control over the money supply and wished to achieve a level of national income of 12.0 in 1997, at what level would you set the money supply? Explain.

1.2 Calculate the regression of income on grade-point average in the example described in this chapter and compare it with the regression of grade-point average on income. Why are the two results different?

1.3 (*a*) Assume that least-squares estimates are obtained for the relationship $Y = a + bX$. After the work is completed, it is decided to multiply the units of the *X* variable by a factor of 10. What will happen to the resulting least-squares slope and intercept?

(*b*) Generalize the result of part (*a*) by evaluating the effects on the regression of changing the units of *X* and *Y* in the following manner:

$$Y^* = c_1 + c_2Y \qquad X^* = d_1 + d_2X$$

What can you conclude?

1.4 What happens to the least-squares intercept and the slope estimate when all observations on the independent variable are identical? Can you explain intuitively why this occurs?

1.5 Prove that the estimated regression line passes through the point of means $(\overline{X}, \overline{Y})$. *Hint:* Show that $\overline{X}$ and $\overline{Y}$ satisfy the equation $Y = a + bX$, where *a* and *b* are defined in Eqs. (1.2) and (1.3).

1.6 How would you interpret the -144.38 value of the intercept in the regression of *Y* on *U* in Example 1.2? Explain why the value of the intercept is not likely to be of much practical interest.

1.7 To test for the sensitivity of least-squares estimates of intercept and slope to the presence of outliers, perform the following calculations:

1. Reestimate the slope and intercept in Example 1.1 under the assumption that the first observation was (21.0, 1.0) rather than (21.0, 4.0).
2. Reestimate the slope and intercept by dropping the first observation from the sample.

(*a*) Describe how the slope and intercept estimates in 1 and 2 compare with those given in the example. A graph of both straight lines would be helpful. Why are least-squares estimates so sensitive to individual data points?

(*b*) Having graphed the least-squares line in case 1, would you conclude that the first data point is an outlier? Discuss.

ELEMENTARY STATISTICS: A REVIEW

The study of econometrics, even in its most applied form, requires a good understanding of statistics. We assume that most readers have studied statistics but realize that this knowledge may need updating. Before continuing our study of econometrics, we will review the statistical ideas that will be used at various stages in the text. To help the reader focus on important ideas rather than details, we have moved most derivations to Appendix 2.1.

2.1 RANDOM VARIABLES

A *random variable* is a variable that takes on alternative values, each with a probability less than or equal to 1. We can describe a random variable by examining the process which generates its values. This process, called a *probability distribution*, lists all possible outcomes and the probability that each will occur. We might define a random variable as a function that assigns to each outcome of an experiment a real number. For example, assume that we assign a value of 1 to a coin toss of heads and a value of 0 to a toss of tails (if we use a fair coin, the probability of heads will be $\frac{1}{2}$). In this case we can interpret the value of the coin toss as a random variable; the process generating the random variable is the *binomial probability distribution.*

It is useful to distinguish between discrete and continuous random variables. A *continuous random variable* may take on any value on the real number line, while a *discrete random variable* may take on only a specific number of real values. Figure 2.1 illustrates discrete and continuous probability functions. With the discrete distribution, we see that the values 10 and 20 occur with probability .25, while the value 40 occurs with a .50 probability. With the continuous distribution, the probability that a particular value lies between any two values

19

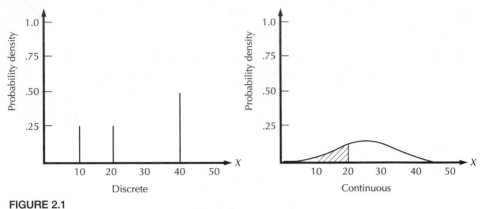

FIGURE 2.1
Probability densities.

of the distribution is determined by the area under the continuous density function between those two values. In this example the probability that values of the distribution lie between 10 and 20 is approximately equal to .30, the shaded area in the figure.

2.1.1   Expected Values

Probability distributions are often described in terms of their means and variances, which in turn are defined in terms of the *expectations operator E*. Since we will work initially with discrete random variables, assume that $X_1, X_2, \ldots,$ X_N represent the N possible outcomes associated with the random variable X. Then the *mean*, or *expected value*, of X is a weighted average of the possible outcomes, where the probabilities of the outcomes serve as the appropriate weights. Specifically, the mean of X, denoted μ_X, is defined by

$$\mu_X = E(X) = p_1X_1 + p_2X_2 + \cdots + p_NX_N = \sum_{i=1}^{N} p_iX_i \qquad (2.1)$$

where p_i is the probability that X_i occurs, $\Sigma p_i = 1$, and $E(\ \ )$ is the expectations operator.

The expected value should be distinguished from the *sample mean*, which tells us the average of the outcomes obtained in a sample in which a number of observations are chosen (usually at random) from the underlying probability distribution. We denote the sample mean of a set of outcomes on X by $\overline{X}$.

The *variance* of a random variable provides a measure of the spread, or dispersion, around the mean. It is denoted σ_X^2, and (in the discrete case) it is defined as

$$\text{Var } (X) = \sigma_X^2 = \sum_{i=1}^{N} p_i[X_i - E(X)]^2 \qquad (2.2)$$

Thus, the variance is a weighted average of the squares of the deviations of outcomes on X from its expected value, with the corresponding probabilities of each outcome occurring serving as weights. The variance in Eq. (2.2) is in itself an expectation, since

$$\sigma_X^2 = E[X - E(X)]^2 \qquad (2.3)$$

The (positive) square root of the variance is called the *standard deviation*.

There are a number of properties of the expectations operator which we will find useful, especially in discussing means and variances of random variables. We encourage the reader to examine carefully the details described in Appendix 2.1. Three of the major results concerning the expectations operator are as follows:

Result 1 $\qquad\qquad E(aX + b) = aE(X) + b$

where X is a random variable and a and b are constants.

Result 2 $\qquad\qquad E[(aX)^2] = a^2 E(X^2)$

Result 3 $\qquad\qquad \text{Var } (aX + b) = a^2 \text{ Var } (X)$

2.1.2 Joint Distributions of Random Variables

It will be useful to study joint distributions of X and a second random variable Y. In the discrete case, joint distributions are described by a list of probabilities of occurrence of all possible outcomes on both X and Y. For example, if Y is a random variable which takes on the value 1 if the head of a household has a college education and 0 if that person does not, while X is the family income variable described earlier, then the *joint* distribution of X and Y might be as follows:

Outcome	Probability	Outcome	Probability
$X = \$5,000, Y = 1$	0	$X = \$10,000, Y = 0$	$\frac{1}{8}$
$X = \$5,000, Y = 0$	$\frac{1}{4}$	$X = \$15,000, Y = 1$	$\frac{1}{3}$
$X = \$10,000, Y = 1$	$\frac{1}{8}$	$X = \$15,000, Y = 0$	$\frac{1}{6}$

Note that all probabilities are nonnegative and sum to 1.

Just as in the case of a single random variable, the expectations operator is useful in describing the important characteristics of joint distributions. We define the *covariance* of X and Y as the expectation of the product of X and Y when both are measured as deviations about their means;

$$\text{Cov }(X, Y) = E[(X - E(X))(Y - E(Y))]$$

$$= \sum_{i=1}^{N} \sum_{j=1}^{N} p_{ij}(X_i - E(X))(Y_j - E(Y)) \qquad (2.4)$$

where p_{ij} represents the joint probability of X and Y occurring.

The covariance is a measure of the linear association between X and Y. If both variables are always above and below their means at the same time, the covariance will be positive, as in Fig. 2.2b. If X is above its mean when Y is below its mean and vice versa, the covariance will be negative, as in Fig. 2.2a. The value of the covariance depends on the units in which X and Y are measured. As a result we will have frequent occasion to use the *correlation coefficient*

$$\rho(X, Y) = \frac{\text{Cov }(X, Y)}{\sigma_X \sigma_Y} \qquad (2.5)$$

where σ_X and σ_Y represent the standard deviations of X and Y, respectively.

Unlike covariance, the correlation coefficient has been normalized and is *scale-free*. It can be shown that the correlation coefficient will always lie between -1 and $+1$. A positive correlation indicates that the variables move in the same direction, while a negative correlation implies that they move in opposite directions.

Several properties of the expectations operator are useful when one is deal-

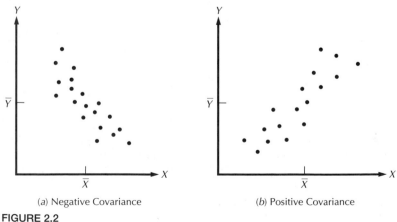

(a) Negative Covariance   (b) Positive Covariance

FIGURE 2.2
Covariance.

ing with joint probability distributions. They are stated here and proved in Appendix 2.1.

Result 4 If X and Y are random variables, $E(X + Y) = E(X) + E(Y)$

Result 5 $\text{Var}(X + Y) = \text{Var}(X) + \text{Var}(Y) + 2\,\text{Cov}(X, Y)$

Example 2.1 Covariance and Correlation The joint probability distribution of income (in thousands of dollars) and education (in years) for the five employees of a small firm is as follows:

Income (X)	5	10	15	20	25
Education (Y)	10	8	10	15	12

The means and variances of each of the variables are

$E(X) = (5 + 10 + 15 + 20 + 25)/5 = 15$
$\text{Var}(X) = [(-10)^2 + (-5)^2 + 0^2 + 5^2 + 10^2]/5 = 50$

$E(Y) = (10 + 8 + 10 + 15 + 12)/5 = 11$
$\text{Var}(Y) = [(-1)^2 + (-3)^2 + (-1)^2 + 4^2 + 1^2]/5 = 5.6$

The covariance between X and Y is then given by

$\text{Cov}(X, Y) = [(-10)(-1) + (-5)(-3) + (0)(-1) + (5)(4) + (10)(1)]/5 = 11$

Finally, the correlation between X and Y is

$$\rho(X, Y) = 11/[(50)(5.6)]^{1/2} = .66$$

2.1.3 Independence and Correlation

In certain cases the probability of an outcome associated with Y will be unrelated to the outcome associated with X, and vice versa. In this case we say that X and Y are *independent* random variables. As an example, consider the tossing of a coin for which the probability of heads and the probability of tails are both $\frac{1}{2}$. Assume that the first five tosses are all heads. The probability of tails occurring on the sixth toss will be $\frac{1}{2}$, and this is independent of the previous tosses.

When two variables are independent, calculations involving the expectations operator become simplified. The result is summed up by Rules 6 and 7 for the expectations operator, which are proved in Appendix 2.1.

Result 6   If X and Y are independent, $E(XY) = E(X)E(Y)$.

Result 7   If X and Y are independent, Cov $(X, Y) = 0$.

Result 7 states that if two random variables are independent, the covariance between them is 0. This makes intuitive sense because independence of X and Y means that there is no relation between the outcomes of one variable and the outcomes of the other variable. If there is no relationship, we would expect deviations in X about its mean to be unrelated to deviations in Y. It is important to realize, however, that the result does not hold in the opposite direction. Two variables may have zero covariance, yet there may be a dependence between the variables. The key is that covariance and correlation measure *linear* dependence; the variables may be related nonlinearly yet have a zero covariance.

As an example, assume that X and Y follow the probability distribution

X	-2	-1	0	1	2
Y	4	1	0	1	4

All observations are assumed to occur with equal probability $(\frac{1}{5})$. In this case $E(X) = 0$, $E(Y) = 2$, and

$$\text{Cov } (X, Y) = 1/5 \sum_{i=1}^{5} X_i(Y_i - 2) = 0$$

However, the random variables are certainly not independent. In fact, all five joint outcomes listed satisfy the relationship $Y = X^2$, so that there is an exact nonlinear relationship between X and Y.

2.2   ESTIMATION

2.2.1   Estimators of Mean, Variance, and Covariance

Means, variances, and covariances can be measured with certainty only if we know about all possible outcomes, i.e., the *population*. Usually, however, when we undertake a study, we have only a *sample* of the population. Then we will want to make inferences about the characteristics of the population from the sample. We will show in this chapter how one can take a sample of N data points, obtain estimates of population characteristics, and then draw conclusions about the relationship between the sample estimates and the corresponding population parameters. Since we cannot know the true mean and variance of a random variable, or the true covariance between two random variables, we use the sample information to obtain the best possible estimates.

Our goal is to determine a rule which will give a sample estimate for each and every possible sample. To distinguish the single estimate from the more general rule, we call the latter an *estimator*. It is common for students to confuse "estimates" and "estimators," but this confusion can be eliminated if we remind ourselves that estimators are rules, while estimates are numbers.

Finding the best estimator for any given sample is a complex issue that is discussed in greater detail in Section 2.3. For the moment, assume that a minimal requirement is that the estimator of a parameter (such as the mean or variation) yield estimates closely approximating that parameter. More specifically, we would like the estimator to be *unbiased* in that the *expected value* of the estimator is equal to the parameter itself. As an example, reconsider the sample mean of a random variable X with mean μ_x. The estimator $\overline{X}$ is defined by

$$\overline{X} = \frac{1}{N} \sum_{i=1}^{N} X_i \qquad (2.6)$$

It is very important to note that $\overline{X}$ is a random variable whose values will vary from sample to sample even though the corresponding population parameter μ remains unchanged. Because the sample estimates vary from sample to sample, we can picture their probability distribution. This *sampling distribution* is obtained by repeatedly obtaining new samples and calculating the sample means and variances each time. The sampling distribution for the mean will measure the probability that the sample mean falls within a series of specified intervals (recall our previous discussion of probability distributions).

Given that $\overline{X}$ has a sampling distribution, it is natural to ask whether the expected value of the estimator $\overline{X}$ is equal to the population mean; in other words, is $\overline{X}$ an unbiased estimator of μ? To show that $\overline{X}$ is unbiased, we prove that $E(\overline{X}) = \mu_x$:

$$E(\overline{X}) = E\left(\frac{1}{N} \sum_{i=1}^{N} X_i\right) = \frac{1}{N} E\left(\sum_{i=1}^{N} X_i\right) = \frac{1}{N} \sum_{i-1}^{N} E(X_i)$$

$$= \frac{1}{N} \sum_{i=1}^{N} \mu_X = \frac{1}{N} N\mu_X = \mu_X$$

A reasonable choice for an estimator of the variance of a random variable is

$$\frac{1}{N} \sum_{i=1}^{N} (X_i - \overline{X})^2$$

The problem is that this estimator is biased. As shown in Appendix 2.1, Result 9, an unbiased estimator of the variance of a random variable (with unknown mean), is given by

$$\widehat{\text{Var}}(X) = \frac{1}{N-1} \sum_{i=1}^{N} (X_i - \overline{X})^2 \qquad (2.7)$$

Why do we divide by $N - 1$ (rather than N) to get an unbiased estimate of the sample variance? The exact answer lies in the proof of the result given in Appendix 2.1, but an intuitive answer can be based on the concept of *degrees of freedom*. Our sample is known to contain N data points. However, in computing the sample variance a necessary first step was the computation of the sample mean. This places a constraint on the N data points that the N observations sum to N times the computed mean $\overline{X}$. This leaves $N - 1$ unconstrained observations with which to estimate the sample variance.

Finally, consider how we might obtain an unbiased estimator of the covariance between two random variables. Since the covariance is defined as

$$\text{Cov}\ (X, Y) = E[(X - E(X))(Y - E(Y))]$$

the covariance could be measured as the average of the product of the deviations of X and Y about their means, i.e.,

$$\frac{1}{N} \sum_{i=1}^{N} (X_i - \overline{X})(Y_i - \overline{Y})$$

However, just as in the previous case, this estimator will be biased. To obtain an unbiased estimator we divide the previous summation by the number of degrees of freedom. In calculating the sum of the product of the deviations in X and Y, there are N observations on the joint outcomes of X and Y and thus N independent pieces of information. However, *one* piece of information is used to calculate the means of X and Y: the constraint that the sum of all N observations equals N times the means of X and Y, respectively. As a result there are $N - 1$ degrees of freedom, and the unbiased estimator is

$$\widehat{\text{Cov}}\ (X, Y) = \frac{1}{N - 1} \sum_{i=1}^{N} (X_i - \overline{X})(Y_i - \overline{Y}) \tag{2.8}$$

The sample covariance is distinguished from the true covariance by placing a hat ($\frown$) above the Cov.

Finally, we can define the *sample* correlation coefficient between two variables to correspond to the population coefficient defined earlier. The sample correlation coefficient is

$$r_{XY} = \frac{\sum_{i=1}^{N} (X_i - \overline{X})(Y_i - \overline{Y})}{\sqrt{\sum_{i=1}^{N} (X_i - \overline{X})^2 \sum_{i=1}^{N} (Y_i - \overline{Y})^2}} \tag{2.9}$$

To distinguish r_{XY} from other, more complex measures of correlation we call it the *simple correlation* between X and Y. Like its population counterpart, r_{XY}

ranges from -1 to $+1$ in value, so that its square lies between 0 and 1. We might note that the simple correlation relates directly to the sample covariance between X and Y as follows:

$$r_{XY} = \frac{\widehat{\text{Cov}}\ (X,\ Y)}{\sqrt{\widehat{\text{Var}}\ (X)\ \widehat{\text{Var}}\ (Y)}}$$

Econometrics involves the study of relationships between variables. Since covariance tells us whether and to what extent two variables are related, it serves as one of the underpinnings of applied econometrics. A positive covariance implies that when X lies above its mean, so will Y, and that when X lies below its mean, so will Y. This suggests (see Fig. 2.2*a*) that the best-fitting line through a set of points with negative covariance will have a negative slope.

We can see this more clearly if we relate the measure of sample covariance to the least-squares slope estimator given in Chapter 1. Rewriting the sample covariance estimator in deviations form, with $x_i = X_i - \overline{X}$ and $y_i = Y_i - \overline{Y}$,

$$\widehat{\text{Cov}}\ (X,\ Y) = \frac{1}{N - 1}\ \Sigma x_i y_i \qquad (2.10)$$

Note that we have dropped the index $i = 1, 2, \ldots, N$ for convenience. Recall also that our sample estimator of the variance of X, sometimes denoted s_X^2, is given by

$$\widehat{\text{Var}}\ (X) = \frac{1}{N - 1}\ \Sigma x_i^2$$

Now consider the expression obtained by dividing the sample covariance by the sample variance:

$$\frac{\widehat{\text{Cov}}\ (X,\ Y)}{\widehat{\text{Var}}\ (X)} = \frac{[1/(N - 1)]\Sigma x_i y_i}{[1/(N - 1)]\Sigma x_i^2} = \frac{\Sigma x_i y_i}{\Sigma x_i^2} \qquad (2.11)$$

This ratio is equal to the estimate of this slope obtained in Eq. (1.6). For any sample, the least-squares slope estimator can be measured by the ratio of covariance, which takes the direction of the line, and the variance, a positive number which serves to normalize the units in which the data are measured.

To apply this, consider the grade-point-average example. Our calculations for the least-squares slope estimate can be used to calculate sample means, variance, and covariance. With the data in deviations form, $\overline{x}$ and $\overline{y} = 0$. The covariance between X and Y is given by

$$\frac{1}{N - 1}\ \Sigma x_i y_i = \frac{19.50}{7} = 2.79$$

while the variance of X is given by

$$\frac{1}{N-1}\sum x_i^2 = \frac{162.00}{7} = 23.14$$

The covariance is positive, indicating a positive slope, and the ratio of sample covariance to sample variance, 2.79/23.14, yields the slope estimate, .12.

2.2.2   The Central Limit Theorem

What happens to the sampling distribution of the mean as the sample size gets large? Intuitively, we would expect that a larger sample size should lead to an estimate of the mean that is on average closer to the population mean. In fact, if the sample becomes arbitrarily large, or equal to the population, the estimate of the sample mean should identically equal the population mean.

This intuition, which holds for probability distributions with finite means and is not limited to the normal, is summed up formally as the *central limit theorem*:

> **Central Limit Theorem**   If the random variable X has mean μ and variance σ^2, then the sampling distribution of $\overline{X}$ becomes approximately normal with mean μ and variance σ^2/N as N increases.

$\varsigma^2 = \sigma^2/N$ in normal distribution.

The central limit theorem provides an important reason for our study of the normal distribution in Section 2.4; we will see that for sufficiently large sample sizes, the normality assumption will allow us to simplify our statistical tests greatly. Before studying this description, we pause briefly to discuss the properties that are desirable in a statistical estimator.

2.3   DESIRABLE PROPERTIES OF ESTIMATORS

We have argued that one useful property of a statistical estimator is that it be unbiased. Since the search for estimators is the heart of the science of econometrics, we will pause here to consider other desirable properties. To tie our discussion in with the analysis of the regression model, we will ask what properties we ought to look for in choosing an estimator for an arbitrary parameter β, such as the slope estimator of a straight line. There are four properties of estimators which are important.

2.3.1   Lack of Bias

One very desirable property associated with an estimated regression parameter is for the distribution of the estimator to have the parameter as its mean value. Then if we could analyze new data, we would be assured of being right on average. We will say that $\hat{\beta}$ is an *unbiased* estimator if the mean or expected value of $\hat{\beta}$ is equal to the true value; that is, $E(\hat{\beta}) = \beta$. The difference between a biased estimator and an unbiased estimator can be seen in Fig. 2.3. To clarify the exposition we define the bias associated with an estimated parameter as follows:

$$\text{Bias} = E(\hat{\beta}) - \beta$$

While lack of bias in an estimator is a desirable property, it implies nothing about the dispersion of the estimator about the true parameter. In general, one would like the estimator to be unbiased and also to have a very small dispersion about the mean. This suggests that one should define a second criterion that allows one to choose among alternative unbiased estimators.

2.3.2   Efficiency

We say that $\hat{\beta}$ is an *efficient* unbiased estimator if for a given sample size the variance of $\hat{\beta}$ is smaller than the variance of any other unbiased estimators. It sometimes is difficult to tell whether an estimator is efficient, so that it is natural to describe estimators in terms of their relative efficiency. One estimator is more efficient than another if it has smaller variance. A relatively efficient estimator and a relatively inefficient estimator are shown graphically in Fig. 2.4. Efficiency is desirable because the greater the efficiency associated with an estimation process, the stronger the *statistical* statements one can make about the estimated parameters. Thus, in the extreme case of an (unbiased) estimator with *zero* variance, we can state with certainty the numerical value of the true regression parameter.

2.3.3   Minimum Mean Square Error

There are many circumstances in which one is forced to trade off bias and variance of estimators. When the goal of a model is to maximize the precision

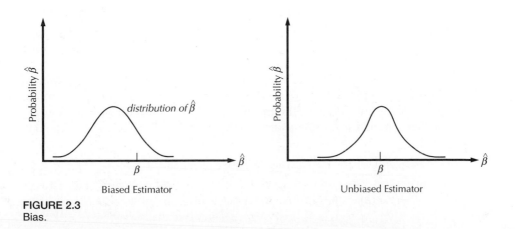

FIGURE 2.3
Bias.

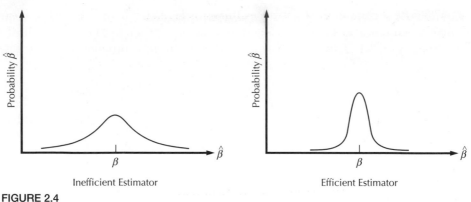

FIGURE 2.4
Efficiency.

of predictions, for example, an estimator with very low variance and some bias may be more desirable than an unbiased estimator with high variance. One criterion which is useful in this regard is the goal of minimizing *mean square error*, which is defined as

$$\text{Mean square error } (\hat{\beta}) = E(\hat{\beta} - \beta)^2$$

It is not difficult to show that this definition is equivalent to[1]

$$\text{Mean square error} = [\text{Bias } (\hat{\beta})]^2 + \text{Var } (\hat{\beta})$$

Thus, the criterion of minimizing mean square error takes into account the variance and the square of the bias of the estimator. When $\hat{\beta}$ is unbiased, the mean square error and variance of $\hat{\beta}$ are equal.

Example 2.2 Mean Square Error   Suppose that one is interested in estimating the mean of a random variable, X, with unknown population mean μ and standard deviation σ and that 10 data points can be collected by random sampling. Because data collection is costly, a researcher proposes to collect only five data points at random. What effect does this more limited sampling procedure have on the properties of the estimator of the mean?

The first complete sample estimator is given by: $\overline{X} = (X_1 + \cdots + X_{10})/10,$

---

[1] If $\overline{\hat{\beta}}$ is the expected value of the estimated regression coefficient,

$$E(\hat{\beta} - \beta)^2 = E[(\hat{\beta} - \overline{\hat{\beta}}) + (\overline{\hat{\beta}} - \beta)]^2 = E(\hat{\beta} - \overline{\hat{\beta}})^2 + E(\overline{\hat{\beta}} - \beta)^2 + 2(\overline{\hat{\beta}} - \beta) E(\hat{\beta} - \overline{\hat{\beta}})$$
$$= \text{Var } (\hat{\beta}) + [\text{Bias } (\hat{\beta})]^2 \quad \text{This follows, since } \overline{\hat{\beta}} = E(\hat{\beta}) \text{ by definition.}$$

while the second limited sample estimator is given by: $\overline{X}' = (X_1 + \cdots + X_5)/5$. Both estimators are unbiased since

$$E(\overline{X}) = [E(X_1) + E(X_2) + \cdots + E(X_{10})]/10 = 10\mu/10 = \mu$$

$$E(\overline{X}') = [E(X_1) + E(X_2) + \cdots + E(X_5)]/5 = 5\mu/5 = \mu$$

However, the first estimator is more efficient than the second because it has lower variance. To see why, note that

$$\text{Var}(\overline{X}) = [\text{Var}(X_1)/10^2 + \cdots + \text{Var}(X_{10})/10^2]$$

$$= 10\sigma^2/100 = \sigma^2/10, \text{ whereas}$$

$$\text{Var}(\overline{X}') = [\text{Var}(X_1)/5^2 + \cdots + \text{Var}(X_5)/5^2] = 5\sigma^2/25 = \sigma^2/5$$

In fact, the estimator of the sample mean which utilizes all the available data (weighted equally) is the most efficient estimator possible.

2.3.4 Consistency

To complete the discussion we consider the properties of estimators as the sample size gets very large, i.e., the *asymptotic*, or large-sample, properties. We would like the estimator $\hat{\beta}$ to get close to the true β as the sample size increases. Specifically, we hope that as the sample size gets very large, the probability that $\hat{\beta}$ will differ from β will get very small. To apply this probabilistic concept to the choice of estimator, we define the probability limit of $\hat{\beta}$ (plim $\hat{\beta}$) as follows:

plim $\hat{\beta}$ is equal to β if, as N approaches infinity, the probability that $|\beta - \hat{\beta}|$ will be less than any arbitrarily small positive number will approach 1.

With this concept it is natural to define the criterion of *consistency* as follows:

$\hat{\beta}$ is a *consistent* estimator of β if the *probability limit* of $\hat{\beta}$ is β.[2]

Roughly speaking, an estimator is consistent if the probability distribution of the estimator collapses to a single point (the true parameter) as the sample size gets arbitrarily large. This is described graphically in Fig. 2.5.

As a rule, econometricians tend to be more concerned with consistency than with lack of bias. A biased yet consistent estimator may not equal the true parameter on average, but it will approximate the true parameter as the sample information grows larger. This is more reassuring from a practical point of view

---

[2] Strictly speaking, $\hat{\beta}$ converges to β in the probability limit if for any $\delta > 0$,

$$\lim_{N \to \infty} \text{Prob}(|\beta - \hat{\beta}| < \delta) = 1$$

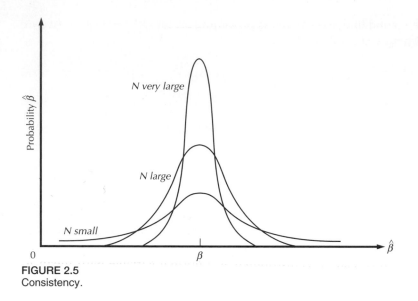

FIGURE 2.5
Consistency.

than the alternative of finding a parameter estimate that is unbiased yet continues to deviate substantially from the true parameter as the sample size gets larger. Figure 2.6 illustrates two parameter estimators, one of which is unbiased with large variance. Because of the large tails, a second estimator, although biased, has sufficiently small variance to have on net a smaller mean square error.

It is natural to consider as an alternative criterion the objective that the *mean square error of the estimator should approach zero as the sample increases.* The mean-square-error criterion implies that the estimator is *unbiased asymptotically* and that its variance goes to zero as the sample size gets very large. It turns out that an estimator with a mean square error that approaches zero will be a consistent estimator but that the reverse need not be true. In most applications consistent

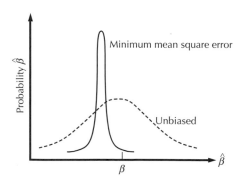

FIGURE 2.6
Mean square error.

estimators have mean square errors approaching zero, and the two criteria are used interchangeably.

2.4 PROBABILITY DISTRIBUTIONS

There are a number of specific probability distributions which will be useful at one or more places in this book. The four distributions covered are the normal, chi-square, t, and F distributions. The discussion which follows is meant to be descriptive, not rigorous.

2.4.1 The Normal Distribution

The normal distribution is a continuous bell-shaped probability distribution, as illustrated in Fig. 2.7. A normal distribution can be fully described by its mean and its variance, so that if X were normally distributed, we would write $X \sim N(\mu_X, \sigma_X^2)$, which is read "$X$ is distributed as a normal variable with mean μ_X and variance σ_X^2."

If X is normally distributed (and $\exp A = e^A$),

$$p(X = X_i) = \frac{1}{\sqrt{2\pi\sigma_X^2}} \exp\left[-\frac{1}{2\sigma_X^2}(X_i - \mu_X)^2\right]$$

For the purposes of statistical testing, it is useful to know that

$$\text{Prob } (\mu_X - 1.96\sigma_X < X_i < \mu_X + 1.96\sigma_X) \approx .95 \qquad (2.12)$$

$$\text{Prob } (\mu_X - 2.57\sigma_X < X_i < \mu_X + 2.57\sigma_X) \approx .99 \qquad (2.13)$$

where μ_X and σ_X are the mean and the standard deviations of the normal random variable X. The probability that a single observation of a normally

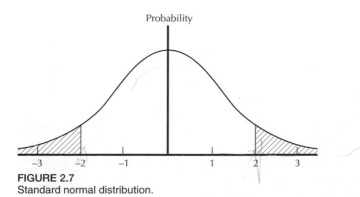

Probability

-3 -2 -1 1 2 3

FIGURE 2.7
Standard normal distribution.

distributed variable X will lie within about 2 standard deviations of its mean is approximately .95. The probability of being within about $2\frac{1}{2}$ standard deviations is about .99. Conversely, the probability that a single observation will be more than 2 ($2\frac{1}{2}$) standard deviations away from the mean is .05 (.01). Figure 2.7 contains an illustration of a normal variable with mean 0 and standard deviation 1. The probability that an observation of the random variable X will be in one or the other of the shaded areas is equal to .05. To illustrate, suppose that the scores on college entrance exams (SATs) are normally distributed with a mean score of 500 and a standard deviation of 100. Then the probability that any particular test score will lie within the range 304 to 696 [500 $\pm$ 1.96(100)] is .95. Correspondingly, only 2.5 percent of the test scores will be greater than 696, while 2.5 percent will be less than 304.

Why study the normal distribution? The normal distribution is a frequent choice of probability distribution for at least two reasons:

1. It is symmetric and bell-shaped, a reasonable way for us to describe the distribution of the parameters, such as slope and intercept, that we hope to estimate.

2. The distribution is fully described by its mean and variance, so that we need not worry about other properties such as skewness and kurtosis.

The following result helps with many of the statistical tests used in econometrics.

Result 10   If two (or more) random variables are normally distributed with identical means and variances, any weighted sum of these variables will be normally distributed.

Example 2.3 Normal Distribution   The distribution of the hourly wage rates of a population of workers is approximately normally distributed with mean $9.60 and standard deviation $5.25. What percentage of the employee population earns more than $20 per hour? Less than $5 per hour? To answer both of these questions, we determine that $20.00 is ($20.00 − $9.60)/ $5.25 = 1.98 standard deviations above the mean, while $5.00 is ($9.60 − $5.00)/$5.25 = .88 standard deviations below the mean. Using Table 1 in the back of the book for the standardized normal distribution, we find that 2.39 percent of the distribution lies to the right of 1.98 standard deviations above the mean, while 18.94 percent lies to the left of .88 standard deviations below the mean. Therefore, approximately 2.39 percent of the employees earn more than $20 per hour, while approximately 18.94 percent earn less than $5 per hour.

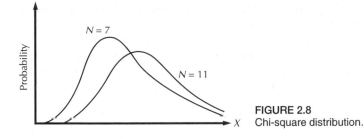

FIGURE 2.8
Chi-square distribution.

2.4.2   Chi-Square Distribution

The chi square is useful for testing hypotheses that deal with *variances* of random variables. Its application is derived from Result 11.

> **Result 11**   The sum of the *squares* of N independently distributed *normal* random variables (with mean 0 and variance 1) is distributed as *chi square* with N degrees of freedom.

Assume, for example, that we calculate the sample variance s^2 of N observations drawn from a normal distribution with variance σ^2. Then it is not difficult to show that $(N - 1)s^2/\sigma^2$ will be distributed as chi square with $N - 1$ degrees of freedom.[3] By examining critical values of the chi-square distribution with the appropriate number of degrees of freedom, we can decide whether to reject the hypothesis that the variance of the random variable equals a given number.

The chi square starts at the origin, is skewed to the right, and has a tail which extends infinitely far to the right (as shown in Fig. 2.8). The exact shape of the distribution depends on the number of degrees of freedom, with the distribution becoming more and more symmetric as the number of degrees of freedom gets larger. When the degrees of freedom get very large, the chi-square distribution approximates the normal. A table of the chi square, often denoted as χ^2, is given at the back of the book (Table 2).

2.4.3   The *t* Distribution

In statistics the variance of a random variable is sometimes assumed to be known. How do we test hypotheses when the variance is not known? The answer lies in the t distribution. The central result which allows us to use the t distribution is as follows.

> **Result 12**   Assume that X is normally distributed with mean 0 and variance 1 and that Z is distributed as chi square with N degrees of freedom. Then if

---

[3] See, for example, W. H. Greene, *Econometric Analysis* (New York: Macmillan, 1990), pp. 62–63.

X and Z are independent, $X/\sqrt{Z/N}$ has a t distribution with N degrees of freedom.

Figure 2.9 illustrates the t distribution. Like the normal, the t is symmetric, and it approximates the normal for large sample sizes. But the t has fatter tails than the normal, an occurrence which is especially pronounced for sample sizes of roughly 30 or less. To see how Result 12 aids us, recall for X normal $(\overline{X} - \mu_X)/(\sigma_X/\sqrt{N})$ is normally distributed with 0 mean and unit variance. But if σ_X is not known, we must replace σ_X^2 by the sample variance s_X^2. Since $(N - 1) s_X^2/\sigma_X^2$ follows a chi-square distribution and $(\overline{X} - \mu_X)/(\sigma_X/\sqrt{N})$ is unit normal, Result 12 tells us that

$$\frac{(\overline{X} - \mu_X)/(\sigma_X/\sqrt{N})}{\sqrt{(N - 1)s_X^2/\sigma_X^2}} \sqrt{N - 1} = \frac{(\overline{X} - \mu_x)\sqrt{N}}{s_X} \tag{2.14}$$

follows a t distribution. Thus, the t distribution can be used to test whether the mean of a random variable is equal to any particular number, even when the variance of the random variable is unknown.

A brief examination of percentiles of the t distribution given in Table 3 at the end of the book might be useful. For a 5 percent significance test, the critical value of the t distribution approaches 1.96, the critical value of the normal distribution, as N gets large. For a sample of 20 or more the critical value of 2.0 is a reasonable approximation. To illustrate, reconsider the SAT example mentioned earlier, but suppose that the sample mean of a distribution of 21 test scores is 500 and that the estimated standard deviation (as opposed to the true standard deviation) is 100. Since the critical value of the t distribution (for a 5 percent significance level) with 20 degrees of freedom is 2.086, the probability that any given test score will be greater than 708 [500 + 2.086(100)] is 2.5 percent.

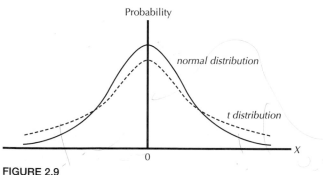

FIGURE 2.9
t distribution.

2.4.4   The F Distribution

There are occasions when we wish to test joint hypotheses involving two or more regression parameters, e.g., the hypothesis that the intercept and slope are both zero against the alternative that one or the other or both are nonzero. The proper test statistic is based on the F distribution and is characterized by two parameters, the first being associated with the number of estimated parameters and the second being associated with the number of degrees of freedom. The F distribution, like the chi square, has a skewed shape and ranges in value from 0 to infinity (see Fig. 2.10).

The F distribution can be used to test the equality of two variances. Its usefulness derives from Result 13.

Result 13   If X and Z are independent and distributed as chi square with N_1 and N_2 degrees of freedom, respectively, then $(X/N_1)/(Z/N_2)$ is distributed according to an F distribution with N_1 and N_2 degrees of freedom.

To see the usefulness of Result 13, assume that we have obtained samples of size N_1 and N_2 from two different normal distributions X and Z. The variance of X is *estimated* as

$$s_X^2 = \frac{1}{N_1 - 1} \sum_{i=1}^{N_1} (X_i - \overline{X})^2$$

and the variance of Z is estimated as

$$s_Z^2 = \frac{1}{N_2 - 1} \sum_{i=1}^{N_2} (Z_i - \overline{Z})^2$$

If we wish to test whether $\sigma_X^2 = \sigma_Z^2$, we can calculate the statistic s_X^2/s_Z^2. If X and Z are independent, then $(N_1 - 1)s_X^2/\sigma_X^2$ is distributed as chi square with

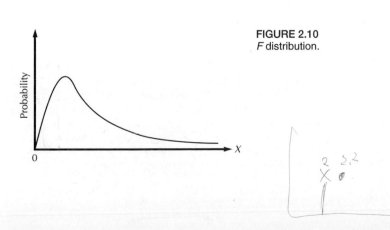

FIGURE 2.10
F distribution.

$N_1 - 1$ degrees of freedom and $(N_2 - 1)s_Z^2/\sigma_Z^2$ is distributed as chi square with $N_2 - 1$ degrees of freedom. Then, using Result 13, we know that the ratio

$$\overset{num.}{\frac{[(N_1 - 1)s_X^2/\sigma_X^2]}{\underset{denom.}{(N_1 - 1)}}} \Bigg/ \frac{[(N_2 - 1)s_Z^2/\sigma_Z^2]}{(N_2 - 1)}$$

will be distributed as an F distribution. Note that if $\sigma_X^2 = \sigma_Z^2$, this reduces to s_X^2/s_Z^2 and the ratio of the estimated variances follows an F distribution with $N_1 - 1$ and $N_2 - 1$ degrees of freedom.

The F statistic is always tabulated with the larger estimate of the variance in the numerator and the smaller estimate in the denominator. The resulting ratio is always greater than 1, and provides information about the upper tail of the F distribution. The greater the difference between the two variances, the greater the F statistic. Thus, a large value of F implies that it is unlikely that the two error variances are equal. In practice, testing is accomplished by choosing a level of significance and then looking up the critical value of the F distribution in a standard F table.

To illustrate, suppose we want to know whether the variance of the SAT mathematics test differs from the variance of the SAT verbal test. Assume also that of the 21 students, all took the verbal test but only 16 took the math test. The sample variance of the mathematics test is 100,000, while the sample variance of the verbal test is 80,000. Assuming that the populations of test scores are normally distributed, the F statistic is 1.25 (100,000/80,000) with 20 and 15 degrees of freedom. Since the 5 percent critical value of the F distribution is 2.33, we cannot rule out the possibility that the true variances are equal ($1.25 < 2.33$). Since we have chosen an F ratio greater than 1 in the upper tail of the distribution, our 5 percent significance test is a *one-tailed test*. If we wished to interpret our results in the context of a *two-tailed test* that allowed the variance of math test scores to be higher or lower than the variance of verbal test scores, we would reach the same conclusion at the 10 percent significance level.[4]

2.5   HYPOTHESIS TESTING AND CONFIDENCE INTERVALS

In this section we review the problem of testing hypotheses. The hypotheses that occur most often in econometrics involve slopes and intercepts of regression lines, but they also may involve variances or covariances of probability distributions. For a simple application, reconsider the grade-point-average example of Chapter 1. The slope of .12 gives us a good guess about the effect of

---

[4] If we chose to do a two-tailed test at the 5 percent significance level using the ratio of the larger to the smaller variance estimate, we could use information about the 2.5 percent significance tests for the F distribution (not available at the back of this book). Alternatively, we could calculate the lower tail of the distribution by reversing the degrees of freedom and using as a critical value the reciprocal of the critical value listed in the table for the reversed degrees of freedom.

family income on grades, but how reliable is that guess? Specifically, how can we be sure that the slope is not really zero, so that income and grade-point average are unrelated? This is a hypothesis-testing problem. Related to hypothesis testing is the concept of a confidence interval. While .12 is a good estimate of the slope, we certainly would not be prepared to argue that .12 measures the slope of the relationship between income and grades of all students. To show how reliable our results are, we need to use data to make probabilistic statements about our slope estimate. Specifically, we might find that we can state that with probability .95 the interval .06 to .18 contains the true slope. The interval .06 to .18 is called *a 95 percent confidence interval* for the slope.

The relationship between hypothesis testing and confidence intervals is a close one. To see this, assume that we wish to test the hypothesis that the slope is 0. We say that the *null hypothesis* is that the slope is 0. However, since we know that 0 lies outside the 95 percent confidence interval, we conclude (with 95 percent confidence) that we can *reject* the null hypothesis of a zero slope.

To continue this review, consider how hypothesis testing and confidence intervals relate to the determination of the mean of a random variable. Specifically, assume that we know the variance of a random variable X (which is normally distributed) but that the true mean is unknown. We wish to make statements about the accuracy with which we have estimated the unknown mean value. Since confidence statements are difficult to make about individual point estimates, we use *confidence intervals*. Assume, for example, that we wish to obtain a 95 percent confidence interval about the sample mean (this is said to be associated with a 5 percent level of *significance*). We obtain the interval by utilizing the fact that $\overline{X}$ is normally distributed with standard deviation $\sigma_X/\sqrt{N}$, where N is the number of observations. The 95 percent confidence interval is

$$\overline{X} - \frac{1.96\sigma_X}{\sqrt{N}} \leq \mu_X \leq \overline{X} + \frac{1.96\sigma_X}{\sqrt{N}}$$

Suppose, for example, that $N = 100$ and $\sigma_X = 10$. Then $\overline{X}$ is normally distributed with a standard deviation of 1. If the point estimate of μ_X is $\overline{X} = 3$, the 95 percent confidence interval will be $1 \leq \mu_X \leq 5$. The 95 percent confidence interval suggests that it is very likely that the (1, 5) interval will contain the true mean μ_X.

The interpretation of the statement that "with 95 percent confidence $1 \leq \mu_X \leq 5$" is as follows. If we could obtain a large number of samples of size $N = 100$, we would obtain many different point estimates of μ_X. If we calculated the interval $\overline{X} \pm 2\sigma_X/\sqrt{N}$ corresponding to each sample's estimate of μ_X, we would have a number of interval statements such as

1. $1 \leq \mu_X \leq 5$ if $\overline{X} = 3$
2. $1.5 \leq \mu_X \leq 5.5$ if $\overline{X} = 3.5$
3. $.7 \leq \mu_X \leq 4.7$ if $\overline{X} = 2.7$

Some of these intervals can be expected to exclude the true mean. However, over a large number of such calculations, 95 percent of the intervals obtained can be expected to contain the true mean.

Confidence intervals can be used to test hypotheses. Consider the null hypothesis that the true mean is equal to zero. For the sample mean of 3 in the above example, we see that the null hypothesis is unlikely to be true, and we reject the null hypothesis (at the 5 percent level of significance) in favor of the alternative—rather vague—hypothesis that the mean is not 0. Note that the null hypothesis has been rejected because it is unlikely that we would have obtained a sample mean of 3 if the true mean had been 0.

As a shortcut for testing the null hypothesis that the mean is 0, we can calculate $Z = \overline{X}/(\sigma_X/\sqrt{N})$. This statistic will be normally distributed with a variance of 1 and, if the null hypothesis is true, a mean of 0. If the statistic is greater than 1.96 in absolute value, we can reject the null hypothesis at the 5 percent level, while if it is greater than 2.57, we can reject it at the 1 percent level (a more powerful statement statistically). Suppose, for example, that we knew that for a given sample the Z value was 2.13. By looking at Table 1 at the back of the book, under the .03 column and on the 2.1 row, we would find that the probability that Z is greater than or equal to 2.13 is equal to .0166. Likewise the probability that Z is less than or equal to -2.13 is also .0166. Taking both into account, we would associate a .0332, or 3.32 percent, significance level with Z. Since Z is greater than 1.96, we can reject the null hypothesis that the true mean of the distribution is zero at the 5 percent level.

We have assumed that the variance of X is known, but it is more likely that the variance will not be known. We therefore need to replace the unknown variance σ_X^2 with the estimated sample variance s_X^2. (Later we will refer to the true error variance as estimated by s^2.) The appropriate test statistic is obtained by subtracting the true mean from the sample mean and dividing the difference by the sample standard deviation:

$$\frac{\overline{X} - \mu_X}{s_X/\sqrt{N}}$$

When we wish to test the null hypothesis that $\mu_X = 0$, this simplifies to

$$\frac{\overline{X}}{s_X/\sqrt{N}}$$

Since this statistic follows a t distribution, we shall call it a t *statistic*.

The t statistic can be used to construct confidence intervals in a manner analogous to the normal distribution. A 95 percent confidence interval would be

$$\overline{X} \pm \frac{t_c s_X}{\sqrt{N}} \tag{2.15}$$

where t_c is the critical value of the t distribution (determined from Table 3 at the back of the book) based on the number of degrees of freedom and the desired level of significance. The number of degrees of freedom equals the number of data points minus the number of constraints placed on the data by the statistical procedure being used. As an example of how to calculate t_c, we must select a value from the table of the t distribution, so that 2.5 percent of the t distribution lies outside either end of the corresponding interval. This is shown in Fig. 2.11 for a t distribution with 60 degrees of freedom. Since we wish 2.5 percent to be in each tail, we select $t_c = 2.00$, reading in the column labeled .05.

To test the hypothesis that the true mean equals a given value μ_X^*, we specify the null hypothesis $\mu_X = \mu_X^*$ and the alternative hypothesis that $\mu_X \neq \mu_X^*$, as well as a level of significance. Using the critical value of the t distribution, we calculate the appropriate confidence interval. If the hypothesized mean μ_X^* lies outside the confidence interval, we reject the null hypothesis. If it lies inside, we fail to reject.

Alternative hypotheses need not be of the two-tailed variety, in which case the true mean may be negative or positive. There are many occasions when *one-tailed tests* are desirable. This involves only minor adjustments in the construction of the confidence intervals. For example, suppose we wish to test the hypothesis that $\mu_X = 0$ but have strong reasons to believe that if μ_X is not equal to 0, then it is positive. Here a one-tailed test is appropriate. The test is as before, but the critical value t_c is chosen so that 5 percent of the distribution lies in one tail, as shown in Fig. 2.12. In the case where the number of degrees of freedom is 60, we read the critical value to be 1.671 from the column of the t table labeled .10.

To illustrate, suppose a sample of 64 SAT mathematics test scores has a mean of 520 and an estimated standard deviation of 100. We wish to test the null hypothesis that the population mean of the SAT scores is 500 at the 5 percent significance level. To do so, we find the critical value of the t distribution with

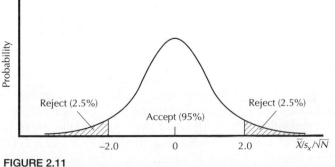

FIGURE 2.11
Two-tailed test.

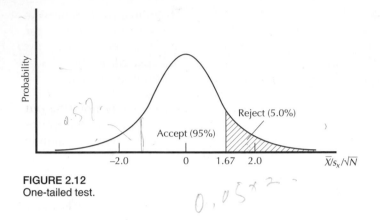

FIGURE 2.12
One-tailed test.

63 degrees of freedom is approximately 2.0. It follows that a 95 percent confidence interval is given by

$$520 \pm 2.00 \left(\frac{100}{8} \right) = 520 \pm 25 = (495, 545)$$

Since 500 lies within the 95 percent confidence interval, we fail to reject the hypothesis that the population mean is equal to 500.

2.5.1   Type I and Type II Errors

The choice of level of significance, usually 1 or 5 percent, corresponding to the choice of the size of confidence interval, is best understood by considering what kinds of errors might be made when hypothesis tests are made. Suppose we test the null hypothesis that $\beta = 0$ and at a 5 percent level of significance *reject* the null hypothesis. It is possible that we will have incorrectly rejected the null hypothesis. This mistake is called a *Type I error,* and the probability of its occurrence is .05. Now suppose we collect a different data set and find a 95 percent confidence interval between $-.02$ and .26. Now we fail to reject the null hypothesis that $\beta = 0$ and thus implicitly accept it as true. However, it is possible that we are making a mistake in this case. The true value of β might be .05, in which case we would have accepted the null hypothesis $\beta = 0$ when it was in fact false. This mistake, called a *Type II error,* is a likely possibility since the confidence interval contains a large number of points.

Suppose we change the level of significance from 5 percent to 1 percent. Then the 95 percent confidence for β will increase to 99 percent. This implies that the probability of incorrectly rejecting the null hypothesis (Type I error) falls from 5 percent to 1 percent, but at the same time the probability of a Type II error increases. Thus, in selecting a level of significance, one faces a trade-off: as we lower the probability of Type I error, we increase the probability of

Type II error. The choice to be made depends on the particular problem, but in econometrics it is usual to choose a rather low level of significance and a low probability of Type I error. ⫮ .

2.5.2   p-Values

Most statistical analyses report tests of statistical significance by pointing out which coefficients are significant at the 1 percent, 5 percent, or other appropriate significance level. However, it is sometimes useful to provide additional information in the form of a *p-value (probability value)*. A p-value describes the exact significance level associated with a particular econometric result. Thus, a p-value of .07 indicates that a coefficient is statistically significant at the .07 level (but not at the 5 percent level). In the context of a two-tailed test using a normal distribution, this means that 7 percent of the *t* distribution lies outside the interval plus or minus 1.96 standard deviations from the mean.

Typically the null hypothesis being tested will be the hypothesis that a particular regression coefficient is equal to 0. The p-value therefore is the probability of getting data that generate a coefficient estimate as large as or larger than the estimated coefficient, given that the null hypothesis of a zero coefficient is true. The smaller the p-value for a given study, the more surprising it will be to see such a result if the null hypothesis is valid. Correspondingly, a large p-value indicates that the data are consistent with the null hypothesis.

The p-value measures the likelihood of a Type I error (as discussed in Section 2.5.1), the probability of incorrectly rejecting a correct null hypothesis. The higher the p-value, the more likely it is that we will err in rejecting the null hypothesis; the lower the p-value, the more comfortable we can feel in rejecting it.

2.5.3   The Power of a Test

A high p-value signifies that a coefficient is not significantly different from zero; as a result the researcher fails to reject the null hypothesis that the coefficient is zero. What are the reasons for this "failure"? One obvious reason could be that the null hypothesis is true. However, an alternative possibility is that the null hypothesis is false but the particular data set used for the test happens to be consistent with the null. (A third possibility—that the model is invalid—will be discussed later in the book.) The statistical concept that helps us evaluate the importance of the second explanation is the *power* of the test. *Power is the probability of rejecting the null hypothesis when it is in fact false.* For any particular null hypothesis, the power is therefore given by 1 minus the probability there will be a Type II error, i.e., 1 minus the probability that one will accept the null hypothesis as true when it is in fact false.

Power depends not only on the size of the effect that has been measured, but also on the size of the data set being studied. Other things being the same, the larger the effect and the larger the sample, the more powerful the test.

When a statistical analysis with relatively low power fails to show a significant p-value, one should not conclude definitively that there is no effect. Rather, one must allow for the fact that the study may be inconclusive because the data set is not sufficient to allow one to distinguish between the null and alternative hypotheses.

A summary of the relationship between Type I and Type II errors and the power of a statistical test is provided in the table below denoting the null hypothesis as H_0. A Type I error occurs when the null hypothesis is true but is rejected by our test; the probability that this will happen is given by the p-value. A Type II error occurs when the null hypothesis is false but we fail to reject it. Its probability is equal to 1 minus the power of the statistical test.

POWER AND TYPE I AND TYPE II ERRORS

Decision	H_0 True	H_0 False
Fail to reject H_0	Correct decision	Type II error (1 − power)
Reject H_0	Type I error (p-value)	Correct decision

Example 2.4 Job Application Success   Suppose that a job applicant pool contains 10,000 men and 10,000 women and that we want to know whether there is a significant difference between the success of women and that of men in obtaining jobs.[5] For a particular sample of 50 men and 50 women, the pass rate was 58 percent for women (29 of 50) and 38 percent for men, so that the differential was 20 percent. The population distribution of differences in pass rates approximates a normal distribution, with a mean of 20 percentage points and a standard deviation of 9.7 percentage points.[6]

Consider the null hypothesis that the men and women have the identical application success rate. With a normal distribution, a 95 percent interval for the pass rate differential is given by $20 \pm 1.96*9.7 = 20 \pm 19.0 = (1.0, 39.0)$. Differentials that are less than 1 percentage point or greater than 39 percentage points have about a 5 percent chance of occurring. The p-value associated with a differential of 0 is somewhat less than 5 percent; in fact, the probability of obtaining a differential less than or equal to 0 (and greater than or equal to 40) is given by the probability that a normal distribution with mean 0 and a standard deviation of 1 takes on values less than $-20/9.7 = -2.06$, or greater than 2.06, which is 4 percent.

---

[5] This example is based on D. Kaye and D. Freedman, "Reference Guide on Statistics," in *Reference Manual on Scientific Evidence* (Washington D.C.: Federal Judicial Center, 1994).

[6] The standard deviation is determined as the standard deviation of a difference in two proportions and for a large population is equal to $[.58 (1 - .58)/50 + .38 (1 - .38)/50]^{.5} = .096$. See, for example, D. Freedman et al., *Statistics* (New York: Norton, 1991), p. 67.

Since the p-value is less than 5 percent, we reject the null hypothesis of equal success rates at the 5 percent level of significance. Because we have just barely rejected the null, it might be interesting to ask about the power of the statistical test. To evaluate the power, we need to specify the alternative hypothesis explicitly. Suppose the alternative is that 55 percent of the women would pass, as would 45 percent of the men, a differential of 10 percentage points. With a normal distribution having a standard deviation of 9.7, only sample differentials larger than approximately 9.7*1.96, or 19.0 points, or smaller than −19.0 points will be deemed to be statistically significant at the 5 percent level. For a normal distribution that is centered on 10 percent (reflecting the alternative hypothesis), we can determine that approximately 18 percent of the distribution lies above 19.0 percentage points and that only a very small percent lies below −19.0. Therefore, the power of the test against the alternative just specified is 18 percent. We see, therefore, that because the test has somewhat limited power against this particular alternative, the probability of rejecting the null hypothesis when the alternative is correct is only 18 percent; there is, of course, an 82 percent chance of accepting the null hypothesis when the alternative is correct.

Now suppose that the sample has doubled in size, from 50 men and 50 women to 100 men and 100 women, and that the pass rates remain the same: 58 percent for women and 38 percent for men. Then the estimated standard deviation of the population falls from 9.7 percentage points to 6.9 percentage points. The 95 percent confidence interval for the pass rate differential is 20 ± 1.96*6.9 = 20 ± 13.5 = (6.5, 33.5). Now the p-value associated with a differential of 0 is about .3 percent, which measures the probability that the actual differential of 20 percentage points (or a greater one) could have resulted from a world in which men and women had equal pass rates. The power of the test has now changed as well. With this larger sample, differential pass rates larger than 6.9*1.96, or 13.5 points, or smaller than −13.5 points will be significant. With a distribution centered at 10 percentage points (associated with the 55 percent, 45 percent alternative hypothesis), the probability that such differential pass rates will occur is the probability that a normal distribution with mean 10 and standard deviation 6.9 will be greater than 13.5 or less than −13.5, which is approximately 31 percent. Therefore, a doubling of the sample size has increased the power of the test against this particular alternative from 18 to 31 percent.

2.6 DESCRIPTIVE STATISTICS

A *histogram* is a useful device for describing the data associated with a particular value. A histogram tabulates the frequency distribution of the data. It typically divides the distance between the minimum and maximum values of the data series into equal intervals and then tabulates the number of observations that fall within each interval.

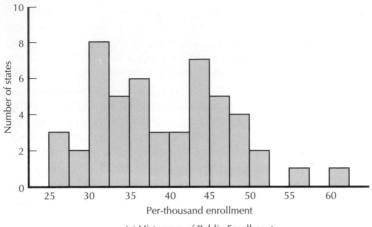

(a) Histogram of Public Enrollment

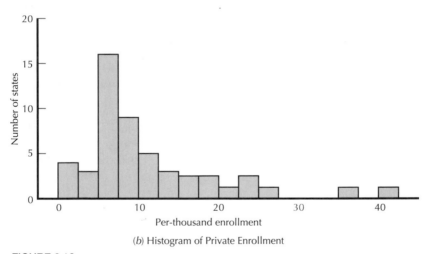

(b) Histogram of Private Enrollment

FIGURE 2.13
Public and private enrollment.

Figure 2.13a presents a histogram that describes the number of individuals per thousand of population enrolled in institutions of public higher education (PUBLIC) in each of the 50 states in the academic year 1984–1985. The corresponding histogram for private per-thousand enrollments (PRIVATE) appears in Fig. 2.13b. In the first figure we see that the three states at the low end of the spectrum enrolled between 25 and 27.5 per thousand in public education (the low was Georgia), while one state (Arizona) enrolled somewhat over 60 per thousand. With respect to private enrollment, the lowest state had no private institutions (Wyoming) while the enrollment in Massachusetts was over 40 per thousand.[7]

Earlier in this chapter we focused on the mean and the standard deviation as descriptive measures of the properties of a data series. The histogram tends to emphasize the minimum and maximum, as well as the distribution of the individual data points. In addition, there are other summary measures of data series that can provide useful descriptive devices generally and which can be particularly helpful when one wishes to evaluate whether a data series approximates a particular probability distribution such as the normal.

The *median* is a measure of central tendency which is more robust to errors or unusually extreme data points than is the mean. For an odd number of observations, the median is the middle observation when the data points are ranked from low to high (or high to low). When the number of observations is even, the median usually is calculated by convention to be the average of the two middle observations.

Skewness is a statistic that provides useful information about the symmetry of a probability distribution. The skewness statistic S for a variable X is given by

$$S = (1/N)\Sigma x_i^3/s^3$$

where s is the standard deviation of X. S is equal to zero for all symmetric distributions including the normal. For nonsymmetric distributions, the skewness statistic is positive when the upper tail of the distribution is thicker than the lower tail, and negative when the lower tail is thicker.

Kurtosis provides a measure of the "thickness" of the tails of a distribution. The kurtosis statistic, K, is given by

$$K = (1/N)\Sigma x_i^4/s^4$$

For a normal distribution K is equal to 3. When the tails of the distribution are thicker than the normal, K will be greater than 3, and vice versa.

It often is useful to test whether a given data series approximates the normal distribution. This can be evaluated informally by checking to see whether the mean and the median are nearly equal, whether the skewness is approximately zero, and whether the kurtosis is close to 3. A more formal test of normality is given by the Jarque-Bera statistic:

$$JB = [N/6][S^2 + (K - 3)^2/4]$$

skewness *kurtosis.*   If normaly S=0 and K-3=0

[7] For further details, see J. Quigley and D. Rubinfeld, "Public Choices in Public Higher Education," in C. Clotfelter and M. Rothschild, eds., *Studies of Supply and Demand in Higher Education* (Chicago: University of Chicago Press, 1993), pp. 243–283.

* For small distributions, need to test if error is normally distributed

The JB statistic follows a chi-square distribution with 2 degrees of freedom. If the JB statistic is greater than the critical value of the chi square, we reject the null hypothesis of normality.

To illustrate these various statistical measures, we have tabulated each of them for the enrollment data series, PUBLIC and PRIVATE, described previously:

	PUBLIC	PRIVATE
Mean	39.29	10.53
Median	38.84	7.84
Standard deviation	8.17	8.24
Skewness	0.38	1.78
Kurtosis	2.61	6.24
Jarque-Bera	1.54	48.26

The public enrollment series has a median which is only slightly lower than the mean and a skewness which is close to zero. As is also suggested by the histogram in Fig. 2.13a, the series is reasonably symmetric. The private enrollment series, by contrast, clearly is not. It has a median which is substantially below the mean, a typical result for a series with a long upper tail. Further, the skewness statistic of 1.78 is substantially greater than 0.

Does either series reasonably approximate a normal distribution? For PRIVATE, the answer clearly is no, since the kurtosis of 6.24 is substantially greater than 3 (thicker than normal tails), and the Jarque-Bera statistic of 48.26 is substantially greater than the critical value of the chi-square distribution, 5.99 (at the 5 percent level of significance). However, we cannot reject the assumption that PUBLIC is approximately normal. While the histogram does not directly mirror the normal, we must take into account the fact that with only 50 observations we would not expect the approximation to be extremely close. Further, the kurtosis of 2.61 is close to 3, and the Jarque-Bera statistic of 1.54 is not significantly different from 0 at the 5 percent significance level.

APPENDIX 2.1 The Properties of the Expectations Operator

This appendix reviews some of the useful properties of the expectations operator.

Result 1 $$E(aX + b) = aE(X) + b \qquad (A2.1)$$

where X is a random variable, and a and b are constants.

Result 2[8] $$E[(aX)^2] = a^2 E(X^2) \qquad (A2.2)$$

---

[8] Note that it is *not true* that $E(X^2) = [E(X)]^2$. To see this in the simplest case, let $X = 1$ where a coin appears heads and $X = 0$ when it appears tails. Then for a fair coin, $p_1 = \frac{1}{2}$ and $p_0 = \frac{1}{2}$, so that $E(X^2) = \frac{1}{2}(1^2) + \frac{1}{2}(0^2) = \frac{1}{2}(1) = \frac{1}{2}$. However, $E(X) = \frac{1}{2}(1) + \frac{1}{2}(0) = \frac{1}{2}$, and $[E(X)]^2 = \frac{1}{4}$.

Result 3 $$\text{Var }(aX + b) = a^2 \text{ Var }(X) \tag{A2.3}$$

PROOF   By definition

$$\text{Var }(aX + b) = E[(aX + b) - E(aX + b)]^2$$

But $E(aX + b) - aE(X) + b$, using Result 1. Therefore,

$$
\begin{aligned}
\text{Var }(aX + b) &= E[aX - E(aX)]^2 = E[aX - aE(X)]^2 \\
&= E[a(X - E(X))]^2 = a^2 E[X - E(X)]^2 \qquad \text{by Result 2} \\
&= a^2 \text{ Var }(X)
\end{aligned}
$$

Now, we can use the expectations operator to prove some results concerning the covariance between two random variables.

Result 4   If X and Y are random variables, then

$$E(X + Y) = E(X) + E(Y) \tag{A2.4}$$

Result 5 $\text{Var }(X + Y) = \text{Var }(X) + \text{Var }(Y) + 2 \text{ Cov }(X, Y)$ (A2.5)

PROOF $\begin{aligned}[t] \text{Var }(X + Y) &= E[(X + Y) - E(X + Y)]^2 \\
&= E[(X + Y) - E(X) - E(Y)]^2 \qquad \text{by Result 4} \\
&= E[(X - E(X)) + (Y - E(Y))]^2 \\
&= E[X - E(X)]^2 + E[Y - E(Y)]^2 \\
&\quad + 2E[(X - E(X))(Y - E(Y))] \\
&= \text{Var }(X) + \text{Var }(Y) + 2 \text{ Cov }(X, Y)
\end{aligned}$

Result 6   If X and Y are independent, then $E(XY) = E(X)E(Y)$.

Result 7   If X and Y are independent, then $\text{Cov }(X, Y) = 0$.

PROOF $\begin{aligned}[t] \text{Cov }(X, Y) &= E[X - E(X)][Y - E(Y)] \\
&= E[XY - E(X)Y - XE(Y) + E(X)E(Y)] \\
&= E(XY) - E(X)E(Y) \\
&= 0 \qquad \text{by Result 6}
\end{aligned}$

Result 8
$$\text{Var}\,(\overline{X}) = \frac{\sigma_X^2}{N}$$

where $\overline{X}$ is the sample mean of a random variable with mean μ and variance σ_X^2.

PROOF $\quad \text{Var}\,(\overline{X}) = \text{Var}\left(\dfrac{1}{N}\sum_{i=1}^{N} X_i\right) \qquad$ by the definition of $\overline{X}$

$$= \left(\frac{1}{N}\right)^2 \text{Var}\left(\sum_{i=1}^{N} X_i\right) \qquad \text{by Result 3}$$

$$= \left(\frac{1}{N}\right)^2 \sum_{i=1}^{N} \text{Var}\,(X_i) \qquad \begin{array}{l}\text{by Results 5 and 7 and the assumption that}\\ \text{each } X_i \text{ is independent of each other } X_i\end{array}$$

$$= \left(\frac{1}{N}\right)^2 \sum_{i=1}^{N} \sigma_X^2 = \left(\frac{1}{N}\right)^2 (N\sigma_X^2) = \frac{\sigma_X^2}{N}$$

Result 8 shows that the variance of the estimator of the mean $\overline{X}$ falls as the sample size increases. Thus, with more and more information, we get more and more accuracy in our estimates of the mean μ.

Result 9
$$E\left[\frac{1}{N-1}\sum_{i=1}^{N}(X_i - \overline{X})^2\right] = \sigma_X^2$$

PROOF $\quad$ First, consider the term involving the summation operator:

$$\sum_{i=1}^{N}(X_i - \overline{X})^2 = \sum_{i=1}^{N}[(X_i - \mu) - (\overline{X} - \mu)]^2$$

$$= \sum_{i=1}^{N}[(X_i - \mu)^2 + (\overline{X} - \mu)^2 - 2(X_i - \mu)(\overline{X} - \mu)]$$

$$= \sum_{i=1}^{N}(X_i - \mu)^2 + \sum_{i=1}^{N}(\overline{X} - \mu)^2 - 2(\overline{X} - \mu)\sum_{i=1}^{N}(X_i - \mu)$$

$$= \sum_{i=1}^{N}(X_i - \mu)^2 + N(\overline{X} - \mu)^2 - 2(\overline{X} - \mu)N(\overline{X} - \mu)$$

$$\text{since } \sum_{i=1}^{N}(X_i - \mu) = \sum_{i=1}^{N}X_i - N\mu = N(\overline{X} - \mu)$$

$$= \sum_{i=1}^{N}(X_i - \mu)^2 - N(\overline{X} - \mu)^2$$

Therefore, taking expected values gives

$$E\left[\frac{1}{N-1}\sum_{i=1}^{N}(X_i - \overline{X})^2\right] = E\left[\frac{1}{N-1}\sum_{i=1}^{N}(X_i - \mu)^2 - \frac{N}{N-1}(\overline{X} - \mu)^2\right]$$

$$= \frac{1}{N-1}E\left[\sum_{i=1}^{N}(X_i - \mu)^2\right] - \frac{N}{N-1}E\left[(\overline{X} - \mu)^2\right]$$

$$= \frac{1}{N-1}\sum_{i=1}^{N}E[(X_i - \mu)^2] - \frac{N}{N-1}\frac{\sigma_X^2}{N} \quad \text{by Results 3 and 8}$$

$$= \frac{1}{N-1}N\sigma_X^2 - \frac{N}{N-1}\frac{\sigma_X^2}{N} \quad\quad\quad \text{by the definition of variance}$$

$$= \frac{N}{N-1}\sigma_X^2 - \frac{1}{N-1}\sigma_X^2 = \sigma_X^2$$

APPENDIX 2.2 Maximum-Likelihood Estimation

Maximum likelihood estimation focuses on the fact that different populations generate different samples; any one sample being scrutinized is more likely to have come from some populations than from others. For example, if one were sampling coin tosses and a sample mean of .5 were obtained (representing half heads and half tails), the most likely population from which the sample was drawn would be a population with a mean of .5. Figure A2.1 illustrates a more general case in which a sample $(X_1, X_2, \ldots, X_8)$ is known to be drawn from a normal population with given variance but unknown mean. Assume that observations come from either distribution A or distribution B. If the true population were B, the probability that we would have obtained the sample shown

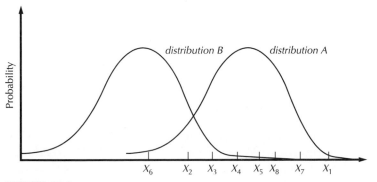

FIGURE A2.1
Maximum-likelihood estimation.

would be quite small. However, if the true population were A, the probability would be substantially larger. Thus, the observations "select" the population A as the most likely to have generated the observed data.

We define the maximum-likelihood estimator of a parameter β as the value of $\hat{\beta}$ which would most likely generate the observed sample observations Y_1, $Y_2, \ldots, Y_N$. In general, if Y_i is normally distributed and each of the Y's is drawn independently, the maximum-likelihood estimator maximizes

$$p(Y_1)p(Y_2) \cdots p(Y_N)$$

where each p represents a probability associated with the normal distribution. Thus, the calculated maximum-likelihood estimate is a function of the *particular* sample of Y's chosen. A different sample would result in a different maximum-likelihood estimate.

$p(Y_1)p(Y_2) \cdots p(Y_n)$ is often referred to as the *likelihood function*. The likelihood function depends not only on the sample values but also on the unknown parameters of the problem. In describing the likelihood function, we often think of the unknown parameters as varying while the Y's are fixed. Maximum-likelihood estimation involves a search over alternative parameter estimators to find those estimators which most likely would generate the sample.

To see how the principle of maximum likelihood can be applied, we note that if X is normally distributed with mean μ and standard deviation σ (Section 2.4.1),

$$p(X = X_i) = \left[\frac{1}{2\pi\sigma^2}\right]^{1/2} \exp\left[-\frac{(x_i - \mu)^2}{2\sigma^2}\right]$$

where exp represents the exponential function. The likelihood function is then given by

$$L(X, \mu, \sigma^2) = \left[\frac{1}{2\pi\sigma^2}\right]^{N/2} \exp\left[-\frac{\Sigma(x_i - \mu)^2}{2\sigma^2}\right]$$

Taking the logarithm of both sides yields the log-likelihood function:

$$\ln L = -N \ln \sigma - N \ln(2\pi)^{1/2} - (1/2\sigma^2) \Sigma(X_i - \mu)^2$$

To obtain the maximum-likelihood estimator of the mean μ, we note that μ enters only in the last term, which is preceded by a negative sign. To maximize the value of the likelihood function, therefore, we minimize $\Sigma(X_i - \mu)^2$, which is accomplished by the least-squares estimator $\overline{X}$, the sample mean. It follows that if X is normally distributed, the sample mean is the maximum-likelihood estimator of the population mean.

To get the maximum-likelihood estimator of σ^2, we differentiate $\ln L$ with respect to σ and equate the result to 0, obtaining

$$-N/\sigma - 1/2 \ \Sigma(X_i - \mu)^2(-2/\sigma^3) = 0$$

Multiplying both sides by $-\sigma^3/N$, we get as an estimator of the population variance

$$\hat{\sigma}^2 = \Sigma(X_i - \mu)^2/N$$

This is a consistent but biased estimator of the variance.

EXERCISES

A number of the following questions pertain to the data set in Table 2.1. Data were collected from a survey of econometrics students, all of whom responded. The variables are defined as

$$\text{RENT} = \text{total monthly rent in dollars}$$

$$\text{NO} = \text{number of persons in apartment}$$

$$\text{RM} = \text{number of rooms}$$

$$\text{SEX} = \begin{cases} 1 & \text{if female} \\ 0 & \text{if male} \end{cases}$$

$$\text{DIST} = \text{distance from center of campus in blocks}$$

$$\text{RPP} = \frac{\text{RENT}}{\text{NO}} = \text{rent per person}$$

2.1 RPP is a measure of rent paid per person. Show that $\overline{(\text{RENT/NO})} = \overline{\text{RPP}}$ is not equal to $\overline{\text{RENT}}/\overline{\text{NO}}$.

2.2 The results from Exercise 2.1 suggest that in general $E(Y/X) \neq E(Y)/E(X)$. Show that for the following example $E(Y/X)$ is positive and $E(Y)/E(X)$ is negative:

$$X = -4 \qquad Y = -8 \qquad \text{Prob} = \tfrac{1}{2}$$

$$X = 2 \qquad Y = 60 \qquad \text{Prob} = \tfrac{1}{2}$$

2.3 Assume that RPP is distributed normally with mean μ_{RPP} and variance σ_{RPP}^2. Test the hypothesis that $\mu_{\text{RPP}} = \$135$ at the 5 percent level of significance if (a) $\sigma_{\text{RPP}}^2 = 2,150$ or (b) σ_{RPP}^2 is unknown. Pay particular attention to your choice of test statistics.

2.4 Now assume that RPP among males is distributed normally with mean μ_{RPP}^m and variance $(\sigma_{\text{RPP}}^m)^2$. RPP among females is also assumed to be distributed normally with mean μ_{RPP}^f and the variance $(\sigma_{\text{RPP}}^f)^2$. Test the hypothesis that $\mu_{\text{RPP}}^m = \mu_{\text{RPP}}^f$ at the 5 percent level of significance when you are given that $\sigma_{\text{RPP}}^{2f} = \sigma_{\text{RPP}}^{2m} = 1,681$.

2.5 (Difficult) Repeat Exercise 2.4, assuming that $\sigma_{\text{RPP}}^{2f} = \sigma_{\text{RPP}}^{2m}$ but that their common value is unknown.

For female (1): M=164.169
s= 34.3206

For male (0) M=126.3523
s=46.3209

TABLE 2.1   N=32
RENTAL DATA

RENT	NO	RM	SEX	DIST	RPP = RENT/NO
$230	2	2	1	7	$115.00
245	2	2	0	24	122.50
190	1	1	1	0	190.00
203	4	2	0	24	50.75
450	3	2	1	4	150.00
280	2	2	1	6	140.00
310	2	2	0	8	155.00
185	2	1	0	8	92.50
218	2	2	0	42	109.00
185	1	1	1	8	185.00
340	2	2	1	3	170.00
230	2	2	0	60	115.00
245	1	1	1	24	245.00
200	2	2	0	36	100.00
125	1	1	0	3	125.00
300	3	3	0	9	100.00
350	2	2	0	16	175.00
100	1	1	0	5	100.00
280	2	2	1	6	140.00
175	2	1	0	4	87.50
310	2	2	0	10	155.00
450	3	2	0	5	150.00
160	2	1	0	12	80.00
285	1	1	0	4	285.00
255	2	2	0	8	127.50
340	4	2	0	3	85.00
300	2	2	0	11	150.00
880	6	6	1	6	146.67
800	5	5	1	10	160.00
450	3	3	0	5	150.00
630	6	6	0	24	105.00
480	3	3	0	24	160.00

2.6 In part (a) of Exercise 2.3 we assumed that RPP was distributed normally with unknown mean σ_{RPP} and known variance $\sigma^2_{RPP} = 2{,}150$. Assuming, as we do in part (b), that σ^2_{RPP} is unknown, test at the 5 percent level of significance that $\sigma^2_{RPP} = 2{,}150$. *Hint:* Under the hypothesis that $\sigma^2_{RPP} = 2{,}150$, find the distribution $(N - 1)s^2/2{,}150$, where

$$s^2 = \frac{1}{N-1} \sum_{i=1}^{N} (RPP_i - \overline{RPP})^2$$

2.7 In Exercise 2.6 we assumed that $(\sigma^m_{RPP})^2 = (\sigma^f_{RPP})^2$. Test this equality at the 5 percent level of significance.

2.8 Assume that X is a normally distributed random variable with mean μ_X and variance σ_X^2. Let $Z = (\overline{X} - \mu_X)/\sigma_X$ be a new random variable. Prove that Z is normally distributed with mean 0 and a variance of $1/N$.

2.9 Assume that X is normally distributed with mean 10 and variance 625. Find the probability that $X \geq 30$.

2.10 A coin is flipped six times. You wish to test the hypothesis that the probability of heads = probability of tails = $\frac{1}{2}$. How do you proceed?

2.11 The sample correlation coefficient between two variables X and Y is denoted (X, Y) and is given by

$$r_{XY} = \frac{\sum_{i=1}^{N}(X_i - \overline{X})(Y_i - \overline{Y})}{\sqrt{\sum_{i=1}^{N}(X_i - \overline{X})^2}\sqrt{\sum_{i=1}^{N}(Y_i - \overline{Y})^2}}$$

Show that if one estimates the regressions

$$Y = a + bX$$

$$X = A + BY$$

the product of the estimates for b and B will equal r_{XY}^2.

2.12 If X is normally distributed with mean μ and variance σ^2, find a transformation of X that has the chi-square distribution with 1 degree of freedom.

2.13 Show that $E(X)^2 = (E(X))^2$ occurs only if X takes on only one value with probability 1.

2.14 Suppose that ε_1 and ε_2 are independent random variables, each with mean 0 and variance σ^2. Suppose you observe X_1 and X_2, which are related to ε_1 and ε_2 as follows:

$$X_1 = \varepsilon_1 \qquad X_2 = \rho\varepsilon_1 + \sqrt{(1 - \rho^2)}\,\varepsilon_2$$

where ρ is a constant, $-1 \leq \rho \leq 1$.

    (a) What is the covariance between X_1 and X_2? The correlation?

    (b) What is the mean of the average $\overline{X} = (X_1 + X_2)/2$ of X_1 and X_2?

    (c) What is the variance of the average $\overline{X}$? Evaluate the variance of $\rho = -1$, $-\frac{1}{2}$, $-\frac{1}{4}$, 0, $\frac{1}{4}$, $\frac{1}{2}$, 1. What do you conclude about the precision of sample averages when the underlying data are not independent random variables?

2.15 Suppose you are a farmer interested in the amount of rainfall on your fields. Let X denote annual rainfall in inches and (by your model) suppose that X is log-normally distributed—that $\log_e X$ is normally distributed with mean μ_X. The observed amounts of rain for the 10-year period from 1988 to 1997 are given as follows:

Year	Rainfall	Year	Rainfall
1988	51.06	1993	35.48
1989	30.06	1994	30.42
1990	31.81	1995	33.09
1991	74.46	1996	30.39
1992	32.41	1997	41.08

(a) Estimate the mean μ_X and variance σ_X^2 of $\log_e X$.

(b) Use a chi-square statistic to test the hypothesis that rainfall amounts vary 20 percent per year (i.e., that the log variance σ_X^2 equals .04).

2.16 Using the rental data in Table 2.1, calculate the mean, median, skewness, and kurtosis of the variable RPP. Using those statistics describe the distribution of rent per capita as fully as possible.

CHAPTER 3

THE TWO-VARIABLE
REGRESSION MODEL

In Chapter 1 we described the method of least squares as one of a number of possible means by which a curve can be fitted to data. Our concern was parameter estimation rather than the statistics of model testing. In this chapter we discuss statistical testing of the least-squares regression model with one dependent variable and one independent variable. First we describe the assumptions underlying the model, and then we analyze the statistical properties of the least-squares estimators. We will see that under certain assumptions least-squares estimators are unbiased, consistent, and efficient. The distribution of the estimated parameters will then be used to construct confidence intervals and to test hypotheses about the model. To complete the chapter we introduce R^2, a measure of the fit of the regression model.

3.1 THE MODEL

To explore the probabilistic nature of the regression model, we allow for the fact that for a given observed value of X (the independent variable), we may observe many possible values of Y (the dependent variable). As an example consider the consumption of an individual who receives an income of $20,000 each year. Because the amount of money spent on food is likely to vary each year, we assume that for each observation X (income), observations on Y (food purchases) will differ randomly. To describe this situation formally, we add a random "error" component to the model, writing it as

$$Y_i = \alpha + \beta X_i + \varepsilon_i \tag{3.1}$$

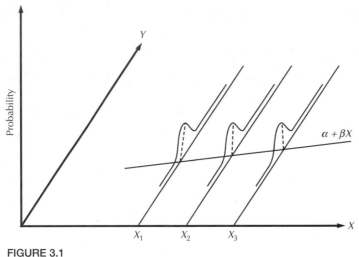

FIGURE 3.1
Two-variable regression model.

where Y is a *random variable*, X is fixed or *nonstochastic*, and ε is a *random error term* whose value is based on an underlying probability distribution. (We have switched our notation to use Greek letters α and β to represent the intercept and slope of the line, i.e., the regression parameters, since our model now contains a random error term.)

The error term may arise through the interplay of several forces.[1] First, errors appear because the model is a simplification of reality. We assume, for example, that price is the sole determinant of the demand for a product. In fact, several omitted variables related to demand, e.g., individual tastes, population, income, and weather, may be included in the error term. If these omitted effects are small, it is reasonable to assume that the error term is random. A second source of error is associated with the collection and measurement of the data. Economic and business data frequently are difficult to measure. For example, an individual firm may not be willing to provide explicit cost information, so that error-free data on costs will not be obtained. Given these sources of error, our decision to represent the relationship in Eq. (3.1) as a *stochastic* one should be clear. For every value X there exists a probability distribution of ε and therefore a probability distribution of the Y's. This is depicted graphically in Fig. 3.1.

We are now in a position to specify fully the *two-variable linear regression model* by listing its important assumptions.

1. The relationship between Y and X is linear, as given by Eq. (3.1).
2. The X's are nonstochastic variables whose values are fixed.

fixed in repeated samples.

[1] The error term must be distinguished from the *residual* ($\hat{\varepsilon}_i = Y_i - \hat{Y}_i$), or the deviation of the dependent variable observation from its fitted value. Errors are associated with the *true* regression model, while residuals arise from the *estimation* process.

3. The error has zero expected value: $E(\varepsilon) = 0$.
4. The error term has constant variance for all observations, i.e.,
$E(\varepsilon^2) = \sigma^2$.
5. The random variables ε_i are statistically independent. Thus,
$E(\varepsilon_i \varepsilon_j) = 0$ for all $i \neq j$.
6. The error term is normally distributed.

Assumptions 1 through 5 constitute the *classical linear regression model*.

Equation (3.1) is often termed the *specification* of the model. Note that we have assumed that Y is related to X rather than vice versa. Also, we have restricted ourselves to one right-hand variable. The assumption that each X is fixed is equivalent to the assumption that each independent variable in question is controlled by the researcher, who can change its value in accordance with experimental objectives. Such an assumption is unrealistic in the study of most business and economic problems; it has been made for expositional purposes.

The assumption that the error term has zero expected value is made in part as a matter of convenience. To see this, assume that the average effect of the omitted variables is equal to α'; that is, $E(\varepsilon_i) = \alpha'$. Then we can write the two-variable model as

$$Y_i = \alpha + \beta X_i + \varepsilon_i + (\alpha' - \alpha') = (\alpha + \alpha') + \beta X_i + (\varepsilon_i - \alpha')$$

$$= \alpha^* + \beta X_i + \varepsilon_i^*$$

where
$$\alpha^* = (\alpha + \alpha') \qquad \varepsilon_i^* = (\varepsilon_i - \alpha')$$

$$E(\varepsilon_i^*) = E(\varepsilon_i - \alpha') = \alpha' - \alpha' = 0$$

Thus, if the error term did have a nonzero mean, the original model would be equivalent to the new model with a different intercept but with an error term having zero mean.

If the error term has a constant variance (as assumed above), we call it *homoscedastic*, but if the variance is changing, we call the error *heteroscedastic*. *Heteroscedasticity* (as opposed to *homoscedasticity*) may arise if one is examining a cross section of firms in an industry. There may be reason to believe that error terms associated with very large firms will have greater variance than will those associated with small firms. Figure 3.2 illustrates two cases of heteroscedasticity. In Fig. 3.2a the variance of the error term decreases as the value of X increases, while in Fig. 3.2b the variance of the errors increases with X.

The assumption that errors corresponding to different observations are independent and therefore uncorrelated is important in both time-series and cross-section studies. When the error terms from different observations are correlated, we say that the error process is *serially correlated*. Figure 3.3 illustrates negative and positive serial correlation in a time-series study (X_t represents the value of X at time t.) Negative serial correlation means that negative errors in one time period are associated with positive errors in the next, and vice versa,

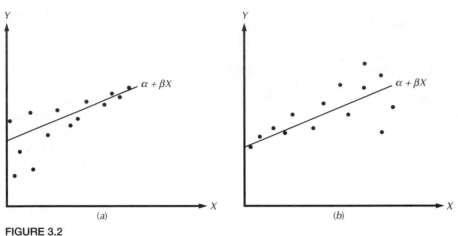

FIGURE 3.2
Heteroscedasticity.

as in Fig. 3.3*a*. When positive serial correlation occurs, as in Fig. 3.3*b*, however, a positive error in one period will tend to be associated with a positive error in the next period.

As a corollary to assumptions stated 2 and 3, we are implicitly assuming that the error term is independent of the X's and therefore uncorrelated with the X's. This follows from the assumption that the X's are nonstochastic. Then

$$E(X_i \varepsilon_i) = X_i E(\varepsilon_i) = 0$$

We shall need this assumption explicitly stated when we cover models in which the X's are stochastic. In addition, assumption 3 allows us to conclude that the

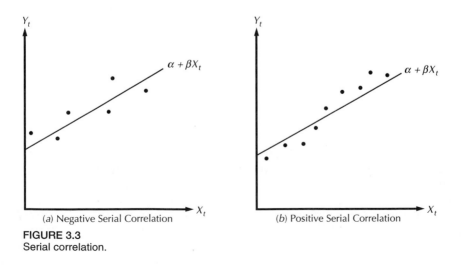

(a) Negative Serial Correlation
(b) Positive Serial Correlation

FIGURE 3.3
Serial correlation.

expected value of the sum of the errors in any sample will be identically zero; i.e.,

$$E(\Sigma\varepsilon_i) = \Sigma E(\varepsilon_i) = 0$$

This follows from the assumption that $E(\varepsilon_i) = 0$, which implies that the expected value of error terms associated with a *particular* X will be identically zero for repeated sampling of Y's associated with that X. We fix each value of X; then we draw samples for the random errors from a population with a known probability distribution. It is the expected value of *each* of these samples of error terms that we assume to be identically zero.

In assumption 4, we have described each error term as having constant variance σ^2. The variance is of course an unknown parameter and must be estimated as part of the regression model. Thus, the regression model described here has three unknown parameters, while the curve-fitting model of Chapter 1 has only two. The assumptions of the model have been given in terms of the error disturbance ε, but we could just as easily have written the assumptions in terms of the probability distribution of Y. In this case they would appear as follows:

3'. The random variable Y has expected value $\alpha + \beta X$:

$$E(Y_i) = E(\alpha + \beta X_i + \varepsilon_i) = \alpha + \beta X_i + E(\varepsilon_i) = \alpha + \beta X_i$$

4'. The random variable Y has constant variance.
5'. The random variables Y_i are independent.

To perform statistical tests on the linear model, we need to specify the probability distribution of the error term. In the *classical normal linear regression model* we add assumption 6, that the error term is normally distributed. This assumption is important for the statistical testing of the model. If one believes that the individual errors are small and independent of each other, the normality assumption is reasonable. Given that the error term ε is normally distributed, it follows that Y is also normally distributed (since X_i is a constant but ε_i is normal).

3.2   BEST LINEAR UNBIASED ESTIMATION

To examine the characteristics of the least-squares parameter estimates, recall that they result from a specific sample of observations of the dependent and independent variables. Since the sample may vary, the estimates may vary as well and thus are associated with a random variable.[2] Because the model is

---

[2] If we select a single sample of Y observations associated with the values of the independent variable, we can obtain an "estimate" of the regression slope. If we replicate the experiment with the same X values, we obtain a new set of observations on Y (because the ε's will differ in the new sample) and thus a new estimate of the slope. If we draw sufficient samples of Y, we obtain a distribution of estimates of the slope.

stochastic, we have shown the formulas for the regression intercept and slope as $\hat{\alpha}$ and $\hat{\beta}$ (where the "hats" over α and β represent estimated values), but it is important to realize that the notation $\hat{\beta}$ serves a double purpose: it refers to the slope *estimate* resulting from a specific sample as well as to the *estimator* (a formula that applies to any sample) that follows a probability distribution.

We hope that the *ordinary least-squares (OLS) estimators* are unbiased and consistent. In fact, one of the nice properties of the ordinary least-squares estimator (which does not require normality of the error term) is that of all estimators which are linear [as in Eq. (3.1)] and which yield unbiased estimates, the estimates resulting from the OLS estimator have the minimum variance. This is the basis of the Gauss-Markov theorem.

> **Gauss-Markov Theorem**   Given assumptions 1 through 5, the estimators $\hat{\alpha}$ and $\hat{\beta}$ are the best (most efficient) linear unbiased estimators of α and β in the sense that they have the minimum variance of all linear unbiased estimators.

To understand the import of the Gauss-Markov theorem, we must first note that $\hat{\beta}$ (and $\hat{\alpha}$) is a *linear* estimator, since $\hat{\beta}$ can be written as a weighted average of the individual observations on Y. There are a large number of possible linear estimators that one might use to estimate the intercept and slope, and a portion of these estimators will be unbiased.[3] However, $\hat{\beta}$ has the additional property that its probability distribution has the smallest variance of all linear estimators that are unbiased. The objective of finding the *best linear unbiased estimator (BLUE)* is one that will pop up again and again in this book. We will see that if certain of the assumptions of the Gauss-Markov theorem do not hold, the least-squares estimators will no longer be BLUE. Our goal will then be to obtain an estimator other than least squares which is BLUE.

It is important to realize that the Gauss-Markov theorem does not apply to nonlinear estimators. A nonlinear estimator may be unbiased and may have lower variance or lower mean square error than the least-squares linear estimator. This suggests that there may be circumstances in which one should use an objective other than "best linear unbiased" when selecting an estimation routine. For example, biased nonlinear estimators with minimum mean square error have a number of useful applications.

We will not attempt to prove the Gauss-Markov theorem at this point (the proof is in Appendix 4.3), but we will find expressions for the mean and variance of the least-squares estimators. To simplify we shall work with the data in deviations form.

From Eq. (3.1), recall that $Y_i = \alpha + \beta X_i + \varepsilon_i$. Summing over all N observations and dividing by N, we find that

$$\bar{Y} = \alpha + \beta \bar{X} + \bar{\varepsilon} \tag{3.2}$$

[3] See Exercise 3.10 for an example.

where $\bar{\varepsilon}$ represents the *sample* mean of the error term. Subtracting Eq. (3.2) from Eq. (3.1) and combining terms gives

$$Y_i - \bar{Y} = \beta(X_i - \bar{X}) + (\varepsilon_i - \bar{\varepsilon})$$

or

$$y_t - \beta x_t + \varepsilon_t \qquad \bar{\varepsilon} \tag{3.3}$$

$\bar{\varepsilon}$ will not equal 0 in the sample, even though $E(\varepsilon_i) = 0$. However, Eq. (3.3) will be used only when we derive results concerning the bias of estimators. Therefore, to simplify we will make the implicit assumption that $\bar{\varepsilon} = 0$ and write the model in deviations form (described in Chapter 1) as

$$y_i = \beta x_i + \varepsilon_i \tag{3.4}$$

The true regression line is $E(y_i) = \beta x_i$. The estimated slope of the line is

$$\hat{\beta} = \frac{\Sigma x_i y_i}{\Sigma x_i^2} \tag{3.5}$$

Because y_i is a random variable, $\hat{\beta}$ will also be random, so that it is natural to determine the properties of the distribution of $\hat{\beta}$. The details are relatively straightforward, but since they are somewhat tedious, we have relegated them to Appendix 3.1. The proofs rely primarily on the results involving the summation and expectations operators, as described in Appendixes 1.1 and 2.1, as well as the assumptions of the classical linear regression model. The first result is that

$$E(\hat{\beta}) = \beta \tag{3.6}$$

so that $\hat{\beta}$ is an *unbiased estimator* of β.

The second result is that

$$\text{Var}(\hat{\beta}) = \frac{\sigma^2}{\Sigma x_i^2} \tag{3.7}$$

so that the variance of $\hat{\beta}$ depends solely on the error variance, the variance of the X's, and the number of observations. In addition, the mean and variance of the estimator of the intercept term are (see Exercise 3.11)

$$E(\hat{\alpha}) = \alpha \tag{3.8}$$

$$\text{Var}(\hat{\alpha}) = \sigma^2 \frac{\Sigma X_i^2}{N\Sigma(X_i - \bar{X})^2} \tag{3.9}$$

Finally, the covariance between $\hat{\alpha}$ and $\hat{\beta}$ is given by

$$\text{Cov}\,(\hat{\alpha}, \hat{\beta}) = \frac{-\overline{X}\sigma^2}{\Sigma x_i^2} \tag{3.10}$$

With information about the means and variances of the least-squares estimators and their covariance, we are ready to discuss statistical testing of the linear model. To do so, we need assumption 6—a normally distributed error term. First, note that since $\hat{\beta}$ is a weighted average of the y's and since the y_i's are normally distributed, *the estimator $\hat{\beta}$ will be normally distributed.* (A linear combination of independent normally distributed variables will be normally distributed.) Even if the y's are not normally distributed, the distribution of $\hat{\beta}$ can be shown to be asymptotically normal (under reasonable conditions) by appeal to the central limit theorem of statistics.[4] To sum up,[5]

$$\hat{\beta} \sim N\!\left(\beta,\ \frac{\sigma^2}{\Sigma x_i^2}\right) \tag{3.11}$$

$$\hat{\alpha} \sim N\!\left(\alpha,\ \sigma^2\,\frac{\Sigma X_i^2}{N\Sigma x_i^2}\right) \tag{3.12}$$

$$\text{Cov}\,(\hat{\alpha}, \hat{\beta}) = \frac{-\overline{X}\sigma^2}{\Sigma x_i^2} \tag{3.13}$$

Note that the variance of $\hat{\beta}$ varies directly with the variance of ε. Thus, other things being equal, we are likely to obtain more precise estimates of the slope when the variance of the error term is small. However, the variance of $\hat{\beta}$ varies inversely with Σx_i^2. Thus, the larger the variance of X_i, the better you are likely to do in estimating β. In fact, it will be difficult to determine the slope accurately when the sample data on the X's are limited to a small interval.

The variance of $\hat{\alpha}$ reaches its minimum of σ^2/N when the mean of X is identically zero. Note also that the sign of the covariance of $\hat{\alpha}$ and $\hat{\beta}$ is opposite in sign to $\overline{X}$. If the mean of X is positive, for example, an overestimate of $\hat{\alpha}$ is likely to be associated with an underestimate of $\hat{\beta}$.

The analysis is not complete, since we need to obtain an estimator of the

---

[4] Roughly speaking, the central limit theorem states that the distribution of the sample mean of an independently distributed variable will tend toward normality as the sample size gets infinitely large. It applies to $\hat{\beta}$ because $\hat{\beta}$ is a linear combination of the y_i's.

[5] Equation (3.11) reads that "$\hat{\beta}$ follows a normal distribution with a mean β and variance $\sigma^2/\Sigma x_i^2$."

population variance σ^2. We will use the following sample estimate of the true variance σ^2:

$$s^2 = \hat{\sigma}^2 = \frac{\Sigma \hat{\varepsilon}_i^2}{N - 2} = \frac{\Sigma (Y_i - \hat{\alpha} - \hat{\beta} X_i)^2}{N - 2} \tag{3.14}$$

where $\hat{\varepsilon}_i = Y_i - \hat{Y}_i$ is the regression *residual*. The *residual variance* $s^?$ is an unbiased as well as consistent estimator of the error variance. (s, and sometimes SER, is called the *standard error of the regression*.) The reader might wonder why the *sum of the squared residuals* $\Sigma \hat{\varepsilon}_i^2$ was divided by $N - 2$ to get an unbiased estimator of the true variance. The answer is that while there are N data points, the estimation of the slope and intercept puts two constraints on the data. This leaves $N - 2$ unconstrained observations with which to estimate the residual variance. For this reason, the divisor of $N - 2$ is referred to as the number of degrees of freedom.

With an estimate of σ^2, we can return to Eqs. (3.11) to (3.13) to obtain sample estimates of the variances associated with the estimated parameters $\hat{\alpha}$ and $\hat{\beta}$ as well as an estimate of the covariance between the two. Each is listed below: $s^2 = \frac{1}{N-2} \Sigma e^2$

$= \frac{1}{N-2} \Sigma (Y_i - a - X_i b)^2$

2d.f since we estimated a and b

$$s_{\hat{\beta}}^2 = \frac{s^2}{\Sigma x_i^2} \tag{3.15}$$

$$s_{\hat{\alpha}}^2 = s^2 \left(\frac{\Sigma X_i^2}{N \Sigma x_i^2} \right) \tag{3.16}$$

$$\widehat{\text{Cov}} (\hat{\alpha}, \hat{\beta}) = -\frac{\overline{X} s^2}{\Sigma x_i^2} \tag{3.17}$$

$s_{\hat{\beta}}$ and $s_{\hat{\alpha}}$, the *standard errors* of the estimated coefficients $\hat{\beta}$ and $\hat{\alpha}$, respectively, provide a measure of the dispersion of the estimates about their means (as do the sample estimates of the variances). They should not be confused with the standard error of the regression s, which measures the dispersion of the error term associated with the regression line.

Example 3.1 Grade-Point Average   Reconsider the grade-point-average example from Chapter 1. The estimated relationship between grade-point average Y and family income X was

$$\hat{Y} = 1.375 + .12X$$

TABLE 3.1
CALCULATION OF s^2
Grade-Point-Average Calculations

(1) x_i	(2) y_i	(3) $\hat{y}_i = \hat{\beta} x_i$	(4) $\hat{\varepsilon}_i = y_i - \hat{y}_i$	(5) $\hat{\varepsilon}_i^2$	(6) x_i^2
7.5	1.0	.90	.10	.0100	56.25
1.5	0	.18	−.18	.0324	2.25
1.5	.5	.18	.32	.1024	2.25
−4.5	−1.0	−.54	−.46	.2116	20.25
−1.5	0	−.18	.18	.0324	2.25
4.5	.5	.54	−.04	.0016	20.25
−7.5	− .5	−.90	.40	.1600	56.25
−1.5	− .5	−.18	− .32	.1024	2.25
				$\Sigma\hat{\varepsilon}_i^2 = .6528$	$\Sigma x_i^2 = 162.00$

$$s^2 = \frac{\Sigma\hat{\varepsilon}_i^2}{N-2} = \frac{.6528}{6} = .109 \qquad s = .33$$

The calculations that allow us to determine s^2 are given in Table 3.1 (see Table 1.2 for preliminary details). In this case, s, the standard error of the regression, is equal to .33. This represents 11 percent of the mean of the grade-point average. (The lower the ratio of s to the mean of the dependent variable, the more closely the data fit the regression line.) Since $\Sigma x_i^2 = 162$, it is easy to calculate the standard error of $\hat{\beta}$. Specifically,

$$s_{\hat{\beta}} = \sqrt{\frac{.109}{162}} = .0259$$

Likewise, Eq. (3.16) can be used to calculate the standard error of $\hat{\alpha}$ as .3688. Assuming normal errors, we determine that $\hat{\beta}$ is normally distributed with mean .12 and standard deviation .026 and that $\hat{\alpha}$ is normally distributed with mean 1.375 and standard deviation .369.

3.3   HYPOTHESIS TESTING AND CONFIDENCE INTERVALS

Given the knowledge of the distributions of $\hat{\alpha}$ and $\hat{\beta}$, it is possible to construct confidence intervals and test hypotheses concerning the regression parameters. Confidence intervals provide a range of values which are likely to contain the true regression parameters. With every confidence interval we associate a *level of statistical significance*. The confidence intervals are constructed so that the probability that the interval contains the true regression parameter is 1 minus the level of significance.

Confidence intervals are particularly useful for testing statistical hypotheses about the estimated regression parameters. We begin with a *null hypothesis,* which usually states that a certain effect is not present. Because we often hope to "accept" the model, the null hypothesis is constructed in a way that makes its rejection possible. To test the validity of a model we set up the null hypothesis that β equals 0. We hope to reject the null hypothesis by obtaining a value of $\hat{\beta}$ which is sufficiently different from 0 to cast significant doubt on the hypothesis that β equals 0. Assume, for example, that $\hat{\beta}$ is .9. If we choose a level of significance of 10 percent, the 90 percent confidence interval for β might be

$$.6 < \beta < 1.2$$

This means that the probability that β is within the range .6 to 1.2 is .90. In addition it means that we can reject the null hypothesis that β equals 0 with 90 percent confidence.

In hypothesis testing some rule for acceptance and rejection must be chosen. One frequently used rule involves the 5 percent level of significance, which uses a criterion that the rejection of the null hypothesis when it is true should occur less than 5 percent of the time. The choice of the significance level depends on the relative importance of two sources of error. Hypothesis testing in classical econometrics deals almost solely with the problem of incorrectly rejecting a true hypothesis (a Type I error). Because of the nature of testable hypotheses which are specified, alternative hypotheses are often ill defined, making it difficult to judge the number of times one will accept the null hypothesis when it is in fact false (a Type II error). For this reason, we will often state that a null hypothesis has been rejected at a 5 percent level of significance while leaving implicit the acceptance of the alternative hypothesis.

It is standard in applied econometric work to examine the test statistics and the standard errors of the coefficients carefully. When rejection of the null hypothesis is valid, the model usually is accepted, at least until further information to the contrary becomes available. The level of significance necessary for model acceptance varies substantially between researchers and between types of models being investigated. For example, a model estimated with a large number of observations may allow one to reject null hypotheses of zero coefficients for many explanatory variables. Thus, we might choose to select a somewhat lower significance level to make rejection of the null hypothesis more difficult.

3.3.1 Tests of Regression Coefficients

The statistical test for rejecting null hypotheses associated with a regression coefficient is usually based on the t distribution. The t distribution is relevant because for statistical testing we need to utilize a sample estimate of the error variance rather than its true value. To use the t distribution to construct 95 percent confidence intervals for the estimated parameters, we first standardize the estimated regression parameter, say $\hat{\beta}$, by subtracting its hypothesized true value β_0 and dividing by the estimate of its standard error. This can be seen most easily when we consider the null hypothesis that $\beta = 0$ or, equivalently, that there is no relationship between the variables X and Y in the two-variable model. In this case the t statistic is given by

$$t_{N-2} = \frac{\hat{\beta}}{s_{\hat{\beta}}}$$

If the t statistic is greater than t_c, *the critical value,* in magnitude, we reject the null hypothesis. Since $t_c = 1.96$ for large samples and a 5 percent significance level, a frequent rule of thumb is that a t value with a magnitude of 2 or larger allows us to reject the null hypothesis.

More generally, we can test the null hypothesis that $\beta = \beta_0$. To do so, we calculate the t statistic:

$$t_{N-2} = \frac{\hat{\beta} - \beta_0}{s_{\hat{\beta}}} \tag{3.18}$$

The standardized variable t_{N-2} also follows a t distribution with $N - 2$ degrees of freedom. With a 5 percent test, the critical value is defined so that

$$\text{Prob} \ (-t_c < t_{N-2} < t_c) \ = .95 \tag{3.19}$$

where Prob denotes probability.

Now, by substituting from Eq. (3.18) we obtain

$$\text{Prob} \left(-t_c < \frac{\hat{\beta} - \beta_0}{s_{\hat{\beta}}} < t_c \right) = .95 \tag{3.20}$$

Modifying Eq. (3.20) slightly,

$$\text{Prob} \ (\hat{\beta} - t_c s_{\hat{\beta}} < \beta_0 < \hat{\beta} + t_c s_{\hat{\beta}}) \ = .95 \tag{3.21}$$

From Eq. (3.21) we obtain a 95 percent confidence interval for β:

$$\hat{\beta} \pm t_c s_{\hat{\beta}} \tag{3.22}$$

Using a similar procedure, we obtain a 95 percent confidence interval for α:

$$\hat{\alpha} \pm t_c s_{\hat{\alpha}} \tag{3.23}$$

It is possible to determine confidence intervals for any level of significance as long as the critical value of the t distribution is correctly chosen. Confidence intervals for the unknown parameters provide us with a statistical statement about the range of values likely to contain the true parameter. Thus, Eq. (3.22) tells us that an interval of t_c standard deviations on either side of the estimated slope parameter has a probability of .95 of containing the true parameter.

Occasionally econometric analyses will provide additional information in the form of a *p-value*. A p-value describes the *exact* significance level associated with an econometric result. Thus, a p-value of .07 indicates that a coefficient is statistically significant at the .07 level (but not at the 5 percent level). In this case 7 percent of the t distribution lies outside an interval of t_c standard deviations from the estimated slope parameter.

Example 3.1 (*continued*) Grade-Point Average   To test the estimated slope parameter in the grade-point-average example, we can use the calculations made in the initial discussion of Example 3.1. We begin by selecting a level of significance—in this case 5 percent. Then we find the critical value of the t distribution (from Table 3 at the back of the book) associated with a probability of .05 and 6 degrees of freedom (there are eight observations and two estimated parameters). In this case.

$$t_c = 2.447$$

Then, a 95 percent confidence interval for the estimated slope parameter would be

$$\hat{\beta} \pm t_c s_{\hat{\beta}} = .12 \pm (2.447)(.026) = .12 \pm .06$$

or

$$.06 < \beta < .18$$

In addition,

$$t = \hat{\beta}/s_{\hat{\beta}} = \frac{.12}{.026} = 4.6$$

We observe that 0 lies *outside* the 95 percent confidence interval for β, allowing us to reject at the 5 percent level of significance the null hypothesis that $\beta = 0$. Equivalently, we can observe that the calculated value of t (4.6) is greater than the critical value of 2.45 and again reject the null hypothesis.

Example 3.2 Consumption Expenditures   Suppose we wish to build a two-variable model that explains the dollar value of aggregate consumption expenditures C, measured in billions of dollars (seasonally adjusted).[6] As an explanatory variable we use aggregate personal disposable income Y, measured in billions of dollars (seasonally adjusted). When C is regressed on Y using quarterly data from the first quarter of 1959 to the second quarter of 1995, we obtain the following result (standard errors are in parentheses):

$$C = -27.53 + .93Y$$
$$\quad\quad (4.45) \quad\quad (.0018)$$

In this case, the intercept of -27.53 is significant at the 5 percent level (the t statistic is -6.18 ($-27.53/4.45$). More important, the t statistic associated with the coefficient of disposable income is 517 ($.93/.0018$). We can clearly reject the null hypothesis of a zero slope in favor of the alternative hypothesis that the slope is nonzero. Rejection of the null hypothesis allows us to accept—at least provisionally—the two-variable regression model. Of course, further research might allow us to find a model of aggregate consumption expenditures that is more suitable than the one just described.

   Suppose (for illustrative purposes) we replace Y as an explanatory variable by a *random* variable. (We chose a variable X that was drawn each time from a normal distribution with a mean of 50 and a variance of 25.) Then we would expect that approximately 1 time in 20 the coefficient on the X variable would be significantly different from zero (at the 5 percent significance level). We found that it took 22 trials before a significantly negative coefficient was obtained. This shows that no matter how reliable or unreliable a statistical estimator is, there is always a statistical chance that one will make incorrect inferences by relying on the regression results.

3.4   ANALYSIS OF VARIANCE AND CORRELATION

3.4.1   Goodness of Fit

Regression residuals can provide a useful measure of the fit between the estimated regression line and the data. A good regression equation is one which helps explain a large proportion of the variance of Y. Large residuals imply a poor fit, while small residuals imply a good fit. The problem with using the residual as a measure of goodness of fit is that its value depends on the units of the dependent variable. To find a measure of goodness of fit which is unit-

---

[6] This example uses data supplied by the Citibase database. The original data (GC and GYD) are seasonally adjusted *at annual rates*.

free, it seems reasonable to use the residual variance divided by the variation of Y.

$$\text{Variation } (Y) = \Sigma(Y_i - \overline{Y})^2$$

Our goal is to divide the variation of Y into two parts, the first accounted for by the regression equation and the second associated with the unexplained portion (the error term) of the model. Assume first that the slope of the linear regression model is known to be 0 and we fit a regression estimating only an intercept. Then the best prediction for Y_i associated with any X_i is given by the sample mean of Y:

$$\hat{Y}_i = \hat{\alpha} + 0 \cdot X_i = \hat{\alpha} = \overline{Y}$$

In this special case we can conclude that the variation of Y measures the square of the difference between the observed values Y_i and the predicted values $\hat{Y}_i = \overline{Y}$.

When the slope is nonzero we can improve our predictions by accounting for Y_i being dependent on X_i,

$$\hat{Y}_i = \hat{\alpha} + \hat{\beta}X_i$$

The additional information will reduce the unexplained portion of the variation in Y. To see this, consider the following identity, which holds for all observations:

$$Y_i - \overline{Y} = (Y_i - \hat{Y}_i) + (\hat{Y}_i - \overline{Y}) \tag{3.24}$$

The term on the left of the equals sign denotes the difference between the sample value of Y and the mean of Y, the first right-hand term gives the residual $\hat{\varepsilon}_i$, and the second right-hand term gives the difference between the predicted value of Y and the mean of Y. This is shown in Fig. 3.4.

To measure variation, we square both sides of Eq. (3.24) and then sum over all observations $i = 1, 2, \ldots, N$:

$$\Sigma(Y_i - \overline{Y})^2 = \Sigma(Y_i - \hat{Y}_i)^2 + \Sigma(\hat{Y}_i - \overline{Y})^2 + 2\Sigma(Y_i - \hat{Y}_i)(\hat{Y}_i - \overline{Y}) \tag{3.25}$$

The last term in Eq. (3.25) can be shown to be identically 0 by using two properties of the least-squares residuals, $\Sigma\hat{\varepsilon}_i = 0$ and $\Sigma\hat{\varepsilon}_iX_i = 0$. All the derivations appear in Appendix 3.2. It follows that

$$
\begin{array}{ccccc}
\Sigma(Y_i - \overline{Y})^2 & = & \Sigma(Y_i - \hat{Y}_i)^2 & + & \Sigma(\hat{Y}_i - \overline{Y})^2 \\
\text{total variation of} & & \text{residual variation of} & & \text{explained variation} \\
Y \text{ (or total sum of} & & Y \text{ (or error sum of} & & \text{of } Y \text{ (or regression} \\
\text{squares)} & & \text{squares)} & & \text{sum of squares)} \\
\text{TSS} & = & \text{ESS} & + & \text{RSS} \tag{3.26}
\end{array}
$$

unexplained.

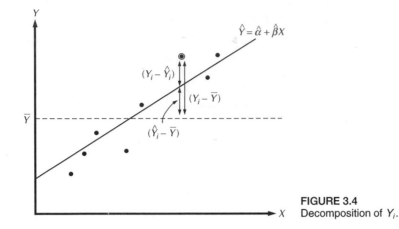

FIGURE 3.4
Decomposition of Y_i.

To normalize, we divide both sides of Eq. (3.26) by the total sum of squares to get

$$1 = \frac{\text{ESS}}{\text{TSS}} + \frac{\text{RSS}}{\text{TSS}}$$

We define the *R-squared* (R^2) of the regression equation as

$$R^2 = 1 - \frac{\text{ESS}}{\text{TSS}} = \frac{\text{RSS}}{\text{TSS}} \qquad (3.27)$$

R^2 is the proportion of the total variation in Y explained by the regression of Y on X. Since the error sum of squares ranges in value between 0 and the total sum of squares, it is easy to see that R^2 ranges in value between 0 and 1. An R^2 of 0 occurs when the *linear* regression model does nothing to help explain the variation in Y. This may occur when the values of Y lie randomly around the horizontal line $Y = \overline{Y}$ or when the sample points lie on a circle (Fig. 3.5*b*). An R^2 of 1 can occur only when all sample points lie on the estimated regression line (Fig. 3.5*a*).

To relate R^2 to the regression parameters estimated earlier in this chapter, we write the predicted values of y_i as

$$\hat{y}_i = \hat{\beta} x_i$$

Then, each dependent variable observation can be subdivided as

$$y_i = \hat{y}_i + \hat{\varepsilon}_i$$

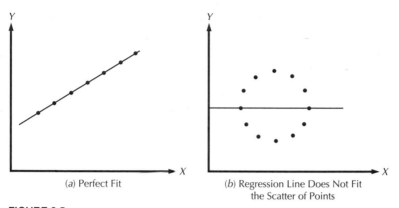

(a) Perfect Fit

(b) Regression Line Does Not Fit
the Scatter of Points

FIGURE 3.5
Measuring *R*-squared.

where $\hat{\varepsilon}_i$ is the regression residual. Now

$$\Sigma y_i^2 = \Sigma \hat{y}_i^2 + \Sigma \hat{\varepsilon}_i^2 \qquad \text{since } \Sigma \hat{y}_i \hat{\varepsilon}_i = \hat{\beta} \Sigma x_i \hat{\varepsilon}_i = 0$$

$$= \hat{\beta}^2 \Sigma x_i^2 + \Sigma \hat{\varepsilon}_i^2$$

from which it follows that

$$R^2 = \frac{\text{RSS}}{\text{TSS}} = \frac{\Sigma \hat{y}_i^2}{\Sigma y_i^2} = \hat{\beta}^2 \frac{\Sigma x_i^2}{\Sigma y_i^2}$$

or

* *All identifications of R^2
are identical.*

$$R^2 = 1 - \frac{\Sigma \hat{\varepsilon}_i^2}{\Sigma y_i^2} \qquad (3.28)$$

Equation (3.28) provides a simple formula for calculating R^2.

Note that R^2 is only a descriptive statistic. Roughly speaking, we associate a high value of R^2 with a good fit of the regression line and associate a low value of R^2 with a poor fit. We must realize, however, that a low value of R^2 can occur for several related reasons. In certain cases X may not be a good explanatory variable. Even though there is reason to believe that X does help in the prediction of Y, unexplained variation in Y may remain even after X has appeared in the equation. In time-series studies, however, one often obtains high values of R^2 simply because any variable that grows over time is likely to do a good job of explaining the variation of any other variable that grows over time. In cross-section studies, by contrast, a lower R^2 may occur even if the model is a satisfactory one because of the large variation across individual units of observation.[7]

It is occasionally useful to summarize the breakdown of the variation in Y in terms of an *analysis of variance*. In such a case the total unexplained and explained variations in Y are converted into *variances* by dividing by the appropriate number of degrees of freedom.[8] Thus, the variance in Y is the total variation divided by $N - 1$, the explained variance is equal to the explained variation (since the regression involves only one additional constraint above the one used to estimate the mean of Y), and the residual variance is the residual variation divided by $N - 2$.

3.4.2   Correlation

Because R^2 is of value in analyzing a model with a causal relationship between the dependent variable Y and the independent variable X, R^2 is interpreted as more than a measure of correlation between two variables. Correlation techniques do not involve an implicit assumption of causality, while regression techniques do. We saw in Chapter 1 that the choice of dependent and independent variables in a regression model is crucial. The dependent variable is the variable to be explained, while the independent variable is the moving force. The least-squares technique is appropriate only if the causal structure of the model can be determined before the data are examined. If a model $Y = \alpha + \beta X$ is specified, one may interpret a significant t statistic on the regression slope parameter as evidence tending to *validate* the model. By contrast, an insignificant statistic would *invalidate* it.

As an example of correlation without causality, consider a series of observations over time that might have been obtained in a nineteenth-century study of medicine in Africa. One might find a high correlation between the number of doctors present in a region and the prevalence of disease in that region, but it would be wrong to infer that the presence of doctors is a cause of spreading disease.

Thus, high correlations do not provide for an inference of causality. One must specify *a priori* (based on previous information) that the number of doctors in a region is a function of the prevalence of disease and test statistically whether such a relationship holds if one is to use regression correctly. Correlation techniques are often used to suggest hypotheses or to confirm previously held

---

[7] This suggests that R^2 alone may not be a suitable measure of the extent to which a model is satisfactory. A better overall measure might be a statistic which describes the predictive power of the model in the face of new data.

[8] The number of degrees of freedom is the number of observations minus the number of constraints placed on the data by the calculation procedure. Thus, an estimate of the variation in Y involves $N - 1$ degrees of freedom because one constraint is placed on the data when deviations are measured about the sample mean (which must in itself be calculated). An additional degree of freedom is used up in the calculation of the slope parameter, leaving $N - 2$ degrees of freedom associated with the unexplained variation in the problem.

suspicions. Such procedures are acceptable as long as one does not infer causality directly from the data. There are numerous cases in economics, business, and other fields in which two variables are highly correlated but both are determined by a third underlying variable. When this is the case, the underlying variable should appear in the regression model as the independent variable.

What happens to the regression slope parameter when an incorrect causal specification is made? Let us compare the slope parameters associated with the following regression models:

i $Y = a + bX + e$
ii $X = A + BY + e'$

The least-squares estimators of b and B are

$$\hat{b} = \frac{\Sigma x_i y_i}{\Sigma x_i^2} \qquad \hat{B} = \frac{\Sigma x_i y_i}{\Sigma y_i^2}$$

The two slopes will yield identical conclusions about the relationship between movement in X and movement in Y only if $\hat{b} = 1/\hat{B}$, or equivalently if $R^2 = 1$ (see Exercise 3.4). Thus, the choice of specification of the regression model will affect our parameter estimates and predictions.

3.4.3   Testing the Regression Equation

The procedure of subdividing the variation in Y into two components suggests a statistical test of the existence of a linear relationship between Y and X. Consider the ratio

$$F_{1,N-2} = \frac{\text{explained variance}}{\text{unexplained variance}} = \frac{\text{RSS}/1}{\text{ESS}/(N-2)} = \frac{\hat{\beta}^2 \Sigma x_i^2}{s^2}$$

Other things being equal, we would expect a strong statistical relationship between X and Y to result in a large ratio of explained to unexplained variance. This test can be applied directly because $F_{1,N-2}$ follows the F distribution with 1 and $N-2$ degrees of freedom. The subscripts on F denote the number of degrees of freedom in the numerator and the denominator, respectively. The value of the F statistic will be 0 only when the explained variance in the regression is 0. One associates a low value with a weak (linear) relationship between X and Y and a high value with a strong (linear) relationship. Fortunately, the numerical distribution of the F statistic is known (see Table 4 at the end of the book for the F distribution). For example, one would reject the null hypothesis of no relationship between Y and X at the 5 percent significance level by looking up the appropriate critical value of the F distribution (5 percent significance) with 1 and $N-2$ degrees of freedom. If the value of $F_{1,N-2}$ calculated from the regression is larger than the critical value, we reject the null hypothesis at the 5 percent level. If the value of $F_{1,N-2}$ is lower than the critical value, we cannot reject the null hypothesis.

The F test bears a close relationship to the t test associated with the null hypothesis that $\beta = 0$. In fact, $F_{1, N-2} = t^2_{N-2}$ for any level of significance. The F test has been introduced here because it will be useful for joint tests of hypotheses, including tests of significance of multiple regression equations.

Example 3.3 Retail Auto Sales   A study was made of the relationship between retail auto sales (dependent variable) and the level of aggregate wages and salaries in the economy (independent variable).[9] One would expect a higher level of wages and salaries to lead to an increase in auto sales. The following is a summary of the regression of retail sales on wages and salaries using quarterly time-series data. The equation to be estimated is

$$S = \alpha + \beta W + \varepsilon$$

where S is the quarterly retail auto sales from the first quarter of 1959 to the second quarter of 1995 in billions of dollars, and W is the quarterly wages for the same time period in billions of dollars. The fitted regression line is listed below. We have included the t statistics in parentheses below the estimated coefficients. We have placed a hat above the dependent variable as a reminder that the equation is used to calculate estimated values of the dependent variable.

$$\hat{S} = 9.48 + .0308\ W \qquad R^2 = .91 \qquad F = 1{,}378$$
$$\phantom{\hat{S} = }(6.96) \qquad (37.1)$$

The positive constant (representing the intercept term) implies that hypothetically if there were no wages in a given month, individuals would still purchase automobiles. The coefficient of the wage variable can be interpreted to mean that a \$1 billion increase in wages and salaries will lead to a \$30.8 million increase in auto sales. (The model could be used to predict the future level of auto sales conditional on future salaries.) Note that the slope coefficient usually is interpreted to measure the change in the dependent variable associated with a *small* change in the independent variable. (In fact, in the linear model, $\hat{\beta} = dS/dW$ holds for all changes in W.) The estimated coefficient is not unit-free. Its value is directly related to the units of measurement of the dependent variable S (billions of dollars) and the independent variable

---

[9] The data were provided by the Citibase database. The variables are quarterly personal consumption expenditures on new autos, seasonally adjusted (GCDAN), and aggregate wages and salaries, seasonally adjusted (GWY).

W (billions of dollars). In this example we have chosen to write the t statistics, rather than the estimated standard errors, in parentheses. Using the t statistics, we can reject the null hypothesis that the intercept and the slope are 0 (taken individually) at the 1 percent as well as the 5 percent level of significance. The R^2 of .91 implies that the regression equation explains 91 percent of the variation in the dependent variable. The F value of 1,378 allows one to reject the null hypothesis that there is no relationship between auto sales and wages and salaries (at the 1 percent level).

If one had reason to believe quite strongly that the graph of auto sales versus wages and salaries should pass through the origin, despite the fact that we have rejected the null hypothesis of a 0 intercept, it would be natural to run the regression without a constant term. The results for the identical sample are

$$\hat{S} = .0354 \ W$$
$$(62.6)$$

While the t test allows one to reject the null hypothesis, the suppression of the significant constant term has lowered the explanatory power of the equation.[10] Thus, we would estimate the regression model with an intercept. Only if there is strong reason to force the equation through the origin should the intercept be equated to 0.

Example 3.4 Using the grade-point-average problem (Example 1.1) we can calculate the following additional statistics:

$$R^2 = .78 \qquad F_{1,6} = 21.57$$

The R^2 of .78 allows us to conclude that the family income variable helps explain 78 percent of the variation in grade-point average for the sample of eight individuals. The F statistic allows us to test the null hypothesis of no relationship between grade-point average and family income. To do so, we use a table of the F distribution to determine the critical value associated with a 5 percent level of significance and 1 and 6 degrees of freedom in the numerator and the denominator, respectively. (The 1 degree of freedom is used because the model includes a single explanatory variable, while the 6 degrees of freedom result from the fact that there are eight observations and two parameters to be estimated.) In this case the critical value of F at the 5

---

[10] When the constant is dropped, the derivation of R^2 must be modified. In this case, a comparison of the predicted values of the dependent variables made it clear that the explanatory power of the equation had declined.

percent level is 5.99. Since the calculated F of 21.57 is greater than the critical value, we reject the null hypothesis at the 5 percent level of significance.

Example 3.5 Public and Private College Enrollment   In Section 2.6 we described two variables that characterize the levels of public (PUBLIC) and private (PRIVATE) enrollment in institutions of higher education (per thousand individuals) in the United States. The earliest colleges in the United States were private eastern schools. Public institutions blossomed at a later time, and consequently their largest growth was in the western United States. Interestingly, states with substantial private enrollments chose not to expand their systems of public education as rapidly as did those with relatively weak private enrollments. This pattern is strongly evidenced in a cross-section regression that relates public enrollments to private enrollments for the 50 states. The regression (with t statistics in parentheses) is as follows:

$$\widehat{\text{PUBLIC}} = 43.97 - .444 \text{ PRIVATE} \qquad R^2 = .20 \qquad F = 12.04$$
$$\phantom{\widehat{\text{PUBLIC}} = } (25.80) \quad (-3.47)$$

There is a statistically significant negative relationship between private and public enrollments. The regression suggests that as private enrollments in a state increase by 1 (per thousand individuals), public enrollments in the state decrease by almost $\frac{1}{2}$. The t statistic of -3.47 and the F statistic of 12.04 both tell us that the negative coefficient on PRIVATE is significantly different from 0 at the 5 percent level of significance.

To evaluate further the validity of the two-variable regression model, we plotted a histogram of the residuals in Fig. 3.6. Because the least-squares residuals sum to zero, it is not surprising that the distribution of residuals centers on 0. Other attributes associated with the distribution of residuals are quite informative, however. They include the following:

Median	.63
Minimum	-15.4
Maximum	19.6
Standard deviation	7.31
Skewness	.21
Kurtosis	2.79
Jarque-Bera	.47

The mean enrollment for public institutions is 39.3 per thousand inhabitants. Seen from this perspective, the residuals, ranging from -15.4 to 19.6, are quite high; this range, along with the relatively high standard deviation

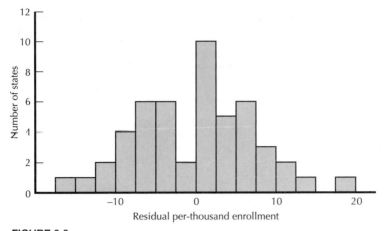

FIGURE 3.6
Histogram of residuals.

of 7.31 is consistent with the low R^2 of .20. Clearly, there is room for improvement in the development of a model that explains public enrollments.

Finally, we can ask whether the assumption of normally distributed errors is a reasonable one. The pattern of the residuals provides helpful information. The median of .63 and the skewness of .21 tell us that the upper tail of the distribution is slightly thicker, with more observations than the lower tail. The kurtosis of 2.79 is only slightly lower than 3.00, telling us that the distribution of residuals has tails that are slightly thinner than the normal. Finally, the Jarque-Bera statistic of .47 is much less than the critical value of the chi-square distribution with 2 degrees of freedom, which is 5.99. We therefore cannot reject the null hypothesis that the residuals are normally distributed and can conclude that the t and F tests we described previously are meaningful.

APPENDIX 3.1 Variance of the Least-Squares Slope Estimator

Result 1

$$E(\hat{\beta}) = \beta$$

PROOF   Recall that $\hat{\beta} = \Sigma x_i y_i / \Sigma x_i^2$. Let

$$c_i = \frac{x_i}{\Sigma x_i^2} \qquad (A3.1)$$

Each c_i is a constant, since the X's are fixed. Substituting into the equation for $\hat{\beta}$, we get

$$\hat{\beta} = \Sigma c_i y_i \qquad \text{(A3.2)}$$

which expresses the estimated slope parameter as a weighted sum of the observations on the dependent variable. (All summations are implicitly assumed to involve observations $i = 1, 2, \ldots, N$.) Then

$$\hat{\beta} = \Sigma c_i y_i = \Sigma c_i(\beta x_i + \varepsilon_i) \qquad \text{since } y_i = \beta x_i + \varepsilon_i$$

$$= \beta \Sigma c_i x_i + \Sigma c_i \varepsilon_i \qquad \text{from Appendix 1.1} \qquad \text{(A3.3)}$$

Therefore, $\quad E(\hat{\beta}) = \beta \Sigma c_i x_i + E(\Sigma c_i \varepsilon_i)$

$$= \beta \Sigma c_i x_i + \Sigma c_i E(\varepsilon_i) \qquad \text{from Appendix 2.1}$$

But $E(\varepsilon_i) = 0$, so that

$$E(\hat{\beta}) = \beta \Sigma c_i x_i = \beta$$

The fact that $\Sigma c_i x_i = 1$ follows directly from the definition of c_i:

$$\Sigma c_i x_i = \Sigma \left(\frac{x_i}{\Sigma x_i^2} \right) x_i = \Sigma \frac{x_i^2}{\Sigma x_i^2} = \frac{\Sigma x_i^2}{\Sigma x_i^2} = 1$$

Result 2
$$\text{Var} (\hat{\beta}) = \frac{\sigma^2}{\Sigma x_i^2}$$

PROOF
$$\text{Var} (\hat{\beta}) = E(\hat{\beta} - \beta)^2$$

But $\quad (\hat{\beta} - \beta) = \beta \Sigma c_i x_i + \Sigma c_i \varepsilon_i - \beta \qquad \text{from Eq. (A3.3)}$

$$= \beta(\Sigma c_i x_i - 1) + \Sigma c_i \varepsilon_i$$

$$= \Sigma c_i \varepsilon_i \qquad \text{from derivation in Result 1}$$

Therefore, $\qquad (\hat{\beta} - \beta)^2 = (\Sigma c_i \varepsilon_i)^2 \qquad \text{(A3.4)}$

and $\text{Var} (\hat{\beta}) = E(\Sigma c_i \varepsilon_i)^2 = E[(c_1 \varepsilon_1)^2 + 2(c_1 c_2 \varepsilon_1 \varepsilon_2) + (c_2 \varepsilon_2)^2 + \cdots + (c_N \varepsilon_N)^2]$

By assumption the ε_i are uncorrelated; that is, $E(\varepsilon_i \varepsilon_j) = 0$ for $i \neq j$. Therefore,

$$\text{Var } (\hat{\beta}) = E(c_1 \varepsilon_1)^2 + E(c_2 \varepsilon_2)^2 + \cdots + E(c_N \varepsilon_N)^2$$
$$= c_1^2 E(\varepsilon_1^2) + c_2^2 E(\varepsilon_2^2) + \cdots + c_N^2 E(\varepsilon_N^2)$$
$$= \Sigma c_i^2 E(\varepsilon_i^2) = \sigma^2 \Sigma c_i^2$$

But

$$\Sigma c_i^2 = \frac{\Sigma x_i^2}{(\Sigma x_i^2)^2} = \frac{1}{\Sigma x_i^2}$$

Therefore,

$$\text{Var } (\hat{\beta}) = \frac{\sigma^2}{\Sigma x_i^2} \tag{A3.5}$$

APPENDIX 3.2 Some Properties of the Least-Squares Residuals

The first two of the following properties hold for the least-squares residuals in both the two-variable and the multiple regression models. Neither result depends on the normality of the error process or on the assumption that the least-squares estimators are BLUE. Rather, they follow directly from the normal equations (A1.18) and (A1.19).

Property 1 $\Sigma \hat{\varepsilon}_i = 0$ (A3.6)

PROOF   In the two-variable model, $\hat{y}_i = \hat{\beta} x_i$. By definition

$$\hat{\varepsilon}_i = y_i - \hat{y}_i = y_i - \hat{\beta} x_i$$

Then $\Sigma \hat{\varepsilon}_i = \Sigma y_i - \hat{\beta} \Sigma x_i = N\bar{y} - \hat{\beta} N\bar{x} = 0$

since $\bar{x} = \bar{y} = 0$ when the data are in deviations form.

Property 2 $\Sigma \hat{\varepsilon}_i X_i = 0$

PROOF $\Sigma \hat{\varepsilon}_i X_i = \Sigma \hat{\varepsilon}_i x_i + \Sigma \hat{\varepsilon}_i \bar{X} = \Sigma \hat{\varepsilon}_i x_i$

(using Property 1). Then

$$\Sigma \hat{\varepsilon}_i x_i = \Sigma (y_i - \hat{\beta} x_i) x_i = \Sigma x_i y_i - \hat{\beta} \Sigma x_i^2$$

But $\hat{\beta}$ is the least-squares estimator, and $\hat{\beta} = \Sigma x_i y_i / \Sigma x_i^2$. Therefore,

$$\Sigma \hat{\varepsilon}_i x_i = \Sigma x_i y_i - \frac{\Sigma x_i y_i}{\Sigma x_i^2} \Sigma x_i^2 = 0$$

Property 3 $\Sigma(Y_i - \hat{Y}_i)(\hat{Y}_i - \overline{Y}) = 0$ from Eq. (3.25)

PROOF $\Sigma(Y_i - \hat{Y}_i)(\hat{Y}_i - Y) = \Sigma\hat{\varepsilon}_i(\hat{Y}_i - \overline{Y})$

$$= \Sigma\hat{\varepsilon}_i\hat{Y}_i - \overline{Y}\Sigma\hat{\varepsilon}_i$$

$$= \Sigma\hat{\varepsilon}_i(\hat{\alpha} + \hat{\beta}X_i) - \overline{Y}\Sigma\hat{\varepsilon}_i$$

$$= \hat{\alpha}\Sigma\hat{\varepsilon}_i + \hat{\beta}\Sigma\hat{\varepsilon}_iX_i - \overline{Y}\Sigma\hat{\varepsilon}_i$$

$$= 0 \qquad\qquad \text{using Properties 1 and 2}$$

Property 4 s^2 is an unbiased estimator of σ^2.

PROOF   Recall that $\hat{\varepsilon}_i = y_i - \hat{\beta}x_i$. But $y_i = \beta x_i + \varepsilon_i$. Therefore,

$$\hat{\varepsilon}_i = \beta x_i + \varepsilon_i - \hat{\beta}x_i = (\beta - \hat{\beta})x_i + \varepsilon_i$$

(As in the text we have implicitly assumed that the errors ε_i have a sample mean of zero.) Squaring and summing over all N observations, we find that

$$\Sigma\hat{\varepsilon}_i^2 = (\hat{\beta} - \beta)^2\Sigma x_i^2 + \Sigma\varepsilon_i^2 - 2(\hat{\beta} - \beta)\Sigma x_i\varepsilon_i$$

Now, taking the expectation of both sides, we get

$$E(\Sigma\hat{\varepsilon}_i^2) = E(\hat{\beta} - \beta)^2\Sigma x_i^2 + E(\Sigma\varepsilon_i^2) - 2E[(\hat{\beta} - \beta)\Sigma x_i\varepsilon_i]$$

But

$$\text{Var}\,(\hat{\beta}) = E(\hat{\beta} - \beta)^2 = \frac{\sigma^2}{\Sigma x_i^2} \qquad \text{see Eq. (A3.5)}$$

$$E(\Sigma\varepsilon_i^2) = (N - 1)\sigma^2 \qquad\qquad \text{see Result 9, Appendix 2.1}$$

In addition $\hat{\beta} - \beta = \Sigma x_i\varepsilon_i/\Sigma x_i^2$. This follows from (A3.3) and the fact that $\Sigma c_i x_i = 1$ so that $\Sigma x_i\varepsilon_i = (\hat{\beta} - \beta)\Sigma x_i^2$, and

$$-2E[(\hat{\beta} - \beta)^2]\Sigma x_i^2 = -2\sigma^2$$

Combining these three results,

$$E(\Sigma\hat{\varepsilon}_i^2) = \sigma^2 + (N - 1)\sigma^2 - 2\sigma^2 = (N - 2)\sigma^2$$

or

$$E(s^2) = \frac{E(\Sigma\hat{\varepsilon}_i^2)}{N - 2} = \sigma^2$$

EXERCISES

3.1 Construct 95 percent confidence intervals for the estimated parameters for Exercise 1.1. Can you reject the null hypothesis that $\beta = 0$? $\beta = 1$?

3.2 Discuss the differences in statistical tests associated with the estimated parameters of a regression when

(a) The error variance is known or not known.

(b) The sample size is finite or infinite.

3.3 Since the standard error of the regression coefficient $\hat{\beta}$ varies inversely with the variance of X, one can improve the significance of the estimated parameter by selecting values of X at the endpoints of the range of possible values. Explain why this is true and discuss whether such a procedure is desirable.

3.4 Prove that the estimated slope of the regression of Y on X will equal the reciprocal of the estimated slope of the regression of X on Y only if $R^2 = 1$.

3.5 Can you give an example of an estimator which is asymptotically unbiased but not consistent?

3.6 When the mean of X is identically 0, the covariance between the estimated slope and intercept is 0. Can you explain intuitively why this is true?

3.7 Suppose you are attempting to build a model that explains aggregate savings behavior as a function of the level of interest rates. Would you rather sample during a period of fluctuating interest rates or a period in which interest rates are relatively constant? Explain.

3.8 Prove that the estimated residuals from the linear regression and the corresponding sample values of X are uncorrelated; that is, $\Sigma X_i \hat{\varepsilon}_i = 0$. *Hint:* The problem will be easier if you work with the data in deviations form.

3.9 Prove that R^2 for the two-variable regression is unchanged if a linear transformation is made on both variables; that is, $Y^* = a_1 + a_2 Y$, $X^* = b_1 + b_2 X$.

3.10 Return once again to the data in Exercise 1.1. Break down the data into two groups of five observations each, according to the order of magnitude of the independent variable (money supply). In other words, the first group should contain the five sample points associated with the five smallest values of the money supply. Calculate the following parameter:

$$B = \frac{\bar{Y}_2 - \bar{Y}_1}{\bar{X}_2 - \bar{X}_1}$$

where the subscript refers to the group number. ($\bar{Y}_2$ is the mean of all Y's in the second group.)

(a) Describe the foregoing process geometrically. In what sense is B an estimated slope parameter?

(b) Compare your estimated parameter to the least-squares slope estimate. Can you prove that B is an unbiased estimator of the true regression slope parameter?

(c) Prove that the variance of the parameter B must be greater than or equal to the variance of the least-squares estimator.

3.11 Prove that

$$E(\hat{\alpha}) = \alpha \quad \text{and} \quad \text{Var}\,(\hat{\alpha}) = \sigma^2 \frac{\Sigma X_i^2}{N\Sigma(X_i - \overline{X})^2}$$

where $\hat{\alpha}$ is the least-squares intercept estimator.

3.12 Prove that

$$\text{Cov}\,(\hat{\alpha}, \hat{\beta}) = \frac{-\overline{X}\sigma^2}{\Sigma x_i^2}$$

where $\hat{\alpha}$ is the intercept estimator and $\hat{\beta}$ is the slope estimator.

CHAPTER 4

THE MULTIPLE
REGRESSION MODEL

In this chapter we discuss the regression model with two or more independent variables (in addition to the constant term), i.e., the *multiple* regression model. We describe the assumptions underlying the classical multiple regression model and show how the least-squares parameter estimates can be obtained. We then discuss the interpretation of regression coefficients. As we will see, problems may arise because of the interaction between the explanatory variables in the regression equation. We place particular emphasis in this chapter on the various regression statistics which aid in the interpretation of the model, including standardized coefficients, elasticities, and partial correlation coefficients.

4.1 THE MODEL

We extend the two-variable model by assuming that the dependent variable Y is a linear function of a series of independent variables $X_1, X_2, \ldots, X_k$ and an error term. This model is a natural extension of the two-variable model, and so it will be unnecessary to derive all our earlier results in full detail.

We write the *multiple regression model* as

$$Y_i = \beta_1 + \beta_2 X_{2i} + \beta_3 X_{3i} + \cdots + \beta_k X_{ki} + \varepsilon_i \tag{4.1}$$

where Y is the dependent variable, the X's are the independent variables, and ε is the error term. X_{2i} represents, for example, the ith observation on explanatory variable X_2. β_1 is the constant term, or intercept, of the equation.

The assumptions of the multiple regression model are quite similar to those of the two-variable model:

1. The relationship between Y and X is linear and is given by Eq. (4.1).
2. The X's are nonstochastic variables. In addition, *no exact linear relationship exists between two or more independent variables.*
3. The error has zero expected value for all observations.
4. The error term has constant variance for all observations.
5. Errors corresponding to different observations are independent and therefore uncorrelated.
6. The error term is normally distributed. $\varepsilon_i \sim N(0, \sigma^2)$

For simplicity we will work with a special case of the multiple regression model, the three-variable model

$$Y_i = \beta_1 + \beta_2 X_{2i} + \beta_3 X_{3i} + \varepsilon_i \tag{4.2}$$

The least-squares procedure is equivalent to searching for parameter estimates which minimize the error sum of squares, defined as

$$\text{ESS} = \Sigma \hat{\varepsilon}_i^2 = \Sigma(Y_i - \hat{Y}_i)^2 \qquad \text{where } \hat{Y}_i = \hat{\beta}_1 + \hat{\beta}_2 X_{2i} + \hat{\beta}_3 X_{3i}$$

Just as we did in Chapter 1, we can find the values of β_1, β_2, and β_3 which minimize ESS. Assuming that there are more than three observations and that the underlying equations are independent, the solution (see Appendix 4.1 for details) is

$$\hat{\beta}_1 = \bar{Y} - \hat{\beta}_2 \bar{X}_2 - \hat{\beta}_3 \bar{X}_3 \tag{4.3}$$

where

$$\bar{X}_2 = \Sigma X_{2i}/N$$

$$\bar{X}_3 = \Sigma X_{3i}/N$$

$$\hat{\beta}_2 = \frac{(\Sigma x_{2i} y_i)(\Sigma x_{3i}^2) - (\Sigma x_{3i} y_i)(\Sigma x_{2i} x_{3i})}{(\Sigma x_{2i}^2)(\Sigma x_{3i}^2) - (\Sigma x_{2i} x_{3i})^2} \tag{4.4}$$

$$\hat{\beta}_3 = \frac{(\Sigma x_{3i} y_i)(\Sigma x_{2i}^2) - (\Sigma x_{2i} y_i)(\Sigma x_{2i} x_{3i})}{(\Sigma x_{2i}^2)(\Sigma x_{3i}^2) - (\Sigma x_{2i} x_{3i})^2} \tag{4.5}$$

In this three-variable model [Eq. (4.2)] the coefficient β_2 measures the change in Y associated with a unit change in X_2 on the assumption that the variable X_3 is held constant. Likewise, the coefficient β_3 measures the change in Y associated with a unit change in X_3 with X_2 held constant. In both cases the assumption that the values of the remaining explanatory variables are constant is crucial to our interpretation of the coefficients. We show in more detail exactly how one holds other variables constant in Appendix 4.2 and encourage the reader to follow the details.

Example 4.1 Auto Sales[1]   To predict quarterly auto sales using a single-equation model, three explanatory variables are likely to be of value. One would expect that sales would move in the same direction as disposable income but would be inversely related to the cost of borrowing money to finance the purchase. We therefore will need the following data for our model:

S = quarterly personal consumption of new autos, billions of current dollars
YP = quarterly personal income, billions of current dollars
R = 3-month Treasury bill rate, in percent per year
CPI = quarterly Consumer Price Index (1983 = 100)

Sales, income, and interest rate variables were deflated by the CPI to be measured in real terms (e.g., SR = S/CPI, YPR = YP/CPI, RR = R/CPI). The equation to be estimated is

$$SR_t = \beta_1 + \beta_2 YPR_t + \beta_3 RR_t + \varepsilon_t$$

where t denotes that the data are measured at time t. Using data from the period 1975 through the second quarter of 1995, the estimated regression is

$$\widehat{SR}_t = .60 + .0070\ YPR_t - 1.366\ RR_t$$

The personal income coefficient means that an increase of $1 billion in real disposable income will lead to a $7.0 million increase in real auto sales, with the effects of all other variables held constant. Also, if the interest rate rises by 1 percentage point, auto sales will drop by $1.366 billion in the following quarter.

4.2   REGRESSION STATISTICS

To test the statistical significance of individual regression coefficients, it is natural to ask whether the Gauss-Markov theorem extends to the multiple re-

---

[1] The data used in this example were obtained from the Citibase database. The original variables were GCDAN, GMPY, FYGN3, and PUNEW. All data are seasonally adjusted. The last three variables are measured monthly. We used quarterly averages in each case.

gression model and whether one can obtain an unbiased estimate of the variance σ^2 as well as information about the distribution of the estimated regression parameters. The derivations of the statistical properties of the multiple regression model are relegated to Appendix 4.3. Here we provide a summary of the important results:

1. Given assumptions 1 through 5 of the multiple regression model, the Gauss-Markov theorem applies; i.e., the ordinary least-squares estimator of each coefficient β_j, $j = 1, 2, \ldots, k$, is BLUE. (When the error term is normally distributed, it is equivalent to the *maximum-likelihood estimator* as well; see Appendix 2.2.)

2. An unbiased and consistent estimate of σ^2 is provided by

$$s^2 = \frac{\Sigma \hat{\varepsilon}_i^2}{N - k}$$

3. When the error is normally distributed, t tests can be applied because

$$\frac{\hat{\beta}_j - \beta_j}{s_{\hat{\beta}_j}} \sim t_{N-k} \qquad \text{for } j = 1, 2, \ldots, k$$

In other words, the estimated regression parameters, which are normalized by subtracting the mean and dividing by the *estimated* standard error, follow the t distribution with $N - k$ degrees of freedom. The *standard errors* of each of the coefficients $s_{\hat{\beta}_1}, s_{\hat{\beta}_2}, \ldots, s_{\hat{\beta}_k}$ are derived in Appendix 4.3 because their calculation involves matrix inversion. Since we will occasionally use the three-variable model for examples, we will reproduce three formulas here; the first two calculate the estimated *variance* of each coefficient, and the third gives the covariance between the two:

$$\widehat{\text{Var}}\,(\hat{\beta}_2) = \frac{s^2}{\Sigma x_{2i}^2 (1 - r^2)} \tag{4.6}$$

$$\widehat{\text{Var}}\,(\hat{\beta}_3) = \frac{s^2}{\Sigma x_{3i}^2 (1 - r^2)} \tag{4.7}$$

$$\widehat{\text{Cov}}\,(\hat{\beta}_2, \hat{\beta}_3) = \frac{-s^2 r}{(1 - r^2)\sqrt{\Sigma x_{2i}^2 \Sigma x_{3i}^2}} \tag{4.8}$$

where $r = \Sigma x_{2i} x_{3i} / \sqrt{\Sigma x_{2i}^2 \Sigma x_{3i}^2}$ is the simple correlation between x_2 and x_3.

4.3   F TESTS, R^2, AND CORRECTED R^2

To use R^2 as a measure of goodness of fit in the multiple regression model, we extend the earlier discussion (Section 3.4) about the decomposition of the variation in the dependent variable Y.

For each observation, we can break down the difference between Y_i and its mean $\bar{Y}$ as follows:

$$(Y_i - \bar{Y}) = (Y_i - \hat{Y}_i) + (\hat{Y}_i - \bar{Y})$$

Squaring both sides and summing over all observations (1 to N), we obtain[2]

$$\Sigma(Y_i - \bar{Y})^2 = \Sigma(Y_i - \hat{Y}_i)^2 + \Sigma(\hat{Y}_i - \bar{Y})^2$$

| Variation in Y | Residual variation | Explained variation |

or, using the terminology introduced in Chapter 3,

TSS	=	ESS	+	RSS
Total sum of squares		Residual sum of squares		Regression sum of squares

Then we define R^2 as

$$R^2 = \frac{\text{RSS}}{\text{TSS}} = \frac{\Sigma(\hat{Y}_i - \bar{Y})^2}{\Sigma(Y_i - \bar{Y})^2} = 1 - \frac{\Sigma\hat{\varepsilon}_i^2}{\Sigma(Y_i - \bar{Y})^2} \qquad (4.9)$$

R^2 measures the proportion of the variation in Y which is "explained" by the multiple regression equation. R^2 is often used informally as a goodness-of-fit statistic and to compare the validity of regression results under alternative specifications of the independent variables in the model. However, there are several problems with the use of R^2. First, *all our statistical results follow from the initial assumption that the model is correct;* we have no procedure that compares alternative specifications. Second, R^2 is sensitive to the number of independent variables included in the regression model. The addition of more independent variables to the regression equation can never lower R^2 and is likely to raise it. (The addition of a new explanatory variable does not alter TSS but is likely to increase RSS.) Thus, one could simply add more variables to an equation if one wished only to maximize R^2. Finally, the interpretation and use of R^2 become difficult when a model is formulated that is constrained to have a 0 intercept. In such a case the ratio of the regression sum of squares to the total sum of squares need not lie within the range of 0 to 1.

R^2 increases with k.

[2] $\Sigma(Y_i - \bar{Y})^2 = \Sigma(Y_i - \hat{Y}_i)^2 + \Sigma(\hat{Y}_i - \bar{Y})^2 + 2\Sigma(\hat{Y}_i - \hat{Y}_i)(\hat{Y}_i - \bar{Y})$ But the last term is identically zero, since

$$\begin{aligned}
\Sigma(Y_i - \hat{Y}_i)(\hat{Y}_i - \bar{Y}) &= \Sigma\hat{\varepsilon}_i(\hat{Y}_i - \bar{Y}) = \Sigma\hat{\varepsilon}_i\hat{Y}_i - \Sigma\hat{\varepsilon}_i\bar{Y} \\
&= \Sigma\hat{\varepsilon}_i(\hat{\beta}_1 + \hat{\beta}_2 X_{2i} + \cdots + \hat{\beta}_k X_{ki}) - \bar{Y}\Sigma\hat{\varepsilon}_i \\
&= \hat{\beta}_1\Sigma\hat{\varepsilon}_i + \hat{\beta}_2\Sigma\hat{\varepsilon}_i X_{2i} + \cdots + \hat{\beta}_k\Sigma\hat{\varepsilon}_i X_{ki} - \bar{Y}\Sigma\hat{\varepsilon}_i \\
&= 0 \qquad \text{since } \Sigma\hat{\varepsilon}_i = 0 \text{ and } \Sigma\hat{\varepsilon}_i X_{ji} = 0 \text{ for } j = 2, 3, \ldots, k
\end{aligned}$$

The difficulty with R^2 as a measure of goodness of fit is that R^2 pertains only to explained and unexplained *variation* in Y and therefore does not account for the number of degrees of freedom. A natural solution is to use *variances*, not variations, thus eliminating the dependence of goodness of fit on the number of independent variables in the model. (Recall that variance equals variation divided by degrees of freedom.) We define $\overline{R}^2$, or *corrected R^2*, as

$$R^2 = 1 - \frac{ESS}{TSS}. \qquad \overline{R}^2 = 1 - \frac{\widehat{\text{Var}}(\varepsilon)}{\widehat{\text{Var}}(Y)}$$

where the sample variances of $\hat{\varepsilon}$ and Y are calculated as follows:[3]

$$\widehat{\text{Var}}(\varepsilon) = s^2 = \frac{\Sigma \hat{\varepsilon}_i^2}{N - k} \qquad \text{Var}(\hat{Y}) = \frac{\Sigma (Y_i - \overline{Y})^2}{N - 1}$$

where k is the number of independent variables. Even though the residual, or error, sum of squares will decrease (or remain the same) as new explanatory variables are added, the residual variance need not. Note that both the numerator and the denominator in the definition of $\widehat{\text{Var}}(\varepsilon)$ change when an additional variable is added to the model. In addition, note [from Eq. (4.9)] that

$$R^2 = 1 - \frac{s^2}{\widehat{\text{Var}}(Y)} \frac{N - k}{N - 1} \qquad (4.10)$$

This allows us to derive a formula[4] for the relationship between R^2 and $\overline{R}^2$:

$$\overline{R}^2 = 1 - (1 - R^2) \frac{N - 1}{N - k} \qquad (4.11)$$

If you examine Eq. (4.11), you will see that

1. If $k = 1$, then $R^2 = \overline{R}^2$.
2. If k is greater than 1, then $R^2 \geq \overline{R}^2$.
3. $\overline{R}^2$ can be negative.

---

[3] We divide by $N - 1$ in calculating the variance of Y because 1 degree of freedom is used when the mean of Y is calculated. However, we divide by $N - k$ when calculating the variance of $\hat{\varepsilon}$ because k parameters of the regression model must be estimated before $\hat{\varepsilon}$ can be calculated (thus the loss of k degrees of freedom from the original N).

[4] From Eq. (4.10) it follows that $1 - R^2 = [s^2/\widehat{\text{Var}}(Y)][(N - k)/(N - 1)]$. But $1 - \overline{R}^2 = s^2/\widehat{\text{Var}}(Y)$. Therefore, $1 - R^2 = (1 - \overline{R}^2)[(N - k)/(N - 1)]$. Solving, we get $\overline{R}^2 = 1 - (1 - R^2)[(N - 1)/(N - k)]$.

$\bar{R}^2$ has a number of properties which make it a more desirable goodness-of-fit measure than R^2. When new variables are added to a regression model, R^2 always increases, while $\bar{R}^2$ may rise or fall.[5] The use of $\bar{R}^2$ eliminates at least some of the incentive for researchers to include numerous variables in a model without much thought about why they should appear. An illustrative example is a model estimated with 25 observations, with a reported R^2 of .8. However, this value resulted only after 17 independent variables were included in the model. The value of $\bar{R}^2$ associated with the same model is only .4. Clearly the corrected R^2 gives a more accurate picture of the limitations of this model.

The F statistic calculated by most regression programs can be used in the multiple regression model to test the significance of the R^2 statistic. The F statistic with $k - 1$ and $N - k$ degrees of freedom allows us to test the hypothesis that *none* of the explanatory variables helps explain the variation of Y about its mean. In other words, the F statistic tests the joint hypothesis that $\beta_2 = \beta_3 = \cdots = \beta_k = 0$. It can be shown that Can do F test if we know R^2

t-test tests only $\beta_2 = 0$

$$F_{k-1, N-k} = \frac{\text{RSS}}{\text{ESS}} \frac{N - k}{k - 1} = \frac{R^2}{1 - R^2} \frac{N - k}{k - 1} \qquad (4.12)$$

F test is testing the joint hypothesis $\beta_2 = 0, \beta_3 = 0, \beta_4 = 0$

If the null hypothesis is true, then we would expect RSS, R^2, and therefore F to be close to 0. Thus, a high value of the F statistic is a rationale for rejecting the null hypothesis. An F statistic not significantly different from 0 lets us conclude that the explanatory variables do little to explain the variation of Y about its mean. In the two-variable model, for example, the F statistic tests whether the regression line is horizontal. In such a case, $R^2 = 0$ and the regression explains none of the variation in the dependent variable. Note that we do not test whether the regression passes through the origin ($\beta_1 = 0$); our objective is simply to see whether we can explain any variation around the mean of Y.

The F test of the significance of a regression equation may allow for rejection of the null hypothesis even though none of the regression coefficients are found to be significant according to individual t tests. This situation may arise, for example, if the independent variables are highly correlated with each other. The result may be high standard errors for the coefficients and low t values, yet the model as a whole may fit the data well.

What if we were to use R^2 to compare the validity of alternative regression models when the dependent variable varies from regression to regression? This occurs in econometric model building when the researcher has little informa-

---

[5] There is a simple rule for one wishing to maximize corrected R^2. If independent variables are left in the regression equation when their t statistic is greater than 1 and are dropped otherwise, then corrected R^2 will be maximized. For details, see P. J. Dhrymes, "On the Game of Maximizing $\bar{R}^2$," *Australian Economic Papers*, vol. 9, December 1970.

tion about the functional form of the dependent variable. Consider the two models

I $Y_i = \beta_1 + \beta_2 X_{2i} + \beta_3 X_{3i} + \varepsilon_i$

II $Y_i - X_{2i} = \beta_1' + \beta_2' X_{2i} + \beta_3' X_{3i} + \varepsilon_i'$

Model I differs from model II only in that the dependent variables differ. (Y might be total local government expenditures, including federal grants, and X_2 might be grants, making the second dependent variable expenditures paid for by locally raised revenues.) It can be shown (see Exercise 4.1) that

1. The R^2 and $\overline{R}^2$ measures associated with models I and II will differ.
2. $\hat{\beta}_1' = \hat{\beta}_1$, $\hat{\beta}_2' = \hat{\beta}_2 - 1$, and $\hat{\beta}_3' = \hat{\beta}_3$.
3. The errors, the least-squares residuals, and the residual variance will be identical in the two models.

Both versions of the model provide identical information, yet the measures of goodness of fit will vary considerably from one case to the other. Thus, R^2 cannot be used *directly* to compare models with different dependent variables.

Example 4.1 (*continued*) Auto Sales   In our earlier auto sales example, the complete regression results are as follows:

Coefficient	Value	Standard error	t statistic
β_1	.60	.14	4.22
β_2	.0070	.0028	2.46
β_3	-1.366	.688	-1.98

Number of variables = 3 (including the constant)
Number of observations = 82   Degrees of freedom = 79
$R^2 = .42$ $\overline{R}^2 = .40$
$F(2, 79) = F_{2, 79} = 28.1$
Standard error of regression(s) = .118
Error sum of squares = ESS = 1.105

All estimated coefficients are significant at the 5 percent level (or marginally significant in the case of the interest rate variable) since all t statistics are greater than or equal to 1.98 in absolute value and there are 79 degrees of freedom. For this reason, none of the variables should be dropped from the regression. The R^2 and $\overline{R}^2$ statistics are very close in magnitude, as expected, since there are a large number of degrees of freedom in the model. The F statistic with 2 and 79 degrees of freedom is highly significant, allowing us to reject the null hypothesis that all explanatory variable coefficients are jointly 0. Finally, the reader should check the relation between the sum of squared residuals and the standard error of the regression: $s^2 = $ ESS/79.

Example 4.2 Interest Rates   In this example we use least squares to estimate a model that explains the movement of monthly interest rates from January 1960 through August 1995. We will return to this interest rate example at various other points in the book, when we treat serial correlation (Chapter 6), single-equation forecasting (Chapter 8), simultaneous equations (Chapter 12), and ARIMA forecasting (Chapter 18).

Interest rates are believed to be determined by the aggregate demand for and supply of liquid assets. The variables that underlie the regression model are as follows:[6]

R = 3-month U.S. Treasury bill rate, in percent per year
IP = Federal Reserve Board index of industrial production (1987 = 100)
$M2$ = nominal money supply, in billions of dollars
PW = producer price index for all commodities (1982 = 100)

The index of industrial production provides a useful measure of the demand for liquid assets; we would expect that increases in production would imply increases in demand, which in turn would increase interest rates. The money supply is an obvious addition to the model, since changes in Federal Reserve policy that cause changes in the money supply directly influence interest rates. A similar story applies to changes in prices, since an increase in the rate of inflation will lead to an increase in interest rates.

The particular money and price change variables used in the regression model were

$$GM2_t = (M2_t - M2_{t-1})/M2_{t-1} \quad \text{and} \quad GPW_t = (PW_t - PW_{t-1})/PW_{t-1}$$

The estimated equation (with t statistics in parentheses) is

$$\hat{R}_t = 1.214 + .0484\ IP_t + 140.33\ GM2_t + 104.58\ GPW_{t-1}$$
$$\quad (2.20) \quad (8.79) \quad\quad (3.89) \quad\quad\quad (6.00)$$

$$R^2 = .22 \quad s = 2.481$$

Industrial production has a strong and significant positive effect on interest rates, as expected. The inflation variable, entering with a 1-month lag, also has the expected sign and is significant. However, the positive sign on the money growth variable GM is directly contrary to our expectations. A further concern is the relatively low R^2 and the relatively high standard error of the regression. The standard error of 2.481 is approximately 40 percent of the mean, which is high for a macroeconomic model of this type.

---

[6] These variables are based on ones taken from the Citibase database: FYGN3, IP, FM2, and PW.

We will see in Chapter 6 that when we improve the specification and use a more efficient method of estimation for this interest rate equation, the sign of the money growth variable will change and the fit of the equation will improve substantially.

Example 4.3 Consumption Function   Three separate regression equations can be used to illustrate some of the econometric issues that arise with the estimation of a simple aggregate consumption function, relating personal consumption (C), savings (S), and disposable personal income (Y). The three models are as follows (data are quarterly, from 1954–1, the first quarter of 1954, to 1995–2, in current dollars:[7]

I $\qquad C_t = \alpha_1 + \beta_1 Y_t + \varepsilon_{1t}$

II $\qquad C_t = \alpha_2 + \beta_2 Y_t + \gamma_2 C_{t-1} + \varepsilon_{2t}$

III $\qquad S_t = \alpha_3 + \beta_3 Y_t + \varepsilon_{3t} \qquad S_t \equiv Y_t - C_t$

The regression results are listed in the following table:

Model	Coefficient	Value	t statistic
I	$\hat{\alpha}_1$	-21.61	-5.75
	$\hat{\beta}_1$	.93	562.5
	$R^2 = .9995$		$s = 31.68$
II	$\hat{\alpha}_2$	$-.066$	$-.047$
	$\hat{\beta}_2$	.18	8.58
	$\hat{\gamma}_2$	.81	35.44
	$R^2 = .9999$		$s = 10.77$
III	$\hat{\alpha}_3$	21.61	5.75
	$\hat{\beta}_3$	.07	44.37
	$R^2 = .9230$		$s = 31.68$

Model I describes the simplest form of the consumption function, in which consumption is determined only by disposable income Y in the same time period. The coefficient of the disposable income variable measures the marginal propensity to consume. In model II a term is added to include the effect of lagged consumption on present consumption. The term is included to

---

[7] The data are from the Citibase database. The variables used are GC and GYD (measured in billions of dollars).

allow current consumption to depend on recent consumption behavior as well as income. The coefficient of the disposable income term must be interpreted differently in model II than in model I. The value of .18 in model II refers to the change in consumption associated with a 1-unit change in disposable income, assuming that consumption in the previous period has remained unchanged. Note that the total effect of a change in disposable income on consumption will take place over time and can be measured only by calculating the long-run marginal propensity to consume, assuming that consumption is unchanged over time.[8] Solving for $C_t = C_{t-1}$, we find that the long-run marginal propensity to consume implied by model II is $.18/(1 - .81) = .95$.

Note the slight increase in R^2 from model I to model II. Since the R^2 for the original equation is already quite high, it is tempting to assume that adding additional variables cannot add much to the explanatory power of the model, but the significant t statistic on the lagged consumption term in model II shows that this is not the case.

Model III represents a savings function, not a consumption function, but a quick examination of the regression results shows the two to be closely related. This is not surprising, since savings is the difference between disposable income and consumption. Note that the estimated coefficients are closely related to each other. The intercepts of models I and III differ only by sign, and the sum of the two slope coefficients is identically 1. The reader can see why this is true by substituting $Y_t - C_t$ for S_t in model III and comparing the results with model I. In addition, the regression sum of squares, the standard error of the regressions, and the residuals are identical in both models.

What appears surprising at first is that the R^2 falls substantially when one moves from model I to model III. The reason for this drop can be seen by recalling that $R^2 = 1 - \text{ESS/TSS}$. Since the estimated residuals are identical in both equations, the error sum of squares is also identical. However, the total sum of squares is different because the dependent variables are different. Thus, models can be alike in almost all respects yet differ substantially in R^2. We will see in Chapter 8 that the standard error of the regression is often more useful as a measure of the predictive power of a regression equation than is R^2.

4.4 MULTICOLLINEARITY

4.4.1 Perfect Collinearity

One of the assumptions of the multiple regression model is that there is no exact linear relationship between any of the independent variables in the model. If such a linear relationship does exist, we say that the independent

---

[8] A detailed analysis of model II is presented in Chapter 9 when distributed lags are discussed.

variables are perfectly *collinear* or that perfect *collinearity* exists. Assume, for example, that the grade-point-average model from Chapter 1 consisted of the following three independent variables:

X_2 = family income, thousands of dollars
X_3 = average hours of study per day
X_4 = average hours of study per week

Variables X_3 and X_4 are perfectly collinear because $X_4 = 7X_3$ for *each and every* student being surveyed. Each parameter makes perfect sense if only one of the collinear variables appears in the model. When both appear, we are faced with an impossible problem. The coefficient of the X_3 variable is a partial regression coefficient measuring the change in Y associated with a unit change in X_3 *with all other variables constant.* Since it is impossible to keep all other variables constant, we are not able to interpret (or even define) the regression coefficient.[9] Perfect collinearity is easy to discover because it will be impossible to calculate least-squares estimates of the parameters. (With collinearity, the system of equations to be solved contains two or more equations which are not independent.)

4.4.2   The Effects of Multicollinearity

In practice, we are often faced with the more difficult problem of having independent variables with a high degree of *multicollinearity.* Multicollinearity arises when two or more variables (or combinations of variables) are highly (but not perfectly) correlated with each other. Suppose two variables are related in this manner. Then it will be possible to obtain least-squares estimates of the regression coefficients, but *interpretation* of the coefficients will be quite difficult. The regression coefficient of the first of the two highly correlated variables is interpreted to measure the change in Y that is due to a change in the variable in question, *other things being equal.* Any time a given change in one variable occurs, the corresponding observation on its highly correlated partner is likely to change in a predictably similar fashion. Thus the presence of multicollinearity implies that there will be very little data in the sample to give one confidence about such an interpretation..

Not surprisingly, the distributions of the estimated regression parameters are quite sensitive to the correlation between independent variables, and also to the magnitude of the standard error of the regression. (Recall that in the two-variable model, the estimated variance of $\hat{\beta}$ is $s^2/\Sigma x_i^2$.) This sensitivity shows up in the form of very high standard errors for the regression parameter. This can be seen if we examine the formulas for the variances of the estimated parameters given in Eqs. (4.6) and (4.7). Both denominators include the term

---

[9] With perfect collinearity, we cannot calculate the least-squares parameter estimates. To see this, reconsider Eqs. (4.3) to (4.5) when X_2 and X_3 are perfectly collinear. In this case Eqs. (4.4) and (4.5) will not be independent, and no solution will exist.

$1 - r^2$. When X_2 and X_3 are uncorrelated in the sample, $r = 0$ and the formulas are essentially identical. However, when r becomes high (close to 1) in absolute value, multicollinearity is present, with the result that the estimated variances of both $\hat{\beta}_2$ and $\hat{\beta}_3$ get very large. This tells us that while $\hat{\beta}_2$ and $\hat{\beta}_3$ will remain unbiased estimators, the reliance that we can place on the value of one or the other will be small. This presents a problem if we believe that one or both of two variables ought to be in a model, but we cannot reject the null hypothesis because of the large estimated standard errors. It may be reasonable in such cases to drop one of the two variables from the equation and reestimate it. We shall see in Chapter 7 that this can cause bias in the reestimated model, but it will help us gauge the effect of the multicollinearity in the original model.[10]

The easiest way to tell whether multicollinearity is causing problems is to examine the standard errors of the coefficients. If several coefficients have high standard errors, and dropping one or more variables from the equation lowers the standard errors of the remaining variables, multicollinearity usually will be the source of the problem. A more sophisticated analysis would take into account the fact that the *covariance* between estimated parameters (as well as the individual standard errors) may be sensitive to multicollinearity. As Eq. (4.8) shows, a high degree of collinearity will be associated with a relatively high (in absolute value) covariance between estimated parameters. This suggests that if one estimated parameter $\hat{\beta}_i$ overestimates the true parameter β_i, a second parameter estimate $\hat{\beta}_j$ is likely to underestimate β_j, and vice versa (assuming $r > 0$).

4.4.3 Indications of Multicollinearity

An estimated model with high standard errors and low t statistics could be indicative of multicollinearity, but it could alternatively suggest that the underlying model is a poor one. How can one test for the presence of multicollinearity?

We have seen that multicollinearity occurs in a particular sample when two or more of the explanatory variables are sufficiently highly correlated to make it difficult to separate the effects of one explanatory variable on the dependent variable from the effects of the other explanatory variables. Explanatory variables are rarely uncorrelated with each other, and so multicollinearity is a matter of degree; consequently, a number of procedures are used to indicate its presence.

1. A relatively high R^2 in an equation with few significant t statistics is one indicator of multicollinearity. In fact, it is possible that the F statistic for the

---

[10] For an additional treatment of tests for multicollinearity, see D. E. Farrar and R. R. Glauber, "Multicollinearity in Regression Analysis: The Problem Re-visited," *Review of Economics and Statistics*, vol. 49, pp. 92–107, 1967. See also D. Belsley, E. Kuh, and R. Welsch, *Regression Diagnostics: Identifying Influential Data and Sources of Collinearity* (New York: Wiley, 1980).

regression equation will be highly significant, while none of the individual t statistics are themselves significant.

2. Relatively high simple correlations between one or more pairs of explanatory variables may indicate multicollinearity. Conclusions about the presence or absence of multicollinearity that are based solely on these correlations must be made with care, however. It is possible that with some data sets, especially those involving time series, correlations among many pairs of variables will be high, yet the data will allow one to separate out the effects of individual explanatory variables on the dependent variable. An additional limitation is that an examination of pairwise simple correlations will not allow one to detect multicollinearity that arises because three or four variables are related to each other.

3. A number of formal tests for multicollinearity have been proposed over the years, but none has found widespread acceptance. One test involves the calculation of a *condition number* associated with the explanatory variable data set. A condition number greater than 20 or 30 is indicative of the presence of multicollinearity.[11]

4.5   STANDARDIZED COEFFICIENTS AND ELASTICITIES

4.5.1   Standardized Coefficients

Standardized coefficients describe the relative importance of the independent variables in a multiple regression model. To calculate standardized coefficients, one simply performs a linear regression in which each variable is *normalized* by subtracting its mean and dividing by its estimated standard deviation. The normalized regression model looks as follows:

$$\frac{Y_i - \overline{Y}}{s_Y} = \beta_2^* \frac{X_{2i} - \overline{X}_2}{s_{X_2}} + \beta_3^* \frac{X_{3i} - \overline{X}_3}{s_{X_3}} + \cdots + \beta_k^* \frac{X_{ki} - \overline{X}_k}{s_{X_k}} + \varepsilon_i \quad (4.13)$$

The standardized coefficients bear a close relationship to the estimated coefficients of the original nonnormalized multiple regression model. It is not difficult to prove that[12]

$$\hat{\beta}_j^* = \hat{\beta}_j \frac{s_{X_j}}{s_Y} \quad j = 2, 3, \ldots, k \quad (4.14)$$

In other words, the standardized coefficient adjusts the estimated slope parameter by the ratio of the standard deviation of the independent variable to the

---

[11] We describe this test only briefly here because it involves matrix algebra. It is spelled out in D. Belsley, E. Kuh, and R. Welsch, *Regression Diagnostics: Identifying Influential Data and Sources of Collinearity* (New York: Wiley, 1980). For a more recent summary, see W. H. Greene, *Econometric Analysis*, 2nd ed. (New York: Macmillan, 1993), Section 9.2.

[12] Writing Eq. (4.13) in deviations form and multiplying both sides by s_Y, we get $y_i = \beta_2^*(s_Y/s_{X_2})x_{2i} + \beta_3^*(s_Y/s_{X_3})x_{3i} + \cdots + \beta_k^*(s_Y/s_{X_k})x_{ki} + \varepsilon_i^*$, from which our result follows directly.

standard deviation of the dependent variable. A standardized coefficient of .7 means that a change of 1 standard deviation in the independent variable will lead to a change of .7 standard deviation in the dependent variable.

Both standardized coefficients and partial correlation coefficients are connected with the variance of Y, the dependent variable. However, the rescaling associated with the normalized regression makes it possible to compare standardized coefficients directly. This cannot be done with the original X's because the dependent variables are in different units with different variances. It is interesting to note that the standardized coefficient of the independent variable in the two-variable model is identically equal to the simple correlation between the two variables. The standardized coefficient of the constant term is undefined, since the constant term drops out as a result of the normalization process.

4.5.2 Elasticity

An elasticity measures the effect on the dependent variable of a 1 percent change in an independent variable. The elasticity of Y with respect to X_2, for example, is the percentage change in Y divided by the percentage change in X_2.

In general, elasticities are not constant but change when measured at different points along the regression line. The elasticities which are usually printed out by computer programs are calculated *at the point of the mean of each of the independent variables.* For the jth coefficient the elasticity is evaluated as

$$E_j = \hat{\beta}_j \frac{X_j}{\bar{Y}} \approx \frac{\partial Y}{\bar{Y}} \bigg/ \frac{X_j}{\bar{X}_j} \tag{4.15}$$

The values of the elasticity are unbounded and may be positive or negative. Elasticities are useful because they are unit-free; i.e., their values are independent of the units in which the variables are measured. For example, if $E_j = 2.0$, we can say that about the mean of the variables a 1 percent increase in X_j will lead to a 2 percent increase in Y. On the other hand, if $E_j = -.5$, a 1 percent increase in X_j will lead to a .5 percent decrease in Y. In general, large elasticities imply that the dependent variable is very responsive to changes in the independent variable.

4.6 PARTIAL CORRELATION AND STEPWISE REGRESSION

In the multiple regression model, it is natural to extend the simple correlation concept to see how much the dependent variable and one independent variable are related after netting out the effect of other independent variables in the model. To do so, we consider the model

$$Y_i = \beta_1 + \beta_2 X_{2i} + \beta_3 X_{3i} + \varepsilon_i$$

The *partial correlation coefficient* between Y and X_2 must be defined in such a way that it measures the effect of X_2 on Y *which is not accounted for by the other variables in the model.* More specifically, the partial correlation coefficient is calculated by eliminating the linear effect of X_3 on Y (as well as the linear effect of X_3 on X_2) and then running the appropriate regression. The steps are as follows:

1. Run the regression of Y on X_3 and obtain fitted values

$$\hat{Y} = \hat{a}_1 + \hat{a}_2 X_3$$

2. Run the regression of X_2 on X_3 and obtain fitted values

$$\hat{X}_2 = \hat{\gamma}_1 + \hat{\gamma}_2 X_3$$

3. Remove the influence of X_3 on both Y and X_2. Let

$$Y^* = Y - \hat{Y} \quad X_2^* = X_2 - \hat{X}_2$$

4. The partial correlation between X_2 and Y is then the simple correlation between Y^* and X_2^*.

To see why the regression of Y^* on X_2^* will give us the desired partial correlation coefficient, note that Y^* and X_2^* are both uncorrelated with X_3 by construction.[13] Then the regression of Y^* on X_2^* relates the part of Y which is uncorrelated with X_3 to the part of X_2 which is uncorrelated with X_3. We denote the partial correlation coefficient and simple correlations as follows:

$r_{YX_2 \cdot X_3}$ = partial correlation of Y and X_2 (controlling for X_3)
r_{YX_2} = simple correlation between Y and X_2
$r_{X_2X_3}$ = simple correlation between X_2 and X_3

Given the definition of partial correlation, it is not difficult to derive the relationship between partial correlation and simple correlation. We state the result without proof, since the details are complicated:

$$r_{YX_2 \cdot X_3} = \frac{r_{YX_2} - r_{YX_3} r_{X_2X_3}}{\sqrt{1 - r_{X_2X_3}^2} \sqrt{1 - r_{YX_3}^2}} \qquad (4.16)$$

[13] The fact that Y^* and X_3 (for example) are uncorrelated follows directly from the fact that Y^* represents the residual of the regression of Y on X_3. We have seen in Chapter 3 that regression residuals are uncorrelated with explanatory variables.

$$r_{YX_3 \cdot X_2} = \frac{r_{YX_3} - r_{YX_2} r_{X_2 X_3}}{\sqrt{1 - r_{X_2 X_3}^2} \sqrt{1 - r_{YX_2}^2}} \tag{4.17}$$

Partial correlations must range in value from -1 to $+1$, just as simple correlations must (recall the derivation of simple correlation). A zero partial correlation between Y and X_2 indicates that there is no linear relationship between Y and X_2 *after the linear effect of X_3 on each has been accounted for.* In such a case we would conclude that X_2 does not have a *direct* effect on Y in the model. In fact, partial correlation coefficients often are used to determine the relative importance of different variables in multiple regression models.

Now let us look at the relationship between partial correlation and R^2. In the two-variable model it is easy to show that one can interpret R^2 as the square of the simple correlation between the dependent and independent variables. It is also possible to interpret the partial correlation between Y and X_2 as the square root of the percentage of variance in Y which is not accounted for by X_3 but which is accounted for by the part of X_2 which is uncorrelated with X_3. Given this fact, it is possible to derive the following relationship between multiple and partial correlation:

$$r_{YX_2 \cdot X_3}^2 = \frac{R^2 - r_{YX_3}^2}{1 - r_{YX_3}^2}$$

or
$$1 - R^2 = (1 - r_{YX_3}^2)(1 - r_{YX_2 \cdot X_3}^2) \tag{4.18}$$

From Eq. (4.18) the partial correlation coefficient can be determined by taking the square root of the percentage of the variance in Y explained by X_2 (with both variables adjusted to eliminate the effect of X_3).

Perhaps the most frequent use of partial correlation occurs in the *stepwise regression* procedure. In stepwise regression one adds variables to a model to maximize $\bar{R}^2$. The partial correlation between each explanatory variable and the dependent variable is useful in determining which variable to add because it tells us whether a given variable affects the dependent variable after the impact of all variables previously included in the model has been eliminated. While stepwise regression can be useful in looking at data when there are a large number of possible explanatory variables, it is of little value when one is attempting to analyze a model statistically. The reason is that t and F tests consider the test of a null hypothesis under the assumption that the model is correctly specified. If we have searched over a large set of variables, selecting the ones that fit well, we are likely to get significant t tests with great frequency. As a result, large t statistics do not allow us to reject the null hypothesis at a given level of significance.

Example 4.4 The Pricing of Scalped Football Tickets[14]   During the 1978 and 1979 seasons, the University of Alabama football team was in a fight for the national championship. Regular season tickets were sold out, and an active market for "scalped" tickets developed. In Alabama, unlike many other states, the resale of tickets to sporting events is legal. Each ticket sold during this period had a list price of $10.00, but actual market prices varied substantially because of changes in the demand for tickets by those without season tickets and changes in the supply of resold tickets by those with season tickets. The regression model relates the average price of resold tickets for each of the 22 games played during the two seasons to a number of demand and supply variables.

The scalped tickets equation is

$$P_i = \beta_1 + \beta_2 SEC_i + \beta_3 TV_i + \beta_4 RANK_i + \beta_5 LWIN_i$$
$$+ \beta_6 WIN_i + \beta_7 HOME_i + \varepsilon_i$$

where P = the average price of a scalped ticket
   SEC = 1 if the opponent is in Alabama's Southeast Conference; 0 if otherwise
   TV = 1 if the game is on television; 0 if otherwise
   $RANK$ = Alabama's previous week ranking in the national football polls
   $LWIN$ = the opponent's win-loss percentage the prior year
   WIN = the opponent's win-loss percentage the current year
   $HOME$ = 1 if the game is at home; 0 if otherwise

The regression results, including the regular and the standardized coefficients, are shown in the following table.

Variable	Coefficient	Standardized coefficient	t statistic (for std. coeff.)
Constant	4.64	19.77	1.83
SEC	5.59	13.05	−2.03
TV	−9.21	−18.10	−2.03
RANK	−1.20	−13.87	−2.05
LWIN	.30	22.10	2.68
WIN	.06	9.57	1.41
HOME	4.97	11.28	1.96

The coefficients in the second column tell us the effect on the dependent variable of a unit change in each of the independent variables. But it is hard to compare the importance of the independent variables in determining

[14] This example is based on Terrence F. Martell and Hassan Tehranian, "The Determinants of Scalped Ticket Prices," *Northeast Journal of Business & Economics*, vol. 14, pp. 33–43, Fall/Winter 1987–1988.

scalped ticket prices, since the units of measurement vary. The standardized coefficients, in the third column, are more appropriate for this purpose. The most important determinant of the scalped price is the opponent's win-loss percentage from the last season (the standardized coefficient is the highest of all the independent variables). The better the opponent's record, the higher the ticket price. All the remaining variables also have the signs we would expect. In order of importance we find that the higher Alabama's ranking, the higher the ticket price (a high ranking means a lower number for the variable RANK), TV coverage lowers the ticket price (since individuals can watch the game at home), Southeast Conference games are more expensive than nonconference games, tickets for home games are more expensive than tickets for away games, and the better the opponent's current record, the higher the ticket price.

Example 4.5 Sales of Durable Goods To predict the monthly sales of durable goods via a linear regression model, the following data are used for the period July 1967 to August 1995:[15]

1. Dependent variable
   SD = monthly retail sales of durable goods (millions of dollars)
2. Independent variables
   DI = retail inventory of department stores in durable goods (millions of dollars)
   IS = inventory sales ratios for all durable goods, retail stores
   I = open market rate on prime 6-month commercial paper (percent)
   E = average hourly gross earnings of workers (dollars)
   P = Consumer Price Index for durable goods (1983 = 100)

The model is specified to be

$$SD_t = \beta_1 + \beta_2 DI_{t-6} + \beta_3 IS_{t-1} + \beta_4 I_{t-1} + \beta_5 E_{t-1} + \beta_6 P_{t-1} + \varepsilon_t$$

The regression results are as follows:

Coefficient	Value	Standard error	t statistic
$\hat{\beta}_1$	22,632	1,775	12.7
$\hat{\beta}_2$	.415	.018	22.9
$\hat{\beta}_3$	− 12,716	1,023	− 12.4
$\hat{\beta}_4$	− 120.5	53.8	− 2.2
$\hat{\beta}_5$	1,530	726	2.15
$\hat{\beta}_6$	− 7.46	50.6	− .15

[15] The following seasonally adjusted variables were used from the Citibase database: RTDR, IVRDR (IS = IVRDR/RTDR), FYCP, LEH, and PUCD.

Coefficient	Partial	Standardized coefficient	Elasticity
$\hat{\beta}_2$	.78	.84	.86
$\hat{\beta}_3$	−.12	−.09	−.77
$\hat{\beta}_4$	−.11	−.02	−.03
$\hat{\beta}_5$	.31	.21	.32
$\hat{\beta}_6$	−.01	−.01	−.02

$$s = 2{,}049 \quad \overline{R}^2 = .990$$

It is not a coincidence that all independent variables have been chosen to be lagged at least one time period. This accounts for lags in response while at the same time making prediction easier. If one wished to predict monthly retail sales of durable goods at time t, one would simply use the regression equation

$$\widehat{SD}_t = 22{,}632 + .415\, DI_{t-6} - 12{,}716\, IS_{t-1} - 120.5 I_{t-1}$$
$$+ 1{,}530 E_{t-1} - 7.46 P_{t-1}$$

To evaluate SD in period $t + 1$, we substitute values for DI given 6 months previously, IS given 1 month previously, etc. If the independent variables were not lagged, some sort of extrapolation process would be needed to forecast their values before a prediction for the dependent variable could be made.

The column labeled *partial* contains the list of partial correlation coefficients, while the column labeled *standardized coefficient* defines itself. In this example, the independent variable coefficients with the largest t statistics in absolute value tend to have the largest standardized and partial correlation coefficients. The standardized coefficient of .21 on lagged earnings means that a 1 standard deviation increase in lagged earnings will lead to a .21 standard deviation increase in the retail sales of durable goods. The partial correlation coefficient of .31 on the same earnings variable implies that 9.4 percent ($.31^2$) of the variance of SD not accounted for by the other independent variables is accounted for by earnings. By examining the elasticities, we see that retail sales of durable goods are sensitive to changes in the gross earnings of workers but not to the Consumer Price Index for durable goods. If earnings were to rise by 1 percent, then we might expect retail sales to increase slightly more than 0.3 percent. But, if the Consumer Price Index were to rise by 1 percent, retail sales would be expected to fall about .02 percent.

APPENDIX 4.1 Least-Squares Parameter Estimation

Our goal is to minimize ESS $= \Sigma(Y_i - \hat{\beta}_1 - \hat{\beta}_2 X_{2i} - \hat{\beta}_3 X_{3i})^2$. We can do this by calculating the partial derivatives with respect to the three unknown parameters β_1, β_2, and β_3, equating each to 0, and solving. To simplify we use the model in derivations form, so that

$$\text{ESS} = \Sigma(y_i - \hat{\beta}_2 x_{2i} - \hat{\beta}_3 x_{3i})^2$$

Then

$$\frac{\partial \text{ESS}}{\partial \beta_2} = 0 \quad \text{or} \quad \Sigma x_{2i} y_i = \beta_2 \Sigma x_{2i}^2 + \beta_3 \Sigma x_{2i} x_{3i} \qquad (A4.1)$$

$$\frac{\partial \text{ESS}}{\partial \beta_3} = 0 \quad \text{or} \quad \Sigma x_{3i} y_i = \beta_2 \Sigma x_{2i} x_{3i} + \beta_3 \Sigma x_{3i}^2 \qquad (A4.2)$$

To solve, we multiply Eq. (A4.1) by Σx_{3i}^2 and multiply Eq. (A4.2) by $\Sigma x_{2i} x_{3i}$ and then subtract the latter from the former:

$$\Sigma x_{2i} y_i \Sigma x_{3i}^2 - \Sigma x_{3i} y_i \Sigma x_{2i} x_{3i} = \beta_2 [\Sigma x_{2i}^2 \Sigma x_{3i}^2 - (\Sigma x_{2i} x_{3i})^2]$$

or

$$\hat{\beta}_2 = \frac{(\Sigma x_{2i} y_i)(\Sigma x_{3i}^2) - (\Sigma x_{3i} y_i)(\Sigma x_{2i} x_{3i})}{(\Sigma x_{2i}^2)(\Sigma x_{3i}^2) - (\Sigma x_{2i} x_{3i})^2}$$

It follows that

$$\hat{\beta}_3 = \frac{(\Sigma x_{3i} y_i)(\Sigma x_{2i}^2) - (\Sigma x_{2i} y_i)(\Sigma x_{2i} x_{3i})}{(\Sigma x_{2i}^2)(\Sigma x_{3i}^2) - (\Sigma x_{2i} x_{3i})^2}$$

Finally, if we set the derivative of ESS with respect to β_1 equal to zero, we find that

$$\hat{\beta}_1 = \bar{Y} - \hat{\beta}_2 \bar{X}_2 - \hat{\beta}_3 \bar{X}_3$$

APPENDIX 4.2 Regression Coefficients

Consider the three-variable multiple regression model

$$Y_i = \beta_1 + \beta_2 X_{2i} + \beta_3 X_{3i} + \varepsilon_i \qquad (A4.3)$$

We argued in the text that β_2 measures the effect of X_2 on Y, with the effect of X_3 held constant. How is this concept actually applied when we obtain least-squares estimates for β_2 (as well as β_3)? The answer is that the estimated coefficient in the three-variable regression model can be calculated by performing two two-variable regressions. (This result generalizes to any multiple regression model.) The first regression adjusts the variable X_2 to "hold X_3 constant," while the second regression estimates the effect of this adjusted variable on Y. The procedure occurs in the following steps.

Step 1   Regress X_2 on X_3. When the equation has been estimated, we can calculate the fitted values and residuals of the model. To simplify, we will work with the data in deviations form, so that the model is

$$x_{2i} = \hat{\alpha} x_{3i} + \hat{\mu}_i \quad \text{or} \quad x_{2i} = \hat{x}_{2i} + \hat{u}_i$$

where $\hat{x}_{2i} = \hat{\alpha} x_{3i}$ $\hat{u}_i = x_{2i} - \hat{\alpha} x_{3i} = x_{2i} - \hat{x}_{2i}$ and $\hat{\alpha} = \dfrac{\Sigma x_{2i} x_{3i}}{\Sigma x_{3i}^2}$

Our interest lies in $\hat{u}_i$, which represents that portion of X_2 which is uncorrelated with X_3. (Recall that the regression residuals are uncorrelated with the right-hand variable.) In fact, holding X_3 constant means eliminating from X_2 the component that is correlated with X_3.

Step 2   Regress Y on $\hat{u}$. The model is

$$y_i = \gamma \hat{u}_i + v_i$$

When it is estimated, we find that

$$\hat{\gamma} = \frac{\Sigma y_i \hat{u}_i}{\Sigma \hat{u}_i^2}$$

$\hat{\gamma}$ represents the effect of "adjusted X_2" on Y and according to our argument should measure the effect of X_2 on Y holding X_3 constant. If we are correct, it must be that $\gamma = \hat{\beta}_2$. To see this we need only perform a few algebraic calculations:

$$\hat{\gamma} = \frac{\Sigma y_i \hat{u}_i}{\Sigma \hat{u}_i^2}$$

But $\hat{u}_i = x_{2i} - \hat{\alpha} x_{3i} = x_{2i} - \dfrac{\Sigma x_{2i} x_{3i}}{\Sigma x_{3i}^2} x_{3i}$

Therefore, $$\frac{\Sigma y_i \hat{u}_i}{\Sigma \hat{u}_i^2} = \frac{\Sigma x_{2i} y_i - \dfrac{\Sigma x_{2i} x_{3i}}{\Sigma x_{3i}^2} \Sigma x_{3i} y_i}{\Sigma x_{2i}^2 + \left(\dfrac{\Sigma x_{2i} x_{3i}}{\Sigma x_{3i}^2}\right)^2 \Sigma x_{3i}^2 - 2 \dfrac{\Sigma x_{2i} x_{3i}}{\Sigma x_{3i}^2} \Sigma x_{2i} x_{3i}}$$

Now, multiplying both sides of the ratio by Σx_{3i}^2 and simplifying, we get

$$\hat{\gamma} = \frac{\Sigma x_{2i} y_i \Sigma x_{3i}^2 - \Sigma x_{2i} x_{3i} \Sigma x_{3i} y_i}{\Sigma x_{2i}^2 \Sigma x_{3i}^2 - (\Sigma x_{2i} x_{3i})^2} = \hat{\beta}_2$$

APPENDIX 4.3 The Multiple Regression Model in Matrix Form

REPRESENTATION OF THE MULTIPLE REGRESSION MODEL

The purpose of this appendix is to present generalizations of important textual items. It would be difficult to accomplish this without using matrix algebra. We presume that the reader has such prior knowledge.

We begin by representing the linear model in matrix form. Recall from the text that the regression model includes $k + 1$ variables—a dependent variable and k independent variables (including the constant term). Since there are N observations, we can summarize the regression model by writing a series of N equations, as follows:

$$Y_1 = \beta_1 + \beta_2 X_{21} + \beta_3 X_{31} + \cdots + \beta_k X_{k1} + \varepsilon_1$$
$$Y_2 = \beta_1 + \beta_2 X_{22} + \beta_3 X_{32} + \cdots + \beta_k X_{k2} + \varepsilon_2 \qquad \text{(A4.4)}$$
$$\cdots\cdots\cdots\cdots\cdots\cdots\cdots\cdots\cdots\cdots\cdots\cdots$$
$$Y_N = \beta_1 + \beta_2 X_{2N} + \beta_3 X_{3N} + \cdots + \beta_k X_{kN} + \varepsilon_N$$

The corresponding matrix formulation of the model is

$$\mathbf{Y} = \mathbf{X}\boldsymbol{\beta} + \boldsymbol{\varepsilon} \qquad \text{(A4.5)}$$

in which

$$\mathbf{Y} = \begin{bmatrix} Y_1 \\ Y_2 \\ \vdots \\ Y_N \end{bmatrix} \quad \mathbf{X} = \begin{bmatrix} 1 & X_{21} & \cdots & X_{k1} \\ 1 & X_{22} & \cdots & X_{k2} \\ \vdots & & & \vdots \\ 1 & X_{2N} & \cdots & X_{kN} \end{bmatrix} \quad \boldsymbol{\beta} = \begin{bmatrix} \beta_1 \\ \beta_2 \\ \vdots \\ \beta_k \end{bmatrix} \quad \boldsymbol{\varepsilon} = \begin{bmatrix} \varepsilon_1 \\ \varepsilon_2 \\ \vdots \\ \varepsilon_N \end{bmatrix} \qquad \text{(A4.6)}$$

where $\mathbf{Y} = N \times 1$ column vector of dependent variable observations
$\mathbf{X} = N \times k$ matrix of independent variable observations
$\boldsymbol{\beta} = k \times 1$ column vector of unknown parameters
$\boldsymbol{\varepsilon} = N \times 1$ column vector of errors

In our representation of the matrix $\mathbf{X}$, each component $\mathbf{X}_{ji}$ has two subscripts, the first signifying the appropriate column (variable) and the second signifying the appropriate row (observation). Each column of $\mathbf{X}$ represents a vector of N observations on a given variable, with all observations associated with the intercept equal to 1.

The assumptions of the classical linear regression model can be represented as follows:

   i. The model specification is given by Eq. (A4.4).
   ii. The elements of $\mathbf{X}$ are fixed and have finite variance. In addition, $\mathbf{X}$ has rank k, which is less than the number of observations N.
   iii. $\boldsymbol{\varepsilon}$ is normally distributed with $E(\boldsymbol{\varepsilon}) = \mathbf{0}$ and $E(\boldsymbol{\varepsilon}\boldsymbol{\varepsilon}') = \sigma^2 \mathbf{I}$, where $\mathbf{I}$ is an $N \times N$ identity matrix.

The assumption that $\mathbf{X}$ has rank k guarantees that perfect collinearity will not be present. With perfect collinearity, one of the columns of $\mathbf{X}$ would be a linear combination of the remaining columns, and the rank of $\mathbf{X}$ would be less than k. The error assumptions are the strongest possible, since they guarantee the statistical as well as arithmetic properties of the ordinary least-squares estimation process. In addition to normality we assume that each error term has mean 0, all variances are constant, and all covariances are 0. The *variance-covariance matrix* $\sigma^2\mathbf{I}$ appears as follows:

$$
E(\boldsymbol{\varepsilon}\boldsymbol{\varepsilon}') = E\left\{ \begin{bmatrix} \varepsilon_1 \\ \varepsilon_2 \\ \cdots \\ \varepsilon_N \end{bmatrix} \begin{bmatrix} \varepsilon_1 & \varepsilon_2 & \cdots & \varepsilon_N \end{bmatrix} \right\}
$$

$$
= \begin{bmatrix} E(\varepsilon_1^2) & E(\varepsilon_1\varepsilon_2) & \cdots & E(\varepsilon_1\varepsilon_N) \\ E(\varepsilon_2\varepsilon_1) & E(\varepsilon_2^2) & \cdots & E(\varepsilon_2\varepsilon_N) \\ E(\varepsilon_N\varepsilon_1) & E(\varepsilon_N\varepsilon_2) & \cdots & E(\varepsilon_N^2) \end{bmatrix}
$$

$$
= \begin{bmatrix} \text{Var}\,(\varepsilon_1) & \text{Cov}\,(\varepsilon_1, \varepsilon_2) & \cdots & \text{Cov}\,(\varepsilon_1, \varepsilon_N) \\ \text{Cov}\,(\varepsilon_1, \varepsilon_2) & \text{Var}\,(\varepsilon_2) & \cdots & \text{Cov}\,(\varepsilon_2, \varepsilon_N) \\ \text{Cov}\,(\varepsilon_1, \varepsilon_N) & \text{Cov}\,(\varepsilon_2, \varepsilon_N) & \cdots & \text{Var}\,(\varepsilon_N) \end{bmatrix} \qquad \text{(A4.7)}
$$

where $\boldsymbol{\varepsilon}'$ is the $1 \times N$ vector transpose of $\boldsymbol{\varepsilon}$.

LEAST-SQUARES ESTIMATION

Our objective is to find a vector of parameters $\hat{\beta}$ which minimize

$$\text{ESS} = \sum_{i=1}^{N} \hat{\varepsilon}_i^2 = \hat{\varepsilon}'\hat{\varepsilon} \tag{A4.8}$$

where
$$\hat{\varepsilon} = \mathbf{Y} - \hat{\mathbf{Y}} \tag{A4.9}$$

and
$$\hat{\mathbf{Y}} = \mathbf{X}\hat{\beta} \tag{A4.10}$$

$\hat{\varepsilon}$ represents the $N \times 1$ vector of regression residuals, while $\hat{\mathbf{Y}}$ represents the $N \times 1$ vector of fitted values for $\mathbf{Y}$. Substituting Eqs. (A4.9) and (A4.10) into Eq. (A4.8), we get

$$\hat{\varepsilon}'\hat{\varepsilon} = (\mathbf{Y} - \mathbf{X}\hat{\beta})'(\mathbf{Y} - \mathbf{X}\hat{\beta}) = \mathbf{Y}'\mathbf{Y} - \hat{\beta}'\mathbf{X}'\mathbf{Y} - \mathbf{Y}'\mathbf{X}\hat{\beta} + \hat{\beta}'\mathbf{X}'\mathbf{X}\hat{\beta}$$
$$= \mathbf{Y}'\mathbf{Y} - 2\hat{\beta}'\mathbf{X}'\mathbf{Y} + \hat{\beta}'\mathbf{X}'\mathbf{X}\hat{\beta} \tag{A4.11}$$

The last step follows because $\hat{\beta}'\mathbf{X}'\mathbf{Y}$ and $\mathbf{Y}'\mathbf{X}\hat{\beta}$ are both scalars and are equal to each other. To determine the least-squares estimators, we minimize ESS as follows:

$$\frac{\partial \text{ESS}}{\partial \hat{\beta}} = -2\mathbf{X}'\mathbf{Y} + 2\mathbf{X}'\mathbf{X}\hat{\beta} = 0$$

$$\hat{\beta} = (\mathbf{X}'\mathbf{X})^{-1}(\mathbf{X}'\mathbf{Y}) \tag{A4.12}$$

The matrix $\mathbf{X}'\mathbf{X}$, called the *cross-product matrix,* is guaranteed to have an inverse because of our assumption that $\mathbf{X}$ has rank k.[16]

Two results concerning the least-squares residuals may be useful in some of the deviations which follow:

$$\mathbf{X}'\hat{\varepsilon} = \mathbf{X}'(\mathbf{Y} - \mathbf{X}\hat{\beta}) = \mathbf{X}'\mathbf{Y} - \mathbf{X}'\mathbf{X}\hat{\beta} = 0 \tag{A4.13}$$

$$\hat{\varepsilon}'\hat{\varepsilon} = \mathbf{Y}'\mathbf{Y} - \hat{\beta}'\mathbf{X}'\mathbf{Y} \quad \text{from (A4.11) and (A4.12)} \tag{A4.14}$$

The first result proves that the sum of the cross-products of the independent variables and the residuals is 0. This is the sample analog of the assumption that $E(\mathbf{X}'\varepsilon) = \mathbf{0}$.

---

[16] The second-order conditions for the minimization of ESS follow from the fact that $\mathbf{X}'\mathbf{X}$ is a positive definite matrix.

Now consider the properties of the least-squares estimator $\hat{\boldsymbol{\beta}}$. First, we can prove that $\hat{\boldsymbol{\beta}}$ is an unbiased estimator of $\boldsymbol{\beta}$:

$$\hat{\boldsymbol{\beta}} = (\mathbf{X'X})^{-1}\mathbf{X'Y} = (\mathbf{X'X})^{-1}\mathbf{X'}(\mathbf{X}\boldsymbol{\beta} + \boldsymbol{\varepsilon})$$

$$= \boldsymbol{\beta} + (\mathbf{X'X})^{-1}\mathbf{X'}\boldsymbol{\varepsilon} = \boldsymbol{\beta} + \mathbf{A}\boldsymbol{\varepsilon} \qquad \text{where } \mathbf{A} = (\mathbf{X'X})^{-1}\mathbf{X'} \quad \text{(A4.15)}$$

$$E(\hat{\boldsymbol{\beta}}) = \boldsymbol{\beta} + E(\mathbf{A}\boldsymbol{\varepsilon}) = \boldsymbol{\beta} + \mathbf{A}E(\boldsymbol{\varepsilon}) = \boldsymbol{\beta}$$

Looking at Eq. (A4.15), we notice that $\mathbf{A}\boldsymbol{\varepsilon} = (\mathbf{X'X})^{-1}\mathbf{X'}\boldsymbol{\varepsilon}$ represents the regression of $\boldsymbol{\varepsilon}$ on $\mathbf{X}$. As long as the effects of missing variables are randomly distributed independently of $\mathbf{X}$ and have 0 mean, the least-squares parameter estimator will be unbiased.

The least-squares estimator will be normally distributed, since $\hat{\boldsymbol{\beta}}$ is a linear function of $\boldsymbol{\varepsilon}$ and $\boldsymbol{\varepsilon}$ is normally distributed. The properties of the variances of the individual $\hat{\beta}_i$'s and their covariances are determined as follows:

$$\mathbf{V} = E[(\hat{\boldsymbol{\beta}} - \boldsymbol{\beta})(\hat{\boldsymbol{\beta}} - \boldsymbol{\beta})']$$

$$= \begin{bmatrix} E(\hat{\beta}_1 - \beta_1)^2 & \cdots & E[(\hat{\beta}_1 - \beta_1)(\hat{\beta}_k - \beta_k)] \\ \cdots\cdots\cdots\cdots\cdots\cdots\cdots\cdots\cdots\cdots\cdots\cdots\cdots\cdots\cdots\cdots \\ E[(\hat{\beta}_k - \beta_k)(\hat{\beta}_1 - \beta_1)] & \cdots & E(\hat{\beta}_k - \beta_k)^2 \end{bmatrix}$$

$$= \begin{bmatrix} \text{Var}(\hat{\beta}_1) & \cdots & \text{Cov}(\hat{\beta}_1, \hat{\beta}_k) \\ \cdots\cdots\cdots\cdots\cdots\cdots\cdots\cdots\cdots\cdots\cdots \\ \text{Cov}(\hat{\beta}_1, \hat{\beta}_k) & \cdots & \text{Var}(\hat{\beta}_k) \end{bmatrix} \qquad \text{(A4.16)}$$

The diagonal elements of $\mathbf{V}$ represent the variances of the estimated parameters, while the off-diagonal terms represent the covariances. We will sometimes write $\mathbf{V} = \text{Var}(\hat{\boldsymbol{\beta}})$. Then

$$\text{Var}(\hat{\boldsymbol{\beta}}) = E[(\hat{\boldsymbol{\beta}} - \boldsymbol{\beta})(\hat{\boldsymbol{\beta}} - \boldsymbol{\beta})'] = E[(\mathbf{A}\boldsymbol{\varepsilon})(\mathbf{A}\boldsymbol{\varepsilon})'] = E(\mathbf{A}\boldsymbol{\varepsilon}\boldsymbol{\varepsilon}'\mathbf{A}')$$

$$= \mathbf{A}E(\boldsymbol{\varepsilon}\boldsymbol{\varepsilon}')\mathbf{A}' = \mathbf{A}(\sigma^2\mathbf{I})\mathbf{A}' = \sigma^2\mathbf{A}\mathbf{A}'$$

since $\mathbf{A}$ and $\mathbf{A}'$ are matrices of fixed numbers. But

$$\mathbf{A}\mathbf{A}' = [(\mathbf{X'X})^{-1}\mathbf{X'}][(\mathbf{X'X})^{-1}\mathbf{X'}]' = [(\mathbf{X'X})^{-1}\mathbf{X'}][\mathbf{X}(\mathbf{X'X})^{-1}]$$

$$= (\mathbf{X'X})^{-1}(\mathbf{X'X})(\mathbf{X'X})^{-1} = (\mathbf{X'X})^{-1}$$

Therefore,
$$E[(\hat{\boldsymbol{\beta}} - \boldsymbol{\beta})(\hat{\boldsymbol{\beta}} - \boldsymbol{\beta})'] = \sigma^2(\mathbf{X'X})^{-1} \qquad \text{(A4.17)}$$

We have already proved that the least-squares estimator is linear and unbiased. In fact, $\hat{\boldsymbol{\beta}}$ is the best linear unbiased estimator of $\boldsymbol{\beta}$ in the sense that it has the minimum variance of all unbiased estimators. To complete the proof of the *Gauss-Markov theorem*, we need to show that any other unbiased linear estimator $\mathbf{b}$ has greater variance than $\hat{\boldsymbol{\beta}}$. Recall that $\hat{\boldsymbol{\beta}} = \mathbf{A}\mathbf{Y}$. Without loss of generality, we can write (for any matrix $\mathbf{C}$)

$$\mathbf{b} = (\mathbf{A} + \mathbf{C})\mathbf{Y} = \mathbf{A}\mathbf{Y} + \mathbf{C}\mathbf{Y} = \hat{\boldsymbol{\beta}} + \mathbf{C}\mathbf{Y} = (\mathbf{A} + \mathbf{C})\mathbf{X}\boldsymbol{\beta} + (\mathbf{A} + \mathbf{C})\boldsymbol{\varepsilon}$$

If **b** is unbiased, then

$$E(\mathbf{b}) = (\mathbf{X'X})^{-1}\mathbf{X'X}\boldsymbol{\beta} + \mathbf{CX}\boldsymbol{\beta} = (\mathbf{I} + \mathbf{CX})\boldsymbol{\beta} = \boldsymbol{\beta} \qquad (\text{A4.18})$$

A necessary and sufficient condition for this to hold for all $\boldsymbol{\beta}$ is for

$$\mathbf{CX} = \mathbf{0}$$

Now examine the matrix Var (**b**). Since $\mathbf{b} - \boldsymbol{\beta} = (\mathbf{A} + \mathbf{C})\boldsymbol{\varepsilon}$,[17]

$$\begin{aligned} \text{Var }(\mathbf{b}) &= E[(\mathbf{b} - \boldsymbol{\beta})(\mathbf{b} - \boldsymbol{\beta})'] = E[(\mathbf{A} + \mathbf{C})\boldsymbol{\varepsilon}][(\mathbf{A} + \mathbf{C})\boldsymbol{\varepsilon}]' \\ &= E[(\mathbf{A} + \mathbf{C})\boldsymbol{\varepsilon}\boldsymbol{\varepsilon}'(\mathbf{A} + \mathbf{C})'] = (\mathbf{A} + \mathbf{C})E(\boldsymbol{\varepsilon}\boldsymbol{\varepsilon}')(\mathbf{A} + \mathbf{C})' \\ &= \sigma^2(\mathbf{A} + \mathbf{C})(\mathbf{A} + \mathbf{C})' \end{aligned}$$

But

$$\begin{aligned} (\mathbf{A} + \mathbf{C})(\mathbf{A} + \mathbf{C})' &= \mathbf{AA'} + \mathbf{CA'} + \mathbf{AC'} + \mathbf{CC'} \\ &= (\mathbf{X'X})^{-1}\mathbf{X'X}(\mathbf{X'X})^{-1} + \mathbf{CX}(\mathbf{X'X})^{-1} \\ &\quad + (\mathbf{X'X})^{-1}\mathbf{X'C'} + \mathbf{CC'} \\ &= (\mathbf{X'X})^{-1} + \mathbf{CC'} \qquad \text{since } \mathbf{CX} = \mathbf{X'C'} = \mathbf{0} \end{aligned}$$

Therefore,

$$\text{Var }(\mathbf{b}) = \sigma^2[(\mathbf{X'X})^{-1} + \mathbf{CC'}] = \text{Var }(\hat{\boldsymbol{\beta}}) + \sigma^2\mathbf{CC'} \qquad (\text{A4.19})$$

We can observe that **CC'** is a positive semidefinite matrix. The only case in which the quadratic form associated with this matrix will be 0 is when $\mathbf{C} = \mathbf{0}$ (all elements are 0). When $\mathbf{C} = \mathbf{0}$, the alternative estimator becomes the ordinary least-squares estimator $\hat{\boldsymbol{\beta}}$ and the theorem is proved.

ESTIMATING σ^2, t TESTS

To calculate the variance-covariance matrix of the estimated parameters, we need to determine an estimate for the scalar σ^2. A natural choice is

$$s^2 = \frac{\hat{\boldsymbol{\varepsilon}}'\hat{\boldsymbol{\varepsilon}}}{N - k} \qquad (\text{A4.20})$$

---

[17] Since $\mathbf{AX} = (\mathbf{X'X})^{-1}\mathbf{X'X} = \mathbf{I}$, $\mathbf{b} - \boldsymbol{\beta} = (\mathbf{A} + \mathbf{C})\mathbf{X}\boldsymbol{\beta} + (\mathbf{A} + \mathbf{C})\boldsymbol{\varepsilon} - \boldsymbol{\beta} = \mathbf{AX}\boldsymbol{\beta} - \boldsymbol{\beta} + \mathbf{CX}\boldsymbol{\beta} + (\mathbf{A} + \mathbf{C})\boldsymbol{\varepsilon} = (\mathbf{A} + \mathbf{C})\boldsymbol{\varepsilon}$.

It is tedious, but not difficult, to prove that s^2 provides an unbiased estimator of σ^2. It follows that $s^2(\mathbf{X'X})^{-1}$ yields an unbiased estimator of Var $(\hat{\boldsymbol{\beta}})$. We rely on the use of the t test when s^2 is used to approximate σ^2. To do so, we use the following statistical results:

1. $\hat{\boldsymbol{\varepsilon}}'\hat{\boldsymbol{\varepsilon}}/\sigma^2$ is distributed as chi square with $N - k$ degrees of freedom.
2. $(N - k)s^2/\sigma^2$ is distributed as chi square with $N - k$ degrees of freedom.
3. $(\hat{\beta}_i - \beta_i)$, for $i = 1, 2, \ldots, k$, is normally distributed with mean 0 and variance $\sigma^2 V_i$, where V_i is the ith diagonal element of $(\mathbf{X'X})^{-1}$.
4. $(N - k)s^2/\sigma^2$ and $\hat{\beta}_i - \beta_i$ are independently distributed.

It follows that
$$t_{N-k} = \frac{\hat{\beta}_i - \beta_i}{s\sqrt{V_i}} \tag{A4.21}$$

is t-distributed with $N - k$ degrees of freedom. This allows us to construct confidence intervals for individual regression parameters in a manner analogous to the procedure described in Chapter 2. To test a hypothesis about a particular value of β_i, we substitute that value into Eq. (A4.21). If the t value is great enough in absolute value, we reject the null hypothesis at the appropriately chosen level of confidence. A 95 percent confidence interval for β_i is given by

$$\hat{\beta}_i \pm t_c(s\sqrt{V_i}) \tag{A4.22}$$

where t_c is the critical value of the t distribution associated with a 5 percent level of significance.

R^2, F TEST

As in the text, we can break down the total variation of Y into two portions, one representing the explained variation and the second representing the unexplained variation. First assume that the Y variable has a 0 mean. In matrix notation, the derivation follows from the fact that we can write the vector $\mathbf{Y}$ as the sum of its predicted values $\hat{\mathbf{Y}} = \mathbf{X}\hat{\boldsymbol{\beta}}$ and the residual vector $\hat{\boldsymbol{\varepsilon}}$:

$$\mathbf{Y} = \mathbf{X}\hat{\boldsymbol{\beta}} + \hat{\boldsymbol{\varepsilon}}$$

Then $\mathbf{Y'Y} = (\mathbf{X}\hat{\boldsymbol{\beta}} + \hat{\boldsymbol{\varepsilon}})'(\mathbf{X}\hat{\boldsymbol{\beta}} + \hat{\boldsymbol{\varepsilon}}) = \hat{\boldsymbol{\beta}}'\mathbf{X'X}\hat{\boldsymbol{\beta}} + \hat{\boldsymbol{\varepsilon}}'\mathbf{X}\hat{\boldsymbol{\beta}} + \hat{\boldsymbol{\beta}}'\mathbf{X'}\hat{\boldsymbol{\varepsilon}} + \hat{\boldsymbol{\varepsilon}}'\hat{\boldsymbol{\varepsilon}}$

$\qquad = \hat{\boldsymbol{\beta}}'\mathbf{X'X}\hat{\boldsymbol{\beta}} + \hat{\boldsymbol{\varepsilon}}'\hat{\boldsymbol{\varepsilon}} \qquad$ since $\mathbf{X'}\hat{\boldsymbol{\varepsilon}} = \mathbf{0}$ and $\hat{\boldsymbol{\varepsilon}}'\mathbf{X} = \mathbf{0}$ $\qquad$ (A4.23)

or   TSS = RSS + ESS

where TSS = total sum of squares
$\qquad$ RSS = regression (explained) sum of squares
$\qquad$ ESS = error (unexplained) sum of squares

Then
$$R^2 = 1 - \frac{\text{ESS}}{\text{TSS}} = 1 - \frac{\hat{\varepsilon}'\hat{\varepsilon}}{\mathbf{Y}'\mathbf{Y}} = \frac{\hat{\boldsymbol{\beta}}'\mathbf{X}'\mathbf{X}\hat{\boldsymbol{\beta}}}{\mathbf{Y}'\mathbf{Y}} \qquad (A4.24)$$

When the dependent variable does not have 0 mean, we must modify our definition of R^2 somewhat. Then $y_i = Y_i - \bar{Y}$, from which it follows that

$$\mathbf{y}'\mathbf{y} = \mathbf{Y}'\mathbf{Y} - N\bar{Y}^2$$

Now, subtracting $N\bar{Y}^2$ from both sides of Eq. (A4.23) and substituting, we find that

$$R^2 = \frac{\text{RSS}}{\text{TSS}} = \frac{\hat{\boldsymbol{\beta}}'\mathbf{X}'\mathbf{X}\hat{\boldsymbol{\beta}} - N\bar{Y}^2}{\mathbf{y}'\mathbf{y}} \qquad (A4.25)$$

To correct for the dependence of goodness of fit on degrees of freedom, we define $\bar{R}^2$ as

$$\bar{R}^2 = 1 - \frac{\hat{\varepsilon}'\hat{\varepsilon}/(N - k)}{\mathbf{y}'\mathbf{y}/(N - 1)} = 1 - \left(\frac{\hat{\varepsilon}'\hat{\varepsilon}}{\mathbf{y}'\mathbf{y}}\right)\left(\frac{N - 1}{N - k}\right) \qquad (A4.26)$$

Now it is appropriate to consider statistical tests on sets of regression coefficients. The most frequently used test involves the test of the joint hypothesis that $\beta_2 = \beta_3 = \cdots = \beta_k = 0$. The appropriate F statistic is

$$F_{k-1,N-k} = \frac{R^2}{1 - R^2} \frac{N - k}{k - 1}$$

Other tests involving combinations of the regression parameters sometimes are used. Again, assume that Y has a 0 mean. In this case we can use the result that

$$F = \frac{(\hat{\boldsymbol{\beta}} - \boldsymbol{\beta})'\mathbf{X}'\mathbf{X}(\hat{\boldsymbol{\beta}} - \boldsymbol{\beta})}{\hat{\varepsilon}'\hat{\varepsilon}} \frac{N - k}{k - 1}$$

is F-distributed with $k - 1$ and $N - k$ degrees of freedom. To test joint hypotheses involving the individual regression parameters, we simply substitute the appropriate test values for $\boldsymbol{\beta}$ and evaluate the F statistic. A sufficiently large value of F allows us to reject the null hypothesis.

EXERCISES

4.1 Consider the following two models:

I $\qquad Y_i = \beta_1 + \beta_2 X_{2i} + \beta_3 X_{3i} + \varepsilon_i$

II $\qquad (Y_i - X_{2i}) = \beta_1' + \beta_2' X_{2i} + \beta_3' X_{3i} + \varepsilon_i'$

(a) Prove that $\hat{\beta}_2' = \hat{\beta}_2 - 1$, $\hat{\beta}_1' = \hat{\beta}_1$, and $\hat{\beta}_3' = \hat{\beta}_3$.

(b) Prove that the least-squares residuals are identical, that is, $\hat{\varepsilon}_i = \hat{\varepsilon}_i'$ for $i = 1, 2, \ldots, N$.

(c) Under what conditions will the R^2 associated with model II be less than the R^2 associated with model I?

4.2 Consider the following two experimental procedures:

1. Run the regression $Y_i = \beta_1 + \beta_2 X_{2i} + \beta_3 X_{3i} + \varepsilon_i$.
2. Run the regression $X_{2i} = \alpha_1 + \alpha_2 X_{3i} + \varepsilon_i'$, calculate the residuals $\hat{\varepsilon}_i'$, and finally run the regression

$$Y_i = \beta_1' + \beta_2'\hat{\varepsilon}_i' + \beta_3'X_{3i} + \varepsilon_i^*$$

Can you prove that $\hat{\beta}_2' = \hat{\beta}_2$? Can you explain intuitively why this result is true?

4.3 A somewhat naive researcher attempts to estimate an aggregate consumption function for the U.S. economy by regressing a consumption variable C on disposable income Y and savings S. The model is

$$C = \beta_1 + \beta_2 Y + \beta_3 S + \varepsilon$$

How good a fit is this researcher likely to get when this equation is run? Can you generalize your conclusion? *Hint:* Note that $C = Y - S$ identically for all observations.

4.4 Assume that the sample variances (and standard deviations) of all the variables in a multiple regression model are identically the same. In this case what is the relationship between the estimated standardized coefficients and the standard regression parameters?

4.5 "Estimated regression parameters, elasticities, standardized coefficients, and partial correlation coefficients will always have the same sign." True or false? Explain.

4.6 Explain the differences between the concepts of simple correlation, partial correlation, and multiple correlation. Why is each one useful?

SINGLE-EQUATION REGRESSION MODELS

Part Two of this book extends the treatment of the single-equation regression model. We begin in Chapter 5 by expanding our discussion of the multiple regression model, focusing on model specification and statistical testing. Topics in this chapter include the use of different functional forms, dummy variables, and t and F tests.

The estimation techniques used in the first part of the book depend crucially on several assumptions relating to the form of the data and the specification of the model. Chapters 6 and 7 deal with several of these assumptions. In Chapter 6 we focus on the possible existence of heteroscedasticity and serial correlation, describing tests for their existence as well as corrections for when they are present. In Chapter 7 we concern ourselves with the difficulties which arise in the regression model. To correct for these problems, we introduce the method of instrumental variables. Because the concerns in this chapter are likely to arise when the model being studied is simultaneous, Chapter 7 serves as an important introduction to the material in Part Three (especially Chapter 12). Chapter 7 also focuses on problems that arise when regression models are incorrectly specified.

Chapter 8 deals with the problem of forecasting with a single-equation model. The means of obtaining a forecast and some measure of the reliability of that forecast are discussed when the explanatory variables are known as well as when they are unknown and when the errors of the regression model are serially correlated. The material in Chapter 8 lays the groundwork for the more advanced analysis of forecasting in Parts Three and Four.

The remaining three chapters in Part Two contain material of a more advanced nature than the material in the first eight chapters of the book. All these chapters deal with extensions of the regression model that can be important in applied econometric work. Chapter 9 contains a treatment of four important topics in econometric modeling: the specification and estimation of distributed lag models, statistical tests of causality, the problem of missing observations, and the use of panel data (pooled cross-section and time-series data).

Chapter 10 deals with nonlinear estimation and maximum-likelihood estimation. Here we allow for models that are nonlinear in the parameters to be estimated. Maximum-likelihood estimation is a powerful technique that is widely used in econometric modeling. This chapter also discusses the specification and estimation of ARCH and GARCH models—models in which the error term is conditionally heteroscedastic and, in particular, the variance of the error term depends on volatilities in previous periods. ARCH and GARCH models, which have found wide application in finance, are estimated by maximum-likelihood techniques.

Chapter 11 deals with the estimation of models in which the variable to be studied is qualitative rather than quantitative. The chapter emphasizes how the linear probability, probit, logit, and censored regression models can be used to study problems involving binary as well as multiple choices. Chapter 11 is self-contained and can be read independently of Chapter 10.

CHAPTER 5

USING THE MULTIPLE
REGRESSION MODEL

We introduced the multiple regression model in Chapter 4, emphasizing how one interprets the estimated coefficients, measures goodness of fit, and performs statistical tests. In this chapter we focus on the use of the multiple regression model. We begin by considering functional form, concentrating on the distinction between linear and nonlinear models. We then consider how the regression model can be applied when one or more of the explanatory variables is a dummy variable. We also consider the appropriate t and F statistics used to perform hypothesis tests involving groups of independent variables.

5.1 THE GENERAL LINEAR MODEL

We have been dealing with equations which are linear combinations of the X's. This specification is not as limiting as it might seem, because the linear regression model can be applied to a more general class of equations that are *inherently linear*. Inherently linear models can be expressed in a form that is linear in the parameters by transforming the variables. *Inherently nonlinear* models, by contrast, cannot be transformed to the linear form. Assume that we begin with the (nonlinear) model

$$Y = F(X_2, X_3, \ldots, X_k, \varepsilon)$$

The model is inherently linear if it can be transformed into

$$f(Y) = \beta_1 + \beta_2 g_2(X_2, \ldots, X_k) + \cdots + \beta_k g_k(X_2, \ldots, X_k) + \varepsilon$$

or $\quad Y^* = \beta_1 + \beta_2 X_2^* + \beta_3 X_3^* + \cdots + \beta_k X_k^* + \varepsilon \qquad (5.1)$

117

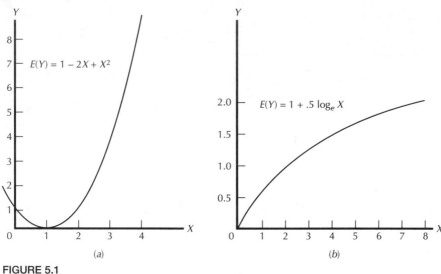

FIGURE 5.1
Nonlinear functional forms.

The relationship in Eq. (5.1) is inherently linear because it is linear with respect to the parameters $\beta_1, \beta_2, \beta_3, \ldots, \beta_k$. We will turn our attention to the estimation of inherently nonlinear models in Chapter 10. For the moment, however, it will be instructive to look at some special cases.

$$I \qquad Y = \beta_1 + \beta_2 X_2 + \beta_3 X_2^2 + \varepsilon \tag{5.2}$$

$$II \qquad \log Y = \alpha_1 + \alpha_2 \log X_2 + \alpha_3 \log X_3 + \varepsilon \tag{5.3}$$

$$III \qquad Y = \gamma_1 X_2^{\gamma_2} X_3^{\gamma_3} \varepsilon^* \tag{5.4}$$

$$IV \qquad Y = \gamma_1 X_2^{\gamma_2} X_3^{\gamma_3} + \varepsilon' \tag{5.5}$$

Model I (the *polynomial model*) provides a means of testing whether the relationship between Y and X_2 is nonlinear (although the model itself is linear in the coefficients). Y is specified to be a *quadratic* function of X_2 (one is shown in Fig. 5.1a). A useful test for nonlinearities is provided by a standard t test of the null hypothesis that $\beta_3 = 0$.

Model II is also linear in the parameters and uses the logarithm of each variable.[1] While the choice of the base of logarithms does not matter substantially (it affects only the constant term in the model), we typically will use natural logarithms to the base e (≈ 2.718) in our analysis. A simple example of the logarithmic function is illustrated in Fig. 5.1b. Model II can be used if one has reason to believe that variables enter into the equation multiplicatively rather than additively. This can most easily be seen by noticing that model II

---

[1] Since $d \log Y/dY = 1/Y$, each parameter $\alpha_2, \alpha_3, \ldots$ is an elasticity.

can be derived from model III (the *multiplicative model*) by taking the logarithms of both sides.[2]

The equivalence of the two models is seen by noting that

$$\alpha_1 = \log \gamma_1 \qquad \alpha_2 = \gamma_2 \qquad \alpha_3 = \gamma_3 \qquad \varepsilon = \log \varepsilon^*$$

Model IV appears to be quite similar to model III, but the similarity is deceptive because no transformation of model IV will provide a new model that is linear in the parameters.

Do not be lulled into a trap when considering transformations which make models linear in the parameters. Something is often lost in the process. For example, consider the transformation from model III to model II. If we assume that the error process ε is normally distributed, the error process in model III (ε^*) will not be normal. We usually assume that ε^* follows a distribution whose logarithm is itself normally distributed; i.e., it will be *lognormal*.[3]

Some additional model specifications that are useful in applied work are as follows:

V   Exponential model: $Y = \exp [(\beta_1 + \beta_2 X_2 + \beta_3 X_3)]\varepsilon$ (5.6)

By taking logarithms of both sides, this model can be written as

$$\log Y = \beta_1 + \beta_2 X_2 + \beta_3 X_3 + \log \varepsilon$$

VI   Reciprocal model: $Y = \dfrac{1}{\beta_1 + \beta_2 X_2 + \beta_3 X_3 + \varepsilon}$ (5.7)

This model can be transformed to

$$\frac{1}{Y} = \beta_1 + \beta_2 X_2 + \beta_3 X_3 + \varepsilon$$

VII   Semilog model: $Y = \beta_1 + \beta_2 \log X_2 + \varepsilon$ (5.8)

VIII   Interaction model: $Y = \beta_1 + \beta_2 X_2 + \beta_3 X_3 + \beta_4(X_2 X_3) + \varepsilon$ (5.9)

Model VIII is worthy of special attention because of the presence of the third right-hand variable, the product of variables X_2 and X_3. To see how such an *interaction term* affects one's interpretation of the regression results, consider the impact of a change in X_2 on Y. If the interaction term were omitted, the effect would be measured by β_2. However, with the interaction, the effect is

---

[2] Note that $\log A^b = b \log A$ and $\log AB = \log A + \log B$ for any A, B, and b.

[3] If ε^* is normal, tests of significance will be invalid when applied to model II since $\log \varepsilon^*$ will not follow the normal distribution.

$\beta_2 + \beta_4 X_3$ [we get this by differentiating Eq. (5.9) with respect to X_2]. Thus, the effect of X_2 on Y depends on the level of the variable X_3. If β_4 is positive, the effect of X_2 on Y will increase as the value of X_3 increases. Of course, this can be accomplished with other forms of equations, but the interaction term is a simple and direct option.[4]

Example 5.1 A Cost Function for the Savings and Loan Industry   An understanding of returns to scale in the savings and loan industry is important for regulators who must decide whether mergers and takeovers are in the public interest, and for managers who must make internal decisions about the efficient size of operations. In both cases the empirical estimation of a cost function can be useful.[5]

The output Q is measured as the total assets (in millions of dollars) of each savings and loan association. Long-run average operating costs, LAC, are measured as the average annual operating expense (in millions of dollars) as a percentage of total assets. Using data for 86 savings and loan associations, the following relationship was obtained:

$$\widehat{LAC} = 238 - .615Q + .00054Q^2$$

The estimated LAC function is U-shaped and reaches its point of minimum average cost when the total assets of the savings and loan association reach $569 million.[6] Because most savings and loans had substantially less than $569 million in assets, the cost-function analysis suggests that an expansion of savings and loans through either growth or mergers could have been valuable.

Example 5.2 Predicting Wine Prices   Traditionally, the process of valuing the quality of new harvests of wine has been left to expert wine tasters. This tradition has been severely shaken by a series of recent econometric analyses of wine pricing showing that one can predict the future value of a vintage (year of harvest) of a wine solely on the basis of the weather. One particularly

---

[4] Interaction terms can be combined with quadratic terms to yield expressions such as $Y = \beta_1 + \beta_2 X_2 + \beta_3 X_3 + \beta_4 X_2 X_3 + \beta_5 X_2^2 + \beta_6 X_3^2 + \varepsilon$. Testing the null hypothesis that $\beta_4 = 0$ provides a test for interaction, and testing the joint hypothesis that $\beta_4 = \beta_5 = \beta_6 = 0$ provides a test of whether nonlinearities are present. These tests are described in Section 5.3.

[5] This example builds on J. Holton Wilson, "A Note on Scale Economies in the Savings and Loan Industry," *Business Economics*, pp. 45–49, January 1981.

[6] This can be seen by graphing the curve or by differentiating the average cost function with respect to Q, setting it equal to 0, and solving for Q.

interesting study involves the pricing of wines harvested at various chateaus in the Bordeaux region of France.[7]

It is well known in the wine industry that the market prices of wines produced at different times from the same chateau vary a great deal. For example, the 1990–1991 London auction prices for a dozen bottles of 1960s Chateau Lafitte wines varied from a low of $223 for the 1968 vintage to a high of $4,335 for the 1961 vintage. There are two reasons for this variability. One is that if older, more mature wines are to be held and sold in the market, they must command an economic return (a higher price) that reflects the opportunity cost of holding the wine. The second reason is that there is substantial variation in the quality of grapes used to make the wine. Grape quality in turn depends heavily on the weather.

In an econometric study of the price of wines for 10 vintages from 1952 to 1980 for 60 different wines from six chateaus, Orley Ashenfelter and his colleagues showed that both reasons are supported by the statistical evidence. The authors estimated a cross-section regression in which the dependent variable, the natural logarithm of the price of a dozen bottles of wine ($PRICE_i$), was regressed against a constant term (not reported here), the age of the vintage (AGE_i), the average temperature over the growing season ($TEMP_i$), the rainfall in September and August ($RAIN_i$), and the rainfall in the months preceding the vintage, from October to March ($WRAIN_i$). They obtained the following results (standard errors are in parentheses):

$$\widehat{PRICE}_i = \underset{(.0075)}{.0240}\ AGE_i + \underset{(.116)}{.608}\ TEMP_i - \underset{(.00095)}{.0038}\ RAIN_i + \underset{(.00051)}{.00115}\ WRAIN_i$$

$$R^2 = .828 \qquad s = .287$$

Each of the regression coefficients is statistically significant at the 5 percent level using a t test. Each of the independent variables has a relatively low correlation with each of the other independent variables, and so multicollinearity is not an issue. The AGE coefficient provides a measure of the real rate of return to holding Bordeaux wines: each additional year of maturity adds about 2.4 percent to the value of the wine. The temperature coefficient has the sign that wine experts would predict: the warmer the growing season, other things equal, the higher the quality of the grapes being harvested. The TEMP variable reflects an additional aspect of the temperature phenomenon: a warm period just before the harvest is especially important for the quality of the vintage grapes. Finally, rain prior to the vintage is a highly

[7] O. Ashenfelter, D. Ashmore, and R. Lalonde, "Bordeaux Wine Vintage Quality and the Weather," *Chance*, vol. 8, no. 4, pp. 7–14, 1995.

significant positive determinant of grape quality, whereas rain just prior to the harvest has a very strong negative effect on quality.

The controversy surrounding the use of regression analysis to predict the price of wine vintages by winery arises because wine quality can be predicted before the harvest is complete and, consequently, before any of the wine is actually tasted. It is not surprising perhaps, that the wine critic Robert Parker, Jr., has called this approach "a Neanderthal way of looking at wine."[8] Econometricians realize that any regression model with a less than perfect fit will generate many predicted values which are greater than the actual value and many which are lower. According to Ashenfelter, *Wine Spectator* magazine apparently did not understand this saying, criticizing the regression approach, "the predictions come exactly true only 3 times in the 27 vintages since 1961. . . . The predicted prices are both under and over the actual prices."

5.2   USE OF DUMMY VARIABLES

Variables used in regression equations usually take values over a continuous range. This need not be the case, however, and at times we may wish to use one or more *independent* variables that take on two or more distinct values. (Estimation when the *dependent* variable is a dummy variable is discussed in Chapter 11.) For example, we may wish to account for the fact that some individuals go to college and others do not. To do so, we create a dummy variable which takes on the value of 1 if the individual goes to college and 0 if the individual does not. Dummy variables are particularly useful when one is dealing with qualitative data.

Suppose a firm uses two types of production processes. On the assumption that the output obtained from each process is normally distributed with different expected values but identical variances, we can represent the production process as a regression equation:

$$Y_i = \beta_1 + \beta_2 X_i + \varepsilon_i \qquad (5.10)$$

where Y_i is the output associated with the ith input process and X_i is a dummy variable

$$X_i = \begin{cases} 1 & \text{if output obtained from machine A} \\ 0 & \text{if output obtained from machine B} \end{cases}$$

In this rather simple example, β_1 measures the expected output associated with machine B while β_2 measures the difference in output associated with a change

---

[8] Robert Parker, Jr., "Wine Equation Puts Some Noses Out of Joint," *New York Times*, March 4, 1995.

from machine B to machine A. This can be seen by taking expected values on both sides of Eq. (5.10) for $X_i = 0$ and $X_i = 1$:

$$E(Y_i) = \begin{cases} \beta_1 & X_i = 0 \\ \beta_1 + \beta_2 & X_i = 1 \end{cases}$$

It should be clear that a test of the null hypothesis that $\beta_2 = 0$ is a test of the hypothesis that there is no difference in the output associated with machines A and B. In fact, the actual least-squares estimates of the regression parameters are the mean output associated with machine B and the difference between the mean outputs of A and B, respectively.

This procedure can easily be modified if more than two distinct values are involved. For example, two dummy variables may be employed to account for the fact that the output produced by each of three processes (A, B, and C) may not be identical. Consider the model

$$Y_i = \beta_1 + \beta_2 X_{2i} + \beta_3 X_{3i} + \varepsilon_i \tag{5.11}$$

where
$$X_{2i} = \begin{cases} 1 & \text{if output obtained from machine A} \\ 0 & \text{otherwise} \end{cases}$$

$$X_{3i} = \begin{cases} 1 & \text{if output obtained from machine B} \\ 0 & \text{otherwise} \end{cases}$$

Thus, the three production processes are represented by the following combination of values taken by the dummy variables:

Machine	X_2	X_3
A	1	0
B	0	1
C	0	0

By taking expected values, we can interpret the regression results:

$$E(Y_i) = \begin{cases} \beta_1 + \beta_2 & X_{2i} = 1, \quad X_{3i} = 0 \\ \beta_1 + \beta_3 & X_{2i} = 0, \quad X_{3i} = 1 \\ \beta_1 & X_{2i} = 0, \quad X_{3i} = 0 \end{cases}$$

β_1 represents the expected value of output associated with machine C. β_2 represents the difference in output associated with a change from machine C to machine A, and β_3 measures the average change in output associated with a change from machine C to machine B. A test of the null hypothesis that $\beta_2 = 0$ provides a test of the hypothesis that there is no difference between the production process associated with machine A and that associated with machine

C, while an analogous test comparing B to C is provided by a t test on the coefficient β_3.

Note that three alternative production processes were represented by two dummy variables (with the third implicit). Representing such a phenomenon by having one variable take on three values, e.g., machine A $= 2$, machine B $= 1$, machine C $= 0$, is not equivalent to the dummy-variable technique unless the differences between outputs associated with the machine B-to-A and machine C-to-B comparisons are identical.

Do not make the mistake of representing the dummy-variable process by using three two-way variables X_2, X_3, and X_4, where X_4 takes on the value 1 when machine C is used and the value 0 otherwise. The introduction of the variable X_4 adds no further information but does add a nonindependent equation in the derivation of the least-squares estimators. In fact, there is *perfect collinearity* in the model because $X_{4i} = 1 - X_{2i} - X_{3i}$ for each observation i.

Suppose we wish to test the null hypothesis that there is no change in output associated with a movement from machine A to machine B. An F test of the null hypothesis that the regression coefficients β_2 and β_3 are equal would be appropriate. However, by rewriting the regression equation, we can do the same test by using the t statistic provided by the standard regression output. Write the regression model as

$$Y_i = \alpha_1 + \alpha_2 X_{2i} + \alpha_3 (X_{3i} + X_{2i}) + \varepsilon_i$$

Then consider the three cases:

$$E(Y_i) = \begin{cases} \alpha_1 + \alpha_2 + \alpha_3 & X_{2i} = 1, \quad X_{3i} = 0 \\ \alpha_1 + \alpha_3 & X_{2i} = 0, \quad X_{3i} = 1 \\ \alpha_1 & X_{2i} = 0, \quad X_{3i} = 0 \end{cases}$$

The test is given by a t test of the null hypothesis that $\alpha_2 = 0$.

We now extend the notion of dummy variables to the more general case in which some of the independent variables are continuous while others are dummies. The classic example is the case of the aggregate consumption function, in which rationing, savings campaigns, and so on, make wartime consumption behavior different from peacetime behavior. We shall distinguish between five different cases of a simple aggregate consumption function in which aggregate consumption is determined by aggregate disposable income with no lags involved.

Case I: $$C_t = \beta_1 + \beta_2 Y_t + \varepsilon_t \qquad\qquad (5.12)$$

This is the case in which peacetime and wartime consumption behavior are assumed to be identical in all respects.

Case II: $$C_t = \beta_1 + \beta_2 Y_t + \alpha D_t + \varepsilon_t \qquad\qquad (5.13)$$

where D_t equals 1 if it is wartime and equals 0 otherwise. Noting that $E(C_t)$ is equal to $\beta_1 + \beta_2 E(Y_t)$ in peacetime and is equal to $(\beta_1 + \alpha) + \beta_2 E(Y_t)$ in wartime, we see that case II corresponds to the assumption that the intercept of the consumption function changes during wartime but that the slope parameter stays the same. A test of whether such a change is statistically significant is provided by a test of the null hypothesis that $\alpha = 0$.

Case III:
$$C_t = \beta_1 + \beta_2 Y_t + \gamma(D_t Y_t) + \varepsilon_t \qquad (5.14)$$

Note that $E(C_t) = \beta_1 + \beta_2 E(Y_t)$ in peacetime and $E(C_t) = \beta_1 + (\beta_2 + \gamma)E(Y_t)$ in wartime, so that case III corresponds to the assumption that the intercept has remained constant but the slope has changed. A test of whether this change is significant is provided by a test of the null hypothesis that the coefficient of $D_t Y_t$ is 0.

Case IV:
$$C_t = \beta_1 + \beta_2 Y_t + \alpha D_t + \gamma(D_t Y_t) + \varepsilon_t \qquad (5.15)$$

Here both the slope and the intercept are allowed to change. Note, however, that the model has still been expressed as a single equation in which the variance of the error term is assumed to be the same in war and peace years. Least-squares estimation yields *unique* estimates of the standard error of the regression and the distributions of the estimated regression parameters.

Case V:
$$C_t = \begin{cases} \beta_1^* + \beta_2^* Y_t + \varepsilon_t^* & \text{war years} \\ \beta_1' + \beta_2' Y_t + \varepsilon_t' & \text{peace years} \end{cases} \qquad (5.16)$$

In this case we have allowed the error variance to vary from war years to peace years. Case V corresponds to running two separate regressions and obtaining separate estimates of the standard errors of the regression. The reader can check to see that the estimated regression parameters in case IV and case V are equivalent ($\hat{\beta}_1' = \hat{\beta}_1$, $\hat{\beta}_1^* = \hat{\beta}_1 + \hat{\alpha}$, $\hat{\beta}_2' = \hat{\beta}_2$, $\hat{\beta}_2^* = \hat{\beta}_2 + \hat{\gamma}$). The choice of model IV or model V depends on whether one believes that the error variance is constant over all model years.[9]

Example 5.3 Wage Differentials
To evaluate whether women are discriminated against in the labor force relative to men, wage differentials can be studied by using cross-section data obtained from the Current Population

---

[9] It is possible to test the null hypothesis that the error variance is constant between war and peace years or, more generally, to decide when it is reasonable to assume that regression models actually switch from one time period to another. See, for example, R. E. Quandt, "Test of the Hypothesis That a Linear Regression System Obeys Two Separate Regimes," *Journal of the American Statistical Association*, vol. 55, pp. 324–330, 1960.

Survey of the U.S. Bureau of the Census. The following variables were included in the multiple regression study:

$$W = \text{wage rate of employed workers in dollars per hour}$$
$$\text{SEX} = 1 \text{ if the person is female, 0 if male}$$
$$\text{ED} = \text{years of education}$$
$$\text{AGE} = \text{age of employee}$$
$$\text{NONWH} = 1 \text{ if the person is non-Hispanic, nonwhite; 0 otherwise}$$
$$\text{HISP} = 1 \text{ if the person is Hispanic; 0 otherwise}$$

Among the regression results obtained for a sample of 206 employees was the following (*t* statistics in parentheses):

$$\hat{W} = \underset{(22.10)}{10.93} - \underset{(-3.86)}{2.73} \text{ SEX}$$

$$R^2 = .068 \qquad F(1,204) = 14.9$$

The dummy variable representing the sex of the employee was significant at the 5 percent level. Since the overall mean hourly wage is $9.60, the dummy variable tells us that the average female wage is $2.73 lower, or $6.87.

The significant wage differential does not disappear when the regression model is expanded to take into account the age and education of the employee as well as that person's race or ethnicity:

$$\hat{W} = \underset{(-3.38)}{-6.41} - \underset{(-4.61)}{2.76} \text{ SEX} + \underset{(8.54)}{.99} \text{ ED} + \underset{(4.63)}{.12} \text{ AGE} - \underset{(-1.07)}{1.06} \text{ NONWH} + \underset{(.22)}{.24} \text{ HISP}$$

$$R^2 = .367 \qquad F(5,200) = 23.2$$

Note that while education and age are significant determinants of the wage rate, the male-female differential remains statistically significant.

Finally, we note that the differential is largely unchanged when the possibility of a nonlinear relationship between AGE and the wage rate is taken into account, as in the following regression:

$$\hat{W} = \underset{(-4.59)}{-14.79} - \underset{(-4.50)}{2.64} \text{ SEX} + \underset{(7.98)}{.92} \text{ ED} - \underset{(-1.22)}{1.18} \text{ NONWH} + \underset{(.28)}{.30} \text{ HISP} + \underset{(3.87)}{.62} \text{ AGE} - \underset{(-3.18)}{.0063} \text{ AGE}^2$$

$$R^2 = .398 \qquad F(6,199) = 21.9$$

The age terms in this regression tell us that, other things being the same, as workers get older, their wage rate increases (.62), but at a decreasing rate (−.0063). A further study of this relationship shows that the wage rate increases until it is maximized at age 49.2 years and then declines steadily thereafter.[10]

---

[10] One can solve for 49.2 by substitution or by using calculus, solving to find the age at which the rate of change of the wage rate is equal to zero.

Example 5.4 Certificates of Deposit In this example an equation is estimated that predicts the total volume of negotiable certificates of deposit (CD)
held by the public on a monthly basis.[11] The equation is a demand relationship, and we would expect the dependent variable to depend on total personal wealth and on the interest rate that individuals receive when part of
that wealth is invested in a certificate of deposit. The primary interest rate
on certificates of deposit (RCDP) was therefore chosen as an explanatory
variable. However, certificates of deposit must compete with other interest-
bearing assets, such as Treasury bills and corporate bonds. Thus, the interest
rates on Treasury bills (RTB) and corporate bonds (RBaa) are also explanatory variables; when these variables increase, the total demand for certificates
of deposit should decrease. These interest-rate variables are multiplied by
personal income (PI), with this last variable serving as a proxy for personal
wealth. The difference between the corporate-bond interest rate and the
interest rate on prime commercial paper (RCP) is also an explanatory variable, representing the difference between long- and short-term interest rates;
when this difference increases, a long-term investment (such as a certificate
of deposit) becomes more attractive. Finally, the lagged dependent variable
is also introduced to reflect lags (Chapter 9).

Since the volume of certificates of deposit, as well as many other financial
variables, displays a definite seasonal behavior, a set of seasonal dummy
variables is introduced to explain as much of this seasonal behavior as possible.
The seasonal variables (denoted $S3$) take the form of monthly dummy variables multiplied by personal income. Since the first seasonal dummy takes on
the value 1 in January and 0 otherwise, the first seasonal variable takes on
the value of personal income in January. There are a total of 12 seasonal
variables in the model, and the constant term has been dropped to eliminate
the collinearity problem. The equation was estimated by using ordinary least
squares with the following results (t statistics in parentheses):

$$\widehat{CD}_t = .72947\ CD_{t-1} - (.00150\ RTB_t)(PI_t) + (.00225\ RCDP_t)(PI_t)$$
$$(14.61)(-2.667)(6.903)$$

$$ - (.00128\ RBaa_t)(PI_t) + .00154\ (RBaa_t - RCP_t)(PI_t) + S3_t$$
$$(-2.453)(2.929)$$

$$R^2 = .9995 \qquad S3_t = \text{seasonal coefficient}_t \times PI_t$$

SEASONAL COEFFICIENTS

Month	Coefficient	t statistic	Month	Coefficient	t statistic	Month	Coefficient	t statistic
Jan.	.01057	2.886	May	.00952	2.656	Sept.	.01113	2.986
Feb.	.00977	2.768	June	.00971	2.659	Oct.	.01179	3.167
Mar.	.00974	2.279	July	.00163	3.137	Nov.	.01117	3.016
Apr.	.00916	2.607	Aug.	.01208	3.265	Dec.	.01147	3.086

[11] This example has been adapted from R. Pindyck and S. Roberts, "Optimal Policies for Monetary Control," *Annals of Economic and Social Measurement*, vol. 3, pp. 207–237, January 1974.

The seasonal coefficients are all significant at the 5 percent level, suggesting that seasonal variations in the volume of certificates of deposit are quite important. The results suggest that August to January are the peak months for public holdings of CDs, while from February to July holdings are relatively lower.

5.3   THE USE OF t AND F TESTS FOR HYPOTHESES INVOLVING MORE THAN ONE PARAMETER

The F distribution can be useful for testing hypotheses in the context of the multiple regression model. The most important example occurs when we wish to test the null hypothesis that a single regression coefficient is equal to zero (or any other number). In this case, the F test reduces to a t test, with the relevant t statistic calculated as the ratio of the estimated coefficient to the estimated standard error. The second use of the F test occurs when we wish to test the null hypothesis that all regression coefficients are equal to zero. While these are the two situations which occur most frequently in econometrics, there are a number of other instances in which the t and/or the F test can be useful:

1. Joint tests on several regression coefficients
2. Tests involving linear functions of the regression coefficients
3. Tests involving the equality of coefficients of different regressions

5.3.1   Joint Tests on Several Regression Coefficients

The F test on R^2 provides a test of the null hypothesis that all regression coefficients are zero, but there are circumstances in which we might want to test the joint significance of a subset of all of the regression coefficients. (Joint F tests for large samples are examples of *Wald tests*, which are described in more detail in Chapter 10.) One case is provided in the discussion of dummy variables. Recall that in case IV in Section 5.2 we included a dummy variable and a dummy interaction term to allow for a shift in the slope and intercept of the consumption function. A second use of the joint test occurs when one wishes to see whether a group of variables explains the variation in the dependent variable. This is often the case for models that include sets of dummy variables, but it also applies much more generally.

To see how the joint test works, reconsider the multiple regression model

$$Y = \beta_1 + \beta_2 X_2 + \cdots + \beta_k X_k + \varepsilon \tag{5.17}$$

We call this model the *unrestricted model (UR)*, since no assumptions have been made about any of the regression coefficients. Suppose we wish to test whether a subset q of the regression coefficients is jointly equal to zero. To do so it is useful to rewrite Eq. (5.17), dividing the variables into two groups, the first containing $k - q$ variables (including the constant) and the second including q variables:

$$Y = \beta_1 + \beta_2 X_2 + \cdots + \beta_{k-q} X_{k-q} + \beta_{k-q+1} X_{k-q+1} + \cdots + \beta_k X_k + \varepsilon \quad (5.18)$$

If all the last q coefficients equal zero, the correct model will be the *restricted* (by the zero coefficients) *model*, denoted R:

$$Y = \beta_1 + \beta_2 X_2 + \cdots + \beta_{k-q} X_{k-q} + \varepsilon \quad (5.19)$$

The null hypothesis, then, is that $\beta_{k-q+1} = \cdots = \beta_k = 0$.

The test of the null hypothesis is straightforward. When we drop the q variables from the model and estimate the restricted model in Eq. (5.19), the error sum of squares ESS_R must be larger than the error sum of squares associated with the unrestricted model ESS_{UR}. (We omit the special case in which $ESS_R = ESS_{UR}$.) This is equivalent to the result that R^2 always increases when additional variables are added to the regression model. If the null hypothesis is correct, dropping the q variables will have little effect on the explanatory power of the equation and ESS_R will be only slightly higher than ESS_{UR}. Of course, any test of the null hypothesis must account for the number of restrictions, i.e., the number of coefficients set equal to zero, and the number of degrees of freedom available in the unrestricted regression model.

The appropriate test statistic is

$$\frac{(ESS_R - ESS_{UR})/q}{ESS_{UR}/(N - k)} \quad (5.20)$$

Here the numerator is the increase in the error sum of squares divided by the number of parameter restrictions implicit in the null hypothesis, and the denominator is the error sum of squares in the original unrestricted model divided by the number of degrees of freedom in the unrestricted model. If the null hypothesis is true, the test statistic given in Eq. (5.20) will have an F distribution with q degrees of freedom in the numerator and $N - k$ in the denominator.[12] The F test on the subset of regression coefficients is carried out just as the F test is on the entire regression equation. We choose a level of significance, say 1 or 5 percent, and then compare the test statistic with the critical value of the F distribution. If the test statistic is larger than the critical value, we reject the null hypothesis and conclude that the subset of variables is statistically significant. As a general rule two separate regression equations must be estimated to apply the test correctly.

---

[12] The F distribution results because (under the null hypothesis) both the numerator and the denominator represent sums of squared variables and are distributed (independently) as chi square.

This F test is not the same as doing a set of individual t tests on each of the variables in the subset. It is not unlikely that all t tests will be insignificant while the joint F test will be significant. We are testing whether the *group* of variables is significant, not individual variables in that group. (We treat the special problem of testing when groups of dummy variables are involved in Appendix 5.1.)

The F test just described is a generalization of the F test on R^2 that was discussed in Chapter 4. To check to see how the two relate, we note first that the F test on a subset of coefficients can be written in terms of the R^2's from the two regression equations. To make the comparison, recall that $R^2 = 1 - \text{ESS/TSS}$, where TSS is the total sum of squares in the regression. Then

$$R^2_{UR} = 1 - \frac{\text{ESS}_{UR}}{\text{TSS}_{UR}} \quad \text{and} \quad R^2_R = 1 - \frac{\text{ESS}_R}{\text{TSS}_R}$$

Both regression equations have the same dependent variable and thus the same total sum of squares, so that $\text{TSS}_{UR} = \text{TSS}_R$. By substituting the two equations above into Eq. (5.20), we find that the test statistic can also be written as

$$F_{q,N-k} = \frac{(R^2_{UR} - R^2_R)/q}{(1 - R^2_{UR})/(N - k)} \tag{5.21}$$

Now the fact that the F test on R^2 is a special case can readily be seen. For the test on R^2, the null hypothesis is that all $k - 1$ variables other than the constant are jointly equal to zero. In this case, the number of parameter restrictions becomes $q = k - 1$. In addition, the restricted model is the regression of Y on a constant. Since R^2 is a measure of the explained variation about the mean, R^2 is identically zero in the restricted case. Substituting both of these pieces of information into Eq. (5.21) shows that $R^2_{UR} = R^2$.

Example 5.5 Demand for Housing   To study the demand for housing, the following regression model was specified:

$$\log Q = \beta_1 + \beta_2 \log P + \beta_3 \log Y + \varepsilon$$

where Q = measure of quantity of housing in square feet consumed by each of 3,120 families per year

P = price of unit of housing in family's locality

Y = measure of family income

The estimation results were (standard errors are in parentheses):

$$\widehat{\log Q} = 4.17 - .247 \log P + .96 \log Y \qquad R^2 = .371$$
$$\phantom{\widehat{\log Q} = } (.11) \quad\;\; (.017) \qquad\;\;\; (.026)$$

The results imply a price elasticity of demand of $-.247$ and an income elasticity of .96. Both elasticities are significantly different from zero, since the t ratios are roughly 14 and 37 in absolute value. However, it is more interesting to ask whether the income elasticity .96 is significantly different from 1. The correct statistic is

$$t_{N-k} = \frac{\hat{\beta}_3 - \beta_3}{s_{\hat{\beta}_3}}$$

or, in this case,

$$t_{3,117} = \frac{.96 - 1}{.026} = -1.54$$

Since the critical value of the t distribution at the 5 percent level is 1.96, we cannot reject the null hypothesis that the income elasticity of demand is 1.

Now suppose that we wish to know whether the demand for housing of blacks differs from that of whites. We thus expand the model to allow for different slopes and intercepts. If we let D represent a dummy variable equal to 1 for black households and 0 otherwise, the expanded model is

$$\log Q = \beta_1 + \alpha_1 D + \beta_2 \log P + \alpha_2 D \log P + \beta_3 \log Y + \alpha_3 D \log Y + \varepsilon$$

When this expanded model was estimated, the results were

$$\widehat{\log Q} = 4.17 - .221 \log P + .920 \log Y + .006\ D - .114\ D \log P$$
$$\qquad\quad (.11) \quad (.02) \qquad\quad (.031) \qquad\quad (.042) \qquad (.061)$$
$$+ .341\ D \log Y \qquad R^2 = .380$$
$$(.120)$$

t tests on the individual coefficients of the terms involving the dummy variables show the first to be insignificant (at the 5 percent level), the second barely insignificant, and the third to be significant. However, we wish to test the null hypothesis that the dummy coefficients are all jointly equal to zero, i.e.,

$$\alpha_1 = \alpha_2 = \alpha_3 = 0$$

Because our information is given in terms of R^2, we apply the formulation given in Eq. (5.21). In terms of that notation, $R^2_{UR} = .380$, $R^2_R = .371$, $N = 3{,}120$, $k = 6$, and $q = 3$. The appropriate F statistic is

$$\frac{(R^2_{UR} - R^2_R)/q}{(1 - R^2_{UR})/(N - k)} = \frac{(.380 - .371)/3}{(1 - .380)/3{,}114} = 15.1$$

This exceeds the critical value of the F distribution at either the 1 percent or the 5 percent level, and so we reject the null hypothesis of identical housing demand for blacks and whites. Note that with a sufficiently large data set it does not take much of an increase in R^2 to allow us to reject the null hypothesis of equality among a subset of coefficients.

5.3.2   Tests Involving Linear Functions of the Regression Coefficients

There are occasions when you may want to test hypotheses involving linear combinations of regression coefficients. Suppose, for example, that you have estimated a consumption function $C = \beta_1 + \beta_2 Y_L + \beta_3 Y_{NL} + \varepsilon$, where Y_L represents labor income and Y_{NL} represents nonlabor income. You might want to test the hypothesis that the marginal propensity to consume is 1; that is, $\beta_2 + \beta_3 = 1$. Or you might want to test whether the two marginal propensities to consume are equal, that is, $\beta_2 = \beta_3$.

We will treat each of these two special cases in this subsection. We begin with the two-variable unrestricted model:

$$Y_i = \beta_1 + \beta_2 X_{2i} + \beta_3 X_{3i} + \varepsilon_i$$

Consider first the null hypothesis that the two regression coefficients are equal. If the null hypothesis is true, we will estimate a restricted least-squares model, given by

$$Y_i = \beta_1 + \beta_2 (X_{2i} + X_{3i}) + \varepsilon_i$$

The appropriate F test is given by Eq. (5.20) or Eq. (5.21), with the number of restrictions q equal to 1.

The same null hypothesis can also be tested by using a t test. To do the test, estimate the equation

$$Y_i = \beta_1 + \beta_2 (X_{2i} + X_{3i}) + \gamma X_{3i} + \varepsilon_i \tag{5.22}$$

If the null hypothesis is true, $\gamma = 0$, which can be tested by using a standard t test of the estimated coefficient on X_3 in Eq. (5.22).

Now suppose you wish to test the hypothesis that $\beta_2 + \beta_3 = 1$. The unrestricted model is as before. To estimate the restricted model, we simply substitute for $\beta_3 = 1 - \beta_2$ in the unrestricted model:

$$Y_i = \beta_1 + \beta_2 X_{2i} + (1 - \beta_2) X_{3i} + \varepsilon_i$$

or

$$Y_i - X_{3i} = \beta_1 + \beta_2 (X_{2i} - X_{3i}) + \varepsilon_i$$

Estimation of this last restricted model (with dependent variable $Y_i - X_{3i}$ and independent variable $X_{2i} - X_{3i}$) provides the necessary input for an F test. Once again there is one restriction, so $q = 1$.

Example 5.6 Demand for Housing   Suppose we have estimated the unrestricted model of Example 5.5 (with an R^2 of .380). We wish to test the null hypothesis that the income elasticity of demand for housing of blacks is equal to 1. Under the null hypothesis $\beta_3 + \alpha_3 = 1$. Substituting $\alpha_3 = 1 - \beta_3$ into the expanded model and rewriting, we obtain the restricted model:

$$\log Q - D\log Y = \beta_1 + \alpha_1 D + \beta_2 \log P + \alpha_2 D \log P + \beta_3(\log Y - D\log Y) + \varepsilon$$

The R^2 associated with the restricted model (which has one restriction) is .3785. From Eq. (5.21), the relevant F statistic is given by

$$F_{1,\,3,114} = \frac{(.380 - .3785)}{(.62/3,114)} = 7.56$$

Since F is greater than the critical value at the 5 percent level of significance, we can reject the null hypothesis.

5.3.3   Tests Involving the Equality of Coefficients of Different Regressions

On occasion one is not sure whether a given model applies to two different data sets. Take, for example, the consumption function used in the earlier discussion of dummy variables. Case IV illustrates the formulation of the model in which one regression model applies in war years and a second model applies in years of peace. It differs from case V since we are assuming that the slope and intercept parameters are distinct but also that the errors in both equations have the same variance. (We will show how to test the identical variance assumption in Chapter 6.)

To test whether the assumption that there are two different regression models is correct, we start with the null hypothesis that the regressions are *identical* and see whether we can reject this hypothesis. To do the *Chow test*, consider the regression models

$$Y_i = \beta_1 + \beta_2 X_{2i} + \cdots + \beta_k X_{ki} + \varepsilon_i \tag{5.23a}$$

$$Y_j = \alpha_1 + \alpha_2 X_{2j} + \cdots + \alpha_k X_{kj} + \varepsilon_j \tag{5.23b}$$

In the first equation we subscript the variables with i to denote observations running from 1 to N.[13] In the second equation we subscript with j the variables running from 1 to M. We have allowed all regression coefficients to differ from Eq. (5.23a) to Eq. (5.23b). Suppose we estimate the model implied by the two equations by applying ordinary least squares to each equation individually. Since no restrictions have been placed on the parameters of the model, we can calculate the unrestricted sum of squares as the sum of the error sums of squares of the individual equations, $ESS_{UR} = ESS_1 + ESS_2$. The number of degrees of freedom is the sum of the number of degrees of freedom in each individual regression, that is, $(N - k) + (M - k) = N + M - 2k$.

Now assume that the null hypothesis is true, that is, $\alpha_1 = \beta_1$, $\alpha_2 = \beta_2, \ldots,$ $\alpha_k = \beta_k$, and $Var(\varepsilon_i) = Var(\varepsilon_j)$. Then the regression model can be written as the single equation

$$Y_i = \beta_1 + \beta_2 X_{2i} + \cdots + \beta_k X_{ki} + \varepsilon_i \qquad (5.24)$$

where the subscript i now runs from observation 1 to observation $N + M$. Now we estimate Eq. (5.24) using ordinary least squares and calculate the restricted error sum of squares ESS_R. If the null hypothesis is true, the restrictions will not hurt the explanatory power of the model and ESS_R will not be much larger than ESS_{UR}. As before, we can perform an F test to see whether the difference between the two error sums of squares is significant. Since there are $N + M - 2k$ degrees of freedom in the unrestricted regression and there are k restrictions, the appropriate F statistic is[14]

$$F_{k, N+M-2k} = \frac{(ESS_R - ESS_{UR})/k}{ESS_{UR}/(N + M - 2k)} \qquad (5.25)$$

If the F statistic is larger than the critical value of the F distribution with k and $N + M - 2k$ degrees of freedom, we can reject the null hypothesis. Here rejection implies that two separate regressions must be estimated: the data cannot be pooled.

Example 5.7 Demand for Housing   Suppose we believe that housing demand is best modeled by two equations, one describing housing demand by

---

[13] This test was devised by Gregory C. Chow in ''Tests of Equality between Sets of Coefficients in Two Linear Regressions,'' *Econometrica*, vol. 28, pp. 591–605, July 1960. See also Franklin M. Fisher, ''Tests of Equality between Sets of Coefficients in Two Linear Regressions: An Expository Note,'' *Econometrica*, vol. 38, pp. 361–366, March 1970.

[14] The statistic follows an F distribution because each error sum of squares follows a chi-square distribution (see Chapter 2), the numerator with k degrees of freedom and the denominator with $N + M - 2k$. Since the two distributions are independent, the ratio follows an F distribution.

blacks and the other describing demand by whites. (This is equivalent to case V in the section on dummy variables.) The model is

$$\log Q = \begin{cases} \beta_1 + \beta_2 \log P + \beta_3 \log Y + \varepsilon & \text{for white households} \\ \gamma_1 + \gamma_2 \log P + \gamma_3 \log Y + u & \text{for black households} \end{cases}$$

We wish to test the null hypothesis that the set of coefficients in the black demand equation is equal to the set of coefficients in the white demand equation. The null hypothesis is that (jointly)

$$\beta_1 = \gamma_1 \qquad \beta_2 = \gamma_2 \qquad \beta_3 = \gamma_3$$

To perform the test we first estimated the model above and added the error sum of squares in each of the equations. We found that $\text{ESS}_{UR} = 13{,}640$. Now assume that the null hypothesis is true. Then the model reduces to

$$\log Q = \beta_1 + \beta_2 \log P + \beta_3 \log Y + \varepsilon \qquad \text{for all households}$$

When we estimated this restricted model, we found the error sum of squares to be $\text{ESS}_R = 13{,}838$. Since there are $k = 3$ restrictions and since $N + M - 2k = 3{,}120 - 6 = 3{,}114$ degrees of freedom, the appropriate F statistic with 3 restrictions and 3,114 degrees of freedom is

$$F_{3,\,3,114} = \frac{(13{,}838 - 13{,}640)/3}{13{,}640/3{,}114} = 15.1$$

Since the value of the F statistic is greater than the critical value of the F distribution at the 5 percent level, we reject the null hypothesis. It is incorrect to assume equal coefficients.

The conclusion of Example 5.7 is not surprising in light of the earlier test results in Examples 5.5 and 5.6. What might seem surprising is that the test statistic here is identical to the statistic calculated in Example 5.5. In the unrestricted model in Example 5.5 we allowed the intercept and all slope coefficients to vary, just as we have done here, by specifying two different demand equations. When estimated using ordinary least-squares estimation, both parameters will be identical, since both models are analytically equivalent. They allow for the same parameter shifts, have the same number of degrees of freedom, and have the same residuals. The error sum of squares in the two-equation specification is the sum of the ESSs for each equation. Thus, while testing subsets of coefficients will not in general be the same as testing for the equality of coefficients between equations, the two are identical when one introduces dummy variables so that *all* parameters in the model change.

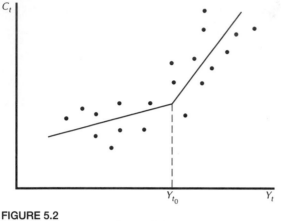

FIGURE 5.2
Piecewise linear regression model.

5.4   PIECEWISE LINEAR REGRESSION

Most of the econometric models we have studied have been continuous, with small changes in one variable having a measurable effect on another variable. This framework was modified when we used dummy variables to account for shifts in slope or intercept or both. It is therefore reasonable to extend the analysis one further step by allowing for changes in slope, with the restriction that the line being estimated be continuous. A simple example is drawn in Fig. 5.2. The true model is continuous, with a *structural break.* If we were explaining consumption as a function of income, for example, the structural break might occur sometime during World War II (or there might be two breaks, one at the beginning and one at the end). Note that there is no discontinuity or shift in the consumption level from year to year. This *piecewise linear model* consists of two straight-line segments.

Piecewise linear models are special cases of a much larger set of models or relationships called *spline functions.* Spline functions have distinct pieces, but the curve representing each piece is a continuous function and not necessarily a straight line. In a typical case, the spline is chosen to be a polynomial of the third degree and the procedure guarantees that the first and second derivatives will be continuous.[15]

To estimate the model given in Fig. 5.2, consider the expression

$$C_t = \beta_1 + \beta_2 Y_t + \beta_3 (Y_t - Y_{t_0}) D_t + \varepsilon_t \tag{5.26}$$

[15] See D. J. Poirier, *The Econometrics of Structural Change* (Amsterdam: North-Holland, 1976), or D. Suits, A. Mason, and L. Chan, "Spline Functions Fitted by Standard Regression Methods," *Review of Economics and Statistics,* vol. LX, pp. 132–139, February 1978.

where C_t = consumption

Y_t = income

Y_{t_0} = income in year in which structural break occurs

and

$$D_t = \begin{cases} 1 & \text{if } t > t_0 \\ 0 & \text{otherwise} \end{cases}$$

For years before and including the break, $D_t = 0$, so that

$$E(C_t) = \beta_1 + \beta_2 Y_t \tag{5.27}$$

However, after the break, $D_t = 1$, so that

$$E(C_t) = \beta_1 + \beta_2 Y_t + \beta_3 Y_t - \beta_3 Y_{t_0}$$

or

$$E(C_t) = (\beta_1 - \beta_3 Y_{t_0}) + (\beta_2 + \beta_3) Y_t \tag{5.28}$$

Before the break the line has slope β_2, but the slope changes to $\beta_2 + \beta_3$ afterward (and the intercept changes as well). Note, however, that there is no discontinuity since

$$E(C_{t_0}) = \beta_1 + \beta_2 Y_{t_0} \qquad \text{from Eq. (5.27)}$$

$$= (\beta_1 - \beta_3 Y_{t_0}) + (\beta_2 + \beta_3) Y_{t_0} = \beta_1 + \beta_2 Y_{t_0} \qquad \text{from Eq. (5.28)}$$

Note also that when $\beta_3 = 0$, the consumption equation reduces to a single straight-line segment, so that a t test of $\hat{\beta}_3 = 0$ provides a simple test for structural change.

What if there were two structural breaks, occurring at times t_0 and t_1? The appropriate model then would be

$$C_t = \beta_1 + \beta_2 Y_t + \beta_3 (Y_t - Y_{t_0}) D + \beta_4 (Y_t - Y_{t_1}) D' + \varepsilon_t$$

where Y_{t_1} represents the income at which a second structural break occurs, and

$$D' = \begin{cases} 1 & \text{if } t > t_1 \\ 0 & \text{otherwise} \end{cases}$$

The equations of each of the three line segments are then

$$E(C_t) = \begin{cases} \beta_1 + \beta_2 Y_t & 0 < t \le t_0 \\ (\beta_1 - \beta_3 Y_{t_0}) + (\beta_2 + \beta_3) Y_t & t_0 \le t \le t_1 \\ (\beta_1 - \beta_3 Y_{t_0} - \beta_4 Y_{t_1}) + (\beta_2 + \beta_3 + \beta_4) Y_t & t > t_1 \end{cases}$$

5.4.1   Switching Regression Method

There may be situations in which it is no longer appropriate to assume that the regression model is continuous. In the more general *switching regression model* the variance of the error term is assumed to be the same throughout the time period being studied but both the intercept and the slope may change at the point of structural break. When the breakpoint is known, the regression model can be written as

$$C_t = \beta_1 + \beta_2 Y_t + \beta_3 D_t + \beta_4 D_t Y_t + \varepsilon_t \qquad (5.29)$$

which is the model that was originally presented as case IV in Section 5.2 on the use of dummy variables.

When the breakpoint is not known, the breakpoint as well as the regression parameters can be estimated by using the method of maximum likelihood.[16] Assuming that the error variance is equal for the entire period of study, this involves estimating Eq. (5.29) for different values of the point of structural break t_0. We choose as the breakpoint the value of t_0 that minimizes the sum-of-squared residuals from the regression (or alternatively that maximizes R^2).

5.5   THE MULTIPLE REGRESSION MODEL WITH STOCHASTIC EXPLANATORY VARIABLES

To this point we have assumed that the independent variables in the multiple regression model were fixed, i.e., nonstochastic. At times, however (as when the researcher samples values for both X and Y), it will be more appropriate to assume that the X's are drawn at random from a probability distribution. Fortunately, we can do this and still maintain most of the previous results. We make the following assumptions:

1. The distribution of each of the explanatory variables is independent of the true regression parameters.

2. Each of the explanatory variables is distributed independently of the errors in the model.

All the basic properties of the least-squares estimators continue to hold. However, we now think of the regression parameters as being estimated *conditional* on the given values of the X's.

If we examine the unconditional properties of the OLS estimator, lack of bias is no longer guaranteed. Fortunately, however, it is still possible to show

---

[16] The method works by maximizing the usual likelihood function (see Appendix 2.2) and by searching over all possible breakpoints. For further details, see S. M. Goldfeld and R. E. Quandt, "The Estimation of Structural Shifts by Switching Regressions," *Annals of Economics and Social Measurement*, vol. 2, pp. 475–485, October 1973. One interesting application that treats markets in disequilibrium is discussed in R. C. Fair and D. M. Jaffee, "Methods of Estimation for Markets in Disequilibrium," *Econometrica*, vol. 40, pp. 497–514, 1972.

that OLS is consistent and for large samples (asymptotically) efficient. Finally, it is also true that least-squares estimators are the maximum-likelihood estimators of the true regression parameters.

Because of the preceding results concerning stochastic explanatory variables (and the fact that estimators are often biased for other reasons), econometricians tend to focus on such large-sample properties of estimators as consistency. We will generally do the same, especially in Chapter 12, where simultaneous-equation models are discussed.

APPENDIX 5.1 Tests Involving Dummy-Variable Coefficients

In multiple regression analysis, the coefficients on each dummy variable measure the differential impact between the included category (receiving a value of 1) and the category or dummy which has been dropped from the regression. As a result, the t test evaluates the null hypothesis that membership in the included and excluded categories will have an identical impact. When there are two or more *sets* of dummy variables, however, the regression results become more difficult to interpret and test. As an example, assume that we are predicting total expenditures on housing as a function of income and number of children, each of which has been classified into a number of categories. To be specific, let

H = annual expenditures on housing

$$I_1 = \begin{cases} 1 & \text{if income} \le \$10,000 \text{ (low income)} \\ 0 & \text{otherwise} \end{cases}$$

$$I_2 = \begin{cases} 1 & \text{if income} > \$10,000 \text{ but} \le \$20,000 \text{ (middle income)} \\ 0 & \text{otherwise} \end{cases}$$

$$I_3 = \begin{cases} 1 & \text{if income} > \$20,000 \text{ (high income)} \\ 0 & \text{otherwise} \end{cases}$$

$$C_1 = \begin{cases} 1 & \text{if no children} \\ 0 & \text{otherwise} \end{cases}$$

$$C_2 = \begin{cases} 1 & \text{if 1 or 2 children} \\ 0 & \text{otherwise} \end{cases}$$

$$C_3 = \begin{cases} 1 & \text{if more than 2 children} \\ 0 & \text{otherwise} \end{cases}$$

When we drop the first dummy variable in each category but include a constant term, the model specification is

$$H = \alpha + \beta_2 I_2 + \beta_3 I_3 + \gamma_2 C_2 + \gamma_3 C_3 + \varepsilon$$

With this specification β_2 measures the differential expenditures on housing for an individual with no children and a middle income relative to an individual with no children and a low income. The t test evaluates the null hypothesis that housing expenditures are equal for both groups. The comparison is thus made relative to *all* categories represented by dummies that have been dropped from the model. Frequently this comparison will not be a particularly useful one. A more constructive analysis might involve the measurement of the differential expenditures on housing of a middle-income individual relative to a low-income individual, both of whom have the same number of children as the *average* of all individuals in the sample.

To see how the multiple regression can be adapted to handle this situation, consider the following variables and the revised model specification:

$$J_1 = \begin{cases} 1 & \text{if low income} \\ 0 & \text{if middle income} \\ -1 & \text{if high income} \end{cases} \qquad J_2 = \begin{cases} 1 & \text{if middle income} \\ 0 & \text{if low income} \\ -1 & \text{if high income} \end{cases}$$

$$D_1 = \begin{cases} 1 & \text{if no children} \\ 0 & \text{if 1 or 2} \\ -1 & \text{if more than 2} \end{cases} \qquad D_2 = \begin{cases} 1 & \text{if 1 or 2 children} \\ 0 & \text{if none} \\ -1 & \text{if more than 2} \end{cases}$$

$$H = a + b_1 J_1 + b_2 J_2 + c_1 D_1 + c_2 D_2 + \varepsilon$$

For all possible combinations of family characteristics the expected value of the dependent variable is as follows:

Category	Expected value $E(H)$
Low income, 0 children	$a + b_1 + c_1$
Middle income, 0 children	$a + b_2 + c_1$
High income, 0 children	$a - b_1 - b_2 + c_1$
Low income, 1 or 2 children	$a + b_1 + c_2$
Middle income, 1 or 2 children	$a + b_2 + c_2$
High income, 1 or 2 children	$a - b_1 - b_2 + c_2$
Low income, more than 2 children	$a + b_1 - c_1 - c_2$
Middle income, more than 2 children	$a + b_2 - c_1 - c_2$
High income, more than 2 children	$a - b_1 - b_2 - c_1 - c_2$

If we then sum over all nine categories, we find that the overall expected value (the average effect) is equal to a, the constant term. If we sum all categories taken in combinations of three (for example, 0 children, 1 or 2 children, more than 2 children), we can find the average effect for each category or group.

The interpretation of the coefficients is straightforward. For example, b_1 measures the extent to which low-income individuals spend differentially on housing *relative to the average individual in the sample.* c_1 measures the differential spending associated with having no children. For individuals with no children and low incomes, the differential is $b_1 + c_1$. The t test associated with b_1 then provides a test of the null hypothesis that the spending of low-income individuals is different from the average, while the t test associated with c_1 tests whether families with no children spend differently from the average.

There is, of course, a close relationship between the coefficients in both models. In particular,

$$\beta_2 = b_2 - b_1 \qquad \beta_3 = -2b_1 - b_2$$

$$\gamma_2 = c_2 - c_1 \qquad \gamma_3 = -2c_1 - c_2 \qquad \alpha = a + b_1 + c_1$$

Which specification of the form for dummy variables should one choose? The answer depends on which null hypothesis one would like to test. In many cases the null hypotheses associated with the alternative specification are more appropriate than are the ones arising directly from the usual dummy-variable specification. In fact, the newer specification can be especially useful when there are large sets of dummy-variable predictors, because it makes their interpretation straightforward. However, when one or more of the predictors is a continuous variable, the interpretation becomes more difficult and the advantage of the procedure is limited.

EXERCISES

5.1 Given the model

$$\log Y = \beta_1 + \beta_2 \log X_2 + \beta_3 \log X_3 + \varepsilon$$

prove that the estimated regression coefficients are the elasticities associated with Y and each of the X's and that these elasticities are constant over the regression line.

5.2 We wish to analyze student housing demand in the Ann Arbor campus area from the rental data given in Table 2.1. As a measure of the demand for a unit's services, construct the variables RENT PER and ROOM PER, defined as follows: RENT PER = RENT (per unit)/NO (number of persons in unit). (RENT PER is listed as RPP in Chapter 2.) ROOM PER = RM (rooms)/NO (number of persons). Then estimate the models:

I   RENT PER $= \beta_1 + \beta_2(\text{SEX}) + \beta_3(\text{ROOM PER}) + \beta_4(\text{DIST}) + \varepsilon$

II   RENT PER $= \beta_1 + \beta_3(\text{ROOM PER}) + \beta_4(\text{DIST}) + \varepsilon$

(In model II, β_2 is constrained to be zero.)   *Check values on Easy reg*

  standard t-test
(a) In model I, test the hypothesis that $\beta_3 = 0$ (as opposed to $\beta_3 > 0$). Is this what you would expect? $T_c = 1.701$ *one tailed test*
(b) In model I, test the hypothesis that $\beta_4 = 0$ (as opposed to $\beta_4 < 0$). Is this what you would expect?   *one tailed test.*
(c) In model I, use a t test to test the hypothesis that $\beta_2 = 0$. Now, using the sum of squared residuals from the estimates of models I and II, do an F test to test the hypothesis that $\beta_2 = 0$. You should recall that if $X = (\text{ESS}_{\text{II}} - \text{ESS}_{\text{I}})/(\text{ESS}_{\text{I}}/(32\text{-}4))$, X follows an F distribution with $(1, 28)$ degrees of freedom. How are the two tests related?

5.3 It is suggested that men and women may not have the same appreciation for spaciousness (as measured by ROOM PER) or for proximity to campus (as measured by DIST). Estimate model III.

III   RENT PER $= \beta_1 + \beta_2(\text{SEX}) + \beta_3(\text{ROOM PER}) + \beta_4(\text{DIST})$

$$+ \beta_5[(\text{ROOM PER})(\text{SEX})] + \beta_6[(\text{DIST})(\text{SEX})] + \varepsilon$$

(a) Test separately the hypotheses that $\beta_5 = 0$ and that $\beta_6 = 0$.
(b) Use an F test to test the joint hypothesis that $\beta_5 = \beta_6 = 0$.
(c) Compute R^2 for models I, II, and III.

5.4 The results from Exercise 5.3 suggest that the demand for housing by men and women is fundamentally different. To see just how different it is, do the following. Divide the data into two groups according to sex and estimate the models:

IV   RENT PER $= \alpha_0 + \alpha_1(\text{ROOM PER}) + \alpha_2(\text{DIST}) + \varepsilon$ males only

V   RENT PER $= \gamma_0 + \gamma_1(\text{ROOM PER}) + \gamma_2(\text{DIST}) + \varepsilon$ females only

(a) Test separately the hypotheses that $\gamma_1 = 0$ and that $\gamma_2 = 0$.
(b) Test the joint hypothesis that $\gamma_1 = \gamma_2 = 0$.

5.5 How can you recover the estimates of γ_0, γ_1, γ_2 (Exercise 5.4) from the estimates of β_1, β_2, β_3, β_4, β_5, and β_6 in model III?

5.6 How would you interpret (economically) the coefficients γ_1 and γ_2 (from Exercise 5.5)? Why might γ_2 be positive?

5.7 In model I (Exercise 5.2), compute the standardized coefficients associated with each explanatory variable.

5.8 In this problem you will study the time-series variation in consumption expenditures in the United States over the period from 1977 (1st quarter) to 1988 (1st quarter). A standard macroeconomic model explains consumption as a general function of disposable income and previous consumption values. However, some opposing points of view are as follows:

1. Consumption is an interstellar process, of which economists know very little, and so it is better to explain consumption by an interstellar activity proxy such as UFO sightings.
2. Changes in consumption are an interstellar activity, so that consumption should be explained by previous consumption values as well as UFO sightings.
3. When people decide how much to spend, they consider only their current income, and so consumption should be explained by disposable income only.
4. People revise their consumption plans via a random process, so that consumption should equal past consumption plus a disturbance.
5. Consumption is a function of both past consumption and income, so that a dollar increase in income has the same effect as a dollar increase in past consumption.

Use the following regression equation to investigate these various views:

$$Y_t = \beta_1 + \beta_2 X_{2t} + \beta_3 X_{3t} + \beta_4 X_{4t} + \varepsilon_t$$

where Y_t = U.S. consumption in time t

$\quad X_{2t}$ = U.S. disposable personal income in time t

$\quad X_{3t}$ = U.S. consumption in time $t - 1$

$\quad X_{4t}$ = U.S. UFO sightings in time t

$\quad \varepsilon_t$ = error term

(a) Estimate the above equation, using the data from Example 4.3 and your own estimate of UFO sightings.

(b) Test the following hypotheses by using the appropriate t tests.
  i. $\beta_4 = 0$ (traditional model)
  ii. $\beta_2 = 0$ (2)

(c) Test the following hypotheses by using the appropriate F tests.
  i. $\beta_2 = \beta_3 = 0$ (View 1)
  ii. $\beta_3 = \beta_4 = 0$ (View 3)
  iii. $\beta_3 = 1, \beta_2 = \beta_4 = 0$ (View 4)
  iv. $\beta_4 = 0, \beta_2 = \beta_3$ (View 5)
  v. $\beta_2 = \beta_3 = \beta_4 = 0$ (No explanatory power from any of the X's)

Indicate the restricted model appropriate for each of these hypotheses.

5.9 You are soon to be interviewed for the position of political analyst for one of the local TV stations. Since all TV stations are devoting a great deal of air time to election coverage, your worldly knowledge will not suffice to land you this position. Consequently, you should consider how to use a regression model to back your opinions regarding the 1996 congressional elections.

To fill up air time, you will need three models. All the models will try to explain differences across states in the percentage of votes received by Democatic candidates among all votes cast for House of Representatives candidates in each state. Therefore, the dependent variable has 50 observations, one for each state. You have four types of explanatory variables:

1. The unemployment rate in each state
2. Regional dummy variables for whether the state is in the northeast, south, midwest, or west
3. A dummy variable for whether Bill Clinton appeared in that state to campaign for congressional candidates
4. Interaction terms between the regional dummies and the Clinton dummy

Your three models differ only in the explanatory variables that they contain:
Model I contains variables (1) and (2).
Model II contains variables (1), (2), and (3).
Model III contains variables (1) and (4).

(a) Write out each model in a regression equation. This can be done in more than one way; pick any formulation you like. Be sure to define all notation, and describe how the explanatory variables will discern the effects of interest, by interpreting the effects to be estimated.

(b) Using the variables in these models, indicate how you would test the following hypotheses. If you propose an F test, give the restricted and unrestricted regression equations.

i. Clinton's appearance doesn't matter.
ii. Regionalism is insignificant: the entire country voted uniformly, with no regional differences.
iii. The northeast and the midwest (the "frostbelt") voted uniformly.
iv. The frostbelt voted uniformly, the "sunbelt" (the south and the west) voted uniformly, but the frostbelt and the sunbelt combined did not necessarily vote uniformly.
v. Clinton's appearance had the same effect in all regions.

CHAPTER 6

SERIAL CORRELATION
AND
HETEROSCEDASTICITY

Now that we have completed a discussion of the classical normal linear regression model, it seems natural to review each of the model's assumptions in turn. Our goal is to determine those situations in which the assumptions are violated and find estimation procedures which improve on the ordinary least-squares procedure when such violations occur. The assumptions are as follows:

1. The model is specified as

$$Y_i = \beta_1 + \beta_2 X_{2i} + \beta_3 X_{3i} + \cdots + \beta_k X_{ki} + \varepsilon_i \tag{6.1}$$

2. The X's are fixed. No linear relationship exists between two or more of the independent variables.

3. The errors are independently distributed from a normal population with 0 expected value and constant variance.

The assumption that the model is correct as specified in Eq. (6.1) is an important one and is the focus of Chapter 7. The problem of collinearity has been detailed in Chapter 4. The third assumption consists of several important parts. Even without normality, it is possible to prove that least-squares regression estimates of the true parameters are unbiased as well as consistent. However, without normality one cannot perform statistical tests using the standard formulas for the t and F distributions. Fortunately, standard statistical tests are approximately correct for reasonably large sample sizes.

While there are statistical methods which allow one to test for normality (see Chapter 2), these tests are not widely used.[1] One reason for this is that the tests are not statistically powerful, in the sense that one often may fail to reject the null hypothesis of normality, even when the error distribution is nonnormal. In addition, if we decided that the normality assumption was invalid, alternative estimation procedures and statistical tests would be more complicated than those associated with the normal classical regression model.

The assumption that the error term has a zero expected value is not serious; if the error has a nonzero expected value, the estimated regression slope parameters will remain unchanged while the intercept will pick up the effect. It will be impossible to differentiate between the true intercept and the nonzero expected value in the error term, while in most econometric applications the intercept term is not of concern. Finally, the assumption of independence of the errors will be considered in Section 6.2, while Section 6.1 will focus on the assumption that the errors have constant variance.

6.1   HETEROSCEDASTICITY

There are occasions in econometric modeling when the assumption of constant error variance, or *homoscedasticity,* is unreasonable. For example, if one is examining a cross section of firms in one industry, error terms associated with very large firms might have larger variances than those error terms associated with smaller firms; sales of larger firms might be more volatile than sales of smaller firms. Or consider a cross-section study of family income and expenditures.[2] It seems plausible to expect that low-income individuals would spend at a rather steady rate, while the spending patterns of high-income families would be relatively volatile. This suggests that in a model in which expenditures are the dependent variable, error variances associated with high-income families would be greater than their low-income counterparts. *Heteroscedasticity,* or unequal variances, usually does not occur in time-series studies because changes in the dependent variable and changes in one or more of the independent variables are likely to be of the same order of magnitude.[3] For example, in the aggregate-consumption-function examples in Chapter 3, both consumption and disposable income grow at about the same rate over time.

For a model with heteroscedastic error disturbances we will assume that each error term ε_i is normally distributed with variance σ_i^2, where the variance $\mathrm{Var}(\varepsilon_i) = E(\varepsilon_i^2) = \sigma_i^2$ is not constant over observations. When heteroscedasticity is present, ordinary least-squares estimation places more weight on the observations with large error variances than on those with smaller error vari-

---

[1] One direct test would proceed as follows. Calculate the standardized residuals from a multiple regression by dividing each residual by the standard error of the regression. If the errors are normal, the distribution of standardized residuals should be unit-normal. See D. A. Belsley, E. Kuh, and R. E. Welsch, *Regression Diagnostics* (New York: Wiley, 1980), pp. 16–18.

[2] This example is studied in detail in S. J. Prais and H. S. Houthakker, *The Analysis of Family Budgets* (Cambridge: Cambridge University Press, 1955).

[3] Of course variances may decrease over time as measurement techniques improve.

ances. The weighting occurs because the sum-of-squared residuals associated with large variance error terms are likely to be substantially greater than the sum-of-squared residuals associated with low variance errors. The regression line will be adjusted to minimize the total sum-of-squared residuals, and this can best be accomplished by guaranteeing a very good fit in the large-variance portion of the data. Because of this implicit weighting, ordinary least-squares parameter estimators are unbiased and consistent, but they are not *efficient;* i.e., the variances of the estimated parameters are not the minimum variances. In addition, the *estimated* variances of the estimated parameters will be biased estimators of the true variance of the estimated parameters.

The fact that the parameter estimators are unbiased can be seen in the context of the two-variable model with the variables measured as deviations about their means. Then

$$\hat{\beta} = \frac{\Sigma x_i y_i}{\Sigma x_i^2} = \frac{\Sigma x_i(\beta x_i + \varepsilon_i)}{\Sigma x_i^2} = \beta + \frac{\Sigma x_i \varepsilon_i}{\Sigma x_i^2}$$

and

$$E(\hat{\beta}) = \beta + \frac{E(\Sigma x_i \varepsilon_i)}{\Sigma x_i^2} = \beta$$

Notice that variances of the error terms play no role in the proof that least-squares estimators are unbiased.

The difficulty with the variances of the estimated parameters also can be seen in the two-variable case. Then, from Chapter 3, we know that

$$\text{Var}(\hat{\beta}) = \frac{\sigma^2}{\Sigma x_i^2} \tag{6.2}$$

The variance of the error was taken out of the summation sign during the derivation because the variance was assumed to be constant. However, when heteroscedasticity is present, the variance is not constant and the derivation does not hold. The result is that the standard formula [Eq. (6.2)] will lead to biased estimates of the variances of each of the estimated parameters. If these biased estimates are used, statistical tests and confidence intervals will be incorrect.

The formula for the correct standard error when the errors are heteroscedastic can be derived in a manner similar to the derivation in the case of the basic linear regression model. The variances of the parameter estimators are given by[4]

$$\text{Var}(\hat{\beta}) = \frac{\Sigma x_i^2 \sigma_i^2}{(\Sigma x_i^2)^2} \tag{6.3}$$

[4] The derivation follows directly from the derivation given in Result 2 of Appendix 3.1. In that derivation, $\text{Var}(\hat{\beta}) = \Sigma c_i^2 E(\varepsilon_i^2)$. Substituting $c_i = x_i / \Sigma x_i^2$ gives the result.

Halbert White has shown that a consistent estimator of the correct variances can be obtained by substituting $\hat{\varepsilon}_i^2$, the square of each regression residual, for σ_i^2 in this formula.[5]

Finally, it is important to bear in mind that the inefficiency of the least-squares estimator arises even if the variances of the parameter estimates are *correctly* determined. In this case, the variances will be larger than the variances associated with an alternative linear unbiased estimator, as is discussed in the following pages.

6.1.1   Corrections for Heteroscedasticity

We discuss the appropriate estimation technique (which is unbiased, consistent, and efficient) in two conceptually separate cases. Each case relies to a different degree on prior and sample information, but both involve relatively simple estimation procedures.

Known Variances   We first assume that sufficient prior knowledge is available for values of each of the error variances to be known. The case of known variances occurs occasionally in econometric work but is especially important here in illustrating how to correct for heteroscedasticity. The appropriate technique, called *weighted least squares,* is a special case of a more general econometric technique known as *generalized least squares.* A matrix derivation of the generalized least-squares procedure appears in Appendix 6.1.

The weighted least-squares estimation procedure, which can be derived from the maximum-likelihood function, is best illustrated in the two-variable model. The appropriate estimator is obtained by minimizing the expression

WLS puts more weight on errors that have lower variance and less on those that have higher variance

$$\sum \left(\frac{Y_i - \hat{\alpha} - \hat{\beta} X_i}{\sigma_i} \right)^2$$

2. the end result is that all errors have same variances.

$\hat{\alpha}$ and $\hat{\beta}$ are, of course, the desired parameter estimates. When the original variables are written in deviations form, the original objective is modified to that of minimizing the expression[6]

$$\sum \left(\frac{y_i - \hat{\beta} x_i}{\sigma_i} \right)^2$$

---

[5] H. White, "A Heteroskedasticity-Consistent Covariance Matrix Estimator and a Direct Test for Heteroskedasticity," *Econometrica,* vol. 48, pp. 817–838, May 1980.

[6] To be correct, the deviations form must be obtained by transforming the model (dividing by σ_i) and then subtracting variable means.

Solving for the least-squares parameter estimates (as in Chapter 1), we find that

$$\hat{\beta} = \frac{\Sigma x_i y_i / \sigma_i^2}{\Sigma x_i^2 / \sigma_i^2} = \frac{\Sigma (x_i/\sigma_i)(y_i/\sigma_i)}{\Sigma (x_i/\sigma_i)^2} = \frac{\Sigma x_i^* y_i^*}{\Sigma (x_i^*)^2} \qquad \text{where } x_i^* = x_i/\sigma_i$$

$$y_i^* = y_i/\sigma_i$$

Thus, the desired estimation procedure is accomplished by weighting the original data and then performing ordinary least-squares estimation on the transformed model.

To use weighted least squares in the multiple regression case, we redefine the variables in the original regression model of Eq. (6.1) as

$$Y_i^* = \frac{Y_i}{\sigma_i} \qquad X_{ji}^* = \frac{X_{ji}}{\sigma_i} \qquad j = 1, 2, \ldots, k \qquad \varepsilon_i^* = \frac{\varepsilon_i}{\sigma_i}$$

In place of the original linear model [Eq. (6.1)] we use the transformed model

$$Y_i^* = \beta_1 X_{1i}^* + \beta_2 X_{2i}^* + \cdots + \beta_k X_{ki}^* + \varepsilon_i^*$$

or, equivalently, $\quad \dfrac{Y_i}{\sigma_i} = \beta_1 \dfrac{1}{\sigma_i} + \beta_2 \dfrac{X_{2i}}{\sigma_i} + \cdots + \beta_k \dfrac{X_{ki}}{\sigma_i} + \dfrac{\varepsilon_i}{\sigma_i}$

Note that the transformed error term is homoscedastic (has constant variance):

$$\text{Var}(\varepsilon_i^*) = \text{Var}\left(\frac{\varepsilon_i}{\sigma_i}\right) = \frac{1}{\sigma_i^2} \text{Var}(\varepsilon_i) = \frac{\sigma_i^2}{\sigma_i^2} = 1$$

Why does this procedure yield efficient parameter estimators? The reason is that the transformed model by construction satisfies all the assumptions of the classical linear regression model (including constant error variance). We therefore know (according to the Gauss-Markov theorem) that the estimators must be efficient.

This analysis is limited because the individual error variances are not always known. In fact, the necessary information for the application of weighted least squares is the *relative* magnitude of the error variances. Since there are many situations in which the relative magnitude of the error variances is not known, it is important to consider special cases in which sufficient sample information is available to make reasonable guesses of the true error variances.

Error Variances Vary Directly with an Independent Variable One possibility is the existence of a relationship between the error variances and the values of one of the explanatory variables in the regression model. Specifically, assume that

$$\text{Var}(\varepsilon_i) = CX_{2i}^2$$

where C is a nonzero constant and X_{2i} is an observation on one of the independent variables in the general linear regression model

$$Y_i = \beta_1 + \beta_2 X_{2i} + \cdots + \beta_k X_{ki} + \varepsilon_i$$

Then we proceed as if the variances are known. To do this, we redefine the variables in the above equation as follows (the value of the constant C does not affect the weighted least-squares procedure):

$$Y_i^* = \frac{Y_i}{X_{2i}} \qquad X_{ji}^* = \frac{X_{ji}}{X_{2i}} \qquad j = 1, 2, \ldots, k \qquad \varepsilon_i^* = \frac{\varepsilon_i}{X_{2i}}$$

The transformed regression equation is

$$\frac{Y_i}{X_{2i}} = \beta_1 \frac{1}{X_{2i}} + \beta_2 + \beta_3 \frac{X_{3i}}{X_{2i}} + \cdots + \beta_k \frac{X_{ki}}{X_{2i}} + \frac{\varepsilon_i}{X_{2i}} \qquad (6.4)$$

We can see that the transformed error term is homoscedastic, since

$$\text{Var}(\varepsilon_i^*) = \text{Var}\left(\frac{\varepsilon_i}{X_{2i}}\right) = \frac{1}{X_{2i}^2}\text{Var}(\varepsilon_i) = C$$

In this particular case the original intercept term has become a variable term, while the slope parameter associated with the variable X_2 has become the new intercept term. Ordinary least-squares regression estimates of the parameters in Eq. (6.4) will yield the appropriate (efficient) parameter estimates, since the errors in the transformed equation are homoscedastic.

Example 6.1 Housing Expenditures   In this example we consider a cross-section study of the annual housing expenditures and annual incomes of four groups of families:

Group	Housing expenditures, $000					Income, $000
1	1.8	2.0	2.0	2.0	2.1	5.0
2	3.0	3.2	3.5	3.5	3.6	10.0
3	4.2	4.2	4.5	4.8	5.0	15.0
4	4.8	5.0	5.7	6.0	6.2	20.0

The housing-expenditure model is hypothesized to be

$$Y_i = \alpha + \beta X_i + \varepsilon_i$$

where Y_i is housing expenditures and X_i is income. An ordinary least-squares regression yields the following regression estimates (t statistics in parentheses):

$$\hat{Y}_i = \underset{(4.4)}{.89} + \underset{(15.9)}{.237} X_i \qquad R^2 = .93 \qquad F = 252.7$$

A graphical examination of the data and knowledge of prior expenditure studies suggests that heteroscedasticity is present in the model.

The housing-expenditure model can be estimated with a correction for heteroscedasticity. The transformed model is

$$\frac{Y_i}{X_i} = \beta + \alpha \frac{1}{X_i} + \varepsilon_i^*$$

and the regression results are

$$\frac{\hat{Y}_i}{X_i} = \underset{(21.3)}{.249} + \underset{(7.7)}{.7529} \frac{1}{X_i} \qquad R^2 = .76 \qquad F = 58.7$$

Note that the revised estimate of the regression coefficient associated with income is .249, an increase over the ordinary least-squares estimate. As expected, the correct use of t and F statistics still allows one to conclude that all regression coefficients are significant at the 5 percent level. Note that the R^2 measure associated with the weighted least-squares procedure is lower than the R^2 associated with the unweighted procedure. The decline in R^2 should not be taken as an indication that the heteroscedasticity correction was incorrect, since the weighted least-squares procedure involves the use of a transformed dependent variable.

The reported R^2 therefore fails to provide a useful measure of goodness of fit for the original model. A better measure would result from the use of the original equation and the efficient parameter estimates to calculate regression residuals $\hat{\varepsilon}_i = Y_i - .7529 - .249\, X_i$. We then have two choices for measuring goodness of fit. First, we can use the standard R^2 formula to calculate $1 - \text{ESS/TSS}$. This R^2 is not necessarily between 0 and 1. For that reason we suggest a second alternative. We use the efficiently estimated parameters to estimate fitted values $\hat{Y}_i = .7529 + .249\, X_i$ and use as our measure of goodness of fit the square of the simple correlation between Y_i and $\hat{Y}_i$. In this particular example both choices yielded measures of fit of .92.

Using Consistent Estimates of Variances   With heteroscedasticity, biased and inconsistent estimation of the variances of the ordinary least-squares parameter estimates causes statistical inferences to be invalid. Hal White has suggested a method for obtaining consistent estimates of variances and covariances of OLS estimates which provides valid statistical tests for large samples.[7] The *heteroscedasticity-consistent estimator* (HCE) is based on the principle of maximum likelihood, which is discussed in detail in Chapter 10.

As an example, recall from Eq. (6.2) that in the two-variable regression model

$$Var(\hat{\beta}) = \frac{\sigma^2}{\Sigma x_i^2}$$

generates a biased estimate of the variance of β. An unbiased estimator, given in Eq. (6.3), is

$$Var(\hat{\beta}) = \frac{\Sigma x_i^2 \sigma_i^2}{(\Sigma x_i^2)^2}$$

The heteroscedasticity-consistent estimator uses Eq. (6.3) as its basis, replacing the unknown σ_i^2 with the squares of the residuals $\hat{\varepsilon}_i^2$. The HCE estimator is currently available in many statistical regression packages. With HCE estimation, the R^2 for the regression will be the same, but all estimates of standard errors and related statistics will change because they are now consistent estimates. While the use of the HCE estimator does generate consistent variance estimates, it does not provide the most efficient parameter estimates. For efficient estimation, one of the weighted least-squares estimation procedures must be used.

Consistent but not efficient.

bias variances for errors

OLS no longer efficient

6.1.2   Tests for Heteroscedasticity

Having discussed modifications of the least-squares procedure in two separate cases, it is natural for us to consider whether appropriate statistical procedures can be found to test for heteroscedasticity. In each case we wish to find a test of the null hypothesis of *homoscedasticity*, that is, $\sigma_1^2 = \sigma_2^2 = \sigma_3^2 = \cdots = \sigma_N^2$, where N is the number of observations. The specific alternative hypothesis against which the null hypothesis is to be tested depends on the estimation procedure that is considered to yield the most desirable correction for heteroscedasticity.

While there are a number of specific tests for heteroscedasticity, a useful first procedure is the informal one of examining the pattern of the residuals to see whether estimated variances differ from observation to observation. To do this,

[7] H. White, "A Heteroskedasticity-Consistent Covariance Matrix Estimator and a Direct Test for Heteroskedasticity," *Econometrica*, vol. 48, pp. 817–838, May 1980.

we suggest calculating the squares of the residuals, $\hat{\varepsilon}_i^2$. If the model in question is a time-series model, a plot of these squared residuals against time will tell us whether, for example, estimated variances increase over time. If the model involves a cross section, a plot of the squared residuals against one or several explanatory variables, or against $\hat{Y}$, will serve the same general purpose.

We now consider a number of formal heteroscedasticity tests, all of which are based in one way or another on the squares of the residuals.

Goldfeld-Quandt Test[8] Assume that we are considering a two-variable model and wish to test the null hypothesis of homoscedasticity against the alternative hypothesis that $\sigma_i^2 = CX_i^2$. The Goldfeld-Quandt test procedure involves the calculation of two least-squares regression lines, one using data thought to be associated with low variance errors and the other using data thought to be associated with high variance errors. If the residual variances associated with each regression line are approximately equal, the homoscedasticity assumption cannot be rejected, but if the residual variance increases substantially, it is possible to reject the null hypothesis. The test can be carried out in the following manner:

1. Order the data by the magnitude of the independent variable X, which is thought to be related to the error variance.

2. Omit the middle d observations. d might be chosen, for example, to be approximately one-fifth of the total sample size.

3. Fit two separate regressions, the first (indicated by subscript 1) for the portion of the data associated with low values of X and the second (indicated by subscript 2) associated with high values of X. Each regression will involve $(N - d)/2$ pieces of data and $[(N - d)/2] - 2$ degrees of freedom. d must be small enough to ensure that sufficient degrees of freedom are available to allow for the proper estimation of each of the separate regressions.

4. Calculate the residual sum of squares associated with each regression: ESS_1, associated with low X's, and ESS_2, associated with high X's. (ESS is described in Chapter 3.)

5. Assuming that the error process is normally distributed (and no serial correlation is present), the statistic $\text{ESS}_2/\text{ESS}_1$ will be distributed as an F statistic with $(N - d - 4)/2$ degrees of freedom in both the numerator and the denominator. We can reject the null hypothesis at a chosen level of significance if the calculated statistic is greater than the critical value of the F distribution.

The Goldfeld-Quandt test can easily be applied to the general linear model by ordering the observations by the magnitude of one of the independent variables. The number of degrees of freedom in the F statistic will be $(N - d - 2k)/2$, where k is the number of independent variables (including a constant term) in in the model. The test works because it allows for the independent regression

[8] S. M. Goldfeld and R. E. Quandt, "Some Tests for Homoscedasticity," *Journal of the American Statistical Society,* vol. 60, pp. 539–547, 1965.

estimation of both high and low observation data. However, there is an important cost involved. Because no restrictions are made on the regression parameters (as well as the error variances) in each of the two regression runs, statistical power is lost. A more powerful test (one that has smaller Type II errors) would take into account the information that the regression parameters are identical for both sets of data and that only the error variance has changed. Finally, the selection of the number of middle observations to eliminate from the test is somewhat arbitrary. If no middle observations are eliminated, the test is still correct, but experience shows that elimination from the test procedure of observations associated with errors of almost equal variance improves the power of the test.

Example 6.2 Goldfeld-Quandt Test   The Goldfeld-Quandt test can be applied to the housing-expenditure example that was used previously. The data are divided into two samples, the first including those with incomes of $5,000 and $10,000 and the second including higher-income families ($15,000 and $20,000). No middle observations are dropped from the sample because a natural break in the data is available without observations being omitted. The output associated with the two separate regression equations is as follows (t statistics in parentheses; data are in thousands of dollars):

I   Low-income families:

$$Y_i = .600 + .276X_i \qquad R^2 = .94 \qquad ESS_1 = .300$$
$$\quad\;\; (3.1) \quad\;\; (11.3)$$

II   High-income families:

$$Y_i = 1.54 + .20X_i \qquad R^2 = .55 \qquad ESS_2 = 2.024$$
$$\quad\;\; (1.4) \quad\;\; (3.1)$$

The F statistic used to test the homoscedasticity assumption is $ESS_2/ESS_1 = 6.7$. Under the null hypothesis this will be distributed as F with 8 degrees of freedom in the numerator and the denominator. Examination of the table of the F distribution shows that the critical value of F at the 5 percent level of significance is 3.44. We conclude that we can reject the null hypothesis in favor of the alternative hypothesis of heteroscedasticity.

Breusch-Pagan Test[9]   The Goldfeld-Quandt test is a natural test to apply when one can order the observations in terms of the increasing variance of the

---

[9] See T. S. Breusch and A. R. Pagan, "A Simple Test for Heteroskedasticity and Random Coefficient Variation," *Econometrica*, vol. 47, pp. 1287–1294, 1979.

error term (or one independent variable). An alternative test which does not require such an ordering and is easy to apply is the *Breusch-Pagan test.*

Consider the following model, which includes a general assumption about the relationship between the true error variance and an independent variable Z:

$$Y_i = \alpha + \beta X_i + \varepsilon_i \tag{6.5}$$

$$\sigma_i^2 = f(\gamma + \delta Z_i) \tag{6.6}$$

Equation (6.6) provides the specification of the form taken by heteroscedasticity if it is indeed present. $f(\ )$ represents a general function that allows, for example, for both linear and logarithmic forms. Z could be the independent variable X, or it could represent a group of independent variables other than X.

To test for heteroscedasticity, we first calculate the least-squares residuals $\hat{\varepsilon}_i$ from the regression in Eq. (6.5). At the same time we use these residuals to estimate:

$$\hat{\sigma}^2 = \frac{\Sigma \hat{\varepsilon}_i^2}{N} \tag{6.7}$$

Now we run the following regression:

$$\frac{\hat{\varepsilon}_i^2}{\hat{\sigma}^2} = \gamma + \delta Z_i + v_i \tag{6.8}$$

If the error term ε in Eq. (6.5) is normally distributed and there is no heteroscedasticity, then one-half of the regression sum of squares, RSS/2, provides a suitable test statistic. Specifically, under the null hypothesis of homoscedasticity,

$$\frac{\text{RSS}}{2} \sim \chi_1^2 \tag{6.9}$$

More generally, when there are p independent Z variables, RSS/2 will follow a chi-square distribution with p degrees of freedom. The higher the value of the regression sum of squares, the more highly correlated Z is with the error variance, and therefore, the less likely the null hypothesis is to hold.

Suppose we do find heteroscedasticity to be present using the Breusch-Pagan test in the case of a single Z variable, as in Eq. (6.8). Then one obvious means of correcting for heteroscedasticity is to transform the original equation by using the Z variable rather than the variable X_2 in Eq. (6.4).[10] When we use more general forms of the Breusch-Pagan test, however, there is no natural way in which to do such a correction.

The White Test[11] The Breusch-Pagan test depends in an important way on the assumption of a normal error term. Hal White has proposed a closely related test that does not depend as crucially on normality. Suppose that instead of Eq. (6.8) we use the regression residuals to run the following regression:

$$\hat{\varepsilon}_i^2 = \gamma + \delta Z_i + v_i$$

from which we calculate the measure of goodness of fit, R^2. The White test is based on the fact that when there is homoscedasticity,

$$NR^2 \sim \chi^2 \tag{6.10}$$

with 1 degree of freedom. More generally, when there are p independent Z variables, the distribution will have p degrees of freedom.

Since the White and Breusch-Pagan tests are so similar, either can be an appropriate choice, depending on the ease of application. Of greater importance for the testing procedure is the choice of Z variables. White suggests, for example, that if the heteroscedasticity is related to a particular variable such as X, one might use variables X and X^2 to allow for nonlinearities. Alternatively, if X and Z were two relevant variables, X^2, Z^2, and XZ might be used.

Example 6.3 Breusch-Pagan and White Tests We applied both the Breusch-Pagan and the White tests to the housing-expenditure example (Example 6.1). In both cases we initially used the assumption that heteroscedasticity took the form

$$\sigma_i^2 = \gamma + \delta X_i$$

[10] A better approach would involve maximum-likelihood estimation. With heteroscedasticity the log-likelihood function is given by

$$\log(L) = -\left(\frac{N}{2}\right) \log(2\pi) - \left(\frac{1}{2}\right) \Sigma \log(\sigma_i^2) - \left(\frac{1}{2}\right) \Sigma \left(\frac{Y_i - \alpha - \beta X_i}{\sigma_i}\right)^2$$

Suppose, for example, that the heteroscedasticity is *multiplicative*, i.e.,

$$\log(\sigma_i^2) = \gamma + \delta \log(Z_i)$$

Substituting this expression into log (L) and maximizing with respect to α, β, γ, and δ yields maximum-likelihood estimates of the regression and heteroscedasticity parameters.

[11] H. White, "A Heteroskedasticity-Consistent Covariance Matrix Estimator and a Direct Test for Heteroskedasticity," *Econometrica*, vol. 48, pp. 817–838, May 1980.

To apply the Breusch-Pagan test, we ran the regression of Y on X and saved the calculated residuals. We found that $\hat{\sigma}^2 = .12523$. Then we regressed the normalized residuals on X to obtain

$$\frac{\hat{\varepsilon}_i^2}{\hat{\sigma}^2} = -.853 + .148X_i + \hat{v}_i$$

The regression sum of squares (which can be calculated from R^2 and the error sum of squares) was equal to 13.732. Therefore, the appropriate test statistic is

$$\frac{RSS}{2} = 6.866$$

which follows a chi-square distribution with 1 degree of freedom. Since the critical value of the chi square is 3.84 at the 5 percent level, we reject the null hypothesis of homoscedasticity in favor of the presence of heteroscedasticity.

The White test is even easier to apply. The R^2 associated with the regression of the normalized residuals is .36. But this is the same R^2 that we would obtain if the equation were not normalized. (Multiplying the dependent variable by a constant does not affect the fit of an equation.) Therefore, the appropriate test statistic is

$$20(R^2) = 7.20$$

which follows a chi-square distribution with 1 degree of freedom. Once again (since 7.20 > 3.84) we reject the null hypothesis of homoscedasticity.

Finally, note that the White test (or the Breusch-Pagan test) can be applied to almost any functional form of X. Using a quadratic form, we calculate the regression of the residuals squared on X and X^2, obtaining the following result:

$$\hat{\varepsilon}_i^2 = .0922 - .0212X_i + .0016X_i^2$$

with an R^2 of .4130. The appropriate test statistic is

$$20(R^2) = 8.260$$

which follows a chi-square distribution with 2 degrees of freedom. The critical value of the chi square with 2 degrees of freedom is 5.99. As before, we reject the null hypothesis of homoscedasticity (since 8.26 > 5.99).

Example 6.4 Correcting for Heteroscedasticity   The consumption of energy over time would be expected to grow as population and income grow, but to decline, other things being equal, as the price of energy increases. Using annual time-series data from 1960 through 1985, we estimated an ordinary least-squares regression using the following variables:[12]

Q = logarithm of quantity of delivered energy [quads (10^{15} BTU)]

YEAR = 1 in 1960, . . . 26 in 1985

P = logarithm of price of a quad (1975 dollars)

INC = logarithm of income per household (1975 dollars)

The regression results (with t statistics in parentheses) were

$$\hat{Q} = -36.84 + .018 \text{ YEAR} - .67 \, P + .55 \text{ INC}$$
$$\phantom{\hat{Q} = }(-1.98) \quad\quad (1.76) \quad\quad (-8.99) \quad\quad (2.03)$$

$$R^2 = .970 \quad\quad\quad s = .032$$

All the coefficients have the expected signs, and the overall regression fits well. Nevertheless, we were concerned about the possibility that the error variances increased over time as energy consumption increased. We performed a Breusch-Pagan test for heteroscedasticity, using the specification that the error variance was directly related to the year of measurement. Specifically, we used the squares of the residuals as the dependent variable (ESQ) and estimated the following equation:

$$\widehat{\text{ESQ}} = -.139 + .000071 \text{ YEAR} \quad\quad R^2 = .165$$
$$\phantom{\widehat{\text{ESQ}} = }(-2.16) \quad\quad (2.17)$$

Our calculated test statistic of 4.28 is greater than the critical value of the chi-square distribution with 1 degree of freedom at the 5 percent level (the critical value is 3.84). Therefore, we reject the null hypothesis of homoscedasticity.

To improve efficiency we reestimated the OLS model by using weighted least squares. Our weights were chosen from the regression above; specifically, we weighted each observation by the inverse of the square root of the predicted values of the regression (any negative predicted values were set equal to a small positive number). The weighted least-squares results are as follows:

$$\hat{Q} = -45.90 + .023 \text{ YEAR} - .68 \, P + .41 \text{ INC}$$
$$\phantom{\hat{Q} = }(-2.71) \quad\quad (2.47) \quad\quad (-9.79) \quad\quad (1.65)$$

$$R^2 = .969 \quad\quad\quad s = .032$$

[12] The data were prepared by the MIT Energy Laboratory. The original sources of the data are the U.S. Department of Commerce Petroleum and Minerals Yearbook and the Energy Information Agency. We wish to thank Daniel McFadden for providing the data series.

The results are quite similar to those we obtained previously. However, the significance of a number of the coefficients has increased, and most important, the standard errors that underlie the significance calculations are the correct ones. Finally, note that R^2 has decreased somewhat, which is to be expected when the statistics are based on the original (unweighted) data.

6.2   SERIAL CORRELATION

The assumption that errors corresponding to different observations are uncorrelated often breaks down in time-series studies. Recall that when the error terms from different (usually adjacent) time periods are correlated, we say that the error term is *serially correlated.* Serial correlation occurs in time-series studies when the errors associated with observations in a given time period carry over into future time periods. For example, if we are predicting the growth of stock dividends, an overestimate in one year is likely to lead to overestimates in succeeding years. This can occur occasionally in cross sections when the units of observation have a natural ordering, e.g., by size or geography.

In this section we deal with the problem of *first-order serial correlation,* in which errors in one time period are correlated directly with errors in the ensuing period.[13] While it is possible that serial correlation can be negative as well as positive, we concern ourselves primarily with the case of positive serial correlation, in which errors in one period are positively correlated with errors in the next period. Positive serial correlation frequently occurs in time-series studies either because of correlation in the measurement error component of the error term or, more likely, because of the high degree of correlation over time that is present in the cumulative effects of omitted variables.

Serial correlation will not affect the unbiasedness or consistency of the ordinary least-squares regression estimators, but it does affect their efficiency.[14] In the case of positive serial correlation, this loss of efficiency will be masked by the fact that the estimates of the standard errors obtained from the least-squares regression will be smaller than the true standard errors. In other words, the regression estimators will be unbiased but the standard error of the regression will be biased downward.[15] This will lead to the conclusion that the parameter estimates are more precise than they actually are. There will be a tendency to reject the null hypothesis when, in fact, it should not be rejected. We shall not prove these results, but one can obtain an intuitive feeling for why they are true by examining Fig. 6.1a and b.

Both graphs illustrate the presence of positive serial correlation in a model with a single explanatory variable. In Fig. 6.1a the error term associated with the first observation happens to be positive. This leads to a series of error terms, the first four of which are positive and the last two of which are negative. In

---

[13] The more general case can be handled with the use of generalized least-squares estimation, as detailed in Appendix 6.1, and with the time-series techniques discussed in Part Four.

[14] If the model includes a lagged dependent variable, the problems are much more severe.

[15] This holds provided that the X's are not negatively serially correlated.

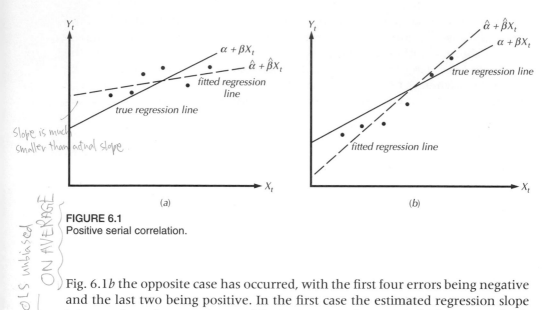

(a)

(b)

Slope is much smaller than actual slope.

OLS unbiased ON AVERAGE

FIGURE 6.1
Positive serial correlation.

Fig. 6.1*b* the opposite case has occurred, with the first four errors being negative and the last two being positive. In the first case the estimated regression slope is lower than the true slope, while in the second case it is higher. Since both cases are equally likely to occur, least-squares slope estimates will be correct on average; i.e., they will be unbiased. However, in both cases the least-squares regression lines fit the observed data points more closely than does the true regression line; this leads to an R^2 that gives an overly optimistic picture of the success of least-squares regression. More important, however, least squares will lead to an estimate of the error variance that is smaller than the true error variance.

6.2.1 Corrections for Serial Correlation

We assume that each of the error terms in a linear regression model is drawn from a normal population with 0 expected value and constant variance but that the errors are not independent over time. Since serial correlation usually is present in time-series data, we use a subscript of t (in place of i) and assume that the total number of observations is T. The model is

$$Y_t = \beta_1 + \beta_2 X_{2t} + \beta_3 X_{3t} + \cdots + \beta_k X_{kt} + \varepsilon_t \tag{6.11}$$

$$\varepsilon_t = \rho \varepsilon_{t-1} + v_t \qquad 0 \le |\rho| < 1 \tag{6.12}$$

where v_t is distributed as $N(0, \sigma_v^2)$ and is independent of other errors over time and ε_t is distributed as $N(0, \sigma_\varepsilon^2)$ but is not independent of other errors over time. The error process as described in Eq. (6.12) is generated by a rule which says that the error in time period t is determined by diminishing the value of the error in the previous period (multiplying by ρ) and then adding the effect of a random variable with 0 expected value. This *first-order autoregressive process,* denoted AR(1), is the most elementary autoregressive error process that is discussed in Part Four of this book.

It is easy to verify that the effect of an error in any given time period is felt in all future time periods, with a magnitude which diminishes over time. We simply calculate the covariances of ε_t with all previous time periods:

$$\text{Var}\,(\varepsilon_t) = E(\varepsilon_t^2) = E[(\rho\varepsilon_{t-1} + v_t)^2] = E(\rho^2\varepsilon_{t-1}^2 + v_t^2 + 2\rho\varepsilon_{t-1}v_t)$$

$$= \rho^2 E(\varepsilon_{t-1}^2) + E(v_t^2) \qquad \text{since } \varepsilon_{t-1} \text{ and } v_t \text{ are independent}$$

$$= \rho^2\,\text{Var}\,(\varepsilon_t) + \sigma_v^2 \qquad \text{since } \varepsilon \text{ is homoscedastic}$$

Solving,

$$\text{Var}\,(\varepsilon_t) = \sigma_\varepsilon^2 = \frac{\sigma_v^2}{1 - \rho^2} \tag{6.13}$$

$$\text{Cov}\,(\varepsilon_t, \varepsilon_{t-1}) = E(\varepsilon_t\varepsilon_{t-1})$$

$$= E[(\rho\varepsilon_{t-1} + v_t)\varepsilon_{t-1}] = E(\rho\varepsilon_{t-1}^2 + v_t\varepsilon_{t-1})$$

$$= \rho E(\varepsilon_{t-1}^2) = \rho\text{Var}\,(\varepsilon_t) = \rho\sigma_\varepsilon^2 \tag{6.14}$$

Likewise, $$\text{Cov}\,(\varepsilon_t, \varepsilon_{t-2}) = E(\varepsilon_t\varepsilon_{t-2}) = \rho^2\sigma_\varepsilon^2 \tag{6.15}$$

$$\text{Cov}\,(\varepsilon_t, \varepsilon_{t-3}) = E(\varepsilon_t\varepsilon_{t-3}) = \rho^3\sigma_\varepsilon^2 \tag{6.16}$$

A useful formula for the first-order serial-correlation coefficient ρ is

$$\rho = \frac{\text{Cov}\,(\varepsilon_t, \varepsilon_{t-1})}{\sigma_\varepsilon^2} = \frac{\text{Cov}\,(\varepsilon_t, \varepsilon_{t-1})}{[\text{Var}\,(\varepsilon_t)]^{1/2}[\text{Var}\,(\varepsilon_{t-1})]^{1/2}} \tag{6.17}$$

since $\sigma_\varepsilon^2 = \text{Var}\,(\varepsilon_t) = \text{Var}\,(\varepsilon_{t-1})$. Thus, ρ measures the correlation coefficient between errors in time period t and errors in time period $t - 1$. When ρ equals 0, no first-order serial correlation is present, while a large value of ρ implies the existence of first-order serial correlation.[16]

If ρ were known, it would be easy to adjust the ordinary least-square regression procedure to obtain efficient parameter estimates. The procedure involves the use of *generalized differencing* to alter the linear model into one in

---

[16] The error term for the first time period is a function of errors in the previous time period for which no data are available. Equation (6.13) suggests that we assume that ε_1 is normally distributed with mean 0 and variance $\sigma_v^2/(1 - \rho^2)$.

which the errors are independent. To describe this procedure, we use the fact that the linear model in Eq. (6.11) holds *for all time periods*. In particular,

$$Y_{t-1} = \beta_1 + \beta_2 X_{2t-1} + \cdots + \beta_k X_{kt-1} + \varepsilon_{t-1} \tag{6.18}$$

Multiplying Eq. (6.18) by ρ and subtracting from Eq. (6.11), we obtain the desired transformation:

$$Y_t^* = \beta_1(1 - \rho) + \beta_2 X_{2t}^* + \cdots + \beta_k X_{kt}^* + v_t \tag{6.19}$$

where

$$Y_t^* = Y_t - \rho Y_{t-1} \qquad X_{2t}^* = X_{2t} - \rho X_{2t-1}$$

$$X_{kt}^* = X_{kt} - \rho X_{kt-1} \qquad v_t = \varepsilon_t - \rho \varepsilon_{t-1}$$

are *generalized differences* of Y_t, X_{2t}, ..., X_{kt}, and ε_t. By construction the transformed equation has an error process which is independently distributed with 0 mean and constant variance. Thus, ordinary least-squares regression applied to Eq. (6.19) will yield efficient estimates of all the regression parameters. Of course, the intercept of the original model must be calculated from the estimated intercept associated with Eq. (6.19).[17]

We have restricted our discussion of serial correlation to the case in which ρ is strictly less than 1. However, the case in which ρ is identically equal to 1 is of particular interest because it leads to a commonly used estimation procedure.[18] The solution process, known as *first-differencing*, is applied if we estimate the transformed equation (by analogy to the generalized differencing procedure):

$$Y_t^* = \beta_2 X_{2t}^* + \beta_3 X_{3t}^* + \cdots + \beta_k X_{kt}^* + v_t \quad \text{where } Y_t^* = Y_t - Y_{t-1} \tag{6.20}$$

$$X_{2t}^* = X_{2t} - X_{2t-1}$$

$$X_{kt}^* = X_{kt} - X_{kt-1}$$

$$v_t = \varepsilon_t - \varepsilon_{t-1}$$

Note that first-differencing eliminates the need for a constant term in the transformed equation. The intercept of the original equation must be calculated

---

[17] The transformed equation is defined only for the time period 2, 3, ..., t. Dropping the initial time period from the regression procedure results in the loss of information. A better solution would take the observations of the first time period into account as follows:

$$Y_1^* = \sqrt{1 - \rho^2}\, Y_1 \qquad X_{21}^* = \sqrt{1 - \rho^2}\, X_{21} \qquad \cdots \qquad X_{k1}^* = \sqrt{1 - \rho^2}\, X_{k1}$$

By construction, $\varepsilon_1^* = (1 - \rho^2)^{1/2}\varepsilon_1$ and $\text{Var}(\varepsilon_1^*) = (1 - \rho^2)\,\text{Var}(\varepsilon_1) = \sigma_v^2$.

[18] Note, however, that as ρ approaches 1, the error variance in the original equation becomes infinitely large, so that the previous analysis does not follow.

by solving in the original equation when the variables are measured at their respective means.[19] If a constant term were included, it would pick up the effect of any time trend present in the initial model.

The generalized differencing procedure would be very useful if the value of ρ were known *a priori*. Because this usually is not the case, we examine some procedures for estimating ρ, each of which has certain computational advantages and disadvantages. These procedures yield estimated parameters with the desired properties when the sample size is large, but little is known about their small-sample properties.[20]

The Cochrane-Orcutt Procedure[21]   This procedure involves a series of iterations, each of which produces a better estimate of ρ than does the previous one. It uses the notion that ρ is a correlation coefficient associated with errors of adjacent time periods. In the first step ordinary least squares is used to estimate the original model [Eq. (6.11)]. The residuals from this equation are then used to perform the regression

$$\hat{\varepsilon}_t = \rho\hat{\varepsilon}_{t-1} + v_t \tag{6.21}$$

The estimated value of ρ is used to perform the generalized differencing transformation process, and a new regression is run. The transformed equation is

$$Y_t^* = \beta_1(1 - \hat{\rho}) + \beta_2 X_{2t}^* + \cdots + \beta_k X_{kt}^* + v_t \quad \text{where } Y_t^* = Y_t - \hat{\rho}Y_{t-1}$$
$$X_{2t}^* = X_{2t} - \hat{\rho}X_{2t-1}$$
$$X_{kt}^* = X_{kt} - \hat{\rho}X_{kt-1}$$

The estimated transformed equation yields parameter values for the original intercept $\hat{\beta}_1$ and all the slope parameters $\hat{\beta}_2, \ldots, \hat{\beta}_k$. These revised parameter estimates are substituted into the *original* equation, and new regression residuals are obtained. The new estimated residuals are

$$\hat{\varepsilon}_t = Y_t - \hat{\beta}_1 - \hat{\beta}_2 X_{2t} - \cdots - \hat{\beta}_k X_{kt}$$

[19] In the two-variable model, for example, $Y_t^* = \beta X_t^*$. To obtain the intercept estimate, we estimate β and then substitute to obtain $\hat{\alpha} = \bar{Y} - \hat{\beta}\bar{X}$.

[20] An appealing alternative that is substantially more difficult computationally is full maximum-likelihood estimation, in which α, β, ρ, and σ_v^2 are chosen to maximize the log-likelihood function:

$$\log (L) = -\left(\frac{1}{2}\right)\log (1 - \rho^2) - \left(\frac{N}{2}\right)\log (2\pi\sigma_v^2) - \left(\frac{1}{2\sigma_v^2}\right)\Sigma v_t^2$$

For further details, see J. Kmenta, *Elements of Econometrics* (New York: Macmillan, 1986), Section 8-3.

[21] D. Cochrane and G. H. Orcutt, "Application of Least-Squares Regressions to Relationships Containing Autocorrelated Error Terms," *Journal of the American Statistical Association*, vol. 44, pp. 32–61, 1949.

If we run the regression

$$\hat{\hat{\varepsilon}}_t = \rho\hat{\hat{\varepsilon}}_{t-1} + v_t$$

these second-round residuals can be used to obtain a new estimate of ρ. The iterative process can be carried on for as many steps as desired. Standard procedure is to stop the iterations when the new estimates of ρ differ from the old ones by less than .01 or .005 or after 10 or 20 estimates of ρ have been obtained. The specific choice made depends on the computational costs involved. Unfortunately, there is no guarantee that the final estimate of ρ will minimize the sum-of-squared residuals, because the iterative technique may lead to a local rather than a global minimum.

The Hildreth-Lu Procedure[22] In this procedure a set of grid values is specified for ρ. These are usually spaced values which are to serve as guesses for the value of ρ. If one knew that positive serial correlation was present, one might choose grid values of ρ equal to 0, .1, .2, .3, .4, .5, .6, .7, .8, .9, 1.0. For each value of ρ the transformed equation

$$Y_t^* = \beta_1(1 - \rho) + \beta_2 X_{2t}^* + \cdots + \beta_k X_{kt}^* + v_t$$

is estimated. The procedure selects the equation with the lowest sum-of-squared residuals as the best equation. The procedure can be continued with new grid values chosen in the neighborhood of the ρ value that is first selected until the desired accuracy is attained. In using the Hildreth-Lu procedure, we may choose any limits and any spacing arrangement for the grid values. The technique is practical and, if used with sufficient care, will make it likely that the maximum likelihood estimate of ρ is approximated. Care should be exercised in the choice of grid values so that the minimum sum of squares obtained is global rather than local.

6.2.2 Tests for Serial Correlation

Durbin-Watson Test We shall now consider a test of the null hypothesis that no serial correlation is present ($\rho = 0$). The alternative hypothesis can be that ρ is nonzero or, in the one-tailed case, that ρ is positive (or negative). By far the most popular test for serial correlation is the *Durbin-Watson test.*[23]

The Durbin-Watson test involves the calculation of a test statistic based on

---

[22] G. Hildreth and J. Y. Lu, "Demand Relations with Autocorrelated Disturbances," *Michigan State University Agricultural Experiment Station Technical Bulletin* 276, November 1960.

[23] J. Durbin and G. S. Watson, "Testing for Serial Correlation in Least-Squares Regression," *Biometrika*, vol. 38, pp. 159–177, 1951. This test is not directly applicable if the regression does not contain a constant term.

the residuals from the ordinary least-squares regression procedure. The statistic is defined as

$$DW = \frac{\sum_{t=2}^{T} (\hat{\varepsilon}_t - \hat{\varepsilon}_{t-1})^2}{\sum_{t=1}^{T} \hat{\varepsilon}_t^2} \tag{6.22}$$

Note that the numerator cannot include a difference for the first observation in the sample since no earlier observation is available. When successive values of $\hat{\varepsilon}_t$ are close to each other, the DW statistic will be low, indicating the presence of positive serial correlation. The DW statistic will lie in the range of 0 to 4, with a value near 2 indicating no first-order serial correlation.[24] By making several approximations, it is possible to show that DW $= 2(1 - \hat{\rho})$. Thus, when there is no serial correlation ($\rho = 0$), the DW statistic will be close to 2. Positive serial correlation is associated with DW values below 2, and negative serial correlation is associated with DW values above 2.

Exact interpretation of the DW statistic is difficult because the sequence of error terms depends not only on the sequence of ε's but also on the sequence of all the X values. For this reason, most tables include test statistics which vary with the number of independent variables and the number of observations.[25] Two limits are given, usually labeled d_l and d_u. If one is investigating the possibility of positive serial correlation, a value for DW below d_l allows one to reject the null hypothesis of no serial correlation. If DW is greater than d_u, the null hypothesis is retained. The range between d_l and d_u leaves us with inconclusive results. For negative serial correlation we simply view matters from the endpoint of 4 instead of the endpoint of 0. The null hypothesis is rejected if the DW statistic is greater than $4 - d_l$, and the hypothesis is accepted if DW is less than $4 - d_u$. Within the range between $4 - d_u$ and $4 - d_l$ the test is inconclusive. (See Table 6.1 for a summary of the Durbin-Watson test.)

TABLE 6.1
RANGE OF THE DURBIN-WATSON STATISTIC

Value of DW	Result
$4 - d_l < DW < 4$	Reject null hypothesis; negative serial correlation present
$4 - d_u < DW < 4 - d_l$	Result indeterminate
$2 < DW < 4 - d_u$	Accept null hypothesis
$d_u < DW < 2$	Accept null hypothesis
$d_l < DW < d_u$	Result indeterminate
$0 < DW < d_l$	Reject null hypothesis; positive serial correlation present

---

[24] The DW statistic cannot be used if the regression equation contains a lagged dependent variable.

[25] Some computer programs calculate the exact statistical significance of the Durbin-Watson statistic.

The region of indeterminacy of the statistical test is due to the fact that the sequence of residuals is influenced by the movement of the independent variables in the regression equation. In this region, it is possible that the seeming correlation of the errors is due to the serial correlation of the independent variable, not to the serial correlation of the error terms.[26] Suppose, for example, that the X's follow a first-order autoregressive process, i.e.,

$$x_t = rx_{t-1} + w_t \qquad (6.23)$$

where $0 \leq r < 1$ and w_t is a random (uncorrelated) error term.

After some additional arithmetic, it is not difficult to show that

$$\text{DW} \approx 2 - 2 \frac{\text{Cov}(\varepsilon_t, \varepsilon_{t-1}) + r(\beta - \hat{\beta})^2 \, \text{Var}(x_t)}{\text{Var}(\varepsilon_t) + (\beta - \hat{\beta})^2 \, \text{Var}(x_t)} \qquad (6.24)$$

If the estimated slope parameter is identically equal to the true parameter, then the presence of serial correlation in the X variable is irrelevant to the calculation of the DW statistic. Despite the fact that $\hat{\beta}$ is an unbiased estimator of β, there will be sampling error involved in the estimation process, and so $\hat{\beta}$ will not be identically equal to β. It should be immediately clear from Eq. (6.24) that, other things being equal, a higher value of r will lead to a lower value of the DW statistic. In fact, a value of r close to 1 may push the DW statistic close to 0, even though the error terms may be uncorrelated themselves. The reason for the upper and lower limits associated with the DW test now becomes clear. If $r = 1$, the d_l limit is the proper one to apply. Anything below d_l indicates positive serial correlation. If $r = -1$, by contrast, the d_u limit should be used. Anything above d_u indicates that positive serial correlation cannot be accepted. In working with time series, the X's are likely to be positively autocorrelated, so that the d_l limit may be the more accurate of the two.

Example 6.5 Bituminous Coal[27]   An attempt was made to explain the demand for bituminous coal (COAL) as a function of the Federal Reserve Board index of iron and steel production (FIS), the Federal Reserve Board index of electrical utility production (FEU), the wholesale price index for coal (PCOAL), and the wholesale price index for natural gas (PGAS). The quantity demanded of bituminous coal has been seasonally adjusted, and the adjusted series was used to perform a linear regression on the explana-

---

[26] For further discussion of the reliability of the Durbin-Watson test, see R. Bartels and J. Goodhew, "The Robustness of the Durbin-Watson Test," *Review of Economics and Statistics*, vol. 63, pp. 136–139, February 1981.

[27] This example was constructed by Dynamics Associates, Cambridge, Mass., and is used with permission.

tory variables listed above. The time series ran monthly from January 1965 to December 1972.

The output from the original regression is as follows (with t statistics in parentheses):

$$\widehat{COAL} = 12{,}262 + 92.34FIS + 118.57FEU - 48.90PCOAL$$
$$\phantom{\widehat{COAL} = }{(3.51)}{(6.46)}{(7.14)}{(-3.82)}$$

$$|\ 118.91PGAS$$
$${(3.18)}$$

$$R^2 = .692 \qquad F(4/91) = 51.0 \qquad DW = .95$$

Although all the t statistics are highly significant, the low DW statistic indicates that serial correlation is likely to be present in the estimated residuals. To correct for the presence of positive first-order serial correlation, the Hildreth-Lu procedure was applied. A series of regressions was run, each with a different chosen value of ρ. The grid search is described by the following table:

ρ	Sum-of-squared residuals (ESS)	ρ	Sum-of-squared residuals (ESS)
−1.0	3.8×10^8	0.0	1.2×10^8
−.8	3.1×10^8	.2	1.0×10^8
−.6	2.5×10^8	.4	9.2×10^7
−.4	2.0×10^8	.6	9.0×10^7
−.2	1.5×10^8	.8	9.6×10^7
		1.0	1.1×10^8

The final value of ρ chosen was .6, the value associated with the smallest sum-of-squared residuals of the regression runs. When ρ was assigned the value of .6, the autoregressive transformation was performed, and the final regression was run, the results were

$$\widehat{COAL^*} = 16{,}245 + 75.29FIS^* + 100.26FEU^* - 38.98PCOAL^*$$
$$\phantom{\widehat{COAL^*} = }{(3.3)}{(4.4)}{(3.7)}{(-2.0)}$$

$$+\ 105.99PGAS^*$$
$${(2.0)}$$

where $COAL^* = COAL - .6COAL_{-1}$ $FEU^* = FEU - .6FEU_{-1}$

$PGAS^* = PGAS - .6PGAS_{-1}$ $FIS^* = FIS - .6FIS_{-1}$

$PCOAL^* = PCOAL - .6PCOAL$ $DW = 2.07$

Note that the DW statistic is substantially higher than in the original regression and that all the estimated regression coefficients continue to be significant at the 5 percent level.

Example 6.6 Interest Rates   In this example we reconsider the attempt (see Example 4.2) to estimate a single-equation model which explains the movement of the Treasury bill rate R_t as a function of industrial production (IP_t), the rate of growth of the money supply ($GM2_t$), and the rate of inflation (GPW_t). Recall that the estimated equation (with t statistics in parentheses) was

$$\hat{R}_t = 1.214 + .0484 \; IP_t + 140.33 \; GM2_t + 104.58 \; GPW_t$$
$$\quad\;\; (2.20) \quad\;\; (8.79) \qquad\quad (3.89) \qquad\qquad (6.00)$$

$$R^2 = .22 \qquad s = 2.481 \qquad DW = .18$$

The low DW statistic of .18 strongly suggests the presence of positive first-order serial correlation. The serial correlation also can be seen graphically by noticing in Fig. 6.2 that the regression residuals are highly correlated. When a residual is positive (negative) during one time period, it is likely to remain positive (negative) during the next. This is especially noticeable during the late 1970s and early 1980s, a period of high nominal interest rates. Unless corrections are made for the presence of serial correlation, not only will parameters be estimated inefficiently, but forecasts are likely to understate the actual interest rate series substantially.

To improve the model we reestimated the interest rate equation by using the Cochrane-Orcutt procedure. The results are as follows:

$$\hat{R}_t = -49.601 + .244 \; IP_t - 62.358 \; GM2_t + 6.210 \; GPW_{t-1}$$
$$\quad\;\;\; (-0.35) \quad\; (6.01) \qquad\quad (-6.55) \qquad\qquad (2.09)$$

$$R^2 = .97 \qquad s = .500 \qquad DW = 1.64 \qquad \hat{\rho} = .99$$

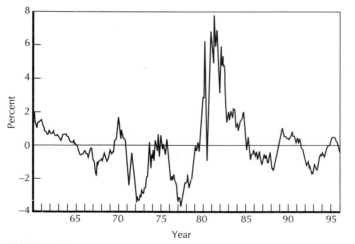

FIGURE 6.2
Interest rate residuals.

This equation fits substantially better than does the uncorrected equation. The t statistics are somewhat lower, but they are the correct, efficiently estimated statistics. (Recall that the original OLS statistics are biased.) Note finally that the DW statistic of 1.64 is substantially below 2. This suggests that more complex forms of correlation among the residuals might be present. We consider this possibility in Part Four.

? , ask slim *?.*

6.2.3 Testing for Serial Correlation When There Is a Lagged Dependent Variable

When one or more lagged endogenous variables are present, the DW statistic will often be close to 2 even when the errors are serially correlated. Of course, one could simply look at the DW statistic as providing an indicator of serial correlation when the DW statistic is low, but this approach is strongly biased against finding serial correlation.[28] Fortunately, a relatively easy alternative test provided by Durbin is strictly valid for large samples of data but can be used for small samples as well. To see how the test is applied, assume that we have estimated Eq. (6.25) using ordinary least squares:

$$Y_t = \alpha + \beta Y_{t-1} + \gamma X_t + \varepsilon_t \tag{6.25}$$

The test statistic to be used is the Durbin h statistic, which is defined as

Compare with t statistic

$$h = \hat{\rho} \sqrt{\frac{T}{1 - T[\text{Var}(\hat{\beta})]}} \tag{6.26}$$

where Var $(\hat{\beta})$ is estimated as the square of the standard error of the coefficient of the lagged endogenous variable, T is the number of observations, and $\hat{\rho}$ is the estimated first-order serial-correlation coefficient. $\hat{\rho}$ can be estimated directly from the DW statistic, since DW $\approx 2(1 - \hat{\rho})$. Solving for $\hat{\rho}$ and substituting, we find that

$$h = \left(1 - \frac{\text{DW}}{2}\right) \sqrt{\frac{T}{1 - T[\text{Var}(\hat{\beta})]}} \tag{6.27}$$

Since Durbin has shown that the h statistic is approximately normally distributed with unit variance, the test for first-order serial correlation can be done directly by using the normal distribution table.

It is important to note that the Durbin h test is not valid when T Var $(\hat{\beta})$ is greater than 1. (We cannot take the square root of a negative number.) In this case Durbin proposes an alternative test which is only slightly more compli-

---

[28] The basic results are derived in J. Durbin, "Testing for Serial Correlation in Least-Squares Regression When Some of the Regressors Are Lagged Dependent Variables," *Econometrica*, vol. 38, pp. 410–421, 1970.

cated. We obtain the residual variable $\hat{\varepsilon}_t$ from the ordinary least-squares regression and also create the lagged residual variable $\hat{\varepsilon}_{t-1}$. To simplify matters, the first observation should be dropped. We estimate Eq. (6.28):

$$\hat{\varepsilon}_t = \alpha + \rho^*\hat{\varepsilon}_{t-1} + \beta^*Y_{t-1} + \gamma^*X_t + u_t \qquad (6.28)$$

We then do a t test of the null hypothesis that ρ^* is not significantly different from 0. If we reject that null hypothesis, we conclude that first-order serial correlation is present.

When there is significant serial correlation in the presence of a lagged dependent variable, parameter estimation becomes more difficult, since ordinary least-squares estimation yields biased results.

Example 6.7 Aggregate Consumption   We estimated a simple, dynamic version of an aggregate-consumption function, in which current consumption C is a function of consumption lagged one quarter C_{-1} and current disposable income YD.[29] The estimated least-squares equation (using quarterly data from the first quarter of 1959 to the third quarter of 1995) is as follows (standard errors are in parentheses):

$$C_t = 1.88 + .086\text{YD}_t + .9114C_{t-1} \qquad DW = 1.569$$
$$ (4.69) \quad (.028) \qquad (.0304) \qquad\qquad R^2 = .999$$

To test for serial correlation we used the Durbin h test. Since the standard error of the lagged dependent variable coefficient is .0304, DW = 1.569, and $T = 147$, we calculate that

$$h = \left[1 - \frac{1.569}{2} \right] \left[\frac{147}{1 - (147)(.0304)^2} \right]^{.5} = 2.79$$

Since 2.79 is greater than the critical value of the normal distribution at the 5 percent level (1.645 for a one-tailed test), we reject the null hypothesis of no serial correlation. As a result, it is important to correct for serial correlation in the estimation of a dynamic aggregate consumption function.

APPENDIX 6.1 Generalized Least-Squares Estimation

In Appendix 4.3 we discussed the matrix generalization of the multiple regression model. Among the assumptions of the classical linear model was the as-

---

[29] We used the Citibase variables GC and GYD, which measure real spending and income in 1982 dollars.

sumption that the error term was not autocorrelated and had constant variance. In matrix notation we wrote

$$E(\varepsilon\varepsilon') = \sigma^2 \mathbf{I}$$

where $\mathbf{I}$ is an $N \times N$ identity matrix.

In this appendix we generalize the linear model to apply to cases in which serial correlation and heteroscedasticity are present. We accomplish this by altering our assumption about the variance-covariance matrix of the error terms. We assume that

$$E(\varepsilon\varepsilon') = \sigma^2 \mathbf{\Omega} \qquad (A6.1)$$

σ^2 is assumed to be unknown, but $\mathbf{\Omega}$ is a known $N \times N$ matrix. This is equivalent to the assumption that the elements of $\mathbf{\Omega}$ are known up to a multiplicative scalar. The only assumption we need to make about the matrix $\mathbf{\Omega}$ is that it is positive definite.[30]

The most general form of the heteroscedasticity case occurs when the error structure is

$$\begin{bmatrix} \sigma_1^2 & 0 & \cdots & 0 \\ 0 & \sigma_2^2 & \cdots & 0 \\ \cdots\cdots\cdots\cdots\cdots\cdots\cdots \\ 0 & 0 & \cdots & \sigma_N^2 \end{bmatrix}$$

Heteroscedasticity differs from the classical model only in the fact that the error variances differ between observations. All error covariances are assumed to be equal to 0. In the first-order serial-correlation example, however, none of the elements of $\mathbf{\Omega}$ are equal to 0. In this case the variance-covariance matrix is

$$\sigma^2 \begin{bmatrix} 1 & \rho & \rho^2 & \cdots & \rho^{N-1} \\ \rho & 1 & \rho & \cdots & \rho^{N-2} \\ \rho^2 & \rho & 1 & \cdots & \rho^{N-3} \\ \cdots\cdots\cdots\cdots\cdots\cdots\cdots\cdots\cdots \\ \rho^{N-1} & \rho^{N-2} & \rho^{N-3} & \cdots & 1 \end{bmatrix}$$

The objective of generalized least-squares estimation is to find parameter estimates for the vector $\boldsymbol{\beta}$ in the most efficient manner possible by accounting for the information provided by the knowledge of the matrix $\mathbf{\Omega}$. Assuming that all other least-squares assumptions hold, we get best linear unbiased parameter estimates if we transform the original data so that the variance-covariance matrix of the transformed errors equals $\sigma^2 \mathbf{I}$. Once this is done, application of

---

[30] A matrix $\mathbf{A}$ is positive definite if and only if $\mathbf{x}'\mathbf{A}\mathbf{x}$ is greater than 0, for all $\mathbf{x}$ not equal to 0, where $\mathbf{x}$ is an $N \times 1$ vector.

the Gauss-Markov theorem will give us our desired result. The assumption that $\mathbf{\Omega}$ is a positive definite matrix is sufficient to guarantee that such a strategy will always succeed. We use a basic theorem of matrix algebra which states that there exists a nonsingular $N \times N$ matrix $\mathbf{H}$ such that

$$\mathbf{H}\mathbf{\Omega}\mathbf{H}' = \mathbf{I} \tag{A6.2}$$

We will find it useful to rewrite Eq. (A6.2) in the form

$$\mathbf{\Omega} = \mathbf{H}^{-1}(\mathbf{H}')^{-1} = (\mathbf{H}'\mathbf{H})^{-1} \tag{A6.3}$$

from which it follows that

$$\mathbf{H}'\mathbf{H} = \mathbf{\Omega}^{-1} \tag{A6.4}$$

We use the matrix $\mathbf{H}$ to transform the original model as follows:

$$\mathbf{H}\mathbf{Y} = \mathbf{H}\mathbf{X}\boldsymbol{\beta} + \mathbf{H}\boldsymbol{\varepsilon} \tag{A6.5}$$

or
$$\tilde{\mathbf{Y}} = \tilde{\mathbf{X}}\boldsymbol{\beta} + \tilde{\boldsymbol{\varepsilon}} \tag{A6.6}$$

where $\qquad \tilde{\mathbf{Y}} = \mathbf{H}\mathbf{Y} \qquad \tilde{\mathbf{X}} = \mathbf{H}\mathbf{X} \qquad \tilde{\boldsymbol{\varepsilon}} = \mathbf{H}\boldsymbol{\varepsilon}$

The error term $\tilde{\boldsymbol{\varepsilon}}$ is consistent since, from Eq. (A6.2),

$$E(\tilde{\boldsymbol{\varepsilon}}\tilde{\boldsymbol{\varepsilon}}') = E(\mathbf{H}\boldsymbol{\varepsilon}\boldsymbol{\varepsilon}'\mathbf{H}') = \sigma^2\mathbf{H}\mathbf{\Omega}\mathbf{H}' = \sigma^2\mathbf{I}$$

Since Eq. (A6.6) obeys the classical assumptions, we know that the estimator

$$\tilde{\boldsymbol{\beta}} = (\tilde{\mathbf{X}}'\tilde{\mathbf{X}})^{-1}\tilde{\mathbf{X}}'\tilde{\mathbf{Y}} \tag{A6.7}$$

will be unbiased and efficient.

In terms of our original data, the generalized least-squares estimator $\tilde{\boldsymbol{\beta}}$ is

$$\tilde{\boldsymbol{\beta}} = [(\mathbf{H}\mathbf{X})'(\mathbf{H}\mathbf{X})]^{-1}(\mathbf{H}\mathbf{X})'(\mathbf{H}\mathbf{Y}) = (\mathbf{X}'\mathbf{H}'\mathbf{H}\mathbf{X})^{-1}\mathbf{X}'\mathbf{H}'\mathbf{H}\mathbf{Y}$$
$$= (\mathbf{X}'\mathbf{\Omega}^{-1}\mathbf{X})^{-1}\mathbf{X}'\mathbf{\Omega}^{-1}\mathbf{Y} \tag{A6.8}$$

The variance-covariance matrix of the estimated parameter vector $\tilde{\boldsymbol{\beta}}$ is

$$E[(\tilde{\boldsymbol{\beta}} - \boldsymbol{\beta})(\tilde{\boldsymbol{\beta}} - \boldsymbol{\beta})'] = \sigma^2(\tilde{\mathbf{X}}'\tilde{\mathbf{X}})^{-1} = \sigma^2(\mathbf{X}'\mathbf{H}'\mathbf{H}\mathbf{X})^{-1}$$
$$= \sigma^2(\mathbf{X}'\mathbf{\Omega}^{-1}\mathbf{X})^{-1} \tag{A6.9}$$

To see that the generalized least-squares results coincide with ordinary least squares when $\boldsymbol{\Omega} = \mathbf{I}$, we substitute for $\boldsymbol{\Omega}$ in Eqs. (A6.8) and (A6.9) and solve.

In order to apply generalized least squares (GLS), we need an estimate of $\boldsymbol{\Omega}$, and in order to perform statistical tests, we need to estimate σ^2. When $\boldsymbol{\Omega}$ is known, we can estimate σ^2 from the residuals of the GLS regression. An unbiased estimate of σ^2 is given by

$$\hat{\sigma}^2 = \frac{1}{N - K} \tilde{\mathbf{u}}' \tilde{\mathbf{u}}$$

where $\tilde{\mathbf{u}}$ is the vector of GLS residuals in this case. Substituting gives

$$\hat{\sigma}^2 = \frac{1}{N - k} (\mathbf{H}\hat{\boldsymbol{\varepsilon}})'(\mathbf{H}\hat{\boldsymbol{\varepsilon}}) = \frac{1}{N - k} (\hat{\boldsymbol{\varepsilon}}' \boldsymbol{\Omega}^{-1} \hat{\boldsymbol{\varepsilon}})$$

so that an unbiased estimate of $E[(\tilde{\boldsymbol{\beta}} - \boldsymbol{\beta})(\tilde{\boldsymbol{\beta}} - \boldsymbol{\beta})']$ is given by

$$\frac{1}{N - k} (\hat{\boldsymbol{\varepsilon}}' \boldsymbol{\Omega}^{-1} \hat{\boldsymbol{\varepsilon}})(\mathbf{X}' \boldsymbol{\Omega}^{-1} \mathbf{X})^{-1} \tag{A6.10}$$

If $\boldsymbol{\varepsilon}$ is normal, $\tilde{\boldsymbol{\beta}}$ is normally distributed, and statistical tests can be applied.

Our final problem is to find a consistent estimate of $\boldsymbol{\Omega}$. Because $\boldsymbol{\Omega}$ is an $N \times N$ matrix with $N(N + 1)/2$ elements, it is impossible to estimate all elements of $\boldsymbol{\Omega}$ from only N observations. The heteroscedasticity and first-order serial-correlation assumptions provide two useful ways of parameterizing the model, although numerous alternatives are available.

Once a consistent estimator of $\boldsymbol{\Omega}$ is used, our estimator will lose the property of being an unbiased estimator but will retain an appropriate large-sample property (something close to consistency). If $\boldsymbol{\Omega}$ is estimated consistently by a matrix $\mathbf{V}$, the GLS estimator and its variance-covariance matrix are

$$\hat{\boldsymbol{\beta}} = (\mathbf{X}' \mathbf{V}^{-1} \mathbf{X})^{-1} \mathbf{X}' \mathbf{V}^{-1} \mathbf{Y} \tag{A6.11}$$

$$E[(\hat{\boldsymbol{\beta}} - \boldsymbol{\beta})(\hat{\boldsymbol{\beta}} - \boldsymbol{\beta})'] = \frac{1}{N - k} (\hat{\boldsymbol{\varepsilon}}' \mathbf{V}^{-1} \hat{\boldsymbol{\varepsilon}})(\mathbf{X}' \mathbf{V}^{-1} \mathbf{X})^{-1}$$

$$= \frac{1}{N - k} (\tilde{\mathbf{u}}' \tilde{\mathbf{u}})(\mathbf{X}' \mathbf{V}^{-1} \mathbf{X})^{-1} \tag{A6.12}$$

where $\hat{\boldsymbol{\varepsilon}}$ are the ordinary least-squares residuals and $\tilde{\mathbf{u}}$ are the generalized least-squares residuals.

To complete this appendix, it will be useful to describe the transformation matrix $\mathbf{H}$ in both the heteroscedasticity and the first-order serial-correlation cases. In the former it is quite easy to choose $\mathbf{H}$ so that $\mathbf{H'H} = \mathbf{\Omega}^{-1}$. The reader should check to see that

$$
\mathbf{H} = \begin{bmatrix}
\dfrac{1}{\sigma_1} & 0 & \cdots & 0 \\
0 & \dfrac{1}{\sigma_2} & \cdots & 0 \\
\multicolumn{4}{c}{\cdots\cdots\cdots\cdots\cdots\cdots} \\
0 & 0 & \cdots & \dfrac{1}{\sigma_N}
\end{bmatrix}
$$

is the correct choice. Transforming the data according to the matrix $\mathbf{H}$ is equivalent to the weighted least-squares procedure described in the text.

The derivation of $\mathbf{H}$ in the first-order serial-correlation case is somewhat more difficult. In this case

$$
\mathbf{H} = (1 - \rho^2)^{-1/2} \begin{bmatrix}
\sqrt{1 - \rho^2} & 0 & 0 & \cdots & 0 & 0 \\
-\rho & 1 & 0 & \cdots & 0 & 0 \\
0 & -\rho & 1 & \cdots & 0 & 0 \\
\multicolumn{6}{c}{\cdots\cdots\cdots\cdots\cdots\cdots\cdots\cdots} \\
0 & 0 & 0 & \cdots & 1 & 0 \\
0 & 0 & 0 & \cdots & -\rho & 1
\end{bmatrix}
$$

The fact that $\mathbf{H}$ is the correct choice can be checked by evaluating $(\mathbf{H'H})^{-1} = \mathbf{\Omega}$. Application of the transformation $\mathbf{H}$ to the data is equivalent to using the generalized differencing process and then applying ordinary least squares. In this sense, corrections for serial correlation involve the use of weighted least-squares estimation just as in the heteroscedasticity case.

What if ordinary least-squares estimation is used even when GLS is appropriate? First we know that if $\mathbf{\Omega}$ is known, OLS and GLS parameter estimates will be unbiased but OLS parameter estimates will have greater variance than do their GLS counterparts. However, it is also true that the OLS estimate of the variance-covariance matrix will be biased. To see this, recall that the OLS variance-covariance matrix is

$$
\sigma^2 (\mathbf{X'X})^{-1} \tag{A6.13}
$$

If the GLS model were in fact correct, the variance-covariance matrix of the parameter vector $\hat{\boldsymbol{\beta}} = (\mathbf{X'X})^{-1}\mathbf{X'Y}$ would be

$$
E[(\hat{\boldsymbol{\beta}} - \boldsymbol{\beta})(\hat{\boldsymbol{\beta}} - \boldsymbol{\beta})'] = E\{[(\mathbf{X'X})^{-1}\mathbf{X'\varepsilon}][(\mathbf{X'X})^{-1}\mathbf{X'\varepsilon}]'\}
$$

since

$$
\hat{\boldsymbol{\beta}} = \boldsymbol{\beta} + (\mathbf{X'X})^{-1}\mathbf{X'\varepsilon}
$$

$$
= (\mathbf{X'X})^{-1}\mathbf{X'}E[(\varepsilon\varepsilon')]\mathbf{X}(\mathbf{X'X})^{-1}
$$

$$
= \sigma^2(\mathbf{X'X})^{-1}\mathbf{X'\Omega X}(\mathbf{X'X})^{-1} \tag{A6.14}
$$

The reported variance-covariance matrix in Eq. (A6.13) may yield a rather poor estimate of the correct variance-covariance matrix for ordinary least-squares parameter estimates as given by Eq. (A6.14).

EXERCISES

6.1 Explain intuitively why weighted least squares yield more efficient parameter estimators than do ordinary least squares when the error term is known to be heteroscedastic.

6.2 You are estimating a cross-section regression for a sample of 100 cities in the United States in which you hope to explain expenditures on education as a function of the median income in the community, the number of school-age children, and the level of state and federal grants received for educational purposes. Would you expect heteroscedasticity to be a problem in this case? If so, would you use the Goldfeld-Quandt test? Why?

6.3 You are estimating the relationship between a firm's sales and advertising expenditures in an industry. It becomes apparent to you that half the firms in the industry are large relative to the other half, and you are concerned about the proper estimation technique in such a situation. Assume that the error variances associated with the large firms are twice the error variances associated with the small firms. Small firm σ^2
Large firm $2\sigma^2$

   (a) If you used ordinary least squares to estimate the regression of sales on advertising (assuming that advertising is an independent variable, uncorrelated with the error term), would your estimated parameters be unbiased? Consistent? Efficient?

   (b) How might you revise the estimation procedure to eliminate or resolve your difficulties? Use WLS :   refer 2 notes .

   (c) Can you test whether the original error-variance assumption is valid?

6.4 Why are the errors in cross-section studies unlikely to be serially correlated? Can you give an example in which serial correlation will be present?

6.5 Can ρ take on an absolute value which is greater than 1? What does this tell you about the stability of the model being studied?

6.6 Using the rental data in Table 2.1, in Exercise 5.2 we estimated the model RENT PER $= \beta_1 + \beta_2(\text{SEX}) + \beta_3(\text{ROOM PER}) + \beta_4(\text{DIST}) + \varepsilon$. Using an F test, test the hypothesis that

$$F\text{-statistic} = \frac{S^2_{male}}{S^2_{female}} = \frac{\text{ESS/df male}}{\text{ESS/df female}}$$

Variance $(\varepsilon_{male}) >$ Variance (ε_{female})

Hint: Run separate regressions of RENT PER $= \beta_1 + \beta_3(\text{ROOM PER}) + \beta_4(\text{DIST}) + \varepsilon$ for males and females. (Why did you drop the SEX variable for these regressions?)

6.7 Using the expenditure data set in Table 6.2, estimate the model

$$\text{EXP} = \beta_1 + \beta_2(\text{POP}) + \beta_3(\text{AID}) + \beta_4(\text{INC}) + \varepsilon$$

using ordinary least squares. Then use a Goldfeld-Quandt test to see if $V(\varepsilon) \sim \text{POP}^2$. If you reject the null hypothesis, reestimate the equation efficiently.

6.8 Using the residuals from the OLS estimation of EXP $= \beta_1 + \beta_2(\text{POP}) + \beta_3(\text{AID}) + \beta_4(\text{INC}) + \varepsilon$, perform a White test and a Breusch-Pagan test for heteroscedasticity, assuming that the error variance is proportional to POP.

TABLE 6.2
EXPENDITURE DATA SET

E, N, S, W = dummy variable equal to 1 if state is in eastern, northern, southern, or western region, respectively; 0 otherwise
EXP = total state and local government expenditures, millions of dollars
PCEXP = per capita state and local government expenditures, dollars
PCAID = per capita federal aid, dollars
POP = population of state, thousands
DEN = population density, thousands per square mile
DPOP = percentage change in population from 1960 to 1970
URB = percentage of population living in metropolitan areas (SMSAs)
PCINC = per capita personal income, dollars
PS = population attending primary or secondary public schools, thousands

State	E	N	S	W	EXP	PCEXP	PCAID	POP	DEN	DPOP	URB	PCINC	PS
Maine	1	0	0	0	704	686.16	186	1,026	.033182	2.5	21.6	3,664	251
N.H.	1	0	0	0	526	679.59	123	774	.085743	21.5	27.3	4,279	168
Vt.	1	0	0	0	411	893.48	235	460	.049639	14.1	0.0	3,703	107
Mass.	1	0	0	0	5,166	891.30	190	5,796	.74061	10.5	84.7	4,825	1,203
R.I.	1	0	0	0	699	721.36	184	969	.92374	10.5	84.7	4,513	190
Conn.	1	0	0	0	2,546	826.62	145	3,080	.63348	19.6	82.6	5,414	665
N.Y.	1	0	0	0	22,750	1,238.60	240	18,367	.38400	8.7	86.5	5,275	3,524
N.J.	1	0	0	0	5,911	804.33	141	7,349	.97713	18.2	76.9	5,379	1,513
Pa.	1	0	0	0	8,840	742.55	136	11,905	.26476	4.2	79.4	4,545	2,362
Ohio	0	1	0	0	6,867	640.46	112	10,722	.26167	9.7	77.7	4,572	2,422
Ind.	0	1	0	0	3,457	653.99	103	5,286	.14644	11.4	61.9	4,364	1,221
Ill.	0	1	0	0	8,935	794.65	156	11,244	.20169	10.2	80.1	5,162	2,349
Mich.	0	1	0	0	7,799	865.31	147	9,013	.15863	13.4	76.7	4,982	2,197
Wisc.	0	1	0	0	3,757	830.09	116	4,526	.083101	11.8	57.6	4,279	995
Minn.	0	1	0	0	3,528	909.98	163	3,877	.048897	11.5	56.9	4,343	910
Iowa	0	1	0	0	2,108	730.93	113	2,884	.051554	2.4	35.6	4,316	647
Mo.	0	1	0	0	3,156	664.84	151	4,747	.068802	8.3	64.1	4,307	1,030
N. Dak.	0	1	0	0	475	749.21	201	634	.009152	-2.3	11.9	4,128	142
S. Dak.	0	1	0	0	521	766.18	195	680	.008953	-2.1	14.3	3,766	162
Neb.	0	1	0	0	1,052	688.48	134	1,528	.019978	5.1	42.8	4,451	330

TABLE 6.2
EXPENDITURE DATA SET (*Continued*)

State	E	N	S	W	EXP	PCEXP	PCAID	POP	DEN	DPOP	URB	PCINC	PS
Kans.	0	1	0	0	1,551	683.86	132	2,268	.027731	3.2	42.3	4,535	475
Del.	0	0	1	0	571	1,000.00	170	571	.28809	22.8	70.4	5,222	134
Md.	0	0	1	0	3,392	837.94	135	4,048	.40926	26.5	84.3	5,017	921
Va.	0	0	1	0	3,037	637.36	131	4,765	.11978	17.2	61.2	4,396	1,069
W. Va.	0	0	1	0	1,250	696.38	252	1,795	.074574	-6.2	31.3	3,624	410
N.C.	0	0	1	0	2,938	562.73	141	5,221	.10699	11.5	37.3	3,868	1,161
S.C.	0	0	1	0	1,512	562.50	153	2,688	.088933	8.7	39.3	3,500	624
Ga.	0	0	1	0	3,197	675.47	178	4,733	.081501	16.4	49.7	3,956	1,090
Fla.	0	0	1	0	4,771	649.38	114	7,347	.13583	37.1	68.6	4,450	1,514
Ky.	0	0	1	0	2,063	624.02	181	3,306	.083380	6.0	40.0	3,634	714
Tenn.	0	0	1	0	2,446	600.69	175	4,072	.098529	10.0	48.9	3,708	892
Ala.	0	0	1	0	2,104	597.56	193	3,521	.069437	5.4	52.3	3,476	784
Miss.	0	0	1	0	1,427	632.54	255	2,256	.047700	1.8	17.7	3,188	526
Ark.	0	0	1	0	1,014	504.98	199	2,008	.038656	7.7	30.9	3,345	462
La.	0	0	1	0	2,691	719.90	196	3,738	.083196	11.9	54.8	3,565	846
Okla.	0	0	1	0	1,767	671.10	190	2,633	.038280	9.9	50.1	3,837	607
Tex.	0	0	1	0	7,246	624.44	141	11,604	.044267	16.9	73.5	4,085	2,738
Mont.	0	0	0	1	587	819.83	252	716	.004918	2.9	24.4	4,083	178
Idaho	0	0	0	1	512	678.15	180	755	.009132	6.9	15.3	3,711	185
Wyo.	0	0	0	1	368	1,063.60	369	346	.003560	0.7	0.	4,269	86
Colo.	0	0	0	1	1,920	812.18	183	2,364	.02782	25.8	71.7	4,600	575
N. Mex.	0	0	0	1	823	764.87	277	1,076	.008862	6.8	31.1	3,512	285
Ariz.	0	0	0	1	1,523	775.85	150	1,963	.017308	36.1	74.5	4,273	485
Utah	0	0	0	1	821	728.48	196	1,127	.013728	18.9	77.6	3,741	306
Nev.	0	0	0	1	543	1,018.80	180	533	.004850	71.3	80.7	5,209	131
Wash.	0	0	0	1	3,070	898.19	184	3,418	.051344	19.5	66.0	4,601	791
Oreg.	0	0	0	1	1,766	808.24	201	2,185	.022717	18.2	61.2	4,339	471
Calif.	0	0	0	1	20,052	982.41	200	20,411	.13054	27.0	92.7	5,087	4,501
Alaska	0	0	0	1	698	2,147.70	570	325	.000574	33.6	0.	5,222	85
Hawaii	0	0	0	1	940	1,152.00	202	816	.12700	21.7	81.9	5,153	182

Source: U.S. Bureau of the Census, Census of Governments and Census of Population, 1970.

177

CHAPTER 7

INSTRUMENTAL VARIABLES AND MODEL SPECIFICATION

In Chapter 6 we focused on the possible failure of two assumptions of the basic regression model: homoscedasticity and no serial correlation. In this chapter we focus on a number of other potential problems with the model.

We begin with the assumption that each of the independent variables is uncorrelated with the error term. When this assumption fails to hold, ordinary least-squares regression no longer yields unbiased and consistent parameter estimators. One source of failure is measurement error in one or more of the independent variables. Another source of failure, when an independent variable is determined in part by the dependent variable, will be discussed in Chapter 12. In the second section of this chapter we show that when there is measurement error, consistent estimators can be obtained if new variables called *instruments* replace the variables that were measured with error. The new "instrumental-variables" estimation technique serves as a replacement for ordinary least squares.

In the third section we consider the problem of specification error, i.e., what happens when the model is invalid, in excluding an appropriate variable, including irrelevant variables, or having the wrong functional form. This serves as a basis for a brief treatment of the trade-offs involved in building econometric models. The fourth section broadens the analysis even further. We describe a series of ad hoc diagnostic tools that can be useful in determining whether one or more data points have an unusually strong influence on the estimated regression line. Finally, in the last section we describe a number of formal statistical tests that help one evaluate whether a model is correctly specified.

7.1 CORRELATION BETWEEN AN INDEPENDENT VARIABLE AND THE ERROR TERM

The difficulties that arise when the independent variables and the error are correlated can best be seen by taking a close look at the two-variable model, with both variables measured in deviations form. The least-squares slope estimator is

$$\hat{\beta} = \frac{\Sigma x_i y_i}{\Sigma x_i^2} \qquad \text{where } y_i = \beta x_i + \varepsilon_i$$

Substituting and expanding terms, we get

$$\hat{\beta} = \frac{\beta \Sigma x_i^2 + \Sigma x_i \varepsilon_i}{\Sigma x_i^2} = \beta + \frac{\Sigma x_i \varepsilon_i}{\Sigma x_i^2} \tag{7.1}$$

The estimator $\hat{\beta}$ is thus proven to be an unbiased estimator of β when the X variable observations are assumed to be fixed in repeated samples. The proof depends heavily on the fact that the expected value of the second term on the right-hand side of Eq. (7.1) is equal to 0. Now suppose we change our initial assumption by assuming that the X's are stochastic (random variables). If we assume further that $E(\Sigma x_i \varepsilon_i) = 0$, the results of the Gauss-Markov theorem are weakened somewhat. It is now true that $\hat{\beta}$ is an unbiased estimator, *conditional on X;* i.e., given particular values of X, $E(\hat{\beta}) = \beta$. In many situations, however, we will be concerned with the properties of $\hat{\beta}$ independent of the values of X. In addition, we may not wish to make the assumption that X and ε are uncorrelated. In this general setting we change our focus; instead of concentrating on the presence or absence of bias, we study the large sample properties of $\hat{\beta}$. Specifically, we look for the assumptions that are necessary to guarantee that $\hat{\beta}$ will be a consistent estimator.

As a general rule there is no guarantee that X and ε will be uncorrelated and therefore no guarantee that $\hat{\beta}$ will be a consistent estimator of β. To see this, consider the case in which X and ε are known to be positively correlated irrespective of the sample size. A quick examination of Eq. (7.1) makes it apparent that the term on the right-hand side of the equation will be positive and that $\hat{\beta}$ will overestimate the true parameter value no matter what the sample size. Thus, correlation between an independent variable and the error term leads in general to inconsistent ordinary least-squares parameter estimates. The particular example just used is depicted graphically in Fig. 7.1. The solid line represents the true regression line, while the dotted line represents the ordinary least-squares regression line. In achieving its objective of minimizing the sum of the squares of the estimated residuals, ordinary least squares

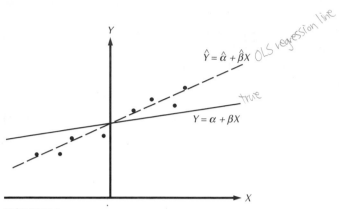

FIGURE 7.1
Correlation between X and ε.

yields biased and inconsistent estimates of the true regression slope parameter. In this case the slope has been overestimated. (The intercept estimate will be a biased and inconsistent estimator of the true intercept, while the estimated standard error of the regression and the standard errors of the coefficients also will be biased and inconsistent.)

7.2 ERRORS IN VARIABLES

We have assumed that all variables used in the regression calculation procedure were measured without error. In practice, measurement errors (as well as errors created by misspecifying the model) are likely to occur, and as we shall see, these errors can substantially alter the properties of the estimated regression parameters. We will work through the problem of measurement error by considering several increasingly complex cases.

7.2.1 Case I: Y Is Measured with Error

Assume that the true regression model (written in deviations form) is

$$y_i = \beta x_i + \varepsilon_i \tag{7.2}$$

where ε_i represents errors associated with the specification of the model (the effects of omitted variables, etc.). Assume in addition that the variable y^*, rather than y, is obtained in the measurement process:

$$y_i^* = y_i + u_i \qquad \text{where } \text{Cov} \,(u_i, x_i) = 0$$

The regression model is estimated with $y*$ as the dependent variable, with no account being taken of the fact that $y*$ is not an accurate measure of y. Adding the measurement error term u_i to each side of Eq. (7.2), we see that this is equivalent to running the regression

$$y_i^* = \beta x_i + (\varepsilon_i + u_i) \tag{7.3}$$

Note that if u_i did not have 0 mean, our estimated regression would need an intercept term. In any case, as long as u_i and x_i are uncorrelated, there is no problem associated with running the regression described in Eq. (7.3). The estimated slope parameter will be unbiased [since $E(u_i x_i) = 0$] and consistent. The only effect of the presence of measurement error in the dependent variable is to increase the error variance. However, the increased error variance will be accounted for in the estimate of s^2, the estimated residual variance, and all statistical tests will apply. (As a general rule, it is impossible to separate out the effects of errors associated with the regression model and measurement error, and no attempt is made to do so.) The situation is not so auspicious, however, when the X variable is measured with error.

7.2.2   Case II: X Is Measured with Error

Assume that $x_i^* = x_i + v_i$, where x_i is the true value and x_i^* is the observed value. The true regression model is

$$y_i = \beta x_i + \varepsilon_i$$

while the actual regression run is

$$y_i = \beta x_i^* + (\varepsilon_i - \beta v_i) = \beta x_i^* + \varepsilon_i^* \tag{7.4}$$

Even if we assume that the measurement error in X is normally distributed with 0 mean, has no serial correlation, and is independent of the error in the true equation, problems arise in using ordinary least squares as a regression technique. This can be most easily seen by noting that the error ε^* and the variable x^* in Eq. (7.4) are correlated (or have a nonzero covariance). In particular,

$$\text{Cov } (\varepsilon_i^*, x_i^*) = E[(\varepsilon_i - \beta v_i)(x_i + v_i)] = -\beta \sigma_v^2$$

Thus, least-squares estimates of the regression parameters will be biased and inconsistent, with the degree of bias and inconsistency being related to the variance of the measurement error.

7.2.3   Case III: X and Y Are Measured with Error

This case contains no new conclusions compared with the previous case, but it will be instructive to examine it in some detail. The assumptions are as follows:

$$y_i^* = y_i + u_i \qquad u_i \sim N(0, \sigma_u^2) \qquad x_i^* = x_i + v_i \qquad v_i \sim N(0, \sigma_v^2) \qquad y_i = \beta x_i$$

u_i and v_i are uncorrelated with each other as well as with x_i, and each error process itself involves no serial correlation. The estimated regression equation will be of the form

$$y_i^* = \beta x_i^* + (u_i - \beta v_i)$$

Now consider the ordinary least-squares estimator $\hat{\beta}$:

$$\hat{\beta} = \frac{\Sigma x_i^* y_i^*}{\Sigma x_i^{*2}} = \frac{\Sigma (x_i + v_i)(y_i + u_i)}{\Sigma (x_i + v_i)^2} = \frac{\Sigma (x_i + v_i)(\beta x_i + u_i)}{\Sigma (x_i + v_i)^2}$$

$$= \frac{\beta \Sigma x_i^2 + \beta \Sigma x_i v_i + \Sigma x_i u_i + \Sigma v_i u_i}{\Sigma x_i^2 + \Sigma v_i^2 + 2\Sigma x_i v_i}$$

Since x_i, u_i, and v_i are all stochastic, it is not easy to evaluate the bias of $\hat{\beta}$. The reason for this is that the expected value of the ratio of two random variables is not equal to the ratio of the expected value of the variables. However, we can evaluate the consistency of $\hat{\beta}$ by evaluating the expression for $\hat{\beta}$ in the limit as the sample size gets large. This calculation is denoted *plim* $\hat{\beta}$. Since u_i and v_i are uncorrelated with each other as well as with x_i, it follows that[1]

$$\text{plim } \hat{\beta} = \text{plim } \frac{\beta \Sigma x_i^2}{\Sigma x_i^2 + \Sigma v_i^2} = \frac{\beta \text{ Var } (x)}{\text{Var } (x) + \sigma_v^2} = \frac{\beta}{1 + \sigma_v^2 / \text{Var } (x)} \qquad (7.5)$$

This suggests that the presence of measurement error of the type in question will lead to an underestimate of the true regression parameter if ordinary least-squares techniques are used.

7.2.4   Instrumental-Variables Estimation

The problem of errors in the measurement of regression variables is quite important, yet econometricians do not have much to offer in the way of useful solutions. As a general rule, we tend to pass over the problem of measurement error, hoping that the errors are small enough not to destroy the validity of the

they are consistent estimators of β but they are inefficient.

---

[1] We have utilized a result that for random variables Z_1 and Z_2, plim (Z_1/Z_2) = plim Z_1/plim Z_2. In this particular case we divide the numerator and the denominator by N and use the fact that plim $\Sigma x_i^2/N$ = Var(x) and plim $\Sigma v_i^2/N$ = σ_v^2.

estimation procedure. One technique which is available and can solve the measurement-error problem is the technique of *instrumental-variables estimation*. We shall briefly outline the concept of instrumental variables, in part because it is likely to be useful with measurement errors, and in part because it is important when one is dealing with models consisting of systems of simultaneous equations.

The method of instrumental variables involves the search for a new variable Z which is highly correlated with the independent variable X and at the same time uncorrelated with the error term in the equation (as well as the errors of measurement of both variables). In practice, we are concerned with the consistency of parameter estimates and therefore concentrate on the relationship between the variable Z and the remaining model variables when the sample size gets large. We define the random variable Z to be an *instrument* if

1. The correlations between Z and ε, u, and v, respectively, in the equation approach zero as the sample size gets large.[2]
2. The correlation between Z and X is nonzero as the sample size gets large.

If we are fortunate enough to be able to choose from several instruments, we simply select the one instrument (or combination of instruments) that has the highest correlation with the X variable.

Assuming for the moment that such a variable can be found, we can alter the least-squares regression procedure to obtain estimated parameters that are consistent. Unfortunately, there is no guarantee that the estimation process will yield unbiased parameter estimates. To simplify matters, consider case II, in which $y_i = \beta x_i + \varepsilon_i$ and only x is measured with error (as $x^* = x + v$). The correct instrumental-variables estimator of the regression slope in the two-variable model is

$$\beta^* = \frac{\Sigma y_i z_i}{\Sigma x_i^* z_i} \tag{7.6}$$

The choice of this particular slope formula is made so that the resulting estimator will be consistent. To see this, we can derive the relationship between the instrumental-variables estimator and the true slope parameter in a manner similar to the derivation in Eq. (7.1):

$$\beta^* = \frac{\Sigma y_i z_i}{\Sigma x_i^* z_i} = \frac{\beta \Sigma x_i^* z_i + \Sigma z_i \varepsilon_i^*}{\Sigma x_i^* z_i} = \beta + \frac{\Sigma z_i \varepsilon_i^*}{\Sigma x_i^* z_i}$$

Clearly, the choice of Z as an instrument guarantees that β^* will approach β as the sample size gets large [Cov(z, ε^*) approaches 0] and will therefore be a consistent estimator of β. One might wonder why the variable x_i^* was not replaced by z_i in the denominator of the instrumental-variables estimator. The

---

[2] Technically speaking, we need to refer to the properties of estimators in the probability limit.

reader should check, using the above procedure, that the estimator $\Sigma y_i z_i / \Sigma z_i^2$ does not yield a consistent estimator of β (see Exercise 7.2).

The technique of instrumental variables appears to provide a simple solution to a difficult problem. We have defined an estimation technique which yields consistent estimates if we can find an appropriate instrument. However, this is likely to be difficult when errors of measurement are present.

A few concluding comments may be instructive. First, the ordinary least-squares estimation technique is actually a special case of instrumental variables. This follows because in the classical regression model X is uncorrelated with the error term and because X is perfectly correlated with itself. Second, if we generalize the measurement-error problem to errors in more than one independent variable, one instrument is needed to replace *each* of the designated independent variables. Finally, we repeat that instrumental-variables estimation guarantees consistent estimation but does not guarantee unbiased estimation.

7.3   SPECIFICATION ERROR

Our discussion of econometrics has relied heavily on the assumption that the model to be estimated is correctly specified. Once the correct specification of the model is assumed, model estimation and model testing become relatively straightforward. In reality, however, we can never be sure that a given model is correctly specified. In fact, researchers usually examine more than one possible specification, attempting to find the specification which best describes the process under study. We attempt to give the reader a feeling for the hazards involved in searching for a model by discussing the costs associated with model misspecification. We concern ourselves with two types of misspecification, the first occurring when relevant variables are omitted from the linear regression and the second occurring when irrelevant variables are added to the equation. Finally, we pause briefly to discuss misspecifications associated with the incorrect choice of functional form.

7.3.1   Omitted Variables

Consider first the case in which a variable is unknowingly omitted from a "true" or correct model specification. Assume that the true model is given by Eq. (7.7),

$$y_i = \beta_2 x_{2i} + \beta_3 x_{3i} + \varepsilon_i \tag{7.7}$$

while the regression model is given by[3]

$$y_i = \beta_2^* x_{2i} + \varepsilon_i^* \tag{7.8}$$

---

[3] We will work with data in deviations form and assume that $\bar{\varepsilon} = 0$ to simplify the derivations. Most, but not all, of the results hold for the intercept of the equation. Since the effect of model misspecifications on the intercept usually is not of paramount importance, we leave the details to the reader (see Exercise 7.3).

All the assumptions of the classical linear model are posited to hold for Eq. (7.7).

As was derived in Chapter 1, the estimated slope parameter is

$$\hat{\beta}_2^* = \frac{\Sigma x_{2i} y_i}{\Sigma x_{2i}^2} \tag{7.9}$$

Substituting y_i, defined as in Eq. (7.7), into Eq. (7.9) and solving, we get

$$\hat{\beta}_2^* = \frac{\Sigma x_{2i}\beta_2 x_{2i} + \Sigma x_{2i}\beta_3 x_{3i} + \Sigma x_{2i}\varepsilon_i}{\Sigma x_{2i}^2}$$

$$= \frac{\beta_2 \Sigma x_{2i}^2 + \beta_3 \Sigma x_{2i} x_{3i} + \Sigma x_{2i}\varepsilon_i}{\Sigma x_{2i}^2}$$

$$= \beta_2 + \beta_3 \frac{\Sigma x_{2i} x_{3i}}{\Sigma x_{2i}^2} + \frac{\Sigma x_{2i}\varepsilon_i}{\Sigma x_{2i}^2}$$

Since X_2 is fixed and $E(\varepsilon_i) = 0$, the last term has expectation zero, so that

$$E(\hat{\beta}_2^*) = \beta_2 + \beta_3 \frac{\Sigma x_{2i} x_{3i}}{\Sigma x_{2i}^2} = \beta_2 + \beta_3 \frac{\text{Cov}(x_2, x_3)}{\text{Var}(x_2)} \tag{7.10}$$

Since there is no guarantee that the second term will be 0, the least-squares slope estimator of Eq. (7.9) will be a *biased* estimator of the true slope parameter β_2. This bias will not disappear as the sample size grows large, so that the omission of a variable from the model also yields an *inconsistent* estimator. The only case in which the bias (and inconsistency) will disappear completely is when $\text{Cov}(x_2, x_3) = 0$, that is, when x_2 and x_3 are uncorrelated in the sample.[4] This result generalizes if there are numerous independent variables. Only when the omitted variable is uncorrelated with all the included independent variables does the bias disappear, and this is extremely unlikely to occur.

The formula in Eq. (7.10) is useful because it tells us that the sign of the bias depends on the correlation between the omitted variable and all included variables as well as depending on the sign of the true slope coefficient β_3. To the extent that x_2 and x_3 are highly correlated, the coefficient of x_2 will include the effect of the x_3 variable and will be biased. When x_2 and x_3 are uncorrelated, x_2 picks up none of the effect of x_3 and no bias occurs. As a practical matter, it is the *extent* of the specification bias which is important. This suggests that a careful researcher will consider not only the question of missing variables but also their possible correlation with included model variables.

To be complete, we should pause to consider the effect of variable omission on the variance of the slope estimator. First consider the case in which x_2 and

---

[4] A high variance for x_2 will lower the amount of bias, but the bias will never reach zero, since we have assumed a finite variance for all sample x's.

x_3 are uncorrelated. Then $\hat{\beta}_2^*$ will be an unbiased estimator of β_2 and will have an identical variance with $\hat{\beta}_2$. The only difficulty with model misspecification arises because the usual *estimator* of the variance of $\hat{\beta}_2^*$ will be biased.[5] However, in the more general case when x_2 and x_3 are correlated, the two estimators will not have identical variances. In the two-variable model, the actual variance of $\hat{\beta}_2^*$ will be less than the actual variance of $\hat{\beta}_2$, even though the model is misspecified.[6]

7.3.2   Presence of an Irrelevant Variable

Now consider the case in which an irrelevant variable has been added to the equation. Assume that the true model is given by

$$y_i = \beta_2 x_{2i} + \varepsilon_i \tag{7.11}$$

and that the regression model is given by

$$y_i = \beta_2^* x_{2i} + \beta_3^* x_{3i} + \varepsilon_i^* \tag{7.12}$$

The presence of the irrelevant variable x_3 implies that we are not taking into account the true parameter restriction $\beta_3^* = 0$. We would expect that not taking into account all the information available about the model would lead to a loss of degrees of freedom and therefore to a loss of efficiency, but no loss of consistency and no bias. To see the latter, we calculate the estimated coefficient of the variable x_2 in Eq. (7.12). Using the derivation described in Chapter 4 [Eq. (4.4)], we find that

$$\hat{\beta}_2^* = \frac{(\Sigma x_{3i}^2)(\Sigma x_{2i} y_i) - (\Sigma x_{2i} x_{3i})(\Sigma x_{3i} y_i)}{(\Sigma x_{2i}^2)(\Sigma x_{3i}^2) - (\Sigma x_{2i} x_{3i})^2}$$

Substituting for y_i from Eq. (7.11) and solving, we get

$$\hat{\beta}_2^* = \beta_2 + \frac{(\Sigma x_{3i}^2)(\Sigma x_{2i} \varepsilon_i) - (\Sigma x_{2i} x_{3i})(\Sigma x_{3i} \varepsilon_i)}{(\Sigma x_{2i}^2)(\Sigma x_{3i}^2) - (\Sigma x_{2i} x_{3i})^2}$$

from which it follows that (taking expected values with x_2 and x_3 fixed)

$$E(\hat{\beta}_2^*) = \beta_2$$

[5] It is cumbersome but not difficult to show that the estimated variance of $\hat{\beta}_2^*$ will be biased upward.

[6] This is shown in P. Rao and R. L. Miller, *Applied Econometrics* (Belmont, Calif.: Wadsworth, 1971).

Thus, the inclusion of an irrelevant variable does not bias the slope parameter estimates of any of the slope variables which appear in the "true" model. It is not difficult to show that the intercept of the equation is unbiased as well and that the estimate of the coefficient of x_3 will have an expected value of 0. We leave both of these proofs to the reader (see Exercises 7.5 and 7.6). (The consistency proofs are similar; you simply need to use probability limits rather than expectations.)

The inclusion of irrelevant variables does affect the efficiency of the least-squares estimator, since the variance of the estimated slope coefficient $\hat{\beta}_2^*$ will in general be larger than the variance of the coefficient $\hat{\beta}_2$. (The only case in which a loss of efficiency will not occur is the special case when x_2 and x_3 are uncorrelated, again an unlikely possibility.) This loss of efficiency makes it more difficult to reject the null hypothesis of a zero slope parameter. However, the estimated variance of $\hat{\beta}_2^*$ will be an unbiased estimator of the true variance of $\hat{\beta}_2$. Thus, the loss of efficiency will be accounted for when the standard error of the regression is calculated.

7.3.3 Nonlinearities

Another specification error can occur when the researcher chooses to estimate a linear regression model that is linear in the explanatory variables when the true regression model is nonlinear. A simple example occurs when the true model is of the polynomial form:

$$y_1 = \beta_2 x_{2i} + \beta_3 x_{2i}^2 + \beta_4 x_{2i}^3 + \varepsilon_i \qquad (7.13)$$

while the estimated model is

$$y_i = \beta_2^* x_{2i} + \varepsilon_i^* \qquad (7.14)$$

Since the model in Eq. (7.14) is a special case of omitted variables, the specification of a linear model when the true model is nonlinear can lead to biased and inconsistent parameter estimates. The same conclusion holds when a polynomial approximation to an inherently nonlinear equation is used (see Section 10.1). For this reason, we often estimate polynomial equations such as Eq. (7.13) as a test for nonlinearity in the independent variables.

7.3.4 Efficiency versus Bias in Model Building

If we are unsure which explanatory variables ought to appear in a model, we face several trade-offs. The analysis shows that the cost of excluding a variable which should appear in the model is bias and inconsistency. The cost of adding one or more irrelevant variables is loss of efficiency. If the number of observations is large, it seems reasonable to opt for the risk of adding irrelevant variables, because the loss of degrees of freedom is unlikely to be serious. If the number of observations is not large, however, loss of efficiency becomes serious.

In general, the choice of model form must be made in terms of the bias-efficiency trade-off, with the result dependent on the objective. If accurate forecasting is the goal, minimizing mean square error is one reasonable objective, since it accounts for both bias and efficiency.[7] Thus, we might estimate each of several alternative models over a given time period and compare the mean square errors associated with each one.

In terms of classical statistics, it is not difficult to test whether irrelevant variables are present. Since the coefficients of irrelevant variables have expected values of 0, we apply standard t tests if we wish to evaluate the relevancy of individual variables and apply an F test if we wish to test the relevancy of a group of variables. This testing fails completely when we are unsure which variables ought to appear in the model. As a result, we must rely on the use of simulation techniques to make such comparisons.[8]

Example 7.1 Demand for Money In a study of the long- and short-run demand for money, Gregory Chow estimated the following demand equation (standard errors are in parentheses, and all data are quarterly):[9]

$$\hat{M}_t = .1365 + 1.069Y_{pt} - .01321Y_t - .7476\,R_t \qquad R^2 = .9965$$
$$\quad\quad\quad\;\; (.148) \quad\quad (.13897) \quad\quad (.0540)$$

where M = natural logarithm of total money stock
Y_p = natural logarithm of permanent income
Y = natural logarithm of current income
R = natural logarithm of rate of interest

Since Chow views the estimated equation as a long-run equation for the demand for money, he concludes that permanent income is more important than current income as the long-run constraint on individual assets. (The Y variable is insignificant, while the Y_p variable is highly significant.) However, one can argue that the estimated equation is in fact a misspecification of the

---

[7] Recall from Chapter 2 that mean square error = variance + bias².

[8] Bayesian econometrics provides a suitable framework in which the limitations of the classical methods of model construction and model testing can be seen. See, for example, A. Zellner, *An Introduction to Bayesian Inference in Econometrics* (New York: Wiley, 1971), and E. Leamer, *Specification Searches in Econometrics* (New York: Wiley, 1979).

[9] G. C. Chow, "On the Long-Run and Short-Run Demand for Money," *Journal of Political Economy*, vol. 74, pp. 111–131, April 1966.

correct long-run demand-for-money equation. Taylor and Newhouse argue that the correct specification is[10]

$$M_t = \beta_1 + \beta_2 Y_{pt} + \beta_3 Y_t + \beta_4 R_t + \beta_5 M_{t-1} + \varepsilon_t \qquad (7.15)$$

If Eq. (7.15) is correct, we would expect the coefficients of Chow's estimated equation to be biased. We can approximate the extent of this bias by using our results on the effects of omitted-variable specification error. Consider the estimated permanent income coefficient, since it is crucial to the policy conclusion which was reached. If the correct model had been

$$M_t = \alpha_1 + \alpha_2 Y_{pt} + \alpha_3 M_{t-1} + u_t$$

then, from Eq. (7.10), we could conclude that the bias in the estimated coefficient $\hat{\alpha}_2$ of the equation $M_t = \alpha_1 + \alpha_2 Y_{pt}$ would be

$$E(\hat{\alpha}_2) - \alpha_2 = \alpha_3 \frac{\text{Cov } (Y_{pt}, M_{t-1})}{\text{Var } (Y_{pt})}$$

While we have not done so in the text, it is possible to extend the formula for specification bias to apply to equations with numerous explanatory variables. In our case the bias in the permanent income term is estimated by

$$E(\hat{\beta}_2) - \beta_2 = \beta_5 d_2$$

where d_2 is the coefficient of Y_{pt} in the auxiliary regression of M_{t-1} on Y_{pt}, Y_t, and R_t, that is,

$$M_{t-1} = d_1 + d_2 Y_{pt} + d_3 Y_t + d_4 R_t + v_t$$

If the variable M_{t-1} is unavailable, we will have to speculate about the extent of any specification bias that is present. However, in this particular example M_{t-1} is available, since it involves a one-period lag of a variable present in the misspecified equation. Since M_{t-1} and Y_{pt} are known to be highly correlated and we expect the sign of M_{t-1} to be positive when the correctly specified equation is run, we would predict that the bias is positive and substantial. In other words, the extent of the importance of permanent income is overstated because of the specification error. This guess is borne out when the correctly specified model is estimated. The results are as follows:

$$\hat{M}_t = .3067 + .06158 Y_{pt} + .3274 Y_t - .3325 R_t + .5878 M_{t-1} \qquad R^2 = .9988$$
$$\qquad\qquad (.14284) \qquad\quad (.0940) \qquad\quad (.0597) \qquad\quad (.0669)$$

---

[10] L. D. Taylor and J. P. Newhouse, "On the Long-Run and Short-Run Demand for Money: A Comment," *Journal of Political Economy*, vol. 77, pp. 851–856, 1969.

The M_{t-1} coefficient is positive and significant, while the Y_{pt} coefficient is positive but is insignificant at the 5 percent level. Thus, the original conclusion ought to be revised to state that current income is more important than permanent income in explaining the long-run demand for money.

7.4   REGRESSION DIAGNOSTICS[11]

The basic linear regression model is prone to a number of possible errors other than the inclusion of irrelevant variables or the omission of relevant ones. We saw in Chapter 6 that serial correlation or heteroscedasticity can lead to inefficient estimators. In fact, any unusual residual pattern, including serial correlation, should be a concern, since it suggests that one or more variables have been improperly omitted from the regression model.

In this section we broaden our analysis of the regression model to consider a number of useful regression diagnostics. These diagnostics are not derived from statistical theory; consequently, they do not provide statistical tests. Rather, they allow us to see whether one or more data points or one or more independent variables have an unusually large influence on the estimated regression parameters. A data point or variable with an unusual influence may reflect a data error—there could have been a mistake in the coding or transcription of the data. In this case an obvious correction would be called for. In most cases, however, data corrections (or the omission of data points) are not necessary. An unusual influence may point to the failure of the regression model to account for a particular event in a particular location or time period, or it may simply reflect the fact that the disturbance term has a large variance.

The detection and evaluation of influential data points and influential variables is complex. To see why, examine Fig. 7.2. The true regression model has a positive slope and is given by $Y_i = \alpha + \beta X_i + \varepsilon_i$. However, a coding error was made on the seventh, largest, data point. That point is clearly very influential, since the estimated regression line, shown by the dashed line $\hat{\alpha} + \hat{\beta} X_i$, has a negative slope. But that data point does not show up as an outlier because, with the quadratic loss function implicit in least squares, the estimated line is forced to lie close to the data point. In the subsections that follow we suggest several diagnostic techniques that can be useful in detecting influential data and influential variables.

---

[11] The material in this section relies heavily on D. A. Belsley, E. Kuh, and R. E. Welsch, *Regression Diagnostics, Identifying Influential Data and Sources of Collinearity* (New York: Wiley, 1980). See also W. S. Krasker, E. Kuh, and R. E. Welsch, "Estimation for Dirty Data and Flawed Models," in Z. Griliches and M. D. Intriligator, eds., *Handbook of Econometrics*, vol. I (Amsterdam: North-Holland, 1983), Chapter 11, and A. R. Pagan and A. D. Hall, "Diagnostic Tests as Residual Analysis," *Econometric Reviews*, vol. 2, pp. 159–218, 1983.

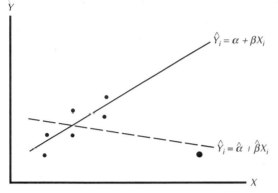

FIGURE 7.2
An influential data point.

7.4.1   Studentized Residuals

Relatively large residuals can be useful as a regression diagnostic. They can warn us that particular observations may be influential. Or, when examined as a group, they can be used to evaluate the assumption that the underlying error distribution is normal. The value of residuals as a diagnostic device is limited, however, because an influential data point can be associated with a small residual. For this reason it is useful to consider the residual that is obtained for each observation *when the regression line is estimated with that particular observation omitted.*

Thus, for our two-variable model, let $\beta(i)$ represent the estimated regression slope when the ith observation has been omitted. We will focus our attention on the residual $\varepsilon(i) = y_i - \beta(i)x_i$. Residuals are most easily interpreted, however, when they are scaled to have unit variance (of course, they also have zero mean). For large samples, we would expect those normalized residuals to follow a normal distribution. Failure to do so, as evidenced by the fact that substantially more than 5 percent of the normalized residuals are more than 2 standard deviations different from the mean of zero, provides evidence that the normality assumption is invalid.

To normalize the residuals, we divide the residual $\varepsilon(i)$ by the estimated standard error of the regression, $s_i(i)$, in which the ith observation has been omitted. The *studentized residual* is thus given by

$$\varepsilon_i^* = \frac{[y_i - \beta(i)x_i]}{s_i(i)} \tag{7.16}$$

Studentized residuals that are greater than 1.96 in absolute value (or more generally greater than the appropriate critical value of the t distribution) can be regarded as outliers and should receive special attention. However, only when there is a higher than expected percentage of such residuals should the assumption of normality be brought into question.

7.4.2   DFBETAS

Frequently, one is interested in the value of a particular parameter of a regression model. In this case, the central question becomes, does any observation have an unusually large influence on the value of the estimated parameter?

The answer is provided by looking at the *DFBETAS* for each observation and each variable. DFBETAS measures the scaled difference between the least-squares estimate and the corresponding parameter that has been estimated with a particular observation omitted. The scale is determined by the estimated standard deviation of $\beta(i)$. For the two-variable model

$$\text{DFBETAS}_i = \frac{[\beta - \beta(i)]}{s_{\beta(i)}} \qquad (7.17)$$

A value of DFBETAS greater than 1.96 in absolute value shows the presence of an influential observation with respect to that value. Assuming that there are no data transcription errors, any conclusions that rely heavily on the estimated value of the particular slope parameter should be qualified. It is true as a general rule that the chance that any particular observation will affect the estimated parameter substantially will decline as the sample size gets larger. Therefore, a better rule of thumb is to look for an observation whose critical value decreases as the sample size gets larger. One possibility is to be concerned when the value of DFBETAS is greater in absolute value than $2/N^{.5}$.

Example 7.2 The Effect of Air Pollution and Crime on Property Values

In a study of property values, Harrison and Rubinfeld used a sample of 506 census tracts in the city of Boston to evaluate the relationship between the quality of life in neighborhoods and property values.[12] The linear regression model related the logarithm of the median value of owner-occupied homes (LMV) to a number of variables (14, including the constant term) that describe the quality of homes in the neighborhood, the accessibility of the neighborhood to nearby work centers, and the quality of life in the neighborhoods. In this example used in the Harrison-Rubinfeld study we report the results of an analysis by Belsley, Kuh, and Welsch of two particular neighborhood variables: the squared level of nitrogen oxides, NOXSQ, and the per-capita crime rate, CRIM.

The relevant portion of the estimated regression equation (with t statistics in parentheses) is

$$\widehat{\text{LMV}} = 9.758 - .00639\text{NOXSQ} - .0119\text{CRIM} + \cdots$$
$$\quad\;\;(65.23)\quad\;(-5.64)\qquad\qquad(-9.53)$$

$$R^2 = .806 \qquad s = .182$$

---

[12] See D. Harrison and D. L. Rubinfeld, "Hedonic Housing Prices and the Demand for Clean Air," *Journal of Environmental Economics and Management,* vol. 5, pp. 81–102, 1978.

Because there are 506 observations, it would require too much space to list all observations for which the studentized residuals were greater than 1.96 or the DFBETAS was greater in absolute value than $2/N^{.5}$. Therefore, we have listed in Table 7.1 the values of the regression diagnostics for the 28 census tracts that exceeded in magnitude one of the following stringent cutoff values:

$$\text{Studentized residual} = 2.5$$

$$\text{DFBETAS} = \frac{3}{\sqrt{N}} = \frac{3}{\sqrt{506}} = .133$$

Of the 18 residuals that are greater than 2.5 in absolute value, tracts 372 and 373 are the highest, with t values of 4.51 and 4.16, respectively. The fact that 18/506, or more than 3 percent, of the residuals have t values

TABLE 7.1
REGRESSION DIAGNOSTICS FOR SELECTED CENSUS TRACTS

Tract	Studentized residual	DFBETAS(NOXSQ)	DFBETAS(CRIM)
149	1.77	.26*	−.014
151	.98	.16*	.002
153	−1.31	−.20*	−.003
215	2.91*	−.08	−.075
359	1.25	.14*	−.006
365	−2.75*	−.18*	.065
368	2.76*	−.19*	−.047
369	2.66*	−.13	−.110
372	4.51*	−.27*	−.129
373	4.16*	−.18*	−.126
381	−2.56*	.10	1.591*
386	−2.56*	.01	−.057
398	−3.21*	−.00	.093
399	−3.30*	−.01	−.577*
400	−3.94*	.01	.122
401	−3.95*	−.02	−.342*
402	−3.99*	−.02	−.064
406	2.14	−.06	−.870*
410	3.16*	−.27*	−.031
411	1.69	−.13	.413*
413	3.52*	−.38*	−.006
414	1.95	−.16*	.178*
417	−2.85*	.05	.110
419	2.32	.03	1.004*
427	−1.96	.14*	.058
490	−3.53*	.30*	.180*
491	−2.02	.18*	.111
506	−3.07*	−.12	−.055

* Indicates that a cutoff has been exceeded.

greater than 2.5 suggests that the assumption of normal errors may not be appropriate. If the errors were normally distributed, only 1.24 percent of the errors would be greater than 2.5 deviations from the mean.

Now consider the DFBETAS. Tract 381 has a very high DFBETAS for the CRIM variable; the removal of this single tract out of a total of 506 would decrease the coefficient on CRIM by 1.59 standard deviations. A check of the data showed that there were no transcription errors, but FBI crime data are notoriously inaccurate, so it is not surprising to find that the coefficient on CRIM is sensitive to particular data points. Fortunately, however, in the original property value study Harrison and Rubinfeld were especially interested in the coefficient on NOXSQ. Tract 381 presents no particular problems for the NOXSQ coefficient, and although there are a number of data points that have DFBETAS that exceed the cutoff point, the highest ($-.38$ for tract 413) is not so substantial as to be of unusual concern.

Overall, the regression diagnostics suggest that the errors may not be normally distributed, so that the significance of particular coefficients is likely to be overstated. There are a number of particularly influential data points which make it dangerous to rely too heavily on the CRIM coefficient. However, the coefficient on NOXSQ is much less sensitive to individual data points and therefore is the more reliable of the two.

7.5   SPECIFICATION TESTS

We have just seen that the consequences of specification errors in econometrics can be very serious. Failure to include a relevant variable in a regression model can lead to biased and inconsistent estimators, while the inclusion of inappropriate variables leads to a loss of efficiency. It is obviously important to be able to test whether a chosen model involves specification errors. In this section we discuss and illustrate a number of tests that apply to specification errors. We begin with some tests that involve omitted variables and that apply to the basic linear regression model. Then we consider a test for measurement error which can be used when it is thought that the error term is correlated with one or more independent variables, or when other assumptions of the basic model may fail.

7.5.1   Testing for Whether Variables Should Be Omitted in the Linear Regression Model

Tests for specification errors have been discussed before. Suppose we believe that the appropriate model is given by

$$y_i = \beta_1 x_{1i} + \beta_2 x_{2i} + \beta_3 x_{3i} + \varepsilon_i \tag{7.18}$$

If we are convinced that the variable x_1 should be in the model but are uncertain about x_2 and x_3, then one appropriate test is the F test involving joint tests of several coefficients (discussed in Section 5.3). The F test evaluates the null hypothesis that $\beta_2 = \beta_3 = 0$ against the alternative that either or both are not zero by asking whether the error sum of squares associated with the restricted model (in which the null hypothesis holds) is significantly larger than the error sum of squares associated with the unrestricted model shown in Eq. (7.18). Similarly, if x_3 were the only uncertain variable, a t test of the null hypothesis that $\beta_3 = 0$ could be done directly by using the regression output when Eq. (7.18) is estimated.

A more general method of doing the same tests that does not utilize least squares and does not rely on the normality of the error term (when the sample size is large) is the *likelihood ratio test*. This test will be discussed more generally in Chapter 10.[13]

In most situations, especially those involving large sample sizes, F tests and likelihood ratio tests should generate very similar results. Depending on the software being used, the likelihood ratio test may be more difficult to apply, but it is more appealing when large samples are involved because it does not require an assumption of normality.[14]

7.5.2   Testing for the Presence or Absence of Measurement Errors

Suppose we are interested in estimating the two-variable regression model

$$y_i = \beta x_i + \varepsilon_i$$

---

[13] Suppose that the value of the log-likelihood function associated with the unrestricted model is given by $L(\beta_1, \beta_2, \beta_3)$, while the (lower) value of the restricted model is given by $L(\beta_1)$. Then, for large samples, it follows that

$$-2[L(\beta_1) - L(\beta_1, \beta_2, \beta_3)] \sim x_2^2$$

where the subscript 2 refers to the number of restrictions that are imposed ($\beta_2 = 0$ and $\beta_3 = 0$).

The likelihood ratio test can be applied quite generally. Whatever the restrictions on the parameters of the model (restrictions that the β's or the error variance take on particular values), it is true that

$$-2[L(\text{restricted}) - L(\text{unrestricted})] \sim x_r^2$$

where r is the number of restrictions involved.

[14] For a general comparison of F tests (a special case of a more general Wald test), likelihood ratio tests, and a third Lagrange multiplier test, see Robert F. Engle, "Wald, Likelihood Ratio, and Lagrange Multiplier Tests in Econometrics," in Z. Griliches and M. D. Intriligator, eds., *Handbook of Econometrics*, vol. II (Amsterdam: Elsevier Science Publishers, 1984), Chapter 13.

but are concerned about the possibility that x might be measured with error.[15] If $x_i = x_i^* - v_i$, then the actual least-squares regression would be

$$y_i = \beta x_i^* + \varepsilon_i^* \tag{7.19}$$

where $\varepsilon_i^* = \varepsilon_i - \beta v_i$.

If x is measured with error, we have seen that a consistent estimator of β can be obtained by using an instrument z which is correlated with x^* but is uncorrelated with ε and v. Suppose the relationship between z and x^* is given by

$$x_i^* = \gamma z_i + w_i \tag{7.20}$$

When estimated using least squares, this relationship becomes

$$\hat{x}_i^* = \hat{\gamma} z_i$$

or

$$x_i^* = \hat{x}_i^* + \hat{w}_i \tag{7.21}$$

where $\hat{w}_i$ are the regression residuals. Substituting Eq. (7.21) into Eq. (7.19) yields the following:

$$y_i = \beta \hat{x}_i^* + \beta \hat{w}_i + \varepsilon_i^* \tag{7.22}$$

Whether or not there is measurement error, the coefficient of $\hat{x}_i^*$ will be consistently estimated by ordinary least squares, since

$$\text{plim} \ (\Sigma \hat{x}_i^* \varepsilon_i^* / N) = \text{plim} \ [\hat{\gamma} \Sigma z_i (\varepsilon_i - \beta v_i) / N] = 0$$

In fact, the least-squares estimator of the coefficient of $\hat{x}_i^*$ in Eq. (7.22) is identically equal to the instrumental-variables estimator,[16] which is given [from Eq. (7.8)] by $\hat{\beta} = \Sigma y_i z_i / \Sigma x_i^* z_i$.

To look at the coefficient of the variable $\hat{w}_i$, note that

$$\text{plim} \ (\Sigma \hat{w}_i \varepsilon_i^* / N) = \text{plim} \ [\Sigma (x_i^* - \hat{\gamma} z_i)(\varepsilon_i - \beta v_i) / N] = \text{plim} \ (-\beta \Sigma x_i^* v_i / N)$$
$$= \text{plim} \ [-\beta \Sigma v_i (x_i + v_i) / N] = -\beta \sigma_v^2$$

---

[15] The same approach applies if we are concerned that x might be correlated with the error term because of simultaneity. For details, see Chapter 12.

[16] The proof involves a substantial amount of algebra and is omitted here.

When there is no measurement error, $\sigma_v^2 = 0$, so that OLS applied to Eq. (7.22) will generate a consistent estimator of the coefficient of $\hat{w}_i$. However, when there is measurement error, the coefficient will be estimated inconsistently.

This suggests a relatively easy measurement-error test. Let δ represent the coefficient of the variable $\hat{w}_i$ in Eq. (7.22). Substituting $\hat{x}_i^* = x_i^* - \hat{w}_i$, we get

$$y_i = \beta x_i^* + (\delta - \beta)\hat{w}_i + \varepsilon_i^*$$

(7.23)

t-test on $(\delta - \beta)$ is Hausman Test.

With no measurement error, $\delta = \beta$, so that the coefficient of $\hat{w}_i$ should equal zero. However, with measurement error, $\delta \neq \beta$, and the coefficient will (in general) be different from zero. We can test for measurement error by doing a simple two-stage procedure. First, we regress x^* on z to obtain the residuals $\hat{w}$. Then, we regress y on x^* and $\hat{w}$ and perform a t test on the coefficient of the $\hat{w}$ variable. If we are concerned with measurement error in more than one variable of a multiple regression model, an equivalent F test could be applied.

The test just described is a special case of a more general test for specification error proposed by Hausman.[17] The Hausman specification test relies on the fact that under the null hypothesis the ordinary least-squares estimator of the parameters of the original Eq. (7.19) is consistent and (for large samples) efficient, but is inconsistent if the alternative hypothesis is true. However, the instrumental-variables estimator [the least-squares estimator of Eq. (7.22)] is consistent whether or not the null hypothesis is true, although it is inefficient if the null is not valid. We will discuss the more general application of the Hausman test when we discuss the use of instrumental variables in the context of simultaneous equations in Chapter 12.

In case of measurement error, δ is biased towards 0 ∴ smaller than actual.

Example 7.3 Testing for Measurement Error in a Model of Public Spending
The expenditures of U.S. state and local governments (EXP) vary substantially by state and by region. Among the important variables that explain differences in spending levels are federal grants-in-aid (AID), the income of states (INC), and the population of states (POP). When a model that relates the dependent variable EXP to the independent variables AID, INC, and POP was estimated by ordinary least squares, using census data for the 50 states (see Table 6.2 for details concerning the data set), the following results were obtained (with t statistics in parentheses):

$$\widehat{\text{EXP}} = -46.81 + .00324\text{AID} + .00019\text{INC} - .597\text{POP}$$

3.233767   0.000190   −0.594075

$$(-.56) \qquad (13.64) \qquad (8.12) \qquad (-5.71)$$

$$R^2 = .993 \qquad F = 2,190$$

[17] See J. A. Hausman, "Specification Tests in Econometrics," *Econometrica*, vol. 46, pp. 1251–1271, November 1978.

There is an important possible source of measurement error in the AID variable. State aid programs involve fixed sums of money, and therefore the monies involved are easy to measure even before state and local budgets are set. Other programs, however, are open-ended, with the actual sum that a state or locality receives being a function of the actual expenditure levels of those governments. As a result, this component of the AID variable can be subject to substantial measurement error.

We can test for the presence of measurement error by using a Hausman specification test. To perform the test, we use the population of primary and secondary school children (PS) as an instrument. (School spending is the largest component of state and local public expenditures, and many school programs are open-ended.) The test proceeds in two stages. In the first stage AID is regressed on PS, and the residual variable $\hat{w}_i$ is calculated as follows:

$$\hat{w}_i = \text{AID} - 77.95 + .845\text{PS} \qquad R^2 = .87$$
$$\phantom{\hat{w}_i = \text{AID} -} (-1.28) \quad (18.02)$$

In the second stage $\hat{w}_i$ is added to the original regression to correct for measurement error. The resulting equation is

$$\widehat{\text{EXP}} = -138.51 + .00174\text{AID} + .00018\text{INC} - .275\text{POP} + 1.372\hat{w}_i$$
$$\phantom{\widehat{\text{EXP}} =} (-1.41) \qquad (1.94) \qquad\qquad (7.55) \qquad\qquad (-1.29) \qquad (1.73)$$

A two-tailed t test of the null hypothesis that there is no measurement error would be accepted at the 5 percent level, since $1.73 < 1.96$. However, measurement error would be deemed to be important if we were using either a one-tailed test, or a two-tailed test at the 10 percent significance level. Note, in any case, that correcting for the possibility of measurement error has substantially lowered the coefficient on the AID variable, suggesting that measurement error causes the effect of AID on public spending to be overstated.

APPENDIX 7.1 Instrumental-Variables Estimation in Matrix Form

The technique of instrumental variables can be used to obtain consistent estimates of $\boldsymbol{\beta}$ when the right-hand variables are known to be correlated with the error term as a result of errors in variables or simultaneous-equation bias. If our original model is

$$\mathbf{Y} = \mathbf{X}\boldsymbol{\beta} + \boldsymbol{\varepsilon} \tag{A7.1}$$

the correlation of one or more X's and the error term ε is summarized as

$$\text{plim}\left(\frac{1}{N}\mathbf{X}'\boldsymbol{\varepsilon}\right) \neq 0 \tag{A7.2}$$

The expression "plim" refers to the probability limit as defined in Chapter 2. To see the difficulty which arises when Eq. (A7.2) holds, premultiply Eq. (A7.1) by the matrix $\mathbf{X}'$ to obtain

$$\mathbf{X}'\mathbf{Y} = \mathbf{X}'\mathbf{X}\boldsymbol{\beta} + \mathbf{X}'\boldsymbol{\varepsilon}$$

If $\text{plim}\,[(1/N)\mathbf{X}'\boldsymbol{\varepsilon}] = 0$, the last term goes to 0 in the probability limit and

$$\hat{\boldsymbol{\beta}} = (\mathbf{X}'\mathbf{X})^{-1}\mathbf{X}'\mathbf{Y} \tag{A7.3}$$

is a consistent estimator of $\boldsymbol{\beta}$. However, when the probability limit is nonzero, ordinary least-squares estimation becomes inconsistent.

Consistent estimates of $\boldsymbol{\beta}$ can be obtained through the use of an $N \times k$ matrix of instruments $\mathbf{Z} = (\mathbf{Z}_1, \mathbf{Z}_2, \ldots, \mathbf{Z}_k)$, where each instrument $\mathbf{Z}_i$ has N observations. $\mathbf{Z}$ satisfies the conditions necessary to be labeled a matrix of instruments if the following conditions hold:[18]

$$\text{plim}\left(\frac{1}{N}\mathbf{Z}'\boldsymbol{\varepsilon}\right) = \mathbf{0} \tag{A7.4}$$

$$\text{plim}\left(\frac{1}{N}\mathbf{Z}'\mathbf{X}\right) = \Sigma \text{ exists and is nonsingular (has an inverse)} \tag{A7.5}$$

$$\text{plim}\left(\frac{1}{N}\mathbf{Z}'\mathbf{Z}\right) = \Sigma^* \text{ exists and is nonsingular} \tag{A7.6}$$

The first condition guarantees that each instrument is uncorrelated with the error term, while the second guarantees a nonzero correlation between the Z's and the X's as well as the fact that all the Z's must be linearly independent. Thus, there is no reason why some of the original X's cannot be used as instruments in the instrumental-variables estimation process.

Given the appropriate instruments, we premultiply Eq. (A7.1) by $\mathbf{Z}'$ to get

$$\mathbf{Z}'\mathbf{Y} = \mathbf{Z}'\mathbf{X}\boldsymbol{\beta} + \mathbf{Z}'\boldsymbol{\varepsilon}$$

from which it follows that

$$\hat{\boldsymbol{\beta}}^* = (\mathbf{Z}'\mathbf{X})^{-1}\mathbf{Z}'\mathbf{Y} \tag{A7.7}$$

---

[18] With errors in variables, $\mathbf{Z}$ must also be unrelated in the probability limit to the measurement error.

will be a consistent estimator of $\boldsymbol{\beta}$. $\hat{\boldsymbol{\beta}}*$ will be consistent because

$$\hat{\boldsymbol{\beta}}* = (\mathbf{Z}'\mathbf{X})^{-1}(\mathbf{Z}'\mathbf{X})\boldsymbol{\beta} + (\mathbf{Z}'\mathbf{X})^{-1}(\mathbf{Z}'\boldsymbol{\varepsilon}) = \boldsymbol{\beta} + (\mathbf{Z}'\mathbf{X})^{-1}(\mathbf{Z}'\boldsymbol{\varepsilon})$$

and $\text{plim } \hat{\boldsymbol{\beta}}* = \boldsymbol{\beta} + \text{plim } [(\mathbf{Z}'\mathbf{X})^{-1}(\mathbf{Z}'\boldsymbol{\varepsilon})]$

$$= \boldsymbol{\beta} + \text{plim } \left[\left(\frac{1}{N}\mathbf{Z}'\mathbf{X} \right)^{-1} \left(\frac{1}{N}\mathbf{Z}'\boldsymbol{\varepsilon} \right) \right] \quad \text{from Eqs. (A7.4) and (A7.5)}$$

$$= \boldsymbol{\beta} + \boldsymbol{\Sigma}^{-1}\mathbf{0} = \boldsymbol{\beta}$$

To find the appropriate distribution of $\hat{\boldsymbol{\beta}}*$, we need to derive $\mathbf{V}$, the asymptotic variance-covariance matrix for $\hat{\boldsymbol{\beta}}*$. To accomplish this, we use the fact that

$$\hat{\boldsymbol{\beta}}* - \boldsymbol{\beta} = (\mathbf{Z}'\mathbf{X})^{-1}(\mathbf{Z}'\boldsymbol{\varepsilon})$$

and $$(\hat{\boldsymbol{\beta}}* - \boldsymbol{\beta})(\hat{\boldsymbol{\beta}}* - \boldsymbol{\beta})' = (\mathbf{Z}'\mathbf{X})^{-1}\mathbf{Z}'\boldsymbol{\varepsilon}\boldsymbol{\varepsilon}'\mathbf{Z}(\mathbf{X}'\mathbf{Z})^{-1}$$

$$\mathbf{V} = \left[\frac{1}{N}\text{plim} \left(\frac{1}{N}\mathbf{Z}'\mathbf{X} \right)^{-1} \right] \left[\text{plim} \left(\frac{1}{N}\mathbf{Z}'\boldsymbol{\varepsilon}\boldsymbol{\varepsilon}'\mathbf{Z} \right) \right] \left[\text{plim} \left(\frac{1}{N}\mathbf{X}'\mathbf{Z} \right)^{-1} \right]$$

from which it follows, using Eqs. (A7.5) and (A7.6), that

$$\mathbf{V} = \frac{1}{N}\sigma^2\boldsymbol{\Sigma}^{-1}\boldsymbol{\Sigma}*\boldsymbol{\Sigma}^{-1\prime} \tag{A7.8}$$

In practice, the true variance-covariance matrix can be consistently estimated by

$$s^2(\mathbf{Z}'\mathbf{X})^{-1}(\mathbf{Z}'\mathbf{Z})(\mathbf{X}'\mathbf{Z})^{-1} \tag{A7.9}$$

where s^2 is a consistent estimate of σ^2:

$$s^2 = \frac{1}{N-k}(\mathbf{Y} - \mathbf{X}\hat{\boldsymbol{\beta}}*)'(\mathbf{Y} - \mathbf{X}\hat{\boldsymbol{\beta}}*)$$

Note that s^2 is calculated from the residuals of the original equation, not from the equation in which the instruments replace the original right-hand variables.

EXERCISES

7.1 Explain briefly why measurement error in the right-hand variables leads to inconsistent and biased parameter estimates while measurement error in the left-hand variables does not.

7.2 Show in the two-variable model that $\hat{\beta} = \Sigma y_i z_i / \Sigma z_i^2$ (where z is an instrument) will not yield a consistent estimate of the true slope parameter. Are there any conditions under which the instrumental-variables estimator described will yield a consistent estimate of β?

7.3 Prove that the omission of a variable from a "true" regression model will lead in general to a biased estimate of the regression intercept. Under what special conditions will the bias become zero?

7.4 Assume that the true regression model is of the form

$$y_i = \beta_2 x_{2i} + \beta_3 x_{2i}^2 + \varepsilon_i$$

If the regression $y_i = \beta_2^* x_{2i} + \varepsilon_i^*$ is run, what can you say about the direction of the bias of the slope coefficient?

7.5 Prove that the coefficient of an irrelevant variable will have an expected value of 0. *Hint:* Using the analog of Eq. (7.12), solve for the estimated parameter $\hat{\beta}_3^*$ and then take expected values.

7.6 Prove that the inclusion of an irrelevant variable does not bias the estimated intercept parameter.

7.7 Suppose you believe that the true model is given by $Y = \beta_2 X_2 + \beta_3 X_3 + \cdots + \beta_k X_k + \varepsilon$. What is gained or lost by running the regression on the model $Y = \beta_1 + \beta_2 X_2 + \beta_3 X_3 + \cdots + \beta_k X_k + \varepsilon$?

7.8 Explain why observations that lie far from the mean of a variable are more likely to have unusual influence than are those that lie close to the mean.

7.9 Consider the regression model $y_i = \beta_1 + \beta_2 x_{2i} + \beta_3 x_{3i} + \varepsilon_i$. Suppose that you are concerned that both x_2 and x_3 are measured with error, and that z_2 and z_3 are considered to be possible instruments for x_2 and x_3, respectively. How would you perform a Hausman specification test to evaluate the presence or absence of measurement error?

FORECASTING WITH A SINGLE-EQUATION REGRESSION MODEL

A principal purpose for constructing single-equation regression models is *forecasting*. A forecast is a quantitative estimate (or set of estimates) about the *likelihood* of future events which is developed on the basis of past and current information. This information is embodied in the form of a model—a single-equation structural model or, as we will discuss in Parts Three and Four of this book, a multi-equation model or a time-series model. By extrapolating our models beyond the period over which they were estimated, we can make forecasts about future events. In this chapter we show how the single-equation regression model can be used as a forecasting tool.

The term *forecasting* is often thought to apply solely to problems in which we predict the future. We shall remain consistent with this notion by orienting our notation and discussion toward time-series forecasting. We stress, however, that most of the analysis applies equally well to cross-section models.

Two types of forecasts can be useful. *Point forecasts* predict a single number in each forecast period, while *interval forecasts* indicate an interval in which we hope the realized value will lie. We begin by discussing point forecasts, after which we consider how confidence intervals (interval forecasts) can be used to provide a margin of error around point forecasts.

The information provided by the forecasting process can be used in many ways. Forecasts frequently are used as guides for public and private policy. A forecast of a high rate of inflation that is based on the assumption of a large budget deficit may lead policy makers to alter their budget plans, or a forecast of an increased world demand for crude oil may lead shipbuilders to invest in

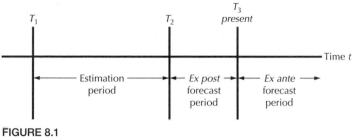

FIGURE 8.1
Types of forecasting.

new supertankers. Forecasts are also useful as guidelines for model building. A forecast which is found to be way off target when actual data become available provides information which may lead to the revision of the model that provided the forecast.

It is useful to distinguish between *ex post* and *ex ante* forecasting. In terms of time-series models, both predict values of a dependent variable beyond the time period used to estimate the model. In an *ex post* forecast, observations on both endogenous variables and the exogenous explanatory variables are already known with certainty during the forecast period. Thus, *ex post* forecasts can be checked against existing data and provide a means of evaluating a forecasting model. An *ex ante* forecast also predicts values of the dependent variable beyond the original estimation period, but uses explanatory variables that may or may not yet be known with certainty. The distinction between *ex post* and *ex ante* forecasting can be seen in Fig. 8.1.

A distinction can also be made between *conditional* and *unconditional* forecasts. In an unconditional forecast, values for all the explanatory variables in the forecasting equation are known with certainty. Any *ex post* forecast is, of course, an unconditional forecast, but *ex ante* forecasts also may be unconditional. Suppose that for some industry, for example, monthly sales $S(t)$ are linearly related to two variables X_1 and X_2, but with lags of 3 and 4 months, respectively.

$$S(t) = a_0 + a_1 X_1(t - 3) + a_2 X_2(t - 4) + \varepsilon(t) \tag{8.1}$$

If this equation were estimated, it could be used to produce unconditional forecasts of $S(t)$ 1, 2, and 3 months in the future. For example, to produce a 3-month forecast of $S(t)$, we would use the current value of X_1 and last month's value of X_2, both of which are known.

In a conditional forecast, values for one or more explanatory variables are not known, so that guesses (or forecasts) must be used to produce a forecast of the dependent variable. If we wanted to use Eq. (8.1) to forecast $S(t)$ four months into the future, we would also have to forecast $X_1(t)$ one month into the future, making our forecast of $S(t)$ *conditional* on our forecast of $X_1(t)$. Of course, if the right-hand side of the forecasting equation contained no lags, e.g., if it were of the form

$$S(t) = a_0 + a_1 X_1(t) + a_2 X_2(t) + \varepsilon(t) \tag{8.2}$$

every *ex ante* forecast generated by the equation would be a conditional forecast.

An important concern in this chapter is the problem of evaluating the nature of the *forecast error* by using the appropriate statistical tests. We define the *best forecast* as the one which yields the forecast error with the *minimum variance*. In the single-equation regression model, ordinary least-squares estimation yields the best forecast among all linear unbiased estimators. We will extend our notion of the best forecast in later chapters when we consider minimum mean-square-error forecasts that are based on nonlinear equations and on estimation procedures that do not guarantee unbiased parameter estimates.

The error associated with a forecasting procedure can come from a combination of four distinct sources. First, the random nature of the additive error process in a linear regression model guarantees that forecasts will deviate from true values even if the model is specified correctly and its parameter values are known. Second, the process of estimating the regression parameters introduces error because estimated parameter values are random variables that may deviate from the true parameter values. Third, in the case of a conditional forecast, errors are introduced when forecasts are made for the values of the explanatory variables for the period in which the forecast is made. Fourth, errors may be introduced because the model specification may not be an accurate representation of the "true" model.

We proceed by discussing the best forecast and the properties of the forecast error found in three different cases. We deal first with unconditional forecasts generated by a linear regression model in which the error process obeys the assumptions of the classical linear model. Next, we treat the problem of unconditional forecasting when the error process is known to be serially correlated. Finally, we consider the added dimension of difficulty which arises when conditional forecasting is attempted.

8.1   UNCONDITIONAL FORECASTING

To produce an unconditional forecast from a regression model, the explanatory variables must be known with certainty for the entire forecast period. One way this can occur is by having the explanatory variables appear with time lags. Even if explanatory variables do not appear with lags, we may be able to forecast them perfectly, thus generating unconditional forecasts for the dependent variable, if they happen to be seasonal variables or demographic or economic variables that change slowly and predictably. For example, monthly forecasts over a 1-year horizon which use population and the month of the year as two explanatory variables will be unconditional, since population growth over this short period can be predicted precisely and since the month of the year is known with certainty.

8.1.1   The Forecast Error

We begin our discussion of unconditional forecasting by considering the simple two-variable regression model·

$$Y_t = \alpha + \beta X_t + \varepsilon_t \qquad t = 1, 2, \ldots, T \tag{8.3}$$

$$\varepsilon_t \sim N(0, \sigma^2)$$

We pose the forecasting problem as follows: Given a *known* value X_{T+1}, what is the best forecast that can be made for Y in period $T + 1$? In solving the problem, we assume that α *and* β *are known.* If this is the case, the appropriate forecast for Y_{T+1} is given by

$$\hat{Y}_{T+1} = E(Y_{T+1}) = \alpha + \beta X_{T+1} \tag{8.4}$$

To see why, consider the *forecast error*

$$\hat{e}_{T+1} = \hat{Y}_{T+1} - Y_{T+1} \tag{8.5}$$

This forecast error has two desirable properties:

1. $E(\hat{e}_{T+1}) = E(\hat{Y}_{T+1} - Y_{T+1}) = E(-\varepsilon_{T+1}) = 0$, so that the forecast of Y_{T+1} is unbiased.
2. The forecast error variance

$$\sigma_f^2 = E[(\hat{e}_{T+1})^2] = E[(\varepsilon_{T+1})^2] = \sigma^2$$

is the minimum variance among all possible forecasts that are based on linear equations.[1]

Since the forecast error is normally distributed with mean 0 and variance σ^2, we can perform significance tests on the forecasted value of Y by calculating the normalized error

$$\lambda = \frac{\hat{Y}_{T+1} - Y_{T+1}}{\sigma} \tag{8.6}$$

---

[1] σ, the square root of the forecast error variance, is called the *standard error of the forecast.*

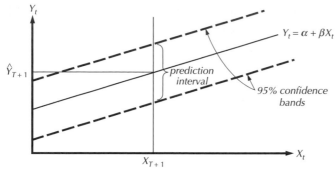

FIGURE 8.2
Forecast when equation parameters are known.

Since λ is normally distributed with mean 0 and standard deviation 1, we determine a 95 percent confidence interval by using the fact that

$$\text{Prob}\left(-\lambda_{.05} \leq \frac{\hat{Y}_{T+1} - Y_{T+1}}{\sigma} \leq \lambda_{.05}\right) = .95 \tag{8.7}$$

where $\lambda_{.05}$ is obtained from a table of the normal distribution (using a 5 percent significance test). We write the confidence interval as

$$\hat{Y}_{T+1} - \lambda_{.05}\sigma \leq Y_{T+1} \leq \hat{Y}_{T+1} + \lambda_{.05}\sigma \tag{8.8}$$

The 95 percent confidence interval for a typical two-variable regression model is shown in Fig. 8.2.

Confidence intervals provide a simple test of the reliability of the regression model. When the actual value of Y_{T+1} is obtained, we can compare it with the previously forecasted value. If Y_{T+1} lies within the 95 percent confidence interval, the model is satisfactory, but if the value lies outside the interval, the model is not performing well. If this poor performance is known to be due to an extraordinary event that is not accounted for by the model, we are likely to wait for a second forecast before concluding that the model is unreliable, but as a general rule we take the poor forecast as evidence of the need to revise the basic model structure.

The use of forecasting as a means of evaluating model reliability is quite distinct from use of the classical t, F, and R^2 statistics described earlier in this book. A single-equation regression model can have significant t statistics and a high R^2 and still forecast very poorly. This may result from a structural change occurring during the forecast period that is not explained by the model. On the other hand, good forecasts can come from regression models that have relatively low R^2's and one or more insignificant regression coefficients. This may happen when there is very little variation in the dependent variable, so that although it is not being explained well by the model, it is easy to forecast.

Usually the parameters of the regression model are random variables that have been estimated. We also do not usually know the error variance σ^2, so this too is an estimated random variable. Let us therefore reconsider the problem of forecasting under the more realistic assumption that both the regression parameters and the error variance must be estimated. The best forecast for Y_{T+1} is then determined from a simple two-stage procedure:

1. Estimate Eq. (8.3) by using ordinary least squares.
2. Choose $\hat{Y}_{T+1} = \hat{\alpha} + \hat{\beta} X_{T+1}$.

The forecast error is then

$$\hat{e}_{T+1} = \hat{Y}_{T+1} - Y_{T+1} = (\hat{\alpha} - \alpha) + (\hat{\beta} - \beta) X_{T+1} - \varepsilon_{T+1} \qquad (8.9)$$

There are two sources of error involved in Eq. (8.9), the first being due to the presence of the additive error term ε_{T+1} and the second being due to the random nature of the estimated regression parameters. While the former error source is due to the variance in the variable Y, the latter error source is sensitive to the estimation process and therefore to the number of degrees of freedom. We will see this as we examine the distribution of the error of forecast.

To begin, the error of forecast is normally distributed, since it is a linear function of $\hat{\alpha}, \hat{\beta}$, and ε_{T+1}, all of which are normally distributed. Second, it has 0 mean, since

$$E(\hat{e}_{T+1}) = E(\hat{\alpha} - \alpha) + E(\hat{\beta} - \beta) X_{T+1} + E(-\varepsilon_{T+1}) = 0 \qquad (8.10)$$

(Remember that $\hat{\alpha}$ and $\hat{\beta}$ are unbiased estimators and that X_{T+1} is known.) Finally, we can determine the variance of $\hat{e}_{T+1}$:

$$\sigma_f^2 = E[(\hat{e}_{T+1})^2] = E[(\hat{\alpha} - \alpha)^2] + E[(\hat{\beta} - \beta)^2] X_{T+1}^2 + E[(\varepsilon_{T+1})^2]$$
$$+ E[(\hat{\alpha} - \alpha)(\hat{\beta} - \beta)] 2X_{T+1} \qquad (8.11)$$

or $\qquad \sigma_f^2 = \text{Var}(\hat{\alpha}) + 2X_{T+1} \text{Cov}(\hat{\alpha}, \hat{\beta}) + X_{T+1}^2 \text{Var}(\hat{\beta}) + \sigma^2 \qquad (8.12)$

Note that all the cross-product terms involving estimated parameters and ε_{T+1} become 0 when expected values are taken, since $\hat{\alpha} - \alpha$ and $\hat{\beta} - \beta$ depend on $\varepsilon_1, \ldots, \varepsilon_T$, all of which are independent of ε_{T+1}. Recall that we previously (Chapter 3) derived the variances of $\hat{\alpha}$ and $\hat{\beta}$ as well as their covariance:

$$\text{Var}(\hat{\alpha}) = \sigma^2 \frac{\Sigma X_t^2}{T \Sigma (X_t - \overline{X})^2} \qquad (8.13)$$

$$\text{Var}(\hat{\beta}) = \frac{\sigma^2}{\Sigma (X_t - \overline{X})^2} \qquad (8.14)$$

$$\text{Cov}(\hat{\alpha}, \hat{\beta}) = \frac{-\overline{X} \sigma^2}{\Sigma (X_t - \overline{X})^2} \qquad (8.15)$$

where the summations run from 1 to T and $\bar{X}$ is the sample mean of X for the first T observations. Substituting Eqs. (8.13) to (8.15) into Eq. (8.12) and manipulating terms, we get

$$\sigma_f^2 = \sigma^2 \left[\frac{\Sigma X_t^2}{T \Sigma (X_t - \bar{X})^2} - \frac{2 \bar{X} X_{T+1}}{\Sigma (X_t - \bar{X})^2} + \frac{X_{T+1}^2}{\Sigma (X_t - \bar{X})^2} + 1 \right] \qquad (8.16)$$

But
$$\frac{\Sigma X_t^2}{T \Sigma (X_t - \bar{X})^2} = \frac{\Sigma (X_t - \bar{X})^2 + T \bar{X}^2}{T \Sigma (X_t - \bar{X})^2} = \frac{1}{T} + \frac{\bar{X}^2}{\Sigma (X_t - \bar{X})^2} \qquad (8.17)$$

Therefore,
$$\sigma_f^2 = \sigma^2 \left[1 + \frac{1}{T} + \frac{\bar{X}^2 - 2 \bar{X} X_{T+1} + X_{t+1}^2}{\Sigma (X_t - \bar{X})^2} \right] \qquad (8.18)$$

or
$$\sigma_f^2 = \sigma^2 \left[1 + \frac{1}{T} + \frac{(X_{T+1} - \bar{X})^2}{\Sigma (X_t - \bar{X})^2} \right] \qquad (8.19)$$

Equation (8.19) tells us that the forecast error is sensitive to the size of the sample used in the estimation process as well as to the variance in X and the distance between X_{T+1} and $\bar{X}$.[2] Other things being equal, then, the larger the sample size and the greater the variance in X, the smaller the error of forecast. In addition, the error of forecast is smallest when X_{T+1} happens to be equal to the sample mean of X, since the last term in brackets in Eq. (8.19) then becomes 0. This suggests that the best forecasts about Y can be made for values of X around which the most sample information is available. This is not surprising; as the new value of X gets farther from the mean, it moves out of the range of experience used to estimate the model and generates less reliable forecasts. In general it is dangerous to extend a model much beyond its range of estimation. When time-series forecasts involve values of X_{T+1} that are substantially different from X, the resulting forecast error may be large.

If σ^2 were known, we could calculate σ_f^2 and then proceed to construct confidence intervals as before, relying on the knowledge that

$$\lambda = \frac{\hat{Y}_{T+1} - Y_{T+1}}{\sigma_f} \sim N(0, 1) \qquad (8.20)$$

However, σ^2 usually is not known, so that as a practical matter we use s^2 as an unbiased and consistent estimator of σ^2:

$$s^2 = \frac{1}{T-2} \Sigma (Y_t - \hat{Y}_t)^2 \qquad (8.21)$$

---

[2] Equation (8.19) shows the error for a point forecast. If we forecast the expected value of the outcome, the equation is modified by omitting the 1 in the bracketed expression. That term adds to the expected value of the forecast the error variance associated with selecting a single forecast from the distribution of possible forecasts.

As we saw in Chapter 3, this allows us to calculate confidence intervals by using the t distribution. Writing the *estimated* forecast error variance

$$s_f^2 = s^2 \left[1 + \frac{1}{T} + \frac{(X_{T+1} - \overline{X})^2}{\Sigma(X_t - \overline{X})^2} \right] \tag{8.22}$$

we know that the normalized error

$$\frac{\hat{Y}_{T+1} - Y_{T+1}}{s_f}$$

will be t-distributed with $T - 2$ degrees of freedom. The 95 percent confidence interval for $\hat{Y}_{T+1}$ is thus given by

$$\hat{Y}_{T+1} - t_{.05}s_f \leq Y_{T+1} \leq \hat{Y}_{T+1} + t_{.05}s_f \tag{8.23}$$

An example of the 95 percent confidence interval is shown in Fig. 8.3.

The principles just discussed also apply to the multiple regression model. Confidence intervals for forecasts generated by a multiple regression model will have the same shape as those in Fig. 8.3. When two or more explanatory variables are present, however, the algebraic derivations of the forecast error distribution and forecast confidence interval become more complex. We will relegate the formal discussion of the multiple regression model to Appendix 8.1.

FIGURE 8.3
Forecast confidence intervals.

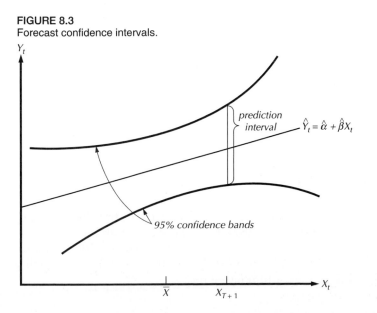

8.1.2   Evaluating Forecasts

After we have estimated a regression model and used it to forecast the dependent variable, how can we evaluate that forecast? One important statistic is the forecast error variance that we just derived and the associated 95 percent confidence interval. This confidence interval provides a good measure of the precision of the forecast.

In addition, we can *simulate* the model by solving it over time, using actual values for the explanatory variables. (If the equation contained a lagged dependent variable, we would use the *predicted* value of that variable, updating it period by period, to create a *dynamic simulation.*) Over the period for which we have data, we could then compare the forecasted series with the actual series. The objective is to see how closely the forecasted variable tracks its corresponding data series.

A number of different statistics can be used to quantitatively measure how closely the forecasted variable tracks the actual data. One measure that is often used is the *rms* (root-mean-square) *forecast error.* The rms error for the variable Y_t is defined as

$$\text{rms error} = \sqrt{\frac{1}{T}\sum_{t=1}^{T}(Y_t^s - Y_t^a)^2} \tag{8.24}$$

where Y_t^s = forecasted value of Y_t

$\quad\quad Y_t^a$ = actual value

$\quad\quad T$ = number of periods

The rms error is a measure of the deviation of the simulated variable from its time path. Of course, the magnitude of this error can be evaluated only by comparing it with the average size of the variable in question.

Another useful statistic is *Theil's inequality coefficient,* which is defined as

$$U = \frac{\sqrt{\dfrac{1}{T}\sum_{t=1}^{T}(Y_t^s - Y_t^a)^2}}{\sqrt{\dfrac{1}{T}\sum_{t=1}^{T}(Y_t^s)^2} + \sqrt{\dfrac{1}{T}\sum_{t=1}^{T}(Y_t^a)^2}} \tag{8.25}$$

Note that the numerator of U is just the rms forecast error, but the scaling of the denominator is such that U will always fall between 0 and 1. If $U = 0$, $Y_t^s = Y_t^a$ for all t and there is a perfect fit; if $U = 1$, the predictive performance of the model is as bad as it could possibly be. Hence, the Theil inequality coefficient measures the rms error in relative terms.

The Theil inequality coefficient can be decomposed in a useful way. It can be shown with a little algebra that

$$\frac{1}{T}\Sigma(Y_t^s - Y_t^a)^2 = (\bar{Y}^s - \bar{Y}^a)^2 + (\sigma_s - \sigma_a)^2 + 2(1 - \rho)\sigma_s\sigma_a \quad (8.26)$$

where $\bar{Y}^s$, $\bar{Y}^a$, σ_s, and σ_a are the means and standard deviations of the series Y_t^s and Y_t^a, respectively, and ρ is their correlation coefficient, that is, $\rho = (1/\sigma_s\sigma_a T) \Sigma(Y_t^s - \bar{Y}^s)(Y_t^a - \bar{Y}^a)$. We can then define the *proportions of inequality* as

$$U^M = \frac{(\bar{Y}^s - \bar{Y}^a)^2}{(1/T) \Sigma(Y_t^s - Y_t^a)^2} \quad (8.27)$$

$$U^S = \frac{(\sigma_s - \sigma_a)^2}{(1/T) \Sigma(Y_t^s - Y_t^a)^2} \quad (8.28)$$

and

$$U^C = \frac{2(1 - \rho)\sigma_s\sigma_a}{(1/T) \Sigma(Y_t^s - Y_t^a)^2} \quad (8.29)$$

The proportions U^M, U^S, and U^C are called the *bias*, the *variance*, and the *covariance proportions* of U, respectively. They are useful as a means of breaking down the simulation error into its characteristic sources. (Note that $U^M + U^S + U^C = 1$.)

The bias proportion U^M is an indication of systematic error, since it measures the extent to which the *average* values of the simulated and actual series deviate from each other. Whatever the value of the inequality coefficient U, we would hope that U^M would be close to zero. A large value of U^M (above .1 or .2) would mean that a systematic bias is present, so that revision of the model is necessary.

The variance proportion U^S indicates the ability of the model to replicate the degree of variability in the variable of interest. If U^S is large, it means that the actual series has fluctuated considerably while the simulated series shows little fluctuation, or vice versa; this would again indicate that the model should be revised. Finally, the covariance proportion U^C measures unsystematic error; i.e., it represents the remaining error after deviations from average values have been accounted for. Since it is unreasonable to expect predictions to be perfectly correlated with actual outcomes, this component of error is less worrisome than the other two. Indeed, for any value of $U > 0$, the ideal distribution of inequality over the three sources is $U^M = U^S = 0$ and $U^C = 1$.

Example 8.1 Forecasting Grade-Point Averages   Reconsider the grade-point-average example discussed in Chapters 1 and 3. In that example we estimated a linear relationship between grade-point average (Y) and family income (X) for a cross section of eight individuals. We are now in a position to forecast the grade-point average of individuals not in the original sample, given only information about their family incomes. In terms of the notation used in Chapter 1, the relevant information is as follows:

Estimated regression line $= \hat{Y}_i = 1.375 + .12X_i$

Estimated error variance $= s^2 = .109 \qquad N = 8$

$\bar{X} = 13.5 \qquad \Sigma(X_i - \bar{X})^2 = 162$

Assume that several individuals not in the original sample report their family income. We wish to predict grade-point average and to calculate confidence intervals. The relevant calculations are summarized in Table 8.1, while 95 percent confidence bands are shown in Fig. 8.4.

In Table 8.1, we see in the first column that the smallest error of forecast is associated with the family income of $13,500, the mean family income of the original sample. For that individual we can be reasonably confident that the final grade-point average will lie in the range of 2.1 to 3.9. The fact that the 95 percent prediction interval is so large, even at the point of minimum forecast error, suggests the limiting nature of the grade-point-average model. A more sophisticated model (with additional explanatory variables) and more sample observations would most likely lead to a smaller forecast interval. We should note also that the error of forecast grows nonlinearly as values for family income increase beyond the mean. In fact, the forecast interval for the last individual (with family income of $27,500) is not only large but also unrealistic, since a grade-point average of 4.675 is not within the experience of the original sample.

TABLE 8.1
GRADE-POINT-AVERAGE FORECAST CALCULATIONS

X_{N+1}	$\hat{Y}_{N+1}$	s_f^2	$\hat{Y}_{N+1} - 2.447s_f$	$\hat{Y}_{N+1} + 2.447s_f$
6.5	2.155	.156	1.189	3.121
10.0	2.575	.131	1.709	3.441
13.5	2.995	.123	2.137	3.853
17.0	3.315	.131	2.429	4.201
20.5	3.835	.156	2.869	4.801
24.0	4.155	.197	3.069	5.241
27.5	4.675	.254	3.442	5.908

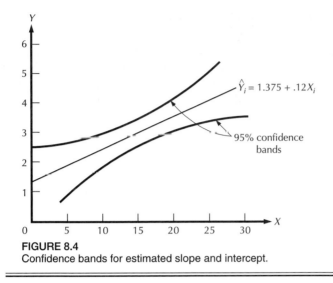

FIGURE 8.4
Confidence bands for estimated slope and intercept.

Example 8.2 Forecasting Interest Rates   In this example we use a simple regression model to forecast the interest rate on 3-month Treasury bills. We will use the model developed in Example 4.2. Recall that this model relates the monthly 3-month Treasury bill rate (R) to the index of industrial production (IP), the rate of growth of the broadly defined money supply $M2$ $(GM2_t = (M2_t - M2_{t-1})/M2_{t-1})$, and the lagged rate of wholesale price inflation, $GPW_t = (PW_t - PW_{t-1})/PW_{t-1}$, where PW is the producer price index for all commodities. In Example 4.2 we estimated this equation by using monthly data over the period January 1960 through August 1995. The OLS estimates (with t statistics in parentheses) were

$$\hat{R}_t = \underset{(2.20)}{1.214} + \underset{(8.79)}{.0484IP_t} + \underset{(3.89)}{140.33GM2_t} + \underset{(6.00)}{104.58GPW_{t-1}}$$

$$R^2 = .22 \qquad s = 2.4810 \qquad DW = .18$$

We will now use this equation to generate a forecast of the Treasury bill rate for the period January 1995 through February 1996. (Note that this forecast extends 6 months beyond the estimation period.) The forecasted path for the interest rate (dashed line) and the original series (solid line) are shown in Fig. 8.5. Note that the equation considerably overpredicts the interest rate throughout the forecast period.

We also calculated the rms forecast error and the Theil inequality coeffi-

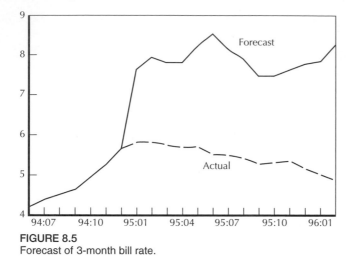

FIGURE 8.5
Forecast of 3-month bill rate.

cient along with its components for this forecast. These statistics, which are helpful in evaluating the forecast, are as follows:

Interest rate forecast evaluation	
Root-mean-squared error	2.504093
Theil inequality coefficient	0.187605
Bias proportion	0.973300
Variance proportion	0.000043
Covariance proportion	0.026657

Observe that the bias proportion of the Theil inequality coefficient is very large (about 97 percent). This simply means that a large systematic bias is present (as we can observe from Fig. 8.5), so that the model is not likely to be reliable for forecasting.

Note that the Durbin-Watson statistic for the regression equation was .18, indicating that the residuals are highly serially correlated. This suggests that the weak forecasting performance of this interest rate model might be improved by taking serial correlation into account. We will explore this possibility in the next section.

8.2 FORECASTING WITH SERIALLY CORRELATED ERRORS

When the error process is serially correlated in time-series models, the problem of determining the best forecast and its appropriate distribution becomes somewhat more difficult. Consider the two-variable model in which the errors are first-order serially correlated:

$$Y_t = \alpha + \beta X_t + \varepsilon_t \qquad \varepsilon_t = \rho\varepsilon_{t-1} + v_t$$

$$|\rho| < 1 \qquad v_t \sim N(0, \sigma_v^2)$$

In the previous section our best forecast for Y_{T+1} was determined by assigning ε_{T+1} the value 0 for the forecast period. This was reasonable, given that the errors had 0 mean and were independent over time. In the serially correlated case, however, we will make use of our knowledge of the errors in periods previous to the forecast period to modify our prediction of the error in period $T + 1$.

To pursue this matter further, assume that the regression parameters α, β, and ρ are known. We proceed by choosing the forecasted value of Y_{T+1} as follows:

$$\hat{Y}_{T+1} = \alpha + \beta X_{T+1} + \hat{\varepsilon}_{T+1} \tag{8.30}$$

Rather than setting $\hat{\varepsilon}_{T+1} = 0$, as in the previous section, we calculate $\hat{\varepsilon}_{T+1}$ from the previous error term. Since $\varepsilon_{T+1} = \rho\varepsilon_T + v_T$, we choose $\hat{\varepsilon}_{T+1} = \rho\hat{\varepsilon}_T$ (since v_t has 0 mean and is uncorrelated over time).[3] Therefore,

$$\hat{Y}_{T+1} = \alpha + \beta X_{T+1} + \rho\varepsilon_T \tag{8.31}$$

If we forecast farther into the future, the information provided by serial correlation becomes less and less useful, since

$$\hat{\varepsilon}_{T+2} = \rho\hat{\varepsilon}_{T+1} = \rho^2\hat{\varepsilon}_T$$

$$\hat{\varepsilon}_{T+3} = \rho\hat{\varepsilon}_{T+2} = \rho^3\hat{\varepsilon}_T$$

$$\cdots\cdots\cdots\cdots\cdots$$

$$\hat{\varepsilon}_{T+s} = \rho^s\hat{\varepsilon}_T$$

and ρ^s approaches zero as s gets arbitrarily large.

Note that the identical prediction of Y_{T+1} is obtained when we write the model in generalized difference form:

$$Y_t^* = \alpha(1 - \rho) + \beta X_t^* + v_t \tag{8.32}$$

where $\qquad Y_t^* = Y_t - \rho Y_{t-1} \qquad$ and $\qquad X_t^* = X_t - \rho X_{t-1}$

---

[3] Since α and β are known, there is no estimation involved, so that $\hat{\varepsilon}_T = \varepsilon_T$.

The appropriate forecast is then

$$\hat{Y}^*_{T+1} = \alpha(1 - \rho) + \beta X^*_{T+1} \tag{8.33}$$

where $\qquad \hat{Y}^*_{T+1} = \hat{Y}_{T+1} - \rho Y_T \qquad$ and $\qquad X^*_{T+1} = X_{T+1} - \rho X_T$

The equivalence of Eqs. (8.33) and (8.31) becomes apparent by writing

$$\begin{aligned} \hat{Y}_{T+1} &= \hat{Y}^*_{T+1} + \rho Y_T = \alpha(1 - \rho) + \beta X^*_{T+1} + \rho Y_T \\ &= \alpha(1 - \rho) + \beta X_{T+1} + \rho(Y_T - \beta X_T) \end{aligned}$$

But $Y_T = \alpha + \beta X_T + \varepsilon_T$. Therefore,

$$\hat{Y}_{T+1} = \alpha(1 - \rho) + \beta X_{T+1} + \rho(\alpha + \varepsilon_T) = \alpha + \beta X_{T+1} + \rho \varepsilon_T$$

which is identical to Eq. (8.31).

If α, β, and ρ are known, the forecast error is given by

$$\begin{aligned} \hat{e}_{T+1} &= \hat{Y}_{T+1} - Y_{T+1} = (\alpha + \beta X_{T+1} + \rho \varepsilon_T) - (\alpha + \beta X_{T+1} + \varepsilon_{T+1}) \\ &= \rho \varepsilon_T - \varepsilon_{T+1} = -v_{T+1} \end{aligned}$$

Thus, the forecast error is normally distributed with 0 mean and has a variance

$$\begin{aligned} \sigma_f^2 &= E[(\rho \varepsilon_T - \varepsilon_{T+1})^2] = \rho^2 E(\varepsilon_T^2) + E(\varepsilon_{T+1}^2) - 2\rho E(\varepsilon_T \varepsilon_{T+1}) \\ &= \rho^2 E(\varepsilon_T^2) + E(\varepsilon_{T+1}^2) - 2\rho^2 E(\varepsilon_T^2) \\ &= (1 - \rho^2)\sigma^2 = \sigma_v^2 \qquad \text{since } E(\varepsilon_{T+1}^2) = E(\varepsilon_T^2) = \sigma^2 \end{aligned}$$

Note that this forecast error is *smaller*, by a factor of $1 - \rho^2$, than would be the case if we did not take serial correlation into account.

In practice all three parameters α, β, and ρ usually are not known, but they can be estimated by using any of the estimation techniques described in Chapter 6. To produce the best forecast, one simply uses the estimated equation in generalized difference form. In other words, we calculate $\hat{Y}_{T+1}$ from

$$\hat{Y}_{T+1} = \hat{\rho} Y_T + \hat{\alpha}(1 - \hat{\rho}) + \hat{\beta}(X_{T+1} - \hat{\rho} X_T) \tag{8.34}$$

It can be proved that the mean of the error of forecast will approach zero as the sample size gets large. It is somewhat difficult to determine an explicit expression for the variance of the error of forecast when all three parameters α, β, and ρ have been estimated, since the estimation process guarantees that the estimated slope and intercept parameters will be correlated with the residuals of the regression. In practice, to calculate the variance of the error of forecast (and thus calculate a confidence interval on the forecast itself), we assume that ρ has been estimated exactly. In this case the forecast variance of

Eq. (8.19) applies to our estimated equation in *generalized difference form* (and thus with an error term v_t instead of ε_t). Once again the error of forecast for $\hat{Y}_{T+1}$ will have a smaller variance (and thus the 95 percent confidence bands will be narrower) than would be the case if serial correlation were not taken into account. We will examine this in the context of the multiple regression model in Appendix 8.1. We now turn to an example of forecasting in the presence of serially correlated errors.

Example 8.3 Forecasting Interest Rates   Let us return to the interest rate forecast from Example 8.2. The forecasting performance of our regression equation on that example was poor, but the low Durbin-Watson statistic suggested that part of the problem might be serial correlation in the error term. In Example 6.6 we reestimated our original interest rate equation from Example 4.2 with a correction for first-order serial correlation. The new regression equation (again estimated over the period January 1960 through August 1995) was

$$\hat{R}_t = -49.601 + .244IP_t - 62.358GM2_t + 6.210GPW_{t-1}$$
$$\quad\quad (-0.35) \quad\quad (6.01) \quad\quad (-6.55) \quad\quad\quad (2.09)$$

$$R^2 = .97 \quad\quad s = .500 \quad\quad DW = 1.64 \quad\quad \hat{\rho} = .99$$

Note that the estimated value of ρ, the serial correlation coefficient, is close to 1. The coefficient for the growth rate of the money supply is now negative (which is more consistent with economic theory) and is highly significant. The standard error of the regression is now much smaller, and the Durbin-Watson statistic is 1.64.

We used this new regression equation to once again generate a forecast of the interest rate for the period January 1995 through February 1996. The forecasted and actual series are shown in Fig. 8.6. Observe that the forecasted series is now much closer to the actual series and that there is no longer any systematic tendency to over- or underpredict the actual data. The improved forecasting performance is also evident from the rms forecast error and the components of the Theil inequality coefficient shown below.

Interest rate forecast evaluation	
Root-mean-squared error	0.309388
Theil inequality coefficient	0.028608
Bias proportion	0.038771
Variance proportion	0.060426
Covariance proportion	0.900803

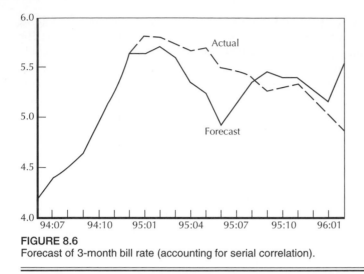

FIGURE 8.6
Forecast of 3-month bill rate (accounting for serial correlation).

Example 8.4 Forecasting Coal Demand[4] In this example we construct and use a forecasting model to predict, on a monthly basis, the demand for bituminous coal. We begin by specifying a linear equation that relates coal demand (COAL) to the Federal Reserve Board index of iron and steel production (FIS), the Federal Reserve Board index of electrical utility production (FEU), the wholesale price index for coal (PCOAL), and the wholesale price index for natural gas (PGAS). We use monthly data over the period January 1965 to December 1972 and a seasonally adjusted series for coal demand. We begin by estimating the equation using ordinary least squares. The regression results are shown below, with t statistics in parentheses:

$$\widehat{\text{COAL}} = 12{,}262 + 92.34\text{FIS} + 118.57\text{FEU} - 48.90\text{PCOAL}$$
$$\phantom{\widehat{\text{COAL}} = 12{,}262 +} (3.51) \qquad (6.46) \qquad\quad (7.14) \qquad\qquad (-3.82)$$

$$+ 118.91\text{PGAS} \qquad\qquad\qquad (8.35)$$
$$ (3.18)$$

$$R^2 = .692 \quad \bar{R}^2 = .675 \quad F(4/91) = 51.0 \quad s = 1{,}200 \quad \text{DW} = .95$$

[4] This example was first discussed in Example 6.5.

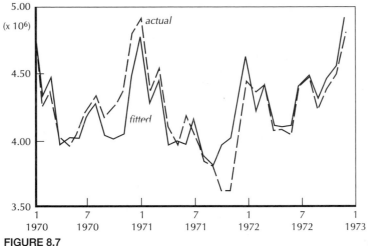

FIGURE 8.7
Coal demand, fitted versus actual. Time bounds: January 1970 to December 1972.

The fit of this equation is quite good, as can be seen both from the statistics and from Fig. 8.7, which compares actual and fitted coal demand over a 3-year period. One problem with the model, however, is the low DW statistic, indicating significant serial correlation.

To improve our forecast, we reestimate the equation by using the Hildreth-Lu regression procedure. In this procedure the equation is transformed using generalized differences:

$$(\text{COAL} - \rho\text{COAL}_{-1}) = c_0(1 - \rho) + c_1(\text{FIS} - \rho\text{FIS}_{-1}) + \cdots$$

Since ρ is not known, Hildreth-Lu performs OLS regressions on this equation by using several different values of ρ. Each time a regression is performed, the sum of squared residuals (ESS) is calculated, and the value of ρ that gives the smallest ESS is used in the final result. The Hildreth-Lu regression results for our coal demand equation are

$$\widehat{\text{COAL}} = 16{,}245 + 75.29\text{FIS} + 100.26\text{FEU} - 38.98\text{PCOAL}$$
$$\phantom{\widehat{\text{COAL}} = }(3.29) \qquad (4.38) \qquad\quad (3.73) \qquad\quad (-2.02)$$

$$+ \ 105.99\text{PGAS} \qquad \hat{\rho} = .60 \tag{8.36}$$
$$(1.96)$$

$$R^2 = .774 \quad \bar{R}^2 = .762 \quad F(4/90) = 77.1 \quad s = 998 \quad DW = 2.07$$

Note that the DW statistic is closer to 2.0 and that the standard error of the equation is smaller (998 versus 1,200 before). All the explanatory variables

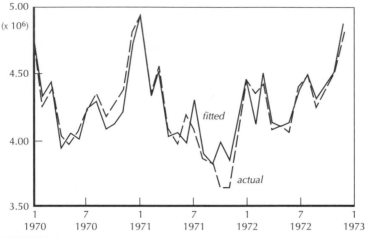

FIGURE 8.8
Coal demand, fitted versus actual with serial-correlation correction. Time bounds: January 1970 to December 1972.

continue to be significant. The fit of the equation can be seen graphically in Fig. 8.8, which compares the actual and fitted series over the 3-year period. A comparison of Fig. 8.8 with Fig. 8.7 shows the better fit afforded by the Hildreth-Lu procedure.

We now generate *ex post* forecasts over the 12-month period January 1973 to December 1973 and compare these forecasts with actual coal demand over that period. First we use Eq. (8.35) which does not account for serial correlation. These forecast results, together with the 95 percent confidence

FIGURE 8.9
Forecast of coal demand using OLS regression. Time bounds: January 1973 to December 1973.

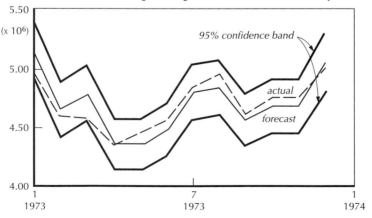

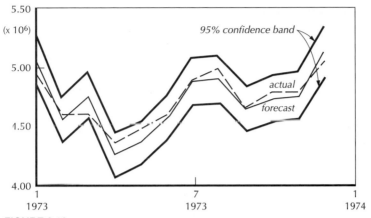

FIGURE 8.10
Forecast of coal demand using serial-correlation correction. Time bounds: January 1973 to December 1973.

band and the actual series for coal demand, are shown in Fig. 8.9. The results are quite good; the actual series always remains within the 95 percent confidence band and in fact is usually quite close to the predicted series.

We can generate even better forecasts, however, by using Eq. (8.36) in its generalized difference form, i.e., by applying Eq. (8.33) or (8.34). These results, again together with the 95 percent confidence band and the actual series, are shown in Fig. 8.10. Note that the 95 percent confidence band is *narrower* when serial correlation has been taken into account; whether our forecasts are *ex ante* or *ex post*, we will have greater confidence in them if we have adjusted our equation to correct for the serial correlation in the error terms. As we would expect, a comparison of the two figures shows that the forecasted series is closer to the actual series (i.e., the resulting forecast errors are indeed smaller) when serial correlation has been accounted for.

8.3 CONDITIONAL FORECASTING

Our previous discussion assumed that the explanatory variables are known without error. This may be an unrealistic assumption during *ex ante* forecasting, since some explanatory variables may have to be predicted into the future. One might expect that the stochastic nature of the predicted value of such X's will lead to forecasts of Y which are less reliable than they are in the fixed-X case. We shall see that the 95 percent confidence intervals for the error of forecast are indeed increased in size when the X's must themselves be predicted. However, because it is quite difficult to derive a formula for the error of forecast in a general setting, we will deal here with a special case which should be instruc-tive.[5]

Consider the following model:

$$Y_t = \alpha + \beta X_t + \varepsilon_t \qquad t = 1, 2, \ldots, T \qquad (8.37)$$

where $\hat{X}_{T+1} = X_{T+1} + u_{T+1}$, $\varepsilon_t \sim N(0, \sigma^2)$, and $u_t \sim N(0, \sigma_u^2)$; ε_t and u_t are uncorrelated. Also,

$$E[(\hat{X}_{T+1} - X_{T+1})(\hat{\beta} - \beta)] = E[(\hat{X}_{T+1} - X_{T+1})(\hat{\alpha} - \alpha)] = 0$$

where $\hat{\alpha}$ and $\hat{\beta}$ are the OLS estimates of α and β.

The model assumes that X_{T+1} is forecasted with a forecast error with 0 mean and constant variance. In addition, the error process associated with the forecast of X_{T+1} is assumed to be independent of the error process associated with each of the Y's in the model. Even though they are stochastic in nature, the X's are still assumed to be uncorrelated with the equation error term. The restrictive-ness of this model becomes clear when we consider the means by which fore-casted values of X_{T+1} might be obtained. One procedure is to extrapolate from the sample values of X. But the likelihood that the X variable is autocorrelated in a time-series model suggests that the error of forecast associated with the extrapolation procedure is itself likely to be serially correlated.

The forecasted value of Y in the time period $T + 1$ is defined by

$$\hat{Y}_{T+1} = \hat{\alpha} + \hat{\beta}\hat{X}_{T+1} \qquad (8.38)$$

The error of forecast is

$$\hat{e}_{T+1} = \hat{Y}_{T+1} - Y_{T+1} = (\hat{\alpha} - \alpha) + (\hat{\beta}\hat{X}_{T+1} - \beta X_{T+1}) - \varepsilon_{T+1} \qquad (8.39)$$

It is easy to see that this error has 0 mean:

$$E(\hat{e}_{T+1}) = E(\hat{\alpha} - \alpha) + E(\hat{\beta}\hat{X}_{T+1}) - \beta X_{T+1} - E(\varepsilon_{T+1})$$
$$= E[\hat{\beta}(X_{T+1} + u_{T+1})] - \beta X_{T+1} = \beta X_{T+1} - \beta X_{T+1} = 0 \qquad (8.40)$$

since $\hat{\beta}$ and u_{T+1} are uncorrelated.

The variance of the error of forecast is somewhat more difficult to derive:

$$\sigma_f^2 = E[(\hat{e}_{T+1})^2] = E[(\hat{\alpha} - \alpha)^2] + E[(\hat{\beta}\hat{X}_{T+1} - \beta X_{T+1})^2] + E[(\varepsilon_{T+1})^2]$$
$$+ 2E[(\hat{\alpha} - \alpha)(\hat{\beta}\hat{X}_{T+1} - \beta X_{T+1})] \qquad (8.41)$$

---

[5] This case is described in M. Feldstein, "The Error of Forecast in Econometric Models When the Forecast-Period Exogenous Variables Are Stochastic," *Econometrica,* vol. 39, pp. 55–60, January 1971.

But
$$\hat{\beta}\hat{X}_{T+1} - \beta X_{T+1} = \hat{\beta}(\hat{X}_{T+1} - X_{T+1}) + X_{T+1}(\hat{\beta} - \beta) \qquad (8.42)$$

Therefore,

$$
\begin{aligned}
E[(\hat{\beta}\hat{X}_{T+1} - \beta X_{T+1})^2] &= E[\hat{\beta}(\hat{X}_{T+1} - X_{T+1}) + X_{T+1}(\hat{\beta} - \beta)]^2 \\
&= E[\hat{\beta}^2(\hat{X}_{T+1} - X_{T+1})^2] + X_{T+1}^2 E[(\hat{\beta} - \beta)^2] \\
&= [\beta^2 + \mathrm{Var}\,(\hat{\beta})]\sigma_u^2 + X_{T+1}^2 \,\mathrm{Var}\,(\hat{\beta}) \qquad (8.43)
\end{aligned}
$$

Note that in arriving at Eq. (8.43) we took advantage of the fact that $u_{T+1} = \hat{X}_{T+1} - X_{T+1}$, that u_{T+1} and $\hat{\beta}$ are uncorrelated, and, finally, that $\hat{\beta}^2 = \beta^2 + \mathrm{Var}\,(\hat{\beta})$. Next, we can use Eq. (8.42) to simplify the last term in Eq. (8.41):

$$
\begin{aligned}
E[(\hat{\alpha} - \alpha)(\hat{\beta}\hat{X}_{T+1} - \beta X_{T+1})] & \\
= E[(\hat{\alpha} - \alpha)\hat{\beta}(\hat{X}_{T+1} - X_{T+1})] &+ X_{T+1}E[(\hat{\alpha} - \alpha)(\hat{\beta} - \beta)] \\
&= X_{T+1}\,\mathrm{Cov}\,(\hat{\alpha}, \hat{\beta}) \qquad (8.44)
\end{aligned}
$$

(The first term on the right is zero by assumption.) Now, by combining terms, we find that

$$
\begin{aligned}
\sigma_f^2 &= \mathrm{Var}\,(\hat{\alpha}) + [\beta^2 + \mathrm{Var}\,(\hat{\beta})]\sigma_u^2 + X_{T+1}^2\,\mathrm{Var}\,(\hat{\beta}) + 2X_{T+1}\,\mathrm{Cov}\,(\hat{\alpha}, \hat{\beta}) + \sigma^2 \\
&= \mathrm{Var}\,(\hat{\alpha}) + \mathrm{Var}\,(\hat{\beta})(X_{T+1}^2 + \sigma_u^2) + 2X_{T+1}\,\mathrm{Cov}\,(\hat{\alpha}, \hat{\beta}) + \sigma^2 + \beta^2\sigma_u^2
\end{aligned}
$$
$$(8.45)$$

When we put this in terms of our least-squares estimators, the formula for the variance of the error of forecast becomes

$$\sigma_f^2 = \sigma^2 \left[1 + \frac{1}{T} + \frac{(X_{T+1} - \bar{X})^2 + \sigma_u^2}{\Sigma(X_t - \bar{X})^2} \right] + \beta^2\sigma_u^2 \qquad (8.46)$$

A comparison of Eq. (8.46) with Eq. (8.19) from Section 8.1 makes it clear that forecasting X increases the forecast error. There are two additional nonnegative terms involved, both of which are minimized only when the forecast of X_{T+1} is exact. Unfortunately, it is difficult to describe the larger confidence intervals for the conditional error of forecast, since $\hat{Y}_{T+1}$ is not normally distributed. (It involves the sum of *products* of normally distributed variables.) While confidence intervals cannot be derived analytically, a rough estimate of the confidence interval might be obtained as follows:

1. Calculate the 95 percent confidence intervals associated with the forecast that would be obtained if we were to select $\hat{X}_{T+1}$ to be 2 standard deviations higher or lower, i.e., the confidence intervals associated with $Y_{T+1}^* = \hat{\alpha} + \hat{\beta}(\hat{X}_{T+1} + 2\sigma_u)$ and $Y_{T+1}^{**} = \hat{\alpha} + \hat{\beta}(\hat{X}_{T+1} - 2\sigma_u)$.

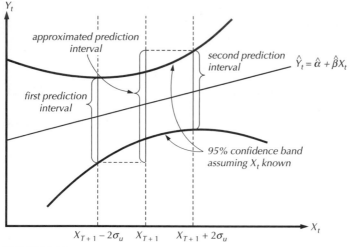

FIGURE 8.11
Approximating the prediction interval for a conditional forecast.

2. The final interval prediction is taken to be the union of the two confidence intervals; i.e., it contains all the values of $\hat{Y}_{T+1}$ common to both confidence intervals.

This process is depicted in Fig. 8.11.

The results of this section help elucidate some of the difficulties involved in the forecasting process. Even if the regression model has a good fit with statistically significant parameters, unconditional forecasts may not be very accurate. Forecasting explanatory variables introduces additional forecast error. A good regression model in terms of unconditional forecasting may perform quite badly when conditional forecasting is attempted. Thus, one should not reject a model with a high forecast error if the primary component of that error is due to an error in prediction involved with the explanatory variables. The problem is even more difficult in macroeconomic forecasting because an accurate initial conditional forecast may lead to a shift in policy and thus to an inaccurate forecast!

APPENDIX 8.1 Forecasting with the Multiple Regression Model

In this appendix we use matrix notation to generalize our discussion of the forecasting problem to the multivariate case. We begin by writing the general linear model in matrix form. The model contains a dependent variable and k independent variables (including the constant term) and is estimated over a total of T observations:

$$\mathbf{Y} = \mathbf{X}\boldsymbol{\beta} + \boldsymbol{\varepsilon} \tag{A8.1}$$

Recall that $\mathbf{Y}$ is a $T \times 1$ column vector of dependent variable observations, $\mathbf{X}$ is a $T \times k$ matrix of independent variable observations, $\boldsymbol{\beta}$ is a $k \times 1$ column vector of unknown parameters, and $\boldsymbol{\varepsilon}$ is a $T \times 1$ column vector of error terms. Then the ordinary least-squares estimate of $\boldsymbol{\beta}$ will be given by

$$\hat{\boldsymbol{\beta}} = (\mathbf{X}'\mathbf{X})^{-1}\mathbf{X}'\mathbf{Y} \tag{A8.2}$$

Now let us examine the characteristics of a forecast made using this estimated equation. Suppose we have a new set of observations (or even forecasts or guesses) for the independent variables for period $T + 1$. Then the forecast for the dependent variable in period $T + 1$ will be given by

$$\hat{Y}_{T+1} = \mathbf{X}_{T+1}\hat{\boldsymbol{\beta}} \tag{A8.3}$$

Note that $\mathbf{X}_{T+1}$ is a $1 \times k$ row vector, so that $\hat{Y}_{T+1}$ is a scalar. Similarly, if we wanted a forecast for period $T + 2$, that would be given by

$$\hat{Y}_{T+2} = \mathbf{X}_{T+2}\hat{\boldsymbol{\beta}} \tag{A8.4}$$

If all the independent variables appeared with lags greater than or equal to two periods, we could simply *observe* $\mathbf{X}_{T+2}$, but if some or all of the independent variables are not lagged, $\mathbf{X}_{T+2}$ will itself have to be forecasted and the forecast of Y_{T+2} will be conditional on the forecast of $\mathbf{X}_{T+2}$.

Since Eqs. (A8.3) and (A8.4) apply for any time period, we will drop the time subscript and rewrite our forecasting equation as

$$\hat{Y} = \tilde{\mathbf{X}}\hat{\boldsymbol{\beta}} \tag{A8.5}$$

where $\hat{Y}$ is a forecast of Y_t for some period and $\tilde{\mathbf{X}}$ is a set of observations on the independent variables for that same period. Finally, denote the *actual* value of Y by $\tilde{Y}$. Then the *forecast error* is given by

$$\hat{e} = \hat{Y} - \tilde{Y} \tag{A8.6}$$

Since the actual value $\tilde{Y}$ of Y can be written as

$$\tilde{Y} = \tilde{\mathbf{X}}\boldsymbol{\beta} + \tilde{\varepsilon} \tag{A8.7}$$

where $\tilde{\varepsilon}$ is the actual value of the additive error term in the forecast period, we can write the forecast error as

$$\hat{e} = \tilde{\mathbf{X}}\hat{\boldsymbol{\beta}} - \tilde{\varepsilon} - \tilde{\mathbf{X}}\boldsymbol{\beta} = -\tilde{\varepsilon} - \tilde{\mathbf{X}}\boldsymbol{\beta} + \tilde{\mathbf{X}}(\mathbf{X}'\mathbf{X})^{-1}\mathbf{X}'\mathbf{Y} \tag{A8.8}$$

Substituting Eq. (A8.1) into Eq. (A8.8), we have

$$
\hat{e} = -\tilde{\varepsilon} - \tilde{\mathbf{X}}\boldsymbol{\beta} + \tilde{\mathbf{X}}(\mathbf{X}'\mathbf{X})^{-1}\mathbf{X}'(\mathbf{X}\boldsymbol{\beta} + \varepsilon) = -\tilde{\varepsilon} - \tilde{\mathbf{X}}\boldsymbol{\beta} + \tilde{\mathbf{X}}\boldsymbol{\beta} + \tilde{\mathbf{X}}(\mathbf{X}'\mathbf{X})^{-1}\mathbf{X}'\varepsilon
$$
$$
= -\tilde{\varepsilon} + \tilde{\mathbf{X}}(\mathbf{X}'\mathbf{X})^{-1}\mathbf{X}\varepsilon \tag{A8.9}
$$

The variance of the forecast error is

$$
\sigma_f^2 = E[\hat{e}^2]
$$
$$
= E[\tilde{\varepsilon}^2] - 2\tilde{\mathbf{X}}(\mathbf{X}'\mathbf{X})^{-1}\mathbf{X}'E[\varepsilon\tilde{\varepsilon}] + \tilde{\mathbf{X}}(\mathbf{X}'\mathbf{X})^{-1}\mathbf{X}'E[\varepsilon\varepsilon']\mathbf{X}(\mathbf{X}'\mathbf{X})^{-1}\tilde{\mathbf{X}}' \tag{A8.10}
$$

We are assuming that the additive error terms are not autocorrelated, and therefore $E[\varepsilon\tilde{\varepsilon}] = 0$. We are also assuming that the error terms are homoscedastic, so that

$$
E[\varepsilon\varepsilon'] = \sigma^2\mathbf{I} \tag{A8.11}
$$

We can thus write the variance of the forecast error as

$$
\sigma_f^2 = \sigma^2 + \sigma^2\tilde{\mathbf{X}}(\mathbf{X}'\mathbf{X})^{-1}\mathbf{X}'\mathbf{I}\mathbf{X}(\mathbf{X}'\mathbf{X})^{-1}\tilde{\mathbf{X}}' = \sigma^2(1 + \tilde{\mathbf{X}}(\mathbf{X}'\mathbf{X})^{-1}\tilde{\mathbf{X}}') \tag{A8.12}
$$

We might now ask what the *smallest possible* forecast error variance could be, i.e., what value of $\tilde{\mathbf{X}}$ would minimize σ_f^2. We can answer this question by solving a *constrained minimization* problem in which we make use of the method of Lagrange multipliers. To minimize σ_f^2 we must minimize the matrix product on the right-hand side of Eq. (A8.12); that is, we want to

minimize $\tilde{\mathbf{X}}(\mathbf{X}'\mathbf{X})^{-1}\tilde{\mathbf{X}}'$ subject to $\tilde{X}_1 = 1$

The constraint that $\tilde{X}_1 = 1$ refers to the fact that the first element of $\tilde{\mathbf{X}}$ is the intercept of the regression equation. We can write the *lagrangian* for this problem as

$$
\mathscr{L} = \tilde{\mathbf{X}}(\mathbf{X}'\mathbf{X})^{-1}\tilde{\mathbf{X}}' - \lambda(\tilde{X}_1 - 1) \tag{A8.13}
$$

where λ is the Lagrange multiplier. Differentiating the lagrangian with respect to $\tilde{\mathbf{X}}$ and setting the derivative equal to 0 gives

$$
\frac{\partial\mathscr{L}}{\partial\tilde{\mathbf{X}}} = 2(\mathbf{X}'\mathbf{X})^{-1}\tilde{\mathbf{X}}' - \lambda\begin{bmatrix} 1 \\ 0 \\ \vdots \\ \vdots \\ 0 \end{bmatrix} = 0 \tag{A8.14}
$$

or
$$\tilde{\mathbf{X}}' = \frac{\lambda}{2} (\mathbf{X}'\mathbf{X}) \begin{bmatrix} 1 \\ 0 \\ \cdot \\ \cdot \\ \cdot \\ 0 \end{bmatrix} \qquad \text{(A8.15)}$$

Thus $\tilde{\mathbf{X}}'$ is proportional to the first column of $\mathbf{X}'\mathbf{X}$:

$$\tilde{\mathbf{X}}' = \frac{\lambda}{2} \begin{bmatrix} T \\ \Sigma X_2 \\ \Sigma X_3 \\ \cdot \\ \cdot \\ \cdot \\ \Sigma X_k \end{bmatrix} \qquad \text{(A8.16)}$$

The summations in Eq. (A8.16) are over the T observations. From the first row of Eq. (A8.16), since $\tilde{X}_1 = 1$,

$$\frac{\lambda}{2} T = 1 \qquad \text{or} \qquad \lambda = \frac{2}{T}$$

We can thus write Eq. (A8.16) as

$$\tilde{\mathbf{X}}' = \begin{bmatrix} 1 \\ \dfrac{\Sigma X_2}{T} \\ \dfrac{\Sigma X_3}{T} \\ \cdot \\ \cdot \\ \cdot \\ \dfrac{\Sigma X_k}{T} \end{bmatrix} \qquad \text{(A8.17)}$$

But note that the right-hand side of Eq. (A8.17) is the *point of means*. Thus, as was the case in the two-variable model, the forecast error variance is minimized when all the new observations on the independent variables are equal to their mean values. What is the value of this minimum forecast error variance? Writing Eq. (A8.17) as

$$\tilde{\mathbf{X}}' = \frac{1}{T} (\mathbf{X}'\mathbf{X}) \begin{bmatrix} 1 \\ 0 \\ \cdot \\ \cdot \\ \cdot \\ 0 \end{bmatrix} \qquad \text{(A8.18)}$$

and substituting this into Eq. (A8.12), we have

$$\min(\sigma_f^2) = \sigma^2 \left\{ 1 + \frac{1}{T}[1 \quad 0 \quad \cdots \quad 0](\mathbf{X'X})(\mathbf{X'X})^{-1}(\mathbf{X'X}) \begin{bmatrix} 1 \\ 0 \\ \cdot \\ \cdot \\ \cdot \\ 0 \end{bmatrix} \frac{1}{T} \right\}$$

$$= \sigma^2 \left(1 + \frac{T}{T^2} \right) = \sigma^2 \left(1 + \frac{1}{T} \right) \tag{A8.19}$$

Now what will our 95 percent confidence regions look like? They will be a multidimensional version of Fig. 8.3. In the case of two independent variables (in addition to the constant term), the 95 percent confidence region will be bounded by two hyperboloids. The confidence interval will be smallest at the mean values of X_1 and X_2.

EXERCISES

8.1 For the regression model $Y_t = \alpha + \beta X_t + \varepsilon_t$:

(a) Suppose α is known. What is the appropriate method for forecasting Y_{T+1}? Show that the error variance of the forecast is given by

$$\sigma^2 \left(1 + \frac{X_{T+1}^2}{\Sigma X_t^2} \right)$$

(b) Suppose β is known. Find the appropriate method for forecasting Y_{T+1} and show that the error variance of the forecast will be

$$\sigma^2 \left(1 + \frac{1}{T} \right)$$

Hint: (1) In the model $Y_t = \alpha + \varepsilon_t$, the least-squares estimator of α is given by $\hat{\alpha} = (1/T)\Sigma Y_i$ and the variance of $\hat{\alpha} = \sigma^2/T$, where $\sigma^2 = \text{Var}(\varepsilon_t)$. (2) In the model $Y_t = \beta X_t + \varepsilon_t$, the least-squares estimator of β is given by $\hat{\beta} = \Sigma X_i Y_i / \Sigma X_i^2$ and the variance of $\hat{\beta} = \sigma^2 / \Sigma X_i^2$.

8.2 In Fig. 8.5 in Example 8.2, the actual series for the interest rate diverges considerably from the forecasted series in 1995. Suggest why the regression model failed during this year.

SINGLE-EQUATION ESTIMATION: ADVANCED TOPICS

In the last eight chapters we completed the development of the core of econometrics, the general linear model. In this chapter we continue our discussion of single-equation estimation by discussing four more advanced topics. The first relates to distributed lag models and their estimation. We focus on two of the most frequently used lag structures: the geometric lag and the polynomial distributed lag.

Next, we show how simple lag models can be used to test for *causality*, i.e., whether changes in one variable can be viewed as a cause of changes in another variable. Third, we consider several means of resolving the dilemma which arises when there are missing observations. The loss of efficiency which results when observations are dropped from the sample is compared with the risks of replacing missing observations with suitable substitutes.

We then provide a brief introduction to the estimation of regression models using a combination of cross-section and time-series data. Several alternative schemes for pooling data are contemplated, and whenever possible the corresponding estimation techniques are described.

9.1 DISTRIBUTED LAG MODELS

In time-series models a substantial period of time may pass between the economic decision-making period and the impact of a change in a policy variable. If the appropriate decision-and-response period is sufficiently long, lagged explanatory variables should be included explicitly in the model. As an example, consider an aggregate consumption function which is to be estimated using quarterly macroeconomic data. One might specify consumption C_t to be a function of aggregate disposable income lagged one quarter Y_{t-1}. The specification of a model's lag structure is a function of the time units of the data. If the same consumption function were specified using annual data, it might be reasonable to drop the lag in the income variable, since the period of measurement is substantially larger than the reaction period.

This simple example assumes that the entire effect of the explanatory variable occurs in one time period. More generally, one would specify that economic changes can be distributed over a number of time periods; this is the basis of the *distributed lag model*, in which a series of lagged explanatory variables accounts for the time-adjustment process. In its most general form the distributed lag model can be written

$$Y_t = \alpha + \beta_0 X_t + \beta_1 X_{t-1} + \beta_2 X_{t-2} + \cdots = \alpha + \sum_{s=0}^{\infty} \beta_s X_{t-s} + \varepsilon_t \quad (9.1)$$

Unless we state otherwise, we will assume that the error term is normally distributed, independent of X, and neither serially correlated nor heteroscedastic. We allow the number of lags to be infinite, although many examples involve a finite lag structure. If the lag structure is infinite, the sequence of lag weights which describe the pattern of the lag response must have a finite sum or the model will not have a finite solution.

If the number of terms in the distributed lag is small, the equation can be estimated by using ordinary least squares. However, when there are many terms and little is known about the form of the lag, direct estimation uses up a large number of degrees of freedom and is likely to lead to imprecise parameter estimates because of multicollinearity. Fortunately, these difficulties can be resolved if one specifies some conditions about the form of the distributed lag. To pursue this topic we describe below two of the most frequently posited lag structures.[1]

9.1.1   Geometric Lag

The geometric lag assumes that the weights of the lagged explanatory variables are all positive and decline geometrically with time. The model is

$$Y_t = \alpha + \beta(X_t + wX_{t-1} + w^2 X_{t-2} + \cdots) + \varepsilon_t$$

$$= \alpha + \beta \sum_{s=0}^{\infty} w^s X_{t-s} + \varepsilon_t \qquad 0 < w < 1 \quad (9.2)$$

---

[1] For a more advanced discussion of distributed lag models, the reader is referred to P. Dhrymes, *Distributed Lags: Problems of Estimation and Formulation* (San Francisco: Holden-Day, 1971); Z. Griliches, "Distributed Lags: A Survey," *Econometrica*, vol. 35, pp. 16–49, 1967; and M. Nerlove, "Lags in Economic Behavior," *Econometrica*, vol. 40, pp. 221–251, 1972.

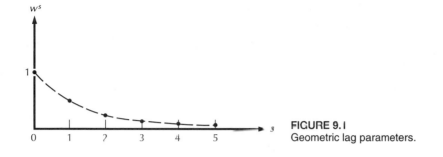

FIGURE 9.1
Geometric lag parameters.

The pattern of parameters associated with the model is depicted in Fig. 9.1 (for $w - \frac{1}{2}$). While the weights of the geometric lag model never become zero, they do diminish, so that beyond a reasonable time the effect of the explanatory variable becomes negligible.

It is useful to describe the lag structure of a distributed lag model in terms of its mean lag and in terms of the long-run response of the dependent variable to a permanent change in one of the explanatory variables. The *long-run response* m is the parameter β times the sum of the lag weights (Σw^s) or $\beta/(1 - w)$, with m measuring the change in Y associated with a 1-unit increase in X which stays in effect for all time.[2] The *mean lag*, by contrast, is defined as a lag-weighted average of time, i.e.,

$$\text{Mean lag} = \frac{\sum\limits_{s=0}^{\infty} s\beta_s}{\sum\limits_{s=0}^{\infty} \beta_s} \qquad \text{where } \beta_s = \beta w^s$$

In the geometric lag model the mean lag is $w/(1 - w)$, since[3]

$$\frac{\sum\limits_{s=0}^{\infty} s\beta_s}{\sum\limits_{s=0}^{\infty} \beta_s} = \frac{\beta\Sigma sw^s}{\beta\Sigma w^s} = \frac{w/(1 - w)^2}{1/(1 - w)} = \frac{w}{(1 - w)}$$

If $w = \frac{1}{2}$, for example, the mean lag of 1 suggests that half the impact of a change in Y will be felt during the first time period.

In its present form the geometric lag model appears difficult to estimate,

---

[2] Recall the sum of an infinite series such as $\Sigma w^s = 1/(1 - w)$. To prove this, let $\Sigma_{s=0}^{\infty} w^s = k$. Multiplying by w implies that $\Sigma_{s=1}^{\infty} w^s = kw$. Subtracting, we get $1 = k(1 - w)$ or $k = 1/(1 - w)$.

[3] The fact that $\Sigma sw^s = w/(1 - w)^2$ follows after some manipulation:

$$\Sigma sw^s = \sum\limits_{s=1}^{\infty} w^s + \sum\limits_{s=2}^{\infty} w^s + \sum\limits_{s=3}^{\infty} w^s + \cdots = \frac{1}{1 - w} \sum\limits_{s=1}^{\infty} w^s = \frac{w}{(1 - w)^2}$$

since it involves an infinite number of regressors. However, the parametric form of the lag weights allows for a substantial simplification of the model. To see this, we rewrite the original model [Eq. (9.2)] with all observations lagged one period:

$$Y_{t-1} = \alpha + \beta(X_{t-1} + wX_{t-2} + \cdots) + \varepsilon_{t-1} \tag{9.3}$$

Then we calculate the expression $Y_t - wY_{t-1}$ to obtain

$$Y_t - wY_{t-1} = \alpha(1 - w) + \beta X_t + u_t \tag{9.4}$$

where $u_t = \varepsilon_t - w\varepsilon_{t-1}$. Rewriting,

$$Y_t = \alpha(1 - w) + wY_{t-1} + \beta X_t + u_t \tag{9.5}$$

Equation (9.5) makes it somewhat easier to measure the effect of a continuous 1-unit change in X on the value of Y. In the first time period the effect is β. However, in the second period Y_{t-1} has increased by β, so that the effect has now become $\beta + \beta w = \beta(1 + w)$. After T periods the effect is $\beta\Sigma_{s=0}^{T-1} w^s = \beta(1 - w^T)/(1 - w)$,[4] while the long-run response is $\beta/(1 - w)$.

It sometimes is useful to calculate the *median lag*, i.e., the value of time T for which the fraction of adjustment completed is equal to $\frac{1}{2}$. To find the median lag we solve

$$\frac{T\text{-period response}}{\text{Long-run response}} = \frac{\beta(1 - w^T)/(1 - w)}{\beta/(1 - w)} = \frac{1}{2}$$

Solving for T, we find that

$$T = \frac{\log \frac{1}{2}}{\log w}$$

Equation (9.5) can be estimated more easily than can Eq. (9.2), since only three parameters remain unknown. However, before further considering the estimation, we need to ascertain whether the model specification is appropriate.

Adaptive Expectations Model   The *adaptive expectations model* postulates that changes in Y are related to changes in the "expected" level of the explanatory variable X. We would write this model as

$$Y_t = \alpha^* + \beta^* X_t^* + \varepsilon_t^* \tag{9.6}$$

---

[4] Again, summing a geometric series.

where X^* represents the desired or expected level of X. For instance, X^* might represent permanent income in the aggregate-consumption example described previously, or an expected price in a microeconometric model. The expected level of X is defined by a second relationship in which expectations are assumed to be altered in every time period as an adjustment between the current observed value of X and the previous expected value of X. The relationship is

$$X_t^* - X_{t-1}^* = \theta(X_t - X_{t-1}^*) \qquad \text{where } 0 < \theta \le 1 \qquad (9.7)$$

It is sometimes more useful to rewrite Eq. (9.7) as

$$X_t^* = \theta X_t + (1 - \theta) X_{t-1}^* \qquad (9.8)$$

This suggests that the expected level of X (permanent income or expected price) is a weighted average of the present level of X and the previous expected level of X. Expected levels of X are adjusted period by period, by taking into account present levels of X. To posit the adaptive expectations model in a form which allows econometric estimation, rewrite Eq. (9.8) by lagging the model period by period while at the same time multiplying by $(1 - \theta)^s$, where s is the number of periods involved in the lag process:

$$(1 - \theta) X_{t-1}^* = \theta(1 - \theta) X_{t-1} + (1 - \theta)^2 X_{t-2}^*$$
$$(1 - \theta)^2 X_{t-2}^* = \theta(1 - \theta)^2 X_{t-2} + (1 - \theta)^3 X_{t-3}^* \qquad (9.9)$$

Now substitute Eq. (9.9) into Eq. (9.8) and combine terms:

$$X_t^* = \theta \left[X_t + (1 - \theta) X_{t-1} + (1 - \theta)^2 X_{t-2} + \cdots \right] = \theta \sum_{s=0}^{\infty} (1 - \theta)^s X_{t-s} \qquad (9.10)$$

Note that the desired level of X is a weighted average of all present and previous values of X, since the weights sum to unity $[\theta \Sigma (1 - \theta)^s = 1]$. Substituting Eq. (9.10) into Eq. (9.6), we get

$$Y_t = \alpha^* + \beta^* \theta \sum_{s=0}^{\infty} (1 - \theta)^s X_{t-s} + \varepsilon_t^* \qquad (9.11)$$

The equivalence of this model to the original geometric lag model [Eq. (9.2)] can be seen by letting

$$\alpha = \alpha^* \qquad \beta = \beta^* \theta \qquad w = (1 - \theta) \qquad \text{and} \qquad \varepsilon_t = \varepsilon_t^*$$

Thus, estimation of the specification associated with the adaptive expectations model is identical to the problem of estimating the geometric lag, with Eq. (9.5) now becoming

$$Y_t = \alpha^*\theta + \beta^*\theta X_t + (1 - \theta) Y_{t-1} + u_t^* \tag{9.12}$$

where $u_t^* = \varepsilon_t^* - (1 - \theta) \varepsilon_{t-1}^*$.

Stock Adjustment Model   The *stock adjustment model* assumes that the desired level of Y is dependent on the current level of X, that is,

$$Y_t^* = \alpha' + \beta'X_t + \varepsilon_t' \tag{9.13}$$

In the consumption example Y_t^* might represent a desired expenditure level, while in the demand example it might represent the desired quantity to be supplied or the desired acreage to be farmed. In any given period the actual value of Y may not adjust completely to obtain the desired level or stock. Lack of knowledge, technical constraints, and other factors may be responsible for this partial adjustment. We can represent the adjustment process as

$$Y_t - Y_{t-1} = \gamma(Y_t^* - Y_{t-1}) \qquad 0 < \gamma < 1 \tag{9.14}$$

The equation specifies that the change in Y will respond only partially to the difference between the desired stock of Y and the past value of Y, with the rate of response being a function of the adjustment coefficient γ. Substituting for Y_t^* in Eq. (9.14) and solving for Y_t yields

$$Y_t = \alpha'\gamma + \gamma\beta'X_t + (1 - \gamma) Y_{t-1} + \gamma\varepsilon_t' \tag{9.15}$$

Once again the stock adjustment model bears a close relationship to the geometric lag model. The two are equivalent in form [see Eq. (9.5)] if we let

$$\alpha = \alpha' \qquad \beta = \gamma\beta' \qquad w = 1 - \gamma \qquad \text{and} \qquad u_t = \gamma\varepsilon_t'$$

However, the equivalence of the models is not complete, because they involve a different set of assumptions about the error structure. To see this, rewrite Eq. (9.15), lagging the model one period and then substituting for Y_{t-1}. Iterating this procedure and collecting terms, we obtain

$$Y_t = \alpha' + \beta'\gamma[X_t + (1 - \gamma) X_{t-1} + (1 - \gamma)^2 X_{t-2} + \cdots] + v_t \tag{9.16}$$

$$v_t = \gamma\varepsilon_t' + \gamma(1 - \gamma)\varepsilon_{t-1}' + \gamma(1 - \gamma)^2\varepsilon_{t-2}' + \cdots$$

or $\qquad Y_t = \alpha' + \beta'\gamma \sum_{s=0}^{\infty} (1 - \gamma)^s X_{t-s} + \gamma \sum_{s=0}^{\infty} (1 - \gamma)^s \varepsilon_{t-s}' \tag{9.17}$

Unlike the original error specification, the error process associated with the stock adjustment model is a moving-average error process.

9.1.2   Geometric Lag Estimation

In this section we briefly outline some of the issues involved in the estimation of the geometric lag model. Recall that such a model can be transformed into a single-equation autoregressive model with a single lagged dependent variable:

$$Y_t = \alpha(1 - w) + wY_{t-1} + \beta X_t + u_t \qquad (9.18)$$

Depending on the model chosen, the error process may follow several alternative assumptions. Consider first the case in which the error term is normally distributed with constant variance and is not serially correlated. As a general rule the geometric lag specification will introduce serial correlation if the original error specified is not autocorrelated. However, the transformation procedure might conceivably eliminate any serial correlation that was originally present.[5] Then the presence of a lagged dependent variable in the model causes ordinary least-squares parameter estimates to be biased, although they remain consistent.

Now consider the estimation problem when the error term follows the pattern suggested by both the geometric lag and the adaptive expectations models: $u_t = \varepsilon_t - w\varepsilon_{t-1}$. In this case ordinary least-squares estimates become inconsistent as well as biased. The difficulty arises because u_t and Y_{t-1} are correlated and the correlation does not disappear as the sample size gets larger (in the probability limit). A number of estimation procedures are available which involve the use of either an instrumental-variables technique or maximum likelihood, but they are too complex to present in detail here.[6] Perhaps the simplest procedure would be to use instrumental-variables estimation with X_{t-1} serving as an instrument for Y_{t-1}. This will yield consistent estimates but is not likely to be very efficient.

Finally, consider a third error specification involving first-order serial correlation, i.e.,

$$u_t = \rho u_{t-1} + \varepsilon_t$$

Once again though, ordinary least-squares parameter estimates will be inconsistent and biased, with the direction of the large sample bias relating directly to the sign of ρ.[7] Both instrumental-variables estimation and maximum-likeli-

---

[5] If $\varepsilon_t = w\varepsilon_{t-1} + u_t$, the transformation process will yield the error process u_t, which is not autocorrelated.

[6] See, for example, J. Kmenta, *Elements of Econometrics* (New York: Macmillan, 1986), Section 11-4.

[7] See Z. Griliches, "A Note on the Serial Correlation Bias in Estimates of Distributed Lags," *Econometrica*, vol. 29, pp. 65–73, 1971.

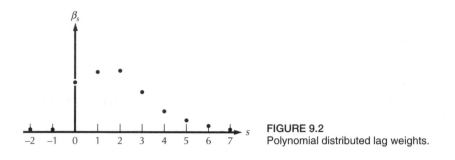

FIGURE 9.2
Polynomial distributed lag weights.

hood estimation are available alternatives. The instrumental-variables estimation process yields consistent estimates, but tends to be inefficient given the known presence of serial correlation. The instrument to replace Y_{t-1} can be obtained by a first-stage regression in which Y_{t-1} is the dependent variable and a series of lagged values of X make up the explanatory variables. The efficiency of this estimator can be improved if the estimated intercept and slope parameters are used to obtain an estimate of the serial-correlation coefficient ρ. We do this by calculating the residuals associated with the estimated intercept and slope parameters. A regression of u_t on u_{t-1} yields an estimate of the serial-correlation coefficient. Once ρ is estimated, the generalized differencing process can be used to reestimate the parameters of the original equation (see Chapter 6).

9.1.3   Polynomial Distributed Lag

The geometric lag formulation is limited because it hypothesizes a declining set of lag weights.[8] A more general formulation is the *polynomial distributed lag* model. The polynomial lag model assumes that the lag weights can be specified by a continuous function, which in turn can be approximated by evaluating a polynomial function at the appropriate discrete points in time. We might assume, for example, that $w_i = c_0 + c_1 i + c_2 i^2$ for $i = 0, 1, 2, 3, \ldots, 6$ and $w_i = 0$ for i less than 0 and greater than 6. This specifies lag weights that are to follow a second-degree polynomial for the first six lagged values and are 0 otherwise. The lag weights might appear as shown in Fig. 9.2.

When specifying a polynomial distributed lag model, we should be sure that the degree of the polynomial is less than the number of terms in the distributed

---

[8] It is possible, of course, to allow the first several lag terms to be estimated freely and to impose the geometric lag assumption on lagged values of the explanatory variable beyond the first several terms.

lag minus 1 or there will be no reduction in the number of lag parameters to be estimated.[9] The choice of endpoint restrictions is an optional one, however. If we do not wish to restrict the lag weights to be 0 outside the lag interval, one or both of the endpoint restrictions may be eliminated.

To understand how the polynomial distributed lag model is estimated, consider the case of a third-degree polynomial with a five-period lag (no endpoint restrictions). The lag specification is

$$Y_t = \alpha + \beta(w_0 X_t + w_1 X_{t-1} + \cdots + w_4 X_{t-4}) + \varepsilon_t \tag{9.19}$$

Assume that

$$w_i = c_0 + c_1 i + c_2 i^2 + c_3 i^3 \qquad i = 0, 1, 2, 3, 4 \tag{9.20}$$

Substituting and rewriting, we get

$$\begin{aligned} Y_t = \alpha &+ \beta c_0 X_t + \beta(c_0 + c_1 + c_2 + c_3) X_{t-1} \\ &+ \beta(c_0 + 2c_1 + 4c_2 + 8c_3) X_{t-2} \\ &+ \beta(c_0 + 3c_1 + 9c_2 + 27c_3) X_{t-3} \\ &+ \beta(c_0 + 4c_1 + 16c_2 + 64c_3) X_{t-4} + \varepsilon_t \end{aligned} \tag{9.21}$$

Combining terms, we have

$$\begin{aligned} Y_t = \alpha &+ \beta c_0 (X_t + X_{t-1} + X_{t-2} + X_{t-3} + X_{t-4}) \\ &+ \beta c_1 (X_{t-1} + 2X_{t-2} + 3X_{t-3} + 4X_{t-4}) \\ &+ \beta c_2 (X_{t-1} + 4X_{t-2} + 9X_{t-3} + 16X_{t-4}) \\ &+ \beta c_3 (X_{t-1} + 8X_{t-2} + 27X_{t-3} + 64X_{t-4}) + \varepsilon_t \end{aligned} \tag{9.22}$$

Equation (9.22) can be estimated by using ordinary least squares. If the error term obeys the classical assumptions of econometrics, the estimated c's will be best linear unbiased estimates.[10] (Once the c's are known, it is a simple procedure to calculate the original lag weights, the w's.) Standard errors for each of the lag weights can be obtained from the variance-covariance matrix of the c's, but the calculations are too involved to include here. In general, statistical tests

---

[9] In addition, the number of observations available must be greater than or equal to the degree of the polynomial plus 2. The two extra observations are needed if the endpoints of the lag are fixed by assumption.

[10] As written, it is impossible to estimate β directly. One simply assumes that $\beta = 1$, allowing the estimated lag weights to incorporate the effect of the true parameter β. To estimate with endpoint restrictions we need to add constraints to Eq. (9.21) before doing the estimation in Eq. (9.22). For example, to set the tail $= 0$, we set $w_5 = 0$ in Eq. (9.20). Then we substitute this constraint in Eq. (9.21) and obtain a new version of Eq. (9.22).

that are performed must be done through the estimated equation [Eq. (9.22)] and not directly through the specified equation [Eq. (9.21)].[11]

9.1.4   Choosing the Number of Lags

When one is specifying a distributed lag model (polynomial or otherwise), how should one decide how many lags to include? This is a question of model specification, and as such, it has no clear or simple answer. Often the number of lags to include on the right-hand side of an equation can be determined, at least roughly, from theory. For example, we might expect that the demand for a product would depend on lagged prices as well as the current price of the product, but that only lagged prices going back as far as 6 months should affect demand.

In many cases, however, it is not clear on the basis of theory alone how many lags to include in an equation. Then we must look to the data to determine the "correct" number of lags. There are a number of ways to do this.

One approach is to use the *corrected* R^2 to determine how many lags to add. Recall from Chapter 4 that a problem with using the ordinary R^2 as a measure of goodness of fit is that it does not account for the number of degrees of freedom. (Adding additional right-hand-side variables to a regression will always increase the R^2.) The corrected R^2 measures the percentage of *variance* in the dependent variable (as opposed to variation) explained by the independent variables:

$$\bar{R}^2 = 1 - \frac{\widehat{\text{Var}}\,(\varepsilon)}{\widehat{\text{Var}}\,(y)}$$

We saw in Chapter 4 that the corrected R^2 is related to the R^2 as follows:

$$\bar{R}^2 = 1 - (1 - R^2)\frac{N - 1}{N - k}$$

where N is the number of observations and k is the number of independent variables. Hence, when one is adding additional independent variables to a regression, $\bar{R}^2$ can increase or decrease. Thus, one approach to selecting the number of lags in a distributed lag model is simply to add additional lags until the corrected R^2 stops increasing.

Another approach is to use the *Akaike information criterion:*

$$\text{AIC} = \log\left(\frac{\Sigma\hat{\varepsilon}_i^2}{N}\right) + \frac{2k}{N}$$

[11] More complex lag formulations can be made with the use of *rational distributed lags.* See A. Pagan, "Rational and Polynomial Lags," *Journal of Econometrics*, vol. 8, pp. 242–254, 1978. The *rational expectations* literature in economics suggests a number of possible lag specifications that all have the property that the parameters of the lag distribution are endogenous and may change over time. See R. J. Barro, "Unanticipated Money Growth and Unemployment in the United States," *American Economic Review*, vol. 67, pp. 101–115, 1977.

where $\Sigma\hat{\varepsilon}_i^2$ is the sum of the squared residuals. The AIC differs from the corrected R^2 in that it penalizes the addition of right-hand-side variables (which reduces the number of degrees of freedom) more heavily. In principle, one could select a lag structure by increasing the number of lags up to the point where the AIC reaches a minimum value.

Another statistic which is closely related to the AIC is the *Schwartz criterion:*

$$SC = \log\left(\frac{\Sigma\hat{\varepsilon}_i^2}{N}\right) + \frac{k\log N}{N}$$

This formula also penalizes the addition of right-hand-side variables more heavily than does the corrected R^2.

Note that neither the corrected R^2, the AIC, nor the SC provides a clear statistical test for the comparison of alternative model specifications. Nonetheless, these statistics provide information which, when combined with judgment, can help determine the specification of a lag structure.

Example 9.1 Consumption Function In modeling the aggregate-consumption function, it is plausible to assume that consumption in the present period C_t is a direct function of personal disposable income Y_t in the present and past periods and the interest rate r_t. We expect that a higher interest rate, other things being equal, will be associated with more savings and less consumption. If we were to regress C_t on Y_t and r_t, a low DW statistic would result, signaling the presence of positive first-order serial correlation. For this reason, a decision was made to estimate an elementary form of the aggregate-consumption function using first differences and a polynomial distributed lag formulation. The model, estimated from the first quarter of 1950 through the first quarter of 1995, is[12]

$$\Delta C_t = \alpha + \beta_0\,\Delta Y_t + \beta_1\,\Delta Y_{t-1} + \cdots + \beta_4\,\Delta Y_{t-4} + \gamma r_t + \varepsilon_t$$

where C_t = quarterly personal consumption expenditures (billions of dollars)
  $\Delta C_t = C_t - C_{t-1}$
  Y_t = quarterly disposable personal income (billions of dollars)
  $\Delta Y_t = Y_t - Y_{t-1}$
  r_t = 3-month average of daily Treasury bill interest rates

A first attempt at model estimation using a five-period third-degree polynomial with no endpoint restrictions yielded the following regression results (t statistics in parentheses):

[12] This example is based on Citibase database variables GC, GYD, and FYGM3.

$$\widehat{\Delta C_t} = 3.106 + .329\ \Delta Y_t + .247\ \Delta Y_{t-1} + .181\ \Delta Y_{t-2} + .121\ \Delta Y_{t-3}$$
$$(11.86)\quad (8.17)\qquad\quad (6.74)\qquad\qquad\quad (6.72)\qquad\qquad\quad (3.18)$$

$$+ .055\ \Delta Y_{t-4} - .055\ r_t$$
$$(1.32)\qquad\quad (-1.48)$$

$$R^2 = .78 \qquad F = 124.8 \qquad DW = 1.95$$

Sum of lag coefficients $= .933$

The coefficients of the lags can be interpreted as follows. An increase of $1 billion in the quarterly change in disposable income in the present time will result in an increase in the change in consumption of $329 million in the first quarter, $247 million in the second quarter, $181 million in the third quarter, etc. The interest rate is inversely related to changes in consumption, but the coefficient is not statistically significant.

If one believes that the effect of changes in personal disposable income on changes in consumption will not be felt after four periods, it is reasonable to set the tail of the lag distribution equal to 0 in period $t - 5$. For illustrative purposes, we have reestimated the model using the zero tail restriction. The results exhibited in the following regression output show that the zero tail restriction has relatively little effect, since the neighboring lag weights are already close to zero. This is a natural consequence of the fact that polynomial functions are continuous.

$$\widehat{\Delta C_t} = 3.105 + .328\ \Delta Y_t + .249\ \Delta Y_{t-1} + .179\ \Delta Y_{t-2} + .117\ \Delta Y_{t-3}$$
$$(1.86)\quad (8.20)\qquad\quad (7.70)\qquad\qquad\quad (7.23)\qquad\qquad\quad (4.41)$$

$$+ .058\ \Delta Y_{t-4} - .54 r_t$$
$$(1.70)\qquad\quad (-1.48)$$

$$R^2 = .78 \qquad F = 156.8 \qquad DW = 1.95$$

Sum of lag coefficients $= .93$

Finally, consider the regression output in which both the tail and the head of the lag distribution are assumed equal to 0:

$$\widehat{\Delta C_t} = 3.197 + .252\ \Delta Y_t + .308\ \Delta Y_{t-1} + .239\ \Delta Y_{t-2} + .117\ \Delta Y_{t-3}$$
$$(1.89)\quad (8.57)\qquad\quad (12.31)\qquad\qquad\quad (18.82)\qquad\qquad\quad (4.34)$$

$$+ .014\ \Delta Y_{t-4} - .54 r_t$$
$$(.45)\qquad\quad (-1.46)$$

$$R^2 = .77 \qquad F = 199.1 \qquad DW = 1.88$$

Sum of lag coefficients $= .93$

The zero restriction on the head of the distribution has altered the pattern of the lag weights somewhat. If graphed, the weights would now approximate an inverted U structure. Once again the zero restriction and the continuity of the polynomial are crucial determinants of the lag pattern.

Example 9.2 Inventory Investment   In this example we construct a single-equation regression model which contains polynomial distributed lags. The example estimates the monthly change in manufacturers' inventories in the durable goods industries IND (end-of-period book value) as a function of shipments SHD, unfilled orders UNOD, and the wholesale price index WHD.[13] Monthly data from January 1983 to May 1987 have been used, and a polynomial distributed lag regression has been performed. The estimation results are shown below, with t statistics in parentheses, and a plot of estimated and actual values of the change in manufacturing durable inventories is presented in Fig. 9.3:

$$\widehat{\Delta IND}_t = -55,670 + \sum_{i=0} a_i SHD_{t-i} - .34 IND_{t-1}$$
$$\quad\quad (5.08) \quad\quad\quad\quad\quad\quad\quad (-5.15)$$

$$+ \ 486 \ \frac{WHD_t - WHD_{t-2}}{2} + .39 \ \frac{UNOD_{t-1} - UNOD_{t-7}}{6}$$
$$\quad\quad (1.21) \quad\quad\quad\quad\quad\quad\quad (2.99)$$

$$R^2 = .80 \quad\quad \bar{R}^2 = .77 \quad\quad F(7/53) = 30.0 \quad\quad DW = 2.65$$

Third-degree polynomial lag coefficients:

$a = -.021$	$a_1 = -.008$	$a_2 = \quad .003$	$a_3 = \quad .013$
(-1.25)	$(-.67)$	$(.41)$	(2.74)
$a_4 = \quad .022$	$a_5 = \quad .029$	$a_6 = \quad .035$	$a_7 - \quad .040$
(6.76)	(6.87)	(5.65)	(4.89)
$a_8 = \quad 0.43$	$a_9 = \quad .044$	$a_{10} = \quad .045$	$a_{11} = \quad .044$
(4.42)	(4.10)	(3.85)	(3.64)
$a_{12} = \quad .042$	$a_{13} = \quad .038$	$a_{14} = \quad .033$	$a_{15} = \quad .027$
(3.45)	(3.25)	(3.04)	(2.76)
$a_{16} = \quad .019$	$a_{17} = \quad .010$	$a_{18} = -.001$	$a_{19} = \quad -.013$
(2.34)	(1.60)	$(-.24)$	(-5.71)
$a_{20} = -0.26$	$a_{21} = -.041$	$a_{22} = -.057$	$a_{23} = (-.074)$
(-6.57)	(-5.49)	(-4.93)	(-4.61)
$a_{24} = -.093$	Sum $= \quad .154$		
(-4.46)	(4.65)		

[13] The following Citibase data series were used: manufacturers' inventories of durable goods (IVMD), shipments of durable goods (MDS), unfilled orders of durable goods (MDU), and the producer price index for all durable goods (PWMD).

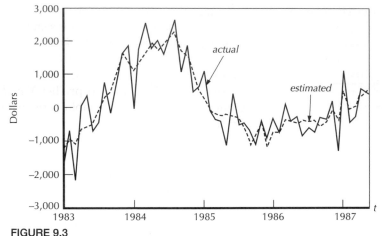

FIGURE 9.3
Change in manufacturer inventories in durable goods industries (millions of dollars).

Note that the final form of the equation expresses the relationship of inventories to shipments as a third-degree polynomial; the polynomial then defines 25 coefficients of current and lagged shipments. The lagged level of inventories is included, the wholesale price index is introduced as the monthly change (averaged over 2 months), and unfilled orders are added by using the monthly change (averaged over 6 months).

An examination of the pattern of the lag coefficients shows that there is a lagged response of manufacturers' inventories to changes in durable goods shipments. Inventories decline initially but then are built up gradually over time, peaking 10 months after an increase in shipments. Inventories then decline continuously through the remaining 14 months. Note from Fig. 9.3 that the predicted values of the regression are to some extent a "smoothed" version of the actual series. This is a typical pattern when a long distributed lag is used as part of a model specification.

9.2   TESTS FOR CAUSALITY

A common problem in economics is determining whether changes in one variable are a cause of changes in another. For example, do changes in the money supply cause changes in GNP, or are GNP and the money supply both endogenously determined? One approach to questions like this is the test for causality introduced by Granger and Sims.[14]

---

[14] See C. W. J. Granger, "Investigating Causal Relations by Econometric Models and Cross-Spectral Methods," *Econometrica*, vol. 37, pp. 424–438, 1969, and C. A. Sims, "Money, Income, and Causality," *American Economic Review*, vol. 62, pp. 540–552, 1972. For an example of its relationship to the rational expectations literature, see T. J. Sargent, "A Classical Macroeconometric Model for the United States," *Journal of Political Economy*, vol. 84, pp. 207–238, 1976, and T. J. Sargent, "Estimation of Dynamic Labor Demand Schedules under Rational Expectations," *Journal of Political Economy*, vol. 86, pp. 1009–1044, 1978.

The basic idea is quite simple: If X causes Y, then changes in X should *precede* changes in Y. In particular, to say that "X causes Y," two conditions should be met. First, X should help to predict Y; i.e., in a regression of Y against past values of Y, the addition of past values of X as independent variables should contribute significantly to the explanatory power of the regression. Second, Y should *not* help to predict X. The reason is that if X helps to predict Y *and* Y helps to predict X, it is likely that one or more other variables are in fact "causing" the observed changes in both X and Y.

To evaluate whether each of these two conditions holds, we want to test the null hypothesis that one variable does not help to predict the other. For example, to test the null hypothesis that "X does not cause Y," we regress Y against lagged values of Y *and* lagged values of X (the "unrestricted" regression) and then regress Y *only* against lagged values of Y (the "restricted" regression). A simple F test can then be used to determine whether the lagged values of X contribute significantly to the explanatory power of the first regression.[15] If they do, we can reject the null hypothesis and conclude that the data are consistent with X causing Y. The null hypothesis that "Y does not cause X" is then tested in the same manner.

To test whether X causes Y, we thus proceed as follows. First, test the null hypothesis "X does not cause Y" by running two regressions:

Unrestricted regression: $$Y = \sum_{i=1}^{m} \alpha_i Y_{t-i} + \sum_{i=1}^{m} \beta_i X_{t-i} + \varepsilon_t \qquad (9.23a)$$

Restricted regression: $$Y = \sum_{i=1}^{m} \alpha_i Y_{t-i} + \varepsilon_t \qquad (9.23b)$$

and use the sum of squared residuals from each regression to calculate an F statistic and test whether the group of coefficients $\beta_1, \beta_2, \ldots, \beta_m$ are significantly different from zero. If they are, we can reject the hypothesis that "X does not cause Y."

Second, test the null hypothesis "Y does not cause X" by running the same regressions as above, but switching X and Y and testing whether lagged values of Y are significantly different from zero. To conclude that X causes Y, we must *reject* the hypothesis "X does not cause Y" and accept the hypothesis "Y does not cause X."

Note that the number of lags m in these regressions is arbitrary and boils

---

[15] Recall from Chapter 4 that the F statistic is as follows:

$$F = (N - k) \frac{(\text{ESS}_R - \text{ESS}_{UR})}{q(\text{ESS}_{UR})}$$

where ESS_R and ESS_{UR} are the sums of squared residuals in the restricted and unrestricted regressions, respectively; N is the number of observations; k is the number of estimated parameters in the unrestricted regression; and q is the number of parameter restrictions. This statistic is distributed as $F(q, N - k)$.

down to a question of judgment. Generally, it is best to run the tests for a few different values of m and make sure that the results are not sensitive to the choice of m. Also, note that a weakness of this test of causality is that a third variable Z might in fact be causing Y but might also be contemporaneously correlated with X. One way to deal with this possibility is to run regressions in which lagged values of Z also appear on the right-hand side.[16]

Example 9.3 Oil and the Economy   During the 1970s and 1980s the world experienced sharp changes in the price of oil. Because of the important role oil plays in industrialized economies, such "oil shocks" can have important macroeconomic implications. Consider, for example, the recessions of 1975 and 1980. The sharp jumps in oil prices that occurred in 1974 and 1979–1980 clearly contributed to those recessions, and they did so in a number of ways. First, they caused a reduction in the real national incomes of oil-importing countries. Second, they led to "adjustment effects"—inflation and a further drop in real income and output resulting from the rigidities that prevented wages and nonenergy prices from coming into equilibrium quickly.[17]

Oil prices had fluctuated prior to the jump that occurred in 1974. In a study of the macroeconomic impact, James Hamilton demonstrated that the data support the hypothesis that changes in oil prices have been a cause of changes in real GNP and other key macroeconomic variables throughout the postwar period.[18] Here we report on his causality tests relating changes in the price of oil, ΔP_t, to percentage changes in real GNP, $\log(\mathrm{GNP}_t/\mathrm{GNP}_{t-1})$. Hamilton ran the OLS regression:

$$z_t = a_0 + a_1 z_{t-1} + \cdots + a_m z_{t-m} + b_1 x_{t-1} + \cdots + b_m x_{t-m} + \varepsilon_t$$

first letting $z_t = \Delta P_t$ and $x_t = \log(\mathrm{GNP}_t/\mathrm{GNP}_{t-1})$ and then vice versa. The results for two pre-1973 samples of quarterly data, first for $m = 4$ and then for $m = 8$, are shown as follows:[19]

---

[16] For a critical examination of Granger-Sims causality tests, see R. L. Jacobi, E. E. Leamer, and M. P. Ward, "The Difficulties with Testing for Causation," *Economic Inquiry*, vol. 17, pp. 401–413, 1979, and E. L. Feige and D. K. Pearce, "The Causal Relationship between Money and Income: Some Caveats for Time Series Analysis," *Review of Economics and Statistics*, vol. 61, pp. 521–533, 1979. Also, for a more general and recent discussion of causal laws and their observation, see C. W. J. Granger, "Some Recent Developments in a Concept of Causality," *Journal of Econometrics*, vol. 39, pp. 199–211, 1988; A. Zellner, "Causality and Causal Laws in Economics," *Journal of Econometrics*, vol. 39, pp. 7–21, 1988; and J. W. Pratt and R. Schlaifer, "On the Interpretation and Observation of Laws," *Journal of Econometrics*, vol. 39, pp. 23–52, 1988.

[17] For a detailed discussion of these effects, see R. S. Pindyck and J. J. Rotenberg, "Energy Shocks and the Macroeconomy," in A. Alm and R. Weiner (eds.), *Managing Oil Shocks*, Cambridge: Ballinger, 1984.

[18] J. D. Hamilton, "Oil and the Macroeconomy since World War II," *Journal of Political Economy*, vol. 91, pp. 228–248, 1983.

[19] The statistics represent an F test of $b_1 = b_2 = \cdots = b_m = 0$.

Null hypothesis	$m = 4, N = 95$ (1949.2–1972.4)		$m = 8, N = 91$ (1950.2–1972.4)	
	$F(4, 86)$	p value	$F(8, 74)$	p value
H_1: GNP $\nrightarrow$ Oil	.58	.68	.71	.68
H_2: Oil $\nrightarrow$ GNP	5.55	.0005	3.28	.003

Observe that hypothesis H_2—oil price changes do not cause changes in real GNP—is strongly rejected in both cases, while hypothesis H_1—changes in real GNP do not cause oil price changes—cannot be rejected. These results, together with the others Hamilton presents, provide evidence of a strong relationship between oil prices and the economy.

Example 9.4 Which Came First: The Chicken or the Egg?

This is a question that has plagued humans since the days of the first omelette. A study by Thurman and Fisher, using causality tests, has finally shed some light on the issue.[20]

The study uses annual data on two variables: total U.S. production of eggs (EGGS) from 1930 to 1983 and total U.S. production of chickens (CHICKENS) for the same period. The test is simple. EGGS is regressed on lagged EGGS and lagged CHICKENS; if the coefficients on lagged CHICKENS are significant as a group, then chickens cause eggs. A symmetric regression is then used to test whether eggs cause chickens. To conclude that one of the two "came first," it is necessary to find unidirectional causality, i.e., to reject the noncausality of one to the other and at the same time to fail to reject the noncausality of the other to the one.

Thurman and Fisher's test results were dramatic. Using lags ranging from 1 to 4 years, they obtained a clear rejection of the hypothesis that eggs do not cause chickens but were unable to reject the hypothesis that chickens do not cause eggs. Thus they were able to conclude that the egg came first!

Thurman and Fisher suggest that this methodology might be applied to other fundamental issues as well. For example, causality tests might be used to test whether it is true that "He who laughs last laughs best" and to test the multivariate "Pride goeth before destruction, and a haughty spirit before a fall." We hope to report on the results of these tests in the next edition of this book.

---

[20] This example is drawn from W. N. Thurman and M. E. Fisher, "Chickens, Eggs, and Causality, or Which Came First?," *American Journal of Agricultural Economics*, pp. 237–238, May 1988.

9.3   MISSING OBSERVATIONS

Our empirical work is often complicated by the fact that observations for one or more variables may be missing. Since there is no best approach in dealing with the problem of missing observations, we proceed by discussing some of the relevant issues and suggesting some possible solutions.

Assume that the regression model is given by

$$Y_i = \beta_1 + \beta_2 X_i + \varepsilon_i \tag{9.24}$$

If N observations on both X and Y are available, the least-squares estimator of the slope is

$$\hat{\beta}_2 = \frac{\sum\limits_{i=1}^{N} (X_i - \overline{X}_N)(Y_i - \overline{Y}_N)}{\sum\limits_{i=1}^{N} (X_i - \overline{X}_N)^2} \tag{9.25}$$

where $\overline{X}_N$ and $\overline{Y}_N$ represent the sample means calculated for the first N observations. Assume that M additional observations are available for the dependent variable but that there are M missing observations for the independent variable.[21] A straightforward solution to the missing-observations problem is simply to drop the last M observations of Y from consideration. If the observations dropped are random, the least-squares slope estimator will remain an unbiased and consistent estimator of β_2, and the only effect of dropping the observations is a loss of efficiency. In general, the closer the missing X's to the sample mean and the smaller the sample variance of the missing X's, the lower the efficiency loss caused by dropping the observations.

If many observations are missing, the potential loss of efficiency necessitates an alternative to simply dropping incomplete observations. If some *a priori* knowledge is available, the best alternative may be to assign values for the missing observations. If no *a priori* information is available, another solution must be found. The most natural approach is to replace the missing observations by the sample mean of the available X observations. This *zero-order approach* is equivalent to regressing X on a constant and assigning to each missing observation the estimated coefficient.

Within the two-variable model it is not difficult to show that the substitution of variable means for missing observations does not change the least-squares slope estimator or its variance. Note, however, that if we were to generalize

---

[21] In most cross-section studies the unavailability of observations on the dependent variable makes any information about the explanatory variables useless. In time-series analysis, missing dependent-variable observations present a serious problem and necessitate a solution.

the model to one containing several independent variables, only one of which has missing observations, the substitution procedure described here *might* yield different slope estimators and an improvement in efficiency.[22]

In practice, the assumption that missing observations are random is unlikely to be realistic. For example, in a study relating automobile expenditures to income, there may be missing observations for low-income individuals, who tend to spend little on automobiles. Dropping observations or using the sample mean of X to replace missing observations is not the correct procedure, because no account is taken of the known correlation between income and expenditures. Equivalently, in doing time-series analysis, we should account for the fact that most time-series variables tend to undergo relatively predictable rates of growth. To do this, we search for proxy variables that are highly correlated with the variables whose observations are missing.

An elementary solution to the time-series problem would involve replacing missing observations with proxy observations obtained by regressing the known values of the independent variable on time and then replacing the missing observations with the fitted values of the regression. This procedure is only one of several ways in which missing observations can be replaced through the interpolation of the X variable. It yields consistent parameter estimates *if the time variable is uncorrelated with the error term in the original equation*. The procedure is most useful because it suggests a more general *first-order approach* to the missing-observations problem.

Suppose a set of "instruments," $Z_2, \ldots, Z_k$, is available with respect to the variable with the missing observations. The instruments are presumed to be highly correlated with the variable X and uncorrelated with error term ε. We can increase the efficiency of the original parameter estimates while maintaining consistency by proceeding as follows.

First, regress X on the set of instruments for all observations with complete information:

$$X_i = \alpha_1 + \alpha_2 Z_{2i} + \cdots + \alpha_k Z_{ki} + u_i \qquad i = 1, 2, \ldots, N \qquad (9.26)$$

Then calculate fitted values for the missing observations:[23]

$$\hat{X}_i = \hat{\alpha}_1 + \hat{\alpha}_2 Z_{2i} + \cdots + \hat{\alpha}_k Z_{ki} \qquad i = N + 1, \ldots, N + M$$

---

[22] See Y. Haitovsky, "Estimation of Regression Equations When a Block of Observations Is Missing," *Proceedings of the American Statistical Association*, Business and Economics Statistics Section, 1968; A. A. Afifi and R. M. Elashoff, "Missing Observations in Multivariate Statistics II. Point Estimates in Simple Linear Regression," *Journal of the American Statistical Association*, vol. 62, pp. 10–29, 1967; and M. G. Dagenais, "The Use of Incomplete Observations in Multiple Regression Analysis," *Journal of Econometrics*, vol. 1, pp. 317–328, 1973.

[23] In time-series analysis it is unlikely that the last set of observations will be missing. The analysis is quite general, however, because we need simply rearrange the numbering of the observations appropriately and all results will follow.

We can then reestimate the original equation as follows:

$$Y_i = \beta_1 + \beta_2 \hat{X}_i + v_i \tag{9.27}$$

where

$$\hat{X}_i = X_i \qquad \text{for } i = 1, 2, \ldots, N$$

$$v_i = \begin{cases} \varepsilon_i & \text{for } i = 1, 2, \ldots, N \\ \varepsilon_i - \beta_2 u_i & \text{for } i = N + 1, \ldots, N + M \end{cases} \tag{9.28}$$

As long as the instruments are correctly chosen, the estimation of Eq. (9.27) will yield a consistent slope estimator.

There are several problems associated with this approach. First, the error variances associated with missing observations will be larger than the remaining error variances [from Eq. (9.28)]:

$$\text{Var } (v_i) = \begin{cases} \sigma^2 & \text{for } i = 1, 2, \ldots, N \\ \sigma^2 + \beta_2^2 \text{ Var } (u_i) & \text{for } i = N + 1, \ldots, N + M \end{cases}$$

A more refined technique would use weighted least squares to adjust for the efficiency loss associated with heteroscedasticity. Second, it is possible that observations will be missing for more than one right-hand variable. Then a series of regressions must be run to fill in the missing observations. Unfortunately, the order of these procedures can affect the estimated parameters. Third, the choice of proper instruments is often difficult. If one or more instruments are correlated with the error term, measurement error (a form of errors in variables) will be introduced when the missing observations are replaced by observations from the constructed proxy variable. For further details the reader should review Chapter 12, in which errors in variables and instrumental variables are discussed.

Example 9.5 Aid to States   To understand how federal aid to states affects their spending decisions, public finance economists often estimate regression models in which state (and/or local) expenditures are determined by a number of important financial and demographic characteristics of a particular state. One rather simple specification of that model is

$$\text{EXP} = \beta_1 + \beta_2 \text{POP} + \beta_3 \text{AID} + \beta_4 \text{INC} + \varepsilon$$

where EXP = aggregate state expenditures in 1972
       POP = state population in 1972
       AID = total federal grants to each state in 1972
       INC = aggregate personal income in the state in 1970

We estimated the expenditure determinants model using data for all 50 states in the United States, obtaining the following result (t statistics in parentheses):

$$\widehat{EXP} = -46{,}816 - .60POP + .0032AID + .00019INC$$
$$\quad\quad\quad (-.56) \quad\quad (-5.7) \quad\quad\quad (13.6) \quad\quad\quad\quad (8.1)$$

Then, as an illustration of how to treat the missing-observations problem, we assumed that the last five observations on INC were not available. We tried three procedures. First, we simply dropped the last five observations from the model. In the second case, we replaced the missing observations with the mean of INC within the known sample of 45 observations. For the third example, we used the suggested first-order process for replacing missing observations by regressing INC on POP and AID within the sample of 45 observations. (The regression was $\widehat{INC} = -1.7 \times 10^9 + 4.63AID + 4{,}162POP$.) We then forecasted INC for the remaining five observations and replaced the missing observations with the forecasted values. The regression results in each of the three correction procedures are included along with the original results in the following table.

	Constant	POP	AID	INC
Original	−46,816	−.60	.0032	.00019
	(−.6)	(−5.7)	(13.6)	(8.1)
Drop missing observations	−97,340	−.62	.0034	.00019
	(−1.1)	(−5.9)	(14.1)	(8.3)
Zero-order approach	−434,550	.10	.0043	.00002
	(−3.9)	(1.6)	(14.1)	(2.6)
First-order approach	−30,526	−.62	.0033	.00019
	(−.4)	(−5.9)	(14.2)	(8.3)

In this particular case (our results will not always hold), we find that the first procedure of omitting the observations has relatively little effect on the regression results. However, replacing the missing observations by the mean of INC has a substantial impact, causing the estimated results to differ from the original. Finally, the first-order procedure yields very good results, with the coefficient on AID becoming very close to the coefficient associated with the full sample. Why did the second procedure work so badly in this case? A partial answer can be obtained by comparing the values used to replace the missing observations with the original data (all values are in billions of dollars).

Observation	INC	Zero-order	First-order
46	15.7	17.9	15.4
47	9.5	17.9	9.4
48	103.8	17.9	102.1
49	1.7	17.9	.5
50	4.2	17.9	2.4

Clearly, in this particular case (with INC varying so widely from state to state), the predicted or forecasted values of INC are much closer to the original than is the mean of INC, and the first-order procedure works better. We stress, however, that this example does not generalize. Which of these elementary techniques is most appropriate depends on the ability of one's model to explain why the missing observations occurred in the first place. In addition, all correction procedures use up sample information and, hence, degrees of freedom. Thus, procedures 2 and 3 overstate the statistical significance of the results because they do not account directly for the fact that preliminary regressions were run to obtain the missing data.

9.4   THE USE OF PANEL DATA

A longitudinal, or *panel data*, set is one that includes a sample of individuals (households, firms, cities, etc.) over a period of time. As a result it may include numerous observations on each individual in the sample. A panel data set can be useful because it allows the researcher to sort out economic effects that cannot be distinguished with the use of either cross-section or time-series data alone.

As an example, suppose we are modeling the profitability of firms in an industry. A regression based on cross-section data for a single year might include such explanatory variables as the quality of management, the amount of physical capital, the employment of labor, and the degree of financial leveraging. This cross-section model can in principle also take into account any scale economies which the firm may enjoy. However, the model cannot account for any increased profitability that may occur over time as technological improvements are made in the industry. In principle, the use of panel data can allow the researcher to separate out the impact of scale economies from the impact of technological change. In effect, the panel data set allows one to study both the changes in profits of a single firm over time and the variation in profits of many firms at a given point in time.

The use of panel data can have a number of other advantages as well. First, panel data sets usually provide an increased number of data points, and that generates additional degrees of freedom. Second, incorporating information relating to both cross-section and time-series variables can substantially diminish the problems that arise when there is an omitted-variables problem.[24] Suppose, for example, a researcher is concerned that firms which enjoy technological improvements are able to increase the use of physical capital in their production. A cross-section analysis, which could not account for technological progress, might inaccurately estimate the effect of increased capital on a firm's

---

[24] For a thorough discussion of panel data, see C. Hsiao, *Analysis of Panel Data* (Cambridge: Cambridge University Press, 1986).

profitability. With panel data, however, the time-series component of the data can be used to incorporate the effect of technological improvement on profitability, and the potential omitted-variables problem thus disappears.

The process of combining cross-section and time-series data to form a panel is called *pooling*. Typically, cross-section parameters may shift over time in a manner that is not reflected in the choice of time-series explanatory variables, or individuals may vary in important ways within the cross-section in a manner that is not reflected in the choice of cross-section variables. As a result, the use of panel data adds a new dimension of difficulty to the problem of model specification; with panel data the disturbance term is likely to consist of time-series-related disturbances, cross-section disturbances, and a combination of both.

In the following subsections we consider a number of alternative specifications that have proven useful in the study of panel data. The presentation is confined to a two-variable regression specification to keep things as simple as possible.

9.4.1   Estimating Models with Panel Data

The first technique for panel data use simply combines, or pools, all the time-series and cross-section data and then estimates the underlying model by utilizing ordinary least squares. A second procedure involves the recognition that omitted variables may lead to changes in the cross-section and time-series intercepts. Models with *fixed effects* add dummy variables to allow for these changing intercepts. A third technique improves the efficiency of the first least-squares estimation process by accounting for cross-section and time-series disturbances. The *random-effects* model is a variation of the generalized least-squares estimation process described in Appendix 6.1. Finally, we consider techniques which account for the fact that the error term may be correlated over time and over cross-section units. Once again a variation of generalized least-squares estimation provides a useful solution to the problem.

Consider the two-variable model:

$$Y_{it} = \alpha + \beta X_{it} + \varepsilon_{it} \qquad \text{for } i = 1, 2, \ldots, N \text{ and } t = 1, 2, \ldots, T$$

where N is the number of cross-section units (individuals) and T is the number of time periods. If all the classical error-term assumptions hold, we could estimate separate cross-section regressions, with each regression involving N observations. For time period $t = 1$ the cross-section regression would be

$$Y_{i1} = \alpha + \beta X_{i1} + \varepsilon_{i1} \qquad i = 1, 2, \ldots, N$$

There would be a total of T such equations. Similarly, we could estimate N time-series regressions with T observations in each one. However, if both α and β are constant over time and over cross-section units, more efficient parameter estimates can be obtained by combining all the data so that one large pooled regression is run with NT observations. In this most elementary pooling technique there will be $NT - 2$ degrees of freedom (since estimation of the two parameters uses up 2 degrees of freedom).

9.4.2   Fixed-Effects Model

The difficulty with the least-squares pooling procedure is that the assumption of constant intercept and slope may be unreasonable. The obvious generalization is to introduce dummy variables that allow the intercept term to vary over time and over cross-section units. If the slopes varied as well, each separate cross-section regression would involve a distinct model and pooling would be inappropriate.[25] We write the *fixed-effects model* as follows:

$$Y_{it} = \alpha + \beta X_{it} + \gamma_2 W_{2t} + \gamma_3 W_{3t} + \cdots + \gamma_N W_{Nt}$$
$$+ \delta_2 Z_{i2} + \delta_3 Z_{i3} + \cdots + \delta_T Z_{iT} + \varepsilon_{it} \qquad (9.29)$$

where

$$W_{it} = \begin{cases} 1 & \text{for } i\text{th individual, } i = 2, \ldots, N \\ 0 & \text{otherwise} \end{cases}$$

$$Z_{it} = \begin{cases} 1 & \text{for } t\text{th time period, } t = 2, \ldots, T \\ 0 & \text{otherwise} \end{cases}$$

We have added $(N - 1) + (T - 1)$ dummy variables to the model and have omitted the remaining two, since their addition would result in perfect collinearity among the explanatory variables. If this model were estimated using ordinary least squares, unbiased and consistent estimates of all parameters (including the slope β) would be obtained. A total of $NT - 2 - (N - 1) - (T - 1)$, or $NT - N - T$, degrees of freedom would be involved. The dummy-variable coefficients would measure the change in the cross-section and time-series intercepts (with respect to the first individual in the first period of time). To see this, we can eliminate the dummy variables and rewrite the model associated with each of the NT observations:

$$Y_{11} = \alpha + \beta X_{11} + \varepsilon_{11}$$
$$Y_{12} = (\alpha + \delta_2) + \beta X_{12} + \varepsilon_{12}$$
$$\cdots\cdots\cdots\cdots\cdots\cdots\cdots\cdots\cdots\cdots\cdots\cdots$$

---

[25] Allowance for random variation in slope parameters is made in the random coefficients model literature. See, for example, W. H. Greene, *Econometric Analysis* (New York: Macmillan, 1990), Section 16.4.

$$Y_{1T} = (\alpha + \delta_T) + \beta X_{1T} + \varepsilon_{1T}$$

$$Y_{21} = (\alpha + \gamma_2) + \beta X_{21} + \varepsilon_{21}$$

$$Y_{22} = (\alpha + \gamma_2 + \delta_2) + \beta X_{22} + \varepsilon_{22}$$

$$\cdots\cdots\cdots\cdots\cdots\cdots\cdots\cdots\cdots\cdots\cdots\cdots\cdots$$

$$Y_{2T} = (\alpha + \gamma_2 + \delta_T) + \beta X_{2T} + \varepsilon_{2T}$$

$$\cdots\cdots\cdots\cdots\cdots\cdots\cdots\cdots\cdots\cdots\cdots\cdots\cdots$$

$$Y_{N1} = (\alpha + \gamma_N) + \beta X_{N1} + \varepsilon_{N1}$$

$$Y_{N2} = (\alpha + \gamma_N + \delta_2) + \beta X_{N2} + \varepsilon_{N2}$$

$$\cdots\cdots\cdots\cdots\cdots\cdots\cdots\cdots\cdots\cdots\cdots\cdots\cdots$$

$$Y_{NT} = (\alpha + \gamma_N + \delta_T) + \beta X_{NT} + \varepsilon_{NT}$$

The effect of the missing δ_1 and γ_1 coefficients is accounted for in the parameter α, the intercept of the first equation. Each of the δ's is then measured in terms of deviations from δ_1 (and the γ's in terms of deviations from γ_1) and thus from the "true" intercept α.

The decision to add dummy variables can be made on the basis of statistical testing. The test involves a comparison of the error sum of squares associated with the two estimation techniques. Since the ordinary least-squares model includes more parameter restrictions than does the fixed-effects model (the intercepts are restricted to be equal over time and over individuals), we would expect the error sum of squares to be higher for the ordinary least-squares model. If the increase in the error sum of squares is not significant when the restrictions are added, we conclude that the restrictions are proper, and ordinary least squares can be applied. If the error sum of squares changes substantially, we opt for the fixed-effects model. The appropriate test statistic is

$$F_{N+T-2,NT-N-T} = \frac{(\text{ESS}_1 - \text{ESS}_2)/(N + T - 2)}{(\text{ESS}_2)/(NT - N - T)}$$

where ESS_1 and ESS_2 are the error sum of squares using the ordinary least-squares model and the fixed-effects model, respectively. On the null hypothesis that the equal-intercept restrictions are correct, the statistic F follows the F distribution with $N + T - 2$ and $NT - N - T$ degrees of freedom.

There are several problems associated with the use of the fixed-effects model. First, the use of dummies does not directly identify what causes the regression line to shift over time and over individuals. Second, the dummy-variable technique uses up a substantial number of degrees of freedom ($N + T - 2$ in our model). For example, the use of dummy variables for a study of 15 firms over a 4-year period would involve a reduction of degrees of freedom from 58 to 41, not an inconsequential number. In part for this reason, researchers often specify models that include only cross-section fixed effects.

9.4.3   Random-Effects Model

Since the inclusion of dummy variables represents a lack of knowledge about the model, it is natural to describe this lack of knowledge through the disturbance term. We might thus wish to choose a pooled cross-section and time-series model in which error terms may be correlated across time and individual units. The *random-effects model* (or error-components model) does so, as follows:[26]

$$Y_{it} = \alpha + \beta X_{it} + \varepsilon_{it} \tag{9.30a}$$

$$\varepsilon_{it} = u_i + v_i + w_{it} \tag{9.30b}$$

where $u_i \sim N(0, \sigma_u^2)$ = cross-section error component
$v_t \sim N(0, \sigma_v^2)$ = time-series error component
$w_{it} \sim N(0, \sigma_w^2)$ = combined error component

We assume also that individual error components are uncorrelated with each other and are not autocorrelated (across both cross-section and time-series units).

The relationship between the random-effects model and the fixed-effects model can be seen by treating the intercept terms in the fixed-effects model as two random variables, one a time-series variable and the other a cross-section variable. If both random variables are assumed to be normally distributed, degrees of freedom are saved because we need to be concerned only with the mean and variance of each of the error components.

The random-effects formulation is obtained from the fixed-effects model by assuming that the mean effect of the random time-series and cross-section variables is included in the intercept term, and the random deviations about the mean are equated to the error components, u_t and v_i, respectively. To see this more clearly, assume no time-series error component. The use of dummy variables would force no restrictions on the pattern of shifting regression intercepts, while the random-effects model would assume that the pattern follows a normal distribution. Specifically, assume that the cross-section intercepts have mean α_u and variance σ_u^2. The combined error component has mean 0 and variance σ_w^2. These two assumptions are equivalent to the assumption that the error component has variance $\sigma_u^2 + \sigma_w^2$, since

$$\text{Var}(\varepsilon_{it}) = \text{Var}(u_i) + \text{Var}(w_{it}) = \sigma_u^2 + \sigma_w^2$$

The effect of the mean of the normally distributed intercepts (α_u) will be accounted for by the inclusion of a constant term in the pooled regression equation. If time-series intercepts had also been random, normally distributed with

[26] See G. S. Maddala, "The Use of Variance Components Models in Pooling Cross Section and Time Series Data," *Econometrica*, vol. 39, no. 2, pp. 341–358, 1971.

mean α_v and variance σ_v^2, we could allow the mean effect of the random intercepts (α_v) to be picked up by the constant term. At the same time the error term would consist of three components and would have variance

$$\text{Var } (\varepsilon_{it}) = \sigma_u^2 + \sigma_v^2 + \sigma_w^2 \tag{9.31}$$

The relationship between the random-effects model and the pooled model using ordinary least squares can be seen directly from Eq. (9.31). If both σ_u^2 and σ_v^2 are 0, the error term consists of a single combined disturbance and the correct procedure is to apply ordinary least-squares regression to the pooled data.

The random-effects model can be estimated as a generalized least-squares regression. The estimation weights observations inversely to their variances. To accomplish the weighting, a two-stage estimation process must be used, since the various error-component variances typically are not known. In the first stage the entire pooled sample is estimated by using ordinary least squares. (The fixed-effects model also could be used.) The ordinary least-squares residuals are used to calculate sample estimates of the variance components. The estimated variances are then used in the second stage, in which the generalized least-squares parameter estimates are obtained.[27] If one is willing to assume that the error components are normally distributed, then all the relevant parameters can be estimated by the method of maximum likelihood, which is described in detail in Section 10.2.

Interestingly, the estimate of the slope parameter obtained when the combined error component σ_w^2 equals zero will approximate the estimate obtained from the fixed-effects model. This result should not be surprising, since the fixed-effects model ignores the possibility of joint cross-section and time-series disturbances. Alternatively, when the combined error component becomes arbitrarily large, the random-effects model approximates the ordinary least-squares pooled data model. This suggests that the random-effects model can be seen as an intermediate model which lies between the extreme of a zero combined error component and an infinitely large combined component.

Which should be preferred, the fixed-effects model or the random-effects model? As we mentioned above, the random-effects model uses up fewer degrees of freedom and has conceptual appeal as a broad characterization of the sources of errors in a large data set with substantial time-series and cross-section variation. However, the fixed-effects model also has advantages. It allows the researcher to analyze the extent to which the dependent variable for each cross-section unit differs from the overall cross-section mean. Further, it does not require the assumption that the individual effects that are incorporated into the error term are uncorrelated with the explanatory variables in

---

[27] For details, see, for example, Greene, op. cit., Section 16.4.3, or Hsiao, op. cit., Section 3.3.2.

the model, an assumption that may not be valid and may therefore cause parameter estimates to be inconsistent.[28]

Example 9.6 Patent Applications and Spending on Research and Development

Firms that are actively involved in the development of new technology often invest substantial sums of money in research and development (R&D). One crude measure of the effectiveness of that expenditure is the number of patent applications a firm makes. (A more meaningful statistic, the net present value of the stream of earnings that R&D generates, is much more difficult to measure.) The relationship between the logarithm of the number of patent applications (P) and the logarithm of R&D expenditures (RND) has been evaluated by using panel data for 45 firms over a 7-year period. The R&D data are lagged 5 years to reflect the long interval that passes before research is translated into an actual patent application. (All firms in the sample had a positive number of patents in every year.)[29]

The basic regression model is given by

$$P_{it} = \beta_0 + \beta_1 \, RND_{i,t-5} + \varepsilon_{it}$$

where i refers to firms and t refers to time. The ordinary least-squares estimation procedure using the pooled data set (with 315 observations) generated the following results (with t statistics in parentheses):

$$\hat{P}_{it} = 1.438 + .845 \, RND_{i,t-5}$$
$$\quad\;\; (14.01) \quad\; (24.17)$$

$$R^2 = .65 \qquad s = .799$$

This regression shows a strong positive relationship between R&D and patent applications. On average in the sample, patent applications increased by .845 percent for every 1 percent increase in R&D expenditures.

Patenting behavior varies considerably across firms, and it is this variation which drives the previous result. Not surprisingly, therefore, a regression of

---

[28] The assumption that the errors are uncorrelated with the explanatory variables can be tested by using a Hausman specification test to compare the parameters estimated using the fixed-effects model to the parameters obtained using the generalized least-squares estimates from the random-effects model.

[29] The patent data were obtained from the Office of Technology Assessment and Forecasting. An earlier version of this study is reported in Bronwyn H. Hall, Zvi Griliches, and Jerry A. Hausman, "Patents and R&D: Is There a Lag?" *International Economic Review*, vol. 27, pp. 265–283, 1986. See also Bound et al., "Who Does Patents and Who Does R&D?" in Z. Griliches, ed., *R&D, Patents, and Productivity* (New York: National Bureau of Economic Research, 1984).

the mean number of patents (averaged over time) on mean R&D yields the following "between-individuals" result:

$$\hat{P}_i = 1.370 + .871 \text{ RND}_i$$
$$\quad\quad (5.53) \quad\quad (10.28)$$

$$R^2 = .71 \quad\quad s = .727$$

Because this second model does not allow for firm-specific patent application differences that are not due to differences in R&D expenditures, it is quite possible that the model overstates the impact of R&D. This hypothesis is confirmed when we add a set of cross-section dummies to the specification, i.e., when a fixed-effects model is estimated. In the fixed-effects model the estimate of the impact of R&D on patents is substantially lower:

$$\hat{P}_{it} = .195 \text{ RND}_{i,t-5}$$
$$\quad\quad (2.38)$$

$$R^2 = .937 \quad\quad s = .366$$

We have not included the individual dummy-variable coefficients associated with each of the firms. However, we did perform an F test of the null hypothesis that all the coefficients are jointly equal to zero. With an F statistic of 27.79 with 24 and 269 degrees of freedom, we rejected this hypothesis at the 5 percent level.

Finally, we estimated a random-effects model allowing for a cross-section error component and a combined error component, with the following results:

$$\hat{P}_{it} = 2.299 + .519 \text{ RND}_{i,t-5}$$
$$\quad\quad (12.13) \quad\quad (8.78)$$

$$\hat{\sigma}_u^2 = .504 \quad\quad \hat{\sigma}_w^2 = .134$$
$$R^2 = .919 \quad\quad s \;\; = .414$$

This model estimates a substantially larger effect than did the fixed-effects model. Which should be preferred? We did a Hausman specification test of the null hypothesis of a random-effects model in comparison to the alternative hypothesis of a fixed-effects model. The resulting chi-square statistic of 32.627 with 1 degree of freedom is significant at the 5 percent level. This supports the conclusion that, of these 4 models, the fixed-effects model most accurately characterizes the relationship between R&D and patent applications.

9.4.4   Time-Series Autocorrelation Model

Random-effects specification has the property that the correlation of disturbances over time is independent of the time gap between the disturbance
terms. An alternative specification would predict a decline in the error correlation over time. This suggests that one ought to consider pooling cross-
section and time-series data under error assumptions involving time-series
(or cross-section) autocorrelation as well as cross-section (or time-series) heteroscedasticity. As an example of how this might be accomplished, consider
the model

$$Y_{it} = \alpha + \beta X_{it} + \varepsilon_{it} \qquad \varepsilon_{it} = \rho_i \varepsilon_{i,t-1} + u_{it} \qquad (9.32)$$

where $\qquad E(\varepsilon_{it}^2) = \sigma^2$

$$E(\varepsilon_{it}\varepsilon_{jt}) = 0 \qquad \text{and} \qquad E(\varepsilon_{i,t-1}u_{jt}) = 0 \qquad i \ne j$$

$$u_{it} \sim N(0, \sigma_u^2)$$

The assumptions imply that while cross-section disturbances are uncorrelated
and have constant variance, time-series disturbances are autocorrelated. We
allow ρ to vary from individual unit to individual unit, but fix each error
structure to involve first-order serial correlation. Efficient parameter estimates
can be obtained by using a variant of generalized least squares. We estimate
each ρ_i and then use the estimated $\hat{\rho}_i$ as a basis for the generalized least-squares
regression. To estimate ρ_i, $i = 1, 2, \ldots, N$, we estimate the entire pooled
sample by using ordinary least squares. Since the parameter estimates are consistent (as well as unbiased), we can use them to calculate the regression
residuals $\hat{\varepsilon}_{it}$. We then estimate each ρ_i consistently as follows:

$$\hat{\rho}_i = \frac{\sum\limits_{t=2}^{T} \hat{\varepsilon}_{it}\hat{\varepsilon}_{i,t-1}}{\sum\limits_{t=2}^{T} \hat{\varepsilon}_{i,t-1}^2} \qquad \text{for } i = 1, 2, \ldots, N$$

We proceed by forming the generalized difference form of the original model:

$$Y_{it}^* = \alpha(1 - \hat{\rho}_i) + \beta X_{it}^* + u_{it}^*$$

where

$$Y_{it}^* = Y_{it} - \hat{\rho}_i Y_{i,t-1} \qquad X_{it}^* = X_{it} - \hat{\rho}_i X_{i,t-1} \qquad u_{it}^* = \varepsilon_{it} - \hat{\rho}_i \varepsilon_{i,t-1}$$

The generalized difference form can now be estimated by applying ordinary
least squares to the pooled model. $NT - N$ observations are used in the esti-

mation, since one observation from each individual unit is dropped in the generalized differencing process. Corrections for heteroscedasticity or cross-section correlation between individual units would proceed in a fashion similar to that just described. If heteroscedasticity had been present in the model of Eq. (9.32), for example, we would use the residuals of the generalized difference model (pooled) to estimate the individual error variances and then apply weighted least squares in the third stage of the estimation process.

Example 9.7 Foreign Aid[30] An important empirical question facing development economists concerns the effect of foreign aid on the investment expenditures of less-developed countries (LDCs). Some economists have argued that inflows of foreign capital to LDCs do not lead to increased investment but instead lead to increased public and private consumption. To deal with this issue, an economic model was developed which accounts for the interrelationship between taxing, spending, and borrowing decisions. The model assumes that local officials seek to maximize an objective function which is influenced by allocative choices between private consumption, public "civil" consumption, public "socioeconomic" consumption, public investment for development purposes, and public borrowing from domestic sources. Maximization of this objective function subject to a budget constraint yields a series of five simultaneous equations which must hold if maximization is to be achieved. To simplify matters we shall examine two of those five equations:

$$T_t = \alpha_1 + \alpha_2 A_{1t} + \alpha_3 A_{2t} + \alpha_4 Y_t + \alpha_5 M_{t-1} + \alpha_6 I_t + \alpha_7 G_{s,t} + \alpha_8 G_{c,t-1} + \varepsilon_{1t}$$

$$I_t = \beta_1 + \beta_2 T_t + \beta_3 A_{1t} + \beta_4 A_{2t} + \beta_5 Y_{t-1} + \varepsilon_{2t}$$

where T_t = level of tax and nontax revenues at time t

I_t = public investment for development purposes at time t

$G_{c,t}$ = public "civil" consumption (government administration, debt service, police, military) at time t

$G_{s,t}$ = public "socioeconomic" consumption (schools, hospitals, roads, agricultural projects) at time t

A_{1t} = grants to the public sector at time t

A_{2t} = loans to the public sector at time t

Y_t = gross domestic product at time t

M_t = imports at time t

---

[30] This example is adapted from P. S. Heller, "A Model of Public Fiscal Behavior in Developing Countries: Aid, Investment, and Taxation," *American Economic Review*, vol. 65, pp. 368–379, June 1975.

The sample of LDCs included 11 African countries: Nigeria, Ghana, Zambia, Kenya, Uganda, Tanzania, Malawi, Liberia, Ethiopia, Tunisia, and Morocco. Time-series data on all variables were available for periods of approximately 6 years. Because the system of equations is simultaneous, the two-stage least-squares technique was chosen to estimate each equation. In addition, a decision was made to use a random-effects model with two error components, a cross-section error term, and a combined error term, $\varepsilon_{it} = u_i + w_{it}$. It was implicitly assumed that time-series intercepts remained constant during the period of study. However, the cross-section error component accounts for the random nature of the cross-section intercepts.

The estimation process proceeded in two steps. First, the reduced form equations were estimated by using ordinary least squares. The fitted values of the right-hand endogenous variables were calculated and substituted in the structural equations. The second stage of this two-step generalized least-squares procedure was then estimated by using a variant of the 2SLS procedure described in the text. For each equation, the ratio of cross section to the combined variance θ was calculated: $\theta = \sigma_u^2/\sigma_w^2$. The estimated equations (with t statistics in parentheses and constant terms dropped) are:

$$\hat{T}_t = -.32A_{1t} - .84A_{2t} + .23Y_t - .39M_{t-1} + 01.03I_t$$
$$\quad (-.58) \quad\quad (-1.98) \quad\quad (4.54) \quad (-3.40) \quad\quad\quad (3.37)$$

$$-.71G_{s,t} + 1.51G_{c,t-1}$$
$$(-2.24) \quad\quad (6.25)$$

$$\theta = .45 \quad\quad N = 57 \quad\quad R^2 = .89$$

and

$$\hat{I}_t = .70A_{1t} + .24A_{2t} + .49\hat{T}_t - .02Y_{t-1}$$
$$\quad (3.21) \quad\quad (1.64) \quad\quad (11.10) \quad (-1.23)$$

$$\theta = .65 \quad\quad N = 61 \quad\quad R^2 = .89$$

The first equation verifies the expected result that higher grants and loans lead to lower domestically raised revenues (although the grants term is insignificant). Government investment and government civil consumption have a strong positive effect on tax revenues, but this is offset to some extent by the negative coefficient on the public socioeconomic consumption term. The results of the second equation indicate that foreign aid has a positive effect on investment, but the value being less than 1 indicates that some of the foreign aid leaks into other expenditure areas. We conclude that the estimated equations verify the fiscal interdependence associated with current and capital budgets. Foreign loans can and do affect public consumption as well as investment.

APPENDIX 9.1 Estimating Confidence Intervals
for Long-Run Elasticities

Assume that we have estimated a distributed lag model with a geometric lag, specified as

$$\log Q_t = \beta_1 + \beta_2 \log P_t + \beta_3 \log Y_t + \beta_4 \log Q_{t-1} + \varepsilon_t \qquad (A9.1)$$

where Q is quantity, P is price, and Y is income. For this equation the short-run price and income elasticities are β_2 and β_3, respectively, but the *long-run* elasticities are[31]

$$\eta^P_{LR} = \frac{\beta_2}{1 - \beta_4} \qquad \text{and} \qquad \eta^Y_{LR} = \frac{\beta_3}{1 - \beta_4}$$

The problem is to estimate *standard errors* (and hence *confidence intervals*) for these elasticity estimates.

The procedure is as follows. Suppose we want to obtain a 90 percent confidence interval for the elasticity estimate given by the ratio $\hat{\beta}_2/(1 - \hat{\beta}_4)$, where $\hat{\beta}_2$ and $\hat{\beta}_4$ are the estimated values of β_2 and β_4. Then form the linear combination

$$\phi = \hat{\beta}_2 - z(1 - \hat{\beta}_4) = \hat{\beta}_2 + z\hat{\beta}_4 - z \qquad (A9.2)$$

where z is yet to be determined. Now note that the variance of this linear combination is

$$\text{Var}\,(\phi) = \text{Var}\,(\hat{\beta}_2) + z^2\,\text{Var}\,(\hat{\beta}_4) + 2z\,\text{Cov}\,(\hat{\beta}_2, \hat{\beta}_4) \qquad (A9.3)$$

If z is the true ratio $\beta_2/(1 - \beta_4)$, then ϕ will have a mean of zero. If the number of degrees of freedom is very large, the distribution of ϕ is approximately normal, so that the probability is 90 percent that the sample value of ϕ is within plus or minus 1.645 times its standard deviation, where 1.645 is obtained from the normal table. Thus,

$$(\hat{\beta}_2 - \hat{\beta}_4 z - z)^2 \leq (1.645)^2[\text{Var}\,(\hat{\beta}) + \text{Var}\,(\hat{\beta}_4)z^2 + 2z\,\text{Cov}\,(\hat{\beta}_2, \hat{\beta}_4)] \qquad (A9.4)$$

---

[31] If Eq. (A9.1) were in *linear* rather than logarithmic form, the elasticities would be given by

$$\eta^P_{LR} = \frac{\beta_2}{1 - \beta_4}\frac{\overline{P}}{\overline{Q}} \qquad \text{and} \qquad \eta^Y_{LR} = \frac{\beta_3}{1 - \beta_4}\frac{\overline{Y}}{\overline{Q}}$$

where a bar indicates the mean value.

with probability 0.90. Now, to obtain the confidence interval, treat Eq. (A9.4) as an equality, i.e., as a *quadratic equation in z*. In other words, substitute the estimates $\hat{\beta}_2$, $\hat{\beta}_4$, Var $(\hat{\beta}_2)$, Var $(\hat{\beta}_4)$, and Cov $(\hat{\beta}_2, \hat{\beta}_4)$ into Eq. (A9.4) and solve the resulting quadratic equation for z. The result will be of the form

$$\hat{z} = \overline{\eta} \pm u$$

where $\overline{\eta}$ is the expected value of the elasticity [and *not* necessarily equal to $\hat{\beta}_2/(1 - \hat{\beta}_4)$] and $\pm u$ is the 90 percent confidence interval.

EXERCISES

9.1 Suppose the equation to be estimated is

$$Y = \beta_1 + \beta_2 X_2 + \beta_3 X_3 + \beta_4 X_4 + \varepsilon$$

The researcher is missing the last five observations for X_4 but has available a variable Z which is known to be highly correlated with X_4. What should the researcher do, and what assumptions must hold for this to be a good procedure?

9.2 Consider the models $Y_t = \alpha + \beta X_t + \varepsilon_t$ and $Z_t = \gamma + \delta Y_t + u_t$.

(a) Suppose you are trying to estimate α and β but the last (Tth) observation on X_t is missing. What should you do?

(b) Suppose now that you are interested in forecasting Z_t and know γ, δ, and X_t for $t \le T$ and Y_t for $t \le T - 1$. What should you do?

9.3 Prove that replacing the missing X observation in the model described in part (a) of Exercise 9.2 by using time t as an instrument will yield a consistent slope estimator. What will happen if the error term is serially correlated?

9.4 Consider the model

$$Y_{it} = \alpha + \beta X_{it} + \varepsilon_{it} \qquad \begin{matrix} i = 1, 2, \ldots, N \\ t = 1, 2, \ldots, T \end{matrix}$$

Assume that it is known that the time-series intercepts are constant. How would you test to see whether the fixed-effects model ought to be used to account for varying cross-section intercepts?

9.5 How would you estimate a pooled time-series cross-section model when the cross-section error component is known to be heteroscedastic? Would a similar method work when it is the time-series component that is known to be heteroscedastic?

9.6 Assume that you are estimating a model with two explanatory variables, each of which has a geometric lag. Derive an equation to be estimated when both lags have identical weights.

9.7 Consider the following model:

$$Y_t = \alpha + \beta(w_0 X_t + w_1 X_{t-1} + w_2 X_{t-2} + w_3 X_{t-3}) + \varepsilon_t$$

Show how to estimate the model using the polynomial distributed lag model and a second-degree polynomial if

(a) There are no endpoint restrictions.

(b) The tail and head of the distribution are assumed equal to 0 ($w_{-1} = w_4 = 0$).

9.8 We wish to examine several alternatives for estimating an equation in the presence of missing data. The model we wish to estimate is

$$EXP = \beta_1 + \beta_2 POP + \beta_3 AID + \beta_4 INC + \varepsilon$$

where it is known (see Chapter 6) that $VAR(\varepsilon) = C(POP^2)$.

(a) Transform each variable, dividing by POP. Define

$$PCEXP = \frac{EXP}{POP} \qquad POP1 = \frac{1}{POP} \qquad PCAID = \frac{AID}{POP} \qquad PCINC = \frac{INC}{POP}$$

Using all the data, find efficient estimates of β_1, β_2, β_3, and β_4 by regressing PCEXP on POP1, PCAID, and PCINC (with a constant term included). These estimates are our reference set for the remainder of the problem. Denote them by β_1^A, β_2^A, β_3^A, β_4^A.

For the remainder of this problem we assume that the last five observations on INC are missing.

(b) Using only the first 45 observations and the transformed data, estimate the model. Label the estimates β_1^B, β_2^B, β_3^B, and β_4^B.

(c) Using observations 1 to 45, find the average of INC; call it $\widehat{INC}$. Define PCINCC by

$$PCINCC_t = \begin{cases} PCINC_t & \text{if } t \le 45 \\ \widehat{INC}/POP_t & \text{if } t \ge 46 \end{cases}$$

Regress PCEXP on POP1, AID, and PCINCC. Label the estimates β_1^C, β_2^C, β_3^C, and β_4^C.

(d) Regress INC on POP and AID using observations 1 to 45. Using the above, predict INC_t for $t = 46$ to 50. Label the predicted values $\widehat{INC}_t$. Define

$$PCINCD_t = \begin{cases} PCINC_t & t \le 45 \\ \dfrac{\widehat{INC}_t}{POP_t} & t \ge 46 \end{cases}$$

and regress PCEXP on POP1, PCAID, and PCINCD. Label the estimated coefficients β_1^D, β_2^D, β_3^D, β_4^D.

(e) Using the first 45 observations, find the average of PCINC. Denote this by $\widehat{PCINC}$. Define

$$PCINCE_t = \begin{cases} PCINC_t & t \le 45 \\ \widehat{PCINC}_t & t \ge 46 \end{cases}$$

Regress PCEXP on POP1, PCAID, and PCINCE. Label the estimates β_1^E, β_2^E, β_3^E, β_4^E, β_5^E.

(f) Using observations 1 to 45, regress PCINC on POP1 and PCAID. Using the above, predict PCINC_t for $t \geq 46$. Call the predicted values $\widehat{\text{PCINC}}_t$. Define

$$\text{PCINCF}_t = \begin{cases} \text{PCINC}_t & t \leq 45 \\ \widehat{\text{PCINC}}_t & t \geq 46 \end{cases}$$

Regress PCEXP on POP1, PCAID, and PCINCF and label the estimated coefficients β_1^F, β_2^F, β_3^F, and β_4^F.

(g) Compare and contrast the results from procedures (a) through (f). Which seem to be the most reasonable methods for dealing with missing observations? Why?

CHAPTER 10

NONLINEAR AND MAXIMUM-LIKELIHOOD ESTIMATION

Advances in the capabilities of computer hardware and software have allowed econometricians to develop and utilize increasingly sophisticated techniques for the estimation of econometric models. Several decades ago the estimation of an inherently nonlinear model could be prohibitively costly, but today such an exercise can be accomplished easily. As a result, econometricians now have access to a much larger set of statistical tools. Of course, choosing the most appropriate technique is still a concern.

In this chapter we focus on three advanced estimation techniques. We begin with an introduction to nonlinear estimation and discuss some alternative techniques for estimating equations that are nonlinear in the parameters. We also show how these equations can be used for forecasting. In the second part of the chapter we describe the technique of maximum-likelihood estimation, a useful alternative to least squares. In the third part we show how nonlinear estimation methods can be used to estimate models in which the error variance depends on the volatility of past errors (ARCH models) and models in which the pattern of past error variances follows a distributed lag (GARCH models). Appendix 10.1 contains a brief introduction to a generalized method of moments estimation, a very general technique that includes nonlinear instrumental-variables estimation and nonlinear generalized least-squares estimation as special cases.

10.1 NONLINEAR ESTIMATION

All the single-equation regression models we have studied to this point have been linear in their coefficients, and thus ordinary least squares or variations on ordinary least squares could be used to estimate them. In this section we examine the problem of estimating equations that are nonlinear in their coefficients. Although procedures for *nonlinear estimation* can be computationally expensive, they greatly increase the scope of model structures that can be used to fit the data.

Our concern will be directed toward equations that are *inherently* nonlinear. For example, the equations

$$Y = \alpha_0 + \alpha_1 X_1^{\beta_1} + \alpha_2 X_2^{\beta_2} + \varepsilon$$

$$Y = \alpha_1 e^{\beta_1 X_1} + \alpha_2 e^{\beta_2 X_2} + \varepsilon$$

cannot be transformed into linear equations and thus do not lend themselves to linear regression. Specifically, we consider equations of the form

$$Y = f(X_1, X_2, \ldots, X_k, \beta_1, \beta_2, \ldots, \beta_p) + \varepsilon \tag{10.1}$$

where f is a nonlinear function of the k independent variables $X_1, \ldots, X_k$ and the p coefficients $\beta_1, \ldots, \beta_p$. The criterion used for determining the estimated values for the coefficients is the same as that used in a linear regression, i.e., minimization of the *sum of squared errors*. If we have T observations on $Y, X_1, \ldots, X_k$, we can write the sum of squared errors as

$$S = \sum_{t=1}^{T} [Y_t - f(X_{1t}, \ldots, X_{kt}, \beta_1, \ldots, \beta_p)]^2 \tag{10.2}$$

We call $\hat{\beta}_1, \ldots, \hat{\beta}_p$ the nonlinear least-squares estimates of $\beta_1, \ldots, \beta_p$, that is, the values of $\beta_1, \ldots, \beta_p$ that minimize the sum of squared errors S.

In the case of a linear regression, obtaining least-squares estimates is computationally straightforward. For a nonlinear equation, however, there are alternative computational approaches to finding coefficient estimates that will minimize the sum of squared errors in Eq. (10.2).

10.1.1   Computational Methods for Nonlinear Estimation

There are three general approaches to the solution of the nonlinear estimation problem. Most numerical estimation methods involve one of these approaches or a combination of two of them. As we will see, the choice of approach depends on the type of equation being estimated.

First, a *direct search* may be used; in this case the sum-of-squared-errors function is evaluated for alternative sets of coefficient values. Those values which result in a minimum are chosen as the estimates. This method may be effective if only one or two coefficients must be estimated. However, if more than two coefficients are involved (which is usually the case), an extremely large number of calculations must be made, and so the method becomes computationally very expensive. For example, if four coefficients must be estimated and 20 alternative values for each coefficient are to be considered, the sum of squared errors must be calculated $(20)^4 = 160,000$ times! As a result, this method is almost never used, and we will not discuss it further.

A second approach involves *direct optimization*. Parameter estimates are obtained by differentiating the sum-of-squared-errors function with respect to each coefficient, setting the derivatives equal to zero (thus defining a minimum), and solving the resulting set of nonlinear equations (which are called the *normal equations*). Taking the derivatives of Eq. (10.2) with respect to β_1, ..., β_p and setting them equal to zero, we find that the normal equations are

$$\sum_{t=1}^{T} 2[Y_t - f(X_{1t}, \ldots, X_{kt}, \beta_1, \ldots, \beta_p)] \frac{\partial f}{\partial \beta_i} = 0 \qquad \text{for } i = 1, \ldots, p$$

These nonlinear equations must be solved simultaneously for $\beta_1, \ldots, \beta_p$, since each equation may contain all p coefficients. As one might expect, this approach can present computational difficulties and therefore is seldom applied directly. One variation of this approach that is computationally feasible is the *steepest-descent method*. The method works by moving from one trial set of coefficient values for $\beta_1, \ldots, \beta_p$ to a new set in such a way that the derivatives $-\partial S/\partial\beta_1, \ldots, -\partial S/\partial\beta_p$ are as large as possible, resulting in rapid progress to the values of $\beta_1, \ldots, \beta_p$ that minimize S (and for which the derivatives are zero).

The third approach to solving nonlinear estimation problems is an *iterative linearization method* in which the nonlinear equation is linearized around some initial set of coefficient values. Then ordinary least squares is performed on this linear equation, generating a new set of coefficient values. The nonlinear equation is relinearized around these new coefficient values, ordinary least squares is again performed to generate new coefficient values, and the equation is relinearized around these values. This iterative process is repeated until *convergence* is attained, i.e., until the coefficient values do not change substantially after each new ordinary least-squares regression.

This approach has certain advantages, the first of which is computational efficiency. If the equation to be estimated is closely approximated by a linear equation, very few iterations may be necessary. A second advantage is that it provides a clear guideline for doing statistical tests that usually are applied only to linear regression. Since a linear regression is performed at each iteration, one can use standard statistical tests (R^2, t statistics, etc.) to evaluate the fit of the final linearized equation. Because this approach has been used in software for econometric modeling, we examine it in more detail below.

We use the fact that any nonlinear function can be expressed as a *Taylor series expansion*. Specifically, we can write Eq. (10.1) in an expansion around a set of initial values $\beta_{1,0}, \ldots, \beta_{p,0}$ for the coefficients $\beta_1, \ldots, \beta_p$. (How these initial values were obtained is not important at this point; let us assume that they represent guesses of the true values.) The expanded equation would be

$$Y = f(X_1, \ldots, X_k, \beta_{1,0}, \ldots, \beta_{p,0}) + \sum_{i=1}^{p} \left(\frac{\partial f}{\partial \beta_i}\right)_0 (\beta_i - \beta_{i,0})$$

$$+ \frac{1}{2} \sum_{i=1}^{p} \sum_{j=1}^{p} \left(\frac{\partial^2 f}{\partial \beta_i \, \partial \beta_j}\right)_0 (\beta_i - \beta_{i,0})(\beta_j - \beta_{j,0}) + \cdots + \varepsilon$$

Here the subscript 0 on the partial derivatives denotes that these derivatives are evaluated at $\beta_1 = \beta_{1,0}, \ldots, \beta_p = \beta_{p,0}$.

A linear approximation to our nonlinear function is provided by the first two terms in the Taylor series expansion. Dropping the second- and higher-order terms and rewriting the equation, we get

$$Y - f(X_1, \ldots, X_k, \beta_{1,0}, \ldots, \beta_{p,0}) + \sum_{i=1}^{p} \beta_{i,0} \left(\frac{\partial f}{\partial \beta_i}\right)_0 = \sum_{i=1}^{p} \beta_i \left(\frac{\partial f}{\partial \beta_i}\right)_0 + \varepsilon$$

$$(10.3)$$

Observe that Eq. (10.3) has the form of a linear regression equation. The left-hand side is a constructed dependent variable. The right-hand side consists (in addition to the additive error term) of a set of unknown coefficients $(\beta_1, \ldots, \beta_p)$ multiplying a set of constructed independent variables. Thus, the coefficients can be estimated by performing ordinary least-squares regression.

The estimated coefficient values for $\beta_1, \ldots, \beta_p$, which are labeled $\beta_{1,1}, \ldots, \beta_{p,1}$, are used as a new set of initial estimates, and the nonlinear equation is *relinearized* around those values. The result is a new linear regression equation

$$Y - f(X_1, \ldots, X_k, \beta_{1,1}, \ldots, \beta_{p,1}) + \sum_{i=1}^{p} \beta_{i,1} \left(\frac{\partial f}{\partial \beta_i}\right)_1 = \sum_{i=1}^{p} \beta_i \left(\frac{\partial f}{\partial \beta_i}\right)_1 + \varepsilon$$

Ordinary least squares is applied to this equation, and a new set of coefficient estimates $\beta_{1,2}, \ldots, \beta_{p,2}$ is obtained. The process of relinearization is repeated until convergence occurs, i.e., until

$$\left|\frac{\beta_{i,j+1} - \beta_{i,j}}{\beta_{i,j}}\right| < \delta \qquad i = 1, 2, \ldots, p \qquad (10.4)$$

where δ is a small number whose choice depends in part on computational expense.

There is no guarantee that this iterative process will converge to the maximum-likelihood estimate of the coefficients. The process may, for example, converge to a local, as opposed to a global, minimum of the sum-of-squared-errors function. One way to see if this has occurred is to repeat the estimation, starting with a different set of initial guesses for the coefficients.

Of crucial importance is the fact that the iterative process may not converge *at all*. Succeeding estimates of the coefficients may differ, and the left-hand side of Eq. (10.4) may grow larger with each new iteration (i.e., the process may *diverge*). If divergence occurs, one can begin the process over again, using a new set of initial guesses for the coefficients. If the process still does not converge, it may be necessary to try a different estimation method.

An alternative method involves a variation on the iterative linearization method. Instead of using the successive estimates resulting from each linearization, estimates are computed from

$$\beta_{i,j+1} = \beta_{i,j} + \alpha(\hat{\beta}_{i,j+1} - \beta_{i,j})$$

where $\hat{\beta}_{i,j+1}$ is the least-squares estimate from the $(j + 1)$st iteration and α is a damping factor $(0 < \alpha < 1)$. The damping factor α can be chosen to avoid overshooting the minimum of the sum-of-squared-errors function.[1]

Other methods of nonlinear estimation are available and may provide convergent estimates when the methods described above fail.[2] There is really no best method, since one may converge more easily while another may involve less computational expense. Often alternative methods are used as a way of checking that the global minimum of the sum-of-squared-errors function has been reached.

10.1.2   Evaluation of Nonlinear Regression Equations

The statistical tests used to evaluate the fit of a linear regression equation are not directly applicable to a nonlinear regression. An F statistic, for example, cannot be used to perform a significance test on the overall fit of a nonlinear regression, nor can t statistics be used in the usual manner. One reason for this is that we cannot obtain an unbiased estimate of σ^2, the true variance of the error term ε, from the regression residuals. Even if ε is normally distributed with 0 mean, the residuals $\hat{\varepsilon}_t$ given by

$$\hat{\varepsilon}_t = Y_t - f(X_{1t}, \ldots, X_{kt}, \hat{\beta}_1, \ldots, \hat{\beta}_p) \tag{10.5}$$

---

[1] The damping factor also can be used to change the step $\beta_{i,j+1} - \beta_{i,j}$ so that its values lie somewhere between that which would be indicated by the linearization method and that which would be indicated by the steepest-descent method. This is the basis for Marquardt's method. See D. W. Marquardt, "An Algorithm for Least Squares Estimation of Nonlinear Parameters," *Journal of the Society of Industrial and Applied Mathematics,* vol. 2, p. 431, 1963.

[2] For a discussion of several alternative estimation methods and their statistical properties, see T. Amemiya, "Nonlinear Regression Models," in Z. Griliches and M. Intriligator (eds.), *Handbook of Econometrics,* vol. 1 (Amsterdam: North-Holland, 1991), Chapter 5.

will not be normally distributed (nor will they have 0 mean). Thus, the sum of squared residuals will not follow a chi-square distribution, the estimated coefficients themselves will not be normally distributed, and standard t tests and F tests cannot be applied.

What we can do, however, is perform t tests and F tests on the *linear* regression that applies to the *final linearization of the iterative process*. We hope that this linearization will provide a reasonable approximation to the nonlinear equation and that it will fit the data. If it does not fit the data (as indicated by the statistics), doubt will be cast on the fit of the nonlinear equation as a whole. In light of this, computer programs that perform nonlinear estimation via the linearization approach usually calculate t statistics and associated standard errors for the last linearization. (These standard errors are consistently estimated.)

Unlike t and F tests, the R^2 can be applied in its conventional sense to a nonlinear regression. Recall that the R^2 is calculated from

$$R^2 = 1 - \frac{\Sigma \hat{\varepsilon}_t^2}{\Sigma y_t^2}$$

(where y_t is measured in deviations form) and represents the fraction of the variation in y_t that is "explained" by the regression. The R^2 will retain this meaning when the equation is nonlinear, if the residuals are calculated from Eq. (10.5).

10.1.3   Forecasting with a Nonlinear Regression Equation

Once a nonlinear regression equation has been estimated, it can be used to obtain forecasts. A forecast of Y_t is given by

$$\hat{Y}_{T+1} = f(X_{1,T+1}, \ldots, X_{k,T+1}, \hat{\beta}_1, \ldots, \hat{\beta}_p) \tag{10.6}$$

We saw in Chapter 8 that for a linear regression such a forecast is unbiased and has the minimum mean square error. This claim cannot be made, however, for a forecast generated from a nonlinear regression, as in Eq. (10.6). The reason for this is that the forecast errors will not be normally distributed with 0 mean as was the case for a linear equation. In such a case we cannot determine whether the forecast error is smaller than the error generated by a different set of coefficient estimates.

Furthermore, the formulas for the standard error of forecast (i.e., the standard deviation of the forecast error) and corresponding confidence intervals that were derived in Chapter 8 for the linear case do not apply to Eq. (10.6). There is in fact no analytic formula that can be used to directly compute forecast confidence intervals for the general nonlinear equation. One solution involves the generation of confidence intervals through the use of Monte Carlo forecasting, as described in Chapter 14. This, however, requires that the coefficients be normally distributed (which is not the case) and that estimates be available for the coefficient standard errors and the standard error of the equation itself (which is also not the case). Thus, Monte Carlo techniques (stochastic simulation) are not directly applicable here.

We suggest the following compromise approach. A Monte Carlo forecast is performed using normally distributed errors for the coefficients and the additive error term, but using the linear regression results from the last iteration to provide estimates for the standard errors. As an illustration, consider the nonlinear regression equation

$$Y_t = \beta_0 + \beta_1 X_t^{\beta_2} + \varepsilon_t$$

After the equation has been estimated and a forecast $\hat{Y}_{T+1}$ has been computed, the standard error of forecast is computed as follows:

1. Rewrite the equation as

$$Y_t = (\beta_0 + \eta_0) + (\beta_1 + \eta_1) X_t^{\beta_2 + \eta_2} + \varepsilon_t$$

where η_0, η_1, η_2, and ε_t are assumed to be normally distributed random variables with 0 mean and standard deviations equal to the *computed standard errors from the linear regression corresponding to the last iteration* of the estimation process.

2. Generate random numbers (from the appropriate normal distributions) for η_0, η_1, η_2, and ε_{T+1} to use for the forecast $\hat{Y}_{T+1}$. Compute this forecast accordingly.

3. Repeat step 2 some 100 or 200 times. Use the sample standard deviation of the resulting distribution of values for $\hat{Y}_{T+1}$ as the standard error of forecast. This approximate standard error of forecast can then be used to calculate confidence intervals.

There is no guarantee that this method will provide even a close approximation to the true standard error of forecast. It does, however, at least provide some measure of forecast confidence.

Example 10.1 Consumption Function   In this example we estimate a *consumption function* that is nonlinear in the coefficients. The objective is to relate aggregate real (constant-dollar) consumption C to aggregate real disposable income YD in the United States, using quarterly time-series data. We would also like to test the hypothesis that the *marginal propensity to consume* (MPC), which is defined as

$$\text{MPC} = \frac{dC}{d\text{YD}}$$

declines as disposable income increases. This hypothesis is easy to support using cross-section data (regressing consumption against income for groups at different income levels), but not using time-series data.

Typically, the following consumption function, which is linear in the coefficients, is estimated:

$$C = \alpha_0 + \alpha_1 YD + \alpha_2 YD^2 + \varepsilon$$

One would expect α_1 to be positive. If the equation is estimated using cross-section data, a significant and negative value of α_2 will usually result, while if time-series data are used, the estimate of α_2 may be positive.

As an alternative, we estimate the following nonlinear consumption function:

$$C = \alpha_0 + \alpha_1 YD^{\alpha_2} + \varepsilon \tag{10.7}$$

The quarterly time-series data being used cover the period 1947-1 to 1995-3. The estimation is performed by using the iterative linearization process. We use the value 1.0 as an initial guess for all three coefficients (we would expect α_1 and α_2 to be close to this value, but we have no expectation regarding the value of α_0).

Convergence occurs after 22 iterations. The estimated nonlinear equation is

$$\hat{C} = 256.33 + .195\ YD^{1.180} \tag{10.8}$$

The standard errors for $\hat{\alpha}_0$, $\hat{\alpha}_1$, and $\hat{\alpha}_2$ are 16.71, .0211, and .0126, respectively. As a result, each of the coefficient estimates is highly significant at the 5 percent level. Furthermore, R^2 is equal to .999.

For comparison, the following linear regression was also estimated (standard errors are in parentheses):

$$\hat{C} = -14.925 + .918\ YD \tag{10.9}$$
$$\phantom{\hat{C} = }\ (7.031) \quad\ (.0030)$$

$$R^2 = .998 \qquad s = 39.23$$

Note that the MPC for this linear equation is a constant, .918. For our nonlinear equation, however, the MPC is

$$MPC = \frac{dC}{dYD} = \alpha_1 \alpha_2\ YD^{\alpha_2 - 1}$$

The mean value of YD is 2165, and at this value MPC is .917. Note that MPC declines as YD increases; for YD equal to 600, MPC is .805.

10.2 MAXIMUM-LIKELIHOOD ESTIMATION

The maximum-likelihood approach was described briefly in Appendix 2.2. In this section we show how this basic principle can be applied broadly to the estimation of econometric models. We saw in Chapters 6 and 7 that ordinary least-squares estimation yields estimators that sometimes are inefficient and at other times are inconsistent. We will see that a great advantage of maximum-likelihood estimation is that under a broad set of conditions parameter estimators are both consistent and (for large samples) asymptotically efficient. The following discussion describes the application of the maximum-likelihood approach to linear models and then nonlinear models.

10.2.1 The Maximum-Likelihood Approach

We begin our analysis with the linear regression model

$$Y_i = \alpha + \beta X_i + \varepsilon_i$$

We know that each Y_i is normally distributed with mean $\alpha + \beta X_i$ and variance σ^2. The probability distribution can be written explicitly as

$$p(Y_i) = \frac{1}{\sqrt{2\pi\sigma^2}} \exp\left[-\frac{1}{2\sigma^2}(Y_i - \alpha - \beta X_i)^2\right]$$

The likelihood function is the product of the individual probabilities taken over all N observations. In this case the likelihood function is

$$L(Y_1, Y_2, \ldots, Y_N, \alpha, \beta, \sigma^2) = p(Y_1)p(Y_2) \cdots p(Y_N)$$
$$= \frac{1}{(2\pi\sigma^2)^N} \cdot \exp\left[-\Sigma\left(\frac{Y_i - \alpha - \beta X_i}{2\sigma^2}\right)^2\right]$$

With maximum-likelihood estimation our goal is to find the values of the parameters α, β, and α^2 which are most likely to generate the sample observations $Y_1, \ldots, Y_N$. This is achieved by maximizing the likelihood function given above with respect to each of the parameters. To do this it is more convenient to work with the logarithm of the likelihood function. The *log-likelihood function* is given by

$$\log L = -(N/2) \log (2\pi) - (N/2) \log (\sigma^2)$$
$$- (\sigma^2/2)\Sigma(Y_i - \alpha - \beta X_i)^2 \tag{10.10}$$

Maximizing log L is equivalent to maximizing L because the logarithmic transformation is monotonic and increasing [for any two values of the function, c_1 and c_2, if $c_1 > c_2$, then $\log(c_1) > \log(c_2)$]. To find the maximum we differentiate the log-likelihood function with respect to each of the three unknown parameters, equate the derivatives to zero, and solve.

Differentiating Eq. (10.10) partially with respect to α, β, and σ^2 and setting the derivatives equal to zero yields

$$\frac{\partial(\log L)}{\partial \alpha} = \frac{1}{\sigma^2} \Sigma(Y_i - \alpha - \beta X_i) = 0 \tag{10.11}$$

$$\frac{\partial(\log L)}{\partial \beta} = \frac{1}{\sigma^2} \Sigma[X_i(Y_i - \alpha - \beta X_i)] = 0 \tag{10.12}$$

$$\frac{\partial(\log L)}{\partial \sigma^2} = \frac{-N}{2\sigma^2} + \frac{1}{2\sigma^4} \Sigma(Y_i - \alpha - \beta X_i)^2 = 0 \tag{10.13}$$

The solution to Eqs. (10.11) to (10.13) yields the following maximum-likelihood estimators:

$$\alpha' = \overline{Y} - \beta'\overline{X} \qquad \beta' = \frac{\Sigma(X_i - \overline{X})(Y_i - \overline{Y})}{\Sigma(X_i - \overline{X})^2} \qquad \sigma^{2\prime} = \frac{\Sigma(Y_i - \alpha' - \beta'X_i)^2}{N}$$

Clearly, the maximum-likelihood estimators of α and β are identical to the least-squares estimators. It follows therefore that α' and β' are best linear unbiased estimators. $\sigma^{2\prime}$, however, is a biased (although consistent) estimator of σ^2. To obtain an unbiased estimator, we need to divide the numerator by $N - 2$, adjusting for degrees of freedom, as discussed in Chapter 3. Now we show how the maximum-likelihood approach can be applied to the estimation of nonlinear models.

Suppose a general model is given by

$$Y = f(X_1, \ldots, X_k, \beta_1, \ldots, \beta_p) + \varepsilon$$

where ε is normally distributed and satisfies all the other assumptions of the basic linear regression model. Then, for each of the N observations on Y and the corresponding X's, we can write the probability distribution of Y, given the X's and β's, as

$$f(Y_i, X_i, \beta) = \left[\frac{1}{2\pi\sigma^2}\right]^{1/2} \exp\left[\left(\frac{-1}{2\sigma^2}\right)(Y_i - f(X_{1i}, \ldots, X_{ki}, \beta_1, \ldots, \beta_p))\right]^2$$

where exp represents the exponential function. Then the log-likelihood function for all N observations is given by

$$L = \Sigma f(Y_i, X_i, \beta) = -\left(\frac{N}{2}\right)\log 2\pi - \left(\frac{N}{2}\right)\log \sigma^2$$

$$- \left(\frac{1}{2\sigma^2}\right)\Sigma(Y_i - f(X_{1i}, \ldots, X_{ki}, \beta_1, \ldots, \beta_p)) \qquad (10.14)$$

(All summations are taken over the observations $i = 1, 2, \ldots, N$.)

By differentiating Eq. (10.14) with respect to each of the β's and σ^2, equating to 0, and solving, we obtain a system of $p + 1$ nonlinear equations with $p + 1$ unknowns. If the equations happen to be linear, as with the basic regression model, it is easy to compute the solutions—the maximum-likelihood estimates for each of the parameters. If the equations are not linear, however, the solution process is more complex and we must use a numerical procedure similar to the one in Section 10.1.1.

Whatever numerical procedure is used to find the solution, the maximum-likelihood estimator has a number of desirable properties:

1. The estimator is consistent.
2. The estimator is asymptotically efficient.
3. Estimates of the (asymptotic) variances of the estimators can be determined as a by-product of the estimation process.

The estimates of the variance of the estimate of each parameter β_i are given by

$$I(\beta_i) = -E[\partial^2 \ln L/\partial\beta_i^2]$$

which is the expected value of the second derivative of the log-likelihood function with respect to β_i. Covariance estimates between estimates of β_i and β_j are obtained similarly by differentiating the log-likelihood function with respect to β_i and then with respect to β_j.

The $I(\cdot)$ function, which describes the components of the *information matrix*, provides a measure of the curvature of the log-likelihood function. The greater the curvature, the higher the estimated variances.

10.2.2 The Likelihood Ratio Test

Suppose we are using maximum-likelihood estimation and wish to test whether certain parameter restrictions are supported by the data. For example, we may want to test the null hypothesis that some of the β's are equal to 0. One useful and very convenient test is the *likelihood ratio test*. To apply the test, suppose that $L(\beta_{UR})$ represents the maximum value of the log-likelihood function when the restrictions do not apply, while $L(\beta_R)$ represents the maximum value when the restrictions do apply.

The likelihood ratio is given by

$$\lambda = \frac{L(\beta_R)}{L(\beta_{UR})}$$

The denominator is based on the unrestricted model; as a result, it must be at least as great as the numerator. Therefore, λ must lie between 0 and 1. If the null hypothesis is true, we expect λ to be close to 1; if it is not true, we expect λ to be close to 0. Intuitively, therefore, we expect to reject the null hypothesis when λ is sufficiently small.

The likelihood ratio test that can be applied to evaluate the null hypothesis builds on the fact that for large sample sizes,

$$-2[L(\beta_R) - L(\beta_{UR})] \sim \chi^2_m$$

where m is the number of restrictions. To do the test we simply compare the calculated value of χ^2_m above with the critical value at, for example, the 5 percent significance level. If χ^2_m is greater than the critical value, we can reject the null hypothesis that the restrictions do not apply, i.e., that the β's are not 0.

As an example, suppose (as in Section 7.5) we are estimating the model

$$y_i = \beta_1 x_{1i} + \beta_2 x_{2i} + \beta_3 x_{3i} + \varepsilon_i \tag{10.15}$$

and wish to test the restrictions that $\beta_2 = 0$ and $\beta_3 = 0$. The restricted model is then given by

$$y_i = \beta_1 x_{1i} + u_i \tag{10.16}$$

The value of $L(\beta_{UR})$ is obtained by maximizing the likelihood function consistent with Eq. (10.15), while the value of $L(\beta_R)$ is given by maximizing the likelihood function associated with Eq. (10.16).

In most situations involving linear models, especially those involving large sample sizes, the more traditional F tests (discussed in Chapter 5) and the likelihood ratio tests should generate very similar results. Depending on the software being used, the likelihood ratio test may be more difficult to apply, but it is more appealing when large samples are involved in part because it need not require an assumption of normality.[3]

---

[3] For a general comparison of F tests (a special case of a more general Wald test), likelihood ratio tests, and Lagrange multiplier tests, see Robert F. Engle, "Wald, Likelihood Ratio, and Lagrange Multiplier Tests in Econometrics," in Z. Griliches and M. D. Intriligator, eds., *Handbook of Econometrics*, vol. II (Amsterdam: Elsevier Science Publishers, 1984), Chapter 13.

10.2.3   An Application: The Box-Cox Model

One interesting nonlinear model, attributed to G. E. P. Box and D. R. Cox, is given for the two-variable model by the following equation:[4]

$$\frac{Y_i^\lambda - 1}{\lambda} = \alpha + \beta \left(\frac{X_i^\lambda - 1}{\lambda}\right) + \varepsilon_i$$

When $\lambda = 1$, this reduces to

$$Y_i - 1 = \alpha + \beta(X_i - 1) + \varepsilon_i$$

which is the basic linear regression model (with dependent variable $Y - 1$ and independent variable $X - 1$).

When $\lambda = 0$, however, the analysis is more complex because $(Y_i^\lambda - 1)/\lambda$ looks indeterminate. Note, however, that we can use a Taylor series expansion to express Y_i^λ as

$$Y_i^\lambda = \exp(\lambda \log Y_i) = 1 + \lambda \log Y_i + \left(\frac{1}{2}\right)(\lambda \log Y_i)^2 + \cdots$$

It follows that

$$\frac{Y_i^\lambda - 1}{\lambda} = \log Y_i + \left(\frac{\lambda}{2}\right)(\log Y_i)^2 + \cdots$$

And, for $\lambda = 0$,
$$\frac{Y_i^\lambda - 1}{\lambda} = \log Y_i$$

Thus, in the special case in which $\lambda = 0$, the Box-Cox transformation yields the log-linear model

$$\log Y_i = \alpha + \beta \log X_i + \varepsilon_i$$

The Box-Cox model is a generalized nonlinear specification, and as such it has several uses. First, one can do maximum-likelihood estimation to find the parameters of a nonlinear model in which the powers of each of the variables are estimated rather than specified arbitrarily. In fact, in a more general model, the parameter λ can be allowed to vary from variable to variable. Second, one can use maximum-likelihood estimation to test whether the linear model or

---

[4] See G. E. P. Box and D. R. Cox, "An Analysis of Transformations," *Journal of the Royal Statistical Society*, Series B, vol. 26, pp. 211–243, 1964.

the log-linear model provides a better model specification. In either case, the appropriate log-likelihood function is given by[5]

$$L = (\lambda - 1) \sum \log Y_i - \left(\frac{N}{2}\right) \log (2\pi) - \left(\frac{N}{2}\right) \log (\sigma^2)$$

$$- \frac{1}{2\sigma^2} \sum \left[\frac{Y_i^\lambda - 1}{\lambda} - \alpha - \beta \frac{X_i^\lambda - 1}{\lambda} \right]^2$$

A comparison of the values of L when $\lambda = 0$ and $\lambda = 1$ allows us to choose the model that best fits the data.

Suppose that a complete maximum-likelihood program is not available and that we are interested in choosing only between the linear and the log-linear models. In this particular case, a least-squares approach can be used to solve the problem. To do so we renormalize the original Y observations by the geometric mean of Y, Y_g. Then Y_g is defined implicitly by the equation

$$\log Y_g = \frac{\sum (\log Y_i)}{N}$$

The normalized Y variables now become

$$Y^* = \frac{Y}{Y_g}$$

We can now compare the best-fitting of the following linear and log-linear models directly (assuming that the errors are normally distributed):

Linear: $Y^* = \alpha' + \beta' X^* + \varepsilon'$

Log-linear: $\log Y^* = \alpha + \beta \log X^* + \varepsilon$

The direct comparison is possible because

$$\sum \log Y^* = \sum \log Y_i - \sum [\log e^{\sum (\log Y_i)/N}] = \sum \log Y_i - N \sum \frac{\log Y_i}{N} = 0$$

It follows that the first term in the log-likelihood function associated with the Box-Cox specification is equal to 0 for the log-linear version of the model. But the first term is also 0 for the linear version, since $\lambda = 1$ in that case. As a result, maximum-likelihood estimation and least squares yield identical out-

---

[5] The first term arises because there is a change of variables in moving from the distribution function of ε to the distribution function for Y. Specifically, $d\varepsilon/dY = Y_i^{\lambda-1}$, so that $\log (d\varepsilon/dY) = (\lambda - 1) \log Y$.

comes when the data are normalized. (The same was shown to be true in Appendix 2.2 when least-squares and maximum-likelihood estimation were compared.) The equation with the smallest error sum of squares or, equivalently, the greatest R^2 will give the best specification.[6]

Example 10.2 Energy, Climate, and the Value of Residential Housing

The value of single-family residences is determined in part by the costs of housing production and in part by the supply and demand for attributes of the houses themselves, of the local neighborhood, and of the region in which the houses are located. As a part of a larger study of the relationship between energy costs, climate, and the demand for housing, J. M. Quigley and D. L. Rubinfeld estimated a housing value model by using a Box-Cox specification.[7]

The model relates the market value of a single-family home V to a set of size and quality attributes h_1; a set of heating, cooling, and related structural attributes h_2; and a pair of climate measures W as follows:

$$\frac{V^\lambda - 1}{\lambda} = \sum_i \beta_i \frac{(h_{1i}^\lambda - 1)}{\lambda} + \sum_j \beta_j \frac{(h_{2j}^\lambda - 1)}{\lambda} + \sum_k \beta_k \frac{(W_k^\lambda - 1)}{\lambda} + \varepsilon$$

The model was estimated using a sample of 5,900 houses (with an average value of $78,000) located in 25 metropolitan areas in 1980. The coefficients and the corresponding t ratios generated by the maximum-likelihood method for the important attributes are given in the table below:

Maximum-likelihood estimates		
Variable	Coefficient	t ratio
Size and quality attributes		
Year built	.115	2.61
Number of baths	.124	2.36
Number of rooms	.194	2.71
Garage (1 yes, 0 no)	.047	2.11
Vermin present (1 yes, 0 no)	.028	1.90
Neighborhood (4 = excellent)	.058	2.27

(continued on the next page)

---

[6] Least-squares techniques such as the one described here generate biased estimates of standard errors. See John J. Spitzer, "Variance Estimates in Models with the Box-Cox Transformation: Implications for Estimation and Hypothesis Testing," *Review of Economics and Statistics,* vol. 66, pp. 645–652, November 1984.

[7] John M. Quigley and Daniel L. Rubinfeld, "Unobservables in Consumer Choice: Residential Energy and the Demand for Comfort," *Review of Economics and Statistics,* vol. 71, pp. 416–425, August 1989.

Maximum-likelihood estimates (*continued*)		
Variable	Coefficient	*t* ratio
Heating and cooling attributes		
Basement (1 yes, 0 no)	.027	2.21
Central air-cond. (1 yes, 0 no)	.059	2.25
Warm-air furnace (1 yes, 0 no)	.045	1.77
Steam heat (1 yes, 0 no)	.084	2.06
Climate attributes		
Hot weather (no. degree days)	.048	1.42
Cold weather (no. degree days)	.042	1.52
Intercept	6.007	6.14
λ	−.10	2.62
$R^2 = .48$		

Most of the individual housing attributes are statistically significant and have the sign one would expect. Additional rooms, bathrooms in particular, add substantially to the value of the house. A central heating system (warm air or steam heat) is quite valuable, as is central air-conditioning. Finally, houses in milder climates are substantially more expensive than are those in very warm or very cold climates.

The estimated value of the Box-Cox parameter λ is rather small, $-.1$, but it is significantly different from 0. This suggests that a log-linear specification would provide a reasonably close approximation to the best-fitting nonlinear model.

10.2.4   Lagrange Multiplier Test

We have discussed two procedures for testing hypotheses: the F test or Wald test (Chapter 5) and the likelihood ratio test. Recall that the Wald test begins with an unrestricted model and asks whether the imposition of a set of restrictions (e.g., that a group of regression parameters are equal to zero) significantly lowers the explanatory power of the regression model. From the perspective of the Wald test, the null hypothesis is given by the restricted model and the alternative hypothesis is given by the unrestricted model. In the linear regression framework, significance is evaluated by using an F test. The likelihood ratio test also provides a test of the null hypothesis given by the restricted model but does so by using a test that relies on the chi-square distribution. The likelihood ratio (LR) test is appealing because it relies on the principle of maximum likelihood.

The Lagrange multiplier (LM) test, the subject of our discussion here, begins with the null hypothesis which is given by the restricted model. It asks whether a movement in the direction of the alternative hypothesis can significantly improve the explanatory power of the restricted model. The LM test is based on the technique of constrained maximization, in which a Lagrange multiplier is used to provide an estimate of the extent to which the imposition of a constraint alters the maximum-likelihood estimates of a set of parameters. Let β_{UR} be the maximum-likelihood estimator of the parameters of the unrestricted model and let β_R represent the parameters associated with the restricted model. Then our objective is to maximize $\ln L(\beta_{UR})$ subject to the restriction that $\beta_{UR} = \beta_R$. This is equivalent to maximizing

$$\ln L(\beta_{UR}) - \lambda(\beta_{UR} - \beta_R)$$

where λ is the Lagrange multiplier. Intuitively, the maximum value of this function will be achieved when the constraint holds exactly. The Lagrange multiplier measures the marginal "valuation" associated with the constraint: the greater is λ, the greater is the reduction in the maximum value of $\ln L(\beta_{UR})$ as the constraint becomes binding.

To see this formally, note that one of the first-order conditions for maximization is

$$\frac{\partial \ln (L)}{\partial \beta_{UR}} = \lambda$$

so that λ is the slope of the likelihood function. If the null hypothesis that the restrictions are valid is not rejected, the restricted parameters will be close to the unrestricted parameters and the value of λ will be small. If, however, the restrictions are significantly binding, the cost of imposing the constraint, which is given by λ, will be large. The LM test, which is based on the magnitude of λ, sometimes is called a *score test*.[8]

The Lagrange multiplier test can be easily applied to the special case in which one is considering the possibility of adding additional explanatory variables to a regression model.[9] Suppose one has estimated the restricted model:

$$Y = \beta_1 + \beta_2 X_2 + \cdots + \beta_{k-q} X_{k-q} + \varepsilon_R \tag{10.17}$$

and is considering the possibility of adding some or all of q additional variables that are contained in the unrestricted model:

$$Y = \beta_1 + \beta_2 X_2 + \cdots + \beta_{k-q} X_{k-q} + \cdots + \beta_k X_k + \varepsilon_{UR} \tag{10.18}$$

---

[8] In general, the test statistic for the LM test is given by

$$\text{LM} = \frac{\lambda(\hat{\beta}_R)^2}{I(\hat{\beta}_R)}$$

where λ and $I(\ )$, the information matrix, are calculated by differentiation of the log-likelihood function.

[9] See, for example, R. Ramanathan, *Statistical Methods in Econometrics* (San Diego: Academic Press, 1993), pp. 276–277.

The Lagrange multiplier test of the hypothesis that each of the additional q variables has a coefficient of 0 is performed by first computing the residuals from the restricted model given by Eq. (10.17). Specifically,

$$\hat{\varepsilon}_R = Y - \hat{\beta}_1 - \hat{\beta}_2 X_2 - \cdots - \hat{\beta}_{k-q} X_{k-q}$$

Now consider the regression of these residuals on all the explanatory variables in the unrestricted model:

$$\hat{\varepsilon}_R = \gamma_1 + \gamma_2 X_2 + \cdots + \gamma_k X_k + u \qquad (10.19)$$

If all the additional variables were "irrelevant," the coefficients would be zero on the $k-q$ variables that are added when we move from the restricted model to the unrestricted model. However, if some or all of the additional variables in the unrestricted model are significant determinants of Y, we expect their coefficients to be statistically significant and thus for Eq. (10.19) to be estimated with a good fit.

The Lagrange multiplier test is determined on the basis of a test of significance of the regression in Eq. (10.19). Specifically, the LM test statistic, which is given by

$$LM = NR_0^2 \qquad (10.20)$$

follows a chi-square distribution with q (the number of restrictions) degrees of freedom. N is the sample size, and R_0^2 is the R^2 associated with the regression in Eq. (10.19).[10]

If the calculated test statistic is greater than the critical value of the chi-square distribution, we reject the null hypothesis that the restricted model is valid. In doing so, we conclude that some of the additional variables should have been included in the regression model. An examination of the t statistics associated with Eq. (10.19) can give an indication of which variables might be chosen, but there is no agreed upon rule of thumb that one should use.

The Lagrange multiplier test often is used as a means of testing for heteroscedasticity; it is given by the White test in Section 6.1. To generalize somewhat from that discussion, suppose one has estimated a linear regression and is concerned about whether the error variance is a function of either of two exogenous variables, X or Z. White suggests that one specify the heteroscedasticity as the following function of the error variances:

$$\sigma^2 = \beta_0 + \beta_1 X + \beta_2 Z + \beta_3 X^2 + \beta_4 Z^2 + \beta_5 XZ + u \qquad (10.21)$$

The null hypothesis of no heteroscedasticity is given by $\beta_1 = \beta_2 = \beta_3 = \beta_4 = \beta_5 = 0$ in Eq. (10.21). To perform the White test we use the square of the

---

[10] For a derivation of this test, see Engle, op. cit.

residuals from the original equation as estimates of σ^2. According to the La-grange multiplier test, we calculate NR^2 from the regression associated with Eq. (10.21). This will follow a chi-square distribution with 5 degrees of freedom, the number of restrictions associated with the null hypothesis.

10.2.5   Comparing the Wald, Likelihood Ratio, and Lagrange Multiplier Tests

In its most general form the Wald test bears a close relationship to both the likelihood ratio test and the Lagrange multiplier test, since it is also based on the difference between the restricted and unrestricted parameter estimates.[11] In the special case of the linear regression model, the Wald test, as described in Chapter 5, simplifies to an F test:

$$F_{q,N-k} = \frac{(R^2_{UR} - R^2_R)/q}{(1 - R^2_{UR})/(N - k)}$$

where R^2_{UR} is R^2 for the unrestricted model and correspondingly for R^2_R. In the very special case in which the unrestricted model is the two-variable linear regression model and $q = 1$, the Wald test further simplifies to

$$W = \frac{NR^2_{UR}}{(1 - R^2_{UR})}$$

In the equivalent case, the LM test is given by

$$LM = NR^2_0$$

where R^2_0 is calculated from the regression of the residuals of a regression of Y on a constant (the deviations in Y) and on the independent variable X.

Finally, the likelihood ratio test in this simple case is given by

$$LR = -N \ln (1 - R^2_{UR})$$

It is important to note that the three tests just described are all asymptotically equivalent; i.e., they will give identical test results if the sample size is allowed to increase without bound. As a general rule, however, they do differ within samples and can generate different and sometimes conflicting tests of signifi-cance.[12] To the extent that the tests differ for a given sample and the model is

---

[11] The Wald test is given by $W = (\hat{\beta}_{UR} - \hat{\beta}_R)^2 I(\hat{\beta}_{UR})$, where $I(\ )$ is the information matrix. The test statistic follows a chi-square distribution with degrees of freedom equal to the number of restrictions.

[12] They are equivalent when the log-likelihood function is quadratic, as, for example, in the case of normally distributed errors.

linear, the Wald test will always give the largest test statistic and the LM test will give the smallest. Therefore, whenever the LM test rejects the null hypothesis that the restricted model is valid, so will the other tests.[13]

When linear models are involved, the Wald test is easily applied because the restricted and unrestricted models can be readily estimated. However, when more general models are involved, the Lagrange multiplier test can provide an appealing alternative, since it relies directly only on the estimation of the restricted model. Further, because it builds on the residuals of the restricted model, it can be used as a means of checking the robustness of the model to a variety of alternatives. We have seen how the LM test can be used as a specification test involving omitted variables. It also can be used as a test for heteroscedasticity, simultaneous equations bias, or the presence of nonlinearities, as the following example illustrates.

Example 10.3 Testing the Linearity of a Consumption Function   In Example 10.1 we showed how to use nonlinear least squares to estimate a nonlinear consumption function of the form

$$C = \alpha_0 + \alpha_1 YD^{\alpha_2} + \varepsilon$$

Suppose we wish to test the null hypothesis that the consumption function is linear, i.e., that $\alpha_2 = 1$.

The Wald test is quite easily applied; in this case the Wald test is equivalent to a t test in which the t value is given by

$$\frac{(\alpha_2 - 1)}{s_{\alpha_2}} = \frac{(1.180 - 1)}{.0126} = 14.25$$

where the standard error is calculated from the last linearized iteration of the nonlinear least-squares estimation procedure. Since this is greater than the critical value of the t distribution, 1.96 for a large-sample two-tailed test at the 5 percent significance level, we reject the null hypothesis of a linear consumption function in favor of the nonlinear specification. This particular Wald test is a special case of a more general chi-square test; we calculated the chi-square statistic to be 202.83, which is approximately equal to the square of 14.25. As in the case of the t test, we reject the null hypothesis of a linear model at the 5 percent significance level.

To test for linearity using a likelihood ratio test, we estimated both the linear and the nonlinear forms of the consumption function by using a

---

[13] See Engle, op. cit., who points out the complexities involved in deciding which of the three tests is the most appropriate.

maximum-likelihood procedure. The LR test is given by

$$-2 \left[\ln L(\beta_R) - L(\beta_{UR}) \right] = 141.04$$

which, while smaller than the chi-square statistic associated with the Wald test, remains highly significant at the 5 percent level with 1 degree of freedom according to the table of the chi-square distribution.

Finally, we undertook an LM test of the linearity assumption. In this case we obtained a chi-square statistic of 194.6, which is also significant.

10.3 ARCH AND GARCH MODELS

In Chapter 6 we discussed the problem of heteroscedasticity and showed how corrections for heteroscedastic error disturbances can lead to more efficient parameter estimates. We focused largely on situations in which the variance of the error term varies directly with one or more independent variables. For example, in the regression equation

$$Y_t = \beta_1 + \beta_2 X_{2t} + \beta_3 X_{3t} + \varepsilon_t \tag{10.22}$$

the variance of ε_t may be proportional to X_{2t}^2. In this case we could use a weighted least-squares procedure in which we divide the left- and right-hand side variables by X_{2t} and then estimate the transformed regression equation

$$\frac{Y_t}{X_{2t}} = \beta_1 \frac{1}{X_{2t}} + \beta_2 + \beta_3 \frac{X_{3t}}{X_{2t}} + \varepsilon_t^*$$

by ordinary least squares. The transformed error term $\varepsilon_t^* = \varepsilon_t / X_{2t}$ is homoscedastic, and so ordinary least squares will yield efficient parameter estimates.

In some applications there may be reason to believe that the variance of the error term is not a function of an independent variable but instead varies over time in a way that depends on how large the errors were in the past. Examples include models of inflation, interest rates, and stock market returns. In these applications there is often evidence of a "clumping" of large and small errors. In modeling interest rates, for example, one is likely to find periods of high volatility (and large errors) followed by periods of low volatility (and smaller errors). In other words, there is a particular kind of heteroscedasticity present in which the variance of the regression error depends on the volatility of the errors in the recent past.

A widely used model of such heteroscedasticity was developed by Robert Engle,[14] who suggested that use of an autoregressive conditional heteroscedas-

---

[14] R. Engle, "Autoregressive Conditional Heteroskedasticity with Estimates of the Variance of U.K. Inflation," *Econometrica*, vol. 50, pp. 987–1008, 1982.

ticity (ARCH) model would lead to increased efficiency. The model works as follows.

We begin with Eq. (10.22) relating a dependent variable to (in this case) two independent variables. We then write a second equation relating the variance of the error term to the amount of volatility observed in recent periods. The simplest such equation would be

$$\sigma_t^2 = \alpha_0 + \alpha_1 \varepsilon_{t-1}^2 \tag{10.23}$$

Equation (10.23) says that the variance of ε_t, σ_t^2, has two components: a constant and last period's news about volatility, which is modeled as last period's squared residual (the ARCH term). Observe that in this model ε_t is heteroscedastic, *conditional* on ε_{t-1}. By taking this information about the conditional heteroscedasticity of ε_t into account, we can obtain more efficient estimates of the parameters β_1, β_2, and β_3.

Estimation of Eqs. (10.22) and (10.23) usually is done by maximum likelihood. Given the low cost of computing power, this is not very difficult. Indeed, most widely used econometrics software packages make it possible to estimate ARCH models of this sort very easily.

Since the variance of ε_t in Eq. (10.23) depends only on last period's volatility, we refer to this model as ARCH(1). More generally, the variance could depend on any number of lagged volatilities. We write the ARCH(p) model as

$$\sigma_t^2 = \alpha_0 + \alpha_1 \varepsilon_{t-1}^2 + \alpha_2 \varepsilon_{t-2}^2 + \cdots + \alpha_p \varepsilon_{t-p}^2 \tag{10.24}$$

Note that in this case the $p + 1$ parameters of the variance process must be estimated along with the parameters β_1, β_2, and β_3 of the regression, again using maximum-likelihood estimation.

Often there is reason to expect that the variance of ε_t will depend on past volatilities going back a large number of periods. (This is particularly true in applications in finance involving the use of daily or weekly data.) The problem in this case is that a large number of parameters must be estimated, and this may be difficult to do with any precision. However, if we recognize that Eq. (10.24) is simply a *distributed lag model* for σ_t^2, we see that we can replace many of these lagged values of ε_t^2 with only one or two lagged values of σ_t^2. (Recall our discussion of the geometric lag model in Chapter 9.) This leads us to the *generalized* autoregressive conditional heteroscedasticity (GARCH) model, which can also be estimated by maximum likelihood.[15]

The simplest GARCH model is the GARCH(1,1) model:

$$\sigma_t^2 = \alpha_0 + \alpha_1 \varepsilon_{t-1}^2 + \lambda_1 \sigma_{t-1}^2 \tag{10.25}$$

[15] This model was introduced by Tim Bollerslev, "Generalized Autoregressive Conditional Heteroscedasticity," *Journal of Econometrics*, vol. 31, pp. 307–327, 1986.

Now the variance of the error term has three components: a constant, last period's volatility (the ARCH term), and last period's variance (the GARCH term). Recall from our discussion of the geometric distributed lag model in Chapter 9 that as long as λ_1 is less than 1, we can rewrite Eq. (10.25) as

$$\sigma_t^2 = \frac{\alpha_0}{1 - \lambda_1} + \alpha_1 \sum_{j=1}^{\infty} \lambda_1^{j-1} \varepsilon_{t-j}^2 \qquad (10.26)$$

In other words, the variance today depends on all past volatilities, but with geometrically declining weights.

In general, we could have any number of ARCH terms and any number of GARCH terms. The GARCH(p,q) model refers to the following equation for σ_t^2:

$$\sigma_t^2 = \alpha_0 + \alpha_1 \varepsilon_{t-1}^2 + \cdots + \alpha_p \varepsilon_{t-p}^2 + \lambda_1 \sigma_{t-1}^2 + \cdots + \lambda_q \sigma_{t-q}^2 \qquad (10.27)$$

Finally, Eq. (10.27) can be generalized even further by including one or more exogenous or predetermined variables as additional determinants of the error variance. For example, if X_{3t} were an exogenous variable, we might include it as part of the following GARCH(1,1) model:

$$\sigma_t^2 = \alpha_0 + \alpha_1 \varepsilon_{t-1}^2 + \lambda_1 \varepsilon_{t-1}^2 + \gamma_1 X_{3t} \qquad (10.28)$$

The addition of exogenous or predetermined variables to the equation for σ_t^2 must be done with care, however. If X_{3t} takes on negative values, it could cause the variance to be negative for some observations.

Just as we can introduce exogenous or predetermined variables on the right-hand side of the equation describing σ_t^2, we can include σ_t^2 (or, alternatively, the standard deviation σ_t) on the right-hand side of the regression equation [Eq. (10.22)]. We may do this, for example, if the purpose of the regression is to explain the return on a financial asset such as a stock or bond. The reason for this is that one would expect the return on a financial asset to be proportional to the asset's riskiness. For example, we might model the nominal return on a stock index, such as the S&P 500 index, (RETURN$_t$), as dependent on a constant term, the rate of inflation, and the conditional variance:

$$\text{RETURN}_t = \beta_1 + \beta_2 \text{INF}_t + \beta_3 \sigma_t^2 + \varepsilon_t \qquad (10.29)$$

We might then describe the variance σ_t^2 as a GARCH(p,q) process, as in Eq. (10.27). A model of this type (in which expected risk is proxied by the conditional variance) is called the ARCH-M (ARCH-in-mean) model.[16]

---

[16] There have been many applications of ARCH and GARCH models in finance. For a survey and overview of these applications, see Tim Bollerslev, Ray Chou, and Kenneth Kroner, "ARCH Modeling in Finance: A Review of the Theory and Empirical Evidence," *Journal of Econometrics*, vol. 52, pp. 5–59, 1992.

Example 10.4 Long-Term Interest Rates   In this example we model the behavior of the AAA corporate bond rate by relating it to current and past values of a short-term risk-free interest rate (the 3-month Treasury bill rate) as well as the Index of Industrial Production and the rate of wholesale price inflation. Figure 10.1 shows the AAA corporate bond rate and the 3-month Treasury bill rate from 1960 through the beginning of 1996. Observe that the bond rate is generally higher than the Treasury bill rate and also tends to smooth out short-term fluctuations in the Treasury bill rate. The bond rate reflects expectations of future values of the Treasury bill rate (and hence should be less volatile than that rate) and also includes a small risk premium reflecting the probability of default.

We regressed the AAA bond rate (RAAA) against current and lagged values of the bill rate ($R3$), current and lagged values of the Index of Industrial Production (IP), the rate of growth of the Producer Price Index for all commodities [GPW = $(PW - PW_{-1})/PW_{-1}$], and the lagged value of the AAA bond rate. (Inclusion of the lagged dependent variable imposes a geometrically declining lag structure which smooths out short-term fluctuations in the other explanatory variables.) After some experimentation, the following equation, estimated by ordinary least-squares, was chosen (t statistics are in parentheses):

$$RAAA_t = .000268 + .2749R3_t - .2685R3_{t-1} + .0325R3_{t-2}$$
$$\quad\quad\quad (0.81)\quad\quad (14.70)\quad\quad\quad (-9.26)\quad\quad\quad (1.73)$$

$$+ .00046IP_t - .00046IP_{t-1} + .0421GPW_t + .9626RAAA_{t-1}$$
$$\quad (2.87)\quad\quad\quad (-2.85)\quad\quad\quad\quad (3.09)\quad\quad\quad\quad (116.72)$$

$$(10.30)$$

$$R^2 = .9954 \quad\quad s = .001830 \quad\quad DW = 1.49 \quad\quad \text{log likelihood} = 2124.0$$

FIGURE 10.1
Three-month Treasury bill rate and AAA corporate bond rate.

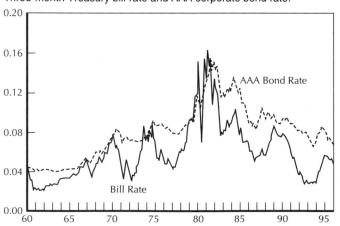

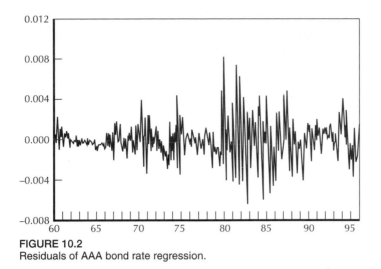

FIGURE 10.2
Residuals of AAA bond rate regression.

Figure 10.2 shows the residuals from this regression. Observe the "clumping" of volatility; there are extended periods in which volatility is quite low (e.g., from 1962 to 1967) and periods in which volatility is quite high (e.g., from 1980 to 1988). This suggests that the error term is conditionally heteroscedastic and thus can be represented by an ARCH or GARCH model.

To explore this possibility, Eq. (10.30) was reestimated using a simple GARCH(1,1) model to represent the variance of the error term. The results are shown below:

$$RAAA_t = .000283 + .2749R3_t - .2685R3_{t-1} + .0325R3_{t-2}$$
$$\quad\;\; (0.26) \qquad\; (7.58) \qquad\quad (-5.97) \qquad\quad (1.06)$$

$$+ .00046IP_t - .00046IP_{t-1} + .0421GPW_t + .9626RAAA_{t-1}$$
$$\quad (1.51) \qquad\quad (-1.50) \qquad\quad (1.52) \qquad\quad (59.29)$$
$$\tag{10.31}$$

$$\sigma_t^2 = .00000011 + .1500\varepsilon_{t-1}^2 - .6000\sigma_{t-1}^2 \tag{10.32}$$
$$\quad\;\; (0.07) \qquad\quad (1.22) \qquad\quad (2.59)$$

$$R^2 = .9954 \qquad s = .001836 \qquad DW = 1.49 \qquad \text{log likelihood} = 2117.2$$

Observe that including this GARCH representation of the error variance had very little impact on any of the coefficient estimates. In addition, only one of the coefficients in the GARCH equation is statistically significant. Also note that the standard error of the regression has increased (from .001830 to .001836). This does not mean that the model does not explain the interest rate as well. It simply reflects the fact that when an equation with heteroscedastic errors is estimated by ordinary least squares (OLS), the estimated standard errors will be biased. (This point was discussed in Chapter 6.)

To explore the pattern of heteroscedasticity further, we added an exogenous variable to the GARCH equation. We retained the GARCH(1,1) structure but also included the change in the lag value of the 3-month Treasury bill rate in this equation. The results of estimating this model are as follows:

$$\text{RAAA}_t = .000028 + .2750R3_t - .2684R3_{t-1} + .0326R3_{t-2}$$
$$\qquad\quad (0.17) \qquad (26.46) \qquad (-20.57) \qquad (3.96)$$

$$+ .00056\text{IP}_t - .00056\text{IP}_{t-1} + .0420\text{GPW}_t + .9629\text{RAAA}_{t-1}$$
$$\quad (7.73) \qquad\quad (-7.63) \qquad\qquad (7.86) \qquad\qquad (301.87)$$

$$\tag{10.33}$$

$$\sigma_t^2 = .00000021 + .1502\varepsilon_{t-1}^2 - .6001\sigma_{t-1}^2 + .000023\Delta R3_{t-1} \qquad (10.34)$$
$$\quad (6.84) \qquad\quad (8.85) \qquad\quad (19.98) \qquad\quad (3.79)$$

$$R^2 = .9954 \qquad s = .001841 \qquad \text{DW} = 1.49 \qquad \text{log likelihood} = 2161.0$$

The lagged change in the 3-month Treasury bill rate adds significantly to the explanation of changes in the variance of the regression error term. In addition, the coefficients on the ARCH and GARCH terms are now highly statistically significant. Finally, there is a small but noticeable change in the magnitude of some of the coefficients in the regression equation, and many of the t statistics have increased.

Example 10.5 Stock Returns   As a second example we study the monthly return on the S&P 500 stock index. We first compute this return by using Citibase data on the S&P 500 Index (FSPCOM) and the dividend yield on the S&P 500 Index (FSDXP). The monthly return then is computed as

$$\text{RETURNSP}_t = \frac{\text{FSPCOM}_t - \text{FSPCOM}_{t-1}}{\text{FSPCOM}_{t-1}} + .01\text{FSDXP}_t/12 \qquad (10.35)$$

We begin by running a simple OLS regression of the return against a constant and two variables that in theory should tend to reduce the return: the change in the 3-month Treasury bill rate, $\Delta R3_t$ (stock prices should reflect the discounted present value of expected future earnings, and so an increase in the discount rate—in this case the Treasury bill rate—should reduce that present value) and the rate of wholesale price inflation, GPW_t (which can reduce after-tax equity returns and in a number of studies has been shown to be negatively correlated with stock returns). The regression equation (with

t statistics in parentheses) is

$$\text{RETURNSP}_t = .0120 - .8270\Delta R3_t - .8551\text{GPW}_t \qquad (10.36)$$
$$\qquad\qquad (6.83) \qquad (-2.70) \qquad (-3.64)$$

$$R^2 = .0549 \qquad s = .0329 \qquad \text{DW} = 1.52 \qquad \text{log likelihood} = 867.1$$

Observe that the R^2 of this regression is low; stock returns—even the returns on a stock index—are very volatile, and very little of the variance of those returns can be explained by economic (or other) variables. Nonetheless, the coefficients of $\Delta R3$ and GPW have the expected signs and are statistically significant.

Figure 10.3 shows the residuals from this regression. Once again there is a "clumping" of volatility. (Perhaps the best known example of such clumping is the increased volatility associated with the stock market crash in October 1987.)

Next we reestimated this model using a GARCH(1,1) specification for the error variance:

$$\text{RETURNSP}_t = .0127 - 1.0833\Delta R3_t - .8009\text{GPW}_t \qquad (10.37)$$
$$\qquad\qquad (8.15) \qquad (-3.62) \qquad (-4.37)$$

$$\sigma_t^2 = .000184 + .1853\varepsilon_{t-1}^2 + .6503\sigma_{t-1}^2 \qquad (10.38)$$
$$\qquad (2.37) \qquad (4.02) \qquad (6.44)$$

$$R^2 = .0527 \qquad s = .0331 \qquad \text{DW} = 1.52 \qquad \text{log likelihood} = 884.3$$

Note that the ARCH and GARCH coefficients are statistically significant and that the coefficients in the regression equation have changed noticeably but

FIGURE 10.3
Return on S&P 500—regression residuals.

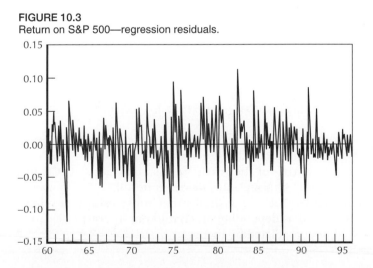

again have the expected negative signs and are statistically significant. The R^2 of the regression has decreased, and the standard error has increased. Since OLS estimation maximizes the R^2, correcting for heteroscedasticity (and thereby obtaining different parameter estimates) can cause the R^2 to fall. (This is an example of how the R^2 can have only limited value in evaluating a regression.) As for the increase in the standard error, remember that with heteroscedastic errors, the estimated standard errors under OLS are biased. The value of the log-likelihood function has increased.

The expected return from holding stocks should compensate investors for the riskiness of stocks. Hence, a logical explanatory variable to add to the regression equation is the standard deviation or variance of the error term itself. We therefore estimated the following GARCH-in-mean model, which includes the standard deviation, σ_t, in the regression equation:

$$RETURNSP_t = -.0017 - .9935\Delta R3_t - .8796GPW_t + .4855\sigma_t \quad (10.39)$$
$$ (-.23) (-3.23) (-4.97) (1.90)$$

$$\sigma_t^2 = .000145 + .1821\varepsilon_{t-1}^2 + .6929\sigma_{t-1}^2 \quad (10.40)$$
$$ (2.28) (4.32) (8.07)$$

$$R^2 = .0507 \quad s = .0332 \quad DW = 1.49 \quad \text{log likelihood} = 886.6$$

Observe that the coefficient of the conditional standard deviation σ_t has the correct sign, although it is only marginally statistically significant.

Finally, we considered a more complicated GARCH structure. After some experimentation the following GARCH(4,2) model was estimated, again with the conditional standard deviation included in the regression equation:

$$RETURNSP_t = .0008 - .9601\Delta R3_t - .8199GPW_t + .3972\sigma_t \quad (10.41)$$
$$ (.21) (-4.52) (-4.85) (3.16)$$

$$\sigma_t^2 = .000242 + .2772\varepsilon_{t-1}^2 + .0065\varepsilon_{t-2}^2 - .0389\varepsilon_{t-3}^2$$
$$ (2.00) (4.57) (.16) (-.48) \quad (10.42)$$
$$ + .1074\varepsilon_{t-4}^2 - .2417\sigma_{t-1}^2 + .6967\sigma_{t-2}^2$$
$$ (1.97) (-2.37) (7.48)$$

$$R^2 = .0452 \quad s = .0334 \quad DW = 1.51 \quad \text{log likelihood} = 893.5$$

Observe that the coefficient on the conditional standard deviation in the regression equation is slightly smaller in magnitude but is now statistically significant. Furthermore, two of the ARCH terms and both GARCH terms are statistically significant. Although this model is not likely to be useful as a predictor of stock returns, it demonstrates that those returns are indeed dependent on risk as well as depending on changes in interest rates and on inflation in a way that is predicted by theory.

APPENDIX 10.1 Generalized Method of Moments Estimation

Recent advances in computer software and technology have helped popularize a nonlinear estimator that ensures consistent parameter estimates under a wide variety of conditions and that does not require the assumption of normality. In this section we give a brief overview of this generalized method of moments (GMM) estimator.[17]

We begin with the most basic *method of moments* estimator, the estimator of the mean of a random variable X. Our goal is to choose an estimator $\hat{X}$ that is consistent. A necessary condition for consistency is that

$$E(X_i - \hat{X}) = 0$$

The sample equivalent of this necessary condition is

$$\left(\frac{1}{N}\right) \Sigma (X_i - \hat{X}) = 0$$

Solving, we find that $\hat{X} = (1/N) \Sigma X_i = \overline{X}$, the sample mean estimator we first discussed in Chapter 2. $\overline{X}$ is a method of moments estimator because it is derived from the necessary condition for consistency associated with the first moment of the probability distribution of X. In this case no other information about the probability distribution (e.g., higher moments, the functional form of the probability distribution) is needed to obtain estimates of the mean.

We can also use the method of moments approach to obtain consistent estimators for the multiple regression model. Suppose we wish to estimate the k-variable regression model

$$Y_i = \beta_0 + \beta_1 X_{1i} + \cdots + \beta_k X_{ki} + \varepsilon_i$$

For each of the parameters β_j, $j = 1, 2, \ldots, k$, to be estimated consistently, the following conditions are required ($X_{1i} = 1$):

$$E[X_{ji}\varepsilon_i] = EX_{ji}[Y_i - \hat{\beta}_j X_{ji}] = 0$$

The sample analog of these theoretical equations is

$$\left(\frac{1}{N}\right) \Sigma X_{ji}\hat{\varepsilon}_{ji} = \left(\frac{1}{N}\right) \Sigma X_{ji} (Y_i - \hat{\beta}_j X_{ji}) = 0$$

---

[17] GMM estimation was originated by Hansen and Singleton. See L. P. Hansen, "Large Sample Properties of Generalized Method of Moments Estimators," *Econometrica*, vol. 60, pp. 1029–1054, 1992, and L. P. Hansen and K. J. Singleton, "Generalized Instrumental Variable Estimation of Nonlinear Rational Expectations Models," *Econometrica*, vol. 56, pp. 1269–1286, 1988. See also J. D. Hamilton, *Time Series Analysis* (Princeton: Princeton University Press, 1994).

These equations may look familiar. Recall that when we derived the ordinary least-squares estimator (Appendices 1.2, 4.1, and 4.3) we solved a series of "normal equations" of the form

$$\Sigma X_{ji} \hat{\varepsilon}_{ji} = \Sigma X_{ji} (Y_i - \hat{\beta}_j X_{ji}) = 0$$

to obtain each of the individual slope parameter estimates $\hat{\beta}_1, \ldots, \hat{\beta}_k$. Once again, because these normal conditions involve the expectation or first moment of a random variable, the resulting estimator, in this case ordinary least squares, is also a GMM estimator.

Instrumental variables estimators are also GMM estimators. To see why, suppose we wish to estimate the k-variable multiple regression model but are concerned (because of simultaneity or measurement error) that the X's might be correlated with the error term. Suppose also that we are aware of one instrument for each X_j, designated Z_j. This amounts to a total of k instruments, each of which is correlated with at least one X_j but uncorrelated with the error term. The necessary conditions for $\hat{\beta}_j$ to be a consistent estimator for each j are as follows:

$$E[Z_{ji} (Y_i - \hat{\beta}_j X_{ji})] = 0$$

The sample analog of these k equations is given by

$$\left(\frac{1}{N}\right) \Sigma Z_{ji} (Y_i - \hat{\beta}_j X_{ji}) = 0$$

These are the "normal equations" associated with the instrumental variables estimation procedure.

As was mentioned above, most of the estimators we have discussed in this book are GMM estimators. For example, maximum-likelihood estimators are method of moments estimators, since they involve the solution to the equations

$$\frac{\partial(\ln L)}{\partial \beta_j} = 0$$

for the likelihood function $L = \Sigma f(Y, X_1, X_2, \ldots, X_k, \beta_1, \beta_2, \ldots, \beta_k)$. These equations can be seen as sample analogs to the underlying moment equations

$$E\left[\frac{\partial \ln f(\ )}{\partial \beta_j}\right] = 0$$

Finally, all generalized least-squares estimators are also method of moments estimators since they can be derived as the solution to a series of normal equations in which the X's are weighted by the inverse of the variance-covariance matrix of the errors (Appendix 6.1).

In all the cases just described, the number of normal equations is exactly equal to the number of parameters to be estimated; i.e., the equations are exactly identified. As a general rule, however, when models are nonlinear, there may be more normal equations than parameters, in which case the model is overidentified. The GMM estimator provides a consistent estimator that uses all the available information in a manner that best accounts for the constraints that are implicit in an overidentified set of equations.

To see more generally how the GMM estimator can be used to estimate a single equation,[18] suppose one wishes to estimate a nonlinear model with k explanatory variables:

$$Y = f(X_1, X_2, \ldots, X_k, \beta_1, \beta_2, \ldots) + \varepsilon$$

Suppose that for any of several possible reasons (e.g., nonlinearity, measurement error, simultaneity) one is concerned that some of the original explanatory variables may be correlated with the error term. Suppose finally that one has the choice of $k + 1$ possible instruments (some of which could include the original explanatory variables). Then, in an ideal world, these $k + 1$ instruments would be used as the basis of "normal equations"

$$\Sigma Z_{ji} \hat{\varepsilon}_j = \Sigma Z_{ji} [Y_i - f_j(\ ) X_{ji}] = 0$$

where f_j represents $\partial f(\ )/\partial X_j$, i.e., the β_j's.

Because this system of equations is overidentified (there are $k + 1$ equations in k unknowns), not all of the equalities can hold exactly. Let u_{ji} represent the "error" associated with each of the normal equations:

$$u_{ji} = \Sigma Z_{ji} [Y_i - f_j(\ ) X_{ji}]$$

Then one possible estimation approach, consistent with ordinary least squares, is to choose the β's that minimize the sum of squares of these errors, with the sum taken over all observations (i) and over all variables (j).

Just as generalized least squares is preferable to ordinary least squares because it weights observations in inverse proportion to the variances of the associated errors, the GMM estimator weights the errors u by their estimated variances. If we let w_{ij} represent the matrix of estimated variances and covariances associated with u_i and u_j, the GMM estimator minimizes $\Sigma u_{ij}^2/w_{ij}$.

It should be clear from the derivation given above that the GMM estimator is a nonlinear instrumental-variables estimator. When the number of instruments is equal to the number of parameters to be estimated, the weighted error sum will be identically equal to zero (since every normal equation will hold exactly). When the equation is overidentified, however, the sum will be positive. We can test the overidentifying restrictions, using the fact that the term min-

---

[18] The GMM estimator has wide applicability as an estimator of a system of simultaneous equations as well.

imized by the GMM estimator follows a chi-square distribution with the number of degrees of freedom equal to the number of overidentifying restrictions. (This is the *Hansen-Singleton J test.*)

The choice of weights when the model is overidentified is more of an art than a science. One reason for this is that the weights to be used with GMM depend on the parameter estimates, which in turn depend on the weights chosen. One procedure is to initialize the model with equal weights and then use the resulting estimate of the parameters to calculate an updated weighting matrix.

EXERCISES

10.1 Expand the consumption function

$$C = a_1 + a_2 YD^{a_3}$$

in a Taylor series expansion around some initial guess for a_1, a_2, and a_3. Set up the linear regression equation. Explain how the equation would be relinearized around the OLS estimates from the first regression.

10.2 Write the sum-of-squared-errors function S for the nonlinear consumption function

$$C = a_0 + a_1 YD^{a_2}$$

Take the derivatives of S with respect to a_0, a_1, and a_2 to obtain the *normal equations.* Describe how these normal equations could be solved to yield estimates of a_0, a_1, and a_2.

10.3 In Example 10.4 the AAA bond rate (RAAA) was specified to be a function of current and lagged values of the Treasury bill rate ($R3$), the Index of Industrial Production (IP), the rate of growth of the Producer Price Index (GPW), and the lagged value of the AAA bond rate. An alternative specification would omit the variable reflecting the Treasury bill rate ($R3$). Using (*a*) a Wald test, (*b*) a likelihood ratio test, and (*c*) a Lagrange multiplier test, determine whether it is appropriate to omit this variable from the model.

10.4 Recall that the GARCH(1,1) model is given by

$$\sigma_t^2 = \alpha_0 + \alpha_1 \varepsilon_{t-1}^2 + \lambda_1 \sigma_{t-1}^2$$

Show that this is equivalent to an ARCH model of infinite order with geometrically declining weights on the past volatilities.

10.5 Recall that in Example 10.4 we estimated regression equations for the AAA corporate bond rate that included a GARCH representation of the error variance. One version of the model had a GARCH(1,1) structure but also included the change in the lagged value of the 3-month Treasury bill rate in the equation for the error variance.

(*a*) Can you improve upon this model by specifying a more complicated GARCH structure, such as GARCH(2,2)? (Use the data supplied in the data diskette that comes with this book.) Also try including additional values of the lagged Treasury bill rate in the equation for the error variance. Are you able to improve on the overall fit and forecasting performance of the model? Why or why not?

(*b*) If the AAA corporate bond rate reflects the riskiness of holding corporate bonds and in particular the volatility of bond prices, the regression equation itself may be improved on by including the lagged variance. Reestimate this model using a GARCH-in-mean specification, which includes either the standard deviation σ_t or the variance σ_{t-1}^2 on the right-hand side of the regression equation. Is the standard deviation or variance statistically significant? Does it improve the fit of the equation?

CHAPTER 11

MODELS OF QUALITATIVE CHOICE

In this chapter we construct models in which the dependent variable involves two or more qualitative choices. These models are valuable in the analysis of survey data. In most surveys the behavioral responses are qualitative: One votes yes or no in an election; uses the subway, the bus, or the automobile; is either in the labor force or out of the labor force, etc.

We discuss initially the specification and estimation of three binary-choice models, the linear probability model, the probit model, and the logit model. Then we direct our attention to extensions of the probit and logit models which involve multiple, rather than binary, choices. We complete the chapter with an analysis of the censored regression model.

11.1 BINARY-CHOICE MODELS

When one or more of the *explanatory* variables in a regression model are binary, we can represent them as dummy variables and proceed as in Chapter 5. However, the application of the linear regression model when the *dependent variable* is binary is more complex. *Binary-choice models* assume that individuals[1] are faced with a choice between two alternatives and that the choice depends on identifiable characteristics. Suppose, for example, that we wish to make predictions about how individuals will vote on a local bond issue. We might expect that individual income is a primary determinant of voting choice and that (other things being equal) high-income individuals are more likely to vote yes on a bond issue than are low-income individuals. Although it is reasonable

---

[1] Households, cities, and firms are all considered individuals in the discussion which follows.

to expect a direct relationship between income and voting behavior, we cannot be sure how each and every individual will vote. A more plausible objective is to predict the *likelihood* that an individual with a given income will vote yes.

Thus, the purpose of a qualitative choice model is to determine the probability that an individual with a given set of attributes will make one choice rather than the alternative. A suitable model is one which allows us to make statements of the following type: "The probability that an individual with an income of \$15,000 will vote yes on the upcoming bond issue is .6." More generally, we wish to find a relationship between a set of attributes describing an individual and the probability that the individual will make a given choice.[2]

To simplify the discussion, we will assume that the probability of an individual making a given choice is a *linear* function of the individual attributes. Alternative model specifications arise because it is possible to make several assumptions about the probabilistic nature of the decision process. We begin with the most elementary specification of a binary-choice model: the linear probability model.

11.1.1   Linear Probability Model

We begin by examining the *linear probability model.* The regression form of the model is

$$Y_i = \alpha + \beta X_i + \varepsilon_i \tag{11.1}$$

where X_i = value of attribute, e.g., income, for ith individual

$$Y_i = \begin{cases} 1 & \text{if first option is chosen (buy a car, vote yes)} \\ 0 & \text{if second option is chosen (not buy, vote no)} \end{cases}$$

ε_i = independently distributed random variable with 0 mean

To interpret Eq. (11.1) we take the expected value of each dependent variable observation Y_i:

$$E(Y_i) = \alpha + \beta X_i \tag{11.2}$$

Since Y_i can take on only two values, 1 and 0, we can describe the probability distribution of Y by letting P_i = Prob $(Y_i = 1)$ and $1 - P_i$ = Prob $(Y_i = 0)$. Then

$$E(Y_i) = 1(P_i) + 0(1 - P_i) = P_i$$

---

[2] The problem of model estimation and its relationship to the theory of choice is described thoroughly in D. McFadden, "Conditional Logit Analysis of Qualitative Choice Behavior," in P. Zarembka (ed.), *Frontiers in Econometrics* (New York: Academic Press, 1973), and T. Domencich and D. McFadden, *Urban Travel Demand: A Behavioral Analysis* (Amsterdam: North-Holland, 1975).

In our example the regression equation describes the probability that an individual will vote yes, given information about his or her income. The slope of the line measures the effect of a unit change in income on the probability of voting yes. The linear probability model often is written in the following form which allows the dependent variable to be interpreted as a probability:

$$P_i = \begin{cases} \alpha + \beta X_i & \text{when} & 0 < \alpha + \beta X_i < 1 \\ 1 & \text{when} & \alpha + \beta X_i \geq 1 \\ 0 & \text{when} & \alpha + \beta X_i \leq 0 \end{cases}$$

The probability distribution of the error term in the model is determined by substituting the values of Y_i (1 and 0) in Eq. (11.1), exhibited in Table 11.1. We can see the relationship between the probability P_i and X_i by using the assumption that the error has 0 mean. It follows that

$$E(\varepsilon_i) = (1 - \alpha - \beta X_i)P_i + (-\alpha - \beta X_i)(1 - P_i) = 0$$

Solving for P_i, we find that

$$P_i = \alpha + \beta X_i$$

$$1 - P_i = 1 - \alpha - \beta X_i$$

The variance of the error term can now be calculated:

$$\begin{aligned} E(\varepsilon_i^2) &= (1 - \alpha - \beta X_i)^2 P_i + (-\alpha - \beta X_i)^2(1 - P_i) \\ &= (1 - \alpha - \beta X_i)^2(\alpha + \beta X_i) + (\alpha + \beta X_i)^2(1 - \alpha - \beta X_i) \\ &= (1 - \alpha - \beta X_i)(\alpha + \beta X_i) = P_i(1 - P_i) \end{aligned}$$

or

$$\sigma_i^2 = E(\varepsilon_i^2) = E(Y_i)[1 - E(Y_i)]$$

This shows that the error term is heteroscedastic. Observations for which P_i is close to 0 or close to 1 will have relatively low variances, while observations with P_i closer to $\frac{1}{2}$ will have higher variances. Heteroscedasticity results in a loss of efficiency, but least squares remains consistent and unbiased.

An obvious way to correct for heteroscedasticity is to estimate the variances of *each* value of Y_i and then apply weighted least-squares estimation. To do this

TABLE 11.1
PROBABILITY DISTRIBUTION OF ε_i

Y_i	ε_i	Probability
1	$1 - \alpha - \beta X_i$	P_i
0	$-\alpha - \beta X_i$	$1 - P_i$

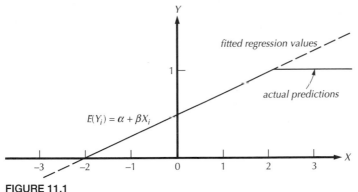

FIGURE 11.1
Prediction with the linear probability model.

we perform ordinary least squares on the original model and estimate each of the error variances as follows:

$$\hat{\sigma}_i^2 = \hat{Y}_i(1 - \hat{Y}_i) \qquad \text{where} \qquad \hat{Y}_i = \hat{\alpha} + \hat{\beta}X_i \qquad (11.3)$$

The difficulty with weighted least squares is that there is no guarantee that the predicted value $\hat{Y}_i$ will lie in the $(0, 1)$ interval. If some values of $\hat{Y}_i$ lie outside the $(0, 1)$ range, the observations must either be dropped from the model or must be arbitrarily set equal to numbers such as .01 and .99. In either case the weighted least-squares procedure will not be efficient for finite samples. Since the weighted least-squares procedure is also sensitive to errors of specification, we advise against its use.

Suppose we wish to use the linear probability model for prediction. A serious weakness of the model arises when the predicted value lies outside the $(0, 1)$ range. This possibility is depicted in Fig. 11.1. Even if the linear probability model is correct, it is possible that a given sample value of X will lie outside the $(-2, 2)$ interval. The fitted value of Y associated with this observation on X will be greater than 1 or less than 0. The obvious correction for this problem is to set extreme predictions equal to 1 or 0, thus constraining predicted probabilities to be within the $(0, 1)$ interval. This is not very satisfying, however, because we might predict an occurrence with a probability of 1 when it is possible that it might not occur, or we might predict an occurrence with a probability of 0 when it might actually occur. While the estimation procedure may well yield unbiased estimates, the predictions obtained from the estimation process are clearly biased.

An alternative approach is to reestimate the parameters α and β subject to the constraint that $0 \le \hat{Y}_i \le 1$. Since there is no guarantee that the estimates will be unbiased,[3] it seems more appropriate to use the ordinary least-squares version of the linear probability model.

[3] See Domencich and McFadden, op. cit., Chapter 5.

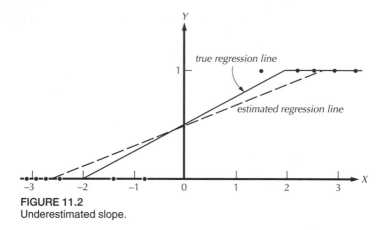

FIGURE 11.2
Underestimated slope.

A final, serious problem arises because observations may be drawn excessively from attributes whose values are extreme. Suppose, for example, that several observations lie outside the $(-2, 2)$ interval shown in Fig. 11.1. This possibility is depicted in Fig. 11.2. In this case, the true regression model associates a probability of 1 with values of X greater than 2 and a probability of 0 with values of X less than -2. The sample contains several X values greater than 2 for which the first option was chosen and several values of X less than -2 for which the second option was chosen. The resulting ordinary least-squares slope estimate will be *biased,* since it will underestimate the true regression slope. However, if the attribute data are bunched somewhat differently, the slope may be overestimated, as shown in Fig. 11.3.

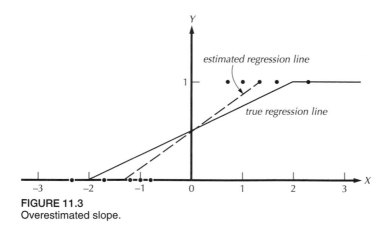

FIGURE 11.3
Overestimated slope.

Example 11.1 Predicting Bond Defaults   A useful means of predicting bond failures is to analyze the factors that correlate highly with actual bond defaults.[4] If we view the decision to default and the decision not to default as two options for local governments, we can estimate the probability of default using the linear probability model. A sample of 35 Massachusetts communities, several of which actually defaulted, was used in a cross-section study using 1930 data [5] The object was to find a set of characteristics of communities which best allows one to predict the probability of default. The model is

$$P_i = \beta_i + \beta_2 TAX_i + \beta_3 INT_i + \beta_4 AV_i + \beta_5 DAV_i + \beta_6 WELF_i + \varepsilon_i$$

where P = 0 if the municipality defaulted and 1 otherwise
   TAX = average of 1929, 1930, and 1931 tax rates
   INT = percentage of budget allocated to interest payments (1930)
    AV = percentage growth in assessed property value (1925–1930)
  DAV = ratio of total debt to total assessed valuation (1930)
WELF = percentage of 1930 budget allocated to charities, pensions, and soldiers' benefits

The regression results were as follows (standard errors are in parentheses):

$$\hat{P} = 1.96 - .029 TAX - 4.86 INT + .063 AV + .007 DAV - .48 WELF$$
$$\quad\;\; (.29) \quad (.009) \qquad (2.13) \qquad (.028) \qquad (.003) \qquad (.88)$$

$$R^2 = .36$$

The R^2 of .36 suggests that a good deal of variance in the model is still unexplained. Nonetheless, one can still use the results of the model to study several economic factors that correlate highly with defaults. The coefficient of the tax rate variable is negative and significant, implying that, *ceteris paribus*, an increase in the tax rate of $1 per thousand will raise the probability of default by .029. The percentage of the budget allocated to interest payments also appears to be a good predictor of defaults, with higher-interest budget shares being positively correlated with the probability of default. The percentage of current budget allocated to welfare bears the same relationship to the probability of default as does the interest budget share but is not significant. The rate of growth of actual assessed valuation is significant and is inversely related to default probability. A growing tax base implies a low probability of default, at least in the short run. Finally, the ratio of debt to assessed valuation is inversely related to default probability. This counter-

---

[4] A bond default occurs when there is a delayed payment of either principal or interest on a bond. Some bondholders are repaid for partial or total loss of interest and payments, but only after some length of time.

[5] See D. L. Rubinfeld, "An Econometric Analysis of the Market for General Obligation Municipal Bonds," unpublished doctoral dissertation, M.I.T., June 1972.

intuitive result suggests that politics, not just economics, is an important predictor of bond defaults.

11.1.2 Probit Model

Given the difficulties associated with the linear probability model, it is natural to transform the original model in such a way that predictions will lie in the (0, 1) interval for all X. The requirement of such a process is that it translate the values of the attribute X, which may range in value over the entire real line, to a probability which ranges in value from 0 to 1. We also would like the transformation to maintain the property that increases in X are associated with increases (or decreases) in the dependent variable for all values of X. These requirements suggest the use of the *cumulative probability function, F.*[6] The resulting probability distribution might be represented as

$$P_i = F(\alpha + \beta X_i) = F(Z_i) \tag{11.4}$$

Under the assumption that we transform the model by using a cumulative *uniform* probability function, we get the constrained version of the linear probability model $P_i = \alpha + \beta X_i$ (see Exercise 11.3). While numerous alternative cumulative probability functions are possible, we shall consider only two: the *normal* and the *logistic.*

The *probit probability model* is associated with the cumulative normal probability function. To understand this model, assume that there exists a theoretical continuous index Z_i which is determined by an explanatory variable X. Thus, we can write

$$Z_i = \alpha + \beta X_i \tag{11.5}$$

Observations on Z_i are not available. Instead, we have data that distinguish only whether individual observations are in one category (high values of Z_i) or a second category (low values of Z_i). Probit analysis solves the problem of how to obtain estimates for the parameters α and β while at the same time obtaining information about the underlying index Z.

To focus on this problem consider an analysis of voter behavior in an election. The individual is assumed to vote yes or no when faced with the choice of one of two candidates for an office. In this case, the index Z_i would represent the strength of feeling of individual i for the first candidate for the office. Suppose we know that the index of strength of feeling is a linear function of income X.

---

[6] Recall that a *cumulative probability function* is defined as having as its value the probability that an observed value of a variable X (for every X) will be less than or equal to a particular X. The range of the cumulative probability function is the (0, 1) interval, since all probabilities lie between 0 and 1.

Then the probit model provides a suitable means of estimating the slope and intercept parameters of the relationship between the index and income.

Let Y represent a dummy variable which equals 1 when the first candidate is selected and 0 when the second candidate is chosen. Then assume that, for each individual voter, Z_i^* represents the critical cutoff value which translates the underlying index into a voting decision. Specifically, the

$$\text{Individual votes for} \begin{cases} \text{first candidate} & \text{if } Z_i > Z_i^* \\ \text{second candidate} & \text{if } Z_i \leq Z_i^* \end{cases} \tag{11.6}$$

The probit model assumes that Z_i^* is a normally distributed random variable, so that the probability that Z_i^* is less than (or equal to) Z_i can be computed from the cumulative normal probability function. The standardized cumulative normal function is written

$$P_i = F(Z_i) = \frac{1}{\sqrt{2\pi}} \int_{-\infty}^{Z_i} e^{-s^2/2} \, ds \tag{11.7}$$

where s is a random variable which is normally distributed with mean zero and unit variance. By construction, the variable P_i will lie in the $(0, 1)$ interval. P_i represents the probability that an event occurs, in this case the probability of the individual's voting for the first candidate. Since this probability is measured by the area under the standard normal curve from $-\infty$ to Z_i, the event will be more likely to occur the larger the value of the index Z_i.

Table 11.2 describes the relationship in Eq. (11.7) for particular values of Z. The cumulative normal function is shown graphically in Fig. 11.4, which compares the probit and linear probability models.

To obtain an estimate of the index Z_i we apply the inverse of the cumulative normal function to Eq. (11.7):

$$Z_i = F^{-1}(P_i) = \alpha + \beta X_i \tag{11.8}$$

We can interpret the probability P_i resulting from the probit model as an estimate of the conditional probability that an individual will vote yes (or an

TABLE 11.2

Z	F(Z)	Z	F(Z)
-3.0	.001	.5	.691
-2.5	.006	1.0	.841
-2.0	.023	1.5	.933
-1.5	.067	2.0	.977
-1.0	.159	2.5	.994
$-.5$	.309	3.0	.999
$.0$	.500	3.5	.999

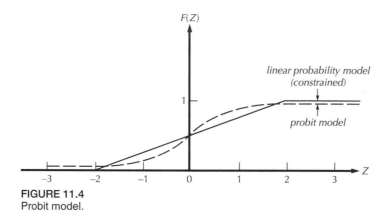

FIGURE 11.4
Probit model.

individual will go to college), given that the individual's income is X_i. This is equivalent to the probability that a standard normal variable will be less than or equal to $\alpha + \beta X_i$.

The slope of the probit function as shown in Fig. 11.4 is larger than the slope of the linear probability function in the middle range but smaller at the extremes of the interval $(-2, 2)$. Outside the $(-2, 2)$ interval the linear probability model has a slope of 0. The graph is suggestive of some of the difficulties associated with a misspecified linear probability model. Assuming that the probit specification is correct, estimation of the linear probability model will lead to the false inference that the slope is constant when in fact the change in probability associated with a change in X is dependent on the value of X selected.

While the probit model is more appealing than the linear probability model, it generally involves nonlinear maximum-likelihood estimation. In addition, the theoretical justification for employing the probit model is somewhat limited. After reviewing the limitations in an example, we shall consider a somewhat more appealing model specification, *the logit model*.

Example 11.2 Voting Behavior   In a study of voting in the 1972 presidential election, a probit model was used to explain the probability of a citizen's voting for George McGovern.[7] The authors assume that there is an underlying index Z_i, "propensity" to vote for McGovern, which is a linear function of the positions that voters support on a number of policy issues. The problem is to transform the linear relation between the index Z_i and the information about policy positions to obtain predicted probabilities of voting for McGovern. The probit results were obtained using a series of data drawn from the 1972 survey of the Center for Political Studies at the University of

---

[7] J. Aldrich and C. F. Cnudde, "Probing the Bounds of Conventional Wisdom: A Comparison of Regression, Probit, and Discriminant Analysis," *American Journal of Political Science*, vol. 19, pp. 571–608, August 3, 1975.

TABLE 11.3
COMPARISON OF LINEAR PROBABILITY AND PROBIT PREDICTIONS:
PROBABILITY OF VOTING FOR MCGOVERN, 1972

7-point issue	Probit model Z_i		Linear probability model	
	Coefficient	SE	Coefficient	SE
Federal jobs	−.375	.002	−.087	.018
Taxation	−.257	.066	−.050	.014
Vietnam	−.593	.092	−.145	.020
Marijuana	−.075	.058	−.019	.014
Busing	−.205	.083	−.067	.019
Women's rights	−.038	.046	−.010	.011
Rights of accused	−.046	.068	−.011	.015
Aid to minorities	−.136	.072	−.030	.017
Liberal or conservative	−.639	.113	−.168	.025
Constant	−.713		.303	
N = 1,130	$R^2 = .530$		$R^2 = .347$	

Michigan. The results of both the probit estimation and the comparable linear probability model regression are shown in Table 11.3. Each of the explanatory variables is a scale representing the individual's own view about how he or she feels about a given issue.

The regression coefficients tell us the linear relationship between the estimated index Z_i and the position variables. (The ratio of the estimated coefficient to the estimated standard error will approximate the normal distribution for large samples, so that the usual normal or t tests can be applied.) The results suggest that a voter's position on federal jobs, taxation, and Vietnam, as well as the self-identified liberal or conservative designation, serve best to explain why the voter may or may not have chosen to vote for McGovern.

These results are not very different from the results of the linear probability model, except for the importance of the busing issue. However, the models yield different results when we interpret the numerical implications of the estimated coefficients. When we look at individual coefficients, what matters is their relative magnitude, not their absolute size. For example, when the linear probability model was estimated, the liberal-conservative coefficient was 3.4 times the size of the taxation coefficient, while the ratio was only 2.5 when probit estimation was used.

11.1.3   Logit Model

The *logit model* is based on the cumulative logistic probability function and is specified as

$$P_i = F(Z_i) = F(\alpha + \beta X_i) = \frac{1}{1 + e^{-Z_i}} = \frac{1}{1 + e^{-(\alpha + \beta X_i)}} \qquad (11.9)$$

TABLE 11.4
VALUES OF CUMULATIVE PROBABILITY FUNCTIONS

	Cumulative normal	Cumulative logistic
z	$P_1(Z) = \dfrac{1}{\sqrt{2\pi}} \displaystyle\int_{-\infty}^{Z} e^{-s^2/2}\, ds$	$P_2(Z) = \dfrac{1}{1 + e^{-z}}$
−3.0	.0013	.0474
−2.0	.0228	.1192
−1.5	.0668	.1824
−1.0	.1587	.2689
− .5	.3085	.3775
.0	.5000	.5000
.5	.6915	.6225
1.0	.8413	.7311
1.5	.9332	.8176
2.0	.9772	.8808
3.0	.9987	.9526

In this notation, e represents the base of natural logarithms, which is approximately equal to 2.718. P_i is the probability that an individual will make a certain choice, given X_i. To get a feeling for the cumulative logistic function, examine Table 11.4. The table shows that the logit and probit formulations are quite similar; the only difference is that the logistic has slightly fatter tails.[8] Because it is similar to the cumulative normal function but easier to use computationally, the logit model often is used as a substitute for the probit.

To show how the model specified in Eq. (11.9) can be estimated, we first multiply both sides of the equation by $1 + e^{-Z_i}$ to get

$$(1 + e^{-Z_i})P_i = 1$$

Dividing by P_i and then subtracting 1 leads to

$$e^{-Z_i} = \frac{1}{P_i} - 1 = \frac{1 - P_i}{P_i}$$

By definition, however, $e^{-Z_i} = 1/e^{Z_i}$, so that

$$e^{Z_i} = \frac{P_i}{1 - P_i}$$

---

[8] E. A. Hanushek and J. E. Jackson, *Statistical Methods for Social Scientists* (New York: Academic, 1977), p. 189, points out that the logistic distribution closely resembles the *t* distribution with 7 degrees of freedom.

Now, by taking the natural logarithm of both sides,

$$Z_i = \log \frac{P_i}{1 - P_i}$$

or [from Eq. (11.9)]

$$\log \frac{P_i}{1 - P_i} = Z_i = \alpha + \beta X_i \qquad (11.10)$$

The dependent variable in this regression equation is the logarithm of the odds that a particular choice will be made. An important advantage of the logit model is that it transforms the problem of predicting probabilities within a (0, 1) interval to the problem of predicting the odds of an event's occurring within the range of the real line. The slope of the cumulative logistic distribution is greatest at $P = \frac{1}{2}$. This implies that changes in independent variables will have their greatest effect on the probability of choosing a given option at the midpoint of the distribution. The low slopes near the endpoints imply that large changes in X are necessary to bring about a small change in probability.

If P_i happens to equal either 0 or 1, the odds, $P_i/(1 - P_i)$, will equal 0 or infinity and the logarithm of the odds will be undefined. Thus, the application of ordinary least-squares estimation to Eq. (11.10) is clearly inappropriate. The correct estimation of the logit model can best be understood by distinguishing between studies in which individual observations are the basic units of analysis and studies in which the analysis involves the use of grouped data.

Consider first the case in which we know the frequency of an event's occurring in a given subgroup of the population but there is no knowledge about the behavior of every individual in that subgroup. Specifically, assume that a single explanatory variable such as income is represented by G different values in the sample (for example, \$5,000, \$10,000), with n_1 individuals having income X_1, n_2 individuals having income X_2, and so forth.[9] Also, let r_1 represent the number of times the first alternative is chosen by individuals with income X_1 (voting yes), r_2 represent the number of times the first alternative is chosen by individuals with income X_2, etc. Then it seems reasonable to utilize a logit model which estimates the probability of each choice *for each group* of identical individuals. Specifically, we approximate P_i as

$$\hat{P}_i = \frac{r_i}{n_i}$$

We can then estimate the logit probability model of Eq. (11.10) by

$$\log \frac{\hat{P}_i}{1 - \hat{P}_i} = \log \frac{r_i/n_i}{1 - r_i/n_i} = \log \frac{r_i}{n_i - r_i} = \alpha^* + \beta^* X_i + \varepsilon_i \quad (11.11)$$

---

[9] For details, see D. R. Cox, *Analysis of Binary Data* (London: Methuen, 1970).

Equation (11.11) is linear in the parameters and can be estimated by using ordinary least squares. For small samples the parameters may be biased, but as the number of observations associated with each of the levels of X increases, the results improve. In fact, the estimated parameters are consistent when *each group* gets arbitrarily large.

This grouping procedure also can be used with individual observations; we divide the independent variable (or variables) arbitrarily into groups and calculate frequencies within each group. For example, assume that we are analyzing voting behavior on the basis of income (low, high) and size of family (small, large).[10] For each voting district we obtain data on the number of registered voters voting for a given candidate associated with each of the four possible combinations of voter characteristics (small family, low income; small family, high income; etc.). The data might be as follows:

$\hat{P}_1$ = fraction of low-income, small-family voters voting for candidate

$\hat{P}_2$ = fraction of low-income, large-family voters voting for candidate

$\hat{P}_3$ = fraction of high-income, small-family voters voting for candidate

$\hat{P}_4$ = fraction of high-income, large-family voters voting for candidate

Since there are four groups, the least-squares regression will have six observations. The dependent-variable observations will be

$$\hat{Z}_1 = \log \frac{\hat{P}_1}{1 - \hat{P}_1} \qquad \hat{Z}_2 = \log \frac{\hat{P}_2}{1 - \hat{P}_2}, \cdots$$

The independent variables will be a series of dummy variables defining the category to which each observation belongs. Thus, if we let

$$X_2 = \begin{cases} 1 & \text{for high-income voters} \\ 0 & \text{otherwise} \end{cases}$$

$$X_3 = \begin{cases} 1 & \text{for large-family voters} \\ 0 & \text{otherwise} \end{cases}$$

the logit model will be *estimated* as

$$\hat{Z}_i = \beta_1 + \beta_2 X_2 + \beta_3 X_3 + \varepsilon_i \tag{11.12}$$

[10] This is equivalent to the logit analysis of contingency tables and is described in H. Theil, "On the Estimation of Relationships Involving Qualitative Variables," *American Journal of Sociology*, vol. 76, pp. 103–154, July 1970, and L. Goodman, "The Multivariate Analysis of Qualitative Data: Interactions among Multiple Classifications," *Journal of the American Statistical Association*, vol. 65, no. 329, pp. 226–256, 1970.

Assuming for the moment that each $\hat{P}_i$ accurately measures the group's frequency in the population, the interpretation of the logit model is straightforward:

$$\hat{Z}_1 \approx Z_1 = \beta_1 = \text{predicted odds of favorable voting by low-income, small-family voters}$$

$$\hat{Z}_2 \approx Z_2 = \beta_1 + \beta_3 = \text{predicted odds of favorable voting by low-income, large-family voters}$$

$$\hat{Z}_3 \approx Z_3 = \beta_1 + \beta_2 = \text{predicted odds of favorable voting by high-income, small-family voters}$$

$$\hat{Z}_4 \approx Z_4 = \beta_1 + \beta_2 + \beta_3 = \text{predicted odds of favorable voting by high-income, large-family voters}$$

Thus, if we want to examine the impact on voting of having a large rather than a small family, independent of income, the effect is measured by the coefficient β_3. Likewise, β_2 measures the difference in the logarithm of the odds of voting between high- and low-income small families.

Because $\hat{P}_i$ does not equal P_i, there are some problems with the use of ordinary least-squares estimation in this grouped-data case. If we assume that each of the individual observations in a group is independent (and follows a binomial probability distribution), the estimated dependent variable, $\log [r_i/(n_i - r_i)]$, will be (for large samples) approximately normally distributed with mean 0 and variance

$$V_i = \frac{n_i}{r_i(n_i - r_i)} \tag{11.13}$$

As a result, the error term in the linear specification of Eq. (11.12) is heteroscedastic. The variance in each of the subgroups will be inversely related to the number of observations in each cell n_i and also will vary with the number of favorable votes r_i. The obvious correction for heteroscedasticity is to use weighted least squares, where each observation is multiplied by the weight $1/\sqrt{V_i}$. However, a number of other corrections have been proposed, mainly to help with the small-sample properties of the estimation process.[11]

---

[11] One adjustment suggested by Cox, op. cit., and by Domencich and McFadden, op. cit., is to use the following equation:

$$\log \frac{r_i + \frac{1}{2}}{n_i - r_i + \frac{1}{2}} = \alpha + \beta X_i$$

If we wish to measure the fit associated with the grouped regression model, we can use the calculated R^2 statistic. However, a preferable statistic looks at the differences between the actual frequencies in each subgroup and the estimated frequencies. Specifically, let P_i^* be the estimated probability calculated for each observation from Eq. (11.9). Then the statistic[12]

$$s = \sum_{i=1}^{G} \frac{n_i(\hat{P}_i - P_i^*)^2}{P_i^*(1 - P_i^*)}$$

is distributed (for large samples) according to the chi-square distribution where the number of degrees of freedom is the number of subcategories G minus the number of estimated parameters. The lower the value of s, the better the fit of the model.

The approximation leading to the specification of Eq. (11.12) is reasonable only when sufficient repetitions occur. In fact, when only one choice is associated with each set of explanatory variables, the left-hand side of Eq. (11.12) is undefined, so that the approximation to Eq. (11.10) is of no use. A useful rule of thumb for the application of the least-squares approximation is that for each value of X, n_i should be at least equal to 5, but a more accurate rule would account for the fact that the least-squares approximation is poorest for levels of X in which the frequency of a given choice is close to 0 or 1. This can be seen in Eq. (11.13). When r_i/n_i approaches either 0 or 1, the expression for V_i gets arbitrarily large. We should note that the approximation implicit in Eq. (11.12) is not strictly appropriate when the explanatory variable is continuous, since the continuous variable must be partitioned, a process which introduces measurement error into the problem.

With continuous variables in models with several attributes serving as explanatory variables, it may be necessary to estimate a logit model in which only *one* choice is associated with each set of independent variables. Fortunately, there is a maximum-likelihood estimation procedure which can be applied to the model in Eq. (11.12). (See Appendix 11.1 for a brief outline of the procedure and the statistical tests associated with it.) Because it is possible to prove that a unique maximum always exists for the logit model, maximum-likelihood estimation is particularly appealing. In fact, maximum-likelihood estimation yields consistent parameter estimators, and the calculation of the appropriate large-sample statistics is not difficult. Thus, the only disadvantage of nonlinear logit estimation is its cost. Small-sample studies suggest that the signs (and frequently the relative magnitudes) of the estimated parameters obtained from the linear probability models and the maximum-likelihood logit estimators usually are the same. This provides some support for the use of the linear probability model, at least as an exploratory technique.

---

[12] See Theil, op. cit., and McFadden, op. cit., for details.

Example 11.3 Voting for a School Budget   The logit model was used to study the voting decisions of 425 individuals in a local school tax referendum in Troy, Michigan, in 1973.[13] The responses to the survey provide a list of attributes of voters as well as estimates of household income and the price of education, measured as the cost to the individual of supporting an additional dollar per pupil of school spending in the community. The model takes the form

$$\log \frac{\text{Prob (yes)}}{1 - \text{Prob (yes)}} = \beta_1 + \beta_2 Z_2 + \cdots + \beta_k Z_k$$

where the Z's represent the voting attributes listed in Table 11.5 and Prob (yes) represents the probability of a voter supporting the tax referendum. The estimated equation appears below, with asymptotic (large sample) standard errors in parentheses (* = significant at the 5 percent level). Note that since the observations are of individuals and are not grouped, the logit model was estimated by using a maximum-likelihood estimation procedure.

$-23.15^* + .24$ SEX $+ 1.13$ MAR $+ 1.09$ OTHER $+ .08$ A35–49
  (3.84)   (.24)   (1.13)   (1.47)   (.30)

  $+ .61$ A50–64 $+ 1.04$ A65 $+ 1.44^*$ PUB1 $+ 1.39^*$ PUB2 $+ 1.30^*$ PUB3
    (.41)   (.79)   (.34)   (.35)   (.42)

  $+ 2.00^*$ PUB4 $+ 2.16^*$ PUB5 $- .56$ PRIV $- .02^*$ YEARS
    (.58)   (.79)   (.42)   (.01)

  $+ 3.07^*$ SCHOOL $+ 2.14^*$ (log INC) $- 1.21^*$ (log PRICE)
    (.84)   (.37)   (.44)

The gender dummy was included to allow for the possibility that because women tend to bear a large share of the responsibility for child care, they might value the benefits associated with the educational system more highly than do men. The coefficient was insignificant here but was significant, as expected, in a later election.

When children are of school age, households are most likely to be aware of the costs and benefits associated with a vote for higher school taxes. The presence of at least one child in public school was expected to and did have a significant positive impact on the probability of a yes vote. The presence of additional school-age children did not increase the probability of a yes vote until, as expected, beyond the fifth child the marginal gain of reallocating the household budget toward private expenditures outweighed the

[13] D. L. Rubinfeld, "Voting in a Local School Election: A Micro Analysis," *Review of Economics and Statistics*, vol. 59, no. 1, pp. 30–42, February 1977.

TABLE 11.5
DEFINITION OF VARIABLES

	1	0
SEX	If female	If male
MAR	If married with spouse present	Otherwise
OTHER	If separated, divorced, or widowed	Otherwise
A35–49	If age 35–49	Otherwise
A50–64	If age 50–64	Otherwise
A65	If age 65 or over	Otherwise
PUB1	If 1 child is in public school	Otherwise
PUB2	If 2 children are in public school	Otherwise
PUB3	If 3 children are in public school	Otherwise
PUB4	If 4 children are in public school	Otherwise
PUB5	If 5 or more children are in public school	Otherwise
PRIV	If the family has 1 or more children in private school	Otherwise
SCHOOL	If individual is employed as a teacher (public or private)	Otherwise

YEARS = number of years living in Troy community
Log INC = natural logarithm of annual household income, dollars
Log PRICE = natural logarithm of price of public schooling, dollars

gain from the public expenditures and the probability of a yes vote declined. The presence of children in private school had a strong negative effect, however. Families that send their children to private school are likely to perceive little benefit from the public school system while facing a substantial tax bill associated with it.

The number of years in residence was also included as an explanatory variable in the logit model. The results suggest that as the time of residence increases, voters tend to vote no, either in criticism of the educational system or possibly in opposition to the growing burden of local taxes.

The highly significant school dummy was included to account for the fact that the sample of respondents was overrepresented by schoolteachers and their spouses. As expected, schoolteachers are more likely to vote yes in the election relative to individuals with otherwise similar attributes.

On the assumption that local school education is a normal good, we expected, other things being equal, that income and the demand for public schools would be positively correlated. In the estimated equations the income variable was positive and significant, consistent with a positive income elasticity of demand for education.

As the price of schooling rose, other things being equal, we expected that the quantity of educational expenditures per pupil demanded would fall, as would the probability of voting yes in the election. Despite the fact that property tax payments are positively correlated with income, we found that the coefficient of the price of schooling variable was negative and significant, consistent with a negative price elasticity of the demand for education.

Example 11.4 Predicting College-Going Behavior   In a study of college choice,[14] a model was constructed to predict whether students attending college would choose to live on campus or to commute, conditional on information about *individual* attributes and attributes of the particular college. The model is

$$\log \frac{P_i}{1 - P_i} = \beta_1 I_1 + \beta_2 I_2 + \beta_3 I_3 + \beta_4 I_4 + \beta_5 D + \beta_6 S + \beta_7 R$$

where P_i = probability that student will choose to live on campus
$\quad Y$ = logarithm (base 10) of family income
$\quad X$ = distance from home to campus
$\quad I_1 = (100 - X)(5 - Y)/500$
$\quad I_2 = X(5 - Y)/500$
$\quad I_3 = (100 - X)Y/500$
$\quad I_4 = XY/500$
$\quad D$ = percentage of students at college who live on campus
$\quad S$ = 1 if female and 0 otherwise
$\quad R$ = 1 if student said he or she preferred to live on campus and 0 otherwise

The logit model was estimated by using the maximum-likelihood estimation routine and a sample of 10,600 students who actually attended college. The estimation results (with standard errors in parentheses) are[15]

$$\log \frac{P_i}{1 - P_i} = -16.59\, I_1 - 8.680\, I_2 - .6277\, I_3 + 10.81\, I_4 + .01929\, D$$
$$\qquad\quad (1.73) \qquad\quad (.90) \qquad\quad (.40) \qquad\quad (.70) \qquad\quad (.0023)$$

$$\qquad -.04789\, S + 1.470\, R$$
$$\qquad\quad (.11) \qquad\quad (.16)$$

The distance-income interaction variables are somewhat difficult to interpret on their own. However, Fig. 11.5 shows that the probability of living on campus increases with distance from campus and is higher at all distances for students with higher family incomes. The probability of campus residency increases with the percentage of students living on campus in the absence of monetary constraints. Finally, there is a slightly higher, but insignificant, probability of living on campus for males than for females.

---

[14] M. G. Kohn, C. F. Manski, and D. S. Mundel, "An Empirical Investigation of Factors Which Influence College Going Behavior," *Rand Corporation Report R1470-NSF*, Santa Monica, CA, September 1974.

[15] We omit the "hat" over the predicted value to simplify the presentation, and will continue to do so throughout the remainder of the book.

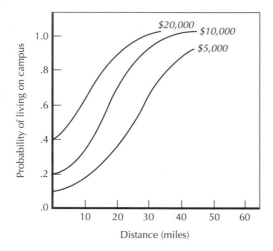

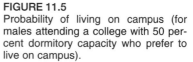

FIGURE 11.5
Probability of living on campus (for males attending a college with 50 percent dormitory capacity who prefer to live on campus).

To interpret the effect of a change in D on the probability of campus residence, we need to solve for the change in probability ΔP as follows:

$$\Delta \log \frac{P_i}{1 - P_i} = .019\, \Delta D$$

To simplify, we utilize the fact that for any continuous variable x, $\Delta \log x \approx \Delta x/x$, and the fact that $\log (x/y) = \log x - \log y$. Then

$$\Delta \log \frac{P_i}{1 - P_i} \approx \left(\frac{1}{P_i} + \frac{1}{1 - P_i}\right)\Delta P_i = \frac{1}{P_i(1 - P_i)}\Delta P_i$$

Since we have chosen $\Delta D = 1$, it follows that

$$\Delta P_i \approx .019[P_i(1 - P_i)]$$

If P_i were equal to .5, for example, ΔP_i would equal .076. Perhaps the most useful single value of P_i to choose for this interpretation is the mean, but an examination of the responses in campus choice for numerous points of the probability distribution can be illuminating.

The campus choice model can easily be used to make predictions. Assume, for example, that we wish to predict the probability that a male student whose family income is $6,000 who has stated a preference for living on campus rather than at home will indeed live on campus. We will assume that the student attends a university near his home at which 50 percent of the students live on campus. To predict the odds of living on campus, we evaluate the right-hand side of the estimated equation when

$$I_1 = .2(5 - \log_{10} 6{,}000) = .2444 \qquad D = 50$$

$$I_3 = .2(\log_{10} 6{,}000) = .7556 \qquad S = 0 \qquad I_2 = I_4 = 0 \qquad R = 1$$

The logarithm (base e) of the odds is -2.10. Taking antilogarithms and solving, we find that $P_i = .108$. Thus, we predict that the student will live on campus with a probability of .108. To see how the probability of the student's living on campus changes as the distance between the university and home increases, we calculate P_i for different values of distance X:

Distance	0	10	20	30	40	50	60	70
Probability of living on campus	.108	.258	.500	.742	.892	.960	.986	.995

Note that once the student's home is more than 50 miles from the campus, he will almost certainly choose to live on campus.

11.1.4 Forecasting: Goodness of Fit

As a general rule, the models developed in this chapter can be applied directly toward forecasting the probability (or the odds) that a given choice will be made. In the voting case, for example, assume that the predicted probability associated with a new observation is .8. We can interpret .8 as measuring our best forecast of the probability that an individual with a given income will vote yes in an election.[16] Of course, if we are forecasting the *explicit* behavior of a single individual, a forecast of .8 can never be correct *ex post*. If we wish to forecast individual choices, we are likely to predict an outcome of 1 (vote yes) if the predicted probability is greater than .5 and an outcome of 0 if the predicted probability is less than .5.

This suggests a problem with the use of R^2 as a measure of fit. In the classical regression model R^2 can range in value between 0 and 1, with a value of close to 1 indicating a good fit. However, the binary dependent-variable model is not likely to yield an R^2 close to 1.[17] If we were to assume, for example, that the true probabilities of an event occurring were uniformly distributed across a given interval, it would be possible to show an upper bound for R^2 of $\frac{1}{3}$. Thus, it is not surprising that in estimating a linear probability model one is likely to obtain[18] a low R^2.

A preferable alternative to R^2 as a measure of goodness of fit is the *likelihood ratio index*. The index builds directly on our discussion of maximum-likelihood estimation in Section 10.2. Let $L(0)$ represent the value of the log-likelihood

---

[16] Assume that our objective is to minimize the variance of the error of forecast. Let $\hat{P}$ be the forecast value of the probability that a given choice will be made. Then the forecast error will be $1 - \hat{P}$ if the event occurs, and $0 - \hat{P}$ otherwise. The variance of the error of forecast is $\sigma_\varepsilon^2 = P(1 - \hat{P})^2 + (1 - P)(-\hat{P})^2$. Minimizing σ_ε^2 with respect to $\hat{P}$ yields $\hat{P} = P$.

[17] This issue is discussed in D. G. Morrison, "Upper Bounds for Correlations between Binary Outcomes and Probabilistic Predictions," *Journal of the American Statistical Association*, vol. 67, 1972.

[18] There are alternative measures of goodness of fit for such models. One useful measure is the average conditional entropy described by H. Theil in *Economics and Informational Theory* (Chicago: Rand McNally, 1967; Amsterdam: North-Holland, 1967).

function when all the parameters are equal to 0 and let $L(\beta^*)$ represent the value when the log-likelihood function has been maximized. Then the likelihood ratio index ρ is defined as

$$\rho = 1 - \frac{L(\beta^*)}{L(0)}$$

By construction, if the maximization procedure suggests that there is no gain from changing any of the estimated parameters from zero, then ρ will equal 0 as well. However, if we were fortunate to estimate a likelihood function that predicted every choice in the sample correctly, the estimated likelihood function would be 1 and the log-likelihood index would be 0. With $L(\beta^*) = 0$, it follows that $\rho = 1$.

Thus, the log-likelihood index ranges from 0 to 1, just as R^2 does. Like R^2, it is unlikely to be close to 1 when binary choices are involved; similarly, any particular numerical value of ρ is difficult to interpret. Nonetheless, the value of ρ does give us some indication of how much can be gained from the addition of new variables to a model.[19]

11.2 MULTIPLE-CHOICE MODELS

We now consider generalizing the results of the previous section to cases in which individuals make choices from three or more mutually exclusive alternatives. There are several ways in which to analyze this problem; we focus here on the case in which alternatives are unranked.

11.2.1 Linear Probability Model

First, consider the extension of the linear probability model to the multiple-choice case. If there are three choices $j = 1, 2, 3$, we write

$$P_{1i} = \alpha_1 + \beta_1 X_i \qquad P_{2i} = \alpha_2 + \beta_2 X_i \qquad P_{3i} = \alpha_3 + \beta_3 X_i \qquad (11.14)$$

P_{ji} is the probability that individual i will choose the jth option, while X_i is the value of X for the ith individual. To estimate each of the three equations in the model by ordinary least squares, it is not necessary to run all three of the linear probability regressions. Since the estimated probabilities are constrained to sum to 1, the estimated intercepts sum to 1 and the slope parameters sum to 0. To prove this, we use the fact that every observation is assigned to one and only one group. Then $P_{1i} + P_{2i} + P_{3i} = 1$. After averaging over all observations in

---

[19] For additional discussion on the measurement of goodness of fit, see Kenneth Train, *Qualitative Choice Analysis* (Cambridge, Mass.: M.I.T. Press, 1986), or G. S. Maddala, *Limited-Dependent and Qualitative Variables in Econometrics* (Cambridge, UK: Cambridge University Press, 1983).

the group, it follows that $\bar{P}_1 + \bar{P}_2 + \bar{P}_3 = 1$ and $p_{1i} + p_{2i} + p_{3i} = 0$ ($p_{ji} = P_{ji} - \bar{P}_j$).

First examine the sum of the least-squares slope estimates:

$$\hat{\beta}_1 + \hat{\beta}_2 + \hat{\beta}_3 - \frac{\Sigma p_{1i} x_i}{\Sigma x_i^2} + \frac{\Sigma p_{2i} x_i}{\Sigma x_i^2} + \frac{\Sigma p_{3i} x_i}{\Sigma x_i^2}$$

$$= \frac{\Sigma (p_{1i} + p_{2i} + p_{3i}) x_i}{\Sigma x_i^2} = 0$$

By contrast, the intercepts sum to 1, since

$$\hat{\alpha}_1 + \hat{\alpha}_2 + \hat{\alpha}_3 = (\bar{P}_1 - \hat{\beta}_1 \bar{X}) + (\bar{P}_2 - \hat{\beta}_2 \bar{X}) + (\bar{P}_3 - \hat{\beta}_3 \bar{X})$$

$$= (\bar{P}_1 + \bar{P}_2 + \bar{P}_3) - \bar{X}(\hat{\beta}_1 + \hat{\beta}_2 + \hat{\beta}_3) = 1$$

Finally,

$$\hat{P}_{1i} + \hat{P}_{2i} + \hat{P}_{3i} = (\hat{\alpha}_1 + \hat{\beta}_1 X_i) + (\hat{\alpha}_2 + \hat{\beta}_2 X_i) + (\hat{\alpha}_3 + \hat{\beta}_3 X_i)$$

$$= (\hat{\alpha}_1 + \hat{\alpha}_2 + \hat{\alpha}_3) + (\hat{\beta}_1 + \hat{\beta}_2 + \hat{\beta}_3) X_i = 1$$

Thus, we need to run only two of the three least-squares regressions. A solution for the parameters of the third equation follows from the first two.

If the X variables in each equation are not identical, the analysis becomes more difficult. The probabilities sum to 1, and ordinary least squares is no longer the most appropriate technique. A useful approach to this problem is provided by Zellner and Lee, who propose that a generalized least-squares estimation procedure be used to account for the correlation between the error terms associated with each equation in the multiple-choice model.[20]

11.2.2 Logit Model

The extension of the logit model in a manner analogous to that of the linear probability model is quite promising.[21] To extend the binary-choice logit model to the three-choice case, for example, we write

$$\log \frac{P_2}{P_1} = \alpha_{21} + \beta_{21} X \quad \log \frac{P_3}{P_1} = \alpha_{31} + \beta_{31} X \quad \log \frac{P_3}{P_2} = \alpha_{32} + \beta_{32} X \quad (11.15)$$

---

[20] See A. Zellner and T. H. Lee, "Joint Estimation of Relationships Involving Discrete Random Variables," *Econometrica*, vol. 33, pp. 382–394, April 1965.

[21] See McFadden, op. cit.; H. Theil, "A Multinomial Extension of the Linear Logit Model," *International Economic Review*, vol. 10, pp. 251–259, 1969; H. Theil, "On the Extension of Relationships Involving Qualitative Variables," *American Journal of Sociology*, vol. 76, pp. 103–154, 1970.

The subscript i, designating individual observations, has been dropped for simplicity. In this case P_j, $j = 1, 2, 3$ indicates the probability that the jth choice will be made. Each equation assumes that the logarithm of the odds of one choice relative to a second choice is a linear function of the attribute X. These odds are dependent on the odds associated with the remaining two equations only in the sense that the system must be constrained so that the sum of the individual probabilities equals 1. As in the linear probability model, it is unnecessary to estimate each of the three equations separately. We can simplify by accounting for the fact that the choice of logit form forces constraints on the model that reduce the number of parameters to be estimated from six to four. To see why, note that

$$\log \frac{P_3}{P_2} = \log \frac{P_3}{P_1} + \log \frac{P_1}{P_2} = \log \frac{P_3}{P_1} - \log \frac{P_2}{P_1}$$

$$= (\alpha_{31} + \beta_{31} X) - (\alpha_{21} + \beta_{21} X) = (\alpha_{31} - \alpha_{21}) + (\beta_{31} - \beta_{21}) X$$

This creates two additional parameter constraints:

$$\alpha_{32} = \alpha_{31} - \alpha_{21} \qquad \beta_{32} = \beta_{31} - \beta_{21}$$

It is somewhat easier to view the logit model's form if we redefine all the unknown parameters as

$$\alpha_{21} = \alpha_2 - \alpha_1 \qquad \alpha_{31} = \alpha_3 - \alpha_1 \qquad \alpha_{32} = \alpha_3 - \alpha_2$$
$$\beta_{21} = \beta_2 - \beta_1 \qquad \beta_{31} = \beta_3 - \beta_1 \qquad \beta_{32} = \beta_3 - \beta_2 \tag{11.16}$$

Then the model system of Eq. (11.15) can be rewritten

$$\log \frac{P_2}{P_1} = (\alpha_2 - \alpha_1) + (\beta_2 - \beta_1) X$$

$$\log \frac{P_3}{P_1} = (\alpha_3 - \alpha_1) + (\beta_3 - \beta_1) X \tag{11.17}$$

$$\log \frac{P_3}{P_2} = (\alpha_3 - \alpha_2) + (\beta_3 - \beta_2) X$$

Since the parameters of the third equation can be calculated once we know the parameters of the first two equations, the third equation need not be estimated.

Suppose sufficient repetitions are available; then we can use the ordinary least-squares approximation to the correct estimation procedure. We estimate the following two equations (i refers to each one of the k levels of X for which repetitions are available, not to the individual observations):

$$\log \frac{r_{2i}/n_i}{r_{1i}/n_i} = \log \frac{r_{2i}}{r_{1i}} = (\alpha_2 - \alpha_1) + (\beta_2 - \beta_1) X_i$$

$$\qquad (11.18)$$

$$\log \frac{r_{3i}/n_i}{r_{1i}/n_i} = \log \frac{r_{3i}}{r_{1i}} = (\alpha_3 - \alpha_1) + (\beta_3 - \beta_1) X_i$$

The estimated parameters will determine the effect of changes in X on the logarithm of the ratios of the probabilities. If actual magnitudes are needed, one must take into account the constraint that the estimated probabilities sum to 1. This can be done by renormalizing the estimated parameter values after the initial least-squares regression has been run. However, the errors are likely to be heteroscedastic. In addition, the cross-equation error correlation ought to be accounted for by using generalized least squares.

If sufficient repetitions are not available, a generalized version of the maximum-likelihood procedure must be used. If computational costs are not a problem, maximum likelihood should be used, because it guarantees consistent parameter estimates and correct large-sample statistics.

Example 11.5 Occupational Attainment   A multiple logit model was constructed to analyze the occupational attainment of individuals.[22] The object was to predict the relative probability that an individual is in each of five occupational categories—professional, white collar, craft, blue collar, or menial—on the basis of the individual's race, gender, education, and labor-market experience; 1,000 observations were used from 1970, each pertaining to a full-time working member of the labor force. The following model was estimated:

$$\log \frac{P_2}{P_1} = \alpha_{21} + \beta_{21} E_i + \gamma_{21} X_i + \delta_{21} R_i + \theta_{21} S_i$$

$$\log \frac{P_3}{P_1} = \alpha_{31} + \beta_{31} E_i + \gamma_{31} X_i + \delta_{31} R_i + \theta_{31} S_i$$

$$\log \frac{P_4}{P_1} = \alpha_{41} + \beta_{41} E_i + \gamma_{41} X_i + \delta_{41} R_i + \theta_{41} S_i$$

$$\log \frac{P_5}{P_1} = \alpha_{51} + \beta_{51} E_i + \gamma_{51} X_i + \delta_{51} R_i + \theta_{51} S_i$$

---

[22] P. Schmidt and R. P. Strauss, "The Prediction of Occupation Using Multiple Logit Models," *International Economic Review*, vol. 16, no. 2, pp. 471–486, 1975.

where subscript 1 = menial occupation
      subscript 2 = blue-collar occupation
      subscript 3 = craft occupation
      subscript 4 = white-collar occupation
      subscript 5 = professional occupation
             E_i = years of schooling of individual i
             X_i = years of work experience of individual i
               (age $- E - 5$)
             R_i = race of individual i (1 if white, 0 if nonwhite)
             S_i = gender of individual i (1 if male, 0 if female)

The estimated coefficients are given in Table 11.6.

The results demonstrate that more education makes it more likely that one will be in a higher-numbered occupation. Presumably, this is what one expects; education enables one to move up the job scale. The only exception is that more education makes it less likely for one to be in a blue-collar position than in a menial position. The effects of labor-market experience are much less strong across occupations and indicate that blue-collar workers tend to have little experience while professionals tend to have much more experience.

The results for gender are apparent. If we order the occupations as follows:

White collar
Menial
Professional
Blue collar
Craft

then, other things being held constant, being *female* (male) makes one more likely to be in any occupational group *lower* (higher) on the list relative to any other occupational group.

TABLE 11.6
ESTIMATED COEFFICIENTS

Dependent variable	Constant	Education	Experience	Race	Gender
log (P_2/P_1)	1.06	−.12*	−.015	.70*	1.25*
log (P_3/P_1)	−3.77*	−.00	.008	1.46*	3.11*
log (P_4/P_1)	−3.30*	.22*	.003	1.76*	− .52*
log (P_5/P_1)	−5.96*	.42*	.008	.98*	.66*
log (P_3/P_2)	−4.82*	.12*	.023*	.76	1.86*
log (P_4/P_2)	−4.36*	.34*	.018*	1.06*	−1.77*
log (P_5/P_2)	−7.01*	.55*	.023*	.28	− .60*
log (P_4/P_3)	.46	.22*	−.005	.30	−3.53*
log (P_5/P_3)	−2.19*	.43*	.000	−.48	−2.46*
log (P_5/P_4)	−2.65*	.20*	.005	−.79	1.18*

* Significant at the 5 percent level.

Finally, if we order the occupations as follows:

Menial
Blue collar
Professional
Craft
White collar

then being *nonwhite* (white) makes it more likely to be in any group *lower* (higher) on the list relative to any other group. Essentially these results show that being nonwhite makes it more likely to be in one of the less economically desirable groups: menial or blue collar. Furthermore, the worst discrimination is encountered in white-collar positions, not, as some might have expected, in the craft positions.

11.2.3   Ordered Probit Model

One interesting extension of the probit model applies to models in which there is an ordering to the categories associated with the dependent variable.[23] Assume, for example, that we are studying a voting process in which three parties offer candidates for office. The first candidate is conservative, the second is liberal, and the third is a socialist. Assume that there is an underlying index Z for each individual voter which measures the extent to which each candidate feels that one ought to rely on the competitive market system. The observed dependent variable is measured as $Y_i = 3$ if conservative, 2 if liberal, and 1 if socialist. The ordered probit model assumes that there are cutoff points Z^* and Z^{**} which define the relationship between the observed and unobserved dependent variables. Specifically, $Z_i = \alpha + \beta X_i$, and

$$Y_i = \begin{cases} 3 & \text{if } Z_i \geq Z^{**} \\ 2 & \text{if } Z^* < Z_i < Z^{**} \\ 1 & \text{if } Z_i \leq Z^* \end{cases}$$

As in the two-category probit model, the parameters are estimated by using maximum likelihood, as are the asymptotic standard errors. Standard normal tests can be applied to test the significance of individual coefficients.

Example 11.6 Congressional Vote on Medicare   McKelvey and Zavoina used an ordered probit model to analyze congressional voting on the 1965 Medicare bill.[24] Before the bill was reported out by the committee, a motion to recommit and thus weaken the bill was rejected. The authors analyzed

---

[23] This technique is discussed in R. D. McKelvey and W. Zavoina, "A Statistical Model for the Analysis of Ordinal Level Dependent Variables," *Journal of Mathematical Sociology*, vol. 4, pp. 103–120, 1975.

[24] McKelvey and Zavoina, op. cit.

TABLE 11.7
COMPARISON OF REGRESSION AND PROBIT ANALYSIS

Variables	Regression analysis			Probit analysis		
	Coefficient	Standardized coefficient	R^2	Coefficient	Standardized coefficient	R^2
Party	− 1.142	−.640	.52	−2.397	−.382	.88
Region	− .747	−.409		−1.730	−.269	
Old	.013	.003		− .001	−.000	
Employment	.055	.131		.204	.136	
Population	.004	.055		.192	.703	

votes on these two separate occasions to determine an index of each representative's position on Medicare. There were three voting combinations: The greatest support position was taken by representatives who voted against recommital and for passage of the bill; the second intermediate position was taken by those who voted for recommital and for passage; and the weakest position was taken by those who voted for recommital and against passage. The explanatory variables used were as follows:

$$\text{Party} = \begin{cases} 1 & \text{if Republican} \\ 2 & \text{if Democrat} \end{cases} \qquad \text{Region} = \begin{cases} 1 & \text{if south} \\ 0 & \text{otherwise} \end{cases}$$

$$\text{Employment} = \text{\% unemployed in the congressional district}$$

$$\text{Old} = \text{\% over 65 years}$$

$$\text{Population} = \text{population density, thousands per square mile}$$

Table 11.7 shows the results of estimating the probit model. As a means of comparison the data also were used to estimate a linear regression model in which the dependent variable was VOTE = 2 if strongly for Medicare as described above, 1 if weakly for, and 0 if against. To compare the resulting coefficients with the probit model, each variable was normalized to have zero mean and unit variance. Note that the relative importance and significance of each variable varies when the standardized probit model, as opposed to the standardized regression model, is used. In the regression analysis, party and region are by far the most important predictors of stance on Medicare, while in the probit analysis, employment and especially population become much more important.

Which analytic technique is preferable? The R^2 statistic calculated for the probit model measures the portion of the variation in the underlying scale explained by the model and is thus roughly comparable to its linear regression counterpart. However, since the linear regression model here has essentially the same defects as the linear probability model discussed earlier, probit is preferable. Indeed, if we were to compare the models on the basis of goodness of fit (R^2), probit would clearly dominate.

11.3 CENSORED REGRESSION MODELS

All the qualitative choice problems we have analyzed in this chapter concern dependent variables that are discrete, usually taking on only two or three values. There are occasions, however, in which the dependent variable has been constructed on the basis of an underlying continuous variable for which there are a number of observations about which we do not have information. Suppose, for example, that we are studying the wages of women. We know the actual wages of those women who are working, but we do not know the "reservation wage" (the minimum wage at which an individual will work) for those who are not. The latter group is simply recorded as not working. Or suppose that we are studying automobile purchasing behavior using a random survey of the population. For those who happened to buy a car, we can record their expenditure, but for those who did not we have no measure of the maximum amount they would have been willing to pay at the time of the survey.

In both of the examples just described, the dependent variable is *censored:* information is missing for the dependent variable, but the corresponding information for the independent variables *is* present. (If both kinds of data are missing, we describe the dependent variable as *truncated.*) In this section we show that ordinary least-squares estimation of the censored regression model will generate biased and inconsistent parameter estimates. We then point to a consistent maximum-likelihood estimator as a preferred alternative.

Suppose the underlying continuous version of the model is given by

$$Y_i^* = \alpha + \beta X_i^* + \varepsilon_i^* \tag{11.19}$$

Y^* might represent the expenditure on automobile purchases for those buying an automobile or the reservation expenditure for those not buying, and X^* might represent household income. For individuals who have not bought an automobile, Y^* cannot be measured and is set equal to 0. As a result, the observed dependent variable is given by

$$Y = Y_i^* \quad \text{for } Y_i^* > 0$$
$$Y = 0 \quad \text{for } Y_i^* \le 0 \tag{11.20}$$

The actual estimated equation will then appear as follows:

$$Y_i = \alpha + \beta X_i + \varepsilon_i \tag{11.21}$$

The model in Eq. (11.21) is sometimes called the *Tobit model,* in recognition of its development by the economist James Tobin. Unfortunately, ordinary least-squares estimation of the Tobit model will yield biased and inconsistent estimates of α and β. This can be seen easily by calculating the mean of ε_i. For least squares to be unbiased and consistent, this mean must equal zero, but we know that $Y_i \ge 0$. It follows directly that $\varepsilon_i \ge -\alpha - \beta X_i$. For any particular

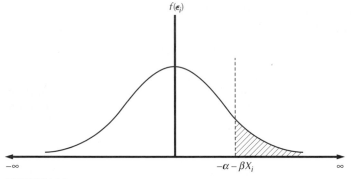

FIGURE 11.6
The probability density function of a normal random variable.

value of X_i, the mean of ε_i can be positive, negative, or zero. The case of a positive mean is shown in Fig. 11.6. Here the probability density function of the true (normally distributed) error term ε is shown, along with the shaded area, which represents all values for which $\varepsilon_i \geq -\alpha - \beta X_i$.

From this figure we can determine the probability density function of the censored error term as follows:

$$f(\varepsilon_i^*) = f(\varepsilon_i | \varepsilon_i \geq -\alpha - \beta X_i) = \frac{f(\varepsilon_i)}{\displaystyle\int_{-\alpha - \beta X_i}^{\infty} f(\theta)\, d\theta}$$

The denominator in the expression on the right is simply the shaded area in the figure. Dividing by this area normalizes the density function so that the total area under the probability density function is equal to 1.

As a final step we can evaluate the mean of the truncated error term. Specifically,

$$E(\varepsilon_i | \varepsilon_i \geq -\alpha - \beta X_i) = \frac{\sigma f(\alpha + \beta X_i)}{F(\alpha + \beta X_i)} = \sigma \lambda_i \tag{11.22}$$

where $\lambda_i = f(\alpha + \beta X_i)/F(\alpha + \beta X_i)$, σ is the standard deviation of the true error term ε_i^*, f is the probability density function of a standard normal variable, and F is the corresponding cumulative distribution function.[25]

λ_i is sometimes called the *hazard rate*. If we have estimates of λ_i, we can use them to normalize the mean of ε_i to zero and hence get consistent estimators of α and β. James Heckman has devised a relatively simple two-stage estimation

---

[25] J. J. Heckman, "Sample Selection Bias as a Specification Error," *Econometrica*, vol. 47, pp. 153–161, January 1979, discusses the derivation of this result.

process that will yield consistent estimates of α and β.[26] In the first stage we estimate λ_i by utilizing the probit model

$$P_i = F(\alpha + \beta X_i) = F(Y_i^*) \tag{11.23}$$

The probit model is estimated by maximum-likelihood estimation (see Appendix 11.1) by distinguishing those observations for which $Y_i^* > 0$ from those for which $Y_i^* \leq 0$. (A linear probability model with $Z_i - 1$ if $Y_i^* > 0$ and $Z_i = 0$ if $Y_i^* \leq 0$ also could be used, but all the difficulties mentioned earlier in this chapter would remain.) From the estimated parameters $\hat{\alpha}$ and $\hat{\beta}$ of the probit model, it is straightforward to calculate $\hat{\lambda}_i$. We either use a table for the normal distribution or rely on a statistical package to do the calculation.

The second stage of the two-stage estimation uses the following model:

$$Y_i = \alpha + \beta X_i + \sigma \hat{\lambda}_i + u_i \tag{11.24}$$

in which $\hat{\lambda}_i$ has been added as an additional explanatory variable. Because $\hat{\lambda}_i$ approaches λ_i as the sample size gets large and λ_i normalizes the mean of ε_i to zero, ordinary least-squares estimation of Eq. (11.24) yields consistent estimates of α and β. Unfortunately, the two-stage estimator (like the linear probability estimator) involves heteroscedastic errors (the error variance depends on X_i as well as whether $Y = 0$), so that the usual t tests are biased. In addition, the estimator is not as efficient as the maximum-likelihood estimator. Therefore, it usually is best to use maximum-likelihood estimation if a program is readily available. The two-stage estimation method can, however, be useful in the model development process.[27]

Example 11.7 The Demand for Public Schooling In Example 11.3 we showed how the logit model could be used to explain the decision to vote yes in a school election as a function of a number of individual and household characteristics. The dependent variable was based on a binary variable YESVM, which was equal to 1 if the individual voted yes and to 0 if the individual voted no.

Using a school-spending equation that relates the logarithm of school spending per pupil to a host of demand variables, we have constructed a new dependent variable, LOGEDUC, which measures the logarithm of each individual's desired level of per-pupil school spending. To simplify the analysis that follows, we have assumed that price (log PRICE) and income (log INC) are the only two explanatory variables.

---

[26] Ibid.

[27] For a more complete discussion of the Tobit model, see T. Amemiya, "Tobit Models: A Survey," *Journal of Econometrics*, pp. 3–61, January/February 1984.

If we knew the desired spending level of all respondents, the demand for school spending per pupil could be estimated using ordinary least squares. Using 95 observations from the Troy, Michigan, study from Example 11.3, we obtained the following results (*t* statistics are in parentheses):

$$\text{LOGEDUC} = 5.89 - .31 \log \text{PRICE} + .38 \log \text{INC}$$
$$\quad\quad (4.23) \quad (-2.07) \quad\quad\quad\quad (3.18)$$

$$R^2 = .11 \quad\quad F = 5.95$$

Suppose, however, that the *only* spending information came from those individuals who actually voted yes in the school election. The truncated dependent variable YSTAR then would be constructed as the product of LOGEDUC and YESVM. If ordinary least squares were used to estimate the truncated model, we would get the following results:

$$\text{YSTAR} = 1.77 - 3.03 \log \text{PRICE} + 2.40 \log \text{INC}$$
$$\quad\quad (.17) \quad (-2.65) \quad\quad\quad\quad (2.63)$$

$$R^2 = .11 \quad\quad F = 5.60$$

The biased one-stage ordinary least-squares estimator performs rather poorly in relation to the true model. Both the price and the income terms have the correct sign, but both are substantially too large, and in addition the price term is too large relative to the income term. (The significant *t* statistics are misleading because the estimator is inconsistent.)

These results are not surprising because the coefficient estimates were both biased and inconsistent. To obtain consistent parameter estimates we used the two-stage procedure suggested by Heckman. In the first stage we estimated the following probit model:

$$\text{Prob(Vote Yes)} = .090 - 2.12 \log \text{PRICE} + .86 \log \text{INC}$$
$$\quad\quad\quad (.022) \quad (-2.41) \quad\quad\quad\quad (2.34)$$

From these regression results we computed the hazard rate $\hat{\lambda}_i$. We then used the estimated hazard rate to compute the second stage of the estimation process, using ordinary least squares, with the following results:

$$\text{YSTAR} = 3.26 - .61 \log \text{PRICE} + .81 \log \text{INC} + .41\hat{\lambda}_i$$
$$\quad\quad (1.15) \quad (-1.32) \quad\quad\quad\quad (1.74) \quad\quad (.69)$$

$$R^2 = .13 \quad\quad F = 2.74$$

Note that the consistent two-stage procedure generates price and income coefficients (these can be interpreted as elasticities) that have the correct sign and the correct relative magnitude. Both, however, are larger than the true coefficients, and both are statistically insignificant at the 5 percent level. Of course, a more accurate and more efficient set of estimates would be obtained if we used maximum-likelihood estimation.

APPENDIX 11.1 Maximum-Likelihood Estimation of the Logit and Probit Models

When one is using either the probit model or the logit model with individual observations, the most suitable estimation technique is maximum likelihood. Assume that we wish to estimate the parameters of the logit model[28]

$$P_i = \frac{1}{1 + e^{-(\alpha + \beta X_i)}} \tag{A11.1}$$

The individual P_i are not observed; instead, we have information for each observation on whether the first or second choice was selected. The measured dependent variable is $Y_i = 1$ if the first choice is made and 0 if the second is made. Our objective is to find parameter estimators for α and β which make it most likely that the choices in the sample would have occurred. If we assume that the first alternative is chosen n_1 times and the second is chosen n_2 times $(n_1 + n_2 = N)$ and if we order the data so that the first n_1 observations are associated with the first alternative, the likelihood function has the form

$$L = \text{Prob } (Y_1, \ldots, Y_N) = \text{Prob } (Y_1) \cdots \text{Prob } (Y_N) \tag{A11.2}$$

Now, by taking into account the fact that the probability of the second alternative being chosen is equal to 1 minus the probability that the first is chosen and using Π to represent the product of a number of factors, the likelihood function reduces to

$$L = P_1 \cdots P_{n_1}(1 - P_{n_1+1}) \cdots (1 - P_N) = \prod_{i=1}^{n_1} P_i \prod_{i=n_1+1}^{N} (1 - P_i)$$

$$= \prod_{i=1}^{N} P_i^{Y_i}(1 - P_i)^{(1-Y_i)}$$

The last expression follows because $Y_i = 1$ for the first n_1 observations and 0 for the last n_2 observations.

---

[28] Maximum-likelihood estimation of the probit model is similar to the logit model, except that P_i represents the probabilities associated with the cumulative normal function rather than the cumulative logistic function.

We maximize the logarithm of L by substituting for the logistic probability function from Eq. (A11.1). Note first that

$$
1 - P_i = 1 - \frac{1}{1 + e^{-(\alpha + \beta X_i)}} = \frac{1 + e^{-(\alpha + \beta X_i)} - 1}{1 + e^{-(\alpha + \beta X_i)}}
$$

$$
= \frac{e^{-\alpha + \beta X_i}}{1 + e^{-(\alpha + \beta X_i)}} = \frac{1}{1 + (1/e^{-(\alpha + \beta X_i)})} = \frac{1}{1 + e^{\alpha + \beta X_i}} \quad \text{(A11.3)}
$$

Then
$$
\log L = \sum_{i=1}^{n_1} \log P_i + \sum_{i=n_1+1}^{N} \log (1 - P_i)
$$

To obtain the slope estimators $\hat{\alpha}$ and $\hat{\beta}$ we differentiate $\log L$ with respect to α and β, set the results equal to zero, and solve:

$$
\frac{\partial(\log L)}{\partial \alpha} = \sum_{i=1}^{n} \frac{\partial P_i/\partial \alpha}{P_i} - \sum_{i=n_1+1}^{N} \frac{\partial P_i/\partial \alpha}{1 - P_i} = 0
$$

$$
\frac{\partial(\log L)}{\partial \beta} = \sum_{i=1}^{n} \frac{\partial P_i/\partial \beta}{P_i} - \sum_{i=n_1+1}^{N} \frac{\partial P_i/\partial \beta}{1 - P_i} = 0
$$

The maximum-likelihood estimation procedure has a number of desirable statistical properties. All parameter estimators are consistent and efficient asymptotically. In addition, all parameter estimators are known to be (asymptotically) normal, so that the analog of the regression t test can be applied. If we wish to test the significance of all or a subset of the coefficients in the logit model or the probit model when maximum likelihood is used, then the likelihood ratio test of Section 10.2 can be applied.

To obtain a measure of goodness of fit analogous to R^2, several options are possible. One is to calculate $1 - L_0/L_{max}$, where L_0 is the initial value of the likelihood function and L_{max} is the highest value. A second option is to calculate residuals $\hat{\varepsilon}_i = Y_i - \hat{P}_i$. These residuals will all be positive for those making the first choice and negative otherwise, as well as being correspondingly smaller in absolute value as the model increasingly better explains the choices being made. From these residuals it is easy to calculate an analog to R^2. Let

$$
\text{ESS} = \sum_{i=1}^{N} \hat{\varepsilon}_i^2 \qquad \text{TSS} = \sum_{i=1}^{N} (Y_i - \bar{Y})^2 \qquad \text{then} \qquad \hat{R}^2 = 1 - \frac{\text{ESS}}{\text{TSS}}
$$

EXERCISES

11.1 In correcting the linear probability model for heteroscedasticity, why can the least-squares residuals not be used directly to calculate an estimate of the error variance σ_i^2 rather than using the formula in Eq. (11.3)?

11.2 What would happen to the coefficients of the linear probability model if the binary dependent variable were represented by a (0, 2) variable rather than by a (0, 1) variable? What does this suggest to you about the interpretation of the estimated least-squares parameters?

11.3 Prove that the transformation of the probability model described in Eq. (11.4) using a cumulative uniform probability function yields the constrained version of the linear probability model.

11.4 Consider the municipal-bond-default example (Example 11.1). Explain how you might reinterpret the bond default issue in terms of the probit model. What are some of the advantages and disadvantages of using the probit specification rather than the linear probability specification?

11.5 The logit model of Eq. (11.9) is linear in the parameters and yet must (usually) be estimated using a nonlinear estimation package. Explain this seeming inconsistency.

11.6 Using the following six data points, estimate a linear probability model using ordinary least squares:

X	-1	-2	0	1	1	1
Y	0	0	0	1	1	1

Calculate R^2 for the model. Then use the estimated model to classify individuals into two categories. Calculate the number of correct classifications by using the following classification rule:

$$\text{Classify} = \begin{cases} \text{first group } (Y = 1) & \text{if } \hat{Y} > \frac{1}{2} \\ \text{second group } (Y = 0) & \text{if } \hat{Y} \leq \frac{1}{2} \end{cases}$$

Discuss the advantages and disadvantages of using R^2 or the percentage of correct classifications as a measure of goodness of fit in the linear probability model.

11.7 Refer to the data set in Table 11.8.

   (a) Using OLS, probit, and logit procedures, estimate the parameters in the model

$$\text{Prob (YESVM = 1)} = F \quad \text{(PUB1\&2, PUB3\&4, PUB5, PRIV,} \\ \text{YEARS, SCHOOL, log INC, PTCON)}$$

How do the results compare?

   (b) Using the OLS estimates, predict YESVM for each case. How many cases actually result in predictions outside the range of 0 to 1? Discuss.

TABLE 11.8
VOTING DATA SET
Variables as in Table 11.5 with addition of PTCON = natural logarithm of property taxes paid per year, dollars; YESVM = dummy variable equal to 1 if individual voted yes in the election and 0 if individual voted no.

Case	PUB1&2	PUB3&4	PUB5	PRIV	YEARS	SCHOOL	log INC	PTCON	YESVM
1	0	1	0	0	10	1	9.7700	7.0475	1
2	0	1	0	0	8	0	10.021	7.0475	0
3	1	0	0	0	4	0	10.021	7.0475	0
4	0	1	0	0	13	0	9.4335	6.3969	0
5	0	1	0	0	3	1	10.021	7.2792	1
6	1	0	0	0	5	0	10.463	7.0475	0
7	0	0	0	0	4	0	10.021	7.0475	0
8	0	1	0	0	5	0	10.021	7.2793	1
9	1	0	0	0	10	0	10.222	7.0475	0
10	0	1	0	0	5	0	9.4335	7.0475	1
11	1	0	0	0	3	0	10.021	7.0475	1
12	1	0	0	0	30	0	9.7700	6.3969	0
13	1	0	0	0	1	0	9.7700	6.7452	1
14	0	1	0	0	3	0	10.021	7.0475	1
15	0	1	0	0	3	0	10.820	6.7452	1
16	0	1	0	0	42	0	9.7700	6.7452	1
17	0	1	0	0	5	1	10.222	7.0475	1
18	1	0	0	0	10	0	10.021	7.0475	0
19	1	0	0	0	4	0	10.222	7.0475	1
20	1	0	0	1	4	0	10.222	6.7452	1
21	0	1	0	0	11	1	10.463	7.0475	1
22	0	0	0	0	5	0	10.222	7.0475	1
23	0	1	0	0	35	0	9.7700	6.7452	1
24	0	1	0	0	3	0	10.463	7.2793	1
25	1	0	0	0	16	0	10.021	6.7452	1
26	0	0	0	1	7	0	10.463	7.0475	0
27	1	0	0	0	5	1	9.7700	6.7452	1
28	1	0	0	0	11	0	9.7700	7.0475	0
29	1	0	0	0	3	0	9.7700	6.7452	0
30	1	0	0	1	2	0	10.222	7.0475	1
31	0	1	0	0	2	0	10.021	6.7452	1
32	1	0	0	0	2	0	9.4335	6.7452	0
33	0	1	0	0	2	1	8.2940	7.0475	0
34	0	0	0	1	4	0	10.463	7.0475	1
35	1	0	0	0	2	0	10.021	7.0475	1
36	0	1	0	0	3	0	10.222	7.2793	0
37	1	0	0	0	3	0	10.222	7.0475	1
38	1	0	0	0	2	0	10.222	7.4955	1
39	0	1	0	0	10	0	10.021	7.0475	0
40	1	0	0	0	2	0	10.222	7.0475	1
41	1	0	0	0	2	0	10.021	7.0475	0
42	1	0	0	0	3	0	10.820	7.4955	0
43	1	0	0	0	3	0	10.021	7.0475	1
44	0	1	0	0	3	0	10.021	7.0475	1
45	1	0	0	0	6	0	10.021	6.7452	1

TABLE 11.8
VOTING DATA SET (*Continued*)

Case	PUB1&2	PUB3&4	PUB5	PRIV	YEARS	SCHOOL	log INC	PTCON	YESVM
46	0	1	0	0	2	0	10.021	7.0475	1
47	1	0	0	0	26	0	9.7700	6.7452	0
48	0	0	0	1	18	0	10.222	7.4955	0
49	0	0	0	0	4	0	9.7700	6.7452	0
50	0	0	0	0	6	0	10.021	7.0475	0
51	0	0	0	0	12	0	10.021	6.7452	1
52	1	0	0	0	49	0	9.4335	6.7452	1
53	1	0	0	0	6	0	10.463	7.2793	1
54	0	0	0	1	18	0	9.7700	7.0475	0
55	1	0	0	0	5	0	10.021	7.0475	1
56	1	0	0	0	6	0	9.7700	5.9915	1
57	1	0	0	0	20	0	9.4335	7.0475	0
58	1	0	0	0	1	1	9.7700	6.3969	1
59	1	0	0	0	3	0	10.021	6.7452	1
60	1	0	0	0	5	0	10.463	7.0475	0
61	1	0	0	0	2	0	10.021	7.0475	1
62	0	0	1	1	5	0	10.820	7.2793	0
63	1	0	0	0	18	0	9.4335	6.7452	0
64	1	0	0	0	20	1	9.7700	5.9915	1
65	0	0	0	0	14	0	8.9227	6.3969	0
66	0	0	1	0	3	0	9.4335	7.4955	0
67	1	0	0	0	17	0	9.4335	6.7452	0
68	1	0	0	0	20	0	10.021	7.0475	0
69	0	1	0	1	3	0	10.021	7.0475	1
70	0	1	0	0	2	0	10.021	7.0475	1
71	0	0	0	0	5	0	10.222	7.0475	1
72	1	0	0	0	35	0	9.7700	7.0475	1
73	0	1	0	0	10	0	10.021	7.2793	0
74	0	1	0	0	8	0	9.7700	7.0475	1
75	1	0	0	0	12	0	9.7700	7.0475	0
76	0	1	0	0	7	0	10.222	6.7452	1
77	1	0	0	0	3	0	10.463	6.7452	1
78	0	1	0	0	25	0	10.222	6.7452	0
79	1	0	0	0	5	1	9.7700	6.7452	1
80	0	1	0	0	4	0	10.222	7.0475	1
81	1	0	0	0	2	0	10.021	7.2793	1
82	0	1	0	0	5	0	10.463	6.7452	1
83	1	0	0	0	3	0	9.7700	7.0475	0
84	1	0	0	0	2	0	10.820	7.4955	1
85	0	0	0	1	6	0	8.9227	5.9915	0
86	1	0	0	1	3	0	9.7700	7.0475	1
87	0	0	1	0	12	0	9.4335	6.3969	0
88	0	0	0	0	3	0	9.7700	6.7452	1
89	0	1	0	0	3	0	10.021	7.0475	1
90	0	0	0	0	3	0	10.021	6.7452	1
91	1	0	0	0	3	0	10.222	7.2793	1
92	0	1	0	0	3	1	10.021	7.0475	1
93	0	0	1	0	5	0	10.021	7.0475	1
94	0	0	0	0	35	1	8.9227	5.9915	1
95	0	1	0	0	3	0	10.463	7.4955	0

PART THREE

MULTI-EQUATION
MODELS

In the next three chapters we concern ourselves with models that consist of more than one equation. In a single-equation regression model the dependent variable is related to a set of explanatory variables; e.g., an interest rate may be related to GNP, the rate of inflation, and the money supply. However, single-equation models do not explain the interdependencies that may exist between the explanatory variables, or show how these explanatory variables are related to other variables. In addition, single-equation models explain causality only in one direction; i.e., explanatory variables determine a dependent variable, but there is no feedback relationship between the dependent variable and the explanatory variables.

Multi-equation simulation models allow us to account for the interrelationships within a set of variables. Often these models consist of a set of regression equations which, after being estimated, are solved simultaneously on a computer. However, simulation models also can include equations which are not estimated, such as accounting identities and behavioral rules of thumb.

In Chapter 12 we describe some of the estimation problems involved in multi-equation models as well as the problem of model identification. We also examine some estimation techniques that have been developed for multi-equation models, including two- and three-stage least squares.

In Chapters 13 and 14 we discuss some general issues involved in the construction, evaluation, and use of simulation models. In Chapter 13 we describe how the simulation of a model is actually carried out, how a simulation model can be evaluated, and how the particular estimation method used for a model affects its simulation performance. We also discuss *vector autoregressions*—nonstructural models in which a set of variables is related to lagged values. In Chapter 14 we examine the dynamic behavior of simulation models, methods of adjusting simulation models, and the use of stochastic simulation to determine confidence intervals for model forecasts.

CHAPTER 12

SIMULTANEOUS-EQUATION ESTIMATION

In the first two parts of this book we concerned ourselves primarily with single-equation models. We found that in many cases ordinary least-squares estimation was the most appropriate estimation procedure. In this chapter we turn our attention to models consisting of several equations, in which the behavior of the variables is jointly determined. Perhaps the simplest example of a simultaneous-equation model is a two-equation model of market demand and supply where price and quantity are both endogenous variables. More complex examples include industrial, regional, and national economic models. All these examples are similar in that each model includes several endogenous variables which are simultaneously determined by an interrelated series of equations.

The presence of two or more endogenous variables necessitates some additional model-building and estimation tools. For example, simultaneity can cause ordinary least-squares parameter estimators to be inconsistent, so that an alternative estimation method must be used. We shall develop these tools by working with simple examples in as comprehensible a fashion as possible. Appendices 12.1 through 12.3 contain a more complete mathematical development of many of the techniques described in the text.

This chapter begins with an explanation of the inconsistency of ordinary least squares when an equation is to be estimated that is part of a system of (two) simultaneously determined equations. The second section discusses the identification problem, with the primary issue being the determination of conditions under which the structural parameters of an equation can be consistently estimated. With this background we describe two-stage least squares, a frequently used type of instrumental-variables estimator. Then we show how to estimate simultaneous-equation models with serial correlation and a lagged dependent variable. Finally, we move to issues involving systems of equations. We describe methods by which all the equations in a model system are estimated simultaneously, thereby providing an improvement in efficiency.

12.1   INTRODUCTION TO SIMULTANEOUS-EQUATION MODELS

Quite frequently in business and economic modeling, the process or processes under study can best be represented by a series of simultaneous interdependent equations. The most common examples of such equations are supply-demand models, in which the price of a product is simultaneously determined by the interaction of producers and consumers in a market, and macroeconomic income determination models, in which aggregate consumption and aggregate disposable income are simultaneously determined. We will use these models to illustrate the fact that the ordinary least-squares estimation of individual equations in a simultaneous-equation model can lead to biased and inconsistent parameter estimators. We will then discuss alternative single-equation estimation procedures which yield consistent parameter estimators.

12.1.1   Simultaneous-Equation Systems

From this point on we will think of models as consisting of a series of equations, with each equation serving to explain one variable which is determined in the model. For this reason it will be useful to replace the terms *independent variable* and *dependent variable* with some new terminology. Consider a three-equation supply-demand model described as follows:

Supply: $$Q_t^S = \alpha_1 + \alpha_2 P_t + \alpha_3 P_{t-1} + \varepsilon_t$$

Demand: $$Q_t^D = \beta_1 + \beta_2 P_t + \beta_3 Y_t + u_t$$

Equilibrium: $$Q_t^D = Q_t^S$$

The supply equation, demand equation, and equilibrium condition determine the market price and the quantity supplied (and demanded) when the market is in equilibrium. For this reason the variables Q_t^D, Q_t^S, and P_t are often called *endogenous* variables; they are determined within the system of equations. The model also contains two variables whose values are not determined directly within the system. These so-called *predetermined variables* help cause the movement of the endogenous variables within the system. P_{t-1} and Y_t are both predetermined variables in the model. There is, of course, an important difference between the two predetermined variables. The first variable P_{t-1} is in fact

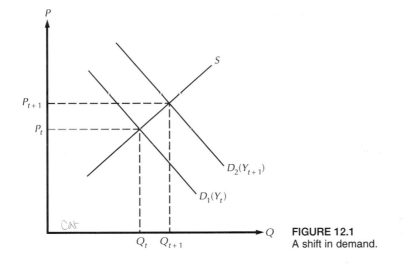

FIGURE 12.1
A shift in demand.

determined within the system—by past values of the variables. Thus, *lagged endogenous* variables are predetermined variables.[1] Finally, the variable Y_t is determined completely outside the model system and is called an *exogenous* variable.

We can see the endogeneity of the P_t and Q_t variables graphically in Fig. 12.1. Demand curve D_1 and supply curve S are shown for time period t and therefore for particular values of the predetermined variables P_{t-1} and Y_t. Now suppose we consider demand and supply in another time period, say $t + 1$, in which income Y_{t+1} has increased. The increase in income will cause the demand curve to shift upward and to the right from D_1 to D_2, which in turn will lead to a higher equilibrium price P_{t+1} and quantity Q_{t+1}.

Because P_t and Q_t are endogenous, applying ordinary least squares to the estimation of the supply (or the demand) equation will generate biased and inconsistent estimators. To see this, we adjust the original model, eliminating the lagged price term from the supply equation and substituting for the equilibrium values of Q_t^S and Q_t^D (represented as Q_t). The model is as follows:

Supply: $\qquad\qquad\qquad\qquad Q_t = \alpha_1 + \alpha_2 P_t + \varepsilon_t$

$$\text{(12.1)}$$

Demand: $\qquad\qquad\qquad\qquad Q_t = \beta_1 + \beta_2 P_t + \beta_3 Y_t + u_t$

---

[1] In most of this chapter we shall consider all lagged endogenous variables as predetermined. This assumption is reasonable as long as there is no serial correlation associated with the error term in the equation containing the lagged endogenous variable. We discuss the specific problems associated with serial correlation and lagged endogenous variables in Section 12.5.

To simplify our analysis, we will have occasion to use the model with all variables measured in deviations form, obtained by substituting $q_t = Q_t - \bar{Q}$, $y_t = Y_t - \bar{Y}$, and $p_t = P_t - \bar{P}$ into Eq. (12.1):

Supply:
$$q_t = \alpha_2 p_t + \varepsilon_t$$

(12.2)

Demand:
$$q_t = \beta_2 p_t + \beta_3 y_t + u_t$$

Such a model is called a *structural model* because its form is given by the under-lying theory. A structural model contains endogenous variables on the left-hand side and (if simultaneous) contains endogenous as well as predetermined variables on the right-hand side.

Our study of the properties of the equation system and the derivations which follow will be aided if we solve the equations in Eq. (12.2) for each of the endogenous variables as a function solely of the predetermined variables in the model. The so-called *reduced form solution* is listed below, first in terms of the original variables [Eq. (12.3)] and second when the variables are measured as deviations about their means [Eq. (12.4)].[2]

$$Q_t = \frac{\alpha_2 \beta_1 - \alpha_1 \beta_2}{\alpha_2 - \beta_2} + \frac{\alpha_2 \beta_3}{\alpha_2 - \beta_2} Y_t + \frac{\alpha_2 u_t - \beta_2 \varepsilon_t}{\alpha_2 - \beta_2}$$

(12.3)

$$P_t = \frac{\beta_1 - \alpha_1}{\alpha_2 - \beta_2} + \frac{\beta_3}{\alpha_2 - \beta_2} Y_t + \frac{u_t - \varepsilon_t}{\alpha_2 - \beta_2}$$

$$q_t = \frac{\alpha_2 \beta_3}{\alpha_2 - \beta_2} y_t + \frac{\alpha_2 u_t - \beta_2 \varepsilon_t}{\alpha_2 - \beta_2} = \pi_{12} y_t + v_{1t}$$

(12.4)

$$p_t = \frac{\beta_3}{\alpha_2 - \beta_2} y_t + \frac{u_t - \varepsilon_t}{\alpha_2 - \beta_2} = \pi_{22} y_t + v_{2t}$$

Using variables measured in deviations form eliminates the constant term in each of the reduced form equations but does not alter the other parameters in any way.

Suppose we estimate the supply equation in Eq. (12.2) by using ordinary least squares. The slope parameter estimate will be

$$\hat{\alpha}_2 = \frac{\Sigma p_t q_t}{\Sigma p_t^2}$$

(12.5)

---

[2] To get the reduced form in the latter case, for example, we set the right-hand side of both equations in Eq. (12.2) equal; that is, $\alpha_2 p_t + \varepsilon_t = \beta_2 p_t + \beta_3 y_t + u_t$. Solving for p_t, we obtain the second equation. Then, substituting this equation into $q_t = \alpha_2 p_t + \varepsilon_t$ in Eq. (12.2), we get the first equation.

Substituting for q_t in equation system (12.2), we find that

$$\hat{\alpha}_2 = \frac{\Sigma p_t(\alpha_2 p_t + \varepsilon_t)}{\Sigma p_t^2} = \alpha_2 + \frac{\Sigma p_t \varepsilon_t}{\Sigma p_t^2} \tag{12.6}$$

If the term $\Sigma p_t \varepsilon_t / \Sigma p_t^2$ on the right-hand side equaled 0 on average, we would know that ordinary least squares was unbiased. Likewise, if the sum approached 0 as the sample size became large, we would know that ordinary least-squares estimation was consistent. Unfortunately, neither of these conditions is true in general. In simultaneous-equation models, where (endogenous) variables in one equation feed back into variables in another equation, the error terms are correlated with the endogenous variables and least squares is both biased and inconsistent.

In the case of the supply-demand model it is not always possible to predict the direction of bias and inconsistency resulting from the use of least-squares estimation. In using least squares to estimate an aggregate-consumption function in a simple model of national income determination, however, the direction of inconsistency is known. Written in deviations form, the structural model is

$$c_t = \beta y_t + \varepsilon_t \qquad y_t = c_t + i_t + g_t \tag{12.7}$$

where c = aggregate consumption
$\quad\ \ i$ = investment
$\quad\ g$ = government spending
$\quad\ y$ = national income
$\quad\ \beta$ = marginal propensity to consume $(0 < \beta < 1)$

i_t and g_t are exogenous variables, and c_t and y_t are endogenous.

The reduced form of the model contains two equations with endogenous variables c_t and y_t on the left-hand side and exogenous variables i_t and g_t on the right. We solve by substituting for y_t in the consumption equation to get

$$c_t = \frac{\beta}{1-\beta} i_t + \frac{\beta}{1-\beta} g_t + \frac{\varepsilon_t}{1-\beta} \qquad y_t = \frac{1}{1-\beta} i_t + \frac{1}{1-\beta} g_t + \frac{\varepsilon_t}{1-\beta}$$

$$\tag{12.8}$$

Thus, using ordinary least squares, we have

$$\hat{\beta} = \frac{\Sigma c_t y_t}{\Sigma y_t^2} = \frac{\Sigma y_t(\beta y_t + \varepsilon_t)}{\Sigma y_t^2} = \beta + \frac{\Sigma y_t \varepsilon_t}{\Sigma y_t^2}$$

and
$$\text{plim } \hat{\beta} = \beta + \text{plim} \frac{\Sigma y_t \varepsilon_t}{\Sigma y_t^2}$$

But

$$\text{plim} \frac{\Sigma y_t \varepsilon_t}{\Sigma y_t^2} = \frac{\text{Cov}\,(i_t,\,\varepsilon_t)\,+\,\text{Cov}\,(g_t,\,\varepsilon_t)\,+\,\text{Var}\,(\varepsilon_t)}{(1\,-\,\beta)\,\text{Var}\,(y_t)}$$

$$= \frac{\text{Var}\,(\varepsilon_t)}{(1\,-\,\beta)\,\text{Var}\,(y_t)} > 0 \quad \text{substituting from Eq. (12.8)}$$

Here, with only one structural equation containing an error term, the direction of bias is clear. Ordinary least squares will overestimate the true value of the marginal propensity to consume.

12.2   THE IDENTIFICATION PROBLEM

Suppose we know the reduced form of a system of equations. Is this sufficient to allow us to discern the value of the parameters in the original set of structural equations? The problem of determining the structural equations, given knowledge of the reduced form, is called the *identification problem*. It is equivalent in our supply-demand example to asking whether we can determine the demand and supply equations if we are given knowledge of P and Q.

Consideration of the identification problem comes before consideration of the estimation problem. Once a structural model has been specified, we must check to see whether we can obtain knowledge of the structural parameters once the reduced form has been estimated.

We say that an equation is *unidentified* if there is no way of estimating all the structural parameters from the reduced form. An equation is *identified* if it is possible to obtain values of the parameters from the reduced form equation system. An equation is *exactly identified* if a unique parameter value exists and is *overidentified* if more than one value is obtainable for some parameters. While we have concentrated on the identification of single equations in a structural system of equations, it is important to realize that within a given structural model some equations may be identified while others may not. In fact, within a single equation it is possible that some parameters may be identified while others may remain unidentified.

Let us continue with our discussion of the identification problem by considering the supply-demand models we described previously. Consider first a supply-demand time-series model in which there are no predetermined variables:

Supply: $Q_t = \alpha_1 + \alpha_2 P_t + \varepsilon_t$

$$(12.9)$$

Demand: $Q_t = \beta_1 + \beta_2 P_t + u_t$

We assume that the market is in equilibrium in each time period so that quantity demanded equals quantity supplied (we have already eliminated the

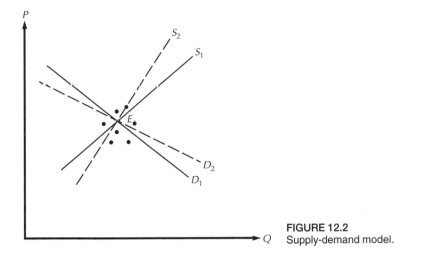

FIGURE 12.2
Supply-demand model.

equilibrium equation by substitution). The key to understanding the identification problem in the context of this model is to focus on the equilibrium
condition. At each period of time there is one value of the price P and one
value of the quantity sold Q. In other words, the only data available to the
econometrician are the market values (for each period of time) of P and Q. The
errors in the equations make it likely that the values of P and Q obtained will
not be identical, but it is likely that all values will lie close to the equilibrium
values of P and Q determined by the direct solution of the equations in the
model. This situation is depicted in Fig. 12.2. Point E represents the supply-
demand equilibrium. When we try to estimate the separate supply and demand
equations using the market data, we obtain meaningless results. There is no
way to ascertain the true supply and demand slopes given only the equilibrium
data. In fact, the only reason why estimation is possible is that errors appear in
both equations. (Otherwise all data points would be at point E.)

The model we are describing is one in which both the supply curve and the
demand curve are unidentified. Neither is identified because there is no way
to obtain the values of the structural parameters (the slopes and intercepts of
the individual supply and demand curves) from the reduced form equations.
(The reduced form is simply the equation describing the point of intersection
of the demand and supply curves with errors attached.) The reduced form
equations for the deviations form are

$$p_t = \frac{u_t - \varepsilon_t}{\alpha_2 - \beta_2} \quad \text{and} \quad q_t = \frac{\alpha_2 u_t - \beta_2 \varepsilon_t}{\alpha_2 - \beta_2}$$

It should be apparent from an examination of Fig. 12.2 that any pair of demand
and supply curves intersecting at point E could just as easily have been the
"true" demand and supply curves. In other words, there are an infinite number

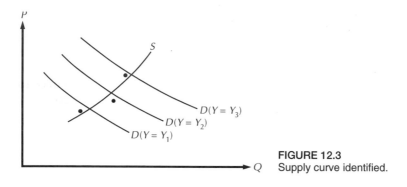

FIGURE 12.3
Supply curve identified.

of structural models (demand and supply curves) which are consistent with the same reduced form (equilibrium value of P and Q). The problem does not involve a lack of data. One could have an infinite number of data points for econometric analysis, but in that case the best one could do would be to estimate the equilibrium values of P and Q with great accuracy; the demand and supply curves would still be unidentified. (Of course, the reduced form equations can be used directly if prediction is the objective, because identification is not required.)

It should be apparent that identification of equations in a model system necessitates further information. Consider the supply-demand system:

Supply: $\qquad\qquad\qquad Q_t = \alpha_1 + \alpha_2 P_t + \varepsilon_t$

$\qquad\qquad\qquad\qquad\qquad\qquad\qquad\qquad\qquad\qquad\qquad$ (12.10)

Demand: $\qquad\qquad\qquad Q_t = \beta_1 + \beta_2 P_t + \beta_3 Y_t + u_t$

Under the assumption that $\beta_3 \neq 0$ and that Y_t varies substantially over time, we cannot plot one demand curve and one supply curve for all time periods. Because income determines demand and income varies over time, we must account for the fact that the demand curve shifts over time. One set of possible demand curves is depicted in Fig. 12.3. (Other sets of demand curves are possible.)

In Fig. 12.3 the equilibrium values trace out the path of the underlying supply curve. The supply curve is identified because the supply parameters can be deduced from the reduced form (the movement of the equilibrium of P and Q). Note that it is the movement of Y over time (or across observations in a cross-section analysis) that is necessary for the identification of the supply equation.

We reiterate that identification is made possible by the existence of prior information about the exogenous variable Y. The supply equation is identified because the exogenous variable Y was excluded from the supply equation. The demand equation is unidentified because prior information is not available which allows for the unique determination of the demand relationship. If we were to consider a model in which the supply relationship is determined by the temperature T in the region and the demand curve is not, then the prior information about the excluded exogenous variable (temperature) in the demand equation would allow us to identify the demand curve.

It is, of course, possible for both the demand curve and the supply curve to be identified. The following supply-demand model has just this property:

Supply:
$$Q_t = \alpha_1 + \alpha_2 P_t + \alpha_3 T_t + \varepsilon_t$$
(12.11)

Demand:
$$Q_t = \beta_1 + \beta_2 P_t + \beta_3 Y_t + u_t$$

If T and Y vary over time (and are not perfectly correlated), both the demand and supply relationships will shift. The movement of the equilibrium values of P and Q is quite complex, since it results from temperature and income changes, but if sufficient data are available we can determine the structural values of the demand and supply parameters uniquely. The shifting of the supply curve associated with changes in T helps us plot out the demand curve at the same time that shifts in demand (changes in Y) allow us to plot out the supply curve.

Finally, consider the situation in which the demand curve is a function not only of income but also of wealth (the two are assumed not to be highly correlated). In this case the demand curve shifts over time as a result of changes in two variables. The supply equation is overidentified because there are two exogenous variables in the supply-demand system of equations which are excluded from the supply equation. This implies that there are at least two ways in which the structural parameters can be obtained from the reduced form parameters.

Our discussion has implicitly involved a search for conditions that are necessary to guarantee the identification of one equation in a two-equation system. This search can be formalized in terms of the *order condition* for identification. The order condition states that if an equation is to be identified, *the number of predetermined variables excluded from the equation must be greater than or equal to the number of included endogenous variables minus 1*. The list of included endogenous variables should contain variables on the left-hand side and the right-hand side of the equation. For some purposes it is useful to express the order condition in a somewhat different but equivalent form: a necessary condition for an equation to be identified is that the number of all variables excluded from the equation be greater than or equal to the number of endogenous variables in the model system minus 1.

The difficulty with the order condition is that it is not a sufficient condition; i.e., it is possible for the condition to be satisfied and for the equation to be unidentified. While the order condition is a satisfactory rule of thumb for identification, there is a possibility that it will fail on occasion. The extension of the order condition to include sufficient as well as necessary conditions for identification is somewhat difficult. Since it involves an understanding of the rank of a matrix, we leave that discussion to Appendix 12.1.

As an example, return to the supply-demand model of Eq. (12.1):

Supply:
$$Q_t = \alpha_1 + \alpha_2 P_t \qquad\qquad + \varepsilon_t$$

Demand:
$$Q_t = \beta_1 + \beta_2 P_t + \beta_3 Y_t + u_t$$

where P is price, Q is quantity, and Y is income. The demand equation is not identified by the order condition, since no predetermined variables are excluded. The necessary condition for the supply curve to be identified is satisfied, since there are two endogenous variables and one excluded predetermined variable. The sufficient condition also will hold when $\beta_3 \neq 0$. This makes intuitive sense, since $\beta_3 = 0$ would imply that the original zero-exclusion restriction has no force in the model. With $\beta_3 = 0$ there is no way to distinguish between the supply and demand equations.

This simple example is useful because it suggests that the problem of identification should not be approached in a rigid manner. Assume, for example, that there is very little variability in the income variable Y and that the associated coefficient is close to 0. While the strict rules for identification will be satisfied, it will still be difficult to distinguish the supply equation from the demand equation. This suggests that attempts to guarantee identifiability in each model equation by adding and deleting variables randomly most likely will lead to problems. While the strict order and rank conditions may be satisfied by such a process, the model is unlikely to have much predictive power, since some or all of the added variables may have little effect on the corresponding endogenous variables.

12.3 CONSISTENT PARAMETER ESTIMATION

Let us return to the supply-demand example of Eq. (12.2) and concentrate on the consistent estimation of the *supply parameters*. For convenience, the structural and reduced form equation systems are reproduced below:

Structural model:

Supply:
$$q_t = \alpha_2 p_t + \varepsilon_t$$

Demand:
$$q_t = \beta_2 p_t + \beta_3 y_t + u_t$$
(12.12)

Reduced form model: $\quad q_t = \pi_{12} y_t + v_{1t} \qquad p_t = \pi_{22} y_t + v_{2t}$

The discussion of instrumental variables in Chapter 7 suggests one approach to the estimation problem. Instrumental-variables estimation is reasonable in the context of simultaneous-equation models because the predetermined variables in the model serve as excellent instrumental variables. The fact that they are present in the model suggests that they are correlated with the endogenous variables, and the fact that they are predetermined guarantees (by assumption) that they are uncorrelated with the error term. In the supply-demand example, the variable y_t would serve as a suitable instrument, yielding the following consistent estimator of the supply slope parameter.

$$\hat{\alpha}_2^* = \frac{\Sigma y_t q_t}{\Sigma p_t y_t}$$

While the use of instrumental variables is appropriate, we are often faced with the problem of choosing among several available instruments. For this reason, we will examine some alternative single-equation estimation techniques, each of which implicitly involves different assumptions about instrument choice. As a first step, consider the reduced form equation system of Eq. (12.4). Since the reduced form equations contain only exogenous variables on the right-hand side, it is clear that ordinary least squares will estimate the reduced form consistently and with a lack of bias. Let us examine these estimated coefficients, $\hat{\pi}_{12}$ and $\hat{\pi}_{22}$, more closely. Note that π_{12}/π_{22} is identically equal to α_2. This suggests that we can estimate α_2 consistently by estimating the reduced form equations using ordinary least squares and then solving to get the estimates of the supply slope parameter $\hat{\alpha}_2^{**} = \hat{\pi}_{12}/\hat{\pi}_{22}$. This procedure, called *indirect least-squares* estimation, can be used to obtain consistent parameter estimates.

When indirect least-squares estimation is possible and a unique estimate of the structural parameter is available, it is not difficult to show that indirect least-squares estimation is *identical* to instrumental-variables estimation with y_t being chosen as the instrument. To see this, substitute for $\hat{\pi}_{12}/\hat{\pi}_{22}$:

$$\hat{\alpha}_2^{**} = \frac{\hat{\pi}_{12}}{\hat{\pi}_{22}} = \frac{\Sigma y_t q_t / \Sigma y_t^2}{\Sigma p_t y_t / \Sigma y_t^2} = \frac{\Sigma y_t q_t}{\Sigma p_t y_t} = \hat{\alpha}_2^*$$

Unfortunately, the example above cannot be generalized. In some cases indirect least squares is not possible, and in other cases it leads to several distinct slope estimates. Consider first the same supply-demand example but assume that we wish to estimate the slope parameter of the *demand equation*. This would involve using the estimated parameters of the reduced form to obtain an estimate of the parameter β_2. But a brief glance at equation system (12.4) will show that this is impossible; there is no way that the structural parameter can be obtained through estimation of the reduced form system. However, consider the supply-demand system when the demand equation has been modified to include a second exogenous variable W (for wealth). The structural equations and reduced form equations are listed below, with all variables measured in deviations form:

Structural model:
$$q_t = \alpha_2 p_t + \varepsilon_t$$

(12.13)

$$q_t = \beta_2 p_t + \beta_3 y_t + \beta_4 w_t + u_t$$

Reduced form model:

$$q_t = \frac{\alpha_2 \beta_3}{\alpha_2 - \beta_2} y_t + \frac{\alpha_2 \beta_4}{\alpha_2 - \beta_2} w_t + \frac{\alpha_2 u_t - \beta_2 \varepsilon_t}{\alpha_2 - \beta_2} = \pi_{12} y_t + \pi_{13} w_t + v_{1t}$$

(12.14)

$$p_t = \frac{\beta_3}{\alpha_2 - \beta_2} y_t + \frac{\beta_4}{\alpha_2 - \beta_2} w_t + \frac{u_t - \varepsilon_t}{\alpha_2 - \beta_2} = \pi_{22} y_t + \pi_{23} w_t + v_{2t}$$

Once again the reduced form equations can be consistently estimated by using ordinary least squares. However, we are faced with two choices of supply slope estimators when we attempt to use the indirect least-squares technique. The two estimators are $\hat{\pi}_{12}/\hat{\pi}_{22}$ (as before) and $\hat{\pi}_{13}/\hat{\pi}_{23}$. In general, both estimators will yield consistent estimates of the true parameter, but the estimates will not be identical in each sample. Thus, if we attempt to use indirect least squares, we are faced with two choices, either one of which may involve a loss of important information about the model being estimated.

In the section that follows we will describe an estimation procedure that avoids any information loss. First, however, it is worth noting that there is one special case in which ordinary least squares does yield consistent parameter estimates. We say that a system of equations is *recursive* if each of the endogenous variables can be determined sequentially and the errors from each equation are independent of each other. Consider the model

Supply:
$$Q_t = \alpha_1 + \alpha_3 P_{t-1} + \varepsilon_t$$

Demand:
$$P_t = \beta_1 + \beta_2 Q_t + \beta_3 W_t + u_t$$

In the supply equation the quantity supplied depends only on the price level in the previous year (as one might expect with farm products). We have written the demand equation with P_t as the dependent variable to show that the market price of the product is determined once the quantity has been supplied. We also make the important assumption that $Cov(\varepsilon_t, u_t) = 0$, i.e., that the two equations are *not* linked by a correlation between the omitted variables.

Although this system of equations may seem simultaneous, it is actually recursive. Given values for P_{t-1}, we can solve directly for Q_t in the supply equation. Then knowing Q_t allows us to solve for P_t in the demand equation. Because the price variable is lagged in the supply equation, there is no direct feedback from the demand equation to the supply equation. In any recursive model of this sort, ordinary least squares (OLS) is the appropriate estimation procedure. OLS is obviously appropriate for the first equation, since P_{t-1} is predetermined and therefore uncorrelated with ε_t. OLS is also appropriate for the second equation because Q_t is uncorrelated with the error term u_t (since the only error term affecting Q_t is ε_t, and ε_t is uncorrelated with u_t).

12.4 TWO-STAGE LEAST SQUARES

Two-stage least squares (2SLS) provides a very useful estimation procedure for obtaining the values of structural parameters in overidentified equations. Two-stage least-squares estimation uses the information available from the specification of an equation system to obtain a unique estimate for each structural parameter. Intuitively, the first stage of 2SLS involves the creation of an instrument, while the second stage involves a variant of instrumental-variables estimation. We describe very briefly the workings of 2SLS and outline some of its properties.

12.4.1 Estimation

Consider the following supply-demand model.

Structural model:

Supply: $q_t = \alpha_2 p_t + \varepsilon_t$

(12.15)

Demand: $q_t = \beta_2 p_t + \beta_3 y_t + \beta_4 w_t + u_t$

Reduced form:

$$q_t = \pi_{12} y_t + \pi_{13} w_t + v_{1t} \qquad p_t = \pi_{22} y_t + \pi_{23} w_t + v_{2t} \qquad (12.16)$$

The supply equation in Eq. (12.15) is clearly overidentified, so that indirect least squares does not yield unique parameter estimates.

Another plausible estimation process is instrumental variables. However, if we were to choose the instrumental-variables approach, we would have a choice between two estimators of the parameter α_2. (The first would use y_t as an instrument, and the second would use w_t.) Since both parameter estimators are consistent, we need a criterion to choose between the two. A reasonable (and efficient) procedure involves choosing as an instrument a weighted average of the two predetermined variables, with the weights being chosen to maximize the correlation between the new instrument and p_t. To get this instrument, we simply regress p_t on y_t and w_t, and calculate the fitted values $\hat{p}_t$. The estimator is then obtained as

$$\alpha_2^* = \frac{\Sigma \hat{p}_t q_t}{\Sigma \hat{p}_t p_t}$$

Formally, the two-stage least-squares process works in the following manner:

1. In the first stage, the reduced form equation for p_t is estimated by using ordinary least squares. In general, this is accomplished by regressing p_t on all the predetermined variables in the equation system. From the first-stage regression, the fitted values of the dependent variable $\hat{p}_t$ are determined.[3] The fitted values $\hat{p}_t$ will by construction be independent of the error terms e_t and u_t (strictly speaking, this independence holds only in large samples, so that we are forced to rely on the consistency property of 2SLS). Thus, the first-stage process allows us to construct a variable which is linearly related to the predetermined model variables (through least-squares estimation) and which is purged of any correlation with the error term in the supply equation.

2. In the second-stage regression, the supply equation of the structural model is estimated by replacing the variable p_t with the first-stage fitted variable $\hat{p}_t$. The use of ordinary least squares in this second stage will yield a consistent estimator of the supply parameter α_2. If additional predetermined variables appeared in the supply equation, two-stage least squares would also estimate those parameters consistently.

By construction, 2SLS eliminates the problem of an oversupply of instruments by using combinations of the predetermined variables to create a new instrument.[4] When an equation is exactly identified, 2SLS estimation is identical to indirect least-squares and instrumental-variables estimation. To see this, reexamine the model depicted in Eqs. (12.2) and (12.4). The 2SLS estimation would proceed as follows:

1. Use OLS to estimate the second part of Eq. (12.4). Then calculate the fitted values

$$\hat{p}_t = \hat{\pi}^*_{22} y_t \qquad \text{when } \hat{\pi}^*_{22} = \frac{\Sigma p_t y_t}{\Sigma y_t^2}$$

2. Use OLS to estimate the equation

$$q_t = \alpha_2 \hat{p}_t + \varepsilon_t$$

Then
$$\hat{\alpha}^{***}_2 = \frac{\Sigma \hat{p}_t q_t}{\Sigma \hat{p}_t^2} = \frac{\Sigma y_t q_t (\Sigma p_t y_t / \Sigma y_t^2)}{\Sigma y_t^2 (\Sigma p_t y_t / \Sigma y_t^2)^2}$$

$$= \frac{\Sigma y_t q_t}{\Sigma p_t y_t} = \begin{cases} \hat{\alpha}^{**}_2 & \text{using indirect least squares} \\ \hat{\alpha}^*_2 & \text{using instrumental variables} \end{cases}$$

---

[3] From Eq. (12.16), $\hat{p}_t = \hat{\pi}_{22} y_t + \hat{\pi}_{23} w_t$, where $\hat{\pi}_{22}$ and $\hat{\pi}_{23}$ are the ordinary least-squares parameter estimates.

[4] When the number of predetermined variables is quite large, the technique of *principal components* can be used to reduce the dimensionality of the problem.

Thus, identical parameter estimates will be obtained *if the equation is exactly identified* when 2SLS, indirect least-squares, and instrumental-variables estimation techniques are used. In the overidentified case we have seen that the indirect least-squares procedure is no longer valid. However, it is still possible to show that 2SLS and instrumental variables are equivalent estimation procedures on the condition that the first stage of two-stage least squares involves all predetermined variables in the system and that the instrument used in the instrumental-variables procedure is the fitted value of the first-stage regression.

What happens to 2SLS when the supply equation is not identified, e.g., when the variables y and w appear in the equation? The answer is that 2SLS is impossible when the equation is unidentified. This is quite easy to visualize if one recalls that the fitted-value variable used in the second-stage regression is a weighted average of the values of the predetermined variables in the system. In our example the supply equation includes the variables y and w. When one attempts to regress q_t on $\hat{p}_t$, y_t, and w_t in the second stage, the perfect collinearity among the variables makes estimation impossible.

Example 12.1 Demand for Electricity   The price elasticity of demand for electricity is an important policy parameter for those concerned with U.S. energy policy. A low elasticity (especially in the long run) means that substantial increases in price will be necessary to discourage consumer demand. The following model of the demand for electricity provides such a price-elasticity estimate.[5] The model is specified as

$$\log Q = \alpha_1 + \alpha_2 \log P + \alpha_3 \log Y + \alpha_4 \log G + \alpha_5 \log D$$
$$+ \alpha_6 \log J + \alpha_7 \log R + \alpha_8 \log H + \varepsilon$$

$$\log P = \beta_1 + \beta_2 \log Q + \beta_3 \log L + \beta_4 \log K + \beta_5 \log F$$
$$+ \beta_6 \log R + \beta_7 \log I + \beta_8 \log T + u$$

where Q = average annual residential electricity sales per customer
P = marginal price of residential electricity (in real terms, i.e., deflated by Consumer Price Index)
Y = annual income per capita (real)
G = price for all types of residential gas
D = heating degree-days
J = average July temperature
R = percentage of population living in rural areas

---

[5] This example is taken from R. Halvorsen, "Residential Demand for Electric Energy," *Review of Economics and Statistics*, vol. 57, pp. 12–18, 1975. We have taken the liberty of simplifying the model and the discussion somewhat to clarify the exposition.

H = average size of household
T = time
L = cost of labor
K = percentage of generation produced by publicly owned utilities
F = cost of fuel per kilowatt-hour of generation
I = ratio of total industrial sales to total residential sales

The first equation is a residential demand equation in which quantity demanded is a function of price and a host of demand-related variables. However, the second equation is not the usual supply relationship one might expect; instead the supply of electricity is assumed to be fixed. The second equation arises because electric energy is sold at block rates, with the price to a customer falling as the volume of sales increases. Thus, the price of electricity is itself a function of the sales. The other variables in the price equation are included to control for factors that affect the price of electricity.

Viewed as a system of equations, the model has two endogenous variables, P and Q, and is simultaneous, since Q appears on the right-hand side of the price equation and P appears on the right-hand side of the demand equation. The demand equation is identified because there are five exogenous variables in the price equation (L, K, F, I, T) which do not appear in the demand equation (in fact, it is overidentified). The price equation is identified because there are five exogenous variables in the demand equation (Y, G, D, J, H) which do not appear in the price equation.

Both equations were estimated using 2SLS. In the first stage the endogenous variables were regressed against all the exogenous variables in the model. In the second stage the structural equations were estimated using the predicted values of the first stage as instruments in place of the right-hand endogenous variables. The data are pooled time-series cross-section data for 48 states for the years 1961 to 1969. Note also that because the model is specified in logarithmic form, all coefficients including the price term are elasticities. The estimated results (with standard errors in parentheses) are

$$\widehat{\log Q} = -0.21 - \underset{(.03)}{1.15} \log P + \underset{(.06)}{.51} \log Y + \underset{(.01)}{.04} \log G - \underset{(.02)}{.02} \log D$$

$$+ \underset{(.12)}{.54} \log J + \underset{(.02)}{.21} \log R - \underset{(.12)}{.24} \log H \qquad R^2 = .91$$

$$\widehat{\log P} = 0.57 - \underset{(.03)}{.60} \log Q + \underset{(.04)}{.24} \log L - \underset{(.01)}{.02} \log K + \underset{(.003)}{.01} \log F$$

$$+ \underset{(.01)}{.03} \log R - \underset{(.01)}{.12} \log I + \underset{(.003)}{.004} \log T \qquad R^2 = .97$$

The results of the two-stage least-squares estimation of the demand equation show that the long-run direct elasticity of demand with respect to the price of electricity is somewhat greater than one (1.15) in absolute value, a much higher elasticity than one would have expected in the short run. On the basis of detailed evidence of the trends in electricity pricing, the results suggest that the past growth of residential demand for electric energy has been due in good part to the decline in the real price of electricity.

Assume that one wished to examine the effect on long-run demand of a tax on the use of electricity. The initial impact will be measured by the demand equation, but the price equation also must be taken into consideration since it measures the secondary effect on price of a change in the quantity of purchases. To measure the *total* long-run elasticity of demand, and thus the long-run change in sales, the elasticity must be calculated from the reduced form equation. When calculated from the reduced form, the total elasticity turns out to be -3.70, a value much larger than the direct effect given by the structural equation.

12.4.2 A Test for Simultaneity

We have seen that when simultaneity is present, one or more of the explanatory variables will be endogenous and therefore will be correlated with the disturbance term. It is therefore natural to test for the presence of simultaneity in the same way that we tested for measurement error in Chapter 7. If there is no simultaneity, ordinary least squares should generate efficient and consistent parameter estimators. Instrumental-variables estimation (including 2SLS), by contrast, will be consistent but inefficient. If there is simultaneity, however, ordinary least squares will be inconsistent, while instrumental-variables estimation will be both consistent and efficient.

We can formulate one version of the appropriate *Hausman specification test* in the context of the supply-demand model of Eq. (12.15).[6] Suppose we are interested in estimating the supply equation:

Supply: $$q_t = \alpha_2 p_t + \varepsilon_t$$

We know (from the specification of the demand equation) that y_t and w_t are exogenous and therefore are appropriate choices for instruments. The null hypothesis of no simultaneity specifies that p_t and ε_t are uncorrelated. Under the alternative hypothesis they are correlated and instrumental-variables estimation is required.

To perform the Hausman test, we take into account the reduced form specification for p_t given by Eq. (12.16). When estimated, this yields

$$\hat{p}_t = \hat{\pi}_{22} y_t + \hat{\pi}_{23} w_t$$

so that
$$p_t = \hat{p}_t + \hat{v}_{2t} \tag{12.17}$$

---

[6] This particular application relies on D. E. Spencer and K. N. Berk, "A Limited Information Specification Test," *Econometrica*, vol. 49, pp. 1079–1085, July 1981. See also J. Kmenta, *Elements of Econometrics* (New York: Macmillan, 1986), p. 718.

Substituting Eq. (12.17) into the supply equation yields the following:

$$q_t = \alpha_2 \hat{p}_t + \alpha_2 \hat{v}_{2t} + \varepsilon_t$$

To do the specification test, we use the residuals from Eq. (12.17) and then estimate the following regression equation:

$$q_t = \alpha_2 \hat{p}_t + \delta \hat{v}_{2t} + \varepsilon_t \tag{12.18}$$

Under the null hypothesis of no simultaneity, the correlation between the residual $\hat{v}_{2t}$ and the error term ε_t will go to zero as the sample size gets large. Thus, when the null hypothesis holds, the estimation of Eq. (12.18) will generate a consistent estimator of α_2. By construction, however, δ, which is equal to α_2, will be consistently estimated as well. α_2 will of course be inefficiently estimated, since one (unnecessary) degree of freedom will have been used up to estimate δ.

This suggests a relatively easy test for simultaneity. Rewrite Eq. (12.18), substituting $\hat{p}_t = p_t - \hat{v}_{2t}$:

$$q_t = \alpha_2 p_t + (\delta - \alpha_2) \hat{v}_{2t} + \varepsilon_t \tag{12.19}$$

Under the null hypothesis, $\delta = \alpha_2$, so that the coefficient on $\hat{v}_{2t}$ should equal 0. However, under the alternative hypothesis, $\delta \neq \alpha_2$ and the coefficient will (in general) be different from 0.

We can therefore test for simultaneity with a simple two-stage procedure. First, we regress p on y and w to obtain the residuals $\hat{v}_2$. Then we regress q on p and $\hat{v}_2$ and perform a t test on the coefficient of the $\hat{v}_2$ variable. If we are concerned with the endogeneity of more than one variable, the analysis becomes somewhat more complicated, but a similar test can be applied.

Finally, note that the identical test can be performed in a somewhat different manner. Substitute $\hat{v}_{2t} = p_t - \hat{p}_t$ into Eq. (12.19) to obtain

$$q_t = \delta p_t - (\delta - \alpha_2) \hat{p}_t + \varepsilon_t \tag{12.20}$$

A t test on the coefficient of the variable $\hat{p}_t$ provides the appropriate specification test. Under the null hypothesis the coefficient will be zero; otherwise it will not.

Example 12.2 Public Spending   In Example 7.3 we estimated a model of state and local government public expenditures (EXP) that took the following form:

$$\text{EXP} = \beta_1 + \beta_2 \text{AID} + \beta_3 \text{INC} + \beta_4 \text{POP} + \varepsilon$$

where AID is the level of federal grants-in-aid, INC is the income of states, and POP is state population. In that example we were concerned with the possibility that AID was measured with error. Suppose that measurement error is not a concern but that simultaneity is, since AID is thought to be determined by the level of public expenditures (for some programs the amount of aid is positively related to state and local effort in raising funds). AID may therefore be determined by EXP itself as well as the population of primary and secondary school children (PS).

If the model is simultaneous, the second equation in the system that determines EXP and AID is given by

$$AID = \gamma_1 + \gamma_2 EXP + \gamma_3 PS + u$$

To test for simultaneity with respect to the AID variable, we proceed as follows. In the first stage AID is regressed on INC, POP, and PS (the reduced form), and the residual variable $\hat{w}$ is calculated (t statistics are in parentheses):

$$\hat{w} = AID - 41.61 + .000036 INC + .175 POP - .833 PS$$
$$\quad\quad\quad (.84) \quad\quad (2.72) \quad\quad\quad (1.39) \quad\quad\quad (-2.16) \quad\quad R^2 = .93$$

In the second stage $\hat{w}$ is added to the original regression to "correct" for simultaneity. The resulting equation is

$$\widehat{EXP} = -89.41 + 4.50 AID - 1.39\hat{w} + .00013 INC - .518 POP$$
$$\quad\quad (-1.04) \quad\quad (5.89) \quad\quad (-1.73) \quad\quad (3.06) \quad\quad\quad (-4.63) \quad\quad R^2 = .99$$

A two-tailed t test of the null hypothesis that there is no simultaneity would be rejected at the 10 percent level. It would not be rejected at the 5 percent level, however. A comparison of the corrected model with the least-squares version of Example 7.3 shows that when simultaneity is taken into account, the AID variable becomes less significant but is greater in magnitude.

12.5 SIMULTANEOUS-EQUATION ESTIMATION WITH SERIAL CORRELATION AND LAGGED DEPENDENT VARIABLES

Many models contain lagged dependent variables to account for adjustments that take place over time. OLS generates consistent but biased estimators when there are lagged dependent variables as long as serial correlation is not present. But serial correlation is very common in time-series models and, unfortunately, neither OLS nor 2SLS is consistent when the equation to be estimated contains a lagged dependent variable and the error term is serially correlated. In this section we suggest why both OLS and 2SLS are inconsistent and in the latter case suggest the use of an alternative consistent estimator originally proposed by Fair.[7]

To begin, consider the following single-equation model (in which the variables appear in deviations form):

$$y_t = \beta y_{t-1} + \varepsilon_t \quad \text{with } \varepsilon_t = \rho \varepsilon_{t-1} + v_t \tag{12.21}$$

In general, if ordinary least squares were used to estimate the slope parameter, inconsistent and biased results would be obtained. Recall that

$$\hat{\beta} = \frac{\Sigma y_t y_{t-1}}{\Sigma y_{t-1}^2} = \beta + \frac{\Sigma y_{t-1} \varepsilon_t}{\Sigma y_{t-1}^2} = \beta + \frac{\text{Cov } (y_{t-1}, \varepsilon_t)}{\text{Var } (y_{t-1})}$$

The covariance of y_{t-1} and ε_t is nonzero, since

$$
\begin{aligned}
\text{Cov } (y_{t-1}, \varepsilon_t) &= E(y_{t-1}\varepsilon_t) = E(\beta y_{t-2} + \varepsilon_{t-1})(\rho \varepsilon_{t-1} + v_t) \\
&= \beta \rho E(\varepsilon_{t-1} y_{t-2}) + \rho E(\varepsilon_{t-1}^2) + \beta E(v_t y_{t-2}) + E(\varepsilon_{t-1} v_t) \\
&= \beta \rho E(\varepsilon_{t-1} y_{t-2}) + \rho E(\varepsilon_{t-1}^2)
\end{aligned}
$$

But $\quad E(\varepsilon_{t-1}^2) = E(\varepsilon_t^2) \quad$ and $\quad E(\varepsilon_{t-1} y_{t-2}) = E(\varepsilon_t y_{t-1})$

Therefore, $\qquad E(y_{t-1}\varepsilon_t) = \beta \rho E(y_{t-1}\varepsilon_t) + \rho E(\varepsilon_t^2)$

$$\text{Cov } (y_{t-1}, \varepsilon_t) = \frac{\rho \text{ Var } (\varepsilon_t)}{1 - \rho\beta} \tag{12.22}$$

The ratio of this covariance to the variance of y_{t-1} will be nonzero even with no serial correlation. (When $\rho = 0$, $\hat{\beta}$ will be biased because $E[\text{Cov}(y_{t-1}, \varepsilon_t)/\text{Var}(y_{t-1})]$ will not equal 0.) Thus, the presence of serial correlation and a lagged dependent variable makes the ordinary least-squares estimator biased and inconsistent. Intuitively, the presence of serial correlation and a lagged dependent variable creates a parameter identification problem. If ordinary least squares is used to estimate Eq. (12.21), it will be impossible to tell to what extent the parameter estimate reflects the presence of a nonzero slope and to what extent there is serial correlation in the model.

Now let us consider what happens in a simultaneous-equations model in which there is a lagged dependent variable and serial correlation. To do so, we reexamine a basic supply-demand model in which the supply equation is iden-

---

[7] R. C. Fair, "The Estimation of Simultaneous Equation Models with Lagged Endogenous Variables and First Order Serially Correlated Errors," *Econometrica*, vol. 38, pp. 507–516, May 1970.

tified and contains an autoregressive error term. The model is given (in deviations form) by

Supply:
$$q_t = \alpha_2 p_t + \alpha_3 q_{t-1} + \varepsilon_t \qquad (12.23)$$

$$\varepsilon_t = \rho \varepsilon_{t-1} + v_t \qquad (12.24)$$

Demand:
$$q_t = \beta_2 p_t + \beta_3 y_t + u_t \qquad (12.25)$$

where u_t and v_t are independent over time and are uncorrelated with each other.

If we substitute Eq. (12.24) into Eq. (12.23) and solve, we get

$$q_t - \rho q_{t-1} = \alpha_2(p_t - \rho p_{t-1}) + \alpha_3(q_{t-1} - \rho q_{t-2}) + v_t \qquad (12.26)$$

Suppose initially that ρ is known. Since p_t is endogenous, OLS estimation of Eq. (12.26) will generate an inconsistent estimate of α_2. But a 2SLS procedure that replaces p_t with an instrument $\hat{p}_t$ (obtained by regressing p_t on q_{t-1}, q_{t-2}, and y_t) will be consistent since by construction $\hat{p}_t$ will be uncorrelated with v_t. Because ρ is not known, however, we must account for the possibility that our estimate of the serial-correlation coefficient, r, will not equal ρ. In this case Eq. (12.26) becomes:

$$q_t - r q_{t-1} = \alpha_2(p_t - r p_{t-1}) + \alpha_3(q_{t-1} - r q_{t-2}) + [v_t + (\rho - r)\varepsilon_{t-1}] \qquad (12.27)$$

Now, a 2SLS procedure which replaces p_t with $\hat{p}_t$ is no longer consistent because ε_{t-1} is correlated with p_{t-1}, and this correlation is not removed when p_t is replaced with its instrument.

To obtain a consistent estimator, Fair proposes the following procedure:

First stage: Estimate the "reduced form" equation

$$p_t = \gamma_2 y_t + \gamma_3 q_{t-1} + \gamma_4 p_{t-1} + \gamma_5 q_{t-2} + w_t \qquad (12.28)$$

and calculate the predicted values $\hat{p}_t$.

Second stage: Estimate the modified "structural" equation

$$q_t - r q_{t-1} = \alpha_2(\hat{p}_t - r p_{t-1}) + [v_t + (\rho - r)\varepsilon_{t-1} + \alpha_2 \hat{w}_t] \qquad (12.29)$$

where $\hat{w}_t = p_t - \hat{p}_t$ is the residual from the first-stage regression. This can be done by using Hildreth-Lu or a similar method that searches over r to find the value that minimizes the sum of squared residuals.

To show why this procedure will generate a consistent estimator for α_2, rewrite Eq. (12.23) lagged one period:

$$\varepsilon_{t-1} = q_{t-1} - \alpha_2 p_{t-1} - \alpha_3 q_{t-2} \tag{12.30}$$

We can see that ε_{t-1} and $\hat{w}_t$ are uncorrelated because each of the right-hand side variables in Eq. (12.30) appears in the first-stage regression. In addition, ε_{t-1} and v_t are uncorrelated by assumption. As a result, the sum of squared residuals in Eq. (12.29) will be minimized when $r = \rho$. The resulting error term, $v_t + \alpha_2 \hat{w}_t$, will be uncorrelated with the right-hand side of Eq. (12.29) for the reasons stated earlier (recall that the first-stage residuals $\hat{w}_t$ are uncorrelated with the first-stage regressors).

Note that it is important that p_{t-1}, q_{t-1}, and q_{t-2} be used in the first-stage regression. If they are not, ε_{t-1} and $\hat{w}_t$ will be uncorrelated, and the minimum sum of squared residuals will not be achieved when $r = \rho$. More generally, if consistency is to be achieved, it is essential when applying the Fair method to include as first-stage "instruments" the lagged dependent variable as well as lagged (one period) values of all included endogenous and exogenous variables. (The lagged dependent variable on the right-hand side will now be lagged two periods.)

The Fair procedure is often of value when simultaneous-equation models are estimated. We illustrate its use in a small macro model in Appendix 14.1.

12.6   MORE ADVANCED ESTIMATION METHODS

We have concentrated to this point on two-equation models that are simultaneous in nature. In the first part of this more advanced section we describe a model that can be estimated efficiently when treated as a system of equations. In the second part we describe estimation procedures that are both consistent and efficient whether or not the equation system is truly simultaneous. Some brief comments on the choice of estimation procedures appear in the third subsection.

12.6.1   The Seemingly Unrelated Model

The *seemingly unrelated regression* (SUR) model is a recursive model which occurs occasionally in business and economic modeling. It consists of a series of endogenous variables that are considered as a group because they bear a close conceptual relationship to each other. An example of such a model is

$$Q_{1t} = \alpha_1 + \alpha_2 P_{1t} + u_{1t}$$

$$Q_{2t} = \beta_1 + \beta_2 P_{2t} + u_{2t}$$

The equations represent a set of two demand equations for related products. If, in fact, the *disturbances* of each equation are uncorrelated, there is no relationship between the equations and OLS estimation is appropriate. If the error terms are correlated, however, efficient estimates can be obtained by using a more sophisticated estimation technique, as we will discuss in the following subsection.

12.6.2 Estimation of Equation Systems

Two-stage least-squares and instrumental-variables estimators yield consistent parameter estimates when equation systems are simultaneous. As a general rule, however, each estimation technique yields inefficient estimates because these techniques apply only to a single equation within the system of equations. Thus, they do take into account the fact that one or more predetermined variables are omitted from the equation to be estimated, but they do not take into account the fact that there may be predetermined variables omitted from other equations as well. An alternative source of inefficiency arises because single-equation estimation does not account for the cross-equation correlation among errors. In either case, the problem of loss of efficiency can be resolved by using any of several methods of estimating systems of equations in which parameters for all equations are determined in a single procedure.

A useful way to understand the complexities of systems estimation is to begin with the special case in which there is cross-equation error correlation but otherwise there is no simultaneity. Thus, we treat the SUR model, which consists of a series of equations that are linked because the error terms across equations are correlated.[8] The SUR method involves generalized least-squares estimation (see Appendix 6.1) and achieves an improvement in efficiency by taking into explicit account the fact that cross-equation error correlations may not be zero.

To see how and why the estimator works, consider the two-equation model

$$y_1 = \alpha x + u_1$$

$$y_2 = \beta z + u_2$$

If the error terms in the two equations were uncorrelated, we would obtain efficient estimates of α and β by performing ordinary least-squares estimation on each separate equation, using N observations for each regression. However, under the assumption that u_1 and u_2 are correlated for identical cross-section units, we can improve on the efficiency of ordinary least squares by writing the equation system as one combined equation, estimating that equation by using generalized least-squares estimation.

---

[8] See A. Zellner, "An Efficient Method of Estimating Seemingly Unrelated Regressions and Tests for Aggregation Bias," *Journal of the American Statistical Association*, vol. 57, pp. 348–368, 1962.

To write the system as one large equation rather than two smaller equations, it is necessary to distinguish between observations associated with the first equation and observations associated with the second equation. To do this we shall relabel the observations, arbitrarily assigning observations 1 to N to the first-equation variables and observations $N + 1$ to $2N$ to the second-equation variables. We now define four new variables:

$$y^* = \begin{cases} y_{1i} & \text{if } i = 1, \ldots, N \\ y_{2i} & \text{if } i = N + 1, \ldots, 2N \end{cases} \qquad x^* = \begin{cases} x_i & \text{if } i = 1, \ldots, N \\ 0 & \text{otherwise} \end{cases}$$

$$z^* = \begin{cases} 0 & \text{if } i = 1, \ldots, N \\ z_i & \text{if } i = N + 1, \ldots, 2N \end{cases} \qquad u^* = \begin{cases} u_{1i} & \text{if } i = 1, \ldots, N \\ u_{2i} & \text{if } i = N + 1, \ldots, 2N \end{cases}$$

Also, $\qquad \sigma_1^2 = \text{Var} (u_1) \qquad \sigma_2^2 = \text{Var} (u_2) \qquad \sigma_{12} = \text{Cov} (u_1, u_2)$

With this new notation the combined equation can be written

$$y^* = \alpha x^* + \beta z^* + u^*$$

Applying the generalized least-squares procedure to this equation allows us to obtain parameter estimates for α and β. Since the algebra involved is substantial (despite the fact that we are working with data in deviations form), we simply present the results here:

$$\hat{\alpha} = \frac{1}{C} (A\sigma_1^2 \Sigma z^2 + B\sigma_{12}\Sigma xz)$$

$$\hat{\beta} = \frac{1}{C} (A\sigma_{12}\Sigma xz + B\sigma_2^2 \Sigma x^2)$$

where

$$A = \sigma_2^2 \Sigma xy_1 - \sigma_{12}\Sigma xy_2$$

$$B = \sigma_1^2 \Sigma zy_2 - \sigma_{12}\Sigma zy_1$$

$$C = \sigma_1^2 \sigma_2^2 \Sigma x^2 \Sigma z^2 - \sigma_{12}^2 (\Sigma xz)^2$$

This example is instructive because it allows us to illustrate the two important cases in which SUR estimation and ordinary least-squares estimation are identical. The first, and most obvious, situation occurs when the cross-equation covariance is identically 0 ($\sigma_{12} = 0$). The second, less obvious, situation occurs when the two explanatory variables (x and z) are identical. The details of these derivations are left to the reader.

The application of generalized least squares necessitates obtaining estimates of the error covariances between equations. These estimates are obtained by first estimating each single equation using ordinary least squares. The variances and covariances of the estimated residuals then provide consistent estimators of the error variances and covariances. In our two-equation example we would estimate σ_1^2, σ_2^2, and σ_{12} as follows:

$$\hat{\sigma}_1^2 = \frac{1}{N-2} \sum_{i=1}^{N} \hat{u}_{1i}^2 \qquad \hat{\sigma}_2^2 = \frac{1}{N-2} \sum_{i=N+1}^{2N} \hat{u}_{2i}^2 \qquad \hat{\sigma}_{12} = \frac{1}{N-2} \sum_{i=1}^{N} \hat{u}_1 \hat{u}_{2,i+N}$$

As a practical matter, SUR estimation is a two-stage estimation procedure. It can be shown to be consistent as well as (asymptotically) efficient.

We can also achieve a gain in efficiency by applying system estimation methods to simultaneous-equation models. The natural extension of SUR estimation is the technique of three-stage least squares (3SLS).[9] 3SLS involves the application of generalized least-squares estimation to a system of equations, each of which has first been estimated using 2SLS. In the first stage of the process the reduced form of the model system is estimated. The fitted values of the endogenous variables are then used to get 2SLS estimates of all the equations in the system. Once the 2SLS parameters have been calculated, the residuals of each equation are used to estimate the cross-equation variances and covariances, just as in the SUR estimation process that was described previously. In the third and final stage of the estimation process, generalized least-squares parameter estimates are obtained. The 3SLS procedure can be shown to yield more efficient parameter estimates than does 2SLS because it takes into account cross-equation correlation.

If one is considering applying 3SLS, several items of information will prove valuable. First, all identities must be removed from the equation system before the estimation process is used. Second, the application of the third stage of the procedure will not alter the 2SLS estimates in the special case in which all the cross-equation covariances are 0. Finally, any equation which is unidentified must be dropped from the equation system before 3SLS is applied. (Recall that 2SLS parameter estimates cannot be obtained for unidentified equations.)

Example 12.3 Public Assistance The growth of public relief payments has long been a concern of professional economists. In an attempt to increase knowledge of the public relief problem, Brehm and Saving used statewide data to study the demand for public assistance.[10] Data were collected on the number of general assistance recipients on an average per month basis, annually by state for the period 1951–1959. One equation which was estimated is of the form

$$N_{ij} = \beta_0 + \beta_1 \frac{P_{ij}}{W_{ij}} + \beta_2 U_{ij} + \beta_3 A_{ij} + \varepsilon_{ij}$$

[9] See A. Zellner and H. Theil, "Three-Stage Least Squares: Simultaneous Estimation of Simultaneous Relations," *Econometrica*, vol. 30, pp. 54–78, 1962.

[10] C. T. Brehm and T. R. Saving, "The Demand for General Assistance Payments," *American Economic Review*, vol. LIX, pp. 1002–1018, 1964.

where $i = 1, 2, \ldots, 48$ refers to observations across states

$j = 1, 2, \ldots, 9$ refers to observations over time

N_{ij} = percentage of ith state's population receiving general assistance payments (GAP) in jth year

P_{ij} = average monthly GAP in ith state for jth year

W_{ij} = average monthly manufacturing wage in ith state for jth year

U_{ij} = unemployment rate in ith state for jth year

A_{ij} = nonagricultural employment as percentage of population in ith state for jth year

The authors were able to predict that the percentage of the population receiving assistance will be directly related to average monthly assistance payments and will be inversely related to the ongoing wage rate. The latter result is expected because higher wages imply a higher opportunity cost of choosing to receive public assistance rather than to work. The unemployment rate appears in the model because it measures the number of individuals whose alternative to general assistance is a zero (or very low) wage. We would expect unemployment rates and public assistance recipient rates to be positively related. Finally, the nonagricultural employment rate is included as a proxy variable for the ease of getting on general assistance rolls. The coefficient is expected to be positive since previous studies have shown a direct relationship between the degree of urbanization in a state and that state's assistance recipient rate.

The authors were concerned with the potential links that might exist between the nine individual cross-section relationships. The primary link is generated by the effect of the migration of individuals from low to high general-assistance-level states that takes place over a period of years. Since no lags are included explicitly in the model, it is reasonable to expect that disturbance terms for one state in a given year will be positively related to disturbance terms for that state in preceding as well as future years. The authors decided to improve the efficiency of the estimation process by using the SUR technique rather than ordinary least squares. The results of their estimations are listed in Table 12.1.

The P/W term is generally the most significant of all the variables (significantly different from 0 at the 5 percent level in all cases but one). In all cases the coefficient has the expected sign. The unemployment variable coefficient is significant in three of the nine years, although it had an unexpected sign only once. Finally, the proxy variable for the ease of becoming a general assistance recipient has the expected sign in every case and is significantly different from 0 in four of the nine cases. The results of the study give additional support to the view that income-related variables such as the ratio of assistance payments to the wage rate are important determinants of recipient levels. The remaining variables have a somewhat lesser effect. The authors concluded that general assistance recipients are not unlike

TABLE 12.1
RESULTS OF SEEMINGLY UNRELATED ESTIMATION

Year	Constant Coeff.	SE	P/W Coeff.	SE	U Coeff.	SE	A Coeff.	SE
1951	−.730	.481	.068	.024	.141	.067	.064	.016
1952	−.812	.423	.031	.019	.195	.051	.066	.014
1953	.067	.555	.080	.025	.093	.076	.017	.019
1954	−.139	.499	.100	.018	.044	.038	.025	.017
1955	−.224	.504	.096	.018	−.042	.051	.043	.016
1956	.210	.498	.072	.017	.040	.046	.025	.014
1957	.286	.537	.073	.017	.058	.039	.019	.016
1958	−.880	.832	.082	.025	.179	.055	.054	.029
1959	−1.030	.901	.095	.027	.218	.089	.051	.033
Mean	−.361		.078		.103		.040	

most consumers in that they react in expected ways to the economic incen-
tives which exist.

Example 12.4 Macroeconomic Model   In their original article dealing
with three-stage least-squares estimation, Zellner and Theil provided an in-
sightful illustrative example in which 2SLS and 3SLS estimates of a simple
macroeconomic model are compared.[11] The model, known as *Klein's Model
I*, includes three behavioral equations and three identities.[12] The behavioral
equations are as follows:

Consumption: $C = \alpha_0 + \alpha_1 \Pi + \alpha_2 (W_1 + W_2) + \alpha_3 \Pi_{-1} + u_1$

Investment: $I = \beta_0 + \beta_1 \Pi + \beta_2 \Pi_{-1} + \beta_3 K_{-1} + u_2$

Demand for labor:

$$W_1 = \gamma_0 + \gamma_1 (Y + T - W_2) + \gamma_2 (Y + T - W_2)_{-1} + \gamma_3 t + u_3$$

where C = consumption
Π = profits
W_1 = private wage bill
W_2 = government wage bill
I = investment

[11] Zellner and Theil, op. cit.
[12] From L. R. Klein, *Economic Fluctuations in the U.S., 1921–1941* (New York: Wiley, 1950).

G = government spending
K = capital stock
Y = national income
T = indirect taxes
t = time, years

The three behavioral equations are linked by three identities:

$$Y + T = C + I + G \qquad Y = W_1 + W_2 + \Pi \qquad K = K_{-1} + I$$

In total, the model includes six endogenous variables and eight predetermined variables. All three behavioral equations are overidentified. The results of the 2SLS and 3SLS estimations are provided in Table 12.2. The reader should pay particular attention to the variances of the coefficient estimators associated with both estimation processes. In all cases (as guaranteed by the estimation process), 3SLS parameter estimates have smaller variances than do their 2SLS counterparts. The gain in efficiency associated with 3SLS is usually in the neighborhood of 5 percent.

TABLE 12.2
THREE-STAGE AND TWO-STAGE LEAST-SQUARES ESTIMATES OF PARAMETERS

		3SLS		2SLS	
Equation	Coefficient of	Coefficient estimate	Variance of coefficient estimator	Coefficient estimate	Variance of coefficient estimator
Consumption	Π	.0479	.0131	.0173	.0139
	$W_1 + W_2$	.8170	.0014	.8102	.0016
	Π_{-1}	.1897	.0109	.2162	.0115
	Constant	16.1923	1.6900	16.5548	1.7450
Investment	Π	.2111	.0285	.1502	.0300
	Π_{-1}	.5667	.0252	.6159	.0264
	K_{-1}	−.1472	.0012	−.1578	.0013
	Constant	17.9210	52.5160	20.2782	56.8920
Demand for labor	$Y + T - W_2$	.4282	.0012	.4389	.0012
	$(Y + T - W_2)_{-1}$	.1543	.0014	.1467	.0015
	t	.1356	.0008	.1304	.0008
	Constant	1.6935	1.3020	1.5003	1.3170

12.6.3   Comparison of Alternative Estimators

We have now completed a survey of several single-equation and system estimation procedures. It is useful to pause for a moment and ask how one selects between alternative estimation techniques. The answer is a difficult one for two reasons. First, the choice of estimation procedure may depend in part on the purpose for which the estimated system of equations is to be used. We shall see in Chapter 13, for example, that the choice of estimation technique can have substantial effects on the dynamic properties of the estimated model. Second, most of our knowledge about the properties of estimators relates to large samples; i.e., we know that these estimators will be consistent and (sometimes) asymptotically efficient. We know little, however, about the small-sample properties of these estimators. Some small-sample studies examine the sensitivity of estimated parameters to different estimation techniques using real world data and previously developed models, while others apply *Monte Carlo* experimentation techniques to known artificial model structures. While the results of the studies are varied and difficult to summarize, it is worthwhile to mention a few of the important issues that arise from them.

Given a truly simultaneous system of equations, we know that ordinary least-squares estimation is inconsistent as well as biased. Two-stage least squares and instrumental variables provide consistent single-equation parameter estimates, but they are biased as well. On the other hand, studies suggest that 2SLS estimates have larger variance than do OLS estimates. Thus, if one's criterion is to minimize mean square error (which combines bias and variance), it is conceivable that OLS estimation will be more suitable than 2SLS and other consistent single-equation techniques. Studies also suggest, however, that systems methods of estimation yield lower variance estimates than do single-equation methods. Since most computer packages allow for the use of generalized least-squares estimation, it is not unusual for one to bear the added expense of performing SUR and 3SLS estimation. The difficulty with all systems estimation techniques, however, is that individual parameter estimates (by construction) are sensitive to the specification of the entire model system. A serious specification error in one equation can affect the parameter estimates in all equations of the model. Thus, the decision to use systems estimation involves a trade-off between the gain in efficiency and the potential costs of specification error.

APPENDIX 12.1 The Identification Problem in Matrix Form

Representation of the Simultaneous-Equation Model

To consider the identification problem in its most general form, we need to distinguish between endogenous and exogenous variables as well as between structural and reduced forms. We assume that the model under investigation consists of G equations. Each equation contains G endogenous variables (some may have coefficients which are known to be equal to 0), K predetermined variables, and a randomly distributed error term. Written equation by equation, the structural form of the model is as follows:[13]

$$
\begin{aligned}
\beta_{11}y_{1i} + \beta_{12}y_{2i} + \cdots + \beta_{1G}y_{Gi} + \gamma_{11}x_{1i} + \gamma_{12}x_{2i} + \cdots + \gamma_{1K}x_{Ki} &= u_{1i} \\
\beta_{21}y_{1i} + \beta_{22}y_{2i} + \cdots + \beta_{2G}y_{Gi} + \gamma_{21}x_{1i} + \gamma_{22}x_{2i} + \cdots + \gamma_{2K}x_{Ki} &= u_{2i} \\
&\cdots \\
\beta_{G1}y_{1i} + \beta_{G2}y_{2i} + \cdots + \beta_{GG}y_{Gi} + \gamma_{G1}x_{1i} + \gamma_{G2}x_{2i} + \cdots + \gamma_{GK}x_{Ki} &= u_{Gi}
\end{aligned}
$$

for $i = 1, 2, \ldots, N$. As noted in the text, the y's are the endogenous variables and the x's are the predetermined variables. In each equation some of the coefficients are equal to 0, and one of the endogenous variables is chosen to have a coefficient of 1. The variable with the coefficient 1 is viewed as the dependent variable. The set of equations given above can be written in matrix form as

$$\mathbf{B}\mathbf{y}_i + \boldsymbol{\Gamma}\mathbf{x}_i = \mathbf{u}_i \tag{A12.1}$$

where
$$
\mathbf{y}_i = \begin{bmatrix} y_{1i} \\ y_{2i} \\ \vdots \\ y_{Gi} \end{bmatrix} \quad
\mathbf{x}_i = \begin{bmatrix} x_{1i} \\ x_{2i} \\ \vdots \\ x_{Ki} \end{bmatrix} \quad
\mathbf{u}_i = \begin{bmatrix} u_{1i} \\ u_{2i} \\ \vdots \\ u_{Gi} \end{bmatrix}
$$

$$
\mathbf{B} = \begin{bmatrix} \beta_{11} & \beta_{12} & \cdots & \beta_{1G} \\ \beta_{21} & \beta_{22} & \cdots & \beta_{2G} \\ \cdots & & & \\ \beta_{G1} & \beta_{G2} & \cdots & \beta_{GG} \end{bmatrix} \quad
\boldsymbol{\Gamma} = \begin{bmatrix} \gamma_{11} & \gamma_{12} & \cdots & \gamma_{1K} \\ \gamma_{21} & \gamma_{22} & \cdots & \gamma_{2K} \\ \cdots & & & \\ \gamma_{G1} & \gamma_{G2} & \cdots & \gamma_{GK} \end{bmatrix}
$$

where $\mathbf{y}_i = G \times 1$ vector of endogenous variables

$\mathbf{x}_i = K \times 1$ vector of predetermined variables

$\mathbf{u}_i = G \times 1$ vector of disturbance terms

$\mathbf{B} = G \times G$ matrix of endogenous variable coefficients

$\boldsymbol{\Gamma} = G \times K$ matrix of predetermined variable coefficients

If we wish to include all N observations available for each y and each x and use the matrix notation, we can rewrite the model as

$$\mathbf{B}\mathbf{Y} + \boldsymbol{\Gamma}\mathbf{X} = \mathbf{U} \tag{A12.2}$$

[13] We have chosen a notation which is most nearly consistent with the notation used in other econometrics textbooks. In this notation lowercase letters do not imply that variables are measured as deviations about their means. See F. M. Fisher, *The Identification Problem in Econometrics* (New York: McGraw-Hill, 1966), for further details.

where $\mathbf{Y} = G \times N$ matrix
$\mathbf{X} = K \times N$ matrix
$\mathbf{U} = G \times N$ matrix

$$\mathbf{Y} = \begin{bmatrix} y_{11} & y_{12} & \cdots & y_{1N} \\ y_{21} & y_{22} & \cdots & y_{2N} \\ \vdots & & & \vdots \\ y_{G1} & y_{G2} & \cdots & y_{GN} \end{bmatrix} \qquad \mathbf{X} = \begin{bmatrix} x_{11} & x_{12} & \cdots & x_{1N} \\ x_{21} & x_{22} & \cdots & x_{2N} \\ \vdots & & & \vdots \\ x_{K1} & x_{K2} & \cdots & x_{KN} \end{bmatrix}$$

$$\mathbf{U} = \begin{bmatrix} u_{11} & u_{12} & \cdots & u_{1N} \\ u_{21} & u_{22} & \cdots & u_{2N} \\ \vdots & & & \vdots \\ u_{G1} & u_{G2} & \cdots & u_{GN} \end{bmatrix}$$

The structural equation contains G equations and G unknowns. If all β's and γ's are known, we can solve for the values of each of the y's, given values of the predetermined x's. To do so, we assume that $\mathbf{B}$ is nonsingular and solve to get the reduced form representation of the model. Premultiplying both sides of Eq. (A12.1) by the matrix $\mathbf{B}^{-1}$, we get

$$\mathbf{y}_i + \mathbf{B}^{-1}\boldsymbol{\Gamma}\mathbf{x}_i = \mathbf{B}^{-1}\mathbf{u}_i$$

or

$$\mathbf{y}_i = \boldsymbol{\pi}\mathbf{x}_i + \mathbf{v}_i$$

where $\boldsymbol{\pi} = -\mathbf{B}^{-1}\boldsymbol{\Gamma}$ is a $G \times K$ matrix of reduced form coefficients

$$\boldsymbol{\pi} = \begin{bmatrix} \pi_{11} & \pi_{12} & \cdots & \pi_{1K} \\ \pi_{21} & \pi_{22} & \cdots & \pi_{2K} \\ \vdots & & & \vdots \\ \pi_{G1} & \pi_{G2} & \cdots & \pi_{GK} \end{bmatrix}$$

and $\mathbf{v}_i = \mathbf{B}^{-1}\mathbf{u}_i$ is a $G \times 1$ vector of reduced form disturbances. The reduced form of the model is

$$y_{1i} = \pi_{11}x_{1i} + \pi_{12}x_{2i} + \cdots + \pi_{1K}x_{Ki} + v_{1i}$$
$$y_{2i} = \pi_{21}x_{1i} + \pi_{22}x_{2i} + \cdots + \pi_{2K}x_{Ki} + v_{2i}$$
$$\cdots \cdots \cdots$$
$$y_{Gi} = \pi_{G1}x_{1i} + \pi_{G2}x_{2i} + \cdots + \pi_{GK}x_{Ki} + v_{Gi}$$

In terms of all N equations, we would rewrite the system of equations as

$$\mathbf{Y} = \boldsymbol{\pi}\mathbf{X} + \mathbf{V} \qquad\qquad (A12.3)$$

where $\mathbf{Y} = G \times N$ matrix $\mathbf{X} = K \times N$ matrix
$\boldsymbol{\pi} = G \times K$ matrix $\mathbf{V} = G \times N$ matrix

To complete our description of the simultaneous-equation model, we need to specify the assumptions involving the error term $\mathbf{u}_i$. We shall assume that

$$E(\mathbf{u}_i) = \mathbf{0}$$

and

$$E(\mathbf{u}_i\mathbf{u}_i') = \mathbf{\Sigma}$$

where $\mathbf{\Sigma}$ is a $G \times G$ matrix of variances and covariances between error terms of identical observations across equations. We also assume that

$$E(\mathbf{u}_i\mathbf{u}_j') = \mathbf{0} \qquad i, j = 1, 2, \ldots, N \qquad i \neq j$$

This assumption eliminates all correlations between errors associated with different observations both within equations and across different equations.

It is also useful to relate the reduced form error term to the structural error term. Reduced form errors have 0 mean since

$$E(\mathbf{v}_i) = E(\mathbf{B}^{-1}\mathbf{u}_i) = \mathbf{B}^{-1}E(\mathbf{u}_i) = \mathbf{0} \qquad i = 1, 2, \ldots, N$$

The variance-covariance matrix of the reduced form errors $\mathbf{\Omega}$ is

$$\mathbf{\Omega} = E(\mathbf{v}_i\mathbf{v}_i') = \mathbf{B}^{-1}E(\mathbf{u}_i\mathbf{u}_i')(\mathbf{B}')^{-1} = \mathbf{B}^{-1}\mathbf{\Sigma}(\mathbf{B}')^{-1} \qquad \text{(A12.4)}$$

Conditions for Identification

The presence of right-hand endogenous variables in the simultaneous-equation model indicates that OLS estimates of the structural form of the model may be inconsistent. However, OLS estimates of the reduced form will be consistent, since only predetermined variables appear on the right-hand side of the reduced form equations. Thus, it is natural to ask whether it is possible to obtain information about structural parameters, given consistent estimates of reduced form parameters. The problem of expressing the β's and γ's in terms of the reduced form coefficients (the π's) is the *identification problem.* We shall say that a structural parameter is identified if and only if it can be uniquely determined from the set of reduced form parameters. In our notation the link between the structural and reduced forms is provided by two equations:

$$\pi = -\mathbf{B}^{-1}\mathbf{\Gamma} \qquad \text{(A12.5)}$$

$$\mathbf{\Omega} = \mathbf{B}^{-1}\mathbf{\Sigma}(\mathbf{B}')^{-1} \qquad \text{(A12.6)}$$

Knowledge of the reduced form is provided by the $G \times K$ elements of π. Unfortunately, one goal is to determine the $G \times G$ elements of $\mathbf{B}$ and the $G \times K$ elements of $\mathbf{\Gamma}$. What is required is information about restrictions on the structural-form parameters. Restrictions may involve linear relationships between structural parameters as well as restrictions on elements of the variance-covariance matrix of the structural disturbances. We shall focus on the most prevalent form of identifying restriction: the zero restriction on structural-form parameters.

We concentrate, without loss of generality, on the identification of the first equation. In addition, we assume that the variables with 0 coefficient restrictions are grouped after the variables with nonzero coefficients. We assume that of the G endogenous variables in the first equation, the first G_* have nonzero coefficients, while the remaining G_{**} are assumed to have 0 coefficients. In addition, K_0 of the predetermined variables have nonzero coefficients, while K_{00} are equal to 0. In other words, the first equation has G_{**} excluded endogenous variables and K_{00} excluded predetermined variables. The first equation can then be written

$$[\beta_{11} \quad \beta_{12} \quad \cdots \quad \beta_{1G_*} \quad 0 \quad 0 \quad \cdots \quad 0] \begin{bmatrix} y_{1i} \\ y_{2i} \\ \vdots \\ y_{Gi} \end{bmatrix}$$

$$+ [\gamma_{11} \quad \gamma_{12} \quad \cdots \quad \gamma_{1K_0} \quad 0 \quad 0 \quad \cdots \quad 0] \begin{bmatrix} x_{1i} \\ x_{2i} \\ \vdots \\ x_{Ki} \end{bmatrix} = \begin{bmatrix} u_{1i} \\ u_{2i} \\ \vdots \\ u_{Gi} \end{bmatrix}$$

It is useful to represent the equation as

$$[\boldsymbol{\beta}^* \quad \boldsymbol{\beta}^{**}] \begin{bmatrix} \mathbf{y}^* \\ \mathbf{y}^{**} \end{bmatrix} + [\boldsymbol{\gamma}_0 \quad \boldsymbol{\gamma}_{00}] \begin{bmatrix} \mathbf{x}_0 \\ \mathbf{x}_{00} \end{bmatrix} = \mathbf{u}_i \tag{A12.7}$$

where $\mathbf{y}^* = G_* \times 1$ vector of observations on included endogenous variables
   $\mathbf{y}^{**} = G_{**} \times 1$ vector of observations on excluded endogenous variables
   $\boldsymbol{\beta}^* = 1 \times G_*$ vector of nonzero coefficients
   $\boldsymbol{\beta}^{**} = 1 \times G_{**}$ vector of 0's
   $\boldsymbol{\gamma}_0 = 1 \times K_0$ vector of nonzero coefficients
   $\boldsymbol{\gamma}_{00} = 1 \times K_{00}$ vector of 0's
   $\mathbf{x}_0 = K_0 \times 1$ vector of observations on included predetermined variables
   $\mathbf{x}_{00} = K_{00} \times 1$ vector of observations on excluded predetermined variables

Dropping the i subscript to simplify the notation, we can rewrite the first equation as

$$\boldsymbol{\beta}^* \mathbf{y}^* + \boldsymbol{\gamma}_0 \mathbf{x}_0 = \mathbf{u} \tag{A12.8}$$

by eliminating the terms with 0 coefficients. Using a similar notation, we can rewrite the reduced form equation as

$$\begin{bmatrix} y^* \\ y^{**} \end{bmatrix} = \begin{bmatrix} \pi_{*,0} & \pi_{*,00} \\ \pi_{**,0} & \pi_{**,00} \end{bmatrix} \begin{bmatrix} x_0 \\ x_{00} \end{bmatrix} + \begin{bmatrix} v_* \\ v_{**} \end{bmatrix}$$

In the partitioned matrix of reduced form coefficients the first subscript refers to the endogenous variables and the second refers to the predetermined variables:

$$\pi_{*,0} = G_* \times K_0 \text{ matrix}$$

$$\pi_{*,00} = G_* \times K_{00} \text{ matrix}$$

$$\pi_{**,0} = G_{**} \times K_0 \text{ matrix}$$

$$\pi_{**,00} = G_{**} \times K_{00} \text{ matrix}$$

$$v_* = G_* \times 1 \text{ vector of the first } G_* \text{ reduced form disturbances}$$

$$v_{**} = G_{**} \times 1 \text{ vector of the remaining reduced form disturbances}$$

Now we can examine the conditions that are necessary and sufficient to identify the structural parameters. To do so, we rewrite Eq. (A12.5) as

$$\mathbf{B}\pi = -\Gamma \tag{A12.9}$$

and then rewrite Eq. (A12.9) only in terms of the first equation of the simultaneous-equation system:

$$[\beta^* \quad 0] \begin{bmatrix} \pi_{*,0} & \pi_{*,00} \\ \pi_{**,0} & \pi_{**,00} \end{bmatrix} = -[\gamma_0 \quad 0]$$

It is useful to divide the previous equation into separate subequations:

$$\beta^* \pi_{*,0} = -\gamma_0 \tag{A12.10}$$

$$\beta^* \pi_{*,00} = 0 \tag{A12.11}$$

We previously normalized one of the β's in the first equation to be equal to 1. Then Eq. (A12.10) has $G_* - 1$ unknown β's and K_0 unknown γ's. Equation (A12.11) involves only the $G_* - 1$ unknown β's. We shall focus for the moment on the second equation, which consists of K_{00} individual equations. We know that a necessary condition for the existence of a solution to Eq. (A12.11) is that there be at least $G_* - 1$ equations. This leads directly to the *order condition* for identification:

$$K_{00} \geq G_* - 1 \tag{A12.12}$$

where K_{00} is the number of excluded predetermined variables and G_* is the number of included endogenous variables. The order condition is not a sufficient condition for identification, because not all the K_{00} equations need be independent of each other. This suggests that a necessary and sufficient condition for identification will be one which guarantees that $G_* - 1$ of the K_{00} equations are in fact independent. This condition, often called the *rank condition*, can be stated as follows:

$$\text{rank } [\boldsymbol{\pi}_{*,00}] = G_* - 1 \qquad (A12.13)$$

Once the $G_* - 1$ unknown β's are determined from Eq. (A12.11), there is no difficulty in solving Eq. (A12.10) for the coefficients of the predetermined variables.

APPENDIX 12.2 Two-Stage Least Squares in Matrix Form

Recall from Appendix 12.1 that the determination of the unknown structural coefficients depends on a solution to the equation

$$\boldsymbol{\beta}^* \boldsymbol{\pi}_{*,00} = \mathbf{0} \qquad (A12.14)$$

Given that one β has been set equal to 1, we seek (directly) to obtain values for the remaining $G_* - 1$ unknown β's. Such a solution will exist if rank $[\boldsymbol{\pi}_{*,00}] = G_* - 1$. If the rank condition is satisfied and $K_{00} = G_* - 1$, the first equation is exactly identified. If $K_{00} > G_* - 1$, however, the equation is overidentified. Overidentification occurs because there are more than $G_* - 1$ equations in Eq. (A12.14) from which we wish to find estimates of the $G_* - 1$ unknown β's. There are several ways to combine the set of equations to obtain the value of $\boldsymbol{\beta}^*$. In the overidentified case, 2SLS becomes an appropriate estimation procedure. 2SLS uses all the information available in the equation system (A12.14) to obtain unique structural parameter estimates.

We shall describe the application of 2SLS to the estimation of the first structural equation, which we assume to be overidentified. To do so, it is useful to alter the notation of Appendix 12.1, expressing the first equation as

$$\mathbf{y}_1 = \mathbf{Y}_1 \boldsymbol{\beta}_1 + \mathbf{X}_1 \boldsymbol{\gamma}_1 + \mathbf{u}_1 \qquad (A12.15)$$

where $\mathbf{y}_1 = N \times 1$ vector of observations on endogenous variable with coefficient of 1 in first equation

$\mathbf{Y}_1 = N \times (G_* - 1)$ matrix of observations on endogenous variables included in first equation (on right-hand side)

$\boldsymbol{\beta}_1 = (G_* - 1) \times 1$ vector of coefficients for included endogenous variables

$\mathbf{X}_1 = N \times K_0$ matrix of observations on included predetermined variables

$\boldsymbol{\gamma}_1 = K_0 \times 1$ vector of predetermined variable coefficients

$\mathbf{u}_1 = N \times 1$ vector of disturbances associated with first equation

As described in the text, the application of ordinary least squares to Eq. (A12.15) will yield inconsistent parameter estimates because of the fact that $\mathbf{Y}_1$ and $\mathbf{u}_1$ are (asymptotically) correlated. 2SLS yields consistent estimates by purging $\mathbf{Y}_1$ of the component which is correlated with $\mathbf{u}_1$ and then rerunning the new regression using OLS.

In the first stage, each of the right-hand endogenous variables is regressed on the *entire* set of predetermined variables in the model. This is equivalent to estimating the reduced form equations associated with the $G_* - 1$ right-hand endogenous variables. We can represent this as

$$\mathbf{Y}_1 = \mathbf{X}_1 \boldsymbol{\pi}_1 + \mathbf{X}_2 \boldsymbol{\pi}_2 + \mathbf{V}$$

or

$$\mathbf{Y}_1 = \mathbf{X}\boldsymbol{\pi} + \mathbf{V}$$

where $\mathbf{X}_2 = N \times K_{00}$ matrix of observations on predetermined variables excluded from first equation

$\boldsymbol{\pi}_1 = K_0 \times (G_* - 1)$ matrix of reduced form coefficients

$\boldsymbol{\pi}_2 = K_{00} \times (G_* - 1)$ matrix of reduced form coefficients

$\mathbf{V} = N \times (G_* - 1)$ matrix of reduced form disturbances

The resulting first-stage estimator is

$$\hat{\boldsymbol{\pi}} = (\mathbf{X}'\mathbf{X})^{-1}\mathbf{X}'\mathbf{Y}_1 \qquad (A12.16)$$

from which we calculate the fitted values for $\mathbf{Y}_1$:

$$\hat{\mathbf{Y}}_1 = \mathbf{X}\hat{\boldsymbol{\pi}} \qquad (A12.17)$$

In the second stage we perform an ordinary least-squares procedure of $\mathbf{y}_1$ on $\hat{\mathbf{Y}}_1$ and $\mathbf{X}_1$. The estimated coefficients are the 2SLS parameter estimates of $\boldsymbol{\beta}_1$ and $\boldsymbol{\gamma}_1$. In terms of our matrix formulation, the second-stage estimators are

$$\begin{bmatrix} \hat{\boldsymbol{\beta}}_1 \\ \hat{\boldsymbol{\gamma}}_1 \end{bmatrix} = \{[\hat{\mathbf{Y}}_1 \quad \mathbf{X}_1]'[\hat{\mathbf{Y}}_1 \quad \mathbf{X}_1]\}^{-1}[\hat{\mathbf{Y}}_1 \quad \mathbf{X}_1]'\mathbf{y}_1 \qquad (A12.18)$$

or

$$\begin{bmatrix} \hat{\boldsymbol{\beta}}_1 \\ \hat{\boldsymbol{\gamma}}_1 \end{bmatrix} = \begin{bmatrix} \hat{\mathbf{Y}}_1'\hat{\mathbf{Y}}_1 & \hat{\mathbf{Y}}_1'\mathbf{X}_1 \\ \mathbf{X}_1'\hat{\mathbf{Y}}_1 & \mathbf{X}_1'\mathbf{X}_1 \end{bmatrix}^{-1} \begin{bmatrix} \hat{\mathbf{Y}}_1'\mathbf{y}_1 \\ \mathbf{X}_1'\mathbf{y}_1 \end{bmatrix} \qquad (A12.19)$$

We can rewrite the 2SLS estimators in a more useful form by taking into account the fact that the residuals of the first-stage regression are uncorrelated with all the predetermined variables, that is,

$$\hat{\mathbf{V}}'\mathbf{X} = \mathbf{0} = \mathbf{X}'\hat{\mathbf{V}} \tag{A12.20}$$

Also,
$$\hat{\mathbf{Y}}_1'\hat{\mathbf{V}} = \mathbf{0} \tag{A12.21}$$

since $\hat{\mathbf{Y}}_1$ is a linear combination of predetermined variables. Thus,

$$\mathbf{Y}_1'\mathbf{Y}_1 = (\hat{\mathbf{Y}}_1 + \hat{\mathbf{V}})'(\hat{\mathbf{Y}}_1 + \hat{\mathbf{V}}) = \hat{\mathbf{Y}}_1'\hat{\mathbf{Y}}_1 + \hat{\mathbf{V}}'\hat{\mathbf{V}}$$

Also,
$$\mathbf{X}_1'\hat{\mathbf{Y}}_1 = \mathbf{X}_1'(\mathbf{Y}_1 - \hat{\mathbf{V}}) = \mathbf{X}_1'\mathbf{Y}_1$$

Therefore, we can rewrite Eq. (A12.19) as

$$\begin{bmatrix} \hat{\boldsymbol{\beta}}_1 \\ \hat{\boldsymbol{\gamma}}_1 \end{bmatrix} = \begin{bmatrix} \mathbf{Y}_1'\mathbf{Y}_1 - \hat{\mathbf{V}}'\hat{\mathbf{V}} & \mathbf{Y}_1'\mathbf{X}_1 \\ \mathbf{X}_1'\mathbf{Y}_1 & \mathbf{X}_1'\mathbf{X}_1 \end{bmatrix}^{-1} \begin{bmatrix} (\mathbf{Y}_1 - \hat{\mathbf{V}})'\mathbf{y}_1 \\ \mathbf{X}_1'\mathbf{y}_1 \end{bmatrix} \tag{A12.22}$$

As a comparison to the 2SLS estimator, the reader may find it useful to examine the inconsistent estimators which would be obtained if OLS were applied to the structural equation directly. The estimators are

$$\begin{bmatrix} \hat{\boldsymbol{\beta}}_1^0 \\ \hat{\boldsymbol{\gamma}}_1^0 \end{bmatrix} = \begin{bmatrix} \mathbf{Y}_1'\mathbf{Y}_1 & \mathbf{Y}_1'\mathbf{X}_1 \\ \mathbf{X}_1'\mathbf{Y}_1 & \mathbf{X}_1'\mathbf{X}_1 \end{bmatrix}^{-1} \begin{bmatrix} \mathbf{Y}_1'\mathbf{y}_1 \\ \mathbf{X}_1'\mathbf{y}_1 \end{bmatrix} \tag{A12.23}$$

Incidentally, it is not difficult to show that 2SLS is an instrumental-variables estimator where the fitted values of the first stage and the included predetermined variables of the first stage are the appropriate instruments. To see this, we write the instrumental-variables estimator as follows:

$$\begin{bmatrix} \hat{\boldsymbol{\beta}}_1^* \\ \hat{\boldsymbol{\gamma}}_1^* \end{bmatrix} = \{[\hat{\mathbf{Y}}_1 \quad \mathbf{X}_1]'[\mathbf{Y}_1 \quad \mathbf{X}_1]\}^{-1}[\hat{\mathbf{Y}}_1 \quad \mathbf{X}_1]'\mathbf{y}_1$$

Expanding terms and simplifying, we find that

$$\begin{bmatrix} \hat{\boldsymbol{\beta}}_1^* \\ \hat{\boldsymbol{\gamma}}_1^* \end{bmatrix} = \begin{bmatrix} \hat{\mathbf{Y}}_1'\mathbf{Y}_1 & \hat{\mathbf{Y}}_1'\mathbf{X}_1 \\ \mathbf{X}_1'\mathbf{Y}_1 & \mathbf{X}_1'\mathbf{X}_1 \end{bmatrix}^{-1} \begin{bmatrix} \hat{\mathbf{Y}}_1'\mathbf{y}_1 \\ \mathbf{X}_1'\mathbf{y}_1 \end{bmatrix}$$

$$= \begin{bmatrix} \mathbf{Y}_1'\mathbf{Y}_1 - \hat{\mathbf{V}}'\hat{\mathbf{V}} & \mathbf{Y}_1'\mathbf{X}_1 \\ \mathbf{X}_1'\mathbf{Y}_1 & \mathbf{X}_1'\mathbf{X}_1 \end{bmatrix}^{-1} \begin{bmatrix} \hat{\mathbf{Y}}_1'\mathbf{y}_1 \\ \mathbf{X}_1'\mathbf{y}_1 \end{bmatrix} = \begin{bmatrix} \hat{\boldsymbol{\beta}}_1 \\ \hat{\boldsymbol{\gamma}}_1 \end{bmatrix}$$

To outline a derivation of the asymptotic variance-covariance matrix of the estimated parameters, we can use the formula for the asymptotic variance-covariance matrix of the instrumental-variables estimator as described in Appendix 7.1. In our notation the variance-covariance matrix is

$$\mathrm{Var}\begin{bmatrix}\hat{\boldsymbol{\beta}}_1 \\ \hat{\boldsymbol{\gamma}}_1\end{bmatrix} = \sigma^2\{[\hat{\mathbf{Y}}_1 \quad \mathbf{X}_1]'[\mathbf{Y}_1 \quad \mathbf{X}_1]\}^{-1}$$

$$\times \{[\hat{\mathbf{Y}}_1 \quad \mathbf{X}_1]'[\hat{\mathbf{Y}}_1 \quad \mathbf{X}_1]\}\{[\mathbf{Y}_1 \quad \mathbf{X}_1]'[\hat{\mathbf{Y}}_1 \quad \mathbf{X}_1]\}^{-1}$$

But

$$\mathbf{Y}_1'\mathbf{X}_1 = (\hat{\mathbf{Y}}_1 + \hat{\mathbf{V}})'\mathbf{X}_1 = \hat{\mathbf{Y}}_1\mathbf{X}_1$$

Expanding the expression for $\mathrm{Var}\begin{bmatrix}\hat{\boldsymbol{\beta}}_1 \\ \hat{\boldsymbol{\gamma}}_1\end{bmatrix}$ using the previous result, we get

$$\mathrm{Var}\begin{bmatrix}\hat{\boldsymbol{\beta}}_1 \\ \hat{\boldsymbol{\gamma}}_1\end{bmatrix} = \sigma^2\{[\hat{\mathbf{Y}}_1 \quad \mathbf{X}_1]'[\mathbf{Y}_1 \quad \mathbf{X}_1]\}^{-1} = \sigma^2\begin{bmatrix}\mathbf{Y}_1'\mathbf{Y}_1 - \hat{\mathbf{V}}'\hat{\mathbf{V}} & \mathbf{Y}_1'\mathbf{X}_1 \\ \mathbf{X}_1'\mathbf{Y}_1 & \mathbf{X}_1'\mathbf{X}_1\end{bmatrix}^{-1}$$

$$\text{(A12.24)}$$

In practice, σ^2 is estimated by

$$s^2 = \frac{\hat{\mathbf{u}}_1'\hat{\mathbf{u}}_1}{N - [(G_* - 1) + K_0]} \qquad \text{where } \hat{\mathbf{u}}_1 = \mathbf{y}_1 - \mathbf{Y}_1\hat{\boldsymbol{\beta}}_1 - \mathbf{X}_1\hat{\boldsymbol{\gamma}}_1$$

Note that the residuals utilized to calculate s^2 do not come from the second-stage regression alone but are calculated from the *original* structural equation with the estimated parameters replacing the true parameters. The variance-covariance matrix, on the other hand, does account for the second-stage use of fitted values for $\mathbf{Y}_1$, as seen by the fact that $\mathbf{Y}_1'\mathbf{Y}_1 - \hat{\mathbf{V}}'\hat{\mathbf{V}}$ $(= \hat{\mathbf{Y}}_1'\hat{\mathbf{Y}}_1)$ appears in the matrix to be inverted (rather than $\mathbf{Y}_1'\mathbf{Y}_1$ alone).

APPENDIX 12.3 Seemingly Unrelated Regression Estimation in Matrix Form

As described in the text, SUR estimation is simply the application of generalized least-squares estimation to a group of seemingly unrelated equations. The equations are related through the nonzero covariances associated with error terms across different equations at a given point in time. We can generalize the seemingly unrelated model by writing the system of G equations as follows:

$$\mathbf{Y}_i = \mathbf{X}_i\boldsymbol{\beta}_i + \mathbf{u}_i \qquad i = 1, 2, \ldots, G \qquad \text{(A12.25)}$$

where $\mathbf{Y}_i = N \times 1$ vector
  $\mathbf{X}_i = N \times K_i$ matrix
  $\boldsymbol{\beta}_i = K_i \times 1$ vector
  $\mathbf{u}_i = N \times 1$ vector

It will be useful to write the model in shorthand form as $\mathbf{Y} = \mathbf{X}\boldsymbol{\beta} + \mathbf{u}$, or

$$
\begin{bmatrix} \mathbf{Y}_1 \\ \mathbf{Y}_2 \\ \cdots \\ \mathbf{Y}_G \end{bmatrix} = \begin{bmatrix} \mathbf{X}_1 & \mathbf{0} & \cdots & \mathbf{0} \\ \mathbf{0} & \mathbf{X}_2 & \cdots & \mathbf{0} \\ \cdots\cdots\cdots\cdots\cdots\cdots \\ \mathbf{0} & \mathbf{0} & \cdots & \mathbf{X}_G \end{bmatrix} \begin{bmatrix} \boldsymbol{\beta}_1 \\ \boldsymbol{\beta}_2 \\ \cdot \\ \boldsymbol{\beta}_G \end{bmatrix} + \begin{bmatrix} \mathbf{u}_1 \\ \mathbf{u}_2 \\ \cdot \\ \mathbf{u}_G \end{bmatrix}
\tag{A12.26}
$$

where $\mathbf{Y} = GN \times 1$ matrix

$$
\mathbf{X} = GN \times \left(\sum_{i=1}^{G} K_i \right) \text{ matrix}
$$

$$
\boldsymbol{\beta} = \left(\sum_{i=1}^{G} K_i \right) \times 1 \text{ matrix}
$$

$$
\mathbf{u} = GN \times 1 \text{ matrix}
$$

According to the assumptions of the seemingly unrelated model, there is no autocorrelation within equations, but cross-equation correlation does exist; i.e.,

$$
E(\mathbf{u}_i\mathbf{u}_j') = \begin{bmatrix} \sigma_{ij} & \mathbf{0} & \cdots & \mathbf{0} \\ \mathbf{0} & \sigma_{ij} & \cdots & \mathbf{0} \\ \cdots\cdots\cdots\cdots\cdots \\ \mathbf{0} & \mathbf{0} & \cdots & \sigma_{ij} \end{bmatrix} = \sigma_{ij}\mathbf{I}
\tag{A12.27}
$$

where $\mathbf{I}$ is an $N \times N$ identity matrix. This relationship applies to the covariances between two arbitrary equations in the system of G equations. To generalize this result in matrix form we write

$$
\boldsymbol{\Omega} = E(\mathbf{u}\mathbf{u}') = \begin{bmatrix} E(\mathbf{u}_1\mathbf{u}_1') & E(\mathbf{u}_1\mathbf{u}_2') & \cdots & E(\mathbf{u}_1\mathbf{u}_G') \\ E(\mathbf{u}_2\mathbf{u}_1') & E(\mathbf{u}_2\mathbf{u}_2') & \cdots & E(\mathbf{u}_2\mathbf{u}_G') \\ \cdots\cdots\cdots\cdots\cdots\cdots\cdots\cdots \\ E(\mathbf{u}_G\mathbf{u}_1') & E(\mathbf{u}_G\mathbf{u}_2') & \cdots & E(\mathbf{u}_G\mathbf{u}_G') \end{bmatrix}
$$

Substituting from Eq. (A12.27), we get

$$
\boldsymbol{\Omega} = \begin{bmatrix} \sigma_{11}\mathbf{I} & \sigma_{12}\mathbf{I} & \cdots & \sigma_{1G}\mathbf{I} \\ \sigma_{21}\mathbf{I} & \sigma_{22}\mathbf{I} & \cdots & \sigma_{2G}\mathbf{I} \\ \cdots\cdots\cdots\cdots\cdots\cdots \\ \sigma_{G1}\mathbf{I} & \sigma_{G2}\mathbf{I} & \cdots & \sigma_{GG}\mathbf{I} \end{bmatrix}
$$

All information about error covariances is contained in the matrix $\boldsymbol{\Omega}$. The most efficient estimation of Eq. (A12.26) is obtained by applying generalized least-squares estimation to get

$$
\hat{\boldsymbol{\beta}} = (\mathbf{X}'\boldsymbol{\Omega}^{-1}\mathbf{X})^{-1}(\mathbf{X}'\boldsymbol{\Omega}^{-1}\mathbf{Y})
\tag{A12.28}
$$

with

$$
E[(\hat{\boldsymbol{\beta}} - \boldsymbol{\beta})(\hat{\boldsymbol{\beta}} - \boldsymbol{\beta})'] = (\mathbf{X}'\boldsymbol{\Omega}^{-1}\mathbf{X})^{-1}
\tag{A12.29}
$$

In practice, the elements of $\boldsymbol{\Omega}$ must be estimated. This is accomplished by using the residuals obtained when OLS estimation is applied to each of the G equations:

$$\hat{\sigma}_{ii} = \frac{\hat{\mathbf{u}}_i \hat{\mathbf{u}}_i'}{N - K_i}$$

$$\hat{\sigma}_{ij} = \frac{\hat{\mathbf{u}}_i \hat{\mathbf{u}}_j'}{\sqrt{(N - K_i)(N - K_j)}}$$

$$\hat{\mathbf{u}}_i = \mathbf{Y}_i - \mathbf{X}_i \hat{\boldsymbol{\beta}}_i$$

There are two important cases in which SUR estimation is equivalent to the equation-by-equation application of OLS. The first case occurs when $\sigma_{ij} = 0$ for every i and j, $i \neq j$. Then $\boldsymbol{\Omega}$ simplifies to

$$\boldsymbol{\Omega} = \begin{bmatrix} \sigma_{11}\mathbf{I} & 0 & \cdots & 0 \\ 0 & \sigma_{22}\mathbf{I} & \cdots & 0 \\ \cdots & \cdots & \cdots & \cdots \\ 0 & 0 & \cdots & \sigma_{GG}\mathbf{I} \end{bmatrix} \qquad \text{(A12.30)}$$

The use of simple matrix algebra [substituting Eq. (A12.30) into Eq. (A12.29)] is sufficient to prove the stated result. A second, less obvious case occurs when $\mathbf{X}_i = \mathbf{X}$ for every $i = 1, 2, \ldots, G$ ($K_i = K$ is implicit). This occurs when the identical set of independent variables appears in each equation. Once again the proof involves a straightforward application of the techniques of matrix algebra.

EXERCISES

12.1 Consider the model

$$C_t = \alpha_1 + \alpha_2 Y_t + \varepsilon_t \qquad I_t = \beta_1 + \beta_2 Y_t + \beta_3 G_{t-1} + u_t \qquad Y_t = C_t + I_t + G_t$$

(a) Construct the reduced form system of the model. From the reduced form determine the response of C in the first two periods to a one-unit change in G.
(b) Is the consumption-function equation identified? Is it overidentified?
(c) Is the investment equation identified? Overidentified?
(d) What would happen to your estimated marginal propensity to consume if it has been estimated by using OLS on an equation of the form $C_t = a + bY_t + \varepsilon_t$?

12.2 Consider the supply-demand model

$$Q_t^S = \alpha_1 + \alpha_2 P_t + \varepsilon_t$$

$$Q_t^D = \beta_1 + \beta_2 P_t + \beta_3 Y_t + \beta_4 P_{t-1} + u_t$$

$$Q_t^D = Q_t^S$$

where $E(\varepsilon_i \varepsilon_j) = 0$, $i \neq j$, and $E(u_i u_j) = 0$, $i \neq j$.

(a) Is the supply equation identified? What would happen if the supply equation were estimated using OLS?

(b) Is the demand equation identified? What would happen if the demand equation were estimated using OLS?

(c) If you were told to estimate the supply equation using instrumental variables, what would you do? Be explicit.

(d) If you were told to estimate the supply equation using 2SLS, what would you do? How does this relate to part (c)?

(e) Could you use indirect least squares to estimate the demand equation? Why or why not?

(f) Would your results be different if you knew that ε was autocorrelated?

12.3 Consider the two-equation model system

$$Y_1 = a_1 Y_2 + a_2 Z_1 + u_1 \qquad Y_2 = b_1 Y_1 + b_2 Z_2 + u_2$$

(Assume that $Z_1 \neq Z_2$.)

(a) Under what conditions will OLS estimation of the first equation lead to consistent parameter estimates? *Hint:* There are two conditions, one relating to parameter values and the other relating to error variances and covariances.

(b) Under what assumptions is the first equation identified? *Hint:* Again there are two conditions, the first relating to parameter values and the second relating to error covariances.

12.4 Consider the two-equation model system

$$Y_1 = a_1 + a_2 Y_2 + u_1 \qquad Y_2 = b_1 + b_2 Y_1 + b_3 Z_1 + b_4 Z_2 + u_2$$

Assess the following approaches to the estimation of the first equation in terms of possible bias, inconsistency, and efficiency. Which of the estimators are instrumental-variables estimators? How does the last estimation process relate to the previous three?

(a) OLS estimation of the first equation

(b) Indirect least-squares estimation of the first equation

(c) Instrumental-variables estimation using Z_1 as an instrument in the first equation

(d) 2SLS estimation of the first equation

(e) Estimating the first equation as $\hat{Y}_1 = c_1 + c_2 Z_1 + c_3 Z_2$

12.5 Explain intuitively (using a three-equation model) why the omission of one variable from each equation in a system of equations is insufficient to guarantee that each equation in the system is identified.

12.6 Prove that the two forms of the order condition for identifiability which are described in the text are equivalent.

12.7 Consider the three-equation model system

$$Y_1 = \alpha_1 + \alpha_2 Y_2 \qquad\qquad + \alpha_4 X_1 + \alpha_5 X_2 + u_1$$

$$Y_2 = \beta_1 \qquad\quad + \beta_3 Y_3 \qquad\qquad + \beta_5 X_2 + u_2$$

$$Y_3 = \gamma_1 + \gamma_2 Y_2 \qquad\qquad\qquad\qquad + u_3$$

Which of the above equations (if any) are unidentified? Exactly identified? Overidentified?

12.8 Consider the following simple macroeconomic model of an economy:

$$C_t = \alpha_1 + \alpha_2 Y_t + \alpha_3 r_t + u_{1t} \qquad I_t = \beta_1 + \beta_2 r_t + \beta_3(Y_t - Y_{t-1}) + u_{2t}$$

$$r_t = \gamma_1 + \gamma_2 I_t + \gamma_3 M_t + u_{3t} \qquad Y_t = C_t + I_t + G_t$$

Which of the equations are identified? Unidentified? How might you estimate the identified equations?

12.9 Consider the following two-equation recursive model:

$$Y_1 = \alpha_1 \qquad\qquad + \alpha_3 X + u_1$$

$$Y_2 = \beta_1 + \beta_2 Y_1 \qquad\qquad + u_2$$

(a) Explain why OLS is the appropriate estimation technique (assuming that u_1 and u_2 are uncorrelated).

(b) Suppose a naive researcher, seeing Y_1 on the right-hand side of the second equation, attempts to estimate it using 2SLS, i.e., regressing Y_2 on the fitted values of Y_1 determined by using OLS on the first equation. What will be the outcome of such an attempt? How might one obtain a value for $\hat{\beta}_2$ if such a procedure is used?

(c) How would the answers to (b) differ if the second equation contained X explicitly as an independent variable?

12.10 Using Example 12.3, prove that seemingly unrelated regression estimation reduces to OLS estimation when the cross-equation error covariance is 0 and when the independent variables in each equation are identical.

12.11 Consider the following two-equation supply-demand model:

Demand: $$P_t = \alpha_1 + \alpha_2 Q_t + u_{1t}$$

Supply: $$Q_t = \beta_1 + \beta_2 P_{t-1} + \beta_3 W_t + u_{2t}$$

(a) Discuss the identifiability of each equation.

(b) Under what condition is the model recursive?

(c) If the model is recursive, how would you estimate the demand equation?

(d) If the model is not recursive, how would you estimate the demand equation?

12.12 Explain why the simple process of lagging all right-hand variables in a simultaneous-equation system does not necessarily make the model recursive.

12.13 Consider the model

$$y_1 = \alpha_2 y_2 + \alpha_3 x + u_1$$

$$y_2 = \beta_1 y_1 + \beta_4 z + \beta_5 w + u_2$$

Assume that you have estimated the reduced form of this model, first using OLS and then using 2SLS estimates of the structural parameters to solve for the reduced form. Explain why these estimates will differ.

CHAPTER 13

INTRODUCTION TO SIMULATION MODELS

In this chapter and Chapter 14 we discuss the construction, evaluation, and analysis of simultaneous-equation simulation models and their use in policy analysis and forecasting. Simulation models have been widely used in the design of public policy.[1] Those who construct or use such models must be able to evaluate them properly and understand their behavior. Most of our examples will be *econometric* simulation models. These models consist of equations which (except for accounting identities) are estimated using the standard econometric techniques described in the preceding chapters. It is important to point out, however, that these model-building techniques also can be applied to other types of models, including models of corporations[2] and models of social or political behavior.[3] In addition to economists, corporate planners, sociologists, political scientists, and others have made increasing use of simulation models as a framework for analysis and prediction.

One of our goals is to explain how a simulation model is constructed, since more is involved than simply putting together several individually estimated single equations. We will see that when individual regression equations, which may fit the historical data very well, are combined to form a simultaneous-equation model, the simulation results may bear little resemblance to reality.

---

[1] For a discussion of policy applications, see M. Greenberger, M. A. Crenson, and B. L. Crissey, *Models in the Policy Process* (New York: Russell Sage Foundation, 1976).

[2] See, for example, J. W. Elliott, *Econometric Analysis for Management Decisions* (Homewood, Ill.: Irwin, 1973), Chapter 13; and T. H. Naylor, *Corporate Planning Models* (Reading, Mass.: Addison-Wesley, 1979), Chapters 4 and 9.

[3] See, for example, R. D. Brunner and G. D. Brewer, *Organized Complexity* (New York: Free Press, 1971).

The difficulty arises because of the dynamic structure of the system that results when individual equations are combined.

To construct and use simulation models, one must be able to compare alternative models of the same process. Thus, we will be concerned at an early stage with evaluating and validating simultaneous-equation simulation models. Model validation presents a less serious problem in the case of single-equation regression, since one can look at a set of statistics such as the R^2 and t statistics to make a judgment about the goodness of fit of the equation. In a multiple-equation model each individual equation may have a very good statistical fit, but the model as a whole may do a poor job of reproducing the historical data. The converse also may be true: the individual equations in a simulation model may have a poor statistical fit, but the model as a whole may reproduce the historical time series very closely.

Another objective is to compare the benefits of a simultaneous-equation model with the costs of building one. If our goal, for example, is to forecast a short-term interest rate, we know that it will be easier to produce a forecast by using a single-equation regression model than by using a multiple-equation simulation model of the money market. The question is whether the added benefit (measured in terms of an improved forecast) of the simultaneous-equation model outweighs the added cost involved in building it.

In this chapter we begin by explaining the simulation process. We then turn to the problem of evaluating simulation models and discuss a number of useful evaluation criteria. Later we will use these criteria to evaluate alternative methods (and examples) of model construction. In the following section we compare alternative methods of estimating a simultaneous-equation model and we examine how the estimation method can affect the model's simulation performance. We next turn to nonstructural models, in particular the estimation and use of *vector autoregressions,* in which a set of variables is regressed against its own lagged values. We end the chapter with a brief discussion of alternative approaches to model building.

13.1   THE SIMULATION PROCESS

Simulation, as we use the word, is simply the mathematical solution to a simultaneous set of difference equations.[4] A *simulation model* refers to that set of equations. As an example, consider the extremely simple macroeconomic model represented by

$$C_t = a_1 + a_2 Y_{t-1} \tag{13.1}$$

$$I_t = b_1 + b_2(Y_{t-1} - Y_{t-2}) \tag{13.2}$$

$$Y_t = C_t + I_t + G_t \tag{13.3}$$

---

[4] A difference equation relates the current value of one variable to current and past values of other variables. Good examples of difference equations are given by the distributed lag models discussed in Chapter 9.

where C = consumption
$\quad$ I = investment
$\quad$ Y = gross national product
$\quad$ G = government spending

and the error terms are suppressed. C, I, and Y are the *endogenous* variables, while G is an *exogenous* variable. This is the standard multiplier-accelerator model described in elementary macroeconomics textbooks. Consumption is proportional to GNP (the multiplier), but investment is proportional to changes in GNP (the accelerator).

If values are given for the parameters a_1, a_2, b_1, and b_2, initial values are specified for the variables C and I, and a time path is given for the exogenous variable G, then the simultaneous solution of these three equations will give us time paths for each of the endogenous variables C, I, and Y. This is what is meant by the simulation process. Given a model whose parameters have been estimated (or its numerical values otherwise supplied), given initial values for the endogenous variables (i.e., base-year values), and given a time series for the exogenous variables (this may be a historical series or may represent hypotheses about the future behavior of the series), the model is solved over some range of time to yield values for each of the endogenous variables.

The model above can be solved analytically by substituting Eqs. (13.1) and (13.2) into Eq. (13.3) and rearranging:

$$Y_t - (a_2 + b_2)\, Y_{t-1} + b_2 Y_{t-2} = (a_1 + b_1) + G_t \qquad (13.4)$$

The result is a second-order difference equation whose solution will depend on two initial conditions as well as all future values of the exogenous variable G_t.[5] We will see in Chapter 14 that the solution for Y_t may not be stable (i.e., it may grow without bound) or it may oscillate. In the case of a simple model, it is easy to determine the conditions that must hold for the model to be stable, while in the case of a more complex model (which may be nonlinear), the conditions for stability may be difficult to ascertain.

Model stability is important because we believe that the real world (or at least most of it) is stable. If, for example, the GNP had moved over the past 20 years according to dotted line A in Fig. 13.1, we would expect a model which explained GNP to yield a solution which moved in the same way, perhaps as represented by solid line B. Solid line C would represent an unstable solution, since it diverges more and more rapidly from the actual range of values of GNP. Other nonrepresentative modes of behavior are possible, such as the dampened oscillations of solid line D in Fig. 13.2 and the explosive oscillations of line E in the same figure. Of course, in some cases nonexplosive oscillations may be a desirable solution—if, for example, the model in question is being used to

---

[5] For an introduction to difference equations and their solution, see A. C. Chiang, *Fundamental Methods of Mathematical Economics* (New York: McGraw-Hill, 1984).

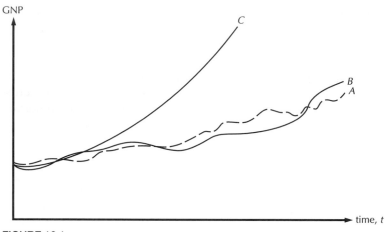

FIGURE 13.1
Stable and unstable solutions.

explain business cycles for some commodity and the frequency of the oscillations closely matches the frequency of the actual cycles.

Solution characteristics are important and will be discussed further in Chapter 14. For now, however, we will limit ourselves to the problem of obtaining
a solution, i.e., performing a simulation. If the parameters are known for a
small model of Eqs. (13.1) to (13.3), the solution can be obtained analytically.
For a larger perhaps nonlinear model, the simultaneous equations must be
solved numerically. Several computer programs exist that make the simulation
of even a very large model quite easy. Most of these programs obtain solutions
by using an iterative procedure in which the nonlinear model is repeatedly
linearized, perhaps renormalized, and then solved.

FIGURE 13.2
Oscillatory solutions.

GNP

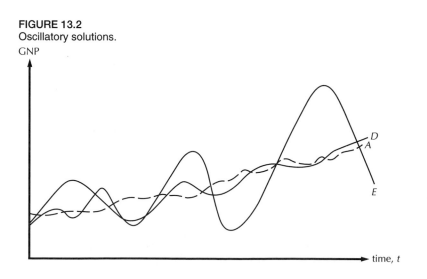

Simulations of a model may be performed for a variety of reasons, including model testing and evaluation, historical policy analysis, and forecasting. Usually the *time horizon* over which the simulation is performed depends on the objective of the simulation.

In Fig. 13.3, T_1 and T_2 represent the time bounds over which the equations of a hypothetical model are estimated (the estimation period). T_3 represents the time today. The first mode of simulation is called an *ex post* or *historical simulation*. The simulation begins in year T_1 and runs forward until year T_2. Historical values in year T_1 are supplied as initial conditions for the endogenous variables, and historical series beginning in T_1 and ending in T_2 are used for the exogenous variables. There is no reinitialization of the endogenous variables; after year T_1 the values for the endogenous variables are determined by the simulation solution. If the model is simulated during a period for which historical data for all variables are available, a comparison of the original data series with the simulated series for each endogenous variable can provide a useful test of the validity of the model. *Ex post* simulations also can be useful in policy analysis. By changing parameter values or letting exogenous policy variables follow different time paths we can examine what might have taken place as a result of alternative policies. One can use a macroeconometric model to examine, for example, the consequences that would have resulted from changes in the level of government spending, tax rates, or the money supply. Similarly, industrywide models can be used to study the effects of alternative government regulatory policies or the impact of macroeconomic growth and fluctuations on the industry.[6]

Forecasting involves a simulation of the model forward in time beyond the estimation period. Of course, before a forecast can be made, one must have time series data for the entire forecast period for all the exogenous variables. In the simple macroeconomic model of Eqs. (13.1) to (13.3), for example, one must first predict (or at least make some assumption about) future values of government

FIGURE 13.3
Simulation time horizons.

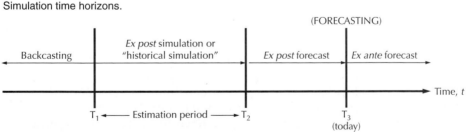

[6] Examples can be found in T. Naylor, *Computer Simulation Experiments with Economic Systems* (New York: Wiley, 1971). For a detailed example of an application of an industrywide econometric model to the analysis of government price regulatory policy, see P. W. MacAvoy and R. S. Pindyck, "Alternative Regulatory Policies for Dealing with the Natural Gas Shortage," *Bell Journal of Economics and Management Science*, vol. 4, Autumn 1973, pp. 454–498, and P. W. MacAvoy and R. S. Pindyck, *The Economics of the Natural Gas Shortage* (Amsterdam. North-Holland, 1975).

spending G_t. Typically, one generates a set of alternative forecasts, each of which is conditional on a set of assumptions about the exogenous variables.

As we saw in Chapter 8, we can distinguish between two types of forecasts. If the estimation period did not extend to the current year (that is, T_2 is less than T_3), one might want to begin the forecast at the end of the estimation period and extend it to the present, perhaps comparing the results with available data. This is called an *ex post forecast* and often is performed to test the forecasting accuracy of a model. A forecast made by beginning the simulation in the current year and extending it into the future is called an *ex ante forecast.*

Forecasting is useful not only for predictive purposes but also for sensitivity analysis and policy analysis. Forecasts can be used to study the effects of changes in exogenous variables or particular parameters and can be used to compare the effects of alternative policies that are stated as movements in controllable exogenous variables (such as G_t in our example) or as changes in the values of policy parameters (such as tax rates).

It is occasionally of interest to simulate a model *backward* in time, beginning at the start of the estimation period. One might do this to test a model's dynamic stability or to analyze hypotheses about events that took place just before the estimation period. In a *backcast* one begins with initial conditions for all variables in period T_1 (see Fig. 13.3 again) and then, using data for the exogenous variables before period T_1, solves the model backward one period at a time.

13.2 EVALUATING SIMULATION MODELS

We have seen that in the case of the single-equation regression model there are statistics (R^2, F test, t tests, etc.) that can be used to judge the significance (in a statistical sense) of the model and its individual estimated coefficients. Other statistics exist (e.g., the DW statistic) to test the underlying assumptions of the model. Even with these tests, however, the choice of whether to accept or reject a single-equation model, particularly in comparison with other single-equation models, is not straightforward. One must decide whether the structural specification of the model is reasonable and whether the estimated coefficients make sense. The model's evaluation also depends on the *purpose* for which the model was built. A model designed for forecasting purposes should have as small a standard error of forecast as possible, while t statistics are more important in a model designed to test a specific hypothesis.

The same considerations apply to a multi-equation simulation model, except that the evaluation criteria become more complicated. With several equations, high statistical significance for some may have to be balanced against low statistical significance for others. More important, the model as a whole will have a dynamic structure which is much richer than that of any one of its individual equations. Thus, even if all the individual equations fit the data well and are statistically significant, the model as a whole, when simulated, may not track those data series closely. Finally, it is possible that in an *ex post* (historical) simulation some of the endogenous variables will track the original data series closely while others will not. As with a single-equation model, the evaluation of a multi-equation model depends on the purpose for which it was built. Some models are built primarily for forecasting, while others are built for descriptive purposes and hypothesis testing, and different criteria will apply.

We will examine criteria that can be used to evaluate multi-equation models, beginning with the individual equations of a model. Do the equations, on a one-by-one basis, fit the data well? This question can be answered by using the same criteria (statistical and otherwise) that were used in the construction and evaluation of single-equation regression models, even if a multi-equation esti- mation procedure was used.

In examining the equations of a model, one typically finds that some of the equations fit the data well while others do not. Thus a judgment must be made as the model is constructed regarding the overall statistical fit. In practice, it may be necessary to use specifications for some of the equations that are less desirable from a statistical point of view but improve the ability of the model to simulate well (according to criteria that we will discuss below). The model builder is thus forced to make compromises, accepting some equations that do not have a good statistical fit in order to build a complete structural model.

Another criterion that is used to evaluate a simulation model is the fit of the individual variables in a *simulation context.* One expects the results of a historical simulation to match the behavior of the real world rather closely, and so one will often perform a historical simulation and then examine how closely each endogenous variable tracks the historical data. It is therefore desirable to have some quantitative measure of how closely individual variables track their cor- responding data series. We saw in Chapter 8, in the context of forecasting with a single-equation model, that a widely used measure is the *rms* (root-mean- square) *simulation error.* Recall that the rms simulation error for the variable Y_t is defined as

$$\text{rms error} = \sqrt{\frac{1}{T} \sum_{t=1}^{T} (Y_t^s - Y_t^a)^2} \qquad (13.5)$$

where Y_t^s = simulated value of Y_t

$\quad Y_t^a$ = actual value

$\quad T$ = number of periods in the simulation

The rms error is a measure of the deviation of the simulated variable from its actual time path. Of course, the magnitude of this error can be evaluated only by comparing it with the average size of the variable in question.

One simulation error statistic which does this is the *rms percent error,* which is defined as

$$\text{rms percent error} = \sqrt{\frac{1}{T} \sum_{t=1}^{T} \left(\frac{Y_t^s - Y_t^a}{Y_t^a} \right)^2} \qquad (13.6)$$

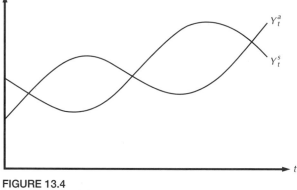

FIGURE 13.4
Low mean simulation error.

Other measures include the *mean simulation error,* which is defined as

$$\text{Mean simulation error} = \frac{1}{T} \sum_{t=1}^{T} (Y_t^s - Y_t^a) \tag{13.7}$$

and the *mean percent error,* which is defined as

$$\text{Mean percent error} = \frac{1}{T} \sum_{t=1}^{T} \frac{Y_t^s - Y_t^a}{Y_t^a} \tag{13.8}$$

The problem with mean errors is that they may be close to 0 if large positive errors cancel out large negative errors. In Fig. 13.4, for example, the mean simulation error would probably be close to 0, while the rms simulation error though large would be a better measure of the simulation performance.[7] However, mean errors are often useful as an indication of a systematic bias.

Sometimes a historical simulation will show some endogenous variables to have a small rms simulation error while others have large errors. In this case model evaluation will involve a consideration of which variables are most critical as well as the *reasons* why large errors have occurred. To do so one can trace through the structure of the model to find out why certain variables diverge from their historical paths during the simulation. The simulation performance of the model often can be improved by substituting new equation forms which may have poorer statistical fits but improve the dynamic structure of the model.

Low rms simulation errors are only one desirable measure of simulation fit. Another important criterion is how well the model simulates *turning points* in the data. Consider Fig. 13.5, where dotted line *A* represents the historical time

---

[7] Mean *absolute* errors (and mean absolute percent errors) also can be calculated to avoid the problem of positive and negative errors canceling, but rms errors are used more often in practice, since they penalize large individual errors more heavily. See Exercise 13.1.

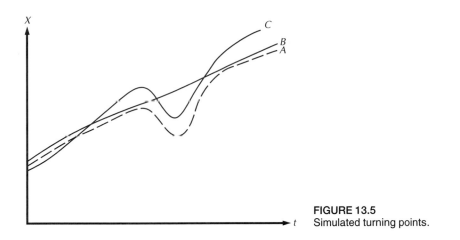

FIGURE 13.5
Simulated turning points.

series for some endogenous variable X and solid lines B and C represent simulated values using two different models. From this figure alone, one would probably prefer the model that produced line C, since despite its larger rms simulation error it duplicates the marked change in variable X that occurred. The model that produced line B did track the historical data closely during the rest of the simulation period, but any simple trend model could have done this.

If the model has been designed for forecasting purposes, the *ex post rms forecast error* is another important criterion for performance. In an *ex post* forecast the results can be compared to recent data. The rms forecast error, i.e., the rms simulation error computed over the forecast range, provides a measure of the ability of the model to forecast. It is possible for some endogenous variables to have large rms forecast errors while others have small errors. Unless the forecasting objective is centered on only one or two variables, all the rms forecast errors must be evaluated jointly.

As we saw in Chapter 8, a useful simulation statistic related to the rms simulation error is *Theil's inequality coefficient:*

$$U = \frac{\sqrt{\dfrac{1}{T} \sum_{t=1}^{T} (Y_t^s - Y_t^a)^2}}{\sqrt{\dfrac{1}{T} \sum_{t=1}^{T} (Y_t^s)^2} + \sqrt{\dfrac{1}{T} \sum_{t=1}^{T} (Y_t^a)^2}} \tag{13.9}$$

Recall that the numerator of U is the rms simulation error, but the scaling of the denominator is such that U will always fall between 0 and 1. If $U = 0$, $Y_t^s = Y_t^a$ for all t and there is a perfect fit. If $U = 1$, the predictive performance of the model is as bad as it possibly could be. When $U = 1$, simulated values are always 0 when actual values are nonzero, or nonzero predictions have been made when actual values are zero and hence easy to predict, or simulated values are positive (negative) when actual values are negative (positive).[8]

We saw in Chapter 8 that the Theil inequality coefficient can be decomposed as follows:

$$\frac{1}{T} \sum (Y_t^s - Y_t^a)^2 = (\overline{Y}^s - \overline{Y}^a)^2 + (\sigma_s - \sigma_a)^2 + 2(1 - \rho)\sigma_s\sigma_a \quad (13.10)$$

where $\overline{Y}^s$, $\overline{Y}^a$, σ_s, and σ_a are the means and standard deviations of the series Y_t^s and Y_t^a, respectively, and ρ is their correlation coefficient.[9] We then define the *proportions of inequality* as

$$U^M = \frac{(\overline{Y}^s - \overline{Y}^a)^2}{(1/T)\Sigma(Y_t^s - Y_t^a)^2} \quad (13.11)$$

$$U^S = \frac{(\sigma_s - \sigma_a)^2}{(1/T)\Sigma(Y_t^s - Y_t^a)^2} \quad (13.12)$$

and

$$U^C = \frac{2(1 - \rho)\sigma_s\sigma_a}{(1/T)\Sigma(Y_t^s - Y_t^a)^2} \quad (13.13)$$

The proportions U^M, U^S, and U^C are called the *bias*, the *variance*, and the *covariance proportions*, respectively, and they let us break the simulation error down into its characteristic sources.

The bias proportion U^M is an indication of systematic error, since it measures the extent to which the *average* values of the simulated and actual series deviate from each other. Whatever the value of the inequality coefficient U, we hope that U^M will be close to zero. A large value of U^M (above .1 or .2) would be quite troubling, since it would mean that a systematic bias is present, so that revision of the model will be necessary.

The variance proportion U^S indicates the ability of the model to replicate the degree of variability in the variable of interest. If U^S is large, it means that the actual series has fluctuated considerably while the simulated series shows little fluctuation, or vice versa. This would also be troubling and might lead us to a revision of the model.

Finally, the covariance proportion measures unsystematic error; i.e., it represents the remaining error after deviations from average values have been accounted for. Since it is unreasonable to expect predictions that are perfectly correlated with actual outcomes, this component of error is less worrisome. Indeed, for any value of $U > 0$, the ideal distribution of inequality over the three sources is $U^M = U^S = 0$ and $U^C = 1$.

---

[8] The inequality coefficient was introduced in H. Theil, *Economic Forecasts and Policy* (Amsterdam: North-Holland, 1961), pp. 30–37, and is discussed in H. Theil, *Applied Economic Forecasting* (Amsterdam: North-Holland, 1966), pp. 26–35. Theil also shows that if U is not large (say, below .3), its variance can be approximated by Var $(U) \approx U^2/T$.

[9] That is, $\rho = (1/\sigma_s\sigma_a T)\Sigma(Y_t^s - \overline{Y}^s)(Y_t^a - \overline{Y}^a)$.

It would be useful to have a measure of performance associated with an *ex ante* forecast for a multi-equation model. We saw in Chapter 8, for example, that for a single-equation regression model a standard error of forecast and a corresponding confidence interval can be computed. Unfortunately, there is no simple way to calculate confidence intervals for the forecast from a multi-equation model, since forecast errors can be compounded in a complex way by the feedback structure of the model. One can, however, calculate confidence intervals by using *stochastic* simulation, as will be discussed in Chapter 14. Often *ex post* rms forecast errors are used as criteria for forecast performance. However, one must remember that the *ex ante* errors are likely to be larger than the *ex post* errors.

Even if a model tracked well, i.e., had small rms simulation and forecast errors for most or all of the endogenous variables, one would also want to investigate whether it responded to stimuli (e.g., large changes in exogenous variables or policy parameters) in a manner consistent with theory and with empirical observation. In the case of a macroeconometric model, for example, the simulation of a \$10 billion increase in government expenditures should result in changes in GNP that roughly match both our theoretical expectations and recent observations. Thus the *dynamic response* of the model (discussed in Chapter 14) is another evaluation criterion.

An additional criterion of model performance is the overall *sensitivity* of the model to factors such as the initial period in which the simulation is begun, minor changes in estimated coefficients, and small changes in the time paths of exogenous variables. If, for example, a model was estimated using data from 1955 to 1995, one would expect the historical simulation to fit well whether it was begun in 1955 or in 1960. We would also expect that small changes in the model's coefficients (at least within one-half of the estimated standard error for the coefficient) would not affect the model's simulation performance very drastically. Another sensitivity test, then, involves resimulating the model after making small changes in individual coefficients. A third sensitivity test involves altering the time paths for exogenous variables over the simulation period. Again, *small* changes in these time paths for exogenous variables should not affect the simulation performance drastically.

We have seen that there are many criteria which can be used to evaluate the performance of a simulation model, but problems may arise in the use of these criteria.[10] What if the rms simulation errors are all very small but the model is very sensitive to the initial starting date in the simulation? What if the *ex post* rms forecast errors are all small but the model fails to reproduce turning points? What if the Theil inequality coefficient U is very small but the bias component U^M is large? Unfortunately, no formulas tell us what to do in cases like these. Part of the art of model building is learning to trade off alternative criteria in different ways.

---

[10] For a detailed treatment of evaluation criteria for econometric models, see D. Belsley, E. Kuh, and R. Welsch, *Regression Diagnostics* (New York: Wiley, 1980).

13.3   A SIMULATION EXAMPLE

As a simple example of a multi-equation simulation model we look at a small linear macroeconomic model, which is given by Eqs. (13.14) to (13.17). (The reader can check that all the equations are identified.)

$$C_t = -9.454 + .0541Y_t + .9260C_{t-1} \tag{13.14}$$
$$ (-2.01) \quad\quad (3.21) \quad\quad\quad (36.73)$$

$$R^2 = .999 \quad\quad s = 11.23 \quad\quad DW = 1.57 \quad\quad \text{Durbin } h = 2.69$$

$$I_t = -66.195 + .1684(Y_{t-1} - Y_{t-2}) + .2181Y_t - 11.256R_{t-4} \tag{13.15}$$
$$ (-8.12) \quad\quad (2.18) \quad\quad\quad\quad\quad\quad\quad (38.53) \quad\quad (-9.20)$$

$$R^2 = .968 \quad\quad s = 23.864 \quad\quad DW = .55$$

$$R_t = -.5561 + .00051Y_t + .0135(Y_t - Y_{t-1}) - .0853(M_t - M_{t-1})$$
$$ (1.83) \quad\quad (2.24) \quad\quad\quad (4.32) \quad\quad\quad\quad\quad (-5.75)$$

$$+ .4259(R_{t-1} + R_{t-2}) \tag{13.16}$$
$$ (16.73)$$

$$R^2 = .934 \quad\quad s = .854 \quad\quad DW = 1.37 \quad\quad \text{Durbin } h = 3.99$$

$$Y_t = C_t + I_t + G_t \tag{13.17}$$

where C = real aggregate personal consumption
$\quad\quad I$ = real gross domestic investment
$\quad\quad Y$ = real GNP (net of exports and imports)
$\quad\quad G$ = real government spending
$\quad\quad M$ = real money stock, narrowly defined (M1)
$\quad\quad R$ = interest rate on 3-month Treasury bills

C, Y, I, and G are all measured in billions of 1982 dollars, while R is given in percent per year. The equations were estimated using quarterly time-series data from 1950 through the end of 1985. The t statistics (in parentheses below each estimated coefficient), the R^2, the standard error, and the DW statistic are shown for each equation. Equations (13.14) and (13.16) contain lagged dependent variables, so their DW statistics are biased toward 2; we therefore also calculate the Durbin h statistic for these equations. Except for Eq. (13.17), which is an identity, the equations were all estimated using ordinary least squares.

Equation (13.14) for aggregate consumption consists of a multiplier with a geometric lag distribution. The investment equation contains both a multiplier and an accelerator, with investment also depending on the short-term interest rate R, with a long time delay. An equation is also estimated for this interest rate, which is positively related to the GNP and changes in GNP, and is negatively related to changes in the money stock. Finally, the model is completed with the addition of the GNP accounting identity in Eq. (13.17). The model

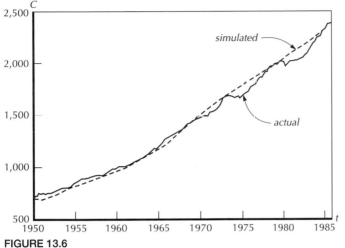

FIGURE 13.6
Historical simulation of consumption.

thus consists of four endogenous variables and four equations as well as two exogenous variables—the money stock and government spending.

Despite the simplicity of this model, its simulation performance is surprisingly good. We performed an *ex post* (historical) simulation over the estimation period 1950-1 to 1985-4, using the historical values for the two exogenous variables—government spending and the money supply. The results are shown graphically in Figs. 13.6 to 13.9, which plot the actual and simulated series for each endogenous variable on the same set of axes.

Looking at Figs. 13.6 to 13.9, we observe that the simulated series do seem to reproduce the general long-run behavior of the actual series, although short-

FIGURE 13.7
Historical simulation of investment.

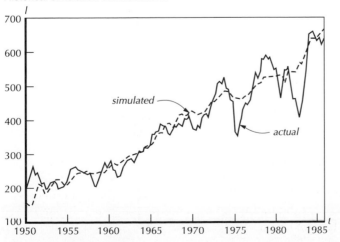

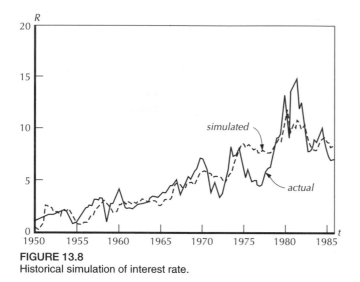

FIGURE 13.8
Historical simulation of interest rate.

run fluctuations in the actual series are not reproduced well and some of the turning points are missed altogether. (Note, for example, that the model fails to reproduce the sharp declines in investment spending that occurred during the recessions of 1975 and 1982.) We can also examine the rms and mean simulation errors and percent simulation errors for each variable, which are shown in Table 13.1 along with the mean value of each variable.

Some of these errors are large (especially for investment and the interest rate), but that is not surprising given the simplistic nature of the model. Recall that the model was estimated using ordinary least squares. We will see in the next section that the use of alternative estimation methods can result in an

FIGURE 13.9
Historical simulation of GNP.

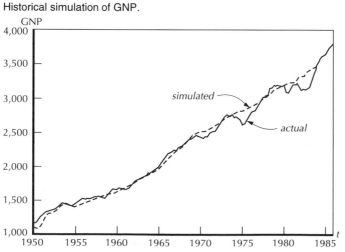

TABLE 13.1
SUMMARY STATISTICS FOR HISTORICAL SIMULATION

	C	I	R	Y
Mean	1,411.2	383.8	5.15	2,306.1
rms error	16.1	39.7	1.11	75.8
rms percent error	3.25%	11.1%	36.11%	3.39%
Mean error	9.01	3.38	.024	12.48
Mean percent error	−.18%	.86%	2.76%	.04%

TABLE 13.2
SUMMARY STATISTICS FOR *EX POST* FORECAST

	C	I	R	Y
Mean	2,479.8	678.7	5.88	3,922.0
rms error	37.0	64.4	1.40	87.9
rms percent error	1.48%	9.67%	23.69%	2.22%
Mean error	18.8	59.5	.99	78.3
Mean percent error	.74%	8.85%	16.71%	1.98%

improved simulation performance. In the meanwhile, we will illustrate the use of this model for forecasting.

We begin with an *ex post* forecast in which the model is simulated forward starting at the end of the estimation period (1985-4) and continuing through the date of the simulation (in this case 1988-1). The results of this simulation are shown in Figs. 13.10 to 13.13. Summary statistics are also shown for each endogenous variable in Table 13.2.

FIGURE 13.10
Ex post forecast of consumption.

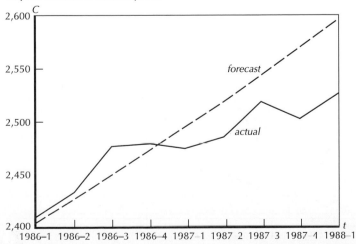

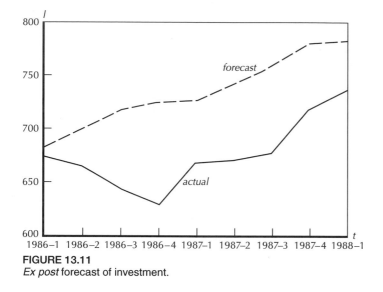

FIGURE 13.11
Ex post forecast of investment.

Note that while the rms errors are sometimes smaller than those for the historical simulation, the mean errors are generally larger in magnitude. For example, the model seriously overpredicts investment for the entire 2 years of the forecast period. This in turn causes it to overpredict GNP and, during 1987, the interest rate.

We can take this example a step further and use the model to produce an *ex ante* forecast. To do this, we begin the simulation in the second quarter of 1988

FIGURE 13.12
Ex post forecast of interest rate.

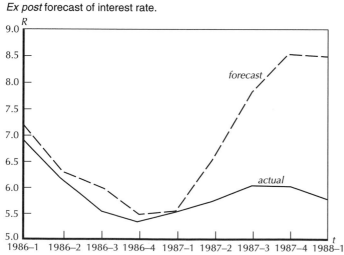

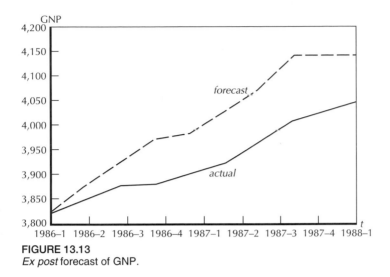

FIGURE 13.13
Ex post forecast of GNP.

and continue through the fourth quarter of 1989. To perform this simulation, however, some forecast or assumption must be made regarding the exogenous variables G_t and M_t. We assumed that G_t would grow at a rate of 3.2 percent per year, which is close to its average historical growth rate. We assumed that M_t would grow at a rate of 1 percent per year, which (in real terms) is a bit below its historical growth rate and hence represents a tight monetary policy.

The results of this forecast are shown for investment and the interest rate in Figs. 13.14 and 13.15. Note that the forecasted interest rate grows steadily, reaching a level above 11 percent. Although the 3-month Treasury bill rate did in fact rise to over 8 percent in 1988 and early 1989, it did not reach the levels

FIGURE 13.14
Ex ante forecast of investment.

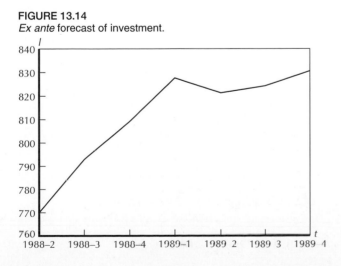

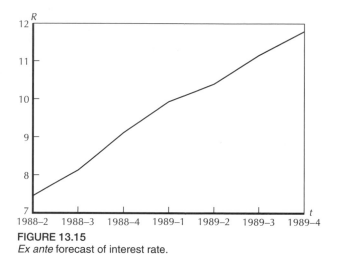

FIGURE 13.15
Ex ante forecast of interest rate.

shown in Fig. 13.15. By the middle of 1989 Federal Reserve monetary policy had eased, and this rate stabilized at about 8 percent.

13.4   MODEL ESTIMATION

In this section we examine how alternative estimation methods can affect the simulation and forecasting performance of a model. The model given by Eqs. (13.14) to (13.17) was estimated using ordinary least squares (OLS), which can result in inconsistent and biased estimates of the coefficients. Let us see how the choice of estimation method affects the performance of the model when it is simulated as a whole.

To do this, we first estimate the model using two-stage least squares (2SLS). Note that the model is *block-recursive* (assuming independent error terms). Specifically, the interest rate appears as an explanatory variable only in the investment equation, and it appears there with a four-quarter lag. As a result, we need not worry about inconsistency in the OLS estimates of the coefficients of the interest rate equation. Only the consumption and investment equations need to be estimated by 2SLS. We do this by using the following instruments: C_{t-1}, $(Y_{t-1} - Y_{t-2})$, Y_{t-1}, G_t, $(M_t - M_{t-1})$, $(R_{t-1} + R_{t-2})$, R_{t-4}. The 2SLS estimates of the consumption and investment equations are

$$C_t = -3.741 + .0282Y_t + .9645C_{t-1}$$
$$(-.75) \qquad (1.54) \qquad (35.33)$$

(13.18)

$$R^2 = .999 \qquad s = 11.32 \qquad DW = 1.63$$

$$I_t = -63.82 + .1793(Y_{t-1} - Y_{t-2}) + .2162Y_t - 10.902R_{t-4}$$
$$(-7.81) \qquad (2.32) \qquad\qquad (38.12) \qquad (-8.89)$$

(13.19)

$$R^2 = .968 \qquad s = 23.87 \qquad DW = .55$$

The use of 2SLS should reduce the possibility of inconsistency introduced by the model's simultaneity. These equations look reasonable, except that Eq. (13.19) for investment has a low DW statistic, indicating serial correlation in the error terms. If this equation could be reestimated using an autoregressive transformation to correct for this serial correlation, more efficient estimates would be obtained. Using an iterative Cochrane-Orcutt procedure to reestimate this equation gives the result shown below:

$$I_t = -46.99 + .0990(Y_{t-1} - Y_{t-2}) + .1992Y_t - 6.165R_{t-4} \quad (13.20)$$
$$\quad (-2.22) \quad (19.88) \quad\quad\quad\quad\quad (2.04) \quad (-3.91)$$

$$R^2 = .985 \quad s = 16.20 \quad DW = 1.80 \quad \hat{\rho} = .78$$

We now have three versions of this model, the first estimated by OLS, the second estimated by 2SLS, and the third combining 2SLS with an autoregressive correction for the investment equation. Each of these models was used to generate an *ex post* forecast over the 2-year period 1986-1 to 1988-1. The rms simulation errors and rms percent errors were computed for each endogenous variable; the results are shown in Table 13.3.

Observe that the forecast generated by the 2SLS version of the model yields smaller rms simulation errors than does the OLS version for every variable. Version 3, which contains the autoregressive correction for serial correlation in the error term of the investment equation, does even better. This correction improves the performance of the model because it adds information to it. Even though we may not know why the additive error term in the investment equation behaves the way it does, we can observe that it is serially correlated and include that information in the model and the forecast.

In Part Four of this book we will discuss time-series models, which describe and predict the behavior of random processes. The autoregressive correction we employed to estimate the third version of our small model makes the implicit assumption that the additive error terms are of the form

$$\varepsilon_t = \rho\varepsilon_{t-1} + \varepsilon_t^* \quad\quad\quad\quad (13.21)$$

TABLE 13.3
SUMMARY STATISTICS FOR *EX POST* FORECAST

	Version 1, OLS		Version 2, 2SLS		Version 3, autoregressive	
	rms error	rms percent error	rms error	rms percent error	rms error	rms percent error
Gross national product Y	87.89	2.22	68.39	1.73	35.03	.89
Consumption C	37.02	1.48	26.70	1.07	23.84	.95
Investment I	64.44	9.60	58.54	8.82	31.05	4.75
Interest rate R	1.40	23.69	1.25	21.26	1.04	17.74

where ε_t^* is the uncorrelated part of ε_t. Equation (13.21) is actually a simple time-series model for ε_t (a first-order autoregressive model, to be exact). If we combine this model with the structural relationships of each equation, the predictive performance of the model as a whole can be improved. In fact, a more complicated time-series model than that of Eq. (13.21) can be used to "explain" the behavior of the additive error term, and we will see in Chapter 19 that the result can be an even greater improvement in model performance.

The important point for now, however, is that the ability of a model to forecast well can depend on the method used to estimate its coefficients. We have examined only two alternatives to OLS, but a variety of other methods are available. R. Fair made a comparison of 10 alternative estimation methods.[11] Each method was used to estimate the seven behavioral equations of a macroeconomic forecasting model that had been previously developed. Historical simulations were then performed with each of the 10 resulting versions of the model, and the rms simulation errors for each endogenous variable were compared. Nine of the estimation methods were as follows:[12]

1. Ordinary least squares (OLS)
2. Two-stage least squares (2SLS)
3. OLS plus first-order autoregressive correction (OLSAUTO1)
4. 2SLS plus first-order autoregressive correction (2SLSAUTO1)
5. OLS plus second-order autoregressive correction (OLSAUTO2)
6. 2SLS plus second-order autoregressive correction (2SLSAUTO2)
7. Full-information maximum likelihood (FIML)
8. FIML plus first-order autoregressive correction (FIMLAUTO1)
9. FIML plus second-order autoregressive correction (FIMLAUTO2)

The rms simulation errors are shown below for one variable, GNP, for the entire sample period (42 observations) and for a four-quarter forecast:

	Entire period	Four quarters
1 OLS	8.45	7.51
2 2SLS	8.07	7.21
3 OLSAUTO1	8.61	6.44
4 2SLSAUTO1	8.27	6.42
5 OLSAUTO2	8.40	6.14
6 2SLSAUTO2	7.78	5.90
7 FIML	7.38	5.34
8 FIMLAUTO1	6.55	4.79
9 FIMLAUTO2	6.99	4.95

[11] See R. Fair, "A Comparison of Alternative Estimators of Macroeconomic Models," *International Economic Review,* vol. 14, no. 2, pp. 261–277, June 1973.

[12] The tenth method was an experimental procedure that accounted for the dynamic structure of the equations on a one-by-one basis. This method has rarely been used, and so we will not describe it here.

Note that it is with the four-quarter forecast that the estimation method used is most critical, with the range of rms errors extending from 7.51 (OLS) to 4.79 (FIMLAUTO1). Since most forecasting is done over the short term, the results for the first four quarters are presented separately from those for the entire sample period. In both cases, however, the use of FIMLAUTO1 seems to yield the best result. This method accounts for correlations between error terms across equations as well as first-order serial correlation in the individual error terms. The results, however, do not prove one method to be better than any other; they simply demonstrate the use of the alternative methods with one particular model.

13.5   NONSTRUCTURAL MODELS: VECTOR AUTOREGRESSIONS

Most of the econometric models we have considered to this point—whether single-equation or multi-equation—are *structural*. By this we mean that the specific relationships between variables are based (either formally or informally) on economic theory. For example, a regression equation to describe or forecast aggregate consumption probably would include disposable income as an explanatory variable, but it also might include a distributed lag of income (or lagged consumption) as well as a measure of wealth in line with the permanent income or life-cycle theories of saving and consumption behavior. Also, the functional form of the equation might be derived as the solution to a consumer's utility maximization problem, or it may simply be specified in a way that is consistent with a theory of consumption behavior. The estimation of such an equation will then provide a means of testing the specific theory.

We have seen that most models are also dynamic. Even in single-equation models, the lag structure and the dynamic adjustment it implies can be an important aspect of model specification and testing. As we will see in Chapter 14, with multi-equation models the lag structure of the individual equations can critically affect the behavior of the model. (For example, in a two-equation supply-demand model of a commodity market the coefficients of lagged variables will determine whether simulations of the model predict cyclical price behavior.) An econometrician can specify alternative lag structures, and the dynamic behavior of the model may to a considerable extent be dictated by this specification. Hence, the econometrician must be sure that the specification is reasonably well grounded in theory.

Unfortunately, economic theory may not be sufficient to determine the right specification. For example, the theory may be too complicated to allow one to precisely derive a specification from first principles, so that some approximate or *ad hoc* specification must be made. Or the theory may be consistent with several alternative lag structures, but these lag structures can result in models with very different dynamic behaviors. Finally, there can be disagreement about what is the right theory. As a result, there are times when one should let the *data*, rather than the econometrician, specify the dynamic structure of a model.

Vector autoregressions (VARs) provide a means of doing this.[13] A VAR makes minimal theoretical demands on the structure of a model. With a VAR, one needs to specify only two things: (1) the *variables* (endogenous and exogenous) that are believed to interact and that hence should be included as part of the economic system one is trying to model and (2) the *largest number of lags* needed to capture most of the effects that the variables have on each other.[14] (For example, if one is modeling the dynamic behavior of a commodity market, the relevant endogenous variables might be price, production, and inventory levels, and the relevant exogenous variables might include aggregate income, the weather, etc. With monthly data, lags up to 6 or 12 months are likely to be sufficient.) The equations of the model are constrained to be linear, and so one need not worry about functional forms.

Letting $x_1, x_2, \ldots, x_n$ be the endogenous variables and $z_1, \ldots, z_m$ be the exogenous variables, a VAR is given by the following set of n linear equations:[15]

$$x_{1,t} = a_{10} + \sum_{j=1}^{p} a_{11j} x_{1,t-j} + \sum_{j=1}^{p} a_{12j} x_{2,t-j} + \cdots + \sum_{j=1}^{p} a_{1nj} x_{n,t-j}$$

$$+ \sum_{j=0}^{r} b_{11j} z_{1,t-1} + \cdots + \sum_{j=0}^{r} b_{1mj} z_{m,t-j} + \varepsilon_{1t}$$

.

.

.   (13.22)

$$x_{n,t} = a_{n0} + \sum_{j=1}^{p} a_{n1j} x_{1,t-j} + \sum_{j=1}^{p} a_{n2j} x_{2,t-j} + \cdots + \sum_{j=1}^{p} a_{nnj} x_{n,t-j}$$

$$+ \sum_{j=0}^{r} b_{n1j} z_{1,t-1} + \cdots + \sum_{j=0}^{r} b_{nmj} z_{m,t-j} + \varepsilon_{nt}$$

[13] Vector autoregressions were introduced as an alternative approach to multi-equation modeling through the work of Sims. See C. A. Sims, "Macroeconomics and Reality," *Econometrica*, vol. 48, pp. 1–48, 1980.

[14] In VARs as formulated by Sims, *all* the variables are assumed to be endogenous. Specifying some of the variables to be exogenous introduces restrictions on the model, because such variables will be able to affect the endogenous variables only directly, not indirectly through feedback from the endogenous variables themselves. A purist would argue that restrictions of this kind are an unwarranted imposition of the modeler's theoretical biases and prevent the data from speaking freely. There is nothing, of course, to prevent one from making all the variables endogenous.

[15] Equation (13.22) can be written much more compactly using matrix notation:

$$\mathbf{x}_t = \mathbf{A}_0 + \mathbf{A}_1 \mathbf{x}_{t-1} + \cdots + \mathbf{A}_p \mathbf{x}_{t-p} + \mathbf{B}_0 \mathbf{z}_t + \mathbf{B}_1 \mathbf{z}_{t-1} + \cdots + \mathbf{B}_r \mathbf{z}_{t-r} + \varepsilon_t$$

where $\mathbf{A}_0$ is an $n \times 1$ vector of intercept terms, $\mathbf{A}_1, \ldots, \mathbf{A}_p$ are $n \times n$ matrices of coefficients that relate lagged values of the endogenous variables to current values of those variables, $\mathbf{B}_0, \ldots, \mathbf{B}_r$ are $n \times m$ matrices of coefficients that relate current and lagged values of the exogenous variables to current values of the endogenous variables, and ε_t is an $n \times 1$ vector of error terms.

Here, p is the number of lags for the endogenous variables and r is the number of lags for the exogenous variables. This model can be estimated by OLS. Since there are no unlagged endogenous variables on the right-hand side and since the right-hand-side variables are the same in each equation, OLS is a consistent and efficient estimator. There would be no gain, for example, from using seemingly unrelated regression estimation.

In choosing p and r, one wants lags long enough to fully capture the dynamics of the system being modeled. On the other hand, the longer the lags, the greater the number of parameters that must be estimated and the fewer the degrees of freedom. [Note that in the equations above there are a total of $n(1 + np + rm)$ parameters. Even with no exogenous variables, if $n = 4$ and $p = 12$, we would have 196 parameters to estimate!] Generally, one must trade off having a sufficient number of lags and having a sufficient number of free parameters. Indeed, this is a weakness of VARs. In practice, one often finds it necessary to constrain the number of lags to be less than what is ideal given the nature of the dynamics. As a result, one can end up having to do just what VARs were intended to avoid—imposing *a priori* (and often ad hoc) structural restrictions on the model.

In our discussion of distributed lag models in Chapter 9 we saw that the determination of the number of lags can be aided by the use of the *corrected R^2*, or the *Akaike information criterion* (AIC). Recall that the AIC is given by

$$\text{AIC} = \log\left(\frac{\Sigma \hat{\varepsilon}_i^2}{N}\right) + \frac{2k}{N}$$

where $\Sigma \hat{\varepsilon}_i^2$ is the sum of squared residuals.

Both the corrected R^2 and the AIC are measures of goodness of fit that correct for the loss of degrees of freedom that results when additional lags are added to a model. These statistics can be used to help determine the number of lags to include in a VAR. Indeed, in many applications of VARs the Akaike information criterion is used as an "objective" way to determine the number of lags to be included.

Example 13.1 Modeling the Dynamics of the Heating Oil Market   Home heating oil is an actively traded commodity in the United States. Because unexpected changes in the weather can have a substantial impact on demand and because the price of crude oil (from which heating oil is made) is volatile, the price of heating oil often fluctuates dramatically.

Suppose one wanted to develop a model of the heating oil market that could be used to forecast prices. One could specify and estimate a structural model that described the dynamics of demand, supply, and inventory holdings, but such a model is likely to be complicated and is unlikely to yield tight forecasts of price, given the uncertainty over future weather patterns and crude oil prices. A vector autoregression provides a much simpler way of modeling the dynamics of this market.

TABLE 13.4
VAR PARAMETER ESTIMATES*

Explanatory variable	Dependent variable, PHO	Dependent variable, QHO	Dependent variable, NHO
PHO_{-1}	.7248 (6.10)	.3041 (3.33)	.4863 (3.46)
PHO_{-2}	.3591 (2.27)	−.2988 (−2.46)	−.2416 (−1.29)
PHO_{-3}	−.3348 (−1.99)	.0062 (.05)	.0320 (.16)
PHO_{-4}	.0633 (.37)	.0536 (.41)	−.2464 (−1.22)
PHO_{-5}	−.0650 (−.39)	−.1256 (−.97)	−.1125 (−.56)
PHO_{-6}	−.0332 (−.20)	−.0629 (−.50)	−.0083 (.04)
PHO_{-7}	.0639 (.42)	−.0106 (−.09)	.1988 (1.10)
PHO_{-8}	.0680 (.61)	.1012 (1.18)	.0282 (.21)
QHO_{-1}	−.0266 (−.18)	.6691 (5.97)	.3880 (2.25)
QHO_{-2}	−.3933 (−2.27)	−.2514 (−1.89)	−.5611 (−2.73)
QHO_{-3}	.0231 (.12)	.1895 (1.26)	.1738 (.75)
QHO_{-4}	.2952 (1.54)	−.0222 (−.15)	.3507 (1.55)
QHO_{-5}	−.2525 (−1.27)	.0576 (.38)	−.0042 (−.02)
QHO_{-6}	−.0163 (−.08)	.0235 (.16)	.2533 (1.09)
QHO_{-7}	−.1017 (−.55)	.2004 (1.40)	.2008 (.91)
QHO_{-8}	−.0291 (−.21)	−.2425 (−2.29)	−.0277 (−.17)
NHO_{-1}	−.1901 (−1.94)	.1112 (1.48)	1.2454 (10.77)
NHO_{-2}	.5132 (3.41)	−.2447 (−2.12)	−.3376 (−1.90)
NHO_{-3}	−.2751 (−1.65)	.0339 (.27)	.0915 (.46)
NHO_{-4}	−.1640 (−.96)	.2161 (1.65)	−.2226 (−1.11)
NHO_{-5}	.2210 (1.27)	−.1608 (−1.21)	−.0406 (−.20)
NHO_{-6}	−.0315 (−.18)	.0074 (.06)	.0251 (.12)
NHO_{-7}	−.0509 (−.30)	−.1331 (−1.01)	−.1287 (−.63)
NHO_{-8}	.0533 (.52)	.1486 (1.87)	.2947 (2.41)
GIP	30.95 (.40)	−23.80 (−.40)	106.57 (1.16)
Constant	40.46 (2.37)	36.13 (2.75)	−63.83 (−3.16)
R^2	.924	.692	.972
DW	2.02	2.09	2.19
s	5.890	4.521	6.967
ESS	2,636	1,553	3,689

* t statistics are in parentheses.

As an example of a VAR, we will relate three endogenous variables to each other: heating oil price (PHO), production (QHO), and inventory (NHO). We will use monthly data covering the period January 1980 through June 1988. (The actual data, which are printed in Table 13.6, at the end of this chapter, begin in January 1979, so as to allow for lags in the model.) We will set the number of lags p at 8. We will also include one exogenous variable—the rate of growth of the Index of Industrial Production (GIP)—unlagged.[16]

---

[16] This is an extremely crude model and is designed only to show how a VAR is estimated and analyzed. Note that for forecasting, the rate of growth of the Index of Industrial Production would itself have to be forecasted, perhaps using a macroeconomic model.

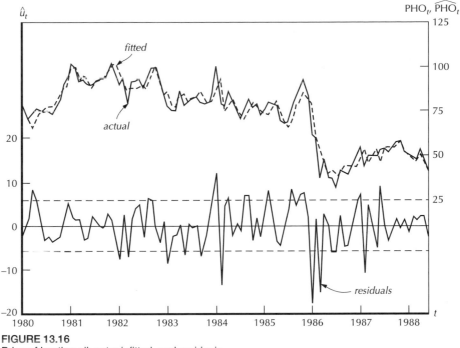

FIGURE 13.16
Price of heating oil: actual, fitted, and residuals.

Because each of the three equations in this VAR contains the same right-hand-side variables, OLS is an efficient estimator. The results of estimating these equations by OLS are shown in Table 13.4. Note that only about a quarter of the lagged variables are significant in each equation. This is typical of a VAR; rather than choose specific lags for each variable, we simply include all the lags (up to eight) for each variable. The exogenous variable GIP is insignificant in all three equations, and so this variable could just as well have been left out of the model. (Or we might have included lags of this variable and introduced alternative exogenous variables, such as the price of crude oil.) Nonetheless, we will work with the model as it stands.

Figure 13.16 shows the actual and fitted values, as well as the residuals, for the price equation. This suggests a good fit, but note that this is not a dynamic simulation; i.e., the actual values of lagged price, production, and inventory are used to calculate the fitted price for each period. A better measure of fit is obtained from a dynamic simulation of all three equations. Figure 13.17 shows the results of such a simulation for the price variable. Observe that the simulated price tracks the actual price for the first 6 months or so but afterward captures only the trend in the actual price and almost none of the short-run fluctuations. This is typical for a VAR, and we would expect the model to be useful only for short-term forecasting. Figures 13.18

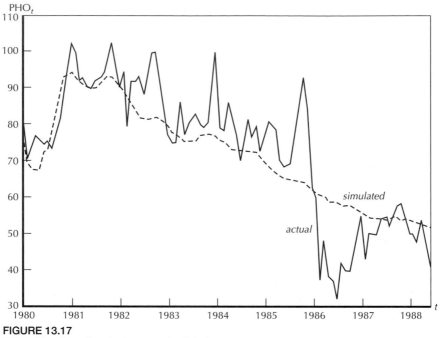

FIGURE 13.17
Price of heating oil: actual versus simulated.

FIGURE 13.18
Price of heating oil: actual versus forecast.

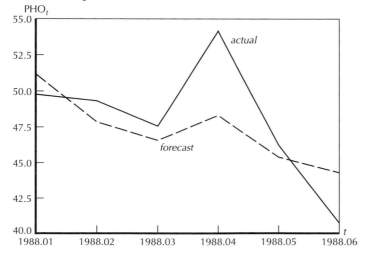

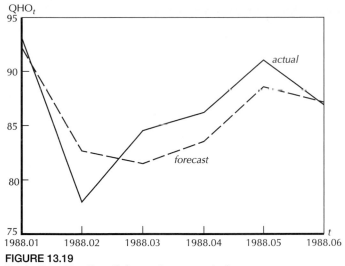

FIGURE 13.19
Production of heating oil: forecast versus actual.

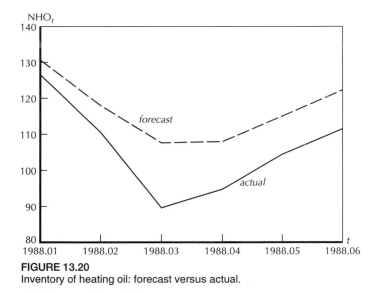

FIGURE 13.20
Inventory of heating oil: forecast versus actual.

through 13.20 show within-sample forecasts of price, production, and inventory for the first 6 months of 1988. Here the model does a better job of capturing the turning points in the data.

13.6   MODELING WITH LIMITED DATA

Our discussion of multi-equation simulation models has focused largely on econometric models. One of the criteria we used to judge or evaluate a simulation model was the degree of statistical fit of the model's individual equations. We said that if the model contained several equations that did not fit the data well or were otherwise statistically insignificant, we might question the validity of the model as a whole. However, this does not mean that econometric estimation is essential to the construction of a simulation model. There are other approaches to modeling.

One important application of multi-equation simulation is in corporate financial planning. In a financial simulation model the equations describe the financial accounting structure of a particular corporation, together with some decision rules that describe dividend payouts, bond issues, etc. Since all the equations are accounting relationships or decision rules (as opposed to behavioral relationships), the model consists of a set of identities and there is no estimation involved. Financial simulation models can be useful for forecasting and analyzing the impact of alternative financial strategies on a company's development. By simulating such a model into the future using different assumptions about capitalization, debt, future revenue streams, etc., one can generate *pro forma* balance sheets and income statements that can provide a useful input for corporate planning.[17]

There may be other situations in which a simulation model is constructed without the use of econometric estimation. Suppose one wanted to construct a model to be simulated over a very long time horizon, perhaps 100 years. Such a model might be used to explain long-run economic growth, changes in population and fertility rates, or some other economic, social, or political process which evolves slowly over a long period. Data might not exist for many of the variables in such a model. One reason for this might be that some of the variables are unobservable and thus unmeasurable; an example would be some attitudinal parameters in a sociological model. On the other hand, the variable may be observable, but perhaps data have never been collected, as is often the case in less-developed countries. Finally, data may be available, but only for a short time period, say 10 or 20 years. Even if the data were used to estimate the coefficients of the model, the resulting estimates might have limited meaning when the model was simulated over a long period.

In this situation the model builder could begin by specifying a set of hypothetical relationships. In the case of an econometric model, those relationships would be estimated and tested by fitting them to available data. If data were not available, one could specify values for the coefficients on the basis of averages, sporadic data points, or perhaps the opinion of "experts."

One of the problems of this modeling technique is that it provides no check on the reasonableness of the individual relationships that make up the model.

---

[17] For an example of a financial simulation model, see J. M. Warren and J. P. Shelton, "A Simultaneous Equation Approach to Financial Planning," *Journal of Finance*, December 1971.

Since the model builder is free to pick the coefficient values instead of fitting them to data, it becomes possible to adjust the coefficients until the model succeeds in reproducing the historical data. In such a case the model may appear to simulate well even though the relationships that go into it are largely invalid, so that the model itself is invalid in terms of its forecasts or policy implications.

Anyone who has constructed an econometric model knows that fitting hypothetical relationships to actual data provides an important check on model builders, forcing them to test statistically each of the originally specified relationships. This check is missing in the dataless approach to modeling, so this approach should be used only with great caution.[18]

Simulation models have found acceptance and application in a wide variety of social science disciplines. Sociological and political simulation models have been constructed by combining econometric estimation methods with the dataless techniques described above. In some cases these modeling efforts have resulted in methodological advances for dealing with situations when data are limited or unreliable. Although the perspective of this book is largely limited to econometric models of the economy, individual markets, and individual firms, the reader should be aware that the applicability of the techniques we are presenting is quite broad.

EXERCISES

13.1 The rms simulation error penalizes heavily for large individual errors. In what cases is it a more or less desirable performance criterion than the mean absolute error (MAE), which is defined as

$$\text{MAE} = \frac{1}{T} \sum_{t=1}^{T} \frac{|Y_t^s - Y_t^a|}{Y_t^a}$$

13.2 The mean error may be small even though the rms error is large if positive and negative errors cancel. In what situation does the mean error provide useful information for evaluating a model that is not provided by the rms error?

13.3 Two sets of actual and predicted series are shown below. Note that the series in the second set are equal to the first set increased by 100.

t	x_t^a	x_t^s	y_t^a	y_t^s
1	-3	-1	97	99
2	5	7	105	107
3	10	7	110	107
4	-4	-1	96	99

[18] One of the more prominent proponents of the dataless approach to modeling has been J. W. Forrester, who has constructed models of, among other things, the dynamics of urban growth and world resource usage. See J. W. Forrester, *Urban Dynamics* (Cambridge, Mass.: M.I.T. Press, 1969); J. W. Forrester, *World Dynamics* (Cambridge, Mass.: Wright-Allen, 1971); and D. Meadows et al., *The Limits to Growth* (Cambridge, Mass.: Wright-Allen, 1972). Forrester's work has been criticized because many of the relationships used in his models have not been substantiated or validated; see, for example, W. D. Nordhaus, "World Dynamics: Measurement without Data," *Economic Journal*, vol. 26, December 1974.

Calculate the rms simulation errors and Theil inequality coefficients for the two variables x_t and y_t. Decompose the inequality coefficients into the proportions U^M, U^S, and U^C and interpret the results.

13.4 Reexamine the historical simulation of the four-equation macroeconometric model in Figs. 13.6 to 13.9. Based on this historical simulation (and the model itself) explain why the *ex post* forecast (Figs. 13.10 to 13.13) overpredicts GNP.

13.5 Specify, estimate, and simulate your own macroeconometric model. Use the data set in Table 13.5. [Equations (13.14) to (13.17) could be used as a starting point.] Produce *ex post* and *ex ante* forecasts and evaluate those forecasts. If possible, experiment with alternative estimation techniques. Attempt to improve on the performance of the four-equation model in the text. (The experience gained in this kind of exercise is invaluable in learning the art of model building.)

13.6 Consider a system of ε equations. Prove that if each of the ε equations has exactly the same set of variables on the right-hand side (including the same number of lags), seemingly unrelated estimation yields the same coefficient estimates as does OLS.

13.7 As you might expect, the demand for heating oil has a strong seasonal component. As a result, a model of the heating oil market (whether structural or a VAR) is likely to perform better if it includes seasonal dummy variables. Using the data set that appears in Table 13.6, construct a VAR for heating oil price, production, and inventory that includes monthly dummy variables for the intercept terms in each of the three equations. Also, experiment with different numbers of lags. To what extent do forecasts of the three endogenous variables change if the number of lags is extended from, say, 8 to 12 months?

TABLE 13.5
MACROECONOMIC DATA SET

Obs.	C	I	R	GNP	G	M
1950-1	711.9	201.9	1.117	1139.7	225.9	449.5
1950-2	725.8	226.1	1.166	1173.3	221.4	453.7
1950-3	754.8	241.6	1.232	1226.0	229.6	450.3
1950-4	740.5	270.3	1.353	1257.2	246.4	445.0
1951-1	754.4	241.6	1.400	1281.9	285.9	432.8
1951-2	740.3	249.0	1.532	1307.6	318.3	433.0
1951-3	747.8	233.8	1.627	1329.6	348.0	439.1
1951-4	752.3	216.2	1.649	1335.3	366.8	439.4
1952-1	754.7	219.9	1.640	1351.7	377.1	442.5
1952-2	768.1	199.9	1.677	1355.6	387.6	445.7
1952-3	772.7	206.6	1.828	1376.0	396.7	447.6
1952-4	790.0	220.8	1.923	1409.1	398.3	452.1
1953-1	799.8	222.3	2.047	1434.0	411.9	453.8
1953-2	803.7	225.1	2.202	1449.0	420.2	455.1
1953-3	803.1	217.4	2.021	1440.9	420.4	455.3
1953-4	803.3	201.5	1.486	1428.3	423.5	454.0
1954-1	807.1	203.2	1.083	1407.7	397.4	450.9
1954-2	814.3	206.4	.814	1399.7	379.0	453.0
1954-3	827.3	215.0	.869	1414.7	372.4	459.1
1954-4	842.3	225.7	1.036	1432.9	364.9	464.6
1955-1	855.3	245.1	1.256	1465.2	364.8	469.6
1955-2	869.1	260.8	1.514	1488.2	358.3	473.0
1955-3	878.0	264.3	1.861	1505.5	363.2	474.6

TABLE 13.5
MACROECONOMIC DATA SET (*Continued*)

Obs.	C	I	R	GNP	G	M
1955-4	892.7	268.9	2.349	1520.6	359.0	474.2
1956-1	895.1	262.1	2.379	1517.2	360.0	475.4
1956-2	896.5	258.3	2.596	1519.7	364.9	472.9
1956-3	899.2	257.1	2.596	1518.7	362.4	468.7
1956-4	908.4	253.8	3.063	1529.8	367.6	467.5
1957-1	914.3	248.6	3.171	1542.3	379.4	464.6
1957-2	916.2	245.3	3.157	1543.1	381.6	461.1
1957-3	922.6	249.2	3.382	1553.9	382.1	457.0
1957-4	925.7	230.3	3.343	1537.2	381.2	453.0
1958-1	916.5	210.9	1.838	1513.9	386.5	447.4
1958-2	926.0	206.2	1.017	1524.9	392.7	449.6
1958-3	939.7	222.2	1.710	1559.0	397.1	454.2
1958-4	949.4	246.4	2.787	1600.5	404.7	458.5
1959-1	964.3	261.7	2.800	1625.3	399.3	464.0
1959-2	977.2	283.1	3.019	1659.1	398.8	466.3
1959-3	986.3	262.4	3.533	1645.8	397.1	467.1
1959-4	989.6	274.1	4.299	1659.0	395.3	460.0
1960-1	997.1	288.7	3.943	1681.0	395.2	459.2
1960-2	1009.8	261.4	3.092	1673.8	402.6	455.7
1960-3	1005.7	258.3	2.390	1670.8	406.8	459.4
1960-4	1007.8	233.6	2.360	1651.5	410.1	455.8
1961-1	1009.5	238.3	2.376	1667.5	419.7	458.0
1961-2	1023.5	249.1	2.324	1695.0	422.4	461.5
1961-3	1024.6	270.5	2.324	1721.8	426.7	462.2
1961-4	1042.9	278.4	2.475	1760.9	439.6	465.4
1962-1	1053.6	287.7	2.739	1787.3	446.0	467.3
1962-2	1063.6	291.2	2.716	1801.7	446.9	468.4
1962-3	1072.8	294.7	2.858	1819.6	452.1	466.4
1962-4	1085.8	280.7	2.803	1819.1	452.6	467.7
1963-1	1094.1	291.9	2.909	1841.2	455.2	471.9
1963-2	1100.2	306.9	2.941	1861.5	454.4	474.8
1963-3	1115.5	315.6	3.280	1895.2	464.1	477.6
1963-4	1123.6	314.0	3.499	1903.1	465.5	479.8
1964-1	1145.2	324.7	3.538	1939.1	469.2	481.8
1964-2	1164.4	323.6	3.481	1960.7	472.7	484.7
1964-3	1184.8	324.5	3.504	1979.6	470.3	491.3
1964-4	1188.0	330.8	3.685	1989.9	471.1	495.5
1965-1	1208.2	362.1	3.899	2039.9	469.6	498.2
1965-2	1221.7	364.3	3.879	2066.8	480.8	497.6
1965-3	1242.3	369.9	3.859	2103.7	491.5	501.7
1965-4	1273.2	371.8	4.158	2150.8	505.8	507.8
1966-1	1287.6	396.9	4.630	2198.0	513.5	511.8
1966-2	1293.1	390.9	4.597	2207.4	523.4	511.8
1966-3	1305.5	389.1	5.047	2236.5	541.9	506.2
1966-4	1309.5	385.2	5.246	2246.4	551.7	503.1
1967-1	1319.4	368.7	4.533	2257.3	569.2	507.1
1967-2	1336.5	361.7	3.657	2271.3	573.1	510.7
1967-3	1343.3	378.8	4.344	2301.2	579.1	518.0
1967-4	1351.5	388.4	4.787	2323.1	583.2	521.3
1968-1	1378.1	387.7	5.064	2355.9	590.1	521.9

TABLE 13.5
MACROECONOMIC DATA SET (*Continued*)

Obs.	C	I	R	GNP	G	M
1968-2	1396.7	397.2	5.510	2394.4	600.5	525.4
1968-3	1421.5	392.0	5.226	2414.5	601.0	528.3
1968-4	1427.1	390.2	5.580	2416.3	599.0	533.7
1969-1	1442.9	412.0	6.137	2448.1	593.2	536.5
1969-2	1451.7	409.1	6.240	2456.8	596.0	532.7
1969-3	1459.9	419.5	7.046	2469.8	590.4	527.6
1969-4	1472.0	400.5	7.317	2457.8	585.3	523.2
1970-1	1481.5	379.9	7.262	2440.0	578.6	521.4
1970-2	1488.1	376.4	6.752	2434.2	569.7	518.0
1970-3	1501.3	390.6	6.374	2463.5	571.6	519.3
1970-4	1497.2	379.3	5.358	2447.1	570.6	521.2
1971-1	1520.9	415.5	3.863	2504.0	567.6	524.7
1971-2	1533.0	423.1	4.206	2520.1	564.0	530.8
1971-3	1541.0	425.9	5.050	2533.8	566.9	534.1
1971-4	1560.1	412.8	4.234	2540.3	567.4	536.5
1972-1	1581.8	439.5	3.435	2597.7	576.4	542.5
1972-2	1607.9	462.3	3.748	2644.3	574.1	547.7
1972-3	1629.8	473.8	4.241	2669.8	566.1	554.3
1972-4	1667.8	486.0	4.851	2719.9	566.1	562.5
1973-1	1689.9	515.7	5.639	2778.1	572.5	565.2
1973-2	1687.2	521.7	6.608	2777.5	568.6	560.0
1973-3	1694.5	511.4	8.388	2761.7	555.8	556.1
1973-4	1686.8	534.2	7.461	2785.2	564.2	548.4
1974-1	1667.5	501.1	7.600	2736.4	567.8	542.1
1974-2	1677.2	496.5	8.268	2753.9	580.2	532.8
1974-3	1686.7	465.5	8.286	2724.8	572.6	522.7
1974-4	1664.7	462.2	7.336	2699.0	572.1	511.9
1975-1	1677.1	370.6	5.873	2625.2	577.5	505.2
1975-2	1706.0	358.1	5.400	2641.3	577.2	506.7
1975-3	1723.9	394.4	6.336	2700.4	582.1	505.4
1975-4	1740.4	410.1	5.684	2737.3	586.8	500.9
1976-1	1777.5	444.7	4.953	2804.6	582.4	502.2
1976-2	1790.4	454.9	5.168	2825.6	580.3	505.5
1976-3	1809.9	452.8	5.168	2842.1	579.4	502.6
1976-4	1837.8	461.8	4.698	2878.6	579.0	505.3
1977-1	1863.7	492.0	4.624	2935.9	580.2	508.1
1977-2	1869.0	519.0	4.828	2975.5	587.5	507.7
1977-3	1888.0	546.9	5.472	3029.8	594.9	509.4
1977-4	1914.2	527.2	6.137	3035.0	593.6	513.0
1978-1	1923.0	544.0	6.408	3059.5	592.5	513.6
1978-2	1960.8	584.6	6.481	3146.7	601.3	514.1
1978-3	1970.3	583.3	7.315	3165.1	611.5	512.5
1978-4	1989.7	595.8	8.680	3196.6	611.1	509.6
1979-1	1997.5	582.2	9.357	3186.4	606.7	503.3
1979-2	1994.1	590.1	9.372	3191.1	606.9	496.1
1979-3	2007.9	575.7	9.631	3194.9	611.3	497.2
1979-4	2018.0	552.9	11.804	3182.6	611.7	487.6
1980-1	2015.4	556.7	13.459	3189.9	617.8	473.9
1980-2	1974.1	499.2	10.049	3098.4	625.1	451.1
1980-3	1996.3	467.7	9.235	3085.1	621.1	464.9

TABLE 13.5
MACROECONOMIC DATA SET (*Continued*)

Obs.	C	I	R	GNP	G	M
1980-4	2015.6	513.5	13.709	3147.0	617.9	465.3
1981-1	2022.9	552.3	14.369	3201.5	626.3	455.3
1981-2	2022.4	551.2	14.829	3200.0	626.4	453.7
1981-3	2031.5	560.7	15.087	3222.4	630.2	448.9
1081 4	2020.0	517.9	12.023	3173.8	635.9	447.1
1982-1	2031.2	464.2	12.895	3130.0	634.6	451.2
1982-2	2041.0	467.5	12.359	3138.2	629.7	447.1
1982-3	2051.8	448.6	9.705	3142.9	642.5	449.1
1982-4	2078.7	408.8	7.935	3147.6	660.1	464.9
1983-1	2094.2	427.1	8.081	3170.5	649.2	475.8
1983-2	2135.1	486.9	8.419	3272.9	650.9	484.3
1983-3	2163.0	524.8	9.186	3341.4	653.6	493.6
1983-4	2191.9	577.2	8.793	3411.3	642.2	496.4
1984-1	2212.1	655.2	9.133	3520.3	653.0	497.4
1984-2	2246.7	658.4	9.843	3585.3	680.2	500.4
1984-3	2257.3	664.2	10.343	3606.0	684.5	501.5
1984-4	2281.1	655.7	8.973	3630.0	693.2	502.1
1985-1	2314.1	632.1	8.183	3649.6	703.4	510.9
1985-2	2337.0	645.7	7.523	3694.8	712.1	518.1
1985-3	2376.1	623.2	7.103	3737.9	738.6	533.8
1985-4	2383.2	643.3	7.146	3780.2	753.7	543.2
1986-1	2409.7	674.4	6.886	3821.7	737.6	553.4
1986-2	2434.3	665.6	6.130	3851.5	751.6	576.7
1986-3	2477.5	645.0	5.533	3879.7	757.2	598.0
1986-4	2480.5	631.0	5.340	3883.3	771.8	620.0
1987-1	2475.9	671.8	5.533	3907.3	759.6	631.8
1987-2	2487.5	673.7	5.733	3927.9	766.7	634.8
1987-3	2520.7	681.9	6.033	3974.3	771.7	630.1
1987-4	2504.6	723.1	6.003	4016.6	788.9	630.5
1988-1	2527.9	741.8	5.760	4035.7	766.0	631.5

TABLE 13.6
HEATING OIL DATA SET

Obs.	Price	Production	Stocks	Obs.	Price	Production	Stocks
1979-01	53.08	94.33	175	1980-02	71.07	80.21	192
1979-02	62.67	80.86	127	1980-03	74.42	79.29	178
1979-03	60.01	93.58	112	1980-04	77.20	73.83	177
1979-04	57.82	88.35	115	1980-05	75.75	76.69	183
1979-05	99.50	95.04	123	1980-06	74.89	79.41	197
1979-06	88.01	94.59	141	1980-07	75.74	83.39	214
1979-07	76.76	102.42	171	1980-08	73.80	76.32	226
1979-08	74.72	102.96	195	1980-09	77.21	80.58	232
1979-09	81.17	100.60	220	1980-10	81.16	80.29	226
1979-10	83.52	100.70	231	1980-11	90.33	81.09	222
1979-11	88.51	97.17	236	1980-12	94.49	89.62	205
1979-12	79.67	99.85	228	1981-01	102.61	92.65	179
1980-01	77.26	93.43	212	1981-02	99.90	78.65	173

TABLE 13.6
HEATING OIL DATA SET (*Continued*)

Obs.	Price	Production	Stocks	Obs.	Price	Production	Stocks
1981-03	92.04	77.00	164	1984-11	79.31	84.78	161
1981-04	92.88	72.54	165	1984-12	72.68	86.73	161
1981-05	90.21	76.07	172	1985-01	75.95	81.56	142
1981-06	90.11	75.03	180	1985-02	80.60	70.11	121
1981-07	92.13	74.24	186	1985-03	79.39	70.27	99
1981-08	92.77	82.33	200	1985-04	78.42	74.70	97
1981-09	94.07	78.30	207	1985-05	70.30	83.26	104
1981-10	98.39	77.03	201	1985-06	68.30	79.41	110
1981-11	102.54	81.48	200	1985-07	68.94	82.02	116
1981-12	98.27	88.53	192	1985-08	76.96	80.35	114
1982-01	89.75	80.32	164	1985-09	82.53	77.82	117
1982-02	94.47	67.95	147	1985-10	87.40	89.96	123
1982-03	79.66	70.92	126	1985-11	93.19	93.06	140
1982-04	91.89	70.74	108	1985-12	84.40	98.45	144
1982-05	91.79	81.15	114	1986-01	61.97	89.86	136
1982-06	93.39	81.87	124	1986-02	59.95	71.76	112
1982-07	88.13	84.75	148	1986-03	37.04	81.93	99
1982-08	93.33	77.71	159	1986-04	48.32	83.64	96
1982-09	99.57	79.71	161	1986-05	37.99	88.59	99
1982-10	99.35	87.97	170	1986-06	36.85	81.87	108
1982-11	89.86	85.80	186	1986-07	31.77	84.01	119
1982-12	83.38	82.30	179	1986-08	42.05	90.58	138
1983-01	77.57	71.95	168	1986-09	39.88	85.95	152
1983-02	75.04	59.78	148	1986-10	39.32	84.22	152
1983-03	74.83	61.78	118	1986-11	43.27	87.51	158
1983-04	86.56	65.13	103	1986-12	48.40	91.23	155
1983-05	77.51	75.76	109	1987-01	55.03	85.99	141
1983-06	80.03	76.38	114	1987-02	43.25	72.07	124
1983-07	81.72	80.72	131	1987-03	50.02	73.90	110
1983-08	83.38	81.06	142	1987-04	49.82	76.59	100
1983-09	80.11	82.17	154	1987-05	49.51	79.51	102
1983-10	78.91	83.11	163	1987-06	53.43	80.67	104
1983-11	80.40	80.40	161	1987-07	53.95	83.70	115
1983-12	86.82	78.18	140	1987-08	51.66	84.04	125
1984-01	99.87	80.32	119	1987-09	53.52	82.50	127
1984-02	79.29	83.14	132	1987-10	57.59	86.11	121
1984-03	78.22	76.84	110	1987-11	58.16	91.29	129
1984-04	86.13	70.26	98	1987-12	53.40	100.42	134
1984-05	80.07	81.34	98	1988-01	49.81	93.24	127
1984-06	76.66	86.40	113	1988-02	49.37	77.80	110
1984-07	70.38	84.28	124	1988-03	47.58	84.32	89
1984-08	77.33	82.49	133	1988-04	54.02	86.07	94
1984-09	81.47	81.21	143	1988-05	46.31	90.86	104
1984-10	76.58	83.42	152	1988-06	40.52	86.79	111

CHAPTER 14

DYNAMIC BEHAVIOR OF SIMULATION MODELS

In this chapter we focus on the dynamic behavior of multi-equation simulation models. Since a simulation model is a set of difference equations that can be solved simultaneously through time, we are interested in the properties of difference-equation solutions. We want to know, for example, what makes the solution to a difference equation (or set of difference equations) oscillate, since oscillatory behavior is important in a model designed to explain (or forecast) cyclical market phenomena. We begin, then, by reviewing difference equations and their solutions.

Simulation models often are used to study and compare the short-run and long-run responses of one variable to another variable. The second section of this chapter deals with *dynamic multipliers* and dynamic response. We may know, for example, that a change in price may result in a change in demand for some good, but how long does it take for that change in demand to occur? We know that an increase in government spending results in an increase in GNP with a multiplier effect, but the size of that multiplier depends on how much time elapses after the level of government spending is increased. By discussing dynamic multipliers and dynamic elasticities, we will see how simulation models can be used as a tool for analyzing the dynamic response of one set of economic variables to changes in other variables. We will also see, in Section 14.3, how the *impulse response function* can be used to analyze the dynamic behavior of a vector autoregression.

In the fourth section of the chapter we describe how a simulation model can be adjusted to improve its forecasting ability or its ability to provide information about policy alternatives. As we will see, misspecification or biased estimation in one part of a model may cause the whole model to perform poorly in a simulation context.

The chapter closes with a brief discussion of *stochastic simulation*. Since the equations of an econometric model are estimated by fitting them to data, the resulting parameter estimates are themselves random variables. Furthermore, each equation has an implicit additive error term associated with it. Stochastic simulation allows us to recognize this random character of the model explicitly, along with the simulation errors it implies. Stochastic simulation is similarly useful when a model is employed for forecasting, as it allows one to obtain confidence intervals for the forecast.

14.1   MODEL BEHAVIOR: STABILITY AND OSCILLATIONS

The structural richness of a multi-equation simulation model makes it somewhat difficult to build, analyze, evaluate, and use. Life is relatively simple in a single-equation world; a regression equation can easily be evaluated on the basis of its statistical fit and can be directly used to produce a forecast. However, things may not be so simple in the case of a simulation model. Each of the regression equations that make up the model may have an excellent statistical fit, but when they are put together and simulated, the results may be meaningless. The reason for this may be that a *structural instability* was built into the model that appears only when the equations are combined and solved simultaneously.

In this section we present the conditions for determining stability (and oscillations) in simple linear models. In particular, we show how these conditions depend not only on the structure of the model but also on the estimated values of the coefficients of the individual equations. We discuss nonlinear models only briefly, since there is little in the way of analytic tools available for exploring their dynamic properties.

14.1.1   Linear Models

We say that a model is *linear* if all the difference equations that constitute it are linear. Sets of linear difference equations can be solved rather easily, and the determination of whether the system is stable is relatively straightforward. We will begin by demonstrating how one can analyze a linear model to determine whether it is stable and/or oscillatory. We will illustrate the method using as an example the simple three-equation multiplier-accelerator model presented at the beginning of Chapter 13:

$$C_t = a_1 + a_2 Y_{t-1} \qquad\qquad a_2 > 0 \qquad\qquad (14.1)$$

$$I_t = b_1 + b_2(Y_{t-1} - Y_{t-2}) \qquad b_2 > 0 \qquad\qquad (14.2)$$

$$Y_t = C_t + I_t + G_t \qquad\qquad (14.3)$$

where C = consumption
 I = investment
 G = government spending (exogenous)
 Y = GNP

The analysis begins by combining the three equations into a *single* difference equation, which we call the *fundamental dynamic equation*. Substituting Eqs. (14.1) and (14.2) into Eq. (14.3), we have as our fundamental dynamic equation the following second-order difference equation for Y_t:

$$Y_t - (a_2 + b_2)Y_{t-1} + b_2Y_{t-2} = (a_1 + b_1) + G_t \qquad (14.4)$$

We are interested in determining if and how the endogenous variable Y_t reaches a new equilibrium value in response to a change in the exogenous variable G_t. In other words, if at time $t = 0$, G_t increases by 1 and then *remains fixed at that higher level*, what will happen to Y_t over all future time? We are thus interested in the pattern by which Y_t reaches a new equilibrium value (if indeed it does reach a new equilibrium value). This pattern, which is called the *transient solution* for Y_t, is found by setting the right-hand side of the fundamental dynamic equation equal to 0:

$$Y_t - (a_2 + b_2)Y_{t-1} + b_2Y_{t-2} = 0 \qquad (14.5)$$

and then *assuming* the solution of this equation to be of the form

$$Y_t = A\lambda^t \qquad (14.6)$$

If Eq. (14.6) is a solution, it should satisfy Eq. (14.5). Substituting Eq. (14.6) into Eq. (14.5) and dividing through the equation by $A\lambda^{t-2}$, we obtain the *characteristic equation* for our model:

$$\lambda^2 - (a_2 + b_2)\lambda + b_2 = 0 \qquad (14.7)$$

The solutions to the characteristic equation, which are called the *characteristic roots* of the model, determine the solution properties of the model. In our example the characteristic equation is quadratic, and so the characteristic roots are easy to find:

$$\lambda_1, \lambda_2 = \frac{(a_2 + b_2) \pm \sqrt{(a_2 + b_2)^2 - 4b_2}}{2} \qquad (14.8)$$

We now have two solutions to our model, $Y_t = A_1\lambda_1^t$ and $Y_t = A_2\lambda_2^t$, where A_1 and A_2 are constants that depend on the initial value that Y_t happens to take. We had assumed that the solutions were of the form $A\lambda^t$, but since λ_1 and λ_2 both satisfy the characteristic equation, we can verify that $A_1\lambda_1^t$ and $A_2\lambda_2^t$ are indeed solutions. If we substitute $A_1\lambda_1^t$ for Y_t in Eq. (14.5), we will obtain the characteristic equation in terms of λ_1, and since λ_1 is known to be a solution to the characteristic equation, we can be sure that $A_1\lambda_1^t$ is a solution. In fact, it is easy to see that if $A_1\lambda_1^t$ and $A_2\lambda_2^t$ are both solutions to Eq. (14.5), the *sum* $Y_t = A_1\lambda_1^t + A_2\lambda_2^t$ is also a solution. The reader can verify this by substituting $A_1\lambda_1^t + A_2\lambda_2^t$ for Y_t in Eq. (14.5).

Depending on the values of a_2 and b_2, the behavior of the solution can be characterized in four possible ways: (1) The solution may be stable, converging without oscillation. This requires that both λ_1 and λ_2 be less than 1 in magnitude and have no imaginary component. (2) The solution may be stable, converging with dampened oscillations. This occurs if the solutions to the characteristic equation are both less than 1 in magnitude but have imaginary components. (3) The solution may be unstable and nonoscillatory. This results if either of the solutions to the characteristic equation is greater than 1 in magnitude but there is no imaginary component. (4) The solution may be unstable and oscillatory (i.e., it exhibits ever-diverging oscillations). This occurs if one or both of the characteristic roots are greater than 1 in magnitude and there is an imaginary component.

It is easy to see how these conditions on the characteristic roots λ_1 and λ_2 determine the behavior of the model if one remembers that the transient solution to the fundamental dynamic equation is given by

$$Y_t = A_1\lambda_1^t + A_2\lambda_2^t$$

Clearly, if either λ_1 or λ_2 is greater than 1 in magnitude, the solution will grow explosively, and if λ_1 and λ_2 are complex (i.e., have imaginary components), the solution will be sinusoidal (i.e., will oscillate).[1]

The type of solution which results will depend on the values of the two parameters a_2 and b_2. For example, if a_2 and b_2 take on the values .6 and .1, respectively, the characteristic roots are given by

$$\lambda_1, \lambda_2 = \frac{.7 \pm \sqrt{.49 - .4}}{2} = .35 \pm .15$$

Since the largest root has a value of .5 and since neither root has an imaginary component, the solution will be stable and nonoscillatory. If a_2 and b_2 have the values .6 and .8, respectively, the characteristic roots will be

$$\lambda_1, \lambda_2 = \frac{1.4 \pm \sqrt{1.96 - 3.2}}{2} \approx .7 \pm .56i$$

---

[1] If the characteristic roots are complex, they will be of the form $\lambda_1, \lambda_2 = \alpha \pm \beta i$. These complex roots, when substituted into $Y_t = A_1\lambda_1^t + A_2\lambda_2^t$, will result in a solution for Y_t that will be a sinusoidal function of time.

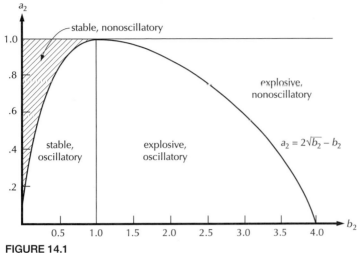

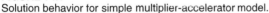

FIGURE 14.1
Solution behavior for simple multiplier-accelerator model.

Now the characteristic roots are both less than 1 in magnitude, but they have an imaginary component, so that the solution will be stable but will oscillate. The reader can see that values of a_2 and b_2 equal to .6 and 1.5, respectively, will result in a solution that is unstable (explosive) and oscillatory, while values of .6 and 3.0 will result in a solution that is unstable and nonoscillatory. In fact, as long as a_2 and b_2 are both less than 1, the solution will be stable, while if either is larger than 1, the solution will be unstable. We can also find an algebraic relationship between a_2 and b_2 that will determine whether the solution is oscillatory. The characteristic roots [see Eq. (14.8)] will have an imaginary component if

$$4b_2 > (a_2 + b_2)^2 \qquad (14.9)$$

or $$a_2 < 2\sqrt{b_2} - b_2 \qquad (14.10)$$

In Fig. 14.1 the plane is divided into regions that indicate the range of parameter values that would result in each of the four types of solutions. The region that indicates the values of a_2 and b_2 that would result in a stable and nonoscillatory solution has been shaded.

In Fig. 14.2 and Table 14.1 we illustrate four solutions for Y_t corresponding to the four pairs of values for a_2 and b_2 from above, that is, $(a_2, b_2) = (.6, .1)$, $(.6, .8)$, $(.6, 1.5)$, and $(.6, 3.0)$. These solutions begin with the initial conditions $C_t = 90$, $I_t = 0$, $G_t = 10$, and $Y_t = 100$. After three periods G_t is increased to 12, and a solution is obtained for the next 30 periods. In each case the values 30 and 0 are used for the parameters a_1 and b_1, respectively.

To obtain the fundamental dynamic equation for our three-equation model

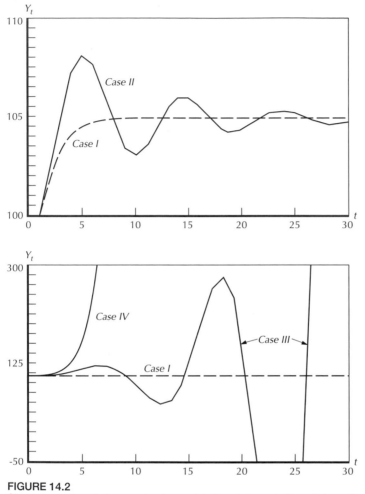

FIGURE 14.2
Simulations of multiplier-accelerator model: Case I: $b_2 = .1$; Case II: $b_2 = .8$;
Case III: $b_2 = 1.5$; Case IV: $b_2 = 3.0$.

(and thus the characteristic equation and characteristic roots), we could have begun by combining the equations of the model for any one endogenous variable. If, for example, we had substituted Eqs. (14.2) and (14.3) into Eq. (14.1) for C_t, we would have the following fundamental dynamic equation in terms of C_t:

$$C_t = a_1 + a_2 C_{t-1} + a_2 b_1 + a_2 b_2 \left(\frac{C_{t-1}}{a_2} - \frac{a_1}{a_2} \right) - a_2 b_2 \left(\frac{C_{t-2}}{a_2} - \frac{a_1}{a_2} \right) + a_2 G_{t-1}$$

$$(14.11)$$

or $$C_t - (a_2 + b_2)C_{t-1} + b_2 C_{t-2} = (a_1 + a_2 b_1) + a_2 G_{t-1} \qquad (14.12)$$

TABLE 14.1
SIMULATIONS OF MULTIPLIER-ACCELERATOR MODEL

t	Case 1 $(b_2 = .1)$	Case II $(b_2 = .8)$	Case III $(b_2 = 1.5)$	Case IV $(b_2 = 3.0)$
0	100	100	100	100
1	100	100	100	100
2	102	102	102	102
3	103.4	104.8	106.2	109.2
4	104.18	107.12	112.02	129.12
5	104.586	108.128	117.942	179.232
6	104.792	107.683	121.648	299.875
7	104.896	106.254	120.548	583.854
8	104.948	104.609	112.679	1,244.25
9	104.974	103.45	97.8034	2,769.74
10	104.987	103.142	78.3680	6,280.3
11	104.993	103.639	59.8696	14,341.9
12	104.997	104.581	50.1727	32,831.8
13	104.998	105.502	57.5584	75,210.9
14	104.999	106.038	87.6135	172,306
15	105	106.052	139.651	394,710
16	105	105.642	203.846	904,080
17	105	105.057	260.601	2.071×10^6
18	105	104.566	283.493	4.742×10^6
19	105	104.347	246.433	1.086×10^7
20	105	104.433	134.27	2.487×10^7
21	105	104.728	-45.6819	5.695×10^7
22	105	105.073	-255.337	1.304×10^8
23	105	105.32	-425.685	2.986×10^8
24	105	105.389	-468.933	6.838×10^8
25	105	105.289	-304.231	1.566×10^9
26	105	105.093	106.513	3.586×10^9
27	105	104.899	722.025	8.210×10^9
28	105	104.784	1,398.48	1.880×10^{10}
29	105	104.779	1,895.77	4.305×10^{10}
30	105	104.863	1,925.4	9.859×10^{10}

It is easy to see that this yields the same characteristic equation as that yielded by Eq. (14.7) and thus the same characteristic roots. The reader can verify that the same characteristic equation would also result if Eqs. (14.1) and (14.3) were substituted into Eq. (14.2) to yield a single fundamental dynamic equation in terms of investment I_t.

Suppose we *estimate* the coefficients of our model and obtain values for a_2 and b_2 that result in an oscillatory (but stable) solution. How should the model then be interpreted? If the oscillations in GNP predicted by the model in a historical simulation bear no resemblance to the actual past behavior of GNP, we should doubt the validity of the model (even if the *individual* equations have good statistical fit). However, if the periodicity and magnitude of the oscillations predicted by the model bear a reasonable resemblance to the actual behavior of the economy, we may conclude that the dynamic structure of the model is representative of that of the actual economy. One might, for example, try to explain the presence of business cycles in the U.S. economy by using a multiplier-accelerator interaction. From Eq. (14.8) a range of values for a_2 and b_2 could be found that would result in oscillations with periodicity close to that observed in business cycles. Statistical tests could then be performed to determine whether data could support values of a_2 and b_2 in that range.

A simple multiplier-accelerator model probably would not suffice to explain the cycles and other fluctuations in the economy. However, the same principles apply for larger and more complicated models.

14.1.2   Analyzing Larger Models

As models become larger, an analysis of their dynamic behavior becomes more difficult and less straightforward. As long as the model remains linear, a characteristic equation can be derived, although a solution to that equation may offer computational problems. Consider, for example, the four-equation macroeconomic model constructed in Chapter 13 [Eqs. (13.14) to (13.17)]. If the equations are combined into a single fundamental dynamic equation for Y, the difference equation will be of the fifth order:

$$Y_t + \alpha_1 Y_{t-1} + \alpha_2 Y_{t-2} + \alpha_3 Y_{t-3} + \alpha_4 Y_{t-4} + \alpha_5 Y_{t-5} = \alpha_6 Z_t \quad (14.13)$$

The characteristic equation will also be fifth order and will have five solutions. A fifth-order equation is harder to solve analytically than is the simple characteristic equation of Eq. (14.7). Thus if the model is large, an analysis of its properties becomes more difficult.

Computer programs can be used to solve characteristic equations of high order. In fact, some of the computer packages that have been written to solve simulation models also provide a solution of the characteristic equation—either directly, if the model is linear, or for a linearization of the model around a particular simulation solution if it is nonlinear. One can thus examine the characteristic roots of a model; those roots which exceed 1 in magnitude will yield instabilities in the model, and those which are complex (i.e., have imaginary components) will contribute to oscillatory behavior.

A large model may have some characteristic roots that are greater than 1 (and some that are complex) but still be useful as a forecasting tool. If a few roots exist that are only slightly larger than 1, their destabilizing effects may be minimal, becoming evident only if the model is simulated over a long time horizon. The importance of stability for a model's forecasting performance thus depends on the length of the forecast.

In the simple model of Eqs. (14.1) to (14.3), it was easy to determine whether the solution was stable and whether a small change in one of the coefficients (that is, a_2 or b_2) would change the solution characteristic from stable to unstable. Suppose, for example, that the estimated values of a_2 and b_2 yield a stable and nonoscillatory solution and we would like to know whether a small change in a_2 will result in unstable behavior. It is very easy to determine analytically whether this would be the case, since one need look only at how the solution to the characteristic equation changes as a result of the change in a_2. Such an analysis is difficult, however, if the model is large. Even if we can determine the characteristic roots for the model, we probably will not be able to determine how those characteristic roots are related to all the individual coefficients in the model. We usually cannot say (without actually performing a simulation) whether a small change in one of the coefficients will move the solution from stable to unstable or from nonoscillatory to oscillatory.

If the model is nonlinear, the situation becomes even more difficult, because we cannot use the solution to a characteristic equation to tell us about the stability of the solution. Most algorithms for nonlinear models involve iterative solutions in which a linearization is made in each iteration. The best one can do is derive a set of characteristic roots based on a linearization about some nominal solution path. If these characteristic roots are all less than 1 in magnitude, the *linearization* of the nonlinear model (i.e., about the particular nominal path) is stable. We still have no guarantee, however, that the full nonlinear model will exhibit stability. Methods for determining the stability of nonlinear models are largely analytic and cannot be applied to models of reasonable size. As a result we have no simple and direct way of determining the stability of a nonlinear model.[2]

How can one determine the solution properties for a medium to large nonlinear simultaneous-equation model? Usually one must resort to performing a series of simulations over different periods of time and using different time paths for the exogenous variables in the model. If the model is nonlinear and complex, the best one can do to determine whether it is stable in the long term is to simulate it over a long period. Similarly, in analyzing the sensitivity of the model to parameter changes, often the simplest thing to do (and the most revealing) is to make trial-and-error experiments with parameter values. After experimenting with models over a period of time, one usually obtains a sense of a model's characteristics and how they are determined.

14.2 MODEL BEHAVIOR: MULTIPLIERS AND DYNAMIC RESPONSE

We often build models to predict how a change in one variable is likely to affect other variables over time. We might construct a macroeconometric model, for

---

[2] Most of the analytic methods come from the field of control theory. An approach that has received some attention by economists (called *Lyapunov's direct method*) provides a sufficient condition for stability in the form of an existence theorem. If a certain function (called a *Lyapunov function*) can be shown to exist for a given model, the model is guaranteed to be stable. For a detailed treatment of the dynamic analysis of linear and nonlinear models, see G. C. Chow, *Analysis and Control of Dynamic Economic Systems* (New York: Wiley, 1975).

example, to determine how changes in government expenditures will affect future values of the GNP and its components: prices, employment, etc. We might construct a microeconometric model of an industry to forecast the future impact on market equilibrium of changes in personal income (or other demand-determining exogenous variables), changes in export demand, or (if the industry is a regulated one) changes in government regulatory policy. In each case we want to make statements about the *dynamic response*—of the macroeconomy, an industry, or a firm—to changes in particular variables. One way to quantify those statements is to calculate and examine the *multipliers* associated with the model's exogenous variables.

In the case of our simple three-equation multiplier-accelerator model, Eqs. (14.1) to (14.3), we can determine what change in Y_t would result from a \$1 increase in G_t (or we could determine the corresponding change in C_t or I_t). Assuming that the model's parameters are such that the simulation solution is stable, we would expect that the initial increase in G_t would result in ever-diminishing increases in Y_t. These changes in Y_t are called *dynamic multipliers.* The initial (first-period) change in Y_t is called the *impact multiplier,* while the *total long-run multiplier* is the sum of all the dynamic multipliers over time. Thus, the long-run multiplier indicates the total long-run change in Y_t that results from a unit change in G_t.

14.2.1   Dynamic Multipliers

Let us return to our simple model of Eqs. (14.1) to (14.3) with parameter values $a_1 = 30$, $a_2 = .6$, $b_1 = 0$, and $b_2 = .1$. We can obtain the dynamic multipliers directly from our simulation of the model in which we increased G_t by 2. Taking the *changes* in Y_t and dividing them by 2 (to correspond to an increase in G_t of 1), we obtain the dynamic multipliers, tabulated in Table 14.2. We also show in Table 14.2 the dynamic multipliers that result for $a_2 = .6$ and $b_2 = .8$, which are oscillatory. The impact multiplier is the initial first-period change in Y_t (1.0), and the total long-run multiplier is the sum of all the dynamic multipliers. Note that in both cases the total long-run multiplier is 2.50. The two solutions are quite different, but they both bring Y_t to the same equilibrium value.

The impact multiplier also can be determined algebraically. First, rewrite Eq. (14.4) as

$$Y_t = (a_2 + b_2)Y_{t-1} - b_2 Y_{t-2} + (a_1 + b_1) + G_t \qquad (14.14)$$

Now, taking first differences across this equation,

$$\Delta Y_t = (a_2 + b_2)\Delta Y_{t-1} - b_2 \, \Delta Y_{t-2} + \Delta G_t \qquad (14.15)$$

we see that for $\Delta G_t = 1$ the first-period change in Y_t will also be 1. In general, one can obtain the impact multipliers directly from the reduced form version

TABLE 14.2
DYNAMIC MULTIPLIERS FOR MULTIPLIER-ACCELERATOR MODEL

t	Case I ($b_2 = .1$)	Case II ($b_2 = .8$)	t	Case I ($b_2 = .1$)	Case II ($b_2 = .8$)
2	1.0	1.0	18	.000023	− .2453
3	.699997	1.39999	19	.000015	− .109543
4	.389999	1.16	20	.000007	.042877
5	.202995	.503998	21	.000004	.147667
6	.103096	− .222397	22	0	.172432
7	.051872	− .714554	23	0	.123268
8	.025993	− .822464	24	0	.03463
9	.013008	− .579803	25	0	− .050133
10	.006508	− .153755	26	0	− .097885
11	.003258	.248581	27	0	− .096931
12	.001625	.471016	28	0	− .057396
13	.000816	.460564	29	0	− .002815
14	.000404	.267975	30	0	.041977
15	.000206	.006714	⋮		
16	.000099	− .204979	Sum	2.5000	2.5000
17	.000053	− .292343			

of a model (the reduced form coefficient of each unlagged exogenous variable is that variable's impact multiplier). The remaining dynamic multipliers, however, cannot be determined by inspection. Instead, one must perform a simulation in which each exogenous variable is increased appropriately and the resulting changes in the endogenous variables are found from the simulation solution.

Keep in mind that if a model is *nonlinear,* the dynamic multipliers will depend on the *size* of the variation of the particular exogenous variable as well as the starting values of all the endogenous variables. The simple model of Eqs. (14.1) to (14.3) is linear, so that the same multipliers would be obtained by increasing G_t by 4 as would be obtained by increasing it by 2 (we would simply divide the changes in Y_t by 4 instead of 2). Furthermore, the multipliers are the same whatever the initial values of Y_t and its components. This would *not* be the case, however, if the model were nonlinear. With a nonlinear model, a large increase in G_t could yield different multipliers than a small increase in G_t, and those multipliers would also differ for different starting values of Y_t. For this reason dynamic multipliers for nonlinear models should be presented together with information about how they were calculated.

Example 14.1 St. Louis Model   An application of dynamic multipliers is provided by the St. Louis model of Andersen and Carlson of the St. Louis

Federal Reserve Bank.[3] They set out to test the monetarist position that only the money supply (and therefore monetary policy) has any long-run impact on the GNP and that government expenditures have almost no long-run impact. The model included as exogenous variables both government expenditures and the money supply. Simulations were used to determine the dynamic and total long-run multipliers corresponding to each of these exogenous variables. The outcome was that the total long-run multiplier for government expenditures was close to zero, while that for the money supply was large.

This result is largely the outcome of only one of the model's eight equations, which relates changes in total spending (in current dollars) ΔY to changes in the money supply ΔM and changes in government expenditures ΔG. The estimated form of that equation uses polynomial distributed lags and constrains each of the independent variables to lie on a fourth-degree polynomial with the head and tail set at 0. The equation is shown below, with t statistics in parentheses:[4]

$$\frac{\widehat{\Delta Y_t}}{Y_t} = \underset{(3.23)}{2.65} + \sum_{i=0}^{4} m_i \frac{\Delta M_{t-i}}{M_{t-i}} + \sum_{i=0}^{4} g_i \frac{\Delta G_{t-i}}{G_{t-i}} \tag{14.16}$$

$$m_0 = .394 \ (2.89) \qquad\qquad g_0 = .071 \ (1.97)$$

$$m_1 = .443 \ (5.69) \qquad\qquad g_1 = .057 \ (2.27)$$

$$m_2 = .289 \ (2.38) \qquad\qquad g_2 = .002 \ (.07)$$

$$m_3 = .071 \ (.91) \qquad\qquad g_3 = -.053 \ (-2.11)$$

$$m_4 = -.071 \ (-.51) \qquad\qquad g_4 = -.067 \ (-1.91)$$

$$\Sigma m_i = 1.127 \ (6.40) \qquad\qquad \Sigma g_i = .010 \ (.14)$$

As can be seen from Eq. (14.16), an increase in G will initially have a small positive impact on Y, but after two or three quarters it will have a negative impact, with a total (long-run) impact that is close to zero. The money supply, by comparison, has a significant long-run impact ($\Sigma m_i = 1.127$).

---

[3] L. C. Andersen and K. M. Carlson, "A Monetarist Model for Economic Stabilization," *Federal Reserve Bank of St. Louis, Monthly Review,* April 1970.

[4] This equation is from the April 1979 version of the model, as estimated over the period 1953-1 through 1978-4. The form of the equation differs only slightly from that in the original model (the three variables are now in percentage change rather than first difference form). For a discussion of changes in the specification, see K. M. Carlson, "Does the St. Louis Model Now Believe in Fiscal Policy?" *Federal Reserve Bank of St. Louis Review,* vol. 60, February 1978.

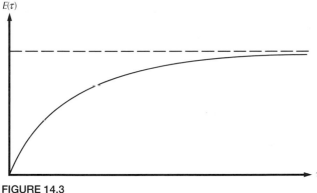

FIGURE 14.3
Dynamic elasticity.

14.2.2   Dynamic Elasticities

In constructing a microeconometric model, we usually are interested in describing the dynamic response of a particular industry. Corresponding to the dynamic multipliers, we calculate *dynamic elasticities*. A dynamic elasticity tells us how the demand for a good will change *over time* in response to a change in price or in consumers' incomes. We often make statements about the price or income elasticity of a good without explicitly recognizing that the value of the elasticity depends on how much time is allowed to elapse after price or income has changed.[5] In fact, it is more meaningful to look at a dynamic elasticity, such as

$$E_p(\tau) = -\frac{P_t}{Q_t}\frac{Q_{t+\tau} - Q_t}{\Delta P_t} \tag{14.17}$$

Here, ΔP_t is a change in price (occurring at time t) and $Q_{t-\tau} - Q_t$ is the change in quantity demanded after a time interval τ has elapsed. Other dynamic elasticities (income, cross-price, etc.) would be defined in the same way.

By simulating the model (with a change in price), we can calculate and plot the elasticity as a function of the time interval τ. We normally would expect the elasticity to grow monotonically and approach some asymptotic value, as in Fig. 14.3. It is quite possible, however, that as a result of the model's structure (which we hope reflects the true market structure) the elasticity would oscillate (still approaching some asymptotic long-run value as long as the model is stable), as in Fig. 14.4.

The behavior of dynamic elasticities is important if a model is being used to

---

[5] By definition, price elasticity of demand $= E_p = -\dfrac{P}{Q}\dfrac{\Delta Q}{\Delta P}$. Income elasticity $= E_t = \dfrac{I}{Q}\dfrac{\Delta Q}{\Delta I}$.
The problem is that given some ΔP (or ΔI), how much time should be allowed to elapse before we measure ΔQ?

$E(\tau)$

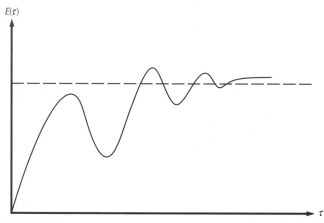

τ

FIGURE 14.4
Oscillating dynamic elasticity.

forecast or analyze the impact of a price increase, or a change in the price of a competing good, on an industry's (or company's) sales. That impact must be described in dynamic terms. It is possible that a price increase will result in a drop in demand, but only after a long period of time has elapsed. However, it may result in an initially large drop in demand but later (after consumers' perceptions of relative prices have changed) an increase in demand, so that the net decrease is small. The time required for these changes to occur is likely to vary considerably from industry to industry. Because of this, a company that is trying to plan its production and marketing in anticipation of a planned change in prices must have some idea of how much time will pass before it experiences a resulting change in sales.

Example 14.2 Automobile Demand   The dynamic characteristics of elasticities are very important in analyzing the demand for automobiles. To see why, let us examine a quarterly model of automobile demand constructed by Saul Hymans.[6]

The demand for cars (a flow variable) will depend on the *stock in circulation* at that time and provides a means of adjusting the stock to some desired or equilibrium level. We therefore begin by writing an equation for the *desired stock* of cars KA*:

$$KA_t^* = a + b(DI_{t-1}) + c(UM_{t-1}) + d(PA_t) + \varepsilon_t \qquad (14.18)$$

[6] S. H. Hymans, "Consumer Durable Spending: Explanation and Prediction," *Brookings Papers on Economic Activity*, no. 2, pp. 173–199, 1970.

where DI = disposable personal income, net of transfers, 1958 dollars
    UM = unemployment rate for males twenty years of age and over,
        percent
    PA = a real (constant-dollar) price index of cars (1958 = 1.0)

Given this desired stock, gross real expenditures on cars (CARK) can be described by

$$\text{CARK}_t = w(\text{KA}_t^* - \text{KA}_{t-1}) + v(\text{KA}_{t-1}) \tag{14.19}$$

where KA = actual car stock
    w = quarterly rate of adjustment between desired and actual stocks
    v = quarterly rate of depreciation of actual stock

Equation (14.18) can then be substituted for KA* in Eq. (14.19) to yield a new equation for CARK. Hymans added a dummy variable to account for strikes against General Motors in 1964 and Ford in 1967 and obtained the following estimated equation using quarterly data over 1954-1 through 1968-4 and a Hildreth-Lu correction for serial correlation:[7]

$$\widehat{\text{CARK}}_t = 19.009 + .206\text{DI}_{t-1} - .753\text{UM}_{t-1} - 25.861\text{PA}_t$$
$$\quad\quad (2.93) \quad\quad (9.14) \quad\quad\quad (-3.73) \quad\quad\quad (-4.40)$$

$$- .157\text{KA}_{t-1} + 1.626\text{STRIKE} \tag{14.20}$$
$$(-6.33) \quad\quad\quad (3.94)$$

To simulate the model and forecast the effects of price or income changes, Eq. (14.20) is combined with the following identity for the stock of cars:

$$\text{KA}_t = (1 - v)\text{KA}_{t-1} + \text{CARK}_t \tag{14.21}$$

Hymans uses a calculated value of .078 for the quarterly depreciation rate v. Equations (14.20) and (14.21) thus constitute a two-equation simulation model for expenditures on cars.

This model implies that long-run price and income elasticities are *smaller* in magnitude than are short-run elasticities. In particular, the short-run (impact) *price* elasticity is −1.07, while the long-run elasticity is −.36. The short-run *income* elasticity is 3.08, while the long-run elasticity is 1.02. The reason, of course, is the *stock adjustment effect*. When prices go up (or income goes down) consumers may initially cut down drastically on purchases of new cars. After a few years go by, however, old cars will have depreciated,

---

[7] STRIKE = −2 in 1964-4, 1 in 1965-1 and 1965-2, −1 in 1967-4, and $\frac{1}{2}$ in 1968-1 and 1968-2.

so that purchases of new cars will pick up, reaching a new equilibrium level that is below, but not that much below, what it was before the price increase.

Example 14.3 Another Macroeconometric Model   For another macro-econometric example, let us look at a quarterly model constructed by Kmenta and Smith.[8] The equations, which were estimated with quarterly data over the period 1954 to 1963, using three-stage least squares, are shown below with standard errors in parentheses:

$$\hat{C}_t = -1.7951 + .1731Y_t + .0421(L_t - .7275L_{t-1}) + .7275C_{t-1} \quad (14.22)$$
$$\quad\quad (.7803) \quad\quad (.0131) \quad\quad (.0277) \quad\quad (.0665) \quad\quad\quad (.0665)$$

$$R^2 = .9968$$

$$\hat{I}^d_t = 2.5624 - .4411r_t + .1381(S_{t-1} - S_{t-2}) + .0237t + .8917I^d_{t-1}$$
$$\quad\quad (1.0759) \quad (.1891) \quad (.0501) \quad\quad\quad\quad (.0110) \quad (.0700) \quad (14.23)$$

$$R^2 = .8961$$

$$\hat{I}^r_t = 3.6083 - .5127r_t + .1267(S_{t-1} - S_{t-2}) + .0218t + .6483I^r_{t-1}$$
$$\quad\quad (.5779) \quad (.1133) \quad (.0335) \quad\quad\quad\quad (.0059) \quad (.0668)$$
$$(14.24)$$

$$R^2 = .8394$$

$$\hat{I}^i_t = 3.0782 - .8934r_t + .3713(S_{t-1} - S_{t-2}) + .0450 + .3178I^i_{t-1}$$
$$\quad\quad (1.3610) \quad (.4089) \quad (.1303) \quad\quad\quad\quad (.0208) \quad (.1181) \quad (14.25)$$

$$R^2 = .5341$$

$$\hat{r}_t = 13.8928 + .0261Y_t - .1501M_t + .0588M_{t-1} \quad\quad\quad (14.26)$$
$$\quad\quad (1.8706) \quad (.0042) \quad (.0335) \quad (.0338)$$

$$R^2 = .8538$$

$$Y_t = C_t + I^d_t + I^r_t + I^i_t + G_t \quad\quad\quad\quad\quad\quad\quad\quad\quad (14.27)$$

$$S_t = Y_t - I^i_t \quad\quad\quad\quad\quad\quad\quad\quad\quad\quad\quad\quad\quad\quad (14.28)$$

$$L_t = M_t + TD_t \quad\quad\quad\quad\quad\quad\quad\quad\quad\quad\quad\quad\quad (14.29)$$

[8] J. Kmenta and P. E. Smith, "Autonomous Expenditures versus Money Supply: An Application of Dynamic Multipliers," *Review of Economics and Statistics,* vol. LV, pp. 299–307, August 1973.

where Y = gross national product

$\quad\quad C$ = consumption expenditures

$\quad\quad I^d$ = producer's outlays on durable plant and equipment

$\quad\quad I^r$ = residential construction

$\quad\quad I^i$ = increase in inventories

$\quad\quad G$ − government purchases of goods and services plus net foreign investment

$\quad\quad S$ = final sales of goods and services

$\quad\quad t$ = time in quarters (first quarter of 1954 = 0)

$\quad\quad r$ = yield on all corporate bonds, percent per annum

$\quad\quad M$ = money supply, i.e., demand deposits plus currency outside banks

$\quad\quad$ TD = time deposits in commercial banks

$\quad\quad L$ = money supply plus time deposits in commercial banks (representing liquid wealth)

All the variables except for t and r are measured in billions of 1958 dollars, and the variables G, M, TD, and t are taken to be exogenous. No prices or wages are included in the model, since during this time period prices were relatively stable.

To examine the dynamic characteristics of this model, we can begin by writing the reduced form equation for GNP. This is found by expressing the current endogenous variables in Eq. (14.27) in terms of the exogenous and lagged endogenous variables. Making those substitutions gives the reduced form equation

$$\hat{Y}_t = -20.8070 + \underset{(.1024)}{.3168M_t} - \underset{(.0755)}{.1242M_{t-1}} + \underset{(.0308)}{.0481L_t} - \underset{(.0224)}{.0350L_{t-1}}$$

$$+ \underset{(.0286)}{1.1427G_t} + \underset{(.0489)}{.1035t} + \underset{(.0356)}{.8313C_{t-1}} + \underset{(.1796)}{.7270(S_{t-1} - S_{t-2})}$$

$$+ \underset{(.0853)}{1.0190I^d_{t-1}} + \underset{(.0802)}{.7409I^r_{t-1}} + \underset{(.1350)}{.3631I^i_{t-1}} \tag{14.30}$$

According to this equation, the impact effect of a \$1 billion increase in government expenditures G_t is to increase GNP by \$1.1427 billion, while the impact effect of a \$1 billion increase in money supply M_t is to increase GNP by \$.3649 billion (.3168 plus .0481, since M_t is a component of L_t).

Before examining the dynamic multipliers, let us determine what type of solution the model will have by finding the characteristic roots. First, by substituting for C_{t-1}, S_{t-1}, S_{t-2}, I^d_{t-1}, I^r_{t-1}, and I^i_{t-1} in Eq. (14.30) we obtain the fundamental dynamic equation, which expresses current GNP in terms of its own lagged values and in terms of current and lagged values of the exogenous variables:

$$Y_t = 3.0716Y_{t-1} - 3.6561Y_{t-2} + 2.0850Y_{t-3} - .5585Y_{t-4} + .0535Y_{t-5}$$
$$+ 1.1427G_t - 2.5300G_{t-1} + 1.3779G_{t-2} + .5853G_{t-3} - .7463G_{t-4}$$
$$+ .1784G_{t-5} + .3168M_t - .7499M_{t-1} + .6253M_{t-2} - .2000M_{t-3}$$
$$+ .0082M_{t-4} + .0046M_{t-5} + .0481L_t - .1065L_{t-1} + .0580L_{t-2}$$
$$+ .0246L_{t-3} - .0314L_{t-4} + .0075L_{t-5} + .1034t - .2050(t - 1)$$
$$+ .1267(t - 2) - .0192(t - 3) - .0032(t - 4) - .5113$$

$$(14.31)$$

From Eq. (14.31) we can determine the characteristic equation of the model:

$$\lambda^5 - 3.0716\lambda^4 + 3.6561\lambda^3 - 2.0850\lambda^2 + .5585\lambda - .0535 = 0 \qquad (14.32)$$

The characteristic roots (i.e., the solutions to this equation) are

$$\lambda_1 = .2081 \qquad \lambda_{2,3} = .8475 \pm .0809i \qquad \lambda_{4,5} = .5843 \pm .1156i$$

Since all the roots are less than 1 in magnitude (λ_2 and λ_3 have a magnitude

TABLE 14.3
DYNAMIC GNP MULTIPLIERS

Lag k	Multipliers of G_{t-k}	M_{t-k}	L_{t-k}	$t - k$
0	1.14271	.31683	.04811	.10341
1	.98001	.22330	.04126	.11262
2	.21029	.15287	.00885	.09459
3	.03086	.11372	.00130	.07525
4	− .01519	.08722	− .00064	.05920
5	− .02878	.06775	− .00121	.04660
6	− .03352	.05291	− .00141	.03679
7	− .03539	.04135	− .00149	.02908
8	− .03604	.03210	− .11052	.02298
9	− .03592	.02487	− .00151	.01808
10	− .03520	.08196	− .00148	.01412
11	− .00396	.01410	− .00143	.01091
12	− .03227	.01036	− .00136	.00820
13	− .03024	.00729	− .00127	.00619
14	− .02795	.00486	− .00188	.00448
15	− .02552	.00295	− .00107	.00312
16	− .02303	.00148	− .00097	.00204
17	− .02056	.00037	− .00086	.00120
18	− .01816	− .00044	− .00076	.00055
19	− .01589	− .00102	− .00067	.00006
. . .	. . .	. . .	. . .	. . .

of .8513) and since four of them are complex, the solution will be stable, and we will observe dampened oscillations. The dynamic multipliers also exhibit dampened oscillations and converge toward 0 as the length of the time lag increases, as can be seen in Table 14.3.

By summing the multipliers listed in the table, we see that the total long-run multiplier for government expenditures is 1.8406, that for the money supply (the combined effect of M_t and L_t) is 1.2270, and that for the time trend is .6363. These results are quite different from those of the St. Louis model and support the view that both government expenditures and the money supply are effective as policy instruments.

14.3 THE IMPULSE RESPONSE FUNCTION AND VECTOR AUTOREGRESSIONS

Dynamic multipliers are one way of characterizing the dynamic behavior of a simulation model, but they only describe the response of the model to changes in exogenous variables. Another approach is to determine how each endogenous variable responds over time to a shock in that variable and in every other endogenous variable. The *impulse response function* traces the response of the endogenous variables to such shocks.

As an example, go back to the simple four-equation (three behavioral identities and one accounting identity) macroeconometric model introduced in Section 13.3. That model can be written as follows:

$$C_t = a_0 + a_1 Y_t + a_2 C_{t-1} + \varepsilon_{1t} \tag{14.33}$$

$$I_t = b_0 + b_1 \Delta Y_t + b_2 Y_{t-1} + b_3 R_{t-4} + \varepsilon_{2t} \tag{14.34}$$

$$R_t = c_0 + c_1 Y_t + c_2 \Delta Y_t + c_3 \Delta M_t + c_4 (R_{t-1} + R_{t-2}) + \varepsilon_{3t} \tag{14.35}$$

$$Y_t = C_t + I_t + G_t \tag{14.36}$$

where consumption C, investment I, the interest rate R, and GNP (net of exports and imports) Y are endogenous variables, and the money supply M and government spending G are exogenous.

Now consider the effects of a shock, or change, in ε_1, ε_2, and ε_3. A change in ε_1 will immediately affect consumption and, through the GNP accounting identity [Eq. (14.36)], Y. As a result, it will also have an immediate effect on I and R, as can be seen from Eqs. (14.34) and (14.35). There will be further changes in all the variables over time as the initial effects of the shock propagate through the model. A change in ε_3, by comparison, will have an immediate effect on R but will affect I, and hence C and Y, only after four periods. Later it will have further effects on R, through the dependence of R on Y, and so on.

The impulse response is the tracing through of these effects. Ideally, we would like to identify shocks with specific endogenous variables so that we can determine how an unexpected change in one variable affects all variables over time. If the model is linear and if the error terms are uncorrelated with each other, this is straightforward. In a nonlinear model it may not be possible, because a single endogenous variable may not appear on the left-hand side of each equation.

Even in a linear model, if the errors are correlated, there is no simple way to unambiguously identify shocks with specific variables. The reason for this is that the errors will have common components that affect more than one variable. When this is the case (as it often is), the usual procedure is to arbitrarily attribute all the effects of such common components to the variable that appears first in the system. For example, if ε_1 and ε_2 happened to be correlated, we would attribute all of the common component of a shock to consumption and none of it to investment. The only problem with this procedure is that impulse responses will depend on the particular ordering of the equations in the model. For example, if the investment equation had appeared first, all the common components of the shock would have been attributed to investment rather than to consumption.

To actually calculate the impulse response, the model should be in a stable equilibrium. (If necessary, hold any exogenous variables constant and simulate the model over a long enough period that all the endogenous variables stop changing.) Now introduce a one-period shock to one of the endogenous variables. For example, increase ε_1 by, say, 1 standard deviation at time $t = 0$. (The shock is maintained for only one period and hence is an "impulse.") To the extent that this endogenous variable (in this case consumption) affects other endogenous variables, the shock will filter through the model, affecting all the variables. In later periods it may even have a greater effect on the original endogenous variable than it did initially because of feedback effects through the other variables.

One then introduces a one-period shock to the next endogenous variable (for example, increasing ε_2 by 1 standard deviation for one period) and again traces through the effects on all the variables in the model, and so on for the other endogenous variables.

This procedure is particularly well suited to studying vector autoregressions. Recall from our discussion in Section 13.5 that a VAR provides a means of letting the data, rather than the econometrician, determine the dynamic structure of a model. Thus, after estimating a VAR, it is important to be able to characterize its dynamic structure clearly. The impulse responses do this by showing how shocks to any one variable filter through the model to affect every other variable and eventually feed back to the original variable itself.

Example 14.4 Dynamic Behavior of the Heating Oil Market In Example 13.1 we developed a vector autoregression to model the market for home heating oil. The VAR we estimated related current and lagged values of price, production, and inventory. To see what that model tells us about the dynamics of the heating oil market, we will study the response of each endogenous variable to shocks in that variable and in the other endogenous variables.

To calculate these impulse responses, we increase—for 1 month only—the error term in the first equation (i.e., the equation for PHO) by 1 standard deviation and then calculate the immediate and future effects of this change on price, production, and inventory. We then repeat this for a 1-standard-deviation increase in the error term in the second equation and finally for the error term in the third equation. We therefore need to know the estimated covariances among the three error terms. The estimated covariances are as follows:

	With		
Covariance of	$\hat{\varepsilon}_1$	$\hat{\varepsilon}_2$	$\hat{\varepsilon}_3$
$\hat{\varepsilon}_1$	25.85	−.0035	−7.28
$\hat{\varepsilon}_2$	−.0035	15.23	6.31
$\hat{\varepsilon}_3$	−7.28	6.31	36.17

Note that the residuals of the third equation are strongly correlated with those of the first two equations. Thus a shock to ε_1, for example, will have a common component with ε_3. As was discussed above, all of this common component is attributed to price.

Figure 14.5 shows the response of each variable to a 1-standard-deviation shock in price, i.e., a one-period increase in ε_1 of $(25.85)^{1/2} = 5.08$ cents per gallon. Initially, of course, price increases by 5.08 cents. Inventory also falls initially because of the negative covariance of ε_1 and ε_3. Over the next 4 or 5 periods price falls and inventory rises, but there is little effect on production until some 14 periods have passed. Ultimately, changes in all the variables approach zero as the effects of the shock dampen out.

Figures 14.6 and 14.7 show the response of each variable to 1-standard-deviation shocks in production and inventory, respectively. Note that although the initial effects of a shock to production are concentrated largely on production, after three or four periods production returns close to its initial value, but there is a sustained effect on inventory. By contrast, the effects of a shock to inventory are confined largely to inventory. This shock induces cycles in inventory, which dampen slowly.

Another way of characterizing the dynamic behavior of the model is through a *variance decomposition*. This breaks down the variance of the forecast error for each variable into components that can be attributed to each of the endogenous variables. Table 14.4 shows the variance decomposition for price. The second column in the table gives the standard errors of forecast for horizons of 1 month, 2 months, etc. For the 1-month forecast, the stan-

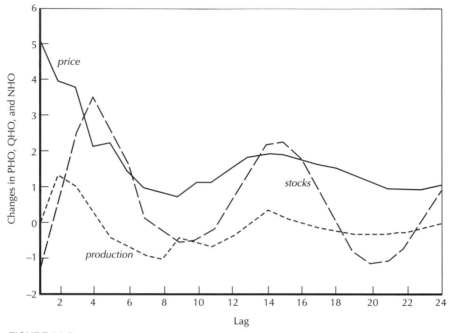

FIGURE 14.5
Response to 1-standard-deviation shock in price.

FIGURE 14.6
Response to 1-standard-deviation shock in production.

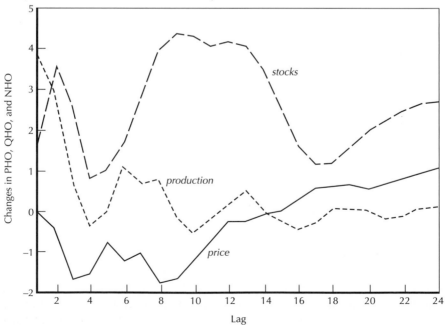

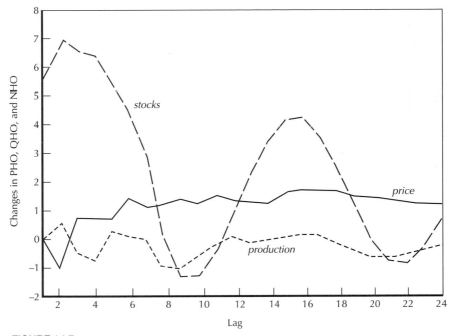

FIGURE 14.7
Response to 1-standard-deviation shock in inventory.

dard error is just 5.08, the standard deviation of ε_1. For the 2-month forecast, the standard error is 6.54, because it includes the effects of uncertainty over the 1-month forecasts of production and inventory.

The third column of Table 14.4 shows the percentage of the price forecast variances that can be attributed to shocks in price alone, as opposed to production and inventory. The fourth column shows the percentage of the price forecast variances that can be attributed to shocks in production, and the fifth column shows the percentage attributable to inventory. For example, if the model is used to make a 5-month forecast of price, 87.9 percent of the forecast variance will be attributable to price shocks, 8.4 percent to production shocks, and 3.7 percent to inventory shocks. Not surprisingly, the greater the forecast horizon, the larger the proportion of forecast variance that will be due to the nonprice variables.

14.4   ADJUSTING SIMULATION MODELS

If one adjusts a simulation model, its forecasting performance sometimes can be improved. The structure of the model may be such that its dynamic behavior verges on being unstable, and minor changes may be sufficient to stabilize the behavior. Or a bias in an individual estimated coefficient may result in consis-

TABLE 14.4
VARIANCE DECOMPOSITION OF PHO

Period	S.E.	PHO	QHO	NHO
1	5.08	100.00	.00	.00
2	6.54	96.95	.39	2.66
3	7.80	91.88	5.30	2.83
4	8.27	88.43	8.26	3.31
5	8.63	87.92	8.38	3.69
6	8.96	84.21	9.75	6.03
7	9.15	81.92	10.64	7.44
8	9.45	77.71	13.64	8.65
9	9.73	73.85	15.91	10.24
10	9.97	71.57	16.98	11.46
11	10.18	69.89	16.94	13.17
12	10.38	69.26	16.35	14.40
13	10.63	69.07	15.65	15.27
14	10.88	69.07	14.96	15.98
15	11.16	68.51	14.22	17.27
16	11.43	67.62	13.63	18.75
17	11.68	66.62	13.25	20.13
18	11.91	65.66	12.97	21.37
19	12.10	64.88	12.84	22.28
20	12.26	64.11	12.68	23.21
21	12.40	63.33	12.65	24.01
22	12.53	62.57	12.76	24.67
23	12.66	61.78	13.00	25.22
24	12.80	61.02	13.32	25.66

tent under- or overprediction by the model as a whole, which can be corrected by an adjustment in the coefficient value.

Suppose we estimated a regression equation to forecast an interest rate. The result might have been Eq. (13.16). The selection of this equation might have been based solely on statistical grounds, i.e., R^2, t statistics, etc. Suppose we use the equation to produce a predicted series for the interest rate over the historical time period. It may be that the predicted series is close to the actual interest rate series during those periods when the interest rate does not change very much, but during periods when the interest rate is changing rapidly, the predicted series misses the turns in the actual series. Thus, although the overall fit of the equation is good, the equation may fail to pick up turns in the variable that is being explained. If this is the case, we may want to change the equation, perhaps by introducing additional explanatory variables or changing the functional form or the lag structure. The result may have an overall statistical fit that is not as good but may be more useful for purposes of prediction or analysis.

Once a single-equation regression model has been built, one probably will not want to change any of the coefficient values that have been estimated (although alternative estimation techniques may be used). This may not be the case with a simulation model. Let us consider as an example the four-equation model from Chapter 13, i.e., Eqs. (13.14) to (13.17).

Suppose we wanted to use this model to forecast the interest rate. We might be satisfied with each of the equations taken by itself, but we might not be happy with the simulation performance of the model as a whole. The model might be overly sensitive to changes in an exogenous variable, or it simply might be unstable or oscillate. One way to improve its performance (as discussed in Chapter 13) is to use alternative estimation methods. Aside from the use of two-stage least squares to ensure consistency (discussed in some detail in Chapter 12), we saw in Section 13.4 that the use of simple single-equation estimation techniques such as an autoregressive correction (for serially correlated error terms) can greatly improve a model's forecasting performance and that the use of full-information techniques can result in even further improvement.

Other techniques are available for making changes in the model, and they are often used interdependently. The first of these techniques involves analyzing all the feedback and feedforward loops in the model. To do this, one begins with a *block diagram* of the model. A block diagram, an example of which is shown for our simple four-equation model in Fig. 14.8, illustrates all the causal flows between variables and blocks of variables. Feedback loops are essentially circular causal flows; an example in Fig. 14.8 is the loop between consumption and GNP; consumption is at least in part determined by GNP, but it is also a component of (and therefore helps determine) GNP.

One can use a block diagram to identify mechanisms in the model that could

FIGURE 14.8
Block diagram for simple four-equation model.

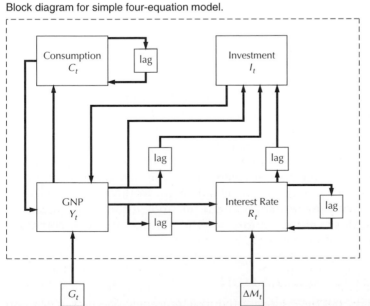

result in an unstable performance. In our four-equation model, for example, consumption and investment both depend on total GNP but at the same time contribute to total GNP. Thus, if the multiplier coefficients in these equations were too large, a feedback loop could result that would continually magnify small changes in consumption or investment demand into very large changes in the GNP. If this is the case, one might want to restructure one of the demand equations to reduce the dependence on total GNP. One could, for example, introduce another explanatory variable that would eliminate some of the dependence on GNP of consumption. Note that the restructuring of individual equations will be done for different reasons than would be the case in a single-equation model. In a single-equation model one is usually concerned only with the statistical fit, either overall or at particular turning points. In a simulation model, however, one is also concerned with the dynamic interaction of the equations which compose the model. Thus, we may want to restructure an equation even though it has a very satisfactory statistical fit.

There is a second method that is often used to make minor adjustments in large econometric models, particularly those used for forecasting purposes. This consists of making small changes in some of the model's coefficients and introducing adjustable parameters at key points in the model to improve its ability to forecast. Suppose, for example, that one of the variables in a model is consistently simulated above its actual values. There may be several reasons for this: One or more of the coefficients in the consumption equation may be biased, some of the coefficients in other equations that feed into the consumption equation may be biased, or the structure of the model may simply build an upward trend into that particular variable. One way of dealing with this problem is to adjust some of the coefficients in the equation for the variable that is simulating badly.

This must be done with care. By adjusting some of the coefficients, the analyst may make the model track the historical data very well even though it is really a very poor representation of the real world, with little predictive value. Coefficients should be adjusted only with great caution and only if they are not statistically significant. A statistically significant coefficient indicates that the data have information to convey, and this information should be accounted for when one is making a forecast.

Related to the problem of adjusting a model to improve its forecasting performance is the question of how literally a model's forecasts should be taken. Forecasters and policy makers usually allow for a considerable amount of interaction between their models and their judgment. In this way a model becomes more than just a mathematical forecasting tool; it serves as a means of processing and making available information that was not originally contained in the model.

14.5 STOCHASTIC SIMULATION

In Chapter 8 we saw that the forecasts produced by a single-equation regression model are subject to four sources of error:

1. The regression equation contains an implicit additive error term.

2. The estimated values of the coefficients of the equation are themselves random variables and will therefore differ from the true values.

3. The exogenous variables have to be forecasted themselves, and those forecasts may contain errors.

4. The equation is misspecified; i.e., the functional form may not be representative of the real world.

We showed in Chapter 8 how we could calculate a confidence interval on a forecast that would account for the first three sources of error. (We cannot account for the fourth source of error, and so all our confidence intervals are calculated under the assumption that the model is correctly specified.)

In the case of a multi-equation simulation model the four sources of error still apply, although now misspecification can occur not only for individual equations but also for the dynamic structure contained in the model as a whole. Furthermore, even if the model is specified correctly, errors in each equation of the first three types may become multiplied across equations and thus be magnified.

As an example, consider again the four-equation model of Eqs. (13.14) to (13.17), along with the corresponding block diagram in Fig. 14.8. When the model is simulated, the consumption equation will generate a prediction of consumption which will be in error as a result of both the implicit additive error term in that equation and the fact that the equation's coefficients are not known with certainty. Since consumption is a component of GNP, the error in consumption will contribute to an error in GNP, and this error in GNP will contribute to the error term in the prediction of investment (together with the additive error term and coefficient errors in the investment equation). Investment is also a component of GNP, so that the error in investment will also contribute to an error in GNP. Similarly, consumption is a function of GNP, so that the error in consumption will become still larger as a result of the accumulated error in GNP.

If the model is linear, the final forecasting error variances associated with each endogenous variable can be calculated exactly, although to do so is not computationally trivial. Generally, a more fruitful approach (particularly for nonlinear models) is to perform a *stochastic simulation* (also called a *Monte Carlo simulation*). This is done by specifying, for each equation of the model, a probability distribution for the additive error term and for each estimated coefficient. Next, a large number (say 1,000) of simulations are performed. In each simulation, values for the additive error terms and estimated coefficients are chosen at random from the corresponding probability distributions. For any particular endogenous variable, the results of the simulation yield points that trace out a probability distribution of that variable's forecasted value. Thus, the dispersion of the forecasts about their mean value can be used to define a forecast confidence interval.

If unbiased and consistent estimates have been obtained for all the model's coefficients, the determination of the appropriate probability distributions for the estimated coefficients is straightforward. For each equation, the additive error can be assumed to be normally distributed with 0 mean and standard deviation equal to the standard error of the regression. The coefficients of each equation can be assumed to follow a *joint* normal distribution, where the mean of each coefficient is given by its estimated value, the standard deviation of each coefficient is given by its estimated standard error, and the covariances between coefficients are given by the estimated covariance matrix.

To illustrate the technique, let us take the four-equation model as an example. To perform a stochastic simulation, the equations of the model would be written

$$C_t = (-9.454 + v_{11}) + (.0541 + v_{12})Y_t + (.9260 + v_{13})C_{t-1} + \varepsilon_{1t} \qquad (14.37)$$

$$I_t = (-66.195 + v_{21}) + (.1684 + v_{22})(Y_t - Y_{t-1}) + (.2181 + v_{23})Y_{t-1}$$
$$- (11.256 + v_{24})R_{t-4} + \varepsilon_{2t} \qquad (14.38)$$

$$R_t = (-.5561 + v_{31}) + (.00051 + v_{32})Y_t + (.0135 + v_{33})(Y_t - Y_{t-1})$$
$$- (.0853 + v_{34})(M_t - M_{t-1}) + (.4259 + v_{35})(R_{t-1} + R_{t-2}) + \varepsilon_{3t} \quad (14.39)$$

$$Y_t = C_t + I_t + G_t \qquad (14.40)$$

In the first equation the "error terms" v_{11}, v_{12}, and v_{13} should be assumed to follow a joint normal distribution. In some situations it may be computationally difficult to generate random numbers from joint distributions, and if the covariances are small, it is reasonable to perform the stochastic simulation under the approximating assumption that the covariances between coefficients are zero. It is important to remember, however, that ignoring the covariances between coefficients will usually lead one to *overestimate* the size of the model's forecast errors. The majority of the estimated covariances are usually negative and cancel part of the variance in each coefficient. Ignoring the covariances thus tends to lead one to overemphasize the degree of fluctuation in the coefficients, and forecast confidence intervals obtained in this way will be somewhat conservative.

Ignoring covariances for the purposes of this example, the error term v_{11} is assumed to be a normally distributed random variable with 0 mean and a standard deviation of 4.70 (which is the estimated standard error of the coefficient -9.454 in the consumption equation). Similarly, v_{12} is normally distributed with 0 mean and a standard deviation of .0169 and v_{13} is normally distributed with 0 mean and a standard deviation of .025. The additive error term ε_{1t} is, *for each period t*, a normally distributed random variable with 0 mean and a standard deviation of 11.23 (the standard error of the equation). The remaining error terms in Eqs. (14.38) and (14.39) are similarly defined.

Now suppose that we would like to obtain a stochastic one-period-ahead forecast of the interest rate R_t (under the assumption that the exogenous variables M_t and G_t are known with certainty). We do this by performing several hundred simulations of the model one period ahead. In each simulation we select at random a value for v_{11} from a normal distribution with mean 0 and standard deviation 4.70, select at random a value for v_{12} from a normal distribution with mean 0 and standard deviation .0169, etc. The result of these simulations will be a range of forecasted values of R_t. This range will have some sample mean, and the several hundred simulated values themselves will determine a probability distribution about this mean (if the model is nonlinear, this probability distribution will not be normal). Next, we can calculate the standard deviation of this sample distribution, which will give us an estimated value for the standard error of the forecast. We can then use this standard error of forecast just as we did in Chapter 8 to determine forecast confidence intervals.

If the model is linear, then as the number of simulations included in the sample becomes large, the sample mean will approach the *deterministic forecast* (the forecast corresponding to all the random parameters set at 0). If the model is nonlinear, however, there is no guarantee that the sample mean will approach the deterministic forecast as the sample size increases, and in fact it usually will not. In addition, it may be necessary for an unacceptably large number of simulations to be performed before the sample means for each variable converge at all. We therefore center our confidence intervals on the deterministic forecast rather than on the sample mean of the stochastic simulations.

The process would be exactly the same if we wanted to forecast over a time horizon longer than one period. For each simulation we simply select a *different* random value for ε_{1t}, ε_{2t}, and ε_{3t} for *each period*, but we use the *same* random value for v_{11}, v_{12}, etc., during the entire simulation (since the equations of the model were specified and estimated under the assumption that the coefficients are constant over time). Furthermore, if the future values of the exogenous variables G_t and M_t were not known with certainty but had to be forecasted themselves, standard errors could be associated with their forecasts. The exogenous variables could then be treated as normally distributed random variables (with means equal to their forecasted values and standard deviations equal to their standard errors of forecast) in our stochastic simulation. For example, Eq. (14.40) could be rewritten to include an error term associated with G_t (which now must itself be forecasted):

$$Y_t = C_t + I_t + (\hat{G}_t + \eta_t) \tag{14.41}$$

Here, $\hat{G}_t$ is a forecast of G_t and η_t is a normally distributed random variable (defined for each period t) with mean 0 and standard deviation equal to the standard error of the forecast $\hat{G}_t$. Note that our forecast is now a *conditional* forecast.

APPENDIX 14.1 A Small Macroeconomic Model

As a more detailed example of model construction and simulation, we present a simplified structural model of the U.S. economy.[9] This is a highly aggregated model of real gross domestic product (GDP) and its major components and is consistent with the traditional IS/LM models presented in a variety of intermediate macroeconomic theory textbooks. While it does not represent the state of the art of macroeconomic modeling and forecasting, it does provide a useful starting point for students interested in the development and use of multi-equation models.

MODEL SPECIFICATION AND ESTIMATION

The model contains 11 behavioral equations and two identities: one for real disposable income and the accounting identity for real GDP. Each equation in the model is estimated using two-stage least squares.[10] Table A14.1 lists all the endogenous and exogenous variables in the model.[11]

Real GDP and its components are all measured in terms of billions of 1992 dollars on a fixed-weight, rather than chain-weight, basis to preserve the GDP accounting identity with which most students are familiar. Both measures of real output are reported quarterly by the Bureau of Economic Analysis (BEA); however, the chain-weighted measure of real GDP is now the measure used by the BEA because of the problems which arise in making long-term comparisons of real GDP when fixed-weight price indices are used in an environment of rapidly changing prices.

FIXED-WEIGHT VERSUS CHAIN-WEIGHTED REAL GDP

Before 1996 the BEA employed a calculation of real GDP using fixed-price weights based on a particular year, e.g., 1987. Every 5 years the BEA rebenchmarks its calculation of the components of real GDP, updating the price weights in the process. In general, measures of constant-dollar GDP calculated by using prices from a more recent base year will increase less than will calculations that are based on prices from an earlier year. This occurs because output grows most rapidly for those products which have the smallest increases in price. When

---

[9] Michael Donihue, Associate Professor of Economics at Colby College, constructed the model and wrote this appendix.

[10] In "The Estimation of Simultaneous Equation Models with Lagged Endogenous Variables and First Order Serially Correlated Errors," *Econometrica*, vol. 38, pp. 507–516, 1970, Ray C. Fair showed that the lagged dependent and independent variables must be included as instruments to obtain consistent parameter estimates when autocorrelated disturbances create a problem. Fair's method was used in Chapter 12 for two-stage estimation of those equations which exhibited serially correlated disturbances.

[11] A complete listing of all of the data can be found on the data disk that accompanies this text.

TABLE A14.1
VARIABLES IN THE MODEL

Variables	Definition	Equation number
Endogenous		
C	Personal consumption expenditures	(A14.4)
GDP	Gross domestic product	(A14.1)
INFL	Rate of growth of CPI	(A14.13)
INR	Nonresidential fixed investment	(A14.6)
INV	Change in business inventories	(A14.8)
IR	Residential fixed investment	(A14.7)
M	Imports of goods and services	(A14.5)
RL	Average yield on AAA corporate bonds	(A14.10)
RS	Interest rate on 3-month Treasury bills	(A14.9)
TAX	Personal and indirect business tax payments	(A14.3)
UR	Civilian unemployment rate	(A14.11)
WINF	Wage inflation	(A14.12)
YPD	Disposable personal income	(A14.2)
Exogenous		
G	Government purchases of goods and services	
GDPPOT	Potential GDP	
M2	Money stock	
NETWRTH	Household net worth	
OIL	Rate of growth of oil prices	
PRFT	Corporate profits	
PROD	Rate of growth of labor productivity	
TR	Transfer payments to persons	
X	Exports of goods and services	

real GDP is calculated using recent prices, goods and services with strong output growth will receive less weight than they would if those goods and services were valued using prices from an earlier time period. Real growth in aggregate output will thus be lower than it would be if earlier prices were used.[12]

Economists have always known that this presents a problem for comparisons of GDP over time. However, the difference in the effect of using one set of prices over an earlier set was generally considered to be so small as to be unimportant. Two factors caused the BEA to rethink its approach toward calculating real GDP. First, the energy price shocks of the 1970s and the more recent fluctuations in food prices were so large that the choice of price weights had a significant impact on the measurement of real GDP growth.

Second, since the mid-1980s dramatic reductions in computer prices have resulted in a difference of 0.3 percent annually in the rate of growth of real GDP when calculated using 1987 price weights versus prices based in 1982. With the 1995 rebenchmarking of the national income and product accounts,

[12] For a thorough discussion of the BEA's new GDP measures, see the article by Allan H. Young listed at the end of this appendix.

the BEA began using a new measure of real GDP which more accurately reflects output growth in an environment of rapidly changing prices. This measure is known as *chain-weighted real GDP.*

One problem confronting economic modelers is that the *level* of chain-weighted real GDP is not equal to the sum of chain-weighted consumption, investment, government spending, and net exports. However, the *rate of growth* of real, chain-weighted GDP does equal the rate of growth of its real, chain-weighted components.[13] To simplify the specification of the model here and preserve the real GDP accounting identity in level terms, the BEA's rebench-marked measure of GDP based on fixed-weight 1992 prices is used.

EQUATIONS OF THE MODEL

The flowchart in Fig. A14.1 provides a blueprint for the specification of the model. Real, fixed-weight GDP is disaggregated into endogenous components that include real consumption (C), real nonresidential (INR) and residential (IR) fixed investment, real inventory investment (INV), and real imports (M). The remaining components—real government purchases (G) and real exports (X)—are treated as exogenous variables. The GDP identity is thus specified as

$$\text{GDP}_t = C_t + \text{INR}_t + \text{IR}_t + \text{INV}_t + G_t + X_t - M_t \qquad \text{(A14.1)}$$

Each behavioral equation in the model is estimated by using quarterly data from the first quarter of 1960 through the last quarter of 1995. As shown in Fig. A14.1, real disposable income is an important variable in the model because it determines personal consumption expenditures, imports of goods and services, and money demand. A near identity, in nominal terms, would calculate disposable income as gross domestic product minus corporate profits, plus transfer payments, and minus business and personal tax payments. For this model, real disposable income is calculated in Eq. (A14.2) using real values for GDP, tax and transfer payments, and corporate profits. Both transfer payments and corporate profits are treated as exogenous variables.

$$\text{YPD}_t = \text{GDP}_t - \text{PRFT}_t + \text{TR}_t - \text{TAX}_t \qquad \text{(A14.2)}$$

The tax mechanism in the model is very simple. Total business and personal taxes are estimated as follows (t statistics are in parentheses):

$$\widehat{\text{TAX}}_t = -39.76 + 0.196\text{GDP}_t \qquad \text{(A14.3)}$$
$$\underset{(-1.218)}{} \quad \underset{(29.17)}{}$$

$$R^2 = 0.995 \qquad s = 17.27 \qquad \text{DW} = 2.425 \qquad \hat{\rho} = 0.832$$

Instruments: constant,C,G,GDPPOT,INFL,INR,INV,IR,M,M2,RL,RS,X,YPD,GDP$_{t-1}$,TAX$_{t-1}$

---

[13] In nominal terms the familiar GDP accounting identity always holds.

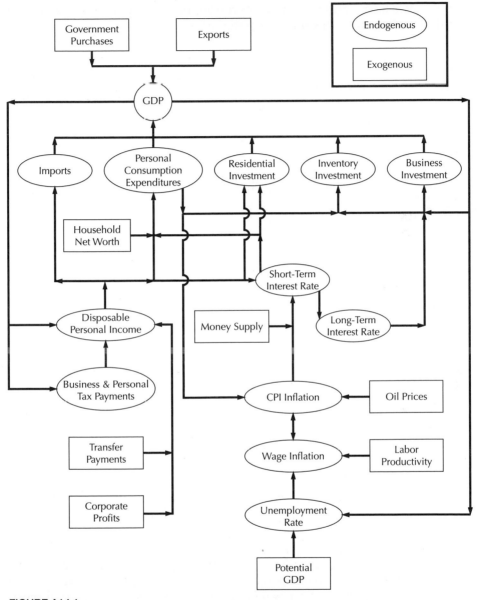

FIGURE A14.1
A small macroeconomic model.

Personal consumption represents two-thirds of GDP and appropriately represents a key behavioral equation in this model. As expected, disposable income is an important determinant of consumption. Household net worth (assets minus liabilities) is also a positive determinant of consumption. By raising the return on savings and increasing the cost of borrowing, higher short-term interest rates have a negative effect on consumption. Thus, the estimated consumption function for this simple macro model is

$$\hat{C}_t = \underset{(0.289)}{2.577} + \underset{(2.104)}{0.100\text{YPD}_t} + \underset{(2.518)}{0.012\text{NETWRTH}_t} - \underset{(-2.131)}{1.785\text{RS}_t} + \underset{(11.522)}{0.817C_{t-1}}$$

(A14.4)

$$R^2 = 0.9997 \qquad s = 17.30 \qquad \text{DW} = 2.102 \qquad \hat{\rho} = 0.240$$

Instruments: constant,G,GDPPOT,INFL,INR,INV,IR,M,M2,RL,WINF,X,C,C_{t-2},NETWRTH$_{t-1}$,YPD$_{t-1}$

Demand for real imports of goods and services is endogenized by relating changes in imports to the level of disposable income. To facilitate simulation of the model, however, we construct our import equation in terms of the level of imports, resulting in the estimated equation

$$\hat{M}_t = M_{t-1} - \underset{(-1.853)}{5.636} + \underset{(3.846)}{0.003\text{YPD}_t}$$

(A14.5)

$$R^2 = 0.997 \qquad\qquad s = 10.79 \qquad\qquad \text{DW} = 1.693$$

Instruments: constant,C,G,GDP,GDPPOT,INFL,INR,INV,M2,RL,RS,X,YPD$_{t-1}$

Turning next to the investment sector, nonresidential investment will depend positively on aggregate economic activity and will depend negatively on the opportunity cost of investment. Thus, real nonresidential fixed investment is estimated to be a positive function of GDP and a negative function of long-term interest rates:

$$\widehat{\text{INR}}_t = -\underset{(-0.364)}{38.62} + \underset{(7.638)}{0.121\text{GDP}_t} - \underset{(-2.065)}{7.244\text{RL}_{t-4}}$$

(A14.6)

$$R^2 = 0.996 \qquad s = 8.871 \qquad \text{DW} = 1.266 \qquad \hat{\rho} = 0.975$$

Instruments: constant,C,G,GDPPOT,INFL,INV,IR,M,M2,X,YPD,GDP$_{t-1}$,INR$_{t-1}$,RL$_{t-5}$

Residential investment is a procyclical variable that reflects household demand for new homes. Therefore, investment in residential structures is estimated as a function of real disposable income and the cost of borrowing. To keep the model simple, short-term interest rates are used as a proxy for mortgage interest rates:

$$\widehat{\text{IR}}_t = \underset{(1.329)}{73.39} + \underset{(3.349)}{0.041\text{YPD}_{t-1}} - \underset{(-4.675)}{6.101\text{RS}_{t-1}}$$

(A14.7)

$$R^2 = 0.962 \qquad s = 8.999 \qquad \text{DW} = 1.124 \qquad \hat{\rho} = 0.952$$

Inst: constant,C,G,GDP,GDPPOT,INFL,INR,INV,IR,M,M2,NETWRTH,RL,X,IR$_{t-1}$,RS$_{t-2}$,YPD$_{t-2}$

The change in business inventories each quarter is equal to the excess of production relative to demand. Research has shown that much of the variation in real output growth over the course of a business cycle can be attributed to variations in the rate of inventory accumulation. Thus, the change in business inventories is estimated as a function of the change in the difference between total output and consumption:

$$\widehat{INV}_t = 2.420 + 0.378\Delta(GDP_t - C_t) + 0.756INV_{t-1} \qquad (A14.8)$$
$$\quad\;\;\,(1.248) \qquad (4.999) \qquad\qquad\quad (13.05)$$

$$R^2 = 0.660 \qquad s = 13.34 \qquad DW = 2.384$$

Instruments: constant,C,G,GDPPOT,INFL,INR,IR,M,M2,RL,RS,X,INV_{t-2},$\Delta(GDP_{t-1} - C_{t-1})$

The monetary sector of our model consists of a standard LM curve and a simple term-structure equation. Short-term interest rates are modeled as a normalization of a traditional money demand equation. Demand for money increases with income but decreases when real short-term interest rates rise as the opportunity cost of holding money increases. Thus, real interest rates should be a positive function of disposable income and a negative function of the money supply. *Ex post*, the real interest rate will equal the nominal interest rate minus the rate of inflation. Thus, short-term interest rates are estimated by

$$\widehat{RS}_t = -23.44 + 0.012YPD_t - 0.011M2_t + 0.157INFL_t \qquad (A14.9)$$
$$\qquad\;\;(-2.564) \qquad (3.484) \qquad\;\; (-3.470) \qquad\;\; (3.903)$$

$$R^2 = 0.912 \qquad s = 0.828 \qquad DW = 1.871 \qquad \hat{\rho} = 0.942$$

Instruments: constant,C,G,INR,INV,IR,M,RL,X,$INFL_{t-1}$,RS_{t-1},$M2_{t-1}$,YPD_{t-1}

Influences on short-term interest rates are passed through contemporaneously and with a lag to long-term rates. The term structure equation of our model is

$$\widehat{RL}_t = 0.256 + 0.112RS_t + 0.887RL_{t-1} \qquad (A14.10)$$
$$\qquad\;\;(2.233) \qquad (4.575) \qquad (36.76)$$

$$R^2 = 0.984 \qquad s = 0.339 \qquad DW = 1.995 \qquad \hat{\rho} = 0.193$$

Instruments: constant,C,G,GDP,GDPPOT,INFL,INR,INV,IR,M,M2,X,YPD,RL_{t-2},RS_{t-1}

The unemployment rate is determined according to a traditional Okun's law equation which relates changes in the unemployment rate to the GDP gap:

$$\widehat{\Delta UR}_t = -0.001 - 0.092(\Delta \log GDP_t - \Delta \log GDPPOT_t) \qquad (A14.11)$$
$$\qquad\;\;(-0.061) \qquad (-9.541)$$

$$R^2 = 0.361 \qquad s = 0.279 \qquad DW = 1.837$$

Instruments: constant,C,G,INFL,INR,INV,IR,M,M2,NETWRTH,RL,RS,WINF,X,YPD

Note that the R^2 statistic for Eq. (A14.11) is much lower than it is in the other equations as a result of the fact that the dependent variable is measured in terms of quarterly changes.[14]

The final two equations in the model predict wage and price inflation. The annual rate of growth in wages will be a positive function of overall price inflation, a negative function of the unemployment rate (excess labor supply puts downward pressure on wage growth), and a positive function of productivity growth. Our estimated equation for overall wage growth is

$$\widehat{WINF}_t = \underset{(4.207)}{3.388} + \underset{(11.00)}{0.751 INFL_t} - \underset{(-2.139)}{0.254 UR_{t-2}} + \underset{(2.822)}{0.272 PROD_t} \qquad (A14.12)$$

$$R^2 = 0.483 \qquad s = 2.039 \qquad DW = 1.796$$

Inst: constant,C,G,GDP,GDPPOT,INFL$_{t-1}$,INR,INV,IR,M,NETWRTH,PRFT,RL,RS,TR,UR,WINF$_{t-1}$,X

The annual rate of growth in the consumer price index is estimated to be a function of wage inflation, consumer demand, and oil prices:

$$\widehat{INFL}_t = \underset{(-1.605)}{-1.935} + \underset{(2.214)}{0.472 WINF_t} + \underset{(2.100)}{0.001 C_{t-1}} + \underset{(3.856)}{0.042 OIL_t} + \underset{(2.894)}{0.465 INFL_{t-1}}$$

$$(A14.13)$$

$$R^2 = 0.701 \qquad s = 1.759 \qquad DW = 2.110$$

Inst: constant,C,C_{t-2},G,GDP$_{t-1}$,GDPPOT,INV,IR,M,NETWRTH,PRFT,RL,RS,TR,WINF$_{t-1}$,X,YPD

SIMULATION OF THE MODEL

The model can now be simulated as a complete system. Two historical simulations and an *ex post* forecast were performed to evaluate the model's ability to replicate the actual data.[15] The first simulation covers the entire estimation period (1960−2 to 1995−4). The second covers the final 10 years of historical data in the sample, from the first quarter of 1986 through the fourth quarter of 1995. Then, to perform an *ex post* forecast, each equation of the model was reestimated using data from the first quarter of 1960 through the fourth quarter of 1993, truncating the sample period by 2 years. Then the model was simulated over the final eight quarters for which data were available (1994−1 to 1995−4), solving for values of the endogenous variables by using actual his-

[14] The R^2 statistic calculated for the *level* of the unemployment rate is equal to 0.966.

[15] The simulations here are dynamic in the sense that simulated (rather than actual) values for the endogenous variables in a given period are used as inputs when the model is solved in future periods.

TABLE A14.2
MODEL SIMULATION ERRORS

	Historical simulations				Ex post simulation	
	1960-2–1995-4		1986-1–1995-4		1994-1–1995-4	
	Mean errors	rms errors	Mean errors	rms errors	Mean errors	rms errors
C	0.712	75.910	−44.838	73.884	1.970	18.524
GDP	0.437	124.857	−104.954	136.777	14.919	34.828
INFL	−0.350	3.440	−1.688	4.695	−4.095	4.378
INR	−5.482	49.027	−90.569	99.722	34.681	40.365
INV	−0.030	23.814	−4.449	27.573	18.707	26.119
IR	0.622	30.825	−17.149	30.887	11.507	12.246
M	−4.615	42.036	−52.050	66.422	51.946	56.455
RL	0.224	1.842	−0.607	1.198	0.735	1.032
RS	0.071	2.491	−1.348	2.444	−0.637	0.715
TAX	−0.166	43.305	−31.290	41.595	−0.870	12.488
UR	0.572	1.121	−0.266	0.763	−0.549	0.590
WINF	−0.438	3.559	−2.047	4.790	−3.780	4.244
YPD	0.603	97.843	−73.664	99.886	15.790	40.429

torical values for the exogenous variables. Table A14.2 summarizes the results of these simulations.

For each experiment, root-mean-square (rms) errors and mean errors are presented. Mean errors provide a measure of the bias of the model's predicted values for each variable; a negative entry corresponds to a positive bias for that variable. Over the full sample period the model produces relatively small mean errors, underpredicting real GDP, consumption, interest rates, and unemployment on average. The rms errors reported here are somewhat larger than what we might expect with the large-scale macroeconometric models used for forecasting and policy analysis, primarily as a result of the lack of detail in the scope of this model and the simplified equation specifications. The errors for the subsample of data are substantially larger as the model tends to exhibit a negative bias (overprediction) for each of the endogenous variables.

Figures A14.2 to A14.11 illustrate actual and simulated values for the endogenous variables in the model for the historical simulation covering the entire sample. These figures illustrate the biases reported by the error statistics in Table A14.2. In Fig. A14.2 we see that the model's predicted values track the actual values for real GDP fairly closely but miss the major business cycle turning points. The model fails to capture the recession of 1990–1991 entirely, overpredicting consumption and nonresidential and residential investment. Economists today generally point to a collapse in business and consumer confidence as a major contributing factor to the last recession—an unobservable component in our model.

Figure A14.11 shows that much of the historical error underlying CPI infla-

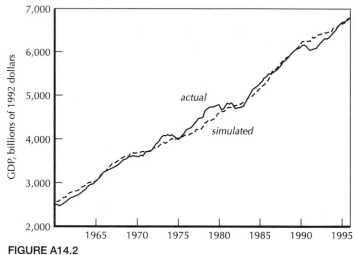

FIGURE A14.2
Historical simulation of GDP.

FIGURE A14.3
Historical simulation of consumption.

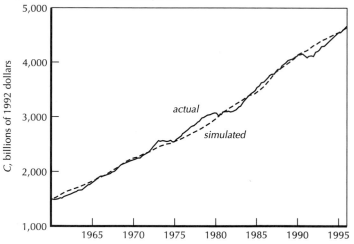

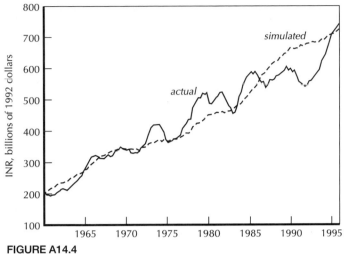

FIGURE A14.4
Historical simulation of nonresidential investment.

FIGURE A14.5
Historical simulation of residential investment.

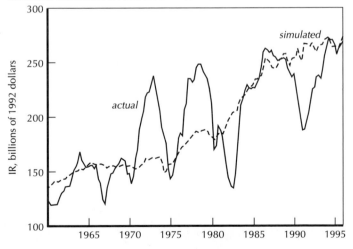

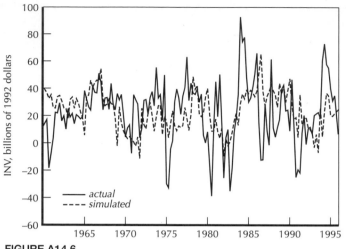

FIGURE A14.6
Historical simulation of inventory investment.

FIGURE A14.7
Historical simulation of short-term interest rate.

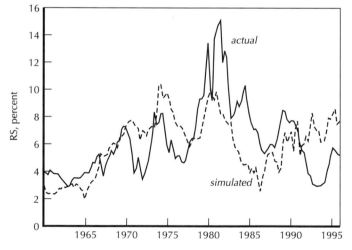

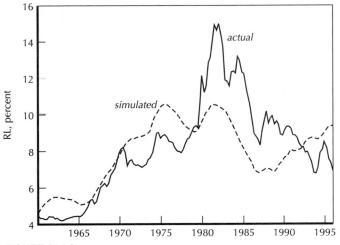

FIGURE A14.8
Historical simulation of long-term interest rate.

FIGURE A14.9
Historical simulation of the unemployment rate.

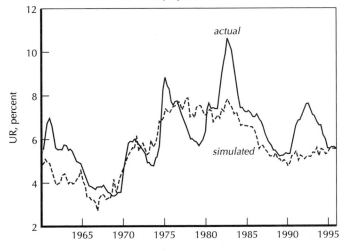

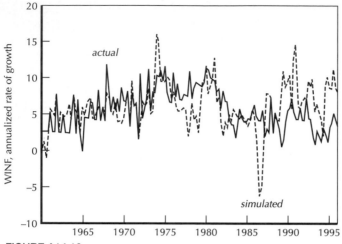

FIGURE A14.10
Historical simulation of wage inflation.

FIGURE A14.11
Historical simulation of CPI inflation.

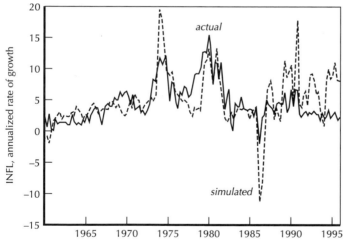

tion is due to overpredictions coinciding with the rapid changes in oil prices which occurred in 1974 and 1986. Figures A14.10 and A14.11 also illustrate the recent breakdown in the historical relationship between wages and prices and demand pressures in the rest of the economy. In the mid-1990s many economists expected wage and price inflation to be much higher than it was because of an extended period of output growth above potential and relatively low rates of unemployment. The *ex post* simulations illustrated in Figs. A14.12 to A14.15 illustrate this fact and present a current puzzle for economists who believe in traditional theories of macroeconomic behavior.

Before using the model to perform some simple policy experiments, it is helpful to calculate the dynamic GDP multipliers that correspond to changes in government spending (G) and the money supply (M2). These total multipliers, which represent the change in GDP after the specified number of periods has elapsed, are shown in Table A14.3. The government spending multipliers were obtained by increasing G in our model by $1 billion above its historical path, beginning in the first quarter of 1986. The simulated values for GDP corresponding to the historical series for government spending were then subtracted from the simulated series for GDP resulting from the higher value of government spending. Note that the initial impact of the change in government spending produces a multiplier of 2.16. The long-run government spending multiplier for this model is about 1.4.

Similarly, the money supply was increased by $1 billion in the first quarter of 1986 and all quarters thereafter, and the corresponding changes in GDP were then calculated. From Fig. A14.1 we see that in this simple model changes in the money supply affect GDP indirectly through the interest-sensitive components of spending. Thus, the initial impact multiplier of a $1 billion change in the money supply is $0.03 billion (1992 dollars). In the long run the change in GDP resulting from a $1 billion change in M2 is about $0.36 billion.

Forecasting and Policy Analysis

Next we demonstrate the use of this model in performing some standard forecasting and policy experiments. In each experiment we simulate the model 3 years into the future, beginning in the first quarter of 1996. The four experiments outlined below are representative of applications of structural macro models that are commonly performed by commercial forecasters and government policy makers.

Experiment 1: Baseline Forecast   Once the model has been specified and estimated, the first step in producing a forecast involves coming up with projections for the exogenous variables in the model. By definition, these variables are determined outside the model, and thus the subjective judgment of the forecaster plays a critical role. Published government budget projections and growth targets for money supply will, for example, aid the forecaster in determining future paths for these variables. Other variables, however, require an

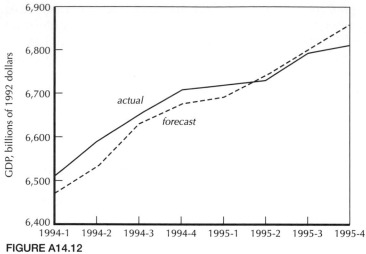

FIGURE A14.12
Ex post forecast of GDP.

FIGURE A14.13
Ex post forecast of short-term interest rate.

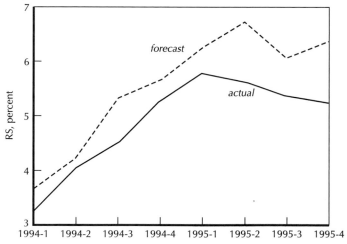

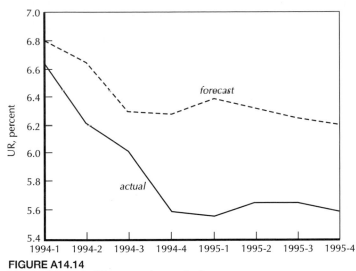

FIGURE A14.14
Ex post forecast of the unemployment rate.

FIGURE A14.15
Ex post forecast of CPI inflation.

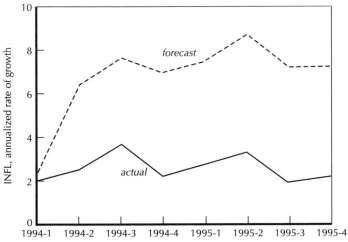

TABLE A14.3
DYNAMIC MULTIPLIERS

	ΔGDP				ΔGDP	
Quarter	From ΔG	From ΔM2	Quarter	From ΔG	From ΔM2
0	2.16	0.03	16	1.45	0.36
2	1.67	0.19	20	1.43	0.36
4	1.54	0.23	24	1.41	0.37
6	1.49	0.27	28	1.39	0.37
8	1.48	0.30	32	1.37	0.36
10	1.47	0.32	36	1.35	0.36
12	1.47	0.34			

The multipliers in this table are dynamic in that they show the change in GDP resulting from a $1 billion change in the exogenous variable within n quarters after the change occurs.

educated guess on the part of the forecaster. As a result, the final forecast will reflect the skill and expertise of the modeler. For our baseline forecast we employ a less subjective approach by estimating a first-order autoregressive model for each of the exogenous variables and then using the resulting equations to produce quarterly forecasts through the end of 1998. (Part Four of this book introduces more subjective time-series models which could be used to forecast these exogenous variables.) The OLS regression equations used for forecasting the exogenous variables are presented in Table A14.4.

TABLE A14.4
FORECAST EQUATIONS FOR EXOGENOUS VARIABLES

Variable	Intercept	Coefficient	R^2
G	9.171 (2.197)	0.995 (237.9)	0.997
GDPPOT	22.62 (6.064)	1.002 (1267)	0.999
M2	12.46 (5.379)	1.007 (843.4)	0.999
NETWRTH	9.398 (0.133)	1.007 (221.7)	0.997
OIL	3.515 (1.043)	0.271 (3.334)	0.074
PRFT	10.67 (1.149)	0.976 (36.66)	0.904
PROD	1.709 (4.975)	0.027 (0.318)	0.001
TR	3.336 (2.052)	1.005 (334.9)	0.999
X	−0.787 (−0.508)	1.018 (243.9)	0.998

The estimates presented in this table correspond to parameter estimates for the autoregressive forecasting equation $Y_t = \alpha + \beta Y_{t-1} + \varepsilon_t$. t statistics are given in parentheses.

Experiment 2: Constant Government Spending   In this experiment real government spending is assumed to remain constant throughout the forecast horizon, equal to its value in the fourth quarter of 1995. All the other exogenous variables follow the same paths that they follow in the baseline forecast. The objective is to examine how a lower level of government spending, with no trend, will affect GDP, prices, and the other variables.

Experiment 3: Ten Percent Money Supply Growth   In the baseline forecast M2 grows at an annual rate of 4 percent each quarter. In this experiment M2 is assumed to grow at an annual rate of 10 percent each quarter. Faster growth of the money supply should be expansionary, resulting in greater output growth, lower interest rates, and higher rates of inflation.

Experiment 4: Tax Cut   In Eq. (A14.3) the estimated average tax rate is 0.196. In this experiment we lower the average tax rate to 0.167 in an attempt to simulate the effect of a 15 percent tax cut. A tax reduction such as this one should be highly expansionary.

The results of these experiments are shown in Figs. A14.16 to A14.19 and are consistent with traditional Keynesian models. In the baseline forecast real government purchases grow at an annual rate of roughly 0.8 percent each quarter. Holding government spending constant in real terms reduces aggregate demand, decreasing GDP and its components. Interest rates fall as a drop in disposable income results in lower money demand while the money supply remains the same as in the baseline forecast. The unemployment rate rises relative to the baseline with the drop in output below potential, and inflation falls slightly.

FIGURE A14.16
Alternative policy forecasts of GDP.

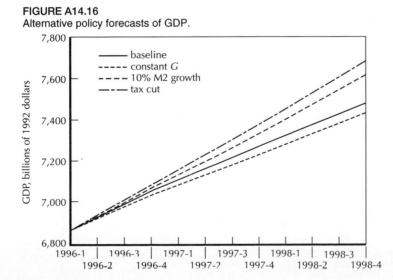

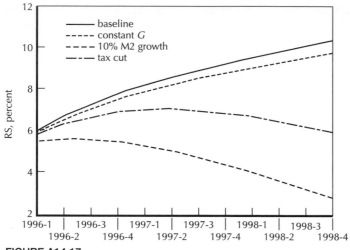

FIGURE A14.17
Alternative policy forecasts of short-term interest rates.

FIGURE A14.18
Alternative policy forecasts of the unemployment rate.

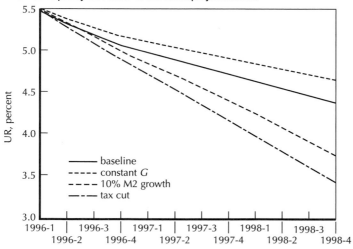

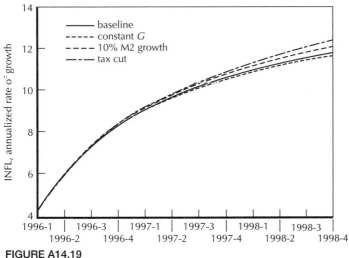

FIGURE A14.19
Alternative policy forecasts of CPI inflation.

Increasing the rate of growth of the money supply lowers both short-term and long-term interest rates substantially, resulting in more investment and consumer spending. GDP rises, and unemployment falls. Greater growth of the money supply also results in higher inflation.

Finally, a 15 percent tax cut would, according to this model, be highly expansionary. Real GDP growth accelerates, unemployment falls, and inflation increases.

FURTHER READING

Donihue, Michael R. "Evaluating the Role Judgment Plays in Forecast Accuracy," *Journal of Forecasting,* vol. 12, no. 2, pp. 81–92, February 1993.

Fair, Ray C. *Specification, Estimation, and Analysis of Macroeconometric Models* (Cambridge, Mass.: Harvard University Press, 1994).

Klein, Lawrence R., ed. *Comparative Performance of U.S. Econometric Models* (New York: Oxford University Press, 1991).

Klein, Lawrence R., and Richard M. Young. *An Introduction to Econometric Forecasting and Forecasting Models* (Lexington, Mass.: Lexington Books, DC Heath, 1980).

Young, Allan H. "Alternative Measures of Change in Real Output and Prices, Quarterly Estimates for 1959–92," *Survey of Current Business,* vol. 73, pp. 31–41, March 1993.

EXERCISES

14.1 Show that if $A_1\lambda_1^t$ and $A_2\lambda_2^t$ are both transient solutions to a model, i.e., both satisfy an equation such as Eq. (14.5), then the sum $A_1\lambda_1^t + A_2\lambda_2^t$ must also be a solution.

14.2 Consider the following simple multiplier-accelerator macroeconomic model:

$$C_t = a_1 + a_2 Y_{t-1} \qquad I_t = b_1 + b_2(C_t - C_{t-1}) \qquad Y_t = C_t + I_t + G_t$$

Note that investment is now a function of changes in consumption rather than a function of changes in total GNP.

(a) Determine the characteristic equation for this model and find the associated characteristic roots.

(b) Find the relationships between values of a_2 and b_2 that determine what kind of solution the model will have. Draw a diagram that corresponds to that of Fig. 14.1.

(c) What is the impact multiplier corresponding to a change in G_t? What is the *total* long-run multiplier corresponding to a change in G_t?

14.3 The following equations describe a simple "cobweb" model of a competitive market:

Demand: $Q_t^D = a_1 + a_2 P_t \qquad a_2 < 0$

Supply: $Q_t^S = b_1 + b_2 P_{t-1} \qquad b_2 > 0$

When the market is in equilibrium, $Q_t^D = Q_t^S$. Now suppose that the market is temporarily out of equilibrium, i.e., that $Q_t^D \neq Q_t^S$ temporarily.

(a) Show that the price will converge in a stable manner to an equilibrium value if $b_2/a_2 < 1$.

(b) Show that the path to equilibrium will be oscillatory if $b_2 > 0$ and will not be oscillatory if $b_2 < 0$.

PART FOUR

TIME-SERIES MODELS

In the first three parts of this book we saw how econometric models—both single-equation regression models and multi-equation models—can be constructed and used to explain and forecast the future movements of one or more variables. In Part Four we are again interested in constructing models and using them for forecasting, but these models are quite different from the ones we worked with earlier. We no longer predict future movements in a variable by relating it to a set of other variables in a causal framework; instead, we base our prediction solely on the past behavior of that variable.

As an example, consider the time series $y(t)$ drawn in the figure on page 464, which might represent the historical performance of an economic or business variable—a stock market index, an interest rate, a production index, or perhaps the daily sales volume for a commodity. $y(t)$ might have moved up or down partly in response to changes in prices, personal income, and interest rates (or so we may believe). However, much of its movement might have been due to factors we cannot explain, such as the weather, changes in taste, or simply seasonal (or aseasonal) cycles in spending.

It may be difficult or impossible to explain the movement of $y(t)$ through the use of a structural model. This may happen if, for example, data are not available for those explanatory variables which are believed to affect $y(t)$. Or if data are available, the estimation of a regression model for $y(t)$ may result in standard errors so large that they make most of the estimated coefficients insignificant and the standard error of forecast unacceptably large.

Even if we can estimate a statistically significant regression equation for $y(t)$, the result may not be useful for forecasting purposes. To obtain a forecast for $y(t)$ from a regression equation, explanatory variables that are not lagged must

463

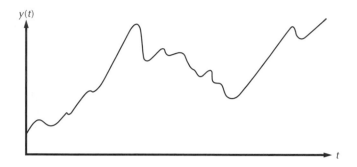

themselves be forecasted, and this may be more difficult than is forecasting $y(t)$ itself. The standard error of forecast may be small for $y(t)$ with known future values of the explanatory variables. However, when the future values of the explanatory variables are unknown, their forecast errors may be so large that they make the total forecast error for $y(t)$ too large to be acceptable.

Thus there are situations in which we seek an alternative means of obtaining a forecast of $y(t)$. Can we observe the time series in the figure and draw some conclusions about its *past* behavior that would allow us to infer something about its probable *future* behavior? For example, is there some kind of overall upward trend in $y(t)$ which, because it has dominated the past behavior of the series, may be expected to dominate its future behavior? Or does the series exhibit cyclical behavior which we can extrapolate into the future? If systematic behavior of this type is present we can attempt to construct a *model* for the time series which does not offer a structural explanation for its behavior in terms of other variables but does replicate its past behavior in a way that may help us forecast its future behavior. A *time-series model* accounts for patterns in the past movements of a variable and uses that information to predict its future movements. In a sense a time-series model is just a sophisticated method of extrapolation. Yet as we will see in this part of the book, it sometimes provides an effective tool for forecasting.

Since time-series analysis builds on the development of the single-equation regression model, we treat time-series models in the last part of the book even though they are the "simplest" class of models in terms of their explanation of the real world. To forecast a short-term interest rate, we might use a regression model to relate that variable to GDP, prices, and the money supply. A time series for interest rates would relate that variable to its past values and to variables that describe the random nature of its past behavior. The model, like most regression models, is an equation containing a set of coefficients that must be estimated. However, the equation is usually nonlinear in the coefficients, making nonlinear estimation necessary.

Part Four begins with a brief survey of simple extrapolation methods (in effect, deterministic models of time series) as well as methods for smoothing and seasonally adjusting time series. Extrapolation techniques have been used widely for many years, and for some applications they provide a simple yet adequate means of forecasting. Smoothing and seasonal adjustment are also useful techniques which in many instances can facilitate the forecasting or interpretation of a time series.

In Chapter 16 we present a brief introduction to the nature of stochastic time series. We discuss how stochastic processes are generated, what they look like, and most important, how they are described. We also discuss some of the characteristics of stochastic processes and in particular develop the concept of stationarity. Then we describe autocorrelation functions and show how they can be used as a means of describing time series and as a tool for testing their properties. Finally, we discuss methods of testing for stationarity and the concept of *co-integrated* time series. The concepts and analytic tools developed in this chapter are essential to the discussion of time-series models in the chapters that follow.

Chapter 17 develops linear models for time series, including moving average models, autoregressive models, and mixed autoregressive–moving average models for stationary time series. We show how some nonstationary time-series models can be differenced one or more times to produce a stationary series. This enables us to develop a general integrated autoregressive–moving average (ARIMA) model. Finally, we show how autocorrelation functions can be used to specify and characterize a time-series model.

Chapter 18 deals with the use of time-series models to make forecasts. The chapter explains how the parameters of a time-series model are estimated and how a specification of the model can be verified. It goes on to discuss how the model can be used to produce a forecast. We also show how time series are adaptive in nature, i.e., how they produce forecasts in a way that adapts to new information. The last part of Chapter 18 deals with forecast errors and shows how confidence intervals can be determined for forecasts.

Chapter 19 develops some examples of applications of time-series modeling. Here we lead the reader through the construction of several time-series models and demonstrate their application to forecasting problems.

CHAPTER 15

SMOOTHING AND EXTRAPOLATION OF TIME SERIES

As was explained in the introduction to Part Four, a time-series model is a sophisticated method of extrapolating data. At times, however, less sophisticated methods of extrapolation can be used for forecasting purposes. For example, projections for a large number of time series may be needed quickly, so that time and resources do not permit the use of formal modeling techniques, or there may be reason to believe that a particular time series follows a simple trend, thus obviating the need for a more complicated model. We therefore begin by discussing some simple (and not so simple) methods of extrapolation. These extrapolation techniques represent *deterministic models* of time series.

At times it is desirable to *smooth* a time series and thus eliminate some of the more volatile short-term fluctuations. Smoothing may be done before making a forecast or simply to make the time series easier to analyze and interpret. Smoothing also may be done to remove seasonal fluctuations, i.e., to *deseasonalize* (or *seasonally adjust*) a time series. We will discuss smoothing and seasonal adjustment in the second section of this chapter.

15.1 SIMPLE EXTRAPOLATION MODELS

We begin with simple models that can be used to forecast a time series on the basis of its past behavior. These models are *deterministic* in that no reference is made to the sources or nature of the underlying randomness in the series. Essentially, the models involve extrapolation techniques that have been standard tools of the trade in economic and business forecasting for years. Although they usually do not provide as much forecasting accuracy as do the modern

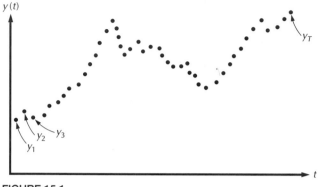

FIGURE 15.1
Discrete time series.

stochastic time-series models, they often provide a simple, inexpensive, and still quite acceptable means of forecasting.

Most of the series we encounter are not continuous in time; instead, they consist of discrete observations made at regular intervals of time. A typical time series might be given by Fig. 15.1. We denote the values of that series by y_t, so that y_1 represents the first observation, y_2 the second, and y_T the *last* observation for the series.[1] Our objective is to model the series y_t and use that model to forecast y_t beyond the last observation y_T. We denote the forecast one period ahead by $\hat{y}_{T+1}$, two periods ahead by $\hat{y}_{T+2}$, and l periods ahead by $\hat{y}_{T+l}$.

If the number of observations is not too large, the simplest and most complete representation of y_t is given by a polynomial whose degree is 1 less than the number of observations; i.e., we can describe y_t by a continuous function of time $f(t)$, where

$$f(t) = a_0 + a_1 t + a_2 t^2 + \cdots + a_n t^n \qquad (15.1)$$

and $n = T - 1$. Such a polynomial (if the a's are chosen correctly) will pass through *every point* in the time series y_t. Thus, we can be sure that $f(t)$ will equal y_t at every time t from 1 to T. Can we, however, have any confidence that a *forecast* of y_t generated by $f(t)$ will be at all close to its actual future value? For example, will the forecast

$$f(T + 1) = a_0 + a_1(T + 1) + a_2(T + 1)^2 + \cdots + a_{T-1}(T + 1)^{T-1} = \hat{y}_{T+1}$$

be close to the actual future value y_{T+1}? Unfortunately, we have no way of answering this question without additional prior information. The difficulty with the model given by Eq. (15.1) is that it does not describe y_t; it merely *reproduces* y_t. It does not capture any characteristics of y_t that might repeat

---

[1] In Part Four of the book we use lowercase letters, for example, y_t, to denote time series.

themselves in the future. Thus, although $f(t)$ correlates perfectly with y_t, it is of little use for forecasting.

15.1.1   Simple Extrapolation Models

A basic characteristic of y_t is its long-run growth pattern. If we believe that this upward trend exists and will continue (and there may not be any reason why we should), we can construct a simple model that describes the trend and can be used to forecast y_t.

The simplest extrapolation model is the *linear trend model.* If we believe that a series y_t will increase in constant absolute amounts in each time period, we can predict y_t by fitting the trend line

$$y_t = c_1 + c_2 t \tag{15.2}$$

where t is time and y_t is the value of y at time t. Usually t is chosen to equal 0 in the base period (first observation) and to increase by 1 during each successive period. For example, if we determine by regression that

$$y_t = 27.5 + 3.2t \tag{15.3}$$

we can predict that the value of y in period $t + 1$ will be 3.2 units higher than the previous value.

It may be more realistic to assume that the series y_t grows with constant percentage increases rather than constant absolute increases. This assumption implies that y_t follows an *exponential growth curve:*

$$y_t = f(t) = Ae^{rt} \tag{15.4}$$

Here A and r would be chosen to maximize the correlation between $f(t)$ and y_t. A forecast one period ahead would then be given by

$$\hat{y}_{T+1} = Ae^{r(T+1)} \tag{15.5}$$

and a forecast l periods ahead by

$$\hat{y}_{T+l} = Ae^{r(T+l)} \tag{15.6}$$

This is illustrated in Fig. 15.2. The parameters A and r can be estimated by taking the logarithms of both sides of Eq. (15.4) and fitting the log-linear regression equation[2]

$$\log y_t = c_1 + c_2 t \tag{15.7}$$

where $c_1 = \log A$ and $c_2 = r$.

---

[2] Note that in the exponential growth model the logarithm of y_t is assumed to grow at a constant rate. If $y_{t+1} = Ae^{rt}$, then $y_{t+1}/y_t = e^r$, and $\log y_{t+1} - \log y_t = r$.

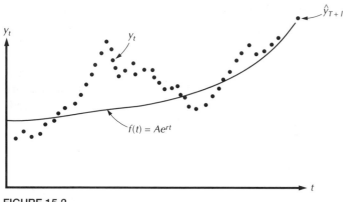

FIGURE 15.2
Exponential growth curve.

A third extrapolation method is based on the *autoregressive trend model*

$$y_t = c_1 + c_2 y_{t-1} \tag{15.8}$$

In using such an extrapolation procedure one has the option of fixing $c_1 = 0$, in which case c_2 represents the rate of change of the series y. If, however, c_2 is set equal to 1, with c_1 not equal to 0, the extrapolated series will increase by the same absolute amount in each time period. The autoregressive trend model is illustrated in Fig. 15.3 for three different values of c_2 (in all cases $c_1 = 1$).

A variation of this model is the *logarithmic autoregressive trend model*

$$\log y_t = c_1 + c_2 \log y_{t-1} \tag{15.9}$$

FIGURE 15.3
Autoregressive trend model.

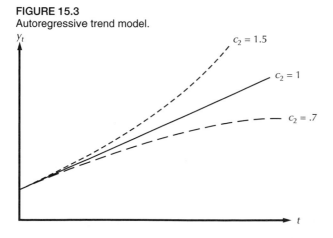

If c_1 is fixed to be 0, the value of c_2 is the compounded rate of growth of the series y. Both linear extrapolation and compound extrapolation based on the autoregressive model are commonly used as a simple means of forecasting.

Note that the four models described above basically involve regressing y_t (or log y_t) against a function of time (linear or exponential) and/or itself lagged. Alternative models can be developed by making the function slightly more complicated. As examples, let us examine two other simple extrapolation models: the *quadratic trend model* and the *logistic growth curve*.

The quadratic trend model is a simple extension of the linear trend model and involves adding a term in t^2

$$y_t = c_1 + c_2 t + c_3 t^2 \tag{15.10}$$

If c_2 and c_3 are both positive, y_t will always be increasing, but even more rapidly as time goes on. If c_2 is negative and c_3 is positive, y_t will at first decrease but later increase. If both c_2 and c_3 are negative, y_t will always decrease. The various cases are illustrated in Fig. 15.4 ($c_1 > 0$ in each case). Note that even if the data show that y_t has generally been increasing over time, estimation of Eq. (15.10) may yield a positive value for c_3 but a negative value for c_2. This can occur (as shown in Fig. 15.4) because the data usually span only a portion of the trend curve.

A somewhat more complicated model, at least in terms of its estimation, is the *logistic curve*, which is given by

$$y_t = \frac{1}{k + ab^t} \qquad b > 0 \tag{15.11}$$

FIGURE 15.4
Quadratic trend model.

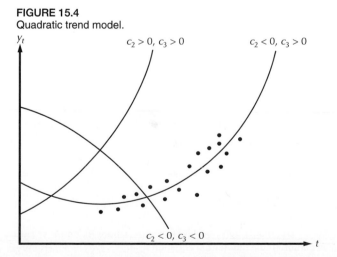

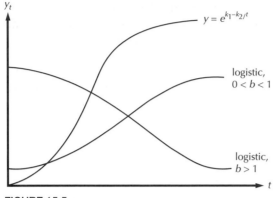

FIGURE 15.5
S-shaped curves.

This equation is nonlinear in the parameters (k, a, and b) and therefore must be estimated using a nonlinear estimation procedure. While this can add computational expense, there are some cases in which it is worth it. As shown in Fig. 15.5, Eq. (15.11) represents an S-shaped curve which may be used to represent the sales of a product that will someday saturate the market (so that the total stock of the good in circulation will approach some plateau or, equivalently, additional sales will approach zero).[3]

Other S-shaped curves can be used in addition to the logistic curve. One very simple function with an S shape that can be used to model sales saturation patterns is given by

$$y_t = e^{k_1 - (k_2/t)} \tag{15.12}$$

Note that if we take the logarithms of both sides, we have an equation that is linear in the parameters α and β and which can be estimated using ordinary least squares:

$$\log y_t = k_1 - \frac{k_2}{t} \tag{15.13}$$

This curve is also shown in Fig. 15.5. Note that it begins at the origin and rises more steeply than does the logistic curve.

---

[3] The following *approximation* to the logistic curve can be estimated using ordinary least squares:

$$\frac{\Delta y_t}{y_{t-1}} = c_1 - c_2 y_{t-1}$$

The parameter c_2 should always be less than 1 and typically is in the vicinity of .05 to .5. This equation is a discrete-time approximation to the differential equation $dy/dt = c_2 y(c_1 - y)$, and the *solution* to this differential equation has the form of Eq. (15.11).

Example 15.1 Forecasting Department Store Sales   In this example simple extrapolation models are used to forecast monthly retail sales for department stores.[4] The time series is listed in the table below, where monthly observations are seasonally adjusted and cover the period from January 1986 to December 1995. The units of measurement are millions of dollars and the source of the data is the U.S. Department of Commerce.

	1986	1987	1988	1989	1990	1991	1992	1993	1994	1995
January	11,181	11,887	12,498	13,471	14,035	14,113	15,358	16,612	17,752	19,409
February	11,258	12,181	12,297	13,055	14,127	14,413	15,666	16,425	18,040	19,229
March	11,459	12,023	12,687	13,388	14,435	14,761	15,421	16,067	18,304	19,324
April	11,508	12,251	12,736	13,555	14,048	14,761	15,433	16,669	18,161	19,344
May	11,519	12,472	12,855	13,567	13,965	14,782	15,636	16,814	18,076	19,485
June	11,621	12,365	12,847	13,675	14,394	14,569	15,607	16,847	18,464	19,656
July	11,769	12,394	12,879	13,717	14,270	14,888	15,681	17,132	18,486	19,766
August	11,834	12,516	12,924	13,743	14,281	14,988	15,936	17,162	18,718	19,614
September	11,836	12,445	13,113	14,014	14,221	14,805	16,017	17,377	18,724	19,776
October	11,766	12,534	13,280	13,915	14,197	14,863	16,188	17,616	19,016	19,531
November	11,655	12,411	13,323	13,990	14,333	15,045	16,242	17,470	19,008	19,795
December	11,723	12,611	13,382	14,079	14,280	15,046	16,382	17,637	19,064	19,685

One might wish to forecast monthly sales for January, February, and the months following in 1996. For this example we extrapolate sales for January 1996. The results of four regressions associated with four of the trend models described above are listed below. Standard regression statistics are shown with t statistics in parentheses:

Linear trend model:

$$\text{SALES}_t = 10{,}765.4 + 71.682t \qquad (15.14)$$
$$\phantom{\text{SALES}_t = }(126.73) \qquad (58.10)$$

$R^2 = .966 \qquad F(1/73) = 3{,}375 \qquad s = 468.2 \qquad \text{DW} = .14$

Logarithmic linear trend model (exponential growth):

$$\log(\text{SALES})_t = 9.322 + .00474t \qquad (15.15)$$
$$\phantom{\log(\text{SALES})_t = }(24.75) \qquad (86.55)$$

$R^2 = .984 \qquad F(1/73) = 7{,}492 \qquad s = .021 \qquad \text{DW} = .32$

Autoregressive trend model:

$$\text{SALES}_t = 37.53 + 1.00226\,\text{SALES}_{t-1} \qquad (15.16)$$
$$\phantom{\text{SALES}_t = }(0.39) \qquad (156.59)$$

$R^2 = .995 \qquad F(1/73) = 24{,}519 \qquad s = 176.3 \qquad \text{DW} = 2.53$

[4] We use the series RT531R in the CITIBASE database.

Logarithmic autoregressive trend model:

$$\log (SALES)_t = 0.0272 + 0.99766 \log (SALES)_{t-1} \qquad (15.17)$$
$$\quad\quad\quad (0.43) \quad\quad (152.81)$$

$$R^2 = .994 \qquad F(1/73) = 23{,}352 \qquad s = .012 \qquad DW = 2.5$$

In the first regression a time variable running from 0 to 118 was constructed and then used as the independent variable. When $t = 119$ is placed in the right-hand side of the equation

$$SALES = 10{,}765.4 + 71.68t \qquad (15.18)$$

the resulting forecast is 19,295.3. The use of the second log-linear equation yields a forecast of 19,648.5. The third regression, based on an autoregressive process, yields an extrapolated value for January 1996 of 19,767.8:

$$19{,}767.8 \approx 37.53 + 1.0023 \times 19{,}685$$

If the constant term were dropped from Eq. (15.17), the extrapolated value would be 19,730.3. The fourth regression result is based on the logarithmic autoregressive model. The extrapolated value in this case is 19,765.1. If one were to calculate a compounded growth rate for the series and extrapolate on the basis that the growth rate remains unchanged, the extrapolated value would be 19,694.7.

The simulated and actual series are plotted for each of the four extrapolation models in Fig. 15.6a and b. One can see from the figures that the two autoregressive models are closer to the actual series at the end of the period. Of course, other trend models could be used to extrapolate the data. For example, the reader might try to calculate a forecast based on a quadratic trend model (see Exercise 15.1).

Simple extrapolation methods such as those used in the preceding example frequently form the basis for making casual long-range forecasts of variables ranging from GNP to population to pollution indices. Although they can be useful as a way of quickly formulating initial forecasts, they usually provide little forecasting accuracy. An analyst who estimates an extrapolation model is at least advised to calculate a standard error of forecast and a forecast confidence interval, following the methods presented in Chapter 8. More important, one should realize that there are alternative models that can be used to obtain forecasts with smaller standard errors.

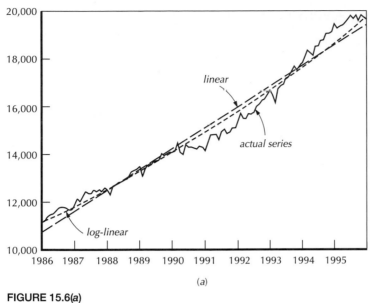

FIGURE 15.6(a)
Simulated and actual sales.

FIGURE 15.6(b)
Simulated and actual sales.

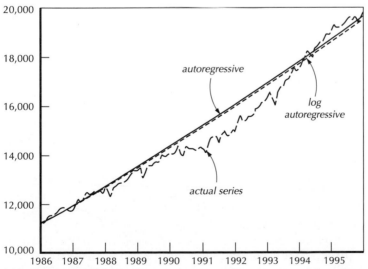

15.1.2   Moving Average Models

Another class of deterministic models that are often used for forecasting consists of *moving average models*. As a simple example, assume that we are forecasting a monthly time series. We might use the model

$$f(t) = \tfrac{1}{12}(y_{t-1} + y_{t-2} + \cdots + y_{t-12}) \tag{15.19}$$

Then, a forecast one period ahead would be given by

$$\hat{y}_{T+1} = \tfrac{1}{12}(y_T + y_{T-1} + \cdots + y_{T-11}) \tag{15.20}$$

The moving average model is useful if we believe that a likely value for our series next month is a simple average of its values over the past 12 months. It may be unrealistic, however, to assume that a good forecast of y_t can be given by a simple average of its past values. It is often more reasonable to have more recent values of y_t play a greater role than do earlier values. In such a case recent values should be weighted more heavily in the moving average. A simple model that accomplishes this is the *exponentially weighted moving average* (EWMA) model:

$$\hat{y}_{T+1} = \alpha y_T + \alpha(1 - \alpha)y_{T-1} + \alpha(1 - \alpha)^2 y_{T-2} + \cdots$$

$$= \alpha \sum_{\tau=0}^{\infty} (1 - \alpha)^{\tau} y_{T-\tau} \tag{15.21}$$

Here α is a number between 0 and 1 that indicates how heavily we weight recent values relative to older ones. With $\alpha = 1$, for example, our forecast becomes

$$\hat{y}_{T+1} = y_T \tag{15.22}$$

and we ignore any values of y that occurred before y_T. As α becomes smaller, we place greater emphasis on more distant values of y. Note that Eq. (15.21) represents a true average, since

$$\alpha \sum_{\tau=0}^{\infty} (1 - \alpha)^{\tau} = \frac{\alpha}{1 - (1 - \alpha)} = 1 \tag{15.23}$$

so that the weights sum to unity.

The reader may suspect that if the series has an upward (downward) trend, the EWMA model will underpredict (overpredict) future values of y_t. This will indeed be the case, since the model averages past values of y_t to produce a forecast. If y_t has been growing steadily in the past, the EWMA forecast $\hat{y}_{T+1}$

will thus be *smaller* than the most recent value y_T, and if the series continues to grow steadily in the future, $\hat{y}_{T+1}$ will be an underprediction of the true value y_{T+1}. Thus one ought to remove any trend from the data before using the EWMA technique. Once an untrended initial forecast has been made, the trend term can be added to obtain a final forecast.

If we want to make a forecast $\hat{y}_{T+1}$ more than one period ahead using an exponentially weighted moving average model, we can modify Eq. (15.21) to include a weighted average of the more recent short-run forecasts $\hat{y}_{T+l-1}$, $\hat{y}_{T+l-2}, \ldots, \hat{y}_{T+1}$. This logical extension of the EWMA model is given by

$$
\begin{aligned}
\hat{y}_{T+l} &= \alpha\hat{y}_{T+l-1} + \alpha(1 - \alpha)\hat{y}_{T+l-2} + \cdots + \alpha(1 - \alpha)^{l-2}\hat{y}_{T+1} \\
&\quad + \alpha(1 - \alpha)^{l-1}y_T + \alpha(1 - \alpha)^{l}y_{T-1} + \alpha(1 - \alpha)^{l+1}y_{T-2} \\
&\quad + \alpha(1 - \alpha)^{l+2}y_{T-3} + \cdots
\end{aligned}
\tag{15.24}
$$

As an example, consider a forecast two periods ahead ($l = 2$), which would be given by

$$
\begin{aligned}
\hat{y}_{T+2} &= \alpha\hat{y}_{T+1} + \alpha(1 - \alpha)y_T + \alpha(1 - \alpha)^2 y_{T-1} + \cdots \\
&= \alpha[\alpha y_T + \alpha(1 - \alpha)y_{T-1} + \cdots] + \alpha(1 - \alpha)y_T \\
&\quad + \alpha(1 - \alpha)^2 y_{T-1} + \cdots \\
&= \alpha^2 \sum_{\tau=0}^{\infty} (1 - \alpha)^{\tau}y_{T-\tau} + \alpha(1 - \alpha) \sum_{\tau=0}^{\infty} (1 - \alpha)^{\tau}y_{T-\tau} \\
&= \alpha \sum_{\tau=0}^{\infty} (1 - \alpha)^{\tau}y_{T-\tau}
\end{aligned}
\tag{15.25}
$$

Note that the two-period forecast is the same as the one-period forecast. The weightings on y_T, $y_{T-1}, \ldots$, in the EWMA model are the same as they were before, but we are now extrapolating the average ahead an extra period. In fact, it is not difficult to show (see Exercise 15.4) that the l-period forecast $\hat{y}_{T+l}$ is also given by Eq. (15.25).

The moving average forecasts represented by Eqs. (15.20), (15.21), and (15.24) are all *adaptive forecasts*. By "adaptive" we mean that they automatically adjust themselves to the most recently available data. Consider, for example, a simple four-period moving average. Suppose y_{20} in Fig. 15.7 represents the most recent data point. Then our forecast will be given by

$$
\hat{y}_{21} = \tfrac{1}{4}(y_{20} + y_{19} + y_{18} + y_{17})
\tag{15.26}
$$

and a forecast two periods ahead will be given by

$$
\hat{y}_{22} = \tfrac{1}{4}(\hat{y}_{21} + y_{20} + y_{19} + y_{18}) = \tfrac{5}{16}y_{20} + \tfrac{5}{16}y_{19} + \tfrac{5}{16}y_{18} + \tfrac{1}{16}y_{17}
\tag{15.27}
$$

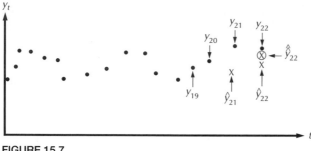

FIGURE 15.7
Adaptive forecasts.

These forecasts are represented by crosses in Fig. 15.7. If y_{21} were known, we would forecast y_{22} one period ahead as

$$\hat{y}_{22} = \tfrac{1}{4}(y_{21} + y_{20} + y_{19} + y_{18})$$

This forecast is represented by a circled cross in Fig. 15.7. Now suppose that the *actual* value of y_{21} turns out to be larger than the predicted value, i.e.,

$$y_{21} > \hat{y}_{21}$$

The actual value of y_{22} is of course not known, but we would expect that $\hat{\hat{y}}_{22}$ would provide a better forecast than $\hat{y}_{22}$ would because of the extra information used in the adaptive process. The EWMA forecast would exhibit the same adaptive behavior.

Although the moving average models described above are certainly useful, they do not provide us with information about *forecast confidence*. The reason for this is that no regression is used to estimate the model, so that we cannot calculate standard errors, nor can we describe or explain the stochastic (or unexplained) component of the time series. It is this stochastic component that creates the error in our forecast. Unless the stochastic component is explained through the modeling process, little can be said about the kinds of forecast errors that can be expected.

15.2   SMOOTHING AND SEASONAL ADJUSTMENT

Smoothing techniques provide a means of removing or at least reducing volatile short-term fluctuations in a time series. This can be useful since it is often easier to discern trends and cyclical patterns and otherwise visually analyze a smoothed series. Seasonal adjustment is a special form of smoothing; it removes seasonal (cyclical) oscillations from the series rather than removing irregular short-term fluctuations.

15.2.1 Smoothing Techniques

In the last section we discussed moving average models (both simple and exponentially weighted) in the context of forecasting, but these models also provide a basis for smoothing time series. For example, one of the simplest ways to smooth a series is to take an *n-period moving average.* Denoting the original series by y_t and the smoothed series by $\tilde{y}_t$, we have

$$\tilde{y}_t = \frac{1}{n} (y_t + y_{t-1} + \cdots + y_{t-n+1}) \tag{15.28}$$

Of course, the larger the n is, the smoother the $\tilde{y}_t$ will be. One problem with moving average is that it uses only *past* (and current) values of y_t to obtain each value of $\tilde{y}_t$. This problem is easily remedied by using a *centered moving average.* For example, a five-period centered moving average is given by

$$\tilde{y}_t - \tfrac{1}{5}(y_{t+2} + y_{t+1} + y_t + y_{t-1} + y_{t-2}) \tag{15.29}$$

Exponential smoothing simply involves the use of the exponentially weighted moving average model for smoothing. (Recall that this model assigns heavier weights to recent values of y_t.) The exponentially smoothed series $\tilde{y}_t$ is given by

$$\tilde{y}_t = \alpha y_t + \alpha(1 - \alpha) y_{t-1} + \alpha(1 - \alpha)^2 y_{t-2} + \cdots \tag{15.30}$$

where the summation in Eq. (15.30) extends all the way back through the length of the series. In fact, $\tilde{y}_t$ can be calculated much more easily if we write

$$(1 - \alpha)\tilde{y}_{t-1} = \alpha(1 - \alpha) y_{t-1} + \alpha(1 - \alpha)^2 y_{t-2} + \cdots \tag{15.31}$$

Now, subtracting Eq. (15.31) from Eq. (15.30), we obtain a recursive formula for the computation of $\tilde{y}_t$:

$$\tilde{y}_t = \alpha y_t + (1 - \alpha)\tilde{y}_{t-1} \tag{15.32}$$

Note that the closer α is to 1, the more heavily the current value of y_t is weighted in generating $\tilde{y}_t$. Thus smaller values of α imply a more heavily smoothed series.

Sometimes one may wish to heavily smooth a series but not give very much weight to past data points. In such a case the use of Eq. (15.32) with a small value of α (say, .1) would not be acceptable. Instead one can apply *double exponential smoothing.* As the name implies, the singly smoothed series $\tilde{y}_t$ from Eq. (15.32) is just smoothed again:

$$\tilde{\tilde{y}}_t = \alpha\tilde{y}_t + (1 - \alpha)\tilde{\tilde{y}}_{t-1} \tag{15.33}$$

In this way a larger value of α can be used, and the resulting series $\tilde{y}_t$ will still be heavily smoothed.

The simple exponential smoothing formula of Eq. (15.32) also can be modified by incorporating average *changes* in the long-run trend (increase or decline) of the series. This is the basis for *Holt's two-parameter exponential smoothing* method.[5] Now the smoothed series $\tilde{y}_t$ is found from two recursive equations and depends on two smoothing parameters, α and γ, both of which must lie between 0 and 1 (again, the smaller are α and γ, the heavier is the smoothing):

$$\tilde{y}_t = \alpha y_t + (1 - \alpha)(\tilde{y}_{t-1} + r_{t-1}) \tag{15.34}$$

$$r_t = \gamma(\tilde{y}_t - \tilde{y}_{t-1}) + (1 - \gamma)r_{t-1} \tag{15.35}$$

Here r_t is a smoothed series representing the trend, i.e., the average rate of increase, in the smoothed series $\tilde{y}_t$. This trend is added in when one is computing the smoothed series $\tilde{y}_t$ in Eq. (15.34), thus preventing $\tilde{y}_t$ from deviating too far from recent values of the original series y_t. This is particularly useful if the smoothing method is going to be used as a basis for forecasting. An l-period forecast can be generated from Eqs. (15.34) and (15.35) using

$$\hat{y}_{T+l} = \tilde{y}_T + lr_T \tag{15.36}$$

Thus the l-period forecast takes the most recent smoothed value $\tilde{y}_T$ and adds in an expected increase lr_T based on the (smoothed) long-run trend. (If the data have been detrended, the trend should be added back to the forecast.)

Smoothing methods tend to be *ad hoc,* particularly when they are used to generate forecasts. One problem is that we have no way of determining the "correct" values of the smoothing parameters, so that their choice becomes somewhat arbitrary. If our objective is simply to smooth the series to make it easier to interpret or analyze, this is not really a problem, since we can choose the parameters to give us the extent of smoothing desired. We must be careful, however, to recognize that when using an equation such as Eq. (15.36) for forecasting that the resulting forecast will be somewhat arbitrary.

Example 15.2 Monthly Housing Starts   The time series for monthly housing starts in the United States provides a good example of the application of smoothing and seasonal adjustment methods.[6] The series fluctuates considerably and also exhibits strong seasonal variation. In this example we smooth the series by using the moving average and exponential smoothing methods.

---

[5] C. C. Holt, "Forecasting Seasonals and Trends by Exponentially Weighted Moving Averages," unpublished research report, Carnegie Institute of Technology, Pittsburgh, 1957.

[6] The original data series is in thousands of units per month and is *not* seasonally adjusted. We have used the series HS6FR in the CITIBASE database.

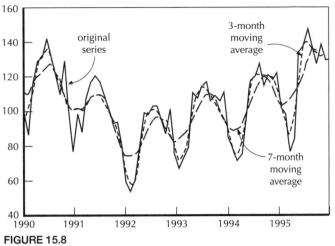

FIGURE 15.8
Smoothing using moving averages.

We begin by using three- and seven-period centered moving averages to smooth the series; i.e., we generate the smoothed series $\tilde{y}_t$ from the original series y_t using

$$\tilde{y}_t = \frac{1}{n} \sum_{i=0}^{n-1} y_{t+(1/2)(n-1)-i} \qquad (15.37)$$

where $n = 3$ or 7. Note that since the moving average is centered, there is no need to detrend the series before smoothing it. The original series, together with the two smoothed series, is shown in Fig. 15.8. Observe that the use of the seven-period moving average heavily smoothes the series and even eliminates some of the seasonal variation.

We now use the exponential smoothing method, i.e., apply Eq. (15.32). Since the original series is growing over time and the exponentially weighted moving average is not centered, the smoothed series will underestimate the original series unless we first detrend the series. To detrend the original series we assumed a linear trend (we could of course test alternative time trends) and ran the following regression over the period January 1986 to October 1995:

$$\hat{y}_t = 142.92 - 0.4192t \qquad R^2 = .227 \qquad (15.38)$$
$$\phantom{\hat{y}_t =} (29.38) \quad (-5.83)$$

The *residuals* u_t from this regression, that is, $u_t = y_t - 142.92 + .4192t$, provide the detrended series.

We next apply exponential smoothing to this detrended series. We use two alternative values of the smoothing parameter: $\alpha = .8$ (light smoothing)

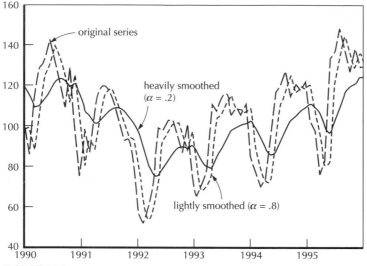

FIGURE 15.9
Smoothing using exponentially weighted moving averages.

and $\alpha = .2$ (heavy smoothing). Finally, we take the smoothed detrended series $\tilde{u}_t$ and add the trend back in; i.e., we compute $\tilde{y}_t = \tilde{u}_t + 142.92 - .4192t$.

The original series and the smoothed series are shown in Fig. 15.9. Observe from the figure that the seasonal variations, while reduced, are pushed forward by heavy exponential smoothing. This occurs because the exponentially weighted moving average is not centered. Thus, if a series shows strong seasonal variations, exponential smoothing should be used only after the series has been seasonally adjusted.

15.2.2   Seasonal Adjustment

Seasonal adjustment techniques are basically ad hoc methods of computing *seasonal indices* (which attempt to measure the seasonal variation in the series), and then using those indices to *deseasonalize* (i.e., seasonally adjust) the series by removing the seasonal variations. National economic data in the United States usually are seasonally adjusted by the *Census II method* (or one of its variants), which was developed by the Bureau of the Census of the U.S. Department of Commerce. The Census II method is a rather detailed and complicated procedure (and is amazingly ad hoc), and we therefore will not attempt to describe it here. Instead, we discuss the basic idea that lies behind all seasonal adjustment methods (including Census II) and present a very simple method that in many cases is quite adequate.

Seasonal adjustment techniques are based on the idea that a time series y_t can be represented as the product of four components:

$$y_t = L \times S \times C \times I \qquad (15.39)$$

where L = value of the long-term secular trend in series
S = value of seasonal component
C = (long-term) cyclical component
I = irregular component

The objective is to eliminate the seasonal component S.

To do this we first try to isolate the combined long-term trend and cyclical components $L \times C$. This cannot be done exactly; instead, an ad hoc smoothing procedure is used to remove (as much as possible) the combined seasonal and irregular components $S \times I$ from the original series y_t. For example, suppose y_t consists of monthly data. Then a *12-month average* $\tilde{y}_t$ is computed:

$$\tilde{y}_t = \tfrac{1}{12}(y_{t+6} + \cdots + y_t + y_{t-1} + \cdots + y_{t-5}) \qquad (15.40)$$

Presumably $\tilde{y}_t$ is relatively free of seasonal and irregular fluctuations and is thus an *estimate* of $L \times C$.

We now divide the original data by this estimate of $L \times C$ to obtain an estimate of the combined seasonal and irregular components $S \times I$:

$$\frac{L \times S \times C \times I}{L \times C} = S \times I = \frac{y_t}{\tilde{y}_t} = z_t \qquad (15.41)$$

The next step is to eliminate the irregular component I as completely as possible in order to obtain the seasonal index. To do this, we *average the values of $S \times I$ corresponding to the same month*. In other words, suppose that y_1 (and hence z_1) corresponds to January, y_2 to February, etc., and that there are 48 months of data. We thus compute

$$\begin{aligned}
\tilde{z}_1 &= \tfrac{1}{4}(z_1 + z_{13} + z_{25} + z_{37}) \\
\tilde{z}_2 &= \tfrac{1}{4}(z_2 + z_{14} + z_{26} + z_{38}) \\
&\;\;\cdots\cdots\cdots\cdots\cdots\cdots\cdots\cdots\cdots \\
\tilde{z}_{12} &= \tfrac{1}{4}(z_{12} + z_{24} + z_{36} + z_{48})
\end{aligned} \qquad (15.42)$$

The rationale here is that when the seasonal-irregular percentages z_t are averaged for each month (each quarter if the data are quarterly), the irregular fluctuations will be largely smoothed out.

The 12 averages $\tilde{z}_1, \ldots, \tilde{z}_{12}$ will then be estimates of the seasonal indices. They should sum close to 12 but will not do so exactly if there is any long-run trend in the data. Final seasonal indices are computed by multiplying the indices in Eq. (15.42) by a factor that brings their sum to 12. (For example, if $\tilde{z}_1, \ldots,$ $\tilde{z}_{12}$ add to 11.7, multiply each one by 12.0/11.7 so that the revised indices will add to 12.) We denote these final seasonal indices by $\bar{z}_1, \ldots, \bar{z}_{12}$.

The deseasonalization of the original series y_t is now straightforward: just divide each value in the series by its corresponding seasonal index, thus removing the seasonal component while leaving the other three components. Thus, the seasonally adjusted series y_t^a is obtained from $y_1^a = y_1/\bar{z}_1$, $y_2^a = y_2/\bar{z}_2$, $\ldots, y_{12}^a = y_{12}/\bar{z}_{12}$, $y_{13}^a = y_{13}/\bar{z}_1$, $y_{14}^a = y_{14}/\bar{z}_2$, etc.

Example 15.3 Monthly Housing Starts   Let us now apply the seasonal adjustment technique to our series for monthly housing starts (see Example 15.2). To do this we first compute a 12-month average $\tilde{y}_t$ of the original series y_t using Eq. (15.40) and then divide y_t by $\tilde{y}_t$, that is, compute $z_t = y_t/\tilde{y}_t$. Note that z_t contains (roughly) the seasonal and irregular components of the original series. We remove the irregular component by averaging the values of z_t that correspond to the same month; i.e., we compute $\tilde{z}_1, \tilde{z}_2,$ $\ldots, \tilde{z}_{12}$ using Eq. (15.42). We then compute the final *seasonal indices* $\bar{z}_1,$ $\bar{z}_2, \ldots, \bar{z}_{12}$ by multiplying $\tilde{z}_1, \ldots, \tilde{z}_{12}$ by a factor that brings their sum to 1. The final seasonal indices are as follows:

	Seasonal indices		
Month	**Index**	**Month**	**Index**
January	.7437	July	1.1466
February	.7508	August	1.1120
March	1.0330	September	1.0544
April	1.1797	October	1.1211
May	1.1848	November	.8836
June	1.2285	December	.7582

FIGURE 15.10
Housing starts: seasonal indices.

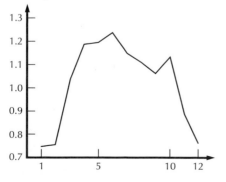

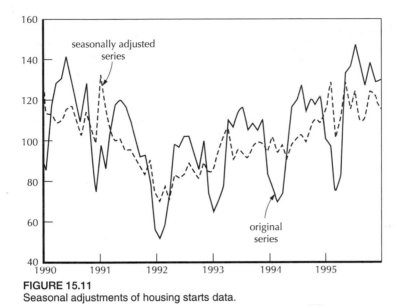

FIGURE 15.11
Seasonal adjustments of housing starts data.

These seasonal indices have been plotted in Fig. 15.10.

To deseasonalize the original series y_t we just divide each value in the series by its corresponding seasonal index, thus removing the seasonal component. The original series y_t and the seasonally adjusted series y_t^a are shown in Fig. 15.11. Observe that the seasonal variation has been eliminated in the adjusted series, while the long-run trend and short-run irregular fluctuations remain.

EXERCISES

15.1 Go back to Example 15.1 and use the data for monthly department store sales to estimate a quadratic trend model. Use the estimated model to obtain an extrapolated value for sales for January 1996. Try to evaluate your model in comparison to the other four estimated in Example 15.1. Explain how and why your forecast for January differs from the other forecasts in the example.

15.2 Which (if any) of the simple extrapolation models presented in Section 15.1 do you think might be suitable for forecasting the GNP? The Consumer Price Index? A short-term interest rate? Annual production of wheat? Explain.

15.3 Show that the exponentially weighted moving average (EWMA) model will generate forecasts that are adaptive in nature.

15.4 Show that the EWMA forecast l periods ahead is the same as the forecast one period ahead, i.e.,

$$\hat{y}_{T+l} = \alpha \sum_{\tau=0}^{\infty} (1 - \alpha)^{\tau} y_{T-\tau}$$

TABLE 15.1
S&P COMMON STOCK PRICE INDEX: COMPOSITE (1941–1943 = 10)

Obs.	Jan/Jul	Feb/Aug	Mar/Sept	Apr/Oct	May/Nov	Jun/Dec
1980.01	110.8700	115.3400	104.6900	102.9700	107.6900	114.5500
1980.07	119.8300	123.5000	126.5100	130.2200	135.6500	133.4800
1981.01	132.9700	128.4000	133.1900	134.4300	131.7300	132.2800
1981.07	129.1300	129.6300	118.2700	119.8000	122.9200	123.7900
1982.01	117.2800	114.5000	110.8400	116.3100	116.3500	109.7000
1982.07	109.3800	109.6500	122.4300	132.6600	138.1000	139.3700
1983.01	144.2700	146.8000	151.8800	157.7100	164.1000	166.3900
1983.07	166.9600	162.4200	167.1600	167.6500	165.2300	164.3600
1984.01	166.3900	157.2500	157.4400	157.6000	156.5500	153.1200
1984.07	151.0800	164.4200	166.1100	164.8200	166.2700	164.4800
1985.01	171.6100	180.8800	179.4200	180.6200	184.9000	188.8900
1985.07	192.5400	188.3100	184.0600	186.1800	197.4500	207.2600
1986.01	208.1900	219.3700	232.3300	237.9800	238.4600	245.3000
1986.07	240.1800	245.0000	238.2700	237.3600	245.0900	248.6100
1987.01	264.5100	280.9300	292.4700	289.3200	289.1200	301.3800
1987.07	310.0900	329.3600	318.6600	280.1600	245.0100	240.9600
1988.01	250.4800	258.1300	265.7400	262.6100	256.1200	270.6800
1988.07	269.0500	263.7300	267.9700	277.4000	271.0200	276.5100
1989.01	285.4100	294.0100	292.7100	302.2500	313.9300	323.7300
1989.07	331.9300	346.6100	347.3300	347.4000	345.9900	348.5700
1990.01	339.9700	330.4500	338.4700	338.1800	350.2500	360.3900
1990.07	360.0300	330.7500	315.4100	307.1200	315.2900	328.7500
1991.01	325.4900	362.2600	372.2800	379.6800	377.9900	378.2900
1991.07	380.3300	389.4000	387.2000	386.8800	385.9200	388.5100
1992.01	416.0800	412.5600	407.3600	407.4100	414.8100	408.2700
1992.07	415.0500	417.9300	418.4800	412.5000	422.8400	435.6400
1993.01	435.2300	441.7000	450.1600	443.0800	445.2500	448.0600
1993.07	447.2900	454.1300	459.2400	463.9000	462.8900	465.9500
1994.01	472.9900	471.5800	463.8100	447.2300	450.9000	454.8300
1994.07	451.4000	464.2400	466.9600	463.8100	461.0100	455.1900
1995.01	465.2500	481.9200	493.1500	507.9100	523.8100	539.3500
1995.07	557.3670	559.1110	578.7700	582.9180	595.5300	614.5700
1996.01	614.4200	649.5400				

Source: Citibase.

15.5 Monthly data for the Standard & Poor 500 Common Stock Price Index are shown in Table 15.1. The data are also plotted in Fig. 15.12.

(a) Using all but the last two data points (i.e., January and February of 1996), exponentially smooth the data, using a value of .9 for the smoothing parameter α. *Hint:* Remember that a moving average is always shorter than the original series. Repeat for a value of .2.

(b) Again using all but the last two data points, smooth the data using Holt's two-parameter exponential smoothing method. Set $\alpha = .2$ and $\gamma = .2$. Explain how and why the results differ from those in (a) above. Now use Eq. (15.36) to forecast the series out 1 and 2 months. How close is your forecast to the actual values of the S&P 500 index for January and February 1996?

15.6 Monthly data for retail auto sales are shown in Table 15.2 on page 488. The data are also plotted in Fig. 15.13.

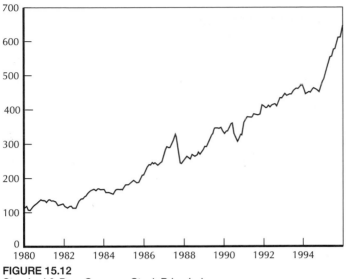

FIGURE 15.12
Standard & Poor Common Stock Price Index.

(*a*) Use a 6-month centered moving average to smooth the data. Is a seasonal pattern evident? Would you expect auto sales to exhibit seasonal regularities?

(*b*) Using the original data in Table 15.2, apply the seasonal adjustment procedure described in the text. Plot the 12 final seasonal indices as a function of time and try to explain the shape of the curve. Also plot the seasonally adjusted series and compare it to the original series.

FIGURE 15.13
Monthly auto sales (thousands of units).

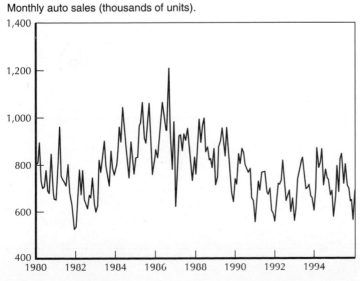

TABLE 15.2
RETAIL SALES: NEW PASSENGER CARS, TOTAL DOMESTICS
PLUS IMPORTS (thousands)

Obs.	Jan/Jul	Feb/Aug	Mar/Sept	Apr/Oct	May/Nov	Jun/Dec
1980.01	805.8000	811.6000	895.2000	743.3000	696.7000	701.9000
1980.07	772.6000	685.5000	674.1000	847.5000	698.2000	649.4000
1981.01	647.5000	764.0000	962.7000	751.3000	733.6000	723.8000
1981.07	706.8000	801.1000	687.2000	648.8000	584.6000	522.9000
1982.01	534.7000	632.5000	777.0000	668.9000	774.3000	651.0000
1982.07	629.5000	608.9000	671.2000	656.0000	743.4000	632.0000
1983.01	595.8000	627.8000	821.4000	761.9000	836.6000	903.8000
1983.07	791.6000	740.7000	704.8000	860.8000	781.7000	751.7000
1984.01	778.5000	841.4000	963.9000	895.6000	1047.0000	952.4000
1984.07	889.8000	814.9000	743.5000	901.5000	802.4000	759.3000
1985.01	829.9000	833.4000	965.0000	983.3000	1068.5000	920.2000
1985.07	892.4000	995.4000	1064.3000	859.1000	758.4000	808.5000
1986.01	866.8000	829.7000	893.8000	969.3000	1068.5000	997.8000
1986.07	949.7000	949.0000	1213.1000	902.1000	778.5000	987.4000
1987.01	621.8000	774.4000	927.0000	931.3000	861.2000	935.1000
1987.07	905.7000	959.2000	896.9000	794.5000	729.2000	834.6000
1988.01	757.2000	880.5000	998.5000	895.1000	966.9000	1002.6000
1988.07	856.0000	878.7000	822.3000	829.0000	786.8000	872.0000
1989.01	711.9000	745.6000	879.2000	904.6000	963.8000	888.8000
1989.07	837.1000	963.5000	829.9000	739.2000	672.3000	640.9000
1990.01	743.3000	716.5000	850.3000	802.1000	872.4000	857.3000
1990.07	803.2000	786.0000	769.0000	787.8000	661.2000	651.1000
1991.01	554.6000	621.5000	730.3000	690.7000	769.5000	771.7000
1991.07	773.2000	690.4000	671.4000	702.0000	606.5000	593.2000
1992.01	560.5000	651.1000	720.4000	715.8000	733.7000	824.8000
1992.07	733.6000	644.8000	673.7000	694.5000	601.0000	660.5000
1993.01	562.2000	593.4000	735.1000	768.7000	812.1000	835.6000
1993.07	763.5000	697.1000	704.0000	717.3000	667.6000	661.1000
1994.01	606.1000	698.6000	876.2000	785.8000	814.5000	871.4000
1994.07	713.2000	782.3000	741.8000	738.0000	670.7000	691.8000
1995.01	581.5000	649.1000	798.7000	685.9000	825.2000	852.8000
1995.07	721.3000	806.4000	714.9000	701.6000	644.5000	654.3000
1996.01	567.0000	690.6000				

Source: Citibase.

CHAPTER 16

PROPERTIES OF STOCHASTIC TIME SERIES

In Chapter 15 we discussed a number of simple extrapolation techniques. In this chapter we begin our treatment of the construction and use of time-series models. Such models provide a more sophisticated method of extrapolating time series in that they are based on the notion that the series that is to be forecasted has been generated by a *stochastic* (or *random*) *process*, with a structure that can be characterized and described. In other words, a time-series model provides a description of the random nature of the process that generated the sample of observations under study. The description is given not in terms of a cause-and-effect relationship (as would be the case in a regression model) but in terms of how that randomness is embodied in the process.

This chapter begins with an introduction to the nature of stochastic time-series models and shows how those models characterize the stochastic structure of the underlying process that generated the particular series. The chapter then turns to the properties of stochastic time series, focusing on the concept of *stationarity*. This material is important for the discussion of model construction in the following chapters. We next present a statistical test (the Dickey-Fuller test) for stationarity. Finally, we discuss *co-integrated* time series—series which are nonstationary but which can be combined to form a stationary series.

16.1 INTRODUCTION TO STOCHASTIC TIME-SERIES MODELS

The time-series models developed in this chapter and the following chapters are all based on the assumption that the series to be forecasted has been generated by a *stochastic process*. In other words, we assume that each value $y_1, y_2,$

. . . , Y_T in the series is drawn randomly from a probability distribution. In modeling such a process, we attempt to describe the characteristics of its randomness. This should help us infer something about the probabilities associated with alternative future values of the series.

To be completely general, we could assume that the observed series $y_1, \ldots, y_T$ is drawn from a set of *jointly distributed random variables.* If we could somehow numerically specify the probability distribution function for our series, we could determine the probability of one or another future outcome.

Unfortunately, the complete specification of the probability distribution function for a time series usually is impossible. However, it usually is possible to construct a simplified model of the time series which explains its randomness in a manner that is useful for forecasting purposes. For example, we may believe that the values of $y_1, \ldots, y_T$ are normally distributed and are correlated with each other according to a simple first-order autoregressive process. The actual distribution may be more complicated, but this simple model may be a reasonable approximation. Of course, the usefulness of such a model depends on how closely it captures the true probability distribution and thus the true random behavior of the series. Note that it need not (and usually will not) match the actual past behavior of the series *since the series and the model are stochastic.* It should simply capture the characteristics of the series' randomness.

16.1.1   Random Walks

Our first (and simplest) example of a stochastic time series is the *random walk* process. In the simplest random walk process each successive change in y_t is drawn independently from a probability distribution with 0 mean. Thus, y_t is determined by

$$y_t = y_{t-1} + \varepsilon_t \qquad (16.1)$$

with $E(\varepsilon_t) = 0$ and $E(\varepsilon_t \varepsilon_s) = 0$ for $t \neq s$. Such a process could be generated by successive flips of a coin, where a head receives a value of $+1$ and a tail receives a value of -1.

Suppose we wanted to make a forecast for such a random walk process. The forecast is given by

$$\hat{y}_{T+1} = E(y_{T+1} | y_T, \ldots, y_1) \qquad (16.2)$$
$$= y_T + E(\varepsilon_{T+1}) = y_T \qquad (16.3)$$

The forecast two periods ahead is

$$\hat{y}_{T+2} = E(y_{T+2} | y_T, \ldots, y_1) = E(y_{T+1} + \varepsilon_{T+2})$$
$$= E(y_T + \varepsilon_{T+1} + \varepsilon_{T+2}) = y_T \qquad (16.4)$$

Similarly, the forecast l periods ahead is also y_T.

Although the forecast $\hat{y}_{T+1}$ will be the same no matter how large l is, the variance of the forecast error will grow as l becomes larger. For one period the forecast error is given by

$$e_1 = y_{T+1} - \hat{y}_{T+1}$$
$$= y_T + \varepsilon_{T+1} - y_T = \varepsilon_{T+1} \tag{16.5}$$

and its variance is just $E(\varepsilon_{T+1}^2) = \sigma_\varepsilon^2$. For the two-period forecast

$$e_2 = y_{T+2} - \hat{y}_{T+2} \tag{16.6}$$
$$= y_T + \varepsilon_{T+1} + \varepsilon_{T+2} - y_T = \varepsilon_{T+1} + \varepsilon_{T+2}$$

and its variance is

$$E[(\varepsilon_{T+1} + \varepsilon_{T+2})^2] = E(\varepsilon_{T+1}^2) + E(\varepsilon_{T+2}^2) + 2E(\varepsilon_{T+1}\varepsilon_{T+2}) \tag{16.7}$$

Since ε_{T+1} and ε_{T+2} are independent, the third term in Eq. (16.7) is 0 and the error variance is $2\sigma_\varepsilon^2$. Similarly, for the l-period forecast, the error variance is $l\sigma_\varepsilon^2$. Thus, the *standard error of forecast* increases with the square root of l. We can thus obtain *confidence intervals* for our forecasts, and these intervals will become wider as the forecast horizon increases. This is illustrated in Fig. 16.1. Note that the forecasts are all equal to the last observation y_T, but the confidence intervals represented by 1 standard deviation in the forecast error increase as the square root of l increases.

The fact that we can generate confidence intervals of this sort is an important advantage of stochastic time-series models. As we explained in Chapter 8, policy makers need to know the margin of error in order to evaluate a particular forecast, and so confidence intervals can be as important as the forecasts themselves.

A simple extension of the random walk process discussed above is the random walk with drift. This process accounts for a trend (upward or downward)

FIGURE 16.1
Forecasting a random walk.

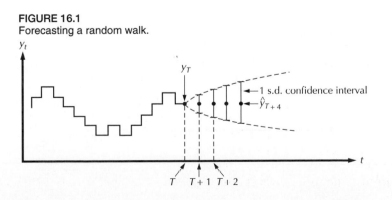

in the series y_t and thus allows us to embody that trend in our forecast. In this process y_t is determined by

$$y_t = y_{t-1} + d + \varepsilon_t \tag{16.8}$$

so that on average the process will tend to move upward (for $d > 0$). Now the one-period forecast is

$$\hat{y}_{T+1} = E(y_{T+1}|y_T, \ldots, y_1) = y_T + d \tag{16.9}$$

and the l-period forecast is

$$\hat{y}_{T+l} = y_T + ld \tag{16.10}$$

The standard error of forecast will be the same as before. For one period,

$$e_1 = y_{T+1} - \hat{y}_{T+1}$$
$$= y_T + d + \varepsilon_{T+1} - y_T - d = \varepsilon_{T+1} \tag{16.11}$$

as before. The process, together with forecasts and forecast confidence intervals, is illustrated in Fig. 16.2. As can be seen in that figure, the forecasts increase linearly with l and the standard error of forecast increases with the square root of l.

In Chapter 17 we examine a general class of stochastic time-series models. Later, we will see how that class of models can be used to make forecasts for a wide variety of time series. First, however, it is necessary to introduce some basic concepts about stochastic processes and their properties.

FIGURE 16.2
Forecasting a random walk with drift.

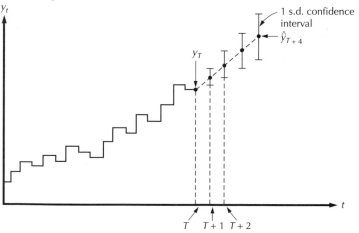

16.1.2 Stationary and Nonstationary Time Series

As we begin to develop models for time series, we want to know whether the underlying stochastic process that generated the series can be assumed to be *invariant with respect to time*. If the characteristics of the stochastic process change over time, i.e., if the process is *nonstationary*, it will often be difficult to represent the time series over past and future intervals of time by a simple algebraic model.[1] By contrast, if the stochastic process is fixed in time, i.e., if it is *stationary*, then one can model the process via an equation with fixed coefficients that can be estimated from past data. This is analogous to the single-equation regression model in which one variable is related to other variables, with coefficients that are estimated under the assumption that the structural relationship described by the equation is invariant over time (i.e., is stationary). If the structural relationship changed over time, we could not apply the techniques of Chapter 8 in using a regression model to forecast.

The models developed in detail in Chapter 17 represent stochastic processes that are assumed to be in equilibrium about a constant mean level. The probability of a given fluctuation in the process from that mean level is assumed to be the same *at any point in time*. In other words, the stochastic properties of the stationary process are assumed to be *invariant with respect to time*.

One would suspect that many of the time series one encounters in business and economics are not generated by stationary processes. The GNP, for example, has for the most part been growing steadily. For this reason alone its stochastic properties in 1997 are quite different from those in 1933. Although it can be difficult to model nonstationary processes, we will see that nonstationary processes can often be transformed into stationary or approximately stationary processes.

16.1.3 Properties of Stationary Processes

We have said that any stochastic time series $y_1, \ldots, y_T$ can be thought of as having been generated by a set of jointly distributed random variables; i.e., the set of data points $y_1, \ldots, y_T$ represents a particular outcome of the joint probability distribution function $p(y_1, \ldots, y_T)$.[2] Similarly, a *future* observation y_{T+1} can be thought of as being generated by a *conditional probability distribution function* $p(y_{T+1}|y_1, \ldots, y_T)$, that is, a probability distribution for y_{T+1} given the past observations $y_1, \ldots, y_T$. We define a *stationary* process, then, as one whose joint distribution and conditional distribution both are *invariant with respect to displacement in time*. In other words, if the series y_t is stationary, then

---

[1] The random walk with drift is an example of a nonstationary process for which a simple forecasting model can be constructed.

[2] This outcome is called a *realization*. Thus, $y_1, \ldots, y_T$ represents one particular realization of the stochastic process represented by the probability distribution $p(y_1, \ldots, y_T)$.

$$p(y_t, \ldots, y_{t+k}) = p(y_{t+m}, \ldots, y_{t+k+m}) \tag{16.12}$$

and
$$p(y_t) = p(y_{t+m}) \tag{16.13}$$

for any t, k, and m.

Note that if the series y_t is stationary, the *mean* of the series, which is defined as

$$\mu_y = E(y_t) \tag{16.14}$$

must also be stationary, so that $E(y_t) = E(y_{t+m})$, for any t and m. Furthermore, the *variance* of the series,

$$\sigma_y^2 = E[(y_t - \mu_y)^2] \tag{16.15}$$

must be stationary, so that $E[(y_t - \mu_y)^2] = E[(y_{t+m} - \mu_y)^2]$, and finally, for any lag k, the *covariance* of the series,

$$\gamma_k = \text{Cov}\,(y_t, y_{t+k}) = E[(y_t - \mu_y)(y_{t+k} - \mu_y)] \tag{16.16}$$

must be stationary, so that $\text{Cov}\,(y_t, y_{t+k}) = \text{Cov}\,(y_{t+m}, y_{t+m+k})$.[3]

If a stochastic process is stationary, the probability distribution $p(y_t)$ is the same for all time t and its shape (or at least some of its properties) can be inferred by looking at a histogram of the observations $y_1, \ldots, y_T$ that make up the observed series. Recall from Chapter 2 that an estimate of the mean μ_y of the process can be obtained from the *sample mean* of the series

$$\bar{y} = \frac{1}{T} \sum_{t=1}^{T} y_t \tag{16.17}$$

and an estimate of the variance σ_y^2 can be obtained from the *sample variance*

$$\hat{\sigma}_y^2 = \frac{1}{T} \sum_{t=1}^{T} (y_t - \bar{y})^2 \tag{16.18}$$

16.2 / CHARACTERIZING TIME SERIES: THE AUTOCORRELATION FUNCTION

While it usually is impossible to obtain a complete description of a stochastic process (i.e., to actually specify the underlying probability distributions), the

---

[3] It is possible for the mean, variance, and covariances of the series to be stationary but not the joint probability distribution. If the probability distributions are stationary, we term the series *strict-sense stationary*. If only the mean, variance, and covariances are stationary, we term the series *wide-sense stationary*. Note that strict-sense stationarity implies wide-sense stationarity but that the converse is not true.

autocorrelation function will prove extremely useful because it provides a partial description of the process for modeling purposes. The autocorrelation function tells us how much correlation there is (and by implication how much interdependency there is) between neighboring data points in the series y_t. We define the *autocorrelation with lag k* as

$$\rho_k = \frac{E[(y_t - \mu_y)(y_{t+k} - \mu_y)]}{\sqrt{E[(y_t - \mu_y)^2]E[(y_{t+k} - \mu_y)^2]}} = \frac{\text{Cov}(y_t, y_{t+k})}{\sigma_{y_t}\sigma_{y_{t+k}}} \qquad (16.19)$$

For a stationary process the variance at time t in the denominator of Eq. (16.19) is the same as the variance at time $t + k$; thus, the denominator is just the variance of the stochastic process, and

$$\rho_k = \frac{E[(y_t - \mu_y)(y_{t+k} - \mu_y)]}{\sigma_y^2} \qquad (16.20)$$

Note that the numerator in Eq. (16.20) is the covariance between y_t and y_{t+k}, γ_k, so that

$$\rho_k = \frac{\gamma_k}{\gamma_0} \qquad (16.21)$$

and thus $\rho_0 = 1$ for *any* stochastic process.

Suppose the stochastic process is simply

$$y_t = \varepsilon_t \qquad (16.22)$$

where ε_t is an independently distributed random variable with zero mean. Then it is easy to see from Eq. (16.20) that the autocorrelation function for this process is given by $\rho_0 = 1$, $\rho_k = 0$ for $k > 0$. The process of Eq. (16.22) is called *white noise*, and there is no model that can provide a forecast any better than $\hat{y}_{T+l} = 0$ for all l. Thus, if the autocorrelation function is zero (or close to zero) for all $k > 0$, there is little or no value in using a model to forecast the series.

Of course the autocorrelation function in Eq. (16.20) is purely theoretical in that it describes a stochastic process for which we have only a limited number of observations. In practice, then, we must calculate an *estimate* of the autocorrelation function, called the *sample autocorrelation function*:

$$\hat{\rho}_k = \frac{\sum_{t=1}^{T-k}(y_t - \bar{y})(y_{t+k} - \bar{y})}{\sum_{t=1}^{T}(y_t - \bar{y})^2} \qquad (16.23)$$

It is easy to see from their definitions that both the theoretical and the estimated autocorrelation functions are symmetrical, i.e., that the correlation for a positive displacement is the same as that for a negative displacement, so that

$$\rho_k = \rho_{-k} \qquad (16.24)$$

Then, in plotting an autocorrelation function (i.e., plotting ρ_k for different values of k), one need consider only positive values of k.

It is often useful to determine whether a particular value of the sample autocorrelation function $\hat{\rho}_k$ is close enough to zero to permit the assumption that the *true* value of the autocorrelation function ρ_k is indeed equal to zero. It is also useful to test whether *all* the values of the autocorrelation function for $k > 0$ are equal to zero. (If they are, we know that we are dealing with white noise.) Fortunately, simple statistical tests can be used to test the hypothesis that $\rho_k = 0$ for a particular k or to test the hypothesis that $\rho_k = 0$ for all $k > 0$.

To test whether a particular value of the autocorrelation function ρ_k is equal to zero we use a result obtained by Bartlett. He showed that if a time series has been generated by a *white noise* process, the sample autocorrelation coefficients (for $k > 0$) are distributed approximately according to a normal distribution with mean 0 and standard deviation $1/\sqrt{T}$ (where T is the number of observations in the series).[4] Thus, if a particular series consists of, say, 100 data points, we can attach a standard error of .1 to each autocorrelation coefficient. Therefore, if a particular coefficient is greater in magnitude than .2, we can be 95 percent sure that the true autocorrelation coefficient is not zero.

To test the *joint hypothesis* that *all* the autocorrelation coefficients are zero we use the Q statistic introduced by Box and Pierce. We will discuss this statistic in some detail in Chapter 18 in the context of performing diagnostic checks on estimated time-series models, and so we mention it here only in passing. Box and Pierce show that the statistic

$$Q = T \sum_{k=1}^{K} \hat{\rho}_k^2 \qquad (16.25)$$

is (approximately) distributed as chi square with K degrees of freedom. Thus, if the calculated value of Q is greater than, say, the critical 5 percent level, we can be 95 percent sure that the *true* autocorrelation coefficients $\rho_1, \ldots, \rho_k$ are not all zero.

In practice, people tend to use the critical 10 percent level as a cutoff for this test. For example, if Q turned out to be 18.5 for a total of $K = 15$ lags, we would observe that this is below the critical level of 22.31 and accept (i.e., fail to reject) the hypothesis that the time series was generated by a white noise process.

---

[4] See M. S. Bartlett, "On the Theoretical Specification of Sampling Properties of Autocorrelated Time Series," *Journal of the Royal Statistical Society*, ser. B8, vol. 27, 1946.

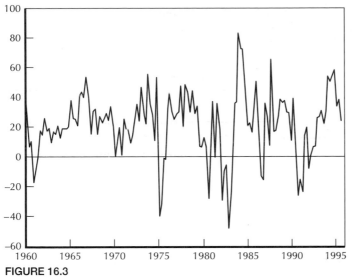

FIGURE 16.3
Nonfarm inventory investment (in 1987 constant dollars).

Let us now turn to an example of an estimated autocorrelation function for a stationary economic time series. We have calculated $\hat{\rho}_k$ for quarterly data on real nonfarm inventory investment (measured in billions of 1987 dollars). The time series itself (covering the period 1960 through 1995) is shown in Fig. 16.3, and the sample autocorrelation function is shown in Fig. 16.4. Note that the autocorrelation function falls off rather quickly as the lag k increases. This is typical of a stationary time series, such as inventory investment. In fact, as we will see, the autocorrelation function can be used to test whether a series is stationary. If $\hat{\rho}_k$ does not fall off quickly as k increases, this is an indication of nonstationarity. We will discuss more formal tests of nonstationarity ("unit root" tests) in Section 16.3.

If a time series is stationary, there exist certain analytic conditions which place bounds on the values that can be taken by the individual points of the autocorrelation function. However, the derivation of these conditions is somewhat complicated and will not be presented at this point. Furthermore, the conditions themselves are rather cumbersome and of limited usefulness in applied time-series modeling. Therefore, we have relegated them to Appendix 16.1. We turn our attention now to the properties of those time series which are nonstationary but which can be transformed into stationary series.

16.2.1   Homogeneous Nonstationary Processes

Probably very few of the time series one meets in practice are stationary. Fortunately, however, many of the nonstationary time series that are encountered (and this includes most of those which arise in economics and business)

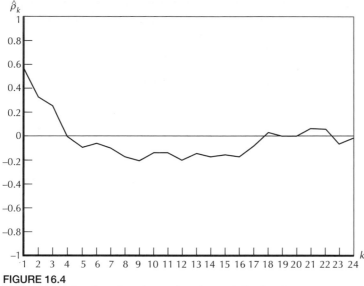

FIGURE 16.4
Nonfarm inventory investment: sample autocorrelation function.

have the desirable property that if they are *differentiated one or more times, the resulting series will be stationary.* Such a nonstationary series is termed *homogeneous.* The number of times the original series must be differenced before a stationary series results is called the *order of homogeneity.* Thus, if y_t is first-order homogeneous nonstationary, the series

$$w_t = y_t - y_{t-1} = \Delta y_t \qquad (16.26)$$

is stationary. If y_t happened to be second-order homogeneous, the series

$$w_t = \Delta^2 y_t = \Delta y_t - \Delta y_{t-1} \qquad (16.27)$$

would be stationary.

As an example of a first-order homogeneous nonstationary process, consider the simple random walk process we introduced earlier:

$$y_t = y_{t-1} + \varepsilon_t \qquad (16.28)$$

Let us examine the variance of this process:

$$\gamma_0 = E(y_t^2) = E[(y_{t-1} + \varepsilon_t)^2] = E(y_{t-1}^2) + \sigma_\varepsilon^2$$
$$= E(y_{t-2}^2) + 2\sigma_\varepsilon^2 \qquad (16.29)$$
$$\vdots$$

or $\qquad\qquad \gamma_0 = E(y_{t-n}^2) + n\sigma_\varepsilon^2 \qquad (16.30)$

Observe from this recursive relationship that the variance is infinite and hence undefined. The same is true for the covariances, since, for example,

$$\gamma_1 = E(y_t y_{t-1}) = E[y_{t-1}(y_{t-1} + \varepsilon_t)] = E(y_{t-1}^2) \qquad (16.31)$$

Now let us look at the series that results from differencing the random walk process, i.e., the series

$$w_t = \Delta y_t = y_t - y_{t-1} = \varepsilon_t \qquad (16.32)$$

Since the ε_t are assumed to be independent over time, w_t is clearly a stationary process. Thus, we see that the random walk process is first-order homogeneous. In fact, w_t is just a white noise process, and it has the autocorrelation function $\rho_0 = 1$, with $\rho_k = 0$ for $k > 0$.

16.2.2   Stationarity and the Autocorrelation Function

The GNP and a series of sales figures for a firm are both likely to be nonstationary. Each has been growing (on average) over time, so that the mean of each series is time-dependent. It is quite likely, however, that if the GNP or the company sales figures are first-differenced one or more times, the resulting series will be stationary. Thus, if we want to build a time-series model to forecast the GNP, we can difference the series one or two times, construct a model for this new series, make our forecasts, and then *integrate* (i.e., undifference) the model and its forecasts to arrive back at GNP.

How can we decide whether a series is stationary or determine the appropriate number of times a homogeneous nonstationary series should be differenced to arrive at a stationary series? We can begin by looking at a plot of an autocorrelation function (called a *correlogram*). Figures 16.5 and 16.6 show autocorrelation functions for stationary and nonstationary series. The autocorrelation function for a stationary series drops off as k, the number of lags, becomes large, but this usually is not the case for a nonstationary series. If we

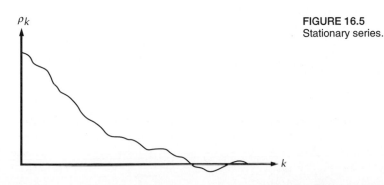

ρ_k

FIGURE 16.5
Stationary series.

k

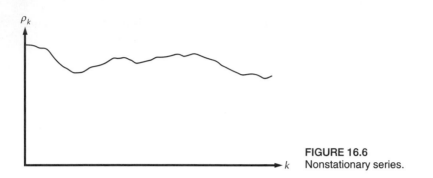

FIGURE 16.6
Nonstationary series.

are differencing a nonstationary series, we can test each succeeding difference by looking at the autocorrelation function. If, for example, the second round of differencing results in a series whose autocorrelation function drops off rapidly, we can determine that the original series is second-order homogeneous. If the resulting series is still nonstationary, the autocorrelation function will remain large even for long lags.

Example 16.1 Interest Rate In applied work it often is not clear how many times a nonstationary series should be differenced to yield a stationary one, and one must make a judgment on the basis of experience and intuition. As an example, we will examine the interest rate on 3-month government Treasury bills. This series, consisting of monthly data from the beginning of 1960 through March 1996, is shown in Fig. 16.7, and its autocorrelation function is shown in Fig. 16.8. The autocorrelation function does decline as the number of lags becomes large, but only very slowly. In addition, the series exhibits an upward trend (so that the mean is not constant over time). We would therefore suspect that this series has been generated by a homogeneous nonstationary process. To check, we difference the series and recalculate the sample autocorrelation function.

The differenced series is shown in Fig. 16.9. Note that the mean of the series is now about constant, although the variance becomes unusually high during the early 1980s (a period when the Federal Reserve targeted the money supply, allowing interest rates to fluctuate). The sample autocorrelation function for the differenced series is shown in Fig. 16.10. It declines rapidly, consistent with a stationary series. We also tried differencing the series a second time. The twice-differenced series, $\Delta^2 R_t = \Delta R_t - \Delta R_{t-1}$, is shown in Fig. 16.11, and its sample autocorrelation function is shown in Fig. 16.12. The results do not seem qualitatively different from the previous case. Our conclusion, then, is that differencing once should be sufficient to ensure stationarity.

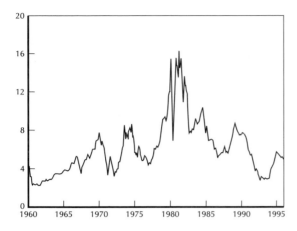

FIGURE 16.7
Three-month Treasury bill rate.

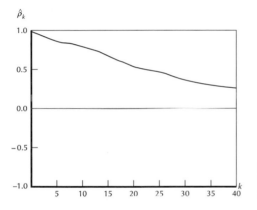

FIGURE 16.8
Three-month Treasury bill rate:
sample autocorrelation function.

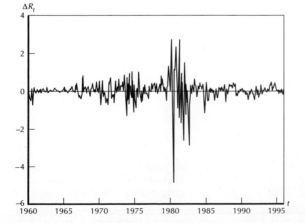

FIGURE 16.9
Three-month Treasury
bill rate—first differences.

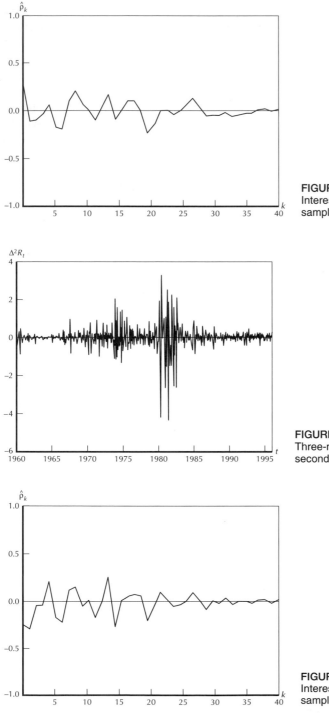

FIGURE 16.10
Interest rate—first differences:
sample autocorrelation function.

FIGURE 16.11
Three-month Treasury bill rate—
second differences.

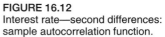

FIGURE 16.12
Interest rate—second differences:
sample autocorrelation function.

Example 16.2 Daily Hog Prices[5]   As a second example, let us examine a time series for the daily market price of hogs. If a forecasting model could be developed for this series, one could conceivably make money by speculating on the futures market for hogs and using the model to outperform the market.

The series consists of 250 daily data points covering all the trading days in 1965. The price variable is the average price in dollars per hundredweight of all hogs sold in the eight regional markets in the United States on a particular day. The sample autocorrelation functions for the original price series and for the first difference of the series are shown in Fig. 16.13.

Observe that the original series is clearly nonstationary. The autocorrelation function barely declines, even after a 16-period lag. The series is, however, first-order homogeneous, since its first difference is clearly stationary.

In fact, not only is the first-differenced series stationary, it appears to resemble white noise, since the sample autocorrelation function $\hat{\rho}_k$ is close to zero for all $k > 0$. To determine whether the differenced series is indeed white noise, we calculated the Q statistic for the first 15 lags. The value of this statistic is 14.62, which, with 15 degrees of freedom, is insignificant at the 10 percent level. We can therefore conclude that the differenced series

FIGURE 16.13
Sample autocorrelation functions of daily hog price data.

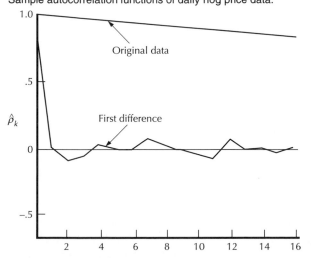

[5] This example is from a paper by R. Leuthold, A. MacCormick, A. Schmitz, and D. Watts, "Forecasting Daily Hog Prices and Quantities: A Study of Alternative Forecasting Techniques," *Journal of the American Statistical Association*, March 1970, Applications Section, pp. 90–107.

is white noise and that the original price series can best be modeled as a
random walk:

$$P_t = P_{t-1} + \varepsilon_t \qquad\qquad (16.33)$$

As is the case with most stock market prices, our best forecast of P_i is its
most recent value, and (sadly) there is no model that can help us outperform
the market.

16.2.3   Seasonality and the Autocorrelation Function

We have just seen that the autocorrelation function can reveal information
about the stationarity of a time series. In the remaining chapters of this book
we will see that other information about a time series can be obtained from its
autocorrelation function. However, we continue here by examining the relationship between the autocorrelation function and the *seasonality* of a time
series.

As was discussed in Chapter 15, seasonality is just a cyclical behavior that
occurs on a regular calendar basis. An example of a highly seasonal time series
would be toy sales, which exhibit a strong peak every Christmas. Sales of ice
cream and iced-tea mix show seasonal peaks each summer in response to
increased demand brought about by warmer weather; Peruvian anchovy production shows seasonal troughs once every 7 years in response to a decreased
supply brought about by cyclical changes in the ocean currents.

Often seasonal peaks and troughs are easy to spot by direct observation of
the time series. However, if the time series fluctuates considerably, seasonal
peaks and troughs may not be distinguishable from the other fluctuations.
Recognition of seasonality is important because it provides information about
"regularity" in the series that can aid us in making a forecast. Fortunately, that
recognition can be made easier with the help of the autocorrelation function.

If a monthly time series y_t exhibits annual seasonality, the data points in the
series should show some degree of correlation with the corresponding data
points which lead or lag by 12 months. In other words, we expect to see some
degree of correlation between y_t and y_{t-12}. Since y_t and y_{t-12} will be correlated,
as will y_{t-12} and y_{t-24}, we also should see correlation between y_t and y_{t-24}.
Similarly, there will be correlation between y_t and y_{t-36}, y_t and y_{t-48}, etc. These
correlations should manifest themselves in the sample autocorrelation function
$\hat{\rho}_k$, which will exhibit peaks at $k = 12, 24, 36, 48$, etc. Thus, we can identify
seasonality by observing regular peaks in the autocorrelation function, even if
seasonal peaks cannot be discerned in the time series itself.

Example 16.3 Hog Production   As an example, look at the time series for the monthly production of hogs in the United States shown in Fig. 16.14. It would take a somewhat experienced eye to easily discern seasonality in that series. The seasonality of the series, however, is readily apparent in its sample autocorrelation function, which is shown in Fig. 16.15. Note the peaks that occur at $k = 12$, 24, and 36, indicating annual cycles in the series.

A crude method of removing the annual cycles ("deseasonalizing" the data) would be to take a 12-month difference, obtaining a new series $z_t =$

FIGURE 16.14
Hog production (in thousands of hogs per month). Time bounds:
January 1962 to December 1971.

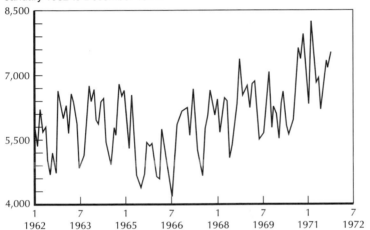

FIGURE 16.15
Sample autocorrelation function for hog production series.

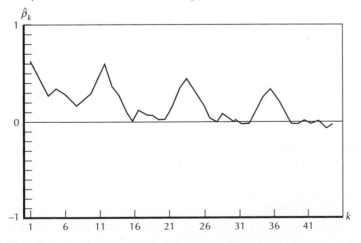

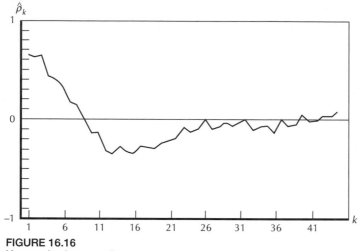

FIGURE 16.16
Hog production: sample autocorrelation function of $y_t - y_{t-12}$.

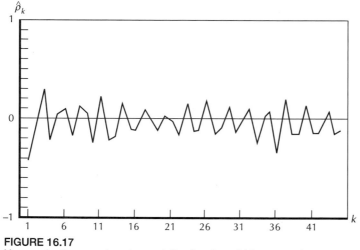

FIGURE 16.17
Hog production sample autocorrelation function of $\Delta(y_t - y_{t-12})$.

$y_t - y_{t-12}$. As can be seen in Fig. 16.16, the sample autocorrelation function for this 12-month differenced series does not exhibit strong seasonality. We will see in later chapters that z_t represents an extremely simple time-series model for hog production, since it accounts only for the annual cycle. We can complete this example by observing that the autocorrelation function in Fig. 16.16 declines only slowly, so that there is some doubt as to whether z_t is a stationary series. We therefore first-differenced this series to obtain $w_t = \Delta z_t = \Delta(y_t - y_{t-12})$. The sample autocorrelation function of this series, which is shown in Fig. 16.17, declines rapidly and remains small, so that we can be confident that w_t is a stationary, nonseasonal time series.

16.3 TESTING FOR RANDOM WALKS

Do economic variables such as GNP, employment, and interest rates tend to revert back to a long-run trend after a shock, or do they follow random walks? This question is important for two reasons. First, if these variables follow random walks, a regression of one against another can lead to spurious results. [The Gauss-Markov theorem would not hold, for example, because a random walk does not have a finite variance. Hence, ordinary least squares (OLS) would not yield a consistent parameter estimator.] Detrending the variables before running the regression will not help; the detrended series will still be nonstationary. Only first-differencing will yield stationary series. Second, the answer has implications for our understanding of the economy and for forecasting. If a variable such as GNP follows a random walk, the effects of a temporary shock (such as an increase in oil prices or a drop in government spending) will not dissipate after several years but instead will be permanent.

In a provocative study, Charles Nelson and Charles Plosser found evidence that GNP and other macroeconomic time series behave like random walks.[6] The work spawned a series of studies that investigate whether economic and financial variables are random walks or are trend-reverting. Several of these studies show that many economic time series do appear to be random walks or at least have random walk components.[7] Most of these studies use *unit root tests* introduced by David Dickey and Wayne Fuller.[8]

Suppose we believe that a variable Y_t, which has been growing over time, can be described by the following equation:

$$Y_t = \alpha + \beta t + \rho Y_{t-1} + \varepsilon_t \tag{16.34}$$

One possibility is that Y_t has been growing because it has a positive trend ($\beta > 0$) but would be stationary after detrending (i.e., $\rho < 1$). In this case Y_t could

---

[6] C. R. Nelson and C. I. Plosser, "Trends and Random Walks in Macroeconomic Time Series: Some Evidence and Implications," *Journal of Monetary Economics,* vol. 10, pp. 139–162, 1982.

[7] Examples of these studies include J. Y. Campbell and N. G. Mankiw, "Are Output Fluctuations Transitory?" *Quarterly Journal of Economics,* vol. 102, pp. 857–880, 1987; J. Y. Campbell and N. G. Mankiw, "Permanent and Transitory Components in Macroeconomic Fluctuations," *American Economic Review Papers and Proceedings,* vol. 77, pp. 111–117, 1987; and G. W. Gardner and K. P. Kimbrough, "The Behavior of U.S. Tariff Rates," *American Economic Review,* vol. 79, pp. 211–218, 1989.

[8] D. A. Dickey and W. A. Fuller, "Distribution of the Estimators for Autoregressive Time-Series with a Unit Root," *Journal of the American Statistical Association,* vol. 74, pp. 427–431, 1979; D. A. Dickey and W. A. Fuller, "Likelihood Ratio Statistics for Autoregressive Time Series with a Unit Root," *Econometrica,* vol. 49, pp. 1057–1072, 1981; and W. A. Fuller, *Introduction to Statistical Time Series* (New York: Wiley, 1976).

be used in a regression, and all the results and tests discussed in Part One of this book would apply. Another possibility is that Y_t has been growing because it follows a random walk with a positive drift (i.e., $\alpha > 0$, $\beta = 0$, and $\rho = 1$). In this case one would want to work with ΔY_t. Detrending would not make the series stationary, and the inclusion of Y_t in a regression (even if detrended) could lead to spurious results.

One might think that Eq. (16.34) could be estimated by OLS and that the t statistic on $\hat{\rho}$ could then be used to test whether $\hat{\rho}$ is significantly different from 1. However, if the true value of ρ is indeed 1, the OLS estimator is biased toward zero. Thus, the use of OLS in this manner can lead one to incorrectly reject the random walk hypothesis.

Dickey and Fuller derived the distribution for the estimator $\hat{\rho}$ that holds when $\rho = 1$ and generated statistics for a simple F test of the random walk hypothesis, i.e., the hypothesis that $\beta = 0$ and $\rho = 1$. The Dickey-Fuller test is easy to perform and can be applied to a more general version of Eq. (16.34). It works as follows.

Suppose Y_t can be described by the following equation:

$$Y_t = \alpha + \beta t + \rho Y_{t-1} + \varepsilon_t \tag{16.35}$$

Using OLS, one first runs the unrestricted regression

$$Y_t - Y_{t-1} = \alpha + \beta t + (\rho - 1)Y_{t-1} \tag{16.36}$$

and then the restricted regression

$$Y_t - Y_{t-1} = \alpha \tag{16.37}$$

Then one calculates the standard F ratio to test whether the restrictions ($\beta = 0$, $\rho = 1$) hold.[9] This ratio, however, is *not* distributed as a standard F distribution under the null hypothesis. Instead, one must use the distributions tabulated by Dickey and Fuller. Critical values for this statistic are shown in Table 16.1.

Note that these critical values are much larger than those in the standard F table. For example, if the calculated F ratio turns out to be 5.2 and there are 100 observations, we would easily reject the null hypothesis of a unit root at the 5 percent level if we used a standard F table (which, with two parameter restrictions, shows a critical value of about 3.1); i.e., we would conclude that there is no random walk. This rejection, however, would be incorrect. Note

---

[9] Recall that F is calculated as follows:

$$F = (N - k)(\text{ESS}_R - \text{ESS}_{UR})/q(\text{ESS}_{UR})$$

where ESS_R and ESS_{UR} are the sums of squared residuals in the restricted and unrestricted regressions, respectively, N is the number of observations, k is the number of estimated parameters in the unrestricted regression, and q is the number of parameter restrictions.

TABLE 16.1
DISTRIBUTION OF F FOR $(\alpha, \beta, \rho) = (\alpha, 0, 1)$ IN $Y_t = \alpha + \beta t + \rho Y_{t-1} + \varepsilon_t$

Sample size N	Probability of a smaller value							
	.01	.025	.05	.10	.90	.95	.975	.99
25	.74	.90	1.08	1.03	5.91	7.24	8.65	10.61
50	.76	.93	1.11	1.37	5.61	6.73	7.81	9.31
100	.76	.94	1.12	1.38	5.47	6.49	7.44	8.73
250	.76	.94	1.13	1.39	5.39	6.34	7.25	8.43
500	.76	.94	1.13	1.39	5.36	6.30	7.20	8.34
∞	.77	.94	1.13	1.39	5.34	6.25	7.16	8.27
Standard error	.004	.004	.003	.004	.015	.020	.032	.058

Source: Dickey and Fuller, op. cit., Table VI, p. 1063, 1981.

that we fail to reject the hypothesis of a random walk using the distribution calculated by Dickey and Fuller (the critical value is 6.49).[10]

One problem with Eq. (16.35) is that it makes the implicit assumption that there is no serial correlation of any kind in the error term ε_t. Often we would like to allow for serial correlation in ε_t and still test for a unit root. This can be done by using the *augmented Dickey-Fuller test*. This test is carried out by expanding Eq. (16.35) to include lagged changes in Y_t on the right-hand side of the equation:

$$Y_t = \alpha + \beta t + \rho Y_{t-1} + \sum_{j=1}^{p} \lambda_j \Delta y_{t-j} + \varepsilon_t \qquad (16.38)$$

where $\Delta Y_t = Y_t - Y_{t-1}$. It is up to the econometrician to specify how many lags (p) to include on the right-hand side of this equation. Usually this is done by experimentation, and one would hope that the test results would come out the same for any reasonable number of lags.

The unit root test is then run the same way as before. Using OLS, one first runs the unrestricted regression

$$Y_t - Y_{t-1} = \alpha + \beta t + (\rho - 1)Y_{t-1} + \sum_{j=1}^{p} \lambda_j \Delta Y_{t-j} \qquad (16.39)$$

and then the restricted regression

$$Y_t - Y_{t-1} = \alpha + \sum_{j=1}^{p} \lambda_j \Delta Y_{t-j} \qquad (16.40)$$

---

[10] For further discussion of the random walk model and alternative tests, see P. Perron, "Trends and Random Walks in Macroeconomic Time Series: Further Evidence from a New Approach," *Journal of Economic Dynamics and Control*, vol. 12, pp. 297–332, 1988, and P. C. B. Phillips, "Time Series Regression with Unit Roots," *Econometrica*, vol. 55, pp. 277–302, 1987.

Then a standard F ratio is calculated to test whether the restrictions ($\beta = 0$, $\rho = 1$) hold. Once again, one must use the distributions tabulated by Dickey and Fuller for this test, which are shown in Table 16.1.

Although the Dickey-Fuller test is widely used, one should keep in mind that its power is limited. It only allows us to reject (or fail to reject) the hypothesis that a variable is *not* a random walk. A failure to reject (especially at a high significance level) provides only weak evidence in favor of the random walk hypothesis.

Example 16.4 Do Commodity Prices Follow Random Walks?   Like stocks and bonds, many commodities are actively traded in highly liquid spot markets. In addition, trading is active in financial instruments, such as futures contracts, that depend on the prices of these commodities. One might therefore expect the prices of these commodities to follow random walks, so that no investor could expect to profit by following some trading rule. (See Example 16.2 on daily hog prices.) Indeed, most financial models of futures, options, and other instruments tied to a commodity are based on the assumption that the spot price follows a random walk.[11]

However, basic microeconomic theory tells us that in the long run the price of a commodity ought to be tied to its marginal production cost. This means that although the price of a commodity may be subject to sharp short-run fluctuations, it ought to tend to return to a "normal" level based on cost. Of course, marginal production cost may be expected to slowly rise (if the commodity is a depletable resource) or fall (because of technological change), but that means that the *detrended* price should tend to revert back to a normal level.

At issue, then, is whether the price of a commodity can best be described as a random walk process, perhaps with trend:

$$P_t = \alpha + P_{t-1} + \varepsilon_t \tag{16.41}$$

where ε_t is a white noise error term, or alternatively as a first-order autoregressive process with trend:

$$P_t = \alpha + \beta t + \rho P_{t-1} + \varepsilon_t \tag{16.42}$$

Since any reversion to long-run marginal cost is likely to be slow, we will be able to discriminate between these two alternative models only with data

---

[11] For a thorough treatment of commodity markets and derivative instruments such as futures contracts, see Darrell Duffie, *Futures Markets* (Englewood Cliffs, N.J.: Prentice-Hall, 1989), and John Hull, *Options, Futures, and Other Derivative Securities* (Englewood Cliffs, N.J.: Prentice-Hall, 1989).

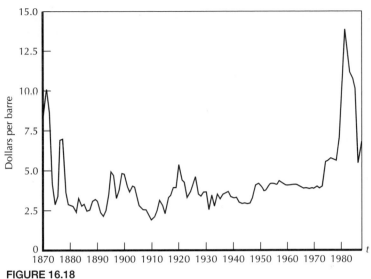

FIGURE 16.18
Price of oil (in 1967 constant dollars).

that cover a long time period (so that short-run fluctuations wash out). Fortunately, more than 100 years of commodity price data are available.

Figures 16.18 through 16.20 show the real (in 1967 dollars) prices of crude oil, copper, and lumber over the 117-year period 1870 to 1987.[12] Observe that the price of oil fluctuated around $4 per barrel from 1880 to 1970 but rose sharply in 1974 and 1980–1981 and then fell during the mid-1980s. Copper prices have fluctuated considerably but show a general downward trend, while lumber prices have tended to increase, at least up to about 1950.

We ran a Dickey-Fuller unit root test on each price series by estimating the unrestricted regression:

$$P_t - P_{t-1} = \alpha + \beta t + (\rho - 1)P_{t-1} + \lambda \Delta P_{t-1} + \varepsilon_t$$

and the restricted regression:

$$P_t - P_{t-1} = \alpha + \lambda \Delta P_{t-1} + \varepsilon_t$$

We tested the restrictions by calculating an F ratio and comparing it to the critical values in Table 16.1. Regression results (with standard errors in parentheses) are shown in Table 16.2.

---

[12] The data for 1870 to 1973 are from Robert Manthy, *A Century of Natural Resource Statistics* (Baltimore, MD: Johns Hopkins University Press, 1978). Data after 1973 are from publications of the Energy Information Agency and the U.S. Bureau of Mines. All prices are deflated by the wholesale price index (now the Producer Price Index).

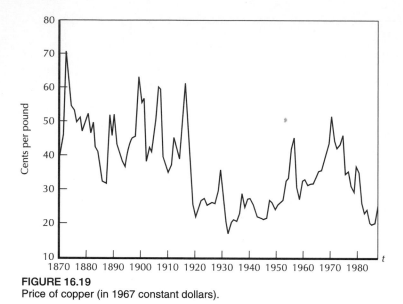

FIGURE 16.19
Price of copper (in 1967 constant dollars).

In each case there are 116 annual observations. Hence, for copper the F ratio is $(112)(4,913.5 - 4,344.8)/(2)(4,344.8) = 7.33$. Comparing this to the critical values for a sample size of 100 in Table 16.1, we see that we can reject the hypothesis of a random walk at the 5 percent level. For lumber the F ratio is 4.64, and for crude oil it is 13.93. Hence, we can easily reject

FIGURE 16.20
Price of lumber (in 1967 constant dollars).

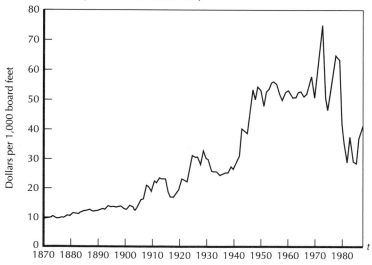

TABLE 16.2
DICKEY-FULLER TESTS

Commodity	α	β	$(\rho - 1)$	λ	ESS
Copper (unrestricted)	11.357	$-.0446$	$-.2417$	.0766	4,344.8
	(3.228)	(.0208)	(.0631)	(.0941)	
Copper (restricted)	$-.1969$			$-.0440$	4,913.5
	(.6098)			(.0934)	
Lumber (unrestricted)	.8825	.0660	$-.1560$	.1392	2,242.8
	(.8689)	(.0263)	(.0515)	(.0958)	
Lumber (restricted)	.2488			.0507	2,428.6
	(.4291)			(.0938)	
Oil (unrestricted)	.4366	.00895	$-.2355$	.2546	100.09
	(.2188)	(.00285)	(.0459)	(.0848)	
Oil (restricted)	$-.0262$			.1760	125.00
	(.0973)			(.0918)	

the hypothesis of a random walk for crude oil but cannot reject this hypothesis for lumber, even at the 10 percent level.

Do commodity prices follow random walks? More than a century of data indicates that copper and crude oil prices are not random walks, but the price of lumber is consistent with the random walk hypothesis.[13]

16.4 CO-INTEGRATED TIME SERIES

Regressing one random walk against another can lead to spurious results in that conventional significance tests will tend to indicate a relationship between the variables when in fact none exists. This is one reason why it is important to test for random walks. If a test fails to reject the hypothesis of a random walk, one can difference the series in question before using it in a regression. Since many economic time series seem to follow random walks, this suggests that one will typically want to difference a variable before using it in a regression. While this is acceptable, differencing may result in a loss of information about the long-run relationship between two variables. Are there situations where one can run a regression between two variables even though both variables are random walks?

There are. Sometimes two variables will follow random walks but a *linear combination* of those variables will be stationary. For example, it may be that the variables x_t and y_t are random walks but the variable $z_t = x_t - \lambda y_t$ is stationary. If this is the case, we say that x_t and y_t are *co-integrated* and call λ the

---

[13] The fact that copper and oil prices do not seem to be random walks does not mean that one can earn an unusually high return by trading these commodities. First, a century is a long time, and so even ignoring transaction costs, any excess return from the use of a trading rule is likely to be very small. Second, the mean-reverting behavior we have found may be due to shifts over time in the risk-adjusted expected return.

co-integrating parameter.[14] One can then estimate λ by running an OLS regression of x_t on y_t. (Unlike the case of two random walks that are not co-integrated, here OLS provides a consistent estimator of λ.) Furthermore, the residuals of this regression then can be used to test whether x_t and y_t are indeed co-integrated.

The theory of co-integration, which was developed by Engle and Granger, is important for reasons that go beyond its use as a diagnostic for linear regression.[15] In many cases economic theory tells us that two variables should be co-integrated, and a test for co-integration is then a test of the theory. For example, although aggregate consumption and disposable income both behave as random walks, we would expect these two variables to move together over the long run, so that a linear combination of the two should be stationary. Another example is the stock market; if stocks are rationally valued the price of a company's shares should equal the present value of the expected future flow of dividends. This means that although dividends and stock prices both follow random walks, the two series should be co-integrated, with the co-integrating parameter equal to the discount rate used by investors to calculate the present value of earnings.[16]

Suppose one determines, using the Dickey-Fuller test described above, that x_t and y_t are random walks but that Δx_t and Δy_t are stationary. It is then quite easy to test whether x_t and y_t are co-integrated. One simply runs the OLS regression (called the *co-integrating regression*):

$$x_t = \alpha + \beta y_t + \varepsilon_t \tag{16.43}$$

and then tests whether the residuals, e_t, from this regression are stationary. (If x_t and y_t are not co-integrated, any linear combination of them will be nonstationary, and hence the residuals e_t will be nonstationary.) Specifically, we test the hypothesis that e_t is not stationary, i.e., the hypothesis of no co-integration.

A test of the hypothesis that e_t is nonstationary can be done in two ways. First, a Dickey-Fuller test can be performed on the residual series. Alternatively,

---

[14] In some situations x_t and y_t will be vectors of variables and λ will be a vector of parameters; λ is then called the *co-integrating vector*. Also, we are assuming that x_t and y_t are both first-order homogeneous nonstationary (also called *integrated of order one*); i.e., the first-differenced series Δx_t and Δy_t are both stationary. More generally, if x_t and y_t are dth-order homogeneous nonstationary (integrated of order d) and $z_t = x_t - \lambda y_t$ is bth-order homogeneous nonstationary, with $b < d$, we say that x_t and y_t are *co-integrated of order d, b*. We will limit our attention to the case of $d = 1$ and $b = 0$.

[15] The theory is set forth in R. F. Engle and C. W. J. Granger, "Co-Integration and Error Correction: Representation, Estimation, and Testing,"*Econometrica,* vol. 55, pp. 251–276, 1987.

[16] For tests of the present-value model of stock pricing, see J. Y. Campbell and R. J. Shiller, "Cointegration and Tests of Present Value Models," *Journal of Political Economy,* vol. 95, pp. 1062–1088, 1987. For other applications, see J. Y. Campbell, "Does Saving Anticipate Declining Labor Income? An Alternative Test of the Permanent Income Hypothesis," *Econometrica,* vol. 55, pp. 1249–1273, 1987, for a study of the co-integration of consumption and income, and R. Meese and K. Rogoff, "Was It Real? The Exchange Rate–Interest Differential Relation over the Modern Floating-Rate Period." *Journal of Finance,* vol. 43, pp. 933–947, 1988, for a study of the co-integration of exchange rates and interest differentials.

TABLE 16.3
CRITICAL VALUES FOR TEST
OF DW = 0

Significance level, %	Critical value of DW
1	.511
5	.386
10	.322

one can simply look at the Durbin-Watson statistic from the co-integrating regression. Recall from Chapter 6 that the Durbin-Watson statistic is given by

$$DW = \frac{\Sigma(e_t - e_{t-1})^2}{\Sigma(e_t)^2}$$

If e_t is a random walk, the expected value of $(e_t - e_{t-1})$ is zero, and so the Durbin-Watson statistic should be close to zero. Thus, one can simply test the hypothesis that DW = 0. For 100 observations, the critical values for this test are shown in Table 16.3.[17] For example, if after running the co-integrating regression we obtain a DW value of .71, we can reject the hypothesis of no co-integration at the 1 percent level.

Example 16.5 The Co-Integration of Consumption and Income   An interesting finding in macroeconomics is that many variables, including aggregate consumption and disposable income, seem to follow random walks. Among other things, this means that the effects of a temporary shock will not tend to dissipate after several years but instead will be permanent. But even if consumption and disposable income are random walks, the two should tend to move together. The reason is that over long periods households tend to consume a certain fraction of their disposable income. Thus, over the long term, consumption and income should stay in line with each other; i.e., they should be co-integrated.

We will test whether real consumption spending and real disposable income are co-integrated, using quarterly data for the first quarter of 1960 through the last quarter of 1995. To do this we first test whether each variable is a random walk, using the augmented Dickey-Fuller test described in the previous section. Running this test, first for consumption and then for disposable income, and in each case including one, two, or four lags for the change in the variable, always yields test statistics that fail to reject the random walk hypothesis, even at the 10 percent level. (We leave it to

---

[17] From Engle and Granger, op. cit., p. 269.

the reader to perform a Dickey-Fuller test for the first differences of these variables and show that in that case we can reject the random walk hypothesis.)

We next run a co-integrating regression of consumption C against disposable income YD.[18] The results are as follows (t statistics are in parentheses):

$$\hat{C}_t = -89.94 + .9346\text{YD}_t \qquad (16.44)$$
$$\quad\ \ (-6.65) \qquad (231.87)$$

$$R^2 = .9974 \qquad s = 48.85 \qquad DW = .325$$

We can use the Durbin-Watson statistic to test whether the residuals in this regression follow a random walk. Comparing the DW of .325 to the critical values in Table 16.3, we see that we can reject the hypothesis of a random walk at the 10 percent level but not at the 5 percent level. Running a Dickey-Fuller test on the residuals of this regression also leads to a rejection of the random walk hypothesis at the 10 percent level but not at the 5 percent level. These results appear to be inconclusive, leaving open the question of whether consumption and disposable income are indeed co-integrated.

It is interesting to compare this result with the example that appeared in the previous edition of this book. In the third edition of the book we ran the same co-integrating regression using quarterly data for the third quarter of 1950 through the first quarter of 1988. The results of that co-integrating regression were as follows:

$$\hat{C}_t = -133.82 + .9651\text{YD}_t \qquad (16.45)$$
$$\quad\ \ (-21.90) \qquad (278.93)$$

$$R^2 = .9981 \qquad s = 23.35 \qquad DW = .4936$$

In this case, the DW of .4936 leads us to reject the hypothesis of a random walk at the 5 percent level. Hence, in the third edition we concluded that "consumption and disposable income are indeed co-integrated." Now we can also conclude that in doing empirical research one must be careful about the sample period and about the stability of the hypothesized relationship.

APPENDIX 16.1 The Autocorrelation Function for a Stationary Process

In this appendix we derive a set of necessary conditions for an autocorrelation function of a stationary process. Let y_t be a stationary process and let L_t be any linear function of y_t and lags in y_t, for example,

$$L_t = \alpha_1 y_t + \alpha_2 y_{t-1} + \cdots + \alpha_k y_{t-k+1} \qquad (A16.1)$$

[18] For readers using CITIBASE data, the corresponding series are GCQ and GYDQ.

Now, since y_t is stationary, the covariances of y_t are stationary, and

$$\text{Cov } (y_{t+i}, y_{t+j}) = \gamma_{|i-j|} \tag{A16.2}$$

independent of t. Then, by squaring both sides of Eq. (A16.1), we see that the variance of L_t is given by

$$\text{Var } (L_t) = \sum_{i=1}^{k+1} \sum_{j=1}^{k+1} \alpha_i \alpha_j \gamma_{|i-j|} \tag{A16.3}$$

If the α's are not all 0, the variance of L_t must be greater than 0, and therefore we must have, for all i and j,

$$\gamma_{|i-j|} > 0 \qquad \text{for } i = j \tag{A16.4}$$

Now, for n observations, write the covariances of y_t as a matrix:

$$\mathbf{\Gamma}_n = \begin{bmatrix} \gamma_0 & \gamma_1 & \gamma_2 & \cdots & \gamma_{n-1} \\ \gamma_1 & \gamma_0 & \gamma_1 & \cdots & \gamma_{n-2} \\ \cdots & \cdots & \cdots & \cdots & \cdots \\ \gamma_{n-1} & \gamma_{n-2} & \gamma_{n-3} & \cdots & \gamma_0 \end{bmatrix} \tag{A16.5}$$

This matrix must be positive definite because the variance of L_t is always greater than zero. Note that

$$\mathbf{\Gamma}_n = \sigma_y^2 \begin{bmatrix} 1 & \rho_1 & \rho_2 & \cdots & \rho_{n-1} \\ \rho_1 & 1 & \rho_1 & \cdots & \rho_{n-2} \\ \cdots & \cdots & \cdots & \cdots & \cdots \\ \rho_{n-1} & \rho_{n-2} & \rho_{n-3} & \cdots & 1 \end{bmatrix} = \sigma_y^2 \mathbf{P}_n \tag{A16.6}$$

where $\mathbf{P}_n$ is the matrix of autocorrelations and is itself positive definite. Thus, the determinant of $\mathbf{P}_n$ and its principal minors must be greater than 0.

As an example, let us consider the case of $n = 2$. The condition on the determinant of $\mathbf{P}_n$ becomes

$$\det \begin{bmatrix} 1 & \rho_1 \\ \rho_1 & 1 \end{bmatrix} > 0$$

which implies that

$$1 - \rho_1^2 > 0$$

or

$$-1 < \rho_1 < 1 \tag{A16.7}$$

Similarly, for $n = 3$, it is easy to see that the following three conditions must all hold:

$$-1 < \rho_1 < 1 \tag{A16.8}$$

$$-1 < \rho_2 < 1 \tag{A16.9}$$

$$-1 < \frac{\rho_2 - \rho_1^2}{1 - \rho_1^2} < 1 \tag{A16.10}$$

Sets of conditions also can be derived for $n = 4$, $n = 5$, etc., but it should become clear that as the number of observations n becomes large, the number of conditions that must hold also becomes quite large. Although these condi-

TABLE 16.4
PRICES OF CRUDE OIL, COPPER, AND LUMBER (in 1967 constant dollars)

Obs.	Oil	Copper	Lumber	Obs.	Oil	Copper	Lumber
1870	8.64	41.61	9.13	1929	3.63	36.86	32.65
1871	10.16	47.54	9.70	1930	3.64	29.21	29.84
1872	8.35	70.64	9.75	1931	2.47	21.54	29.39
1873	4.24	61.57	9.98	1932	3.50	16.77	25.42
1874	2.81	54.68	9.93	1933	2.71	20.59	24.97
1875	3.37	53.37	9.45	1934	3.52	21.76	24.97
1876	6.90	49.60	9.60	1935	3.17	20.82	23.51
1877	6.95	51.15	9.74	1936	3.48	22.78	24.34
1878	3.74	47.17	9.75	1937	3.55	29.66	25.12
1879	2.84	49.50	10.43	1938	3.65	24.69	24.59
1880	2.80	52.68	10.09	1939	3.32	27.71	26.55
1881	2.74	46.39	10.90	1940	3.26	27.90	25.38
1882	2.26	49.85	11.11	1941	3.28	26.16	27.47
1883	3.27	42.64	11.05	1942	3.01	23.18	29.98
1884	2.66	41.67	11.79	1943	2.89	22.18	39.74
1885	2.95	35.62	12.02	1944	2.91	22.01	38.76
1886	2.42	32.53	12.32	1945	2.89	21.61	37.78
1887	2.44	31.96	12.44	1946	2.92	22.12	45.31
1888	2.97	52.03	12.03	1947	3.27	27.45	52.84
1889	3.18	45.61	12.03	1948	4.09	26.57	48.76
1890	3.00	52.41	12.28	1949	4.19	24.40	53.94
1891	2.33	43.75	12.19	1950	4.05	25.92	52.30
1892	2.08	41.26	12.60	1951	3.67	26.56	46.18
1893	2.44	38.18	12.55	1952	3.77	27.34	51.13
1894	3.24	36.84	13.72	1953	4.07	32.99	52.86
1895	4.90	41.43	13.07	1954	4.21	33.94	54.91
1896	4.58	44.17	13.67	1955	4.18	42.71	55.48
1897	3.17	45.42	13.17	1956	4.09	46.09	54.20
1898	3.64	46.00	13.32	1957	4.38	31.73	50.88
1899	4.80	63.20	13.68	1958	4.23	27.27	48.78
1900	4.72	55.17	12.59	1959	4.11	32.95	51.24

TABLE 16.4
PRICES OF CRUDE OIL, COPPER, AND LUMBER (in 1967 constant dollars)
(*Continued*)

Obs.	Oil	Copper	Lumber	Obs.	Oil	Copper	Lumber
1901	4.00	57.19	12.53	1960	4.07	33.83	52.57
1902	3.59	38.16	13.95	1961	4.10	31.64	50.89
1903	4.04	43.00	13.42	1962	4.10	32.28	49.43
1904	3.83	40.91	11.95	1963	4.11	32.38	50.03
1905	2.90	49.03	13.77	1964	4.09	33.79	51.58
1906	2.66	60.50	15.80	1965	3.99	36.23	52.09
1907	2.50	59.52	16.01	1966	3.89	36.27	50.46
1908	2.50	40.74	20.49	1967	3.90	38.20	51.17
1909	2.18	37.36	20.17	1968	3.83	40.78	53.99
1910	1.85	34.99	18.29	1969	3.90	44.60	57.65
1911	2.03	37.01	22.12	1970	3.89	52.26	49.09
1912	2.39	45.79	20.98	1971	4.00	45.13	57.88
1913	3.19	42.50	23.25	1972	3.84	42.49	65.20
1914	2.79	38.75	22.56	1973	3.99	43.73	74.21
1915	2.20	48.19	22.95	1974	5.56	46.81	50.57
1916	3.22	61.68	18.98	1975	5.64	35.11	45.27
1917	3.42	44.88	16.34	1976	5.82	36.22	52.35
1918	3.90	36.34	16.51	1977	5.71	32.48	57.54
1919	3.90	26.15	17.86	1978	5.61	30.23	64.23
1920	5.40	21.96	19.15	1979	6.98	37.77	62.77
1921	4.39	24.85	22.84	1980	10.34	35.99	41.17
1922	4.21	26.85	22.53	1981	13.94	27.22	32.09
1923	3.24	27.75	21.91	1982	12.34	23.37	27.71
1924	3.58	25.69	26.13	1983	11.26	24.80	37.21
1925	4.10	26.22	31.33	1984	10.86	20.76	28.27
1926	4.67	26.74	29.94	1985	10.15	20.47	27.58
1927	3.50	26.22	30.12	1986	5.46	20.91	35.70
1928	3.37	29.26	26.75	1987	6.57	25.61	39.91

tions can provide an analytic check on the stationarity of a time series, in applied work it is more typical to judge stationarity from a visual examination of both the series itself and the sample autocorrelation function. For our purposes it will be sufficient to remember that for $k > 0$, $-1 < \rho_k < 1$ for a stationary process.

EXERCISES

16.1 Show that the random walk process with drift is first-order homogeneous nonstationary.

16.2 Consider the time series 1, 2, 3, 4, 5, 6, . . . , 20. Is this series stationary? Calculate the sample autocorrelation function $\hat{\rho}_k$ for $k = 1, 2, . . . , 5$. Can you explain the shape of this function?

16.3 The data series for the prices of crude oil, copper, and lumber are printed in Table 16.4.

(*a*) Calculate the sample autocorrelation function for each series and determine whether those functions are consistent with the Dickey-Fuller test results in Example 16.4. Specifically, do the sample autocorrelation functions for crude oil and copper prices exhibit stationarity? Does the sample autocorrelation function for the price of lumber indicate that the series is nonstationary?

(*b*) How robust are the Dickey-Fuller test results to the sample size? Divide the sample in half and for each price series repeat the Dickey-Fuller tests for each half of the sample.

16.4 Go back to the data for the S&P 500 Common Stock Price Index at the end of Chapter 15. Would you expect this index to follow a random walk? Perform a Dickey-Fuller test to see whether it indeed does.

16.5 Calculate the sample autocorrelation function for retail auto sales. (Use the data in Table 15.2 at the end of Chapter 15.) Does the sample autocorrelation function indicate seasonality?

CHAPTER 17

LINEAR TIME-SERIES
MODELS

We turn now to the construction of time-series models. Our objective is to develop models that "explain" the movement of a time series by relating it to its own past values and to a weighted sum of current and lagged random disturbances.

While many functional forms can be used, we will focus on linear models. This will allow us to make quantitative statements about the stochastic properties of the models and the forecasts generated by them (e.g., to calculate confidence intervals). In addition, our models apply both to stationary processes and to homogeneous nonstationary processes (which can be differenced one or more times to yield stationary processes). Finally, the models are written as equations with fixed estimated coefficients, representing a stochastic structure that does not change over time. (Although models with time-varying coefficients of nonstationary processes have been developed, they are beyond the scope of this book.)

In the first two sections of the chapter we examine simple moving average and autoregressive models for stationary processes. In a moving average model, the process is described completely by a weighted sum of current and lagged random disturbances. In the autoregressive model, the process depends on a weighted sum of its past values and a random disturbance term. In the third section we introduce mixed autoregressive–moving average models. In these models the process is a function of both its past values and lagged random disturbances, as well as a current disturbance term. Even if the original process is nonstationary, it often can be differenced one or more times to produce a new series that is stationary and for which a mixed autoregressive–moving average model can be constructed. This model can be used to produce a forecast one or more periods into the future, after which the forecasted stationary series can be integrated one or more times to yield a forecast for the original time series. The integrated autoregressive-moving average model provides a general framework for the modeling of homogeneous nonstationary time series.

In building an integrated autoregressive–moving average model for a nonstationary time series, we must specify how many times the series is to be differenced before a stationary series results. We also must specify the number of autoregressive terms and lagged disturbance terms that will be included. We have seen in Chapter 16 that the autocorrelation function can be used to tell us how many times we must difference a homogeneous nonstationary process to produce a stationary process. Here we will see how the autocorrelation function can also be used to help determine how many lagged disturbance terms and autoregressive terms should be included in the model.

17.1   MOVING AVERAGE MODELS

In the *moving average process of order q* each observation y_t is generated by a weighted average of random disturbances going back q periods. We denote this process as MA(q) and write its equation as

$$y_t = \mu + \varepsilon_t - \theta_1\varepsilon_{t-1} - \theta_2\varepsilon_{t-2} - \cdots - \theta_q\varepsilon_{t-q} \qquad (17.1)$$

where the parameters $\theta_1, \ldots, \theta_q$ may be positive or negative.[1]

In the moving average model (and also in the autoregressive model, which will follow) the random disturbances are assumed to be independently distributed across time, i.e., generated by a *white noise* process. In particular, each disturbance term ε_t is assumed to be a normal random variable with mean 0, variance σ_ε^2, and covariance $\gamma_k = 0$ for $k \neq 0$.[2] White noise processes may not occur very often, but as we will see, weighted sums of a white noise process can provide a good representation of processes that are nonwhite.

The reader should observe that the *mean* of the moving average process is independent of time, since $E(y_t) = \mu$. Each ε_t is assumed to be generated by the same white noise process, so that $E(\varepsilon_t) = 0$, $E(\varepsilon_t^2) = \sigma_\varepsilon^2$, and $E(\varepsilon_t\varepsilon_{t-k}) = 0$

---

[1] Following convention, we put a minus sign in front of $\theta_1, \ldots, \theta_q$. In some textbooks the MA(q) model is written as

$$y_t = \mu + \varepsilon_t + \theta_1\varepsilon_{t-1} + \cdots + \theta_q\varepsilon_{t-q}$$

Be aware of this when you are reading and interpreting computer output and as you proceed through the rest of this book.

[2] As we saw in Chapter 16, the autocorrelation function for a white noise process is

$$\rho_k = \begin{cases} 1 & \text{for } k = 0 \\ 0 & \text{for } k \neq 0 \end{cases}$$

for k $\neq$ 0. The process MA(q) is thus described by exactly $q + 2$ parameters, the mean μ, the disturbance variance σ_ε^2, and the parameters $\theta_1, \theta_2, \ldots, \theta_q$ that determine the weights in the moving average.

Let us now look at the *variance*, denoted by γ_0, of the moving average process of order q:

$$
\begin{aligned}
\text{Var } (y_t) = \gamma_0 &= E[(y_t - \mu)^2] \\
&= E(\varepsilon_t^2 + \theta_1^2\varepsilon_{t-1}^2 + \cdots + \theta_q^2\varepsilon_{t-q}^2 - 2\theta_1\varepsilon_t\varepsilon_{t-1} - \cdots) \\
&= \sigma_\varepsilon^2 + \theta_1^2\sigma_\varepsilon^2 + \cdots + \theta_q^2\sigma_\varepsilon^2 \\
&= \sigma_\varepsilon^2(1 + \theta_1^2 + \theta_2^2 + \cdots + \theta_q^2)
\end{aligned}
\tag{17.2}
$$

Note that the expected values of the cross terms are all 0, since we have assumed that the ε_t's are generated by a white noise process for which $\gamma_k = E(\varepsilon_t\varepsilon_{t-k}) = 0$ for $k \neq 0$.

Equation (17.2) imposes a restriction on the values that are permitted for $\theta_1, \ldots, \theta_q$. We would expect the variance of y_t to be finite, since otherwise a realization of the random process would involve larger and larger deviations from a fixed reference point as time increased. This in turn would violate our assumption of stationarity, since stationarity requires that the probability of being some arbitrary distance from a reference point be invariant with respect to time. Thus, if y_t is the realization of a stationary random process, we must have

$$
\sum_{i=1}^{q} \theta_i^2 < \infty
\tag{17.3}
$$

In a sense this result is trivial, since we have only a finite number of θ_i's, and thus their sum is finite. However, the assumption of a fixed number of θ_i's can be considered to be an approximation to a more general model. A complete model of most random processes would require an infinite number of lagged disturbance terms (and their corresponding weights). Then, as q, the order of the moving average process, becomes infinitely large, we must require that the sum $\sum_{i=0}^{\infty}\theta_i^2$ converge. Convergence usually will occur if the θ's become smaller as i becomes larger. Thus, if we are representing a process, believed to be stationary, by a moving average model of order q, we expect the θ_i's to become smaller as i becomes larger. We will see later that this implies that if the process is stationary its correlation function ρ_k will become smaller as k becomes larger. This is consistent with our result in Chapter 16 that one indicator of stationarity is an autocorrelation function that approaches zero.

Now we examine some simple moving average processes, calculating the mean, variance, covariances, and autocorrelation function for each. These statistics are important first because they provide information that helps characterize the process and second because they will help us identify the process when we actually construct models in Chapter 18.

We begin with the simplest moving average process, the moving average process of order 1. The process is denoted by MA(1), and its equation is

$$y_t = \mu + \varepsilon_t - \theta_1\varepsilon_{t-1} \tag{17.4}$$

This process has mean μ and variance $\gamma_0 = \sigma_\varepsilon^2(1 + \theta_1^2)$. Now let us derive the *covariance* for a one-lag displacement, γ_1:

$$\gamma_1 = E[(y_t - \mu)(y_{t-1} - \mu)] = E[(\varepsilon_t - \theta_1\varepsilon_{t-1})(\varepsilon_{t-1} - \theta_1\varepsilon_{t-2})]$$
$$= -\theta_1\sigma_\varepsilon^2 \tag{17.5}$$

In general we can determine the covariance for a k-lag displacement to be

$$\gamma_k = E[(\varepsilon_t - \theta_1\varepsilon_{t-1})(\varepsilon_{t-k} - \theta_1\varepsilon_{t-k-1})] = 0 \qquad \text{for } k > 1 \tag{17.6}$$

Thus, the MA(1) process has a covariance of 0 when the displacement is more than one period. We say, then, that the process has a *memory* of only one period; any value y_t is correlated with y_{t-1} and with y_{t+1} but with no other time-series values. In effect, the process forgets what happened more than one period in the past. In general, the limited memory of a moving average process is important. It suggests that a moving average model provides forecasting information only a limited number of periods into the future.

We can now determine the autocorrelation function for the process MA(1):

$$\rho_k = \frac{\gamma_k}{\gamma_0} = \begin{cases} \dfrac{-\theta_1}{1 + \theta_1^2} & k = 1 \\ 0 & k > 1 \end{cases} \tag{17.7}$$

An example of a first-order moving average process might be given by

$$y_t = 2 + \varepsilon_t + .8\varepsilon_{t-1} \tag{17.8}$$

The autocorrelation function for y_t is shown in Fig. 17.1, and a typical realization is shown in Fig. 17.2.

Now let us proceed by examining the moving average process of order 2. The process is denoted by MA(2), and its equation is

$$y_t = \mu + \varepsilon_t - \theta_1\varepsilon_{t-1} - \theta_2\varepsilon_{t-2} \tag{17.9}$$

This process has mean μ, variance $\sigma_\varepsilon^2(1 + \theta_1^2 + \theta_2^2)$, and covariances given by

$$\gamma_1 = E[(\varepsilon_t - \theta_1\varepsilon_{t-1} - \theta_2\varepsilon_{t-2})(\varepsilon_{t-1} - \theta_1\varepsilon_{t-2} - \theta_2\varepsilon_{t-3})]$$
$$= -\theta_1\sigma_\varepsilon^2 + \theta_2\theta_1\sigma_\varepsilon^2 = -\theta_1(1 - \theta_2)\sigma_\varepsilon^2 \tag{17.10}$$

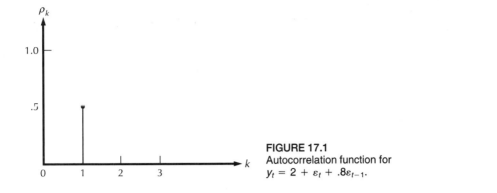

FIGURE 17.1
Autocorrelation function for
$y_t = 2 + \varepsilon_t + .8\varepsilon_{t-1}$.

$$\gamma_2 = E[(\varepsilon_t - \theta_1\varepsilon_{t-1} - \theta_2\varepsilon_{t-2})(\varepsilon_{t-2} - \theta_1\varepsilon_{t-3} - \theta_2\varepsilon_{t-4})] \qquad (17.11)$$
$$= -\theta_2\sigma_\varepsilon^2$$

and $\qquad \gamma_k = 0 \qquad$ for $k > 2$ $\qquad\qquad\qquad\qquad\qquad\qquad\qquad$ (17.12)

The autocorrelation function is given by

$$\rho_1 = \frac{-\theta_1(1 - \theta_2)}{1 + \theta_1^2 + \theta_2^2} \qquad\qquad\qquad (17.13)$$

$$\rho_2 = \frac{-\theta_2}{1 + \theta_1^2 + \theta_2^2} \qquad\qquad\qquad (17.14)$$

and $\qquad\qquad\qquad \rho_k = 0 \qquad$ for $k > 2$ $\qquad\qquad\qquad$ (17.15)

FIGURE 17.2
Typical realization of $y_t = 2 + \varepsilon_t + .8\varepsilon_{t-1}$.

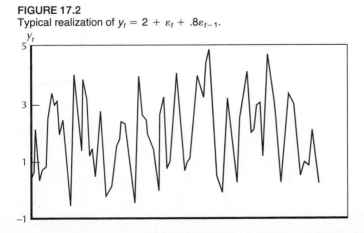

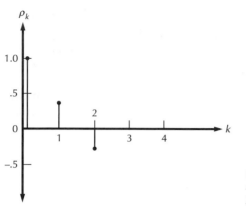

FIGURE 17.3
Autocorrelation function for
$y_t = 2 + \varepsilon_t + 6\varepsilon_{t-1} - .3\varepsilon_{t-2}.$

The process MA(2) has a memory of exactly two periods, so that the value of y_t is influenced only by events that took place in the current period, one period back, and two periods back.

An example of a second-order moving average process might be

$$y_t = 2 + \varepsilon_t + .6\varepsilon_{t-1} - .3\varepsilon_{t-2} \tag{17.16}$$

The autocorrelation function is shown in Figure 17.3, and a typical realization is shown in Fig. 17.4.

We leave to the reader a proof that the moving average process of order q has a memory of exactly q periods and that its autocorrelation function ρ_k is given by the following (see Exercise 17.3):

$$\rho_k = \begin{cases} \dfrac{-\theta_k + \theta_1\theta_{k+1} + \cdots + \theta_{q-k}\theta_q}{1 + \theta_1^2 + \theta_2^2 + \cdots + \theta_q^2} & k = 1, \ldots, q \\ 0 & k > q \end{cases} \tag{17.17}$$

FIGURE 17.4
Typical realization of $y_t = 2 + \varepsilon_t + .6\varepsilon_{t-1} - .3\varepsilon_{t-2}.$

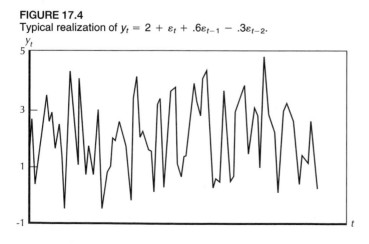

We can now see why the sample autocorrelation function can be useful in specifying the order of a moving average process (assuming that the time series of concern is generated by a moving average process). The autocorrelation function ρ_k for the MA(q) process has q nonzero values and is 0 for $k > q$. As we proceed through this and the next two chapters, we will attempt to give the reader an understanding of how the sample autocorrelation function can be used to identify the stochastic process that may have generated a particular time series.

17.2   AUTOREGRESSIVE MODELS

In the *autoregressive process of order p* the current observation y_t is generated by a weighted average of past observations going back p periods, together with a random disturbance in the current period. We denote this process as AR(p) and write its equation as

$$y_t = \phi_1 y_{t-1} + \phi_2 y_{t-2} + \cdots + \phi_p y_{t-p} + \delta + \varepsilon_t \qquad (17.18)$$

Here δ is a constant term which relates (as we will see) to the mean of the stochastic process.

17.2.1   Properties of Autoregressive Models

If the autoregressive process is stationary, then its mean, which we denote by μ, must be invariant with respect to time; that is, $E(y_t) = E(y_{t-1}) = E(y_{t-2}) = \cdots = \mu$. The mean μ is thus given by

$$\mu = \phi_1 \mu + \phi_2 \mu + \cdots + \phi_p \mu + \delta \qquad (17.19)$$

or

$$\mu = \frac{\delta}{1 - \phi_1 - \phi_2 - \cdots - \phi_p} \qquad (17.20)$$

This formula for the mean of the process also gives us a condition for stationarity. If the process is stationary, the mean μ in Eq. (17.20) must be finite. If this were not the case, the process would drift farther and farther away from any fixed reference point and could not be stationary. (Consider the example of the random walk with drift, that is, $y_t = y_{t-1} + \delta + \varepsilon_t$. Here $\phi_1 = 1$ and $\mu = \infty$ and, if $\delta > 0$, the process continually drifts upward.) If μ is to be finite, it is necessary that

$$\phi_1 + \phi_2 + \cdots + \phi_p < 1 \qquad (17.21)$$

This condition is not sufficient to ensure stationarity, since there are other necessary conditions that must hold if the AR(p) process is to be stationary. We discuss these additional conditions in more detail in Appendix 17.1.

Now let us examine the properties of some simple autoregressive processes. Again we will determine the mean, covariances, etc., for each. We begin with the first-order process AR(1):

$$y_t = \phi_1 y_{t-1} + \delta + \varepsilon_t \tag{17.22}$$

This process has mean

$$\mu = \frac{\delta}{1 - \phi_1} \tag{17.23}$$

and is stationary if $|\phi_1| < 1$. Again, recall that the random walk with drift is a first-order autoregressive process that is *not* stationary. In that process $\phi_1 = 1$, and as we saw in Chapter 16, the variance of the process becomes larger and larger with time.

Let us now calculate γ_0, the variance of this process about its mean. Assuming stationarity, so that we know that the variance is constant (for $|\phi_1| < 1$), and setting $\delta = 0$ (to scale the process to one that has zero mean), we have[3]

$$\gamma_0 = E[(\phi_1 y_{t-1} + \varepsilon_t)^2] = E(\phi_1^2 y_{t-1}^2 + \varepsilon_t^2 + 2\phi_1 y_{t-1}\varepsilon_t) = \phi_1^2 \gamma_0 + \sigma_\varepsilon^2$$

so that

$$\gamma_0 = \frac{\sigma_\varepsilon^2}{1 - \phi_1^2} \tag{17.24}$$

We can also calculate the covariances of y_t about its mean:

$$\gamma_1 = E[y_{t-1}(\phi_1 y_{t-1} + \varepsilon_t)] = \phi_1 \gamma_0 = \frac{\phi_1 \sigma_\varepsilon^2}{1 - \phi_1^2} \tag{17.25}$$

$$\gamma_2 = E[y_{t-2}(\phi_1^2 y_{t-2} + \phi_1 \varepsilon_{t-1} + \varepsilon_t)] = \phi_1^2 \gamma_0 = \frac{\phi_1^2 \sigma_\varepsilon^2}{1 - \phi_1^2} \tag{17.26}$$

Similarly, the covariance for a k-lag displacement is

$$\gamma_k = \phi_1^k \gamma_0 = \frac{\phi_1^k \sigma_\varepsilon^2}{1 - \phi_1^2} \tag{17.27}$$

---

[3] Setting $\delta = 0$ is equivalent to measuring y_t in terms of deviations about its mean, since if y_t follows Eq. (17.22), then the series $\tilde{y}_t = y_t - \mu$ follows the process $\tilde{y}_t = \phi_1 \tilde{y}_{t-1} + \varepsilon_t$. The reader can check to see that the result in Eq. (17.24) is also obtained (although with more algebraic manipulation) by calculating $E[(y_t - \mu)^2]$ directly.

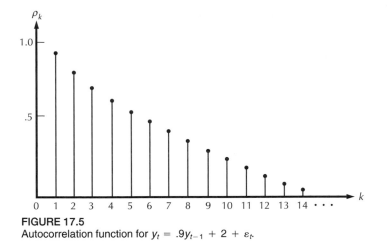

FIGURE 17.5
Autocorrelation function for $y_t = .9y_{t-1} + 2 + \varepsilon_t$.

The autocorrelation function for AR(1) is thus particularly simple—it begins at $\rho_0 = 1$ and then declines geometrically:

$$\rho_k = \frac{\gamma_k}{\gamma_0} = \phi_1^k \qquad (17.28)$$

Note that this process has an *infinite memory*. The current value of the process depends on *all past values,* although the magnitude of this dependence declines with time.[4]

An example of a first-order autoregressive process would be the process defined by

$$y_t = .9y_{t-1} + 2 + \varepsilon_t \qquad (17.29)$$

The autocorrelation function for this process is shown in Fig. 17.5, and a typical realization is shown in Fig. 17.6. The realization differs from that of a first-order moving average process in that each observation is highly correlated with those surrounding it, resulting in discernible overall up-and-down patterns.

---

[4] It can be shown that if the AR(1) process is stationary, it is equivalent to a moving average process of *infinite order* (and thus with infinite memory). In fact, for any stationary autoregressive process of any order there exists an equivalent moving average process of infinite order (so that the autoregressive process is *invertible* into a moving average process). Similarly, if certain *invertibility conditions* are met (and these will be discussed in Appendix 17.1), any finite-order moving average process has an equivalent autoregressive process of infinite order. For a more detailed discussion of invertibility, the reader is referred to G. E. P. Box and G. M. Jenkins, *Time Series Analysis* (San Francisco: Holden-Day, 1970); C. Nelson, *Applied Time Series Analysis* (San Francisco: Holden-Day, 1973), Chapter 3; and C. W. J. Granger and P. Newbold, *Forecasting Economic Time Series* (New York: Academic, 1986).

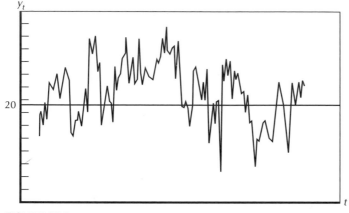

FIGURE 17.6
Typical realization of the process $y_t = .9y_{t-1} + 2 + \varepsilon_t$.

Let us now look at the second-order autoregressive process AR(2):

$$y_t = \phi_1 y_{t-1} + \phi_2 y_{t-2} + \delta + \varepsilon_t \tag{17.30}$$

The process has mean

$$\mu = \frac{\delta}{1 - \phi_1 - \phi_2} \tag{17.31}$$

and a necessary condition for stationarity is that $\phi_1 + \phi_2 < 1$.

Let us now calculate the variances and covariances of y_t (when y_t is measured in deviations form):

$$\gamma_0 = E[y_t(\phi_1 y_{t-1} + \phi_2 y_{t-2} + \varepsilon_t)] = \phi_1 \gamma_1 + \phi_2 \gamma_2 + \sigma_\varepsilon^2 \tag{17.32}$$

$$\gamma_1 = E[y_{t-1}(\phi_1 y_{t-1} + \phi_2 y_{t-2} + \varepsilon_t)] = \phi_1 \gamma_0 + \phi_2 \gamma_1 \tag{17.33}$$

$$\gamma_2 = E[y_{t-2}(\phi_1 y_{t-1} + \phi_2 y_{t-2} + \varepsilon_t)] = \phi_1 \gamma_1 + \phi_2 \gamma_0 \tag{17.34}$$

and in general, for $k \geq 2$,

$$\gamma_k = E[y_{t-k}(\phi_1 y_{t-1} + \phi_2 y_{t-2} + \varepsilon_t)] = \phi_1 \gamma_{k-1} + \phi_2 \gamma_{k-2} \tag{17.35}$$

We can solve Eqs. (17.32), (17.33), and (17.34) simultaneously to get γ_0 in terms of ϕ_1, ϕ_2, and σ_ε^2. Equation (17.33) can be rewritten as

$$\gamma_1 = \frac{\phi_1 \gamma_0}{1 - \phi_2} \tag{17.36}$$

Substituting Eq. (17.34) into Eq. (17.32) yields

$$\gamma_0 = \phi_1\gamma_1 + \phi_2\phi_1\gamma_1 + \phi_2^2\gamma_0 + \sigma_\varepsilon^2 \tag{17.37}$$

Now using Eq. (17.36) to eliminate γ_1 gives us

$$\gamma_0 = \frac{\phi_1^2\gamma_0}{1 - \phi_2} + \frac{\phi_2\phi_1^2\gamma_0}{1 - \phi_2} + \phi_2^2\gamma_0 + \sigma_\varepsilon^2$$

which, after rearranging, yields

$$\gamma_0 = \frac{(1 - \phi_2)\sigma_\varepsilon^2}{(1 + \phi_2)[(1 - \phi_2)^2 - \phi_1^2]} \tag{17.38}$$

These equations can also be used to derive the autocorrelation function ρ_k. From Eqs. (17.34) and (17.36),

$$\rho_1 = \frac{\phi_1}{1 - \phi_2} \tag{17.39}$$

$$\rho_2 = \phi_2 + \frac{\phi_1^2}{1 - \phi_2} \tag{17.40}$$

From Eq. (17.35) one can see that for $k \geq 2$,

$$\rho_k = \phi_1\rho_{k-1} + \phi_2\rho_{k-2} \tag{17.41}$$

and this can be used to calculate the autocorrelation function for $k > 2$.

A comment is in order regarding Eqs. (17.39) and (17.40), which are called the *Yule-Walker equations*. Suppose we have the sample autocorrelation function for a time series which we believe was generated by a second-order autoregressive process. We could then measure ρ_1 and ρ_2 and substitute those numbers into Eqs. (17.39) and (17.40). We would then have two algebraic equations which could be solved simultaneously for the two unknowns ϕ_1 and ϕ_2. Thus, we could use the Yule-Walker equations to obtain estimates of the autoregressive parameters ϕ_1 and ϕ_2.

Let us look at an example of a second-order autoregressive process:

$$y_t = .9y_{t-1} - .7y_{t-2} + 2 + \varepsilon_t \tag{17.42}$$

The autocorrelation function for this process is shown in Fig. 17.7. Note that it is a sinusoidal function that is geometrically dampened. As we will see from further examples, autocorrelation functions for autoregressive processes (of order greater than 1) are typically geometrically dampened, oscillating, sinusoidal functions.

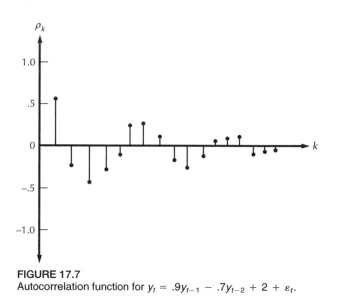

FIGURE 17.7
Autocorrelation function for $y_t = .9y_{t-1} - .7y_{t-2} + 2 + \varepsilon_t$.

The reader should note that *realizations* of second-order (and higher-order) autoregressive processes may or may not be cyclical, depending on the numerical values of the parameters ϕ_1, ϕ_2, etc. Equation (17.30), for example, is a second-order difference equation in y_t (with an additive error term). We saw in Chapter 14 that the values of ϕ_1 and ϕ_2 determine whether the solution to this difference equation is oscillatory.

17.2.2   The Partial Autocorrelation Function *(need know property)*

One problem in constructing autoregressive models is identifying the *order* of the underlying process. For moving average models this is less of a problem, since if the process is of order q, the sample autocorrelations should all be close to zero for lags greater than q. (Bartlett's formula provides approximate standard errors for the autocorrelations, so that the order of a moving average process can be determined from significance tests on the sample autocorrelations.) Although some information about the order of an autoregressive process can be obtained from the oscillatory behavior of the sample autocorrelation function, much more information can be obtained from the *partial autocorrelation function*.

To understand what the partial autocorrelation function is and how it can be used, let us first consider the covariances and autocorrelation function for the autoregressive process of order p. First, notice that the covariance with displacement k is determined from

$$\gamma_k = E[y_{t-k}(\phi_1 y_{t-1} + \phi_2 y_{t-2} + \cdots + \phi_p y_{t-p} + \varepsilon_t)] \qquad (17.43)$$

Now letting $k = 0, 1, \ldots, p$, we obtain the following $p + 1$ difference equations which can be solved simultaneously for $\gamma_0, \gamma_1, \ldots, \gamma_p$:

$$
\begin{aligned}
\gamma_0 &= \phi_1\gamma_1 + \phi_2\gamma_2 + \cdots + \phi_p\gamma_p + \sigma_\varepsilon^2 \\
\gamma_1 &= \phi_1\gamma_0 + \phi_2\gamma_1 + \cdots + \phi_p\gamma_{p-1} \\
&\cdots\cdots\cdots\cdots\cdots\cdots\cdots\cdots\cdots\cdots\cdots \\
\gamma_p &= \phi_1\gamma_{p-1} + \phi_2\gamma_{p-2} + \cdots + \phi_p\gamma_0
\end{aligned}
\tag{17.44}
$$

For displacements k greater than p the covariances are determined from

$$
\gamma_k = \phi_1\gamma_{k-1} + \phi_2\gamma_{k-2} + \cdots + \phi_p\gamma_{k-p}
\tag{17.45}
$$

By dividing the left-hand and right-hand sides of the equations in Eq. (17.44) by γ_0, we can derive a set of p equations that together determine the first p values of the autocorrelation function:

$$
\begin{aligned}
\rho_1 &= \phi_1 + \phi_2\rho_1 + \cdots + \phi_p\rho_{p-1} \\
&\cdots\cdots\cdots\cdots\cdots\cdots\cdots\cdots\cdots\cdots\cdots \\
\rho_p &= \phi_1\rho_{p-1} + \phi_2\rho_{p-2} + \cdots + \phi_p
\end{aligned}
\tag{17.46}
$$

For displacements k greater than p we have, from Eq. (17.45),

$$
\rho_k = \phi_1\rho_{k-1} + \phi_2\rho_{k-2} + \cdots + \phi_p\rho_{k-p}
\tag{17.47}
$$

The equations in Eq. (17.46) are the Yule-Walker equations; if $\rho_1, \rho_2, \ldots, \rho_p$ are known, the equations can be solved for $\phi_1, \phi_2, \ldots, \phi_p$.

Unfortunately, solution of the Yule-Walker equations as presented in Eq. (17.46) requires knowledge of p, the order of the autoregressive process. Therefore, we solve the Yule-Walker equations for *successive values of p*. In other words, suppose we begin by hypothesizing that $p = 1$. Then Eq. (17.46) boils down to $\rho_1 = \phi_1$ or, using the sample autocorrelations, $\hat{\rho}_1 = \hat{\phi}_1$. Thus, if the calculated value $\hat{\phi}_1$ is significantly different from zero, we know that the autoregressive process is *at least* order 1. Let us denote this value $\hat{\phi}_1$ by a_1.

Now consider the hypothesis that $p = 2$. To do this we solve the Yule-Walker equations [Eq. (17.46)] for $p = 2$. Doing this gives us a new set of estimates $\hat{\phi}_1$ and $\hat{\phi}_2$. If ϕ_2 is significantly different from zero, we can conclude that the process is *at least* order 2, while if $\hat{\phi}_2$ is approximately zero, we can conclude that $p = 1$. Let us denote the value $\hat{\phi}_2$ by a_2.

We now repeat this process for successive values of p. For $p = 3$ we obtain an estimate of $\hat{\phi}_3$ which we denote by a_3, for $p = 4$ we obtain $\hat{\phi}_4$ which we denote by a_4, etc. We call this series $a_1, a_2, a_3, \ldots$ the *partial autocorrelation function* and note that we can infer the order of the autoregressive process from its behavior. In particular, if the true order of the process is p, we should observe that $a_j \approx 0$ for $j > p$.

To test whether a particular a_j is zero, we can use the fact that it is approximately normally distributed, with mean zero and variance $1/T$. Hence, we can check whether it is statistically significant at, say, the 5 percent level by determining whether it exceeds $2/\sqrt{T}$ in magnitude.

Example 17.1 Inventory Investment   In Chapter 16 we examined the behavior of real nonfarm inventory investment over the period 1960 through 1995. (The series itself is shown in Fig. 16.3, and its sample autocorrelation function is shown in Fig. 16.4.) We concluded that the series is stationary because the sample autocorrelation function falls toward zero quickly as the number of lags increases.

Figure 17.8 shows the partial autocorrelation function for our inventory investment series. Observe that the partial autocorrelations become close to zero after about four lags. Since there are 144 data points in the sample, a partial autocorrelation is statistically significant at the 5 percent level only if it is larger in magnitude than $2/\sqrt{144} = .167$. There are no partial autocorrelations beyond four lags that are this large (except at a lag of 23). We can conclude from this that to the extent that inventory investment follows an autoregressive process, the order of that process should not be greater than 4. We will take this information into account when we construct a time-series model for inventory investment in Chapter 19.

FIGURE 17.8
Nonfarm inventory investment: partial autocorrelation function.

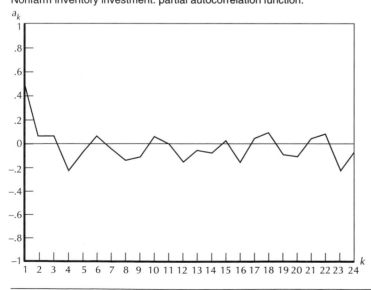

17.3 MIXED AUTOREGRESSIVE—MOVING AVERAGE MODELS

Many stationary random processes cannot be modeled as purely moving average or as purely autoregressive, since they have the qualities of both types of processes. The logical extension of the models presented in the last two sections is the *mixed autoregressive–moving average process of order* (p, q). We denote this process as ARMA(p, q) and represent it by

$$y_t = \phi_1 y_{t-1} + \cdots + \phi_p y_{t-p} + \delta + \varepsilon_t - \theta_1 \varepsilon_{t-1} - \cdots - \theta_q \varepsilon_{t-q} \quad (17.48)$$

We assume that the process is stationary, so that its mean is constant over time and is given by

$$\mu = \phi_1 \mu + \cdots + \phi_p \mu + \delta$$

or
$$\mu = \frac{\delta}{1 - \phi_1 - \cdots - \phi_p} \quad (17.49)$$

This gives a necessary condition for the stationarity of the process, that is,

$$\phi_1 + \phi_2 + \cdots + \phi_p < 1 \quad (17.50)$$

Now let us consider the simplest mixed autoregressive–moving average process, the process ARMA$(1, 1)$:

$$y_t = \phi_1 y_{t-1} + \delta + \varepsilon_t - \theta_1 \varepsilon_{t-1} \quad (17.51)$$

The variances and covariances of this process are determined jointly as follows (setting $\delta = 0$):

$$\gamma_0 = E[y_t(\phi_1 y_{t-1} + \varepsilon_t - \theta_1 \varepsilon_{t-1})] = E[(\phi_1 y_{t-1} + \varepsilon_t - \theta_1 \varepsilon_{t-1})^2]$$
$$= \phi_1^2 \gamma_0 - 2\phi_1 \theta_1 E[y_{t-1} \varepsilon_{t-1}] + \sigma_\varepsilon^2 + \theta_1^2 \sigma_\varepsilon^2 \quad (17.52)$$

Since $E(y_{t-1} \varepsilon_{t-1}) = \sigma_\varepsilon^2$, we have

$$\gamma_0(1 - \phi_1^2) = \sigma_\varepsilon^2(1 + \theta_1^2 - 2\phi_1 \theta_1) \quad (17.53)$$

so that the variance is given by[5]

$$\gamma_0 = \frac{1 + \theta_1^2 - 2\phi_1 \theta_1}{1 - \phi_1^2} \sigma_\varepsilon^2 \quad (17.54)$$

---

[5] For $|\phi_1| < 1$.

We can now determine the covariances γ_1, γ_2, ..., recursively:

$$\gamma_1 = E[y_{t-1}(\phi_1 y_{t-1} + \varepsilon_t - \theta_1 \varepsilon_{t-1})] = \phi_1 \gamma_0 - \theta_1 \sigma_\varepsilon^2 \qquad (17.55)$$

$$= \frac{(1 - \phi_1 \theta_1)(\phi_1 - \theta_1)}{1 - \phi_1^2} \sigma_\varepsilon^2 \qquad (17.56)$$

$$\gamma_2 = E[y_{t-2}(\phi_1 y_{t-1} + \varepsilon_t - \theta_1 \varepsilon_{t-1})] = \phi_1 \gamma_1$$

and similarly,

$$\gamma_k = \phi_1 \gamma_{k-1} \qquad k \geq 2 \qquad (17.57)$$

The autocorrelation function, then, is given by

$$\rho_1 = \frac{\gamma_1}{\gamma_0} = \frac{(1 - \phi_1 \theta_1)(\phi_1 - \theta_1)}{1 + \theta_1^2 - 2\phi_1 \theta_1} \qquad (17.58)$$

and for displacement k greater than 1,

$$\rho_k = \phi_1 \rho_{k-1} \qquad k \geq 2 \qquad (17.59)$$

Thus, the autocorrelation function begins at its starting value ρ_1 (which is a function of both ϕ_1 and θ_1) and then decays geometrically from that starting value. This reflects the fact that the moving average part of the process has a memory of only one period.

Let us examine the autocorrelation functions of some typical ARMA(1, 1) processes. The autocorrelation function for the process

$$y_t = .8y_{t-1} + 2 + \varepsilon_t - .9\varepsilon_{t-1} \qquad (17.60)$$

is shown in Fig. 17.9. The starting value ρ_1 is negative, and the function decays toward 0 from this value.

FIGURE 17.9
Autocorrelation function for $y_t = .8y_{t-1} + 2 + \varepsilon_t - .9\varepsilon_{t-1}$.

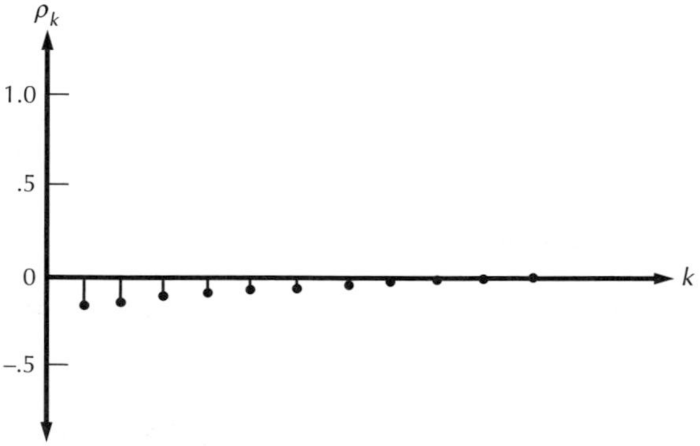

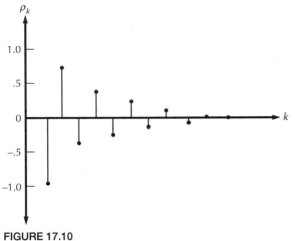

FIGURE 17.10
Autocorrelation function for $y_t = -.8y_{t-1} + 2 + \varepsilon_t + .9\varepsilon_{t-1}$.

The autocorrelation function for the process

$$y_t = -.8y_{t-1} + 2 + \varepsilon_t + .9\varepsilon_{t-1} \qquad (17.61)$$

will exhibit oscillatory behavior, as shown in Fig. 17.10. Note that it oscillates between positive and negative values, since ϕ_1 is negative.

For higher-order processes, i.e., the general ARMA(p, q) process, the variance, covariances, and autocorrelation function are solutions to difference equations that usually cannot be solved by inspection. It can be shown easily, however, that

$$\gamma_k = \phi_1\gamma_{k-1} + \phi_2\gamma_{k-2} + \cdots + \phi_p\gamma_{k-p} \qquad k \geq q + 1 \qquad (17.62)$$

and thus $\quad \rho_k = \phi_1\rho_{k-1} + \phi_2\rho_{k-2} + \cdots + \phi_p\rho_{k-p} \qquad k \geq q + 1 \qquad (17.63)$

Note that q is the memory of the moving average part of the process, so that for $k \geq q + 1$ the autocorrelation function (and covariances) exhibits the properties of a purely autoregressive process.

This completes our discussion of models for stationary stochastic processes. Before we turn to models for homogeneous nonstationary processes, it will be useful to introduce a new notational device. Often it is convenient to write or describe time lags by using the *backward shift operator B*. The operator B imposes a one-period time lag each time it is applied to a variable. Thus, $B\varepsilon_t = \varepsilon_{t-1}$, $B^2\varepsilon_t = \varepsilon_{t-2}, \ldots, B^n\varepsilon_t = \varepsilon_{t-n}$. Using this operator, we can now rewrite Eq. (17.1) for the MA(q) process as

$$y_t = \mu + (1 - \theta_1 B - \theta_2 B^2 - \cdots - \theta_q B^q)\varepsilon_t = \mu + \theta(B)\varepsilon_t \qquad (17.64)$$

where $\theta(B)$ denotes a polynomial function of the operator B. Similarly, Eq. (17.18) for the AR(p) process can be rewritten as

$$(1 - \phi_1 B - \phi_2 B^2 - \cdots - \phi_p B^p) y_t = \delta + \varepsilon_t \tag{17.65}$$

or

$$\phi(B) y_t = \delta + \varepsilon_t \tag{17.66}$$

Finally, Eq. (17.48) for the ARMA(p, q) process can be rewritten as

$$(1 - \phi_1 B - \phi_2 B^2 - \cdots - \phi_p B^p) y_t = \delta + (1 - \theta_1 B - \theta_2 B^2 - \cdots - \theta_q B^q) \varepsilon_t \tag{17.67}$$

or

$$\phi(B) y_t = \delta + \theta(B) \varepsilon_t \tag{17.68}$$

17.4   HOMOGENEOUS NONSTATIONARY PROCESSES: ARIMA MODELS

know concept

In practice, many of the time series we work with are nonstationary, so that the characteristics of the underlying stochastic process change over time. In this section we construct models for those nonstationary series which can be transformed into stationary series by differencing them one or more times. We say that y_t is *homogeneous nonstationary of order d* if

$$w_t = \Delta^d y_t \tag{17.69}$$

is a stationary series. Here Δ denotes differencing, i.e.,

$$\Delta y_t = y_t - y_{t-1} \qquad \Delta^2 y_t = \Delta y_t - \Delta y_{t-1}$$

and so forth. A discussion of the autoregressive characteristics of homogeneous nonstationary series appears in Appendix 17.1.

Observe that if we have a series w_t, we can get back to y_t by *summing* w_t a total of d times. We write this as

$$y_t = \Sigma^d w_t \tag{17.70}$$

where Σ is the summation operator:

$$\Sigma w_t = \sum_{i=-\infty}^{t} w_i \tag{17.71}$$

$$\Sigma^2 w_t = \sum_{j=-\infty}^{t} \sum_{i=-\infty}^{j} w_i \tag{17.72}$$

and so forth. Note that the summation operator Σ is just the *inverse* of the difference operator Δ. Since $\Delta y_t = y_t - y_{t-1}$, we can write that $\Delta = 1 - B$, and thus $\Sigma = \Delta^{-1} = (1 - B)^{-1}$.

In computing this sum for an actual time series, we begin with the first observation on the original undifferenced series (y_0) and then add successive values of the differenced series. Thus, if $w_t - \Delta y_t$, we would compute y_t from

$$y_t = \sum w_t = \sum_{i=-\infty}^{t} w_i = \sum_{i=-\infty}^{0} w_i + \sum_{i=1}^{t} w_i = y_0 + w_1 + w_2 + \cdots + w_t$$

$$(17.73)$$

If y_t had been differenced twice, so that $w_t = \Delta^2 y_t$, we could compute y_t from w_t by summing w_t twice.[6]

After we have differenced the series y_t to produce the stationary series w_t, we can model w_t as an ARMA process. If $w_t = \Delta^d y_t$ and w_t is an ARMA(p, q) *process, then we say that y_t is an integrated autoregressive–moving average process of order (p, d, q), or simply ARIMA(p, d, q). We can write the equation for the* process ARIMA(p, d, q), using the backward shift operator, as

$$\phi(B)\Delta^d y_t = \delta + \theta(B)\varepsilon_t \qquad (17.74)$$

with $$\phi(B) = 1 - \phi_1 B - \phi_2 B^2 - \cdots - \phi_p B^p \qquad (17.75)$$

and $$\theta(B) = 1 - \theta_1 B - \theta_2 B^2 - \cdots - \theta_q B^q \qquad (17.76)$$

We call $\phi(B)$ the *autoregressive operator* and $\theta(B)$ the *moving average operator.*

Note that the mean of $w_t = \Delta^d y_t$ is given by

$$\mu_w = \frac{\delta}{1 - \phi_1 - \phi_2 - \cdots - \phi_p} \qquad (17.77)$$

Thus, if δ is not equal to 0, the *integrated series* y_t will have a built-in *deterministic trend*. Suppose, for example, that $d = 1$ and $\delta > 0$. Then $y_t = \Sigma w_t$ will grow linearly over time. An example of such a series might be the one drawn in Fig. 17.11. The series has a linear time trend that is independent of the random

---

[6] Summing w_t the first time gives us Δy_t:

$$\Delta y_t = \sum w_t = \sum_{i=-\infty}^{0} w_i + \sum_{i=1}^{t} w_i = \Delta y_0 + w_1 + w_2 + \cdots + w_t$$

Now summing Δy_t yields y_t:

$$y_t = \Sigma(\Delta y_t) = \Sigma(\Delta y_0 + w_1 + w_2 + \cdots + w_t) = y_0 + (\Delta y_0 + w_1) + (\Delta y_0 + w_1 + w_2) + \cdots$$
$$+ (\Delta y_0 + w_1 + w_2 + \cdots + w_t)$$

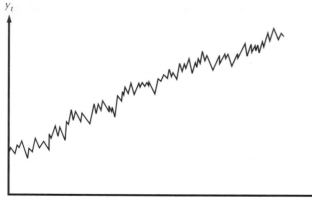

FIGURE 17.11
An ARIMA process with $d = 1$.

disturbances, i.e., that is deterministic. The series drawn in Fig. 17.12, by contrast, has an average slope that is increasing linearly in time. This series might have been generated by a process that is ARIMA with $d = 2$ and $\delta > 0$. Thus $w_t = \Delta^2 y_t$ will have no time trend, $\Sigma w_t = \Delta y_t$ will have a linear time trend, and $\Sigma\Sigma w_t = y_t$ will have a time trend whose rate of increase is constant.

It is possible that the stationary series w_t will not be mixed, i.e., will be completely autoregressive or moving average. If w_t is just AR(p), we call y_t an integrated autoregressive process of order (p, d) and denote it as ARI(p, d, 0). If w_t is just MA(q), we call y_t an integrated moving average process of order (d, q) and denote it as IMA(0, d, q).

FIGURE 17.12
An ARIMA process with $d = 2$.

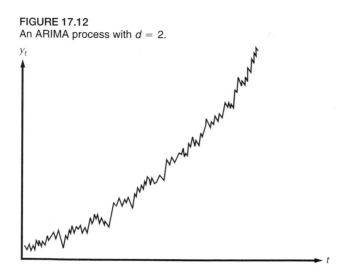

17.5 SPECIFICATION OF ARIMA MODELS

We have seen that any homogeneous nonstationary time series can be modeled as an ARIMA process of order (p, d, q). The practical problem is to choose the most appropriate values for p, d, and q, that is, to *specify* the ARIMA model. This problem is partly resolved by examining both the autocorrelation function and the partial autocorrelation function for the time series of concern.

Given a series y_t that one would like to model, the first problem is to determine the degree of homogeneity d, that is, the number of times the series must be differenced to produce a stationary series. To do this, we make use of the fact that *the autocorrelation function ρ_k for a stationary series must approach 0 as the displacement k becomes large.* To see why, consider a stationary ARMA process of order (p, q). We know that the autocorrelation function for the *moving average part* of this process becomes 0 for $k > q$, as the process has a memory of only q periods. Thus, if y_t is MA(q), then $\rho_k = 0$ for $k > q$. We also know that the autocorrelation function for the *autoregressive part* of a stationary ARMA process is geometrically dampened (see the examples in Figs. 17.5 to 17.7). Finally, the autocorrelation function for the complete ARMA process has moving average characteristics for the first $q - p$ periods, but after that it is autoregressive in character; i.e., it has an envelope that declines geometrically.

To specify d, first examine the autocorrelation function of the original series y_t and determine whether it is stationary. If it is not, difference the series and examine the autocorrelation function for Δy_t. Repeat this process until a value for d is reached such that $\Delta^d y_t$ is stationary; i.e., the autocorrelation function goes to 0 as k becomes large.[7] One should also examine the time series itself; if it appears to have an overall trend, it probably is not stationary.

After d is determined, one can work with the stationary series $w_t = \Delta^d y_t$ and examine both its autocorrelation function and its partial autocorrelation function to determine possible specifications for p and q. For low-order processes this is not too difficult, since the autocorrelation functions for processes such as AR(1), AR(2), MA(1), MA(2), and ARMA(1, 1) are easy to recognize and distinguish from each other (see Figs. 17.1 to 17.10). However, if the time series cannot be modeled as a low-order ARMA process, the specification of p and q becomes more difficult and requires close inspection of the full and partial autocorrelation functions. For example, spikes in the autocorrelation function are indicative of moving average terms, and the partial autocorrelation function can be used for guidance in determining the order of the autoregressive portion of the process.

If both the autoregressive and moving average parts of the process are of high order, one may at best be able to make only a tentative guess for p and q.

---

[7] Remember that in practice we have no guarantee that the time series being modeled is homogeneous nonstationary. If the time series is *nonhomogeneous* nonstationary, no matter how many times it is differenced, the autocorrelation function will not dampen down to 0.

As we will see later, however, it is possible to check that guess after the parameters in the ARMA(p, q) model have been estimated. As a first step in this process of *diagnostic checking* one can calculate the autocorrelation function for the residuals of the estimated ARMA(p, q) model and determine whether those residuals appear to be white noise. If they do not, a new specification can be tried. This process of diagnostic checking will be discussed in more detail in Chapter 18.

Example 17.2 Price of Newsprint   As a first example of model specification, let us examine a quarterly series for the average price of newsprint in the United States over the period 1965-2 through 1977-3 (50 data points). The series itself (not shown here) rises steadily over time, indicating that it is nonstationary. However, the differenced series Δy_t does appear to be stationary, as can be seen from its sample autocorrelation function in Fig. 17.13. The autocorrelation function has the dampened sinusoidal shape of a second-order autoregressive process and no spikes indicative of moving average terms. The partial autocorrelation function, which is shown in Fig. 17.14, has significant spikes at lags 1 and 2, confirming a second-order autoregressive interpretation of the differenced series. We might thus estimate an ARI(2, 1, 0) model.

FIGURE 17.13
Newsprint price: autocorrelation function of Δy_t.

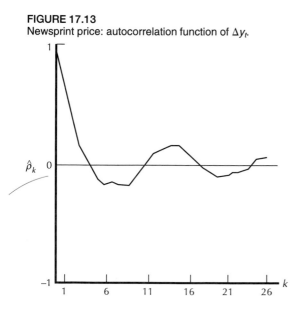

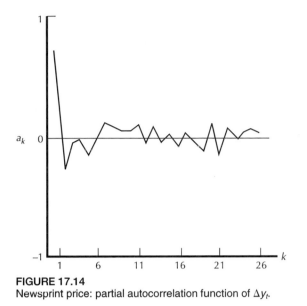

FIGURE 17.14
Newsprint price: partial autocorrelation function of Δy_t.

Example 17.3 Interest Rates As a second example of model specification, go back to the series for the 3-month Treasury bill rate that we examined in Chapter 16. After differencing the series and examining the sample auto-correlation functions, we established that it was probably first-order homogeneous nonstationary, so that d equals 1 in a specification of an ARIMA model. Now, if we examine the autocorrelation function for Δy_t in Fig. 16.10 in more detail, we see that it exhibits moving-average properties that are first or second order; i.e., it begins decaying after the point $k = 1$.

What about the autoregressive properties of the interest rate series? For $k \geq 1$ none of the sample autocorrelations exceed .25 in magnitude, suggesting that only a few autoregressive terms might suffice. Hence, one could begin by estimating an ARIMA(2, 1, 2) model. However, the sample autocorrelations remain significantly different from zero even for large values of k, suggesting that many more autoregressive terms may be necessary. We explore this possibility in Chapter 18, where we estimate and compare an ARIMA(2, 1, 2) model, an ARIMA(8, 1, 2) model, and ARIMA models that include additional moving average terms.

Example 17.4 Hog Production A third example is the monthly series for hog production, which was also examined in Chapter 16. We took a 12-month difference of the series to eliminate seasonal cycles and then found

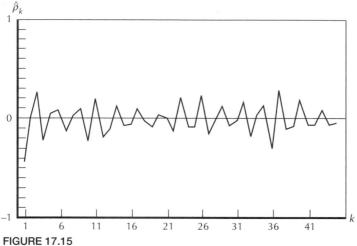

FIGURE 17.15
Monthly hog production: autocorrelation function of $(1 - B)(1 - B^{12})y_t$.

that differencing once was sufficient to ensure stationarity. The autocorrelation function for $(1 - B)(1 - B^{12})y_t$ is shown again in Fig. 17.15. Observe that the sample autocorrelation function begins declining immediately at $k = 1$ and has peaks roughly once every three periods. We might thus suspect that $(1 - B)(1 - B^{12})y_t$ is autoregressive of order 3, so that y_t could be specified by the model:

$$(1 - \phi_1 B - \phi_2 B^2 - \phi_3 B^3)(1 - B)(1 - B^{12})y_t = \varepsilon_t \qquad (17.78)$$

Readers should not be disturbed at this point if they find this process of model specification somewhat bewildering. We will go through several more examples in Chapter 19.

APPENDIX 17.1 Stationarity, Invertibility, and Homogeneity

We saw before that a necessary condition for an ARMA(p, q) process to be stationary is that

$$\phi_1 + \phi_2 + \cdots + \phi_p < 1 \qquad (A17.1)$$

We now present a necessary and sufficient condition for stationarity and use it to demonstrate a particular property of homogeneous nonstationary processes. Note that the process ARMA(p, q) can be written in the form

$$(1 - \phi_1 B - \cdots - \phi_p B^p)\tilde{y}_t = (1 - \theta_1 B - \cdots - \theta_q B^q)\varepsilon_t \qquad (A17.2)$$

or
$$\phi(B)\tilde{y}_t = \theta(B)\varepsilon_t \tag{A17.3}$$

where B is the backward shift operator and $\tilde{y}_t$ is the deviation of y_t from its mean, that is,

$$\tilde{y}_t = y_t - \mu \tag{A17.4}$$

Now let us rewrite Eq. (A17.3) as

$$\tilde{y}_t = \phi^{-1}(B)\theta(B)\varepsilon_t \tag{A17.5}$$

If y_t is a stationary process, then $\phi^{-1}(B)$ must converge. This requires that the roots of the *characteristic equation*

$$\phi(B) = 0 \tag{A17.6}$$

all be *outside* the unit circle. Thus, the solutions $B_1, \ldots, B_p$ to Eq. (A17.6) must all be greater than 1 in magnitude.

Now suppose that the process $\tilde{y}_t$ in Eq. (A17.3) is *nonstationary,* but in such a way that exactly d of the roots of $\phi(B)$ are on the unit circle and the remainder are outside the unit circle. This process can then be rewritten in the form

$$\omega(B)(1 - B)^d \tilde{y}_t = \theta(B)\varepsilon_t \tag{A17.7}$$

where $\omega(B)$ is a stationary autoregressive operator of order $p - d$ and the operator $(1 - B)^d$ has d roots all equal to unity. But $1 - B$ is a *first-difference* operator, that is,

$$(1 - B)\tilde{y}_t = \Delta\tilde{y}_t = \tilde{y}_t - \tilde{y}_{t-1} \tag{A17.8}$$

Thus Eq. (A17.7) can be rewritten as

$$\omega(B)\Delta^d \tilde{y}_t = \theta(B)\varepsilon_t \tag{A17.9}$$

or
$$\omega(B)w_t = \theta(B)\varepsilon_t \tag{A17.10}$$

where $w_t = \Delta^d \tilde{y}_t$ is stationary, since it resulted from differencing $\tilde{y}_t$ d times. We call $\tilde{y}_t$ *homogeneous nonstationary with order d,* and we note the conclusion that such a process has an autoregressive operator $\phi(B)$ such that

$$\phi(B) = \omega(B)(1 - B)^d \tag{A17.11}$$

where the roots of $\omega(B)$ are all outside the unit circle.

Analogous to the stationarity condition for the autoregressive operator is the *invertibility condition* for the moving average operator. We say that y_t is invertible if we can write Eq. (A17.3) as

$$\theta^{-1}(B)\phi(B)\tilde{y}_t = \varepsilon_t \tag{A17.12}$$

i.e., if the moving average part of the ARMA process can be inverted into a purely autoregressive process. Now, if y_t is invertible $\theta^{-1}(B)$ must converge. This requires that the roots of the *characteristic equation*

$$\theta(B) = 1 - \theta_1 B - \theta_2 B^2 - \cdots - \theta_q B^q = 0 \tag{A17.13}$$

must all lie outside the unit circle; i.e., the solutions $B_1, B_2, \ldots, B_q$ to Eq. (A17.13) must all be greater than 1 in absolute value.

As an example, consider the first-order moving average process (that is, $q = 1$), whose characteristic equation is

$$1 - \theta_1 B = 0 \tag{A17.14}$$

Then the invertibility condition becomes

$$|B| = \frac{1}{|\theta_1|} > 1 \tag{A17.15}$$

or

$$|\theta_1| < 1$$

For the second-order moving average process ($q = 2$) the characteristic equation is

$$1 - \theta_1 B - \theta_2 B^2 = 0 \tag{A17.16}$$

and

$$B = \frac{-\theta_1 \pm \sqrt{\theta_1^2 + 4\theta_2}}{2\theta_2} \tag{A17.17}$$

Both of these values of B must be outside the unit circle, implying that

$$\theta_2 + \theta_1 < 1 \tag{A17.18}$$

$$\theta_2 - \theta_1 < 1 \tag{A17.19}$$

and

$$|\theta_2| < 1 \tag{A17.20}$$

EXERCISES

17.1 Calculate the covariances γ_k for MA(3), the moving average process of order 3. Determine the autocorrelation function for this process. Plot the autocorrelation function for the MA(3) process

$$y_t = 1 + \varepsilon_t + .80_{t-1} \quad .5\varepsilon_{t-2} + .3\varepsilon_{t-3}$$

17.2 What characteristics would one expect of a realization of the following MA(1) process?

$$y_t = 1 + \varepsilon_t + .8\varepsilon_{t-1}$$

How would these characteristics differ from those of a realization of the following MA(1) process?

$$y_t = 1 + \varepsilon_t - .8\varepsilon_{t-1}$$

17.3 Show that the covariances γ_k of MA(q), the moving average process of order q, are given by

$$\gamma_k = \begin{cases} (-\theta_k + \theta_1\theta_{k+1} + \cdots + \theta_{q-k}\theta_q)\sigma_\varepsilon^2 & k = 1, \ldots, q \\ 0 & k > q \end{cases}$$

and that the autocorrelation function for MA(q) is given by

$$\rho_k = \begin{cases} \dfrac{-\theta_k + \theta_1\theta_{k+1} + \cdots + \theta_{q-k}\theta_q}{1 + \theta_1^2 + \theta_2^2 + \cdots + \theta_q^2} & k = 1, \ldots, q \\ 0 & k > q \end{cases}$$

as in Eq. (17.17)

17.4 Derive the autocorrelation function for the ARMA(2, 1) process

$$y_t = \phi_1 y_{t-1} + \phi_2 y_{t-2} + \varepsilon_t - \theta_1\varepsilon_{t-1}$$

that is, determine ρ_1, ρ_2, etc., in terms of ϕ_1, ϕ_2, and θ_1. Draw this autocorrelation function for $\phi_1 = .6$, $\phi_2 = .3$, and $\theta_1 = .9$. Repeat for $\phi_1 = .6$, $\phi_2 = .3$, and $\theta_1 = -.9$. Repeat for $\phi_1 = .6$, $\phi_2 = -.3$, and $\theta_1 = -.9$.

17.5 Show that the autocorrelation function for the general ARMA(p, q) process is given by

$$\rho_k = \phi_1\rho_{k-1} + \phi_2\rho_{k-2} + \cdots + \phi_p\rho_{k-p} \quad k \geq q + 1$$

as in Eq. (17.63).

17.6 Suppose that y_t is first-order homogeneous nonstationary and that $w_t = \Delta y_t$ can be represented by the ARMA$(1, 1)$ model

$$w_t = .9w_{t-1} + \varepsilon_t - .6\varepsilon_{t-1} + 1$$

If $y_t = 0$ for $t = 0$, what is $E(y_t)$ as a function of time?

17.7 Relate the summation operator to the backward shift operator by showing that

$$\Sigma = (1 - B)^{-1} = 1 + B + B^2 + B^3 + \cdots$$

17.8 Refer to the time series for nonfarm inventory investment in Fig. 16.3, its sample autocorrelation function in Fig. 16.4, and its partial autocorrelation function in Fig. 17.8. Can you suggest one or more ARMA(p, q) processes that might have generated that time series?

CHAPTER 18

ESTIMATING AND FORECASTING WITH TIME-SERIES MODELS

In this chapter we show how the parameters of an ARIMA model are estimated. As we shall see, if the model contains moving average terms, this involves the application of a nonlinear estimation method similar to the one described in Chapter 10. After this we describe *diagnostic checking,* a procedure used to test whether the model has been specified correctly (i.e., whether p, d, and q have been chosen correctly).

Once a time-series model has been estimated and checked, it can be used for forecasting. In this chapter we explain how to use the general ARIMA model

$$\phi(B)\Delta^d y_t = \theta(B)\varepsilon_t$$

to obtain a forecast of y_t for period $T + l$ (that is, l periods ahead, with $l \geq 1$). We denote this forecast by $\hat{y}_T(l)$ and call it the *origin-T forecast for lead time l.* We will first assume that the true parameters of the model are known and examine the properties both of the forecast and of the forecast error. Then we will see how imperfect knowledge of the true parameter values increases the forecast error.

18.1 MODEL ESTIMATION

Suppose a tentative specification of the time-series model has been made, i.e., values of p, d, and q have been chosen for the ARIMA model,[1]

$$\phi(B)\Delta^d y_t = \phi(B)w_t = \theta(B)\varepsilon_t \tag{18.1}$$

[1] We assume for simplicity here that $\delta = 0$, that is, that w_t is measured as a deviation from its mean value.

549

with $\phi(B) = 1 - \phi_1 B - \phi_2 B^2 - \cdots - \phi_p B^p$ and $\theta(B) = 1 - \theta_1 B - \theta_2 B^2 - \cdots - \theta_q B^q$. Now estimates must be obtained for the p autoregressive parameters $\phi_1, \ldots, \phi_p$ and the q moving average parameters $\theta_1, \ldots, \theta_q$. As in the case of the regression model, we choose parameter values that will minimize the sum of squared differences between the actual time series $w_t = \Delta^d y_t$ and the fitted time series $\hat{w}_t$.

To put this another way, rewrite Eq. (18.1) in terms of the error term series ε_t:[2]

$$\varepsilon_t = \theta^{-1}(B)\phi(B)w_t \tag{18.2}$$

The objective in estimation is to find a set of autoregressive parameters ($\phi_1, \ldots, \phi_p$) and a set of moving average parameters ($\theta_1, \ldots, \theta_q$) that *minimize the sum of squared errors*

$$S(\phi_1, \ldots, \phi_p, \theta_1, \ldots, \theta_q) = \sum_t \varepsilon_t^2 \tag{18.3}$$

We denote the sets of parameters that minimize Eq. (18.3) by ($\hat{\phi}_1, \ldots, \hat{\phi}_p$) and ($\hat{\theta}_1, \ldots, \hat{\theta}_q$) and denote the residuals associated with these parameter values by $\hat{\varepsilon}_t$, so that $\hat{\varepsilon}_t = \hat{\theta}^{-1}(B)\hat{\phi}(B)w_t$. Thus,

$$S(\hat{\phi}_1, \ldots, \hat{\phi}_p, \hat{\theta}_1, \ldots, \hat{\theta}_q) = \sum_t \hat{\varepsilon}_t^2 \tag{18.4}$$

If moving average terms are present, Eq. (18.2) is nonlinear in the parameters, and so a method of nonlinear estimation must be used in the minimization of Eq. (18.3). In addition, the first error term in the series, ε_1, depends on the past and unobservable values $w_0, w_{-1}, \ldots, w_{-p+1}$ and $\varepsilon_0, \varepsilon_{-1}, \ldots, \varepsilon_{-q+1}$. Thus, some method must be used to initialize the series (i.e., choose numbers for these unobservable values).

After the model has been estimated, a procedure of *diagnostic checking* is used to test whether the initial specification was correct. We would expect the *residuals* $\hat{\varepsilon}_t$, $t = 1, \ldots, T$, to resemble closely the true errors ε_t, which by assumption are uncorrelated. We then test whether these residuals are indeed uncorrelated. If they are not, we will want to respecify the model (i.e., choose new values for p, d, and q), estimate this new model, and perform another diagnostic check. Once the model has been checked to our satisfaction, it can be used for forecasting.

Let us examine the estimation procedure in more detail. We assume that a total of $T + d$ observations are available for the homogeneous nonstationary time series of order d, y_t, and we denote these observations as $y_{-d+1}, \ldots, y_0, y_1, \ldots, y_T$. After differencing this series d times, we obtain a stationary series

---

[2] It should be more clear now why we were concerned with the invertibility of $\theta(B)$ in Appendix 17.1.

w_t with T observations $w_1, \ldots, w_T$. The problem is to estimate the parameters for the ARMA(p, q) model which has been specified for the series w_t. To do this, we utilize the fact that (by assumption) the error terms $\varepsilon_1, \ldots, \varepsilon_T$ are all *normally distributed* and independent, with mean 0 and variance σ_ε^2. Then the *conditional log-likelihood function* associated with the parameter values ($\phi_1, \ldots, \phi_p, \theta_1, \ldots, \theta_q, \sigma_\varepsilon$) is given by

$$L = -T \log \sigma_\varepsilon - \frac{S(\phi_1, \ldots, \phi_p, \theta_1, \ldots, \theta_q)}{2\sigma_\varepsilon^2} \qquad (18.5)$$

We say that L is the *conditional* logarithmic likelihood function because the sum of squared errors S depends on the past and unobservable values $w_0, w_{-1}, \ldots, w_{-p+1}, \varepsilon_0, \varepsilon_{-1}, \ldots, \varepsilon_{-q+1}$. This can be seen by writing the equation for the first observable error term ε_1 in the expanded form of the ARMA model:

$$\varepsilon_1 = w_1 - \phi_1 w_0 - \phi_2 w_{-1} - \cdots - \phi_p w_{-p+1} + \theta_1 \varepsilon_0 + \cdots + \theta_q \varepsilon_{-q+1} \qquad (18.6)$$

Setting aside for the moment the problem of determining the past values of w_t and ε_t, Eq. (18.5) makes it clear that the maximum-likelihood estimate of the model's parameters is given by the *minimization* of the sum of squared residuals S. Thus, under the assumption of normally distributed errors, the maximum-likelihood estimate is the same as the *least-squares* estimate.

18.1.1   Initialization of the Series

Because the sum-of-squares function $S(\phi_1, \ldots, \phi_p, \theta_1, \ldots, \theta_q)$ and thus the likelihood function L are both conditional on the past unobservable values of w_t and ε_t ($w_0, \ldots, w_{-p+1}$ and $\varepsilon_0, \ldots, \varepsilon_{-q+1}$), the least-squares estimates we obtain depend on the choice of values made for $w_0, w_{-1}, \ldots$. For this reason we must choose initial starting values for $w_0, w_{-1}, \ldots$, to be used in the minimization of the conditional sum-of-squares function.

The most common solution to this problem is to set $w_0, \ldots, w_{-p+1}$ and $\varepsilon_0, \ldots, \varepsilon_{-q+1}$ equal to their *unconditional expected values*. The unconditional expected values of $\varepsilon_0, \ldots, \varepsilon_{-q+1}$ are all 0, and if $\delta = 0$, the unconditional expected values of $w_0, \ldots, w_{-p+1}$ are 0 as well. This will provide a reasonably good approximation to the correct procedure if the actual values of $\phi_1, \ldots, \phi_p$ are not very close to 1 and if the number of observations T is large relative to p and q.[3]

---

[3] An alternative method of initializing the series is to determine *conditional expected values* for $w_0, \ldots, w_{-p+1}$, that is, values that are conditional on the observed values of $w_1, \ldots, w_T$ and the estimated values of $\varepsilon_1, \ldots, \varepsilon_T$. This procedure is technically difficult, and its benefits may not be substantial. We recommend using the unconditional expected values for $w_0, \ldots, w_{-p+1}$, that is, setting them equal to 0 (when $\delta = 0$).

18.1.2   Nonlinear Estimation of Model Parameters

Our estimation problem is to find values of the parameters $\phi_1, \ldots, \phi_p, \theta_1, \ldots, \theta_q$ that minimize the sum of squared errors. Assuming that the initialization of the series is based, as we suggest, on the unconditional expected values (which are all 0) of $w_0, \ldots, w_{-p+1}$ and $\varepsilon_0, \ldots, \varepsilon_{-q+1}$, the time bounds will be $t = 1$ to T. Thus, the problem is to pick $\hat{\phi}_1, \ldots, \hat{\phi}_p, \hat{\theta}_1, \ldots, \hat{\theta}_q$ to minimize

$$S = \sum_{t=1}^{T} [\varepsilon_t | \hat{\phi}_1, \ldots, \hat{\phi}_p, \hat{\theta}_1, \ldots, \hat{\theta}_q]^2 \tag{18.7}$$

Now suppose the model is purely autoregressive, i.e., is of the form

$$\phi(B)w_t = \varepsilon_t \tag{18.8}$$

or

$$w_t = \phi_1 w_{t-1} + \cdots + \phi_p w_{t-p} + \varepsilon_t \tag{18.9}$$

Observe that since Eq. (18.9) is of the general form

$$y_t = \beta_0 + \beta_1 x_{1t} + \beta_2 x_{2t} + \cdots + \varepsilon_t \tag{18.10}$$

it can be estimated simply as a linear regression. Although for a purely autoregressive model the estimation process is essentially a linear regression, the problem is more difficult if the model contains a moving average component as well. In that case we can represent the model as

$$\theta^{-1}(B)\phi(B)w_t = \varepsilon_t \tag{18.11}$$

Clearly, this "regression equation" is nonlinear in the parameters and thus cannot be estimated by a simple application of ordinary least squares. However, it can be estimated by a general iterative nonlinear estimation routine. The process is nearly identical to that discussed in Chapter 10 and is used in standard nonlinear regression programs.

The nonlinear estimation process typically uses the first two terms in a Taylor series expansion to linearize Eq. (18.11) around an initial guess for the parameter values. A linear regression is then performed on this linearized equation, least-squares estimates of $\phi_1, \ldots, \phi_p, \theta_1, \ldots, \theta_q$ are obtained, and a new linearizaton of Eq. (18.11) is made around these estimates. Again, a linear regression is performed, a second set of parameter estimates is obtained, and a new linearization of Eq. (18.11) is made around this second set of estimates. This process is repeated iteratively until convergence occurs, i.e., until the estimates of the parameters do not change after repeated iterations.

18.1.3   Obtaining an Initial Guess for the Parameter Values

Before a nonlinear estimation can be performed on Eq. (18.11), an initial guess must be made for the parameter values. Convergence of the estimation process may be faster if the initial guess is a good one, i.e., close to the "true" parameter values. On the other hand, if the initial guess is very poor, it is possible that the iterative process will not converge at all.

The sample autocorrelation function sometimes can be used to help produce the initial guess, at least if the time-series model is of low order. For example, if the series w_t is modeled as first-order autoregressive, one need only look at the sample value of ρ_1. If that value is, say, .9, a reasonable first guess for ϕ_1 is $\phi_{1,0} = .9$. If, however, our model for w_t is complex, this inspection method is unlikely to be helpful.

Even if we cannot determine the initial guess by simply inspecting a correlogram, we can still use the numerical values for the sample autocorrelation function to obtain the initial guess. As we demonstrated in Chapter 17, the theoretical autocorrelation function can be related to the theoretical parameter values through a series of equations. If these equations are inverted, they can be used to solve for the parameter values *in terms of the autocorrelation function*. This is straightforward in the case of a purely autoregressive model. As an example, consider the autoregressive process of order p and recall from Eq. (17.47) that the difference equation for its autocorrelation function is given by

$$\rho_k = \phi_1\rho_{k-1} + \phi_2\rho_{k-2} + \cdots + \phi_p\rho_{k-p}$$

Using the fact that $\rho_k = \rho_{-k}$, we can rewrite this equation as a set of p simultaneous linear equations relating the parameters $\phi_1, \ldots, \phi_p$ to $\rho_1, \ldots, \rho_p$:

$$
\begin{aligned}
\rho_1 &= \phi_1 \quad\; + \phi_2\rho_1 + \cdots + \phi_p\rho_{p-1} \\
\rho_2 &= \phi_1\rho_1 + \phi_2 \quad\; + \cdots + \phi_p\rho_{p-2} \\
&\cdots\cdots\cdots\cdots\cdots\cdots\cdots\cdots\cdots\cdots\cdots\cdots \\
\rho_p &= \phi_1\rho_{p-1} + \phi_2\rho_{p-2} + \cdots + \phi_p
\end{aligned}
\tag{18.12}
$$

Using these *Yule-Walker equations* to solve for the parameters $\phi_1, \ldots, \phi_p$ in terms of the estimated values of the autocorrelation function, we arrive at the *Yule-Walker estimates* of the parameters. These estimates can be used to provide a reasonable first guess for the parameter values.[4] This first guess is, however, of limited value, since the purely autoregressive model can be estimated by ordinary least squares.

If the time-series model contains a moving average part, the Yule-Walker equations that relate the values of the autocorrelation function to the values

---

[4] Writing Eq. (18.12) in matrix notation, $\rho = \mathbf{P}\phi$, we can solve for ϕ as simply $\phi = \mathbf{P}^{-1}\rho$.

of the parameters will not be linear. Recall, for example, that the process MA(1) has the autocorrelation function

$$
\rho_k = \begin{cases} \dfrac{-\theta_1}{1 + \theta_1^2} & k = 1 \\ 0 & k > 1 \end{cases}
$$

Suppose in this example that $\rho_1 = .4$ in the sample autocorrelation function. Then

$$
\theta_1 = \frac{-1 \pm \sqrt{1 - 4\rho_1^2}}{2\rho_1} = \frac{-1 \pm .6}{.8} \tag{18.13}
$$

Thus, the first estimate for θ_1 is -2 or $-.5$. Since invertibility necessitates that $|\theta_1| < 1$, we select the value $\theta_{1,0} = -.5$ for our first guess in the nonlinear estimation process. Unfortunately, the solution for the θ's in terms of the ρ's becomes more difficult as the moving average order q becomes larger. In fact, to get initial estimates for the model MA(q), it is necessary to solve q simultaneous nonlinear equations. As a result, we often try several initial guesses and see whether our estimates converge to the same final parameter values.

One might ask why parameter values based on the Yule-Walker equations are not sufficient for practical purposes. This would eliminate the use of nonlinear estimation. One reason is that the sample autocorrelation function is only an *estimate* of the actual autocorrelation function and thus is subject to error. In fact, for small samples the sample autocorrelation function will be biased (downward) from the true autocorrelation function. A second reason is that the sample autocorrelation function does not contain as much information as does the actual time series. To use as much information as possible, we estimate the model's parameters on the basis of the actual time series.

18.2 DIAGNOSTIC CHECKING

After a time-series model has been estimated, one must test whether the specification was correct. This process of diagnostic checking usually involves two steps. First, the autocorrelation function for the simulated series (i.e., the time series generated by the model) can be compared with the sample autocorrelation function of the original series. If the two autocorrelation functions seem very different, we may doubt the validity of the model and a respecification may be in order. If the two autocorrelation functions are not markedly different (and this will most often be the case), one can analyze the *residuals* of the model.

Remember that we have assumed that the random error terms ε_t in the actual process are normally distributed and *independent*. Then, if the model has been specified correctly, the *residuals* $\hat{\varepsilon}_t$ should resemble a white noise process. In particular, we would expect the residuals to be *nearly uncorrelated* with each other, so that a *sample autocorrelation function* of the residuals would be close to 0 for displacement $k \geq 1$.

Recall that the residuals of the model are

$$\hat{\varepsilon}_t = \hat{\theta}^{-1}(B)\hat{\phi}(B)w_t \tag{18.14}$$

Let us denote the sample autocorrelation function (for displacement k) of the residuals as $\hat{r}_k$. It is calculated by

$$\hat{r}_k = \frac{\sum\limits_t \hat{\varepsilon}_t \hat{\varepsilon}_{t-k}}{\sum\limits_t \hat{\varepsilon}_t^2} \tag{18.15}$$

As we mentioned in Chapter 16, a very convenient test based on statistical results obtained by Box and Pierce can be applied to this sample autocorrelation function.[5] *If the model is correctly specified, then for large displacements k (for example, $k > 5$ for low-order models) the residual autocorrelations $\hat{r}_k$ are themselves uncorrelated, normally distributed random variables with mean 0 and variance $1/T$,* where T is the number of observations in the time series. This fact makes it possible to devise a simple diagnostic test.

Consider the statistic Q composed of the first K residual autocorrelations $\hat{r}_1$, $\ldots$, $\hat{r}_K$:[6]

$$Q = T \sum_{k=1}^{K} \hat{r}_k^2 \tag{18.16}$$

This statistic is a sum of squared independent normal random variables, each with mean 0 and variance $1/T$, and is therefore itself approximately distributed as *chi-square* (see Chapter 2). We say "approximately" because the first few autocorrelations r_1, r_2, etc., will have a variance slightly less than $1/T$ and may themselves be correlated. Box and Pierce demonstrate that the approximation is quite close and that the statistic Q will be distributed as $\chi^2(K - p - q)$, i.e., chi square with $K - p - q$ degrees of freedom.[7] Therefore, a statistical hypothesis test of the model's accuracy can be performed by comparing the observed value of Q with the appropriate points from a chi-square table.

---

[5] G. E. P. Box and D. A. Pierce, "Distribution of Residual Autocorrelations in Autoregressive-Integrated Moving Average Time Series Models," *Journal of the American Statistical Association*, vol. 65, December 1970.

[6] For low-order models, K equal to 15 or 20 is sufficient.

[7] In Chapter 16 we said that the Q statistic is chi square with K degrees of freedom. Note, however, that this definition was in reference to a test of the hypothesis that the *original data series* (as opposed to the residuals from our estimated ARMA model) is white noise. For the original data series, $p = q = 0$.

Suppose, for example, that we have specified an ARMA(1, 1) model for a series w_t, that the model has been estimated, and that the statistic Q has been calculated to be 31.5 with $K = 20$. From a chi-square table we see that the 90 percent point for $K - p - q = 18$ degrees of freedom is 26.0 and the 95 percent point is 28.9. Thus, the statistic Q is too large and we can reject the model, since the probability that the residuals are not white noise is at least 95 percent. Suppose that a new model, ARMA(2, 2), is specified and estimated and that the statistic Q is now 22.0, again with $K = 20$. From the chi-square table we see that the 90 percent point for 16 degrees of freedom is 23.5. Thus we need not reject the hypothesis that the residuals are white noise, and this second model is acceptable.[8] To determine the "best" specification we may want to specify and estimate some other ARMA models to see whether a lower chi-square statistic can be obtained.

If the calculated value of Q is between the 90 and 95 percent points of the chi-square tail, some doubt will be thrown on the model. At the very least a second test should be applied. This second test would involve observing the individual values of $\hat{r}_k$ for all k between, say, $K/4$ and K (in our example, between $k = 5$ and $k = 20$). Since these $\hat{r}_k$ are normal with variance $1/T$, we can test to see whether they are all within 2 or 3 standard deviations from their means of 0. If several of the $\hat{r}_k$ are larger than $2/\sqrt{T}$ (2 standard deviations of the normal variable), evidence exists that the model is misspecified. In addition, the evidence may suggest how the model should be respecified. For example, if for an ARMA(2, 1) model $\hat{r}_3$ is very much larger than $2/\sqrt{T}$, this indicates that the model should be respecified with the inclusion of a third-order moving average term.

In constructing a time-series model one often estimates several alternative specifications. It may be the case that two or more specifications pass the diagnostic checks described above. In this case additional tests must be used to determine the "best" specification. One test is to compare the "simulated series" (i.e., the time series generated by the model) for each specification with the original series. The specification that yields the smallest rms simulation error will then be retained. However, unless one specification has a markedly lower rms error, we suggest retaining all the specifications that pass the diagnostic checks and then choosing among them on the basis of their *forecasting* performance.

Example 18.1 Interest Rates   In the last two chapters we began analyzing a time series of monthly data for the interest rate on 3-month U.S. govern-

---

[8] Note that this chi-square test is a "weak" hypothesis test. A value of Q below the 90 percent point on the chi-square distribution indicates that it is not necessary to reject the hypothesis that the residuals are white, since the probability that the hypothesis is true is less than 90 percent. It is thus only an *indirect* test of the hypothesis that the residuals are not white.

ment Treasury bills from the beginning of 1960 through March 1996, and a time series of monthly data for U.S. hog production from 1960 through 1967. Let us now estimate some alternative ARIMA models for these two time series. We will begin with the interest rate series.

Review the sample autocorrelation functions in Figs. 16.8, 16.10, and 16.12 for the series undifferenced, differenced once, and differenced twice. We explained that these autocorrelation functions suggest that the series is first-order homogeneous nonstationary, i.e., can be modeled as ARIMA $(p, 1, q)$. But as we discussed in Chapter 17, a specification for p and q is difficult to determine from the sample autocorrelations. A low-order model such as ARIMA(2,1,2) may suffice, but the fact that the sample autocorrelations remain significantly different from zero even for large lags suggests that it may be necessary to estimate models of higher order.

We begin with a low-order specification and estimate an ARIMA(2,1,2) model. The result is

ARIMA(2,1,2):

$$(1 - .5590B - .1366B^2)\Delta y_t = .00446 + (1 - .2338B - .4721B^2)\varepsilon_t$$
$$\text{(18.17)}$$

$$R^2 = .120 \qquad \chi^2(4, 36) = 120.36$$

Note that while the R^2 of this equation is low, this does not necessarily mean that the specification is a poor one. Remember that the R^2 measures fit in terms of the dependent variable of the regression, which in this case is the *monthly change* in the interest rate. A more revealing statistic is the chi square, which is 120.36. With 32 degrees of freedom (36 lags minus 4 estimated AR and MA parameters), this value is far above the critical 95 percent level. Thus one can conclude that the residuals from this model are autocorrelated, and higher-order terms are needed.

As a next step, we increase the number of parameters and estimate an ARIMA(4,1,4) model. The result is

ARIMA(4,1,4):

$$(1 - .6648B + .5871B^2 - .3981B^3 - .4365B^4)\Delta y_t$$
$$= .00360 + (1 - .3453B + .2755B^2 - .1833B^3 - .7130B^4)\varepsilon_t$$
$$\text{(18.18)}$$

$$R^2 = .181 \qquad \chi^2(8, 36) = 80.42$$

While the chi-square statistic has dropped, it is still highly significant, leading us to reject this specification.

We now try specifications that are of much higher order:

ARIMA(8,1,2):

$$(1 - .8370B + .7152B^2 - .2286B^3 + .1830B^4 - .1972B^5 + .3275B^6$$
$$- .0867B^7 - .0635B^8)\Delta y_t = .00133 + (1 - .5106B + .3764B^2)\varepsilon_t$$

$$\tag{18.19}$$

$$R^2 = .205 \qquad \chi^2(10, 36) = 57.22$$

ARIMA(8,1,4):

$$(1 - .4564B + .7676B^2 - .3146B^3 + .7932B^4 - .3351B^5 + .3661B^6$$
$$+ .0172B^7 - .0367B^8)\Delta y_t = .00167 + (1 - .1142B$$
$$+ .5613B^2 - .1381B^3 + .6309B^4)\varepsilon_t \tag{18.20}$$

$$R^2 = .228 \qquad \chi^2(12, 36) = 47.18$$

The chi-squared statistics have dropped considerably but are still significant at the 95 percent level. It may be that we need an even higher-order specification. The results of estimating an ARIMA(8,1,6) model are as follows:

ARIMA(8,1,6):

$$(1 - .4974B - .0584B^2 + .0025B^3 + .1201B^4 - .0980B^5 - .3310B^6$$
$$+ .2920B^7 - .3395B^8)\Delta y_t = .00269 + (1 - .1549B - .2930B^2$$
$$- .0993B^3 + .0959B^4 + .0761B^5 - .5854B^6)\varepsilon_t \tag{18.21}$$

$$R^2 = .231 \qquad \chi^2(14, 36) = 46.87$$

Compared with the ARIMA(8,1,4) model, the chi-squared statistic is slightly lower (46.87 versus 47.14), but it is more significant because there are two additional parameters and hence two fewer degrees of freedom ($36 - 14 = 22$ versus $36 - 12 = 24$). Hence, adding two additional moving average terms does not improve the model. The reader can verify that adding additional autoregressive terms also does not improve the model.

Although the results of diagnostic checking are not good, the ARIMA (8,1,4) model seems to be the most promising. We will use this model to produce forecasts in the next section.

Example 18.2 Hog Production   Let us now turn to the series for monthly hog production. Recall from Chapter 17 that we suggested that an appropriate model for the series might be

$$(1 - \phi_1 B - \phi_2 B^2 - \phi_3 B^3)(1 - B)(1 - B^{12}) y_t = \varepsilon_t$$

This model was estimated over the period January 1960 to December 1967, with the results

$$(1 + .6681B + .2015B^2 - .1298B^3)(1 - B)(1 - B^{12}) y_t = .0014 + \varepsilon_t$$

$$(18.22)$$

$$R^2 = .365 \qquad \chi^2(3, 20) = 12.83$$

The model is acceptable, but the reader might wonder whether another specification would provide a better fit to the data. Perhaps, for example, the addition of moving average terms would improve the model. To test this, we estimated a model that includes first- and second-order moving average terms:

$$(1 + .6626B + .3945B^2 - .0179B^3)(1 - B)(1 - B^{12}) y_t$$
$$= .0015 + (1 + .0168B - .2191B^2)\varepsilon_t \qquad (18.23)$$

$$R^2 = .349 \qquad \chi^2(5, 20) = 13.01$$

Inclusion of the moving average terms results in a slightly lower value for the R^2. Of greater importance, however, is the fact that the estimated values of ϕ_1, ϕ_2, and ϕ_3 add up to a number greater than 1. The result is a nonstationary model for a series that we believe to be stationary. We would thus reject this model and retain the model of Eq. (18.22).

18.3   MINIMUM MEAN-SQUARE-ERROR FORECASTS

We turn now to forecasting. Our objective is to predict future values of a time series subject to as little error as possible. For this reason we consider the optimum forecast to be that forecast which has the *minimum mean-square forecast error*. Since the forecast error is a random variable, we minimize the *expected value*. Thus, we wish to choose our forecast $\hat{y}_T(l)$ so that $E[e_T^2(l)] = E\{[y_{T+1} - \hat{y}_T(l)]^2\}$ is minimized. We show that this forecast is given by the *conditional* expectation of y_{T+l}, that is, by

$$\hat{y}_T(l) = E(y_{T+l}|y_T, y_{T-1}, \ldots, y_1) \tag{18.24}$$

To prove that the minimum mean-square-error forecast is given by Eq. (18.24), we begin by rewriting the ARIMA model in Eq. (18.1) as

$$\phi(B)(1 - B)^d y_t = \theta(B)\varepsilon_t \tag{18.25}$$

since $\Delta = 1 - B$. Therefore,

$$y_t = \phi^{-1}(B)(1 - B)^{-d}\theta(B)\varepsilon_t = \psi(B)\varepsilon_t = \sum_{j=0}^{\infty} \psi_j \varepsilon_{t-j} \tag{18.26}$$

Here we have expressed the ARIMA model as a purely moving average process of infinite order.[9] Then

$$y_{T+l} = \psi_0\varepsilon_{T+l} + \psi_1\varepsilon_{T+l-1} + \cdots + \psi_l\varepsilon_T + \psi_{l+1}\varepsilon_{T-1} + \cdots$$

$$= \psi_0\varepsilon_{T+l} + \psi_1\varepsilon_{T+l-1} + \cdots + \psi_{l-1}\varepsilon_{T+1} + \sum_{j=0}^{\infty} \psi_{l+j}\varepsilon_{T-j} \tag{18.27}$$

In Eq. (18.27) we have divided the infinite sum into two parts, with the second part beginning with the term $\psi_l\varepsilon_T$ and thus describing information up to and including time period T.

Of course, the forecast $\hat{y}_T(l)$ can be based only on information available up to time T. Our objective is to compare this forecast with the actual value y_{T+l} as expressed in Eq. (18.27). To do so, we write the forecast as a weighted sum of those error terms *which we can estimate*, namely, $\varepsilon_T, \varepsilon_{T-1}, \ldots$. Then the desired forecast is

$$\hat{y}_T(l) = \sum_{j=0}^{\infty} \psi_{l+j}^* \varepsilon_{T-j} \tag{18.28}$$

where the weights ψ_{l+j}^* are to be chosen optimally to minimize the mean-square forecast error. We can now write an expression for the forecast error, $e_T(l)$ by using Eqs. (18.27) and (18.28):

[9] Any ARIMA process can be equivalently expressed as purely moving average or as purely autoregressive. We could have, for example, rewritten Eq. (18.25) as $\phi(B)(1 - B)^d\theta^{-1}(B)y_t = \varepsilon_t$, or $\xi(B)y_t = \varepsilon_t$. This is a purely autoregressive process of infinite order. We do not originally specify the ARIMA process as purely autoregressive or purely moving average (of infinite order) because we would then have an infinite number of parameters to estimate.

$$e_T(l) = y_{T+l} - \hat{y}_T(l) = \psi_0 \varepsilon_{T+l} + \psi_1 \varepsilon_{T+l-1} + \cdots + \psi_{l-1}\varepsilon_{T+1}$$

$$+ \sum_{j=0}^{\infty} (\psi_{l+j} - \psi_{l+j}^*)\varepsilon_{T-j} \qquad (18.29)$$

Since by assumption $E(\varepsilon_i \varepsilon_j) = 0$ for $i \neq j$, the mean square forecast error is

$$E[e_T^2(l)] = (\psi_0^2 + \psi_1^2 + \cdots + \psi_{l-1}^2)\sigma_\varepsilon^2 + \sum_{j=0}^{\infty} (\psi_{l+j} - \psi_{l+j}^*)^2 \sigma_\varepsilon^2 \quad (18.30)$$

Clearly, this expression is minimized by setting the "optimum" weights ψ_{l+j}^* equal to the true weights ψ_{l+j}, for $j = 0, 1, \ldots$. But then our optimum forecast $\hat{y}_T(l)$ is just the conditional expectation of y_{T+l}. This can be seen by taking the conditional expectation of y_{T+l} in Eq. (18.27). The expected values of ε_{T+l}, $\ldots$, ε_{T+1} are all 0, while the expected values of ε_T, ε_{T-1}, $\ldots$, are just the residuals from the estimated equation. Thus, we have

$$\hat{y}_T(l) = \sum_{j=0}^{\infty} \psi_{l+j} \hat{\varepsilon}_{T-j} = E(y_{T+l}|y_T, \ldots, y_1) \qquad (18.31)$$

This provides the basic principle for calculating forecasts from our ARIMA models. Now we apply this principle to the actual computation of forecasts.

18.4 COMPUTING A FORECAST

The computation of the forecast $\hat{y}_T(l)$ can be done recursively by using the estimated ARIMA model. This involves first computing a forecast one period ahead, then using this forecast to compute a forecast two periods ahead, and continuing until the l-period forecast has been reached. Let us write the ARIMA (p, d, q) model as

$$w_t = \phi_1 w_{t-1} + \cdots + \phi_p w_{t-p} + \varepsilon_t - \theta_1 \varepsilon_{t-1} - \cdots - \theta_q \varepsilon_{t-q} + \delta \quad (18.32)$$

with $$y_t = \Sigma^d w_t$$

To compute the forecast $\hat{y}_T(l)$, we begin by computing the *one-period* forecast of w_t, $\hat{w}_T(1)$. To do so, we write Eq. (18.32) with the time period modified:

$$w_{T+1} = \phi_1 w_T + \cdots + \phi_p w_{T-p+1} + \varepsilon_{T+1} - \theta_1 \varepsilon_T - \cdots - \theta_q \varepsilon_{T-q+1} + \delta$$

$$(18.33)$$

We then calculate our forecast $\hat{w}_T(1)$ by taking the conditional expected value of w_{T+1} in Eq. (18.33):

$$\hat{w}_T(1) = E(w_{T+1}|w_T, \ldots) = \phi_1 w_T + \cdots + \phi_p w_{T-p+1}$$
$$- \theta_1 \hat{\varepsilon}_T - \cdots - \theta_q \hat{\varepsilon}_{T-q+1} + \delta \tag{18.34}$$

where the $\hat{\varepsilon}_T$, $\hat{\varepsilon}_{T-1}$, etc., are observed residuals. Note that the expected value of ε_{T+1} is 0. Now, using the one-period forecast $\hat{w}_T(1)$, we can obtain the *two-period* forecast $\hat{w}_T(2)$:

$$\hat{w}_T(2) = E(w_{T+2}|w_T, \ldots)$$
$$= \phi_1 \hat{w}_T(1) + \phi_2 w_T + \cdots + \phi_p w_{T-p+2} - \theta_2 \hat{\varepsilon}_T - \cdots - \theta_q \hat{\varepsilon}_{T-q+2} + \delta$$
$$\tag{18.35}$$

The two-period forecast is then used to produce the three-period forecast, and so on until the *l*-period forecast $\hat{w}_T(l)$ is reached:

$$\hat{w}_T(l) = \phi_1 \hat{w}_T(l - 1) + \cdots + \phi_l w_T + \cdots + \phi_p w_{T-p+l} \tag{18.36}$$
$$- \theta_l \hat{\varepsilon}_T - \cdots - \theta_q \hat{\varepsilon}_{T-q+l} + \delta$$

Note that if $l > p$ and $l > q$, this forecast will be

$$\hat{w}_T(l) = \phi_1 \hat{w}_T(l - 1) + \cdots + \phi_p \hat{w}_T(l - p) \tag{18.37}$$

Once the differenced series w_t has been forecasted, a forecast can be obtained for the original series y_t simply by applying the summation operation to w_t, that is, by summing w_t d times. Suppose, for example, that $d = 1$. Then our *l*-period forecast of y_t is given by

$$\hat{y}_T(l) = y_T + \hat{w}_T(1) + \hat{w}_T(2) + \cdots + \hat{w}_T(l) \tag{18.38}$$

However, if the model for y_t were ARIMA with $d = 2$, the *l*-period forecast $\hat{y}_T(l)$ would be given by

$$\hat{y}_T(l) = y_T + [\Delta y_T + \hat{w}_T(1)] + [\Delta y_T + \hat{w}_T(1) + \hat{w}_T(2)] + \cdots$$
$$+ [\Delta y_T + \hat{w}_T(1) + \cdots + \hat{w}_T(l)]$$
$$= y_T + l \Delta y_T + l \hat{w}_T(1) + (l - 1)\hat{w}_T(2) + \cdots + \hat{w}_T(l) \tag{18.39}$$

Here the summation operator has been applied twice. The procedure is similar for larger values of d.

18.5 THE FORECAST ERROR

As we saw before, if we express the ARIMA model as a purely moving average process of infinite order, the forecast error l periods ahead is given by

$$e_T(l) = y_{T+l} - \hat{y}_T(l) = \psi_0 \varepsilon_{T+l} + \psi_1 \varepsilon_{T+l-1} + \cdots + \psi_{l-1} \varepsilon_{T+1} \quad (18.40)$$

Remember that the weights ψ_j are determined from

$$\psi(B) = \phi^{-1}(B)(1 - B)^{-d}\theta(B) \quad (18.41)$$

We assume that the model parameters $\phi_1, \ldots, \phi_p$ and $\theta_1, \ldots, \theta_q$ are known exactly, and therefore the weights $\psi_0, \psi_1, \ldots,$ are also known exactly. In this case the *variance* of the forecast error is given by

$$E[e_T^2(l)] = (\psi_0^2 + \psi_1^2 + \cdots + \psi_{l-1}^2)\sigma_\varepsilon^2 \quad (18.42)$$

Therefore, the algebraic form for the forecast error variance depends on the particular ARIMA specification that has been adopted. In the next section we examine the forecast error in more detail for some simple ARIMA models. For now, however, there are two things that the reader should observe.

First, we know from the definition of $\psi(B)$ above that $\psi_0 = 1$.[10] Therefore, for *any* ARIMA specification we know that the forecast error *one period* ahead is just

$$e_T(1) = \varepsilon_{T+1} \quad (18.43)$$

and this has variance σ_ε^2. Thus, the forecast error variance one period ahead is the variance of the error term.

Second, we must keep in mind the fact that our calculation of the forecast error was based on the assumption that we knew the parameter values $\phi_1, \ldots, \phi_p$ and $\theta_1, \ldots, \theta_q$ with certainty. However, the parameters are estimated via a nonlinear least-squares regression, and the estimates are random variables with means and variances. Therefore, the *actual* forecast error variance will be *larger* than the variance calculated above. To determine exactly *how much larger*, we must know the variances of the parameter estimates in the ARIMA model. Because the parameters are estimated nonlinearly, we would calculate standard errors based on the *last iteration* of the nonlinear estimation procedure.

The difficulty here is that the standard errors for the linearization in the last iteration may not be "true" estimates of the actual standard errors for the parameter values. As a practical matter, one has the choice of using these

---

[10] Remember that the ARIMA model (with 0 mean) is $w_t = \phi_1 w_{t-1} + \cdots + \phi_p w_{t-p} + \varepsilon_t - \theta_1 \varepsilon_{t-1} - \cdots - \theta_q \varepsilon_{t-q}$. The only unlagged term on the right-hand side is ε_t (which has a weight of 1). Thus, ψ_0 must equal 1 in Eq. (18.26).

standard errors in the calculation of the forecast error variance or ignoring them and simply calculating the forecast error variance based on Eq. (18.42).

18.6 FORECAST CONFIDENCE INTERVALS

Before we can calculate a confidence interval for our forecast, we need an estimate $\hat{\sigma}_\varepsilon^2$ for the variance of the disturbance term. This estimate would logically be based on the sum of squared residuals $S(\hat{\phi}_1, \ldots, \hat{\phi}_p, \hat{\theta}_1, \ldots, \hat{\theta}_q)$ obtained after final estimates of the parameters have been obtained:

$$
\hat{\sigma}_\varepsilon^2 = \frac{S}{T - p - q} = \frac{\sum_{t=1}^{T} \hat{\varepsilon}_t^2}{T - p - q} \tag{18.44}
$$

Here $T - p - q$ is the number of degrees of freedom in the linear regression. We see from Eq. (18.42) and the fact that $\psi_0 = 1$ that a *confidence interval of n standard deviations* around a forecast l periods ahead would be given by

$$
C_n = \hat{y}_T(l) \pm n \left(1 + \sum_{j=1}^{l-1} \psi_j^2 \right)^{1/2} \hat{\sigma}_\varepsilon \tag{18.45}
$$

As expected, this interval gets larger as the lead time l becomes larger, although the exact pattern depends on the weights ψ_j.

Forecasts of y_t, together with a typical 66 percent confidence interval ($n = 1$) and a 95 percent confidence interval ($n = 2$), are shown for a hypothetical ARMA model ($d = 0$) in Fig. 18.1. Note that the forecasts (denoted by crosses) first are increasing but then decline to the constant mean level of the series. We know that the forecast will approach the mean of the series as the lead

FIGURE 18.1
Forecasts and confidence intervals for a stationary ARMA process.

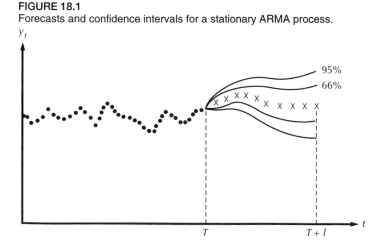

time l becomes large because the process is stationary. The confidence intervals, of course, increase as the forecast lead time becomes longer.

18.7   PROPERTIES OF ARIMA FORECASTS

We now examine the properties of the forecasts derived from some simple ARIMA models. In all the cases that follow we assume that the parameters of the particular ARIMA model are known with certainty.

18.7.1   The AR(1) Process

Let us begin with the stationary first-order autoregressive process, AR(1):

$$y_t = \phi_1 y_{t-1} + \delta + \varepsilon_t \tag{18.46}$$

For this process the one-period forecast is

$$\hat{y}_T(1) = E(y_{T+1}|y_T, \dots, y_1) = \phi_1 y_T + \delta \tag{18.47}$$

Similarly, $\hat{y}_T(2) = \phi_1 \hat{y}_T(1) + \delta = \phi_1^2 y_T + (\phi_1 + 1)\delta \tag{18.48}$

And the l-period forecast is

$$\hat{y}_T(l) = \phi_1^l y_T + (\phi_1^{l-1} + \phi_1^{l-2} + \cdots + \phi_1 + 1)\delta \tag{18.49}$$

Note that in the limit as l becomes large, the forecast converges to the value

$$\lim_{l \to \infty} \hat{y}_T(l) = \delta \sum_{j=0}^{\infty} \phi_1^j = \frac{\delta}{1 - \phi_1} = \mu_y \tag{18.50}$$

We see, then, that the forecast tends to the mean of the series as l becomes large [recall Eq. (17.23) for the mean of the AR(1) process]. Of course this is not surprising, since the series is stationary. As the lead time l becomes very large, there is essentially no useful information in recent values of the time series, y_T, y_{T-1}, etc., that can be used to adjust the forecast away from the mean value. Thus, for a very large lead time the best forecast is the stationary mean of the series.

Let us now calculate the forecast error for this process. The forecast error l periods ahead is given by

$$
\begin{aligned}
e_T(l) = y_{T+l} - \hat{y}_T(l) &= \phi_1 y_{T+l-1} + \delta + \varepsilon_{T+l} - \hat{y}_T(l) \\
&= \phi_1^2 y_{T+l-2} + (\phi_1 + 1)\delta + \varepsilon_{T+l} + \phi_1 \varepsilon_{T+l-1} - \hat{y}_T(l) \\
&\cdots\cdots\cdots\cdots\cdots\cdots\cdots \\
&= \phi_1^l y_T + (\phi_1^{l-1} + \phi_1^{l-2} + \cdots + \phi_1 + 1)\delta \\
&\quad + \varepsilon_{T+l} + \phi_1 \varepsilon_{T+l-1} + \cdots + \phi_1^{l-1} \varepsilon_{T+1} - \hat{y}_T(l)
\end{aligned}
$$

Now substituting Eq. (18.49) for $\hat{y}_T(l)$, we get

$$e_T(l) = \varepsilon_{T+l} + \phi_1\varepsilon_{T+l-1} + \cdots + \phi_1^{l-1}\varepsilon_{T+1} \qquad (18.51)$$

which has a variance

$$E[e_T^2(l)] = (1 + \phi_1^2 + \phi_1^4 + \cdots + \phi_1^{2l-2})\sigma_\varepsilon^2 \qquad (18.52)$$

Note that this forecast error variance increases (nonlinearly) as l becomes larger.

18.7.2   The MA(1) Process

Now let us examine the simple first-order moving average process, MA(1):

$$y_t = \delta + \varepsilon_t - \theta_1\varepsilon_{t-1} \qquad (18.53)$$

The one-period forecast for this process is

$$\hat{y}_T(1) = E(y_{T+1}|y_T, \ldots, y_1) = \delta - \theta_1\hat{\varepsilon}_T \qquad (18.54)$$

where $\hat{\varepsilon}_T$ is the actual residual from the current (and most recent) observation. By comparison, the l-period forecast, for $l > 1$, is just

$$\hat{y}_T(l) = E(y_{T+l}|y_T, \ldots, y_1) = E(\delta + \varepsilon_{T+l} - \theta_1\varepsilon_{T+l-1}) = \delta \qquad (18.55)$$

This is also as expected, since the process MA(1) has a memory of only one period. Thus, recent data are of no help in making a forecast two or more periods ahead, and the best forecast is the mean of the series, δ.

The variance of the forecast error for MA(1) is σ_ε^2 for the one-period forecast, and for the l-period forecast, $l > 1$, it is given by

$$E[e_T^2(l)] = E\{[y_{T+l} - \hat{y}_T(l)]^2\} = E[(\varepsilon_{T+l} - \theta_1\varepsilon_{T+l-1})^2] = (1 + \theta_1^2)\sigma_\varepsilon^2$$

$$(18.56)$$

Thus the forecast error variance is the same for a forecast two periods ahead, three periods ahead, etc. The forecast confidence intervals would appear as shown in Fig. 18.2.

18.7.3   The ARMA(1, 1) Process

Let us now calculate and examine the forecasts generated by the simplest mixed autoregressive–moving average process, ARMA(1, 1):

$$y_t = \phi_1 y_{t-1} + \delta + \varepsilon_t - \theta_1\varepsilon_{t-1} \qquad (18.57)$$

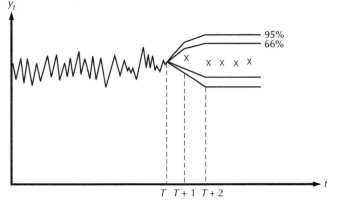

FIGURE 18.2
Forecasts and confidence intervals for an MA(1) process.

The one-period forecast for the ARMA(1, 1) model is given by

$$\hat{y}_T(1) = E(\phi_1 y_T + \delta + \varepsilon_{T+1} - \theta_1 \varepsilon_T) = \phi_1 y_T + \delta - \theta_1 \hat{\varepsilon}_T \quad (18.58)$$

The two-period forecast is

$$\hat{y}_T(2) = E(\phi_1 y_{T+1} + \delta + \varepsilon_{T+2} - \theta_1 \varepsilon_{T+1}) = \phi_1 \hat{y}_T(1) + \delta$$
$$= \phi_1^2 y_T + (\phi_1 + 1)\delta - \phi_1 \theta_1 \hat{\varepsilon}_T \quad (18.59)$$

Finally, the l-period forecast is

$$\hat{y}_T(l) = \phi_1 \hat{y}_T(l - 1) + \delta$$
$$= \phi_1^l y_T + (\phi_1^{l-1} + \cdots + \phi_1 + 1)\delta - \phi_1^{l-1} \theta_1 \hat{\varepsilon}_T \quad (18.60)$$

Note that the limiting value of the forecast as l becomes large is again the mean of the series:

$$\lim_{l \to \infty} \hat{y}_T(l) = \frac{\delta}{1 - \phi_1} = \mu_y \quad (18.61)$$

Examining these forecasts for different lead times, we see that the current disturbance helps determine the one-period forecast and in turn serves as a starting point from which the remainder of the forecast profile, which is autoregressive in character, decays toward the mean $\delta/(1 - \phi_1)$.

The fact that forecasts from ARMA models approach the (constant) mean value of the series as the lead time becomes large indicates a limitation of these models. As we will see in the examples in this chapter and Chapter 19, time-series models are best for short-term forecasting. For a long forecasting horizon a structural econometric model is likely to be more useful.

18.7.4 The ARI(1, 1, 0) Process

Now we examine a simple nonstationary process, the integrated autoregressive process ARI(1, 1, 0):

$$w_t = \phi_1 w_{t-1} + \delta + \varepsilon_t \tag{18.62}$$

with $$w_t = \Delta y_t = y_t - y_{t-1}$$

Forecasts for y_t are related to forecasts of the differenced series w_t as follows:

$$\hat{y}_T(1) = y_T + \hat{w}_T(1) \tag{18.63}$$

and $$\hat{y}_T(l) = y_T + \hat{w}_T(1) + \cdots + \hat{w}_T(l) \tag{18.64}$$

Since the differenced process w_t is AR(1), its forecasts are given by

$$\begin{aligned}
\hat{w}_T(l) &= \phi_1^l w_T + (\phi_1^{l-1} + \phi_1^{l-2} + \cdots + \phi_1 + 1)\delta \\
&= \phi_1^l y_T - \phi_1^l y_{T-1} + (\phi_1^{l-1} + \cdots + \phi_1 + 1)\delta \tag{18.65}
\end{aligned}$$

Then the one-period forecast for y_t is

$$\hat{y}_T(1) = y_T + \phi_1(y_T - y_{T-1}) + \delta = (1 + \phi_1)y_T - \phi_1 y_{T-1} + \delta \tag{18.66}$$

The two-period forecast for y_t is

$$\begin{aligned}
\hat{y}_T(2) &= y_T + \hat{w}_T(1) + \hat{w}_T(2) = \hat{y}_T(1) + \hat{w}_T(2) \\
&= \hat{y}_T(1) + \phi_1^2 w_T + (\phi_1 + 1)\delta \\
&= (1 + \phi_1 + \phi_1^2)y_T - (\phi_1 + \phi_1^2)y_{T-1} + (\phi_1 + 1)\delta + \delta \tag{18.67}
\end{aligned}$$

A more instructive way to look at this forecast, however, is in terms of its *changes*. Since

$$\hat{w}_T(2) = \phi_1 \hat{w}_T(1) + \delta \tag{18.68}$$

we can write the forecast $\hat{y}_T(2)$ as

$$\hat{y}_T(2) = \hat{y}_T(1) + \phi_1 \hat{w}_T(1) + \delta \tag{18.69}$$

Similarly, $$\hat{y}_T(l) = \hat{y}_T(l-1) + \phi_1 \hat{w}_T(l-1) + \delta \tag{18.70}$$

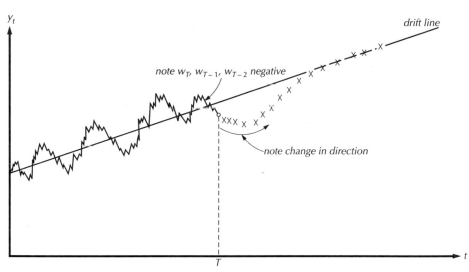

FIGURE 18.3
Hypothetical forecasts for an ARI(1, 1, 0) process.

Now let us examine the properties of this forecast. Since w_t is an AR(1) process, we know from Eq. (18.50) that

$$\lim_{l \to \infty} \hat{w}_T(l) = \frac{\delta}{1 - \phi_1} \qquad (18.71)$$

Thus, as the forecast horizon l becomes large, the forecast profile approaches a straight line with slope $\delta/(1 - \phi_1)$. In other words, as the horizon becomes large, the forecast becomes dominated by the *deterministic drift* of the process. For a short forecast horizon this would not be true. It might have been the case, for example, that the last few differences w_T, w_{T-1}, w_{T-2} were negative although δ was positive, so that the series had an overall upward drift. In this case the short-term forecasts $\hat{w}_T(1)$ and $\hat{w}_T(2)$ might be negative, even though $\hat{w}_T(l)$ would tend toward $\delta/(1 - \phi_1)$ as l became larger. The forecasts for y_t, then, would first be decreasing but then would *change direction*, ultimately approaching a straight line with slope $\delta/(1 - \phi_1)$. This hypothetical ARI (1, 1, 0) forecast is shown graphically in Fig. 18.3.

One thing that becomes immediately clear about ARIMA forecasts is that they are *adaptive*. As can be seen from Fig. 18.3, the forecast makes use of the most recent data and adapts accordingly. Another example of the adaptive nature of ARIMA forecasts is shown in Fig. 18.4. This process is also ARI(1, 1, 0) and is identical to the process in Fig. 18.3 for $t \leq T$. The crosses in Fig. 18.4 represent the forecasts made at time T. Now suppose that the series *increases* in periods $T + 1$, $T + 2$, and $T + 3$ and that a *new* set of forecasts is made in period $T + 3$. These forecasts are denoted by circles, and as can be seen in Fig.

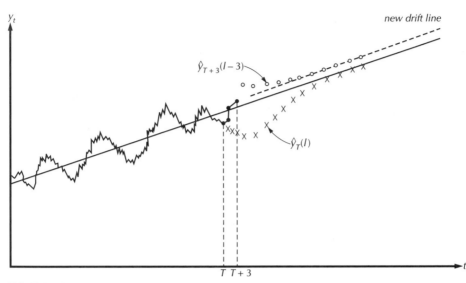

FIGURE 18.4
Adaptive nature of ARI(1, 1, 0) forecast.

18.4, they first *increase* and then *decrease*. Ultimately they will also approach a drift line. This new drift line will have the same slope as before but will be slightly higher as a result of the new data points. What we observe, then, is that the forecast has "adapted" to the new data that became available in periods $T + 1$, $T + 2$, and $T + 3$. Note that the values of this forecast for a long lead time have adapted as well.

18.7.5   Confidence Intervals for the ARI(1, 1, 0) Forecast

We now calculate the forecast error and its variance for the ARI(1, 1, 0) process so that we can obtain a forecast confidence interval. As we will see, the forecast confidence interval for y_t is related to the forecast confidence interval for the differenced series w_t.

We begin with the forecast error for the one-period forecast, $\hat{y}_T(1)$:

$$e_T(1) = y_{T+1} - \hat{y}_T(1) = y_T + w_{T+1} - y_T - \hat{w}_T(1) \qquad (18.72)$$
$$= w_{T+1} - \hat{w}_T(1) = \varepsilon_{T+1}$$

which has a variance σ_ε^2. The two-period forecast error is given by

$$e_T(2) = y_{T+2} - \hat{y}_T(2) = y_T + w_{T+1} + w_{T+2} - y_T - \hat{w}_T(1) - \hat{w}_T(2)$$
$$= [w_{T+1} - \hat{w}_T(1)] + [w_{T+2} - \hat{w}_T(2)]$$
$$= (1 + \phi_1)\varepsilon_{T+1} + \varepsilon_{T+2} \qquad (18.73)$$

and this has a variance

$$E[e_T^2(2)] = \sigma_\varepsilon^2[(1 + \phi_1)^2 + 1] \tag{18.74}$$

Note that this forecast error (and its variance) is cumulative; i.e., it is equal to the two-period error for $\hat{w}_T(2)$ in *addition* to the one-period error for $\hat{w}_T(1)$. Thus, the error in $\hat{y}_T(2)$ is an *accumulation* of the errors in $\hat{w}_T(1)$ and $\hat{w}_T(2)$. Now observe this cumulative phenomenon in the *l*-period forecast:

$$
\begin{aligned}
e_T(l) &= [w_{T+1} - \hat{w}_T(1)] + [w_{T+2} - \hat{w}_T(2)] + \cdots + [w_{T+l} - \hat{w}_T(l)] \\
&= \varepsilon_{T+1} + (\varepsilon_{T+2} + \phi_1\varepsilon_{T+1}) + \cdots \\
&\quad + (\varepsilon_{T+l} + \phi_1\varepsilon_{T+l-1} \\
&\quad\quad + \cdots + \phi_1^{l-1}\varepsilon_{T+1}) \\
&= (1 + \phi_1 + \phi_1^2 + \cdots + \phi_1^{l-1})\varepsilon_{T+1} + (1 + \phi_1 + \cdots + \phi_1^{l-2})\varepsilon_{T+2} \\
&\quad + \cdots + (1 + \phi_1)\varepsilon_{T+l-1} + \varepsilon_{T+l} \\
&= \sum_{i=1}^{l} \varepsilon_{T+i} \sum_{j=0}^{l-i} \phi_1^j \tag{18.75}
\end{aligned}
$$

and this has a variance

$$E[e_T^2(l)] = \sigma_\varepsilon^2 \sum_{i=1}^{l} \left(\sum_{j=0}^{l-i} \phi_1^j \right)^2 \tag{18.76}$$

Thus the error in $\hat{y}_T(l)$ is an accumulation of errors in $\hat{w}_T(1)$, $\hat{w}_T(2)$, . . . , $\hat{w}_T(l)$. This can be seen graphically in Figs. 18.5 and 18.6, which compare confidence intervals for forecasts of the differenced series w_t with confidence intervals for forecasts of y_t. Note the relationship between the forecasts of the differenced series w_t and the forecasts of y_t. w_{T-2} and w_{T-1} are decreasing, and w_T is negative, so that $\hat{w}_T(1)$ and $\hat{w}_T(2)$ are also negative [$\hat{y}_T(1)$ and $\hat{y}_T(2)$ are decreasing], $\hat{w}_T(3)$, $\hat{w}_T(4)$, etc., are positive [$\hat{y}_T(3)$ is larger than $\hat{y}_T(2)$], and finally $\hat{w}_T(l)$ approaches

FIGURE 18.5
Confidence interval for $\hat{w}_T(l)$ for ARI(1, 1, 0) process.

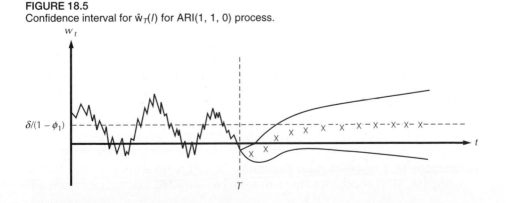

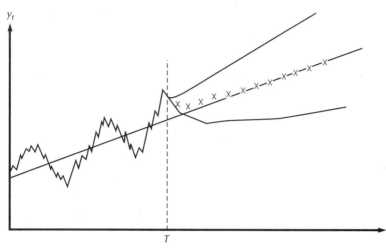

FIGURE 18.6
Confidence interval for $\hat{y}_T(l)$ for ARI(1, 1, 0) process.

the mean $\delta/(1 - \phi_1)$ as l becomes large so that $\hat{y}_T(l)$ approaches the drift line. Observe that the confidence interval for $\hat{y}_T(l)$ grows rapidly, since it must account for the accumulation of forecast errors in the differenced series.

We have examined the forecast properties of only the simplest ARIMA models, but some of our conclusions apply to more complicated (i.e., higher-order) models. In particular, note that a moving average model of order q has a memory of only q periods, so that the observed data will affect the forecast only if the lead time l is less than q. An autoregressive model has a memory of infinite length, so that all past observations will have some effect on the forecast, even if the lead time l is long. But although all past observations have *some* effect on the forecast, only more recent observations have a large effect. Thus even with autoregressive (or mixed autoregressive—moving average) models, past observations have little effect on the forecast if the lead time is long. Thus ARIMA models are best suited to *short-term forecasting*, i.e., forecasting with a lead time l not much longer than $p + q$.

18.8   TWO EXAMPLES

Earlier in this chapter we estimated ARIMA models for the interest rate on 3-month Treasury bills and for monthly hog production in the United States. We now generate forecasts of the interest rate and hog production using ARIMA models.

Example 18.3 Interest Rate Forecast   Recall from Example 18.1 that an ARIMA(8, 1, 4) model for the 3-month Treasury bill rate was estimated by

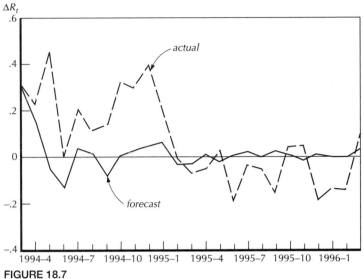

FIGURE 18.7
Monthly changes in Treasury bill rate, 24-month forecast versus actual.

using data that ran through March 1996. In this example, we use that model to generate a series of forecasts of the bill rate.

A 24-month *ex post* forecast (from April 1994 to March 1996) is shown in Fig. 18.7, a 12-month forecast (April 1995 to March 1996) in Fig. 18.8, and

FIGURE 18.8
Monthly changes in Treasury bill rate, 12-month forecast versus actual.

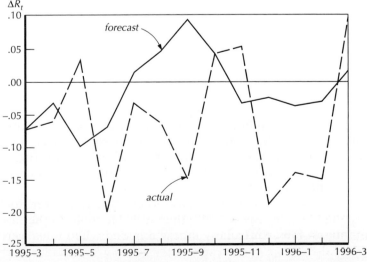

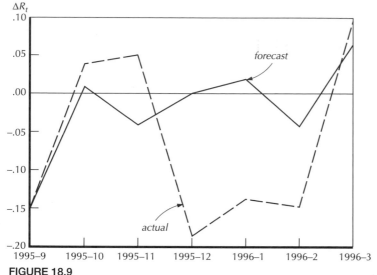

FIGURE 18.9
Monthly changes in Treasury bill rate, 6-month forecast versus actual.

a 6-month forecast (October 1995 to March 1996) in Fig. 18.9. Note that all these figures show the forecasted and actual series for the monthly *change* in the interest rate, not its level.

An evaluation of this model as a forecasting tool is somewhat difficult given the volatility of interest rates. What we can see, however, is that the ARIMA model captures trends but fails to predict sharp turns, especially for the longer forecasts. For example, the 24-month forecast failed to capture the sharp increases in the interest rate that occurred during 1994 and the (somewhat smaller) decreases that occurred during 1995. Likewise, the 12-month forecast failed to predict the sharp declines that occurred during the year. Even the 6-month forecast tends to underpredict changes in the interest rate. This can also be seen in Fig. 18.10, which plots the 6-month forecast and actual values in terms of the *level* of the interest rate rather than first differences.

Figure 18.11 shows an *ex ante* 18-month forecast that extends from October 1995 to March 1997. (This figure is again in terms of first differences.) Here the cyclical changes in the interest rate that occurred (and were predicted by the model) for the first 6 months are predicted to continue occurring through the following 12 months. We leave it to the reader to check the data and determine how accurate this forecast was.

The usefulness of an ARIMA model such as this one as a forecasting tool can be evaluated only in comparison with other available tools. In the case of a short-term interest rate, particularly during a period when rates were

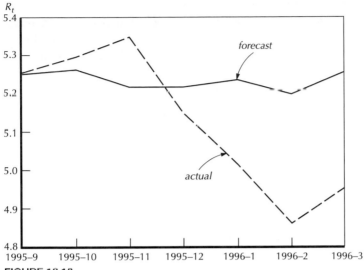

FIGURE 18.10
Three-month Treasury bill rate, 6-month forecast versus actual.

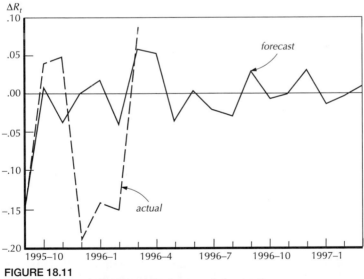

FIGURE 18.11
Monthly changes in Treasury bill rate, *ex ante* forecast.

fluctuating considerably, one might expect a structural regression model to show a better forecasting performance than would a time-series model. In Chapter 19 we will see how a time-series model can be combined with a regression model to improve the forecasting of interest rates.

Example 18.4 Hog Production Forecast   Recall that the ARIMA model for hog production in Eq. (18.22) was estimated using data from the beginning of 1960 to the end of 1967. We generate our forecast out over a 2-year horizon, beginning in January 1968 and ending in January 1970. We then compare the 25 months of forecasted production with the actual data.

The forecasted and actual series for hog production are shown in Fig. 18.12. Observe that our model has generated forecasts which are quite accurate. The model not only correctly forecasts changing trends in the series but also picks up the broad seasonal cycle (as it should, since the model includes a twelfth-difference of the series to explain seasonality). Usually the forecast is within 10 or 15 percent of the actual series and reproduces most of the turning points. This model would be quite acceptable as a forecasting tool. Unlike our interest rate example, hog production probably can be forecasted better using a time-series model than by using a single-equation regression model. The reason for this is that the complicated economics of hog production cannot be represented easily by a single structural equation. Although hog production probably could be modeled rather well by a multi-equation simulation model, constructing such a model would likely be difficult and time-consuming. The time-series model, by contrast, can be constructed easily and quickly and does a reasonable job of forecasting.

FIGURE 18.12
Two-year (25 month) forecast of hog production. Time bounds: January 1968 to January 1970.

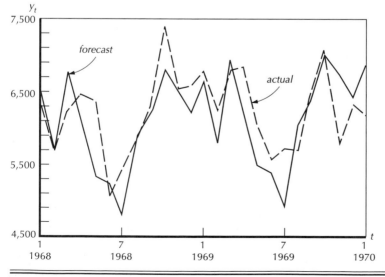

In Chapter 19 we will look at some other examples of time-series models as they are applied to problems in economic and business forecasting. In each case we will go through the process of specifying, estimating, and checking an ARIMA model, and we will then use the model to produce forecasts. This should provide the reader with more of a feeling for the properties and characteristics of time-series models and forecasts.

EXERCISES

18.1 Suppose an ARMA(0, 2) model has been estimated for a time series that has been generated by an ARMA(1, 2) process.

(a) How would the diagnostic test indicate that the model has been misspecified?

(b) What will the residual autocorrelations $\hat{r}_k$ look like? What characteristics of these autocorrelations might indicate that ARMA(1, 2) is a more correct specification?

18.2 Repeat Exercise 18.1 for an ARMA(0, 2) model estimated for a time series that has been generated by an ARMA(2, 3) process.

18.3 Suppose a particular homogeneous nonstationary time series y_t can be modeled as a stochastic process that is ARIMA(1, 1, 1).

(a) How would you calculate the sample autocorrelation functions for y_t and its differences and use them to verify that ARIMA(1, 1, 1) is indeed a proper specification for y_t?

(b) Suppose you did not have access to a computer package for nonlinear estimation. How would you use a *linear regression* to obtain *approximate* estimates of the parameters in the model? (Explain the steps involved clearly.)

18.4 Using data for the 3-month Treasury bill rate (or some other short-term interest rate), specify and estimate alternative models to those in Example 18.1. Experiment with higher-order ARIMA(p, 1, q) models and also with ARIMA(p, 2, q) models. How sensitive are your estimates to the choice of sample period?

18.5 Write the equation that determines the forecast $\hat{y}_T(l)$ in terms of $\hat{w}_T(1)$, $\hat{w}_T(2)$, ..., for a third-order homogeneous nonstationary process; i.e., derive the equivalent of Eq. (18.39) for an ARIMA model with $d = 3$.

18.6 Does it seem reasonable that for any ARIMA specification the forecast error variance one period ahead is always the variance of the error term? Offer an intuitive explanation for why Eq. (18.43) must always hold.

18.7 Derive expressions for the one-, two-, and three-period forecasts, $\hat{y}_T(1)$, $\hat{y}_T(2)$, and $\hat{y}_T(3)$, for the second-order moving average process MA(2). What are the variances of the errors for these forecasts? What is the variance of the error for the l-period forecast, with $l > 3$?

18.8 Derive expressions for the one-, two-, and three-period forecasts for the second-order autoregressive process AR(2). What are the error variances of these forecasts?

18.9 Repeat Exercise 18.8 for the ARMA(2, 1) process.

18.10 Suppose a particular nonstationary time series y_t can be modeled as a stochastic process that is ARIMA(1, 1, 1).

(a) After you have estimated the model's parameters, how would you forecast y_t one period ahead? Express this one-period forecast, $\hat{y}_t(1)$, as a function of observable data. In what sense is this forecast adaptive?

(b) How would you calculate the standard error of the one-period forecast $\hat{y}_t(1)$ *assuming that the parameters of the model are known perfectly*? Note that this is analogous to calculating the standard error of a regression forecast under the assumption that the coefficients β are known perfectly.

(c) What will be the *difference* between the *l*-period forecast $\hat{y}_t(l)$ and the $(l + 1)$-period forecast $\hat{y}_t$ $(l + 1)$ *when l is very large?*

18.11 In Exercise 18.4 we asked you to estimate alternative ARIMA models for the 3-month Treasury bill rate. Now use your models to generate forecasts comparable to those in Example 18.3. Have you been able to construct a model whose forecasting performance is better?

CHAPTER 19

APPLICATIONS OF TIME-SERIES MODELS

We have seen that econometric model building is in part an art. Even with a simple single-equation model one must make judgments about which explanatory variables to include, the functional form for the equation, how the statistical fit of the model should be interpreted, and how useful the resulting model is for forecasting or explanatory purposes. The situation is much the same with time-series models. It is usually not obvious what the proper specification for an ARIMA model should be. Many different specifications may be reasonable for a single time series and its autocorrelation function, so that sound judgment must be used together with a certain amount of experimentation. As in the regression case, one will often specify and estimate more than one ARIMA model and check each one individually. In general, the usefulness of an ARIMA model for forecasting purposes is difficult to ascertain. While confidence intervals can be determined for a model's forecasts, one still must decide whether any significant structural change in the determination of the variable under study might occur and thus alter the future movement of the time series.

In this chapter we present several examples of the construction and use of time-series models. We hope that these examples will help convey a better understanding of the modeling process and acquaint the reader with the usefulness of time-series models in applied forecasting problems. We will see that time-series models can be used in forecasting applications not only by themselves but also in combination with regression models.

We will begin with a model for an aggregate economic variable—nonfarm inventory investment—and then turn to a model for forecasting seasonal telephone data. One might argue that inventory investment can be better explained by a structural econometric model, but such a model can be difficult and time-consuming to build. The seasonal telephone data we examine are cyclical, highly fluctuating, and difficult to explain using a structural econometric model, so that a time-series model provides a natural vehicle for forecasting.

As a final application we show in two examples how it is possible to combine a time-series model with a structural econometric model. To do so, we first construct a regression model and then develop a time-series model for the regression residuals (i.e., for the unexplained noise). This combined regression–time-series model is sometimes called a *transfer function* model, and if it is used properly, it can be a very effective forecasting tool.

19.1   REVIEW OF THE MODELING PROCESS

We begin by briefly reviewing the steps involved in the construction, evaluation, and use of time-series models. One begins with a model *specification*. This first requires a decision about the degree of homogeneity in the time series, i.e., how many times it must be differenced to yield a stationary series. This decision is made by looking at the autocorrelation functions for the series and its differences. (We have seen, however, that the degree of homogeneity is not always obvious.) Then the order of the moving average and autoregressive parts of the model must be determined. One can get some guidance from the total and partial sample autocorrelation functions, but often the correct choice is not clear and several alternative specifications must be estimated.

Once a model (or a group of models) has been specified, it must be *estimated*. If the number of observations in the time series is large relative to the order of the model, this estimation process involves a straightforward nonlinear regression. Afterward, one performs a *diagnostic check.* This involves looking at the autocorrelation function of the residuals from the estimated model. A simple chi-square test can be performed to determine whether the residuals are themselves uncorrelated. In addition, one should check that the parameter estimates are consistent with *stationarity*, e.g., that the autoregressive parameters sum to a number smaller than 1 in magnitude.

The model must then be *evaluated* to determine its ability to forecast accurately and to provide a better understanding of its forecasting properties. For example, the model may pass a diagnostic check but have a very poor statistical fit, and this will limit its usefulness for forecasting. If the model's estimated parameters have large standard errors, the standard error of forecast will be large.

One means of model evaluation and analysis is to perform a *historical simulation* beginning at different points in time. One can then examine statistics such as the rms simulation error and the Theil inequality coefficient and its decomposition. (See Chapters 8 and 13 for a review of these and other model evaluation statistics.) In addition, one can perform an *ex post forecast*, comparing the forecast to actual data to evaluate its performance. This can help one decide how far into the future the model can be used for forecasting. This is particularly important if a time-series model is to be used in conjunction with a structural econometric model. Typically, the time-series model will provide a better forecast over the very short term but the structural econometric model will provide a better forecast over the longer term.

19.2 MODELS OF ECONOMIC VARIABLES: INVENTORY INVESTMENT

In this section we construct and examine some time-series models for the level of real (1987 constant dollar) nonfarm inventory investment. This variable is difficult to explain and forecast using structural econometric models, and so the construction of an ARIMA model seems appropriate.

Our sample consists of quarterly data from the first quarter of 1960 through the last quarter of 1995. However, to evaluate the forecasting performance of our ARIMA models, we will estimate the models using data only through the last quarter of 1994. The time series is shown in Fig. 16.3, and its sample autocorrelation function is shown in Fig. 16.4. When we examined the series and its autocorrelation function in Chapter 16, we noted that the sample autocorrelation function exhibits the properties of a stationary series. (After a displacement lag k of 3, it quickly falls toward zero.) Also, the series itself seems to be stationary since there are no long-run trends either upward or downward.

Nonetheless, as a check we also difference the series once. The differenced series and its sample autocorrelation function are shown in Figs. 19.1 and 19.2. Note that the autocorrelation function drops immediately to about $-.25$, rises

FIGURE 19.1
Inventory investment: first differences (in 1987 constant dollars).

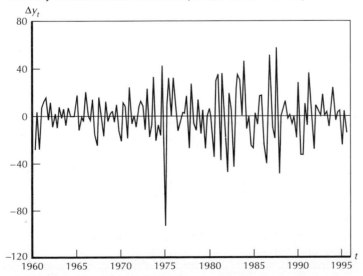

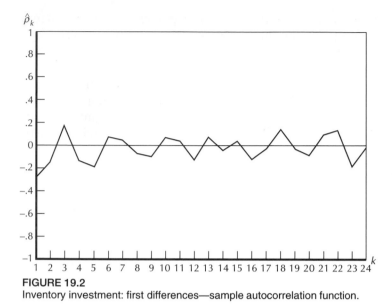

FIGURE 19.2
Inventory investment: first differences—sample autocorrelation function.

to .2, and then oscillates between values of roughly $\pm.1$. There is little in the way of a pattern here, making it difficult to specify an ARIMA model. It seems reasonable to assume that our series is stationary, i.e., to specify and estimate ARIMA $(p, 0, q)$ models.

In Example 17.1 we examined the partial autocorrelation function for this inventory investment series. We noted that the partial autocorrelations became small after four lags, suggesting that the autoregressive component of the ARIMA model could be limited to fourth-order. The fact that the sample auto-correlation function also becomes small by $k = 3$ or 4 suggests that any moving average terms should also be of low order. We therefore begin by estimating the following three specifications: ARIMA(2, 0, 2), ARIMA(4, 0, 0), and ARIMA(4, 0, 2). The results are as follows:

ARIMA(2, 0, 2):
$$(1 + .2432B - .5639B^2)y_t = 21.485 + (1 + .8187B - .1695B^2)\varepsilon_t \quad (19.1)$$

$$R^2 = .335 \quad \chi^2(4, 24) = 27.12$$

ARIMA(4, 0, 0):
$$(1 - .5191B - .0157B^2 - .1994B^3 + .2289B^4)y_t = 21.985 + \varepsilon_t \quad (19.2)$$

$$R^2 = .334 \qquad \chi^2(4, 24) = 26.89$$

ARIMA(4, 0, 2):
$$(1 - .4910B + .7799B^2 - .5565B^3 + .1071B^4)y_t =$$
$$22.349 + (1 + .0332B + .9796B^2)\varepsilon_t \qquad (19.3)$$

$$R^2 = .393 \qquad \chi^2(6, 24) = 15.09$$

All these chi-square statistics (with 20, 20, and 18 degrees of freedom, respectively) are insignificant at the 90 percent level, allowing us in each case to accept the hypothesis that the residuals are white noise. It is clear that inventory investment can be described by a low-order ARIMA model. The ARIMA(4, 0, 2) model seems to be the most promising because it has a much lower chi-square statistic than do the other two models, even after adjusting for degrees of freedom. Nonetheless, it is useful to explore whether adding more AR and MA terms to the model can improve its fit. Hence, we also estimated ARIMA(4, 0, 4) and ARIMA(6, 0, 4) models.

ARIMA(4, 0, 4):

$$(1 - 1.1077B + .6858B^2 - .8389B^3 + .4214B^4)y_t =$$
$$21.586 + (1 - .6239B + .4020B^2 - .5130B^3 - .2412B^4)\varepsilon_t \quad (19.4)$$

$$R^2 = .405 \qquad \chi^2(8, 24) = 16.05$$

ARIMA(6, 0, 4)

$$(1 - .4356B - .0922B^2 - .1927B^3 - .5020B^4 + .4587B^5 + .0419B^6)y_t =$$
$$21.536 + (1 + .0480B + .0064B^2 - .0474B^3 - .9541B^4)\varepsilon_t \quad (19.5)$$

$$R^2 = .455 \qquad \chi^2(10, 24) = 9.87$$

While the ARIMA(4, 0, 4) model does not differ much from the ARIMA(4, 0, 2) model, the ARIMA(6, 0, 4) model has a substantially better fit. The R^2 has increased by about .05, and more important, the chi-square statistic has fallen considerably, even after adjusting for degrees of freedom. Figure 19.3 shows the actual and fitted series, along with the residuals, for this model. The model does not capture the extent of the inventory downturns during the recessions of 1975, 1980, and 1982, but otherwise the fit is good, and the residuals show

FIGURE 19.3
Actual, fitted, and residuals for ARIMA(6, 0, 4) model.

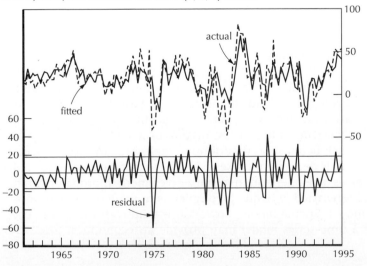

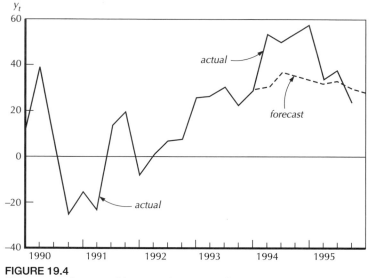

FIGURE 19.4
Eight-quarter forecast of inventory investment: forecast versus actual.

no apparent serial correlation or heteroscedasticity. Hence, we will use the ARIMA(6, 0, 4) model to forecast inventory investment.

We first generate an eight-quarter forecast for 1994 and 1995. The forecasted and actual series are shown in Fig. 19.4. Although the forecast follows the overall trend in inventory investment, it does not capture the sharp increase that occurred during 1994. Might a shorter forecast perform better? Figure 19.5 shows a five-quarter forecast for 1995 and the first quarter of 1996. In this case the forecasted series closely replicates the drop in inventory investment that actually occurred in 1995.

Finally, Fig. 19.6 shows an *ex ante* forecast that extends from 1996-1 to 1997-4. Note that the forecast is close to the mean value of inventory investment during the estimation period and shows little fluctuation. We leave it to the reader to determine the accuracy of this forecast.

The inability of our ARIMA model to predict sharp downturns and upturns in inventory investment limits its value for forecasting. However, before it is discarded as a forecasting tool, it must be compared with the alternative forecasting tools that are available. Many single- and multi-equation regression models have been constructed to forecast inventory investment, some with a performance not much better than that of our simple ARIMA model. Because inventory investment is dependent on several other macroeconomic variables, which are themselves dependent on inventory investment, it probably can best be explained and forecasted by using a complete simultaneous-equation macroeconometric model. Such a model, however, is time-consuming and costly to build, so that a time-series model may provide an economical forecasting alternative.

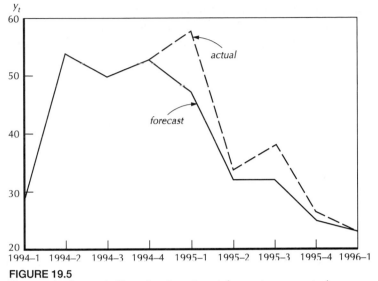

FIGURE 19.5
Five-quarter forecast of inventory investment: forecast versus actual.

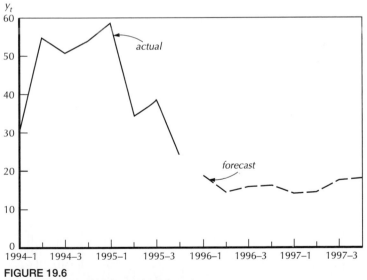

FIGURE 19.6
Ex ante forecast of inventory investment.

19.3   FORECASTING SEASONAL TELEPHONE DATA

An article by Thompson and Tiao provides another interesting case study of
time-series analysis.[1] In the study, forecasting models were constructed for the

---

[1] H. E. Thompson and G. C. Tiao, "Analysis of Telephone Data: A Case Study of Forecasting
Seasonal Time Series." *Bell Journal of Economics and Management Science*, vol. 2, no. 2, Autumn 1971.

inward and outward station movements of the Wisconsin Telephone Company, using monthly data from January 1951 to October 1966. The inward station movement in a given month is the sum of residence and business telephone installations, while the outward station movement consists of removals and disconnects of telephones. It is important to the telephone company to obtain reasonably accurate forecasts of station movements, since these forecasts are used as fundamental inputs to both short- and long-term company planning. The difference between inward and outward station movements represents the net increase (or decrease) of telephones in service, so that an expected positive difference would lead to a sequence of capital expenditures. Underestimating the difference might create a shortage in the supply of telephones and associated facilities, while overestimating it would result in a premature expansion of facilities and thus result in added cost to the company.

The data used by Thompson and Tiao for inward and outward station movements are shown in Figs. 19.7 and 19.8. The data show a very distinct seasonal pattern, with a peak and a trough reached each year. Note that the *level* of each series tends to increase over time *and that the variance of the data tends to increase as the level increases.* To reduce this dependence of the variance on the level, the authors applied a logarithmic transformation to both series. Thus, the analysis that follows is given in terms of transformed logarithmic data. (Logarithmic transformations often are used in time-series analysis as a means of removing growth over time in the variance of the data.)

Time-series models can easily be constructed to account for seasonality; in fact, we treated seasonality earlier when we constructed a time-series model for hog production. It is reasonable to expect a seasonal pattern in station movements, i.e., similarities in observations of the same month in different years. Thus, we would expect observations 12 periods apart to be highly cor-

FIGURE 19.7
Monthly inward station movements, January 1951 to October 1966.

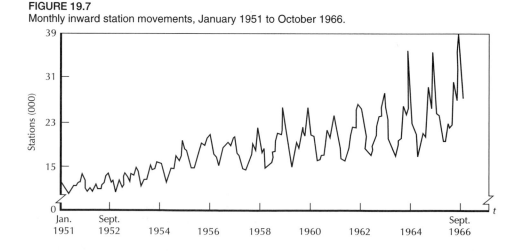

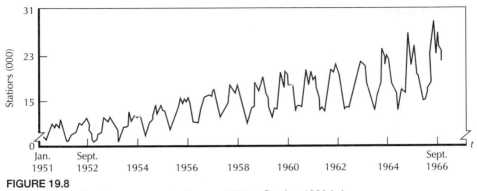

FIGURE 19.8
Monthly outward station movements, January 1951 to October 1966 (y_t).

related (as in our hog production example). We can express this seasonal relationship with the simple autoregressive model

$$(1 - \phi^* B^{12})y_t = e_t \tag{19.6}$$

where e_t is a random shock. While this equation explains the dependence of observations between years, observations in successive months also may be dependent. This dependence may be represented by a second autoregressive model:

$$(1 - \phi B)e_t = \varepsilon_t \tag{19.7}$$

where ε_t is a random shock. Equation (19.6) can be substituted into Eq. (19.7) to eliminate e_t:

$$(1 - \phi^* B^{12})(1 - \phi B)y_t = \varepsilon_t \tag{19.8}$$

or

$$y_t - \phi y_{t-1} - \phi^* y_{t-12} + \phi \phi^* y_{t-13} = \varepsilon_t \tag{19.9}$$

Equation (19.9) is a simple autoregressive model. It serves to describe, however, both seasonal and nonseasonal dependence between observations.[2]

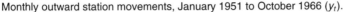

[2] This equation can be generalized to yield a class of models for seasonal series:

$$\phi_{p1}^*(B^{12})\phi_p(B)(1 - B^{12})^{d_1}(1 - B)^d(y_t - \mu) = \theta_q(B)\varepsilon_t$$

where $\phi_{p1}^*(B^{12})$ is a polynomial in B^{12} of order p_1 and $\phi_p(B)$ is a polynomial of order p. The parameters $\phi_1^*, \ldots, \phi_{p1}^*$ can be called seasonal autoregressive parameters. In the preliminary model-building stage particular attention is given to peaks in the sample autocorrelation functions which occur at multiples of 12 lags. Generally, differencing 12 periods apart (one or more times) is needed when ρ_k is persistently large for $k - 12, 24, 36, \ldots$.

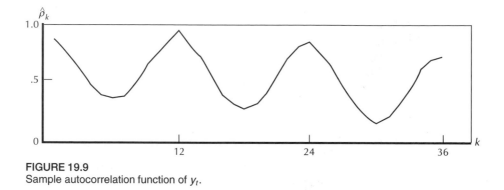

FIGURE 19.9
Sample autocorrelation function of y_t.

In this case we present Thompson and Tiao's model of the *logarithmic outward series*. (Readers interested in the rest of their results may refer to the original paper.) We represent the logarithm of monthly outward station movements by the variable y_t. The sample autocorrelation function of y_t is shown in Fig. 19.9. Note that this autocorrelation function peaks at $k = 12$, 24, and 36; this is not surprising in view of the seasonal pattern in the data. We thus calculate 12-period differences in the series and call this new series w_t:

$$w_t = (1 - B^{12})y_t \tag{19.10}$$

The sample autocorrelation function for w_t is shown in Fig. 19.10. Note that the seasonal dependence between years has been removed and that the magnitude of the autocorrelations has been dampened considerably. Also, note that this autocorrelation function has peaks at every third lag, thus suggesting the autoregressive model[3]

$$(1 - \phi_3 B^3)w_t = \varepsilon_t \tag{19.11}$$

Thompson and Tiao fitted a third-order autoregressive model to the series w_t and then calculated the autocorrelation function for the residuals of this model. They found peaks at $k = 9$, 12, and 13, suggesting the addition of three moving average parameters. Thus, their final ARIMA model for y_t was of the form

$$(1 - \phi_3 B^3)(1 - \phi_{12}B^{12})y_t = (1 - \theta_9 B^9 - \theta_{12}B^{12} - \theta_{13}B^{13})\varepsilon_t \tag{19.12}$$

---

[3] Cycles every third period also could be generated by a second-order autoregressive model (with the proper parameter values). The authors may have tested a second-order model and found Eq. (19.11) to be preferable. In general, however, if a distinct peak occurs in the autocorrelation function at every nth lag, we suggest including an nth-order autoregressive term in the specification of the ARIMA model.

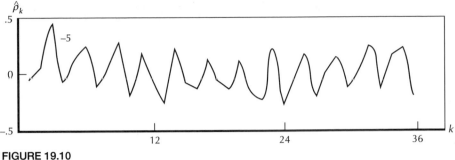

FIGURE 19.10
Sample autocorrelation function for w_t.

The five parameters ϕ_3, ϕ_{12}, θ_9, θ_{12}, and θ_{13} were estimated, and the resulting model was used to forecast the logarithmic outward series for the 36 months from November 1966 to October 1969. The forecast, together with the 95 percent confidence interval, is shown in Fig. 19.11.

Note that the model does a rather good job of forecasting outward station movements, even over a period of 36 months. In fact, it seems to perform considerably better than did our models of inventory investment. The reason for this is that the telephone data used in Thompson and Tiao's study were particularly amenable to time-series analysis. Time-series analysis works best when a persistent pattern (seasonal or otherwise) exists in the data, and such a pattern is present in the telephone data.

FIGURE 19.11
Forecasts of log outward series for the 36 months, November 1966 to October 1969, made in October 1966.

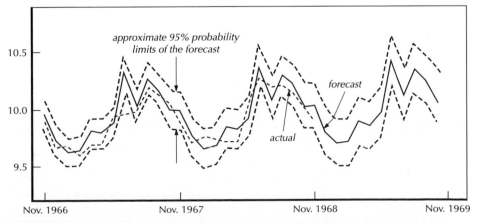

19.4 COMBINING REGRESSION ANALYSIS WITH A TIME-SERIES MODEL: TRANSFER FUNCTION MODELS

In Chapter 18 we estimated a time-series model for a short-term interest rate. Although we used the model to produce a forecast, we suggested that a better forecast could have been obtained by using a single-equation structural regression model (as in Chapter 8). In fact, time-series analysis and regression analysis can be combined to produce a better forecast than would be possible with the use of either of these techniques alone.

Suppose we would like to forecast the variable y_t by using a regression model. Presumably, such a model would include those independent variables which can explain movements in y_t but are not themselves collinear. Suppose our regression model contains two independent variables, x_1 and x_2, as follows:

$$y_t = a_0 + a_1 x_{1t} + a_2 x_{2t} + \varepsilon_t \tag{19.13}$$

This equation has an additive error term that accounts for *unexplained* variance in y_t; that is, it accounts for that part of the variance of y_t which is not explained by x_1 and x_2. The equation can be estimated, and an R^2 will result which (unless by some chance y_t is perfectly correlated with the independent variables) will be less than 1. The equation can then be used to forecast y_t. As we saw in Chapter 8, one source of forecast error would come from the additive noise term whose future values cannot be predicted.

One effective application of time-series analysis is to construct an ARIMA model for the residual series u_t of this regression. We would then substitute the ARIMA model for the implicit error term in the original regression equation. In using the equation to forecast y_t, we would also be able to make a forecast of the error term ε_t using the ARIMA model. The ARIMA model provides some information about what future values of ε_t are likely to be; i.e., it helps "explain" the unexplained variance in the regression equation. The combined regression–time-series model is

$$y_t = a_0 + a_1 x_{1t} + a_2 x_{2t} + \phi^{-1}(B)\theta(B)\eta_t \tag{19.14}$$

where η_t is a normally distributed error term which may have a different variance from ε_t. This model is likely to provide better forecasts than would the regression equation in Eq. (19.13) alone or a time-series model alone since it includes both a structural (economic) explanation of that part of the variance of y_t which can be explained structurally and a time-series "explanation" of that part of the variance of y_t which cannot be explained structurally.

Equation (19.14) is an example of what is sometimes referred to as a *transfer function model* or, alternatively, a *multivariate autoregressive–moving average model* (MARMA model). A transfer function model relates a dependent variable to lagged values of itself, current and lagged values of one or more independent variables, and an error term which is partially "explained" by a time-series model. Thus, the general form for a univariate (only one independent variable) transfer function model can be written as

$$y_t = \nu^{-1}(B)\omega(B)x_t + \phi^{-1}(B)\theta(B)\eta_t \tag{19.15}$$

The technique of transfer function modeling involves examination of partial and total autocorrelation functions for the independent variable x_t as well as the dependent variable y_t in an effort to specify the lag polynomials $\nu(B)$, $\omega(B)$, $\phi(B)$, and $\theta(B)$.[4] One problem with the technique, however, is that the specification of the structural part of the model, i.e., the polynomials $\nu(B)$ and $\omega(B)$, is done mechanically rather than by appeal to economic theory and logic. Structural models that are consistent with intuition and economic theory usually are more reliable (and defensible) than models in which the structure is arrived at mechanically. For this reason we suggest that when models of the form of Eq. (19.15) are used that the structural part of the model be arrived at through the mixture of economic theory and econometric method discussed in Part One, while the time-series part of the model, that is, $\phi(B)$ and $\theta(B)$, be arrived at through an analysis of the residuals of the structural model.

Let us now turn back to the simple model of Eq. (19.14). First, note that specifying a time-series model for the error term is just a generalization of the technique described in Chapter 8 for forecasting with regression models that have serially correlated errors. [If the time-series model is AR(1), it is exactly equivalent to forecasting with first-order serially correlated errors.] Second, note that the parameters a_0, a_1, and a_2 of the structural regression equation and the parameters $\phi_1, \ldots, \phi_p$ and $\theta_1, \ldots, \theta_q$ of the time-series model should be estimated *simultaneously*. (Failure to estimate all the parameters simultaneously can lead to a loss of efficiency.) Unfortunately, the simultaneous estimation of all the parameters is sometimes computationally difficult and in such cases is often not done.

This combined use of regression analysis with a time-series model of the error term is an approach to forecasting that in some cases can provide the best of both worlds. To demonstrate the technique and its use, we turn to two examples.

19.5 A COMBINED REGRESSION–TIME-SERIES MODEL TO FORECAST SHORT-TERM SAVINGS DEPOSIT FLOWS

Our first example that combines time-series analysis with regression analysis is based on a study by Ludwig[5] to forecast the monthly flow of deposits into

[4] The techniques are discussed in detail in G. E. P. Box and G. M. Jenkins, *Time Series Analysis* (San Francisco: Holden-Day, 1970), Chapters 10 and 11, and generally C. W. J. Granger and P. Newbold, *Forecasting Economic Time Series*, 2d ed. (New York: Academic Press, 1986).

[5] R. S. Ludwig, "Forecasting Short-Term Savings Deposit Flows: An Application of Time Series Models and a Regional Analysis," unpublished master's thesis, Sloan School of Management, M.I.T., June 1974.

Massachusetts mutual savings banks. A regression model is first constructed (to explain deposit flows), and then a time-series model is developed to "explain" the residual series (i.e., the error term) in the regression equation.[6]

We begin with a regression equation that provides a structural explanation of mutual savings deposit flows. Ludwig used the ratio of deposit flows S to personal wealth W as the dependent variable, and he chose monthly Massachusetts personal income as a proxy variable for wealth. His best regression equation had three explanatory variables: the effective percentage return (including dividends) on mutual savings deposits r_{ms}, the interest rate on 3-month Treasury bills r_m, and the ratio of the previous month's stock of mutual savings deposits A_{-1} to the wealth variable. His equation, estimated using monthly data for the state of Massachusetts over the period February 1968 to June 1973, is

$$\frac{S}{W} = \underset{(1.89)}{.16} + \underset{(2.98)}{.019 r_{ms}} - \underset{(-5.27)}{.011 r_m} - \underset{(-2.23)}{.032} \frac{A_{-1}}{W} \tag{19.16}$$

$$R^2 = .41 \qquad SER = .016 \qquad F = 14.42 \qquad DW = 1.55$$

As one would expect, there is a positive relationship between savings deposit flows and the effective percentage return on deposits. The interest rate on 3-month Treasury bills, used as a market rate of interest, represents the return on competing risk-free investment alternatives for savings and thus should have a negative impact on savings deposit flows. Finally, the negative relationship between deposit flows and the stock of deposits represents a stock adjustment effect; savings deposits should be proportional to that part of personal wealth which has not already been placed in a savings bank; i.e.,

$$S_t = A_t - A_{t-1} = a(W_t - A_{t-1}) \tag{19.17}$$

so that

$$\frac{S_t}{W_t} = a - a\frac{A_{t-1}}{W_t} \tag{19.18}$$

A historical simulation of Eq. (19.16) is shown in Fig. 19.12, and an *ex post* forecast over the period July 1973 to October 1973 is shown in Fig. 19.13. The historical simulation has an rms *percent* error of 75.1, and the *ex post* forecast has an rms percent error of 157. Observe that the simulation tracks the general movement of the series but leaves much of the variance unexplained. The regression model does well in forecasting deposit flows in July 1973 but fails to capture the sharp drop in deposits in August of that year.

Let us now try to improve the forecast by constructing a time-series model

---

[6] At the time this study was done, simultaneous estimation of the regression and time-series parameters was computationally difficult and so was not performed.

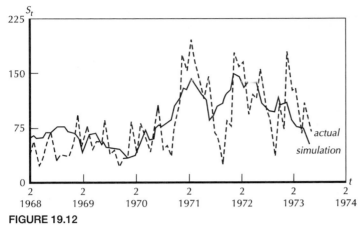

FIGURE 19.12
Historical simulation of Eq. (19.16) for deposit flows.

for the residual series of the regression equation. The sample autocorrelation function for the residual series is shown in Fig. 19.14. Observe that high-order correlations dampen toward 0, so that the residual series can be considered stationary. The autocorrelation function does, however, contain peaks at monthly lags which are multiples of 12, indicating annual seasonality. Figure 19.15 shows the sample autocorrelation function for a 12-month difference of the original residual series, i.e., for the series $(1 - B^{12})u_t$. This autocorrelation function has a dampened sinusoidal shape which is indicative of a purely autoregressive process of order 2 or greater.

Ludwig estimated a variety of autoregressive models for this residual series and found the best one to be

$$(1 - \phi_{12}B^{12})(1 - \phi_1 B - \phi_2 B^2 - \phi_3 B^3 - \phi_4 B^4 - \phi_5 B^5 - \phi_6 B^6)u_t = \eta_t$$

FIGURE 19.13
Ex post forecast of deposit flows.

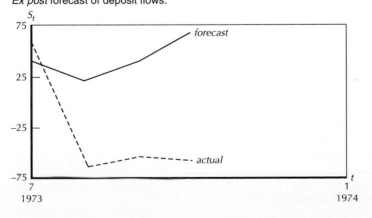

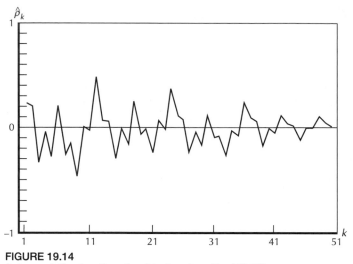

FIGURE 19.14
Autocorrelation function of residuals u_t from Eq. (19.16).

which in its expanded and estimated form is

$$(1 - .736B - .025B^2 - .055B^3 - .009B^4 + .310B^5 - .128B^6 - .782B^{12}$$
$$+ .532B^{13} + .081B^{14} + .125B^{15} - .213B^{16} - .103B^{17} - .060B^{18})u_t = \eta_t$$

$$(19.19)$$

$$R^2 = .78 \qquad \chi^2 = 14.5$$

FIGURE 19.15
Autocorrelation function of 12-month difference of residuals $(1 - B^{12})u_t$.

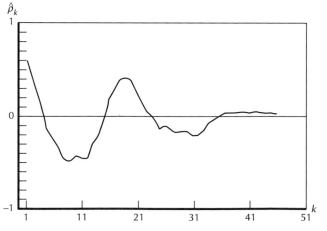

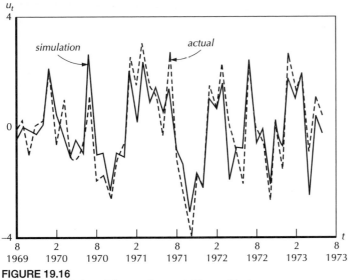

FIGURE 19.16
Historical simulation of time-series model for residuals.

A historical simulation of the time-series model alone is shown in Fig. 19.16. Observe that the residual series is reproduced closely.

Now the time-series model for the residual series can be combined with the regression model of Eq. (19.16). A historical simulation of the combined regression–time-series model is shown in Fig. 19.17. Note that savings deposits are tracked much more closely than before. Indeed, the rms percent error has been reduced by a factor of more than 3, to 29.3.

FIGURE 19.17
Historical simulation of combined regression—time-series model for savings deposit flows.

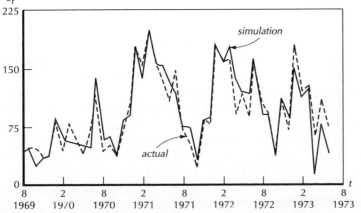

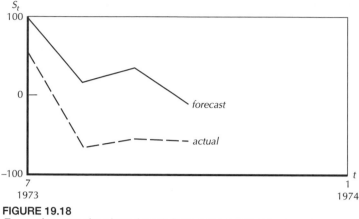

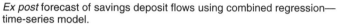

FIGURE 19.18
Ex post forecast of savings deposit flows using combined regression—
time-series model.

Finally, an *ex post* forecast of savings flows is made using the combined regression–time-series model, again for the 4-month period July 1973 to October 1973. This forecast, which is shown in Fig. 19.18, is closer to the actual data than was the case when the regression model alone was used. (The rms percent error has been reduced from 157 to 118.) Although the forecast does not capture the extent of the downturn in savings deposit flows in August 1973, it does capture general movements in the variable.

19.6 A COMBINED REGRESSION–TIME-SERIES MODEL TO FORECAST INTEREST RATES

As a second example of the combined use of regression analysis with time-series models, we construct a model to forecast, on a monthly basis, the interest rate on 3-month Treasury bills. We will start with a regression model that explains the interest rate as a function of industrial production, inflation, and the rate of growth of the money supply. We will then examine the residuals of that model and fit an ARIMA model to them. Finally, we will reestimate all the parameters of the combined regression–time-series model simultaneously (a step that we did not take in the previous example).

We begin with the interest rate regression we developed in Example 8.2. Recall that in that regression we related the 3-month Treasury bill rate (R3) to the index of industrial production (IP), the rate of growth of the broadly defined money supply M2 [$GM2_t = (M2_t - M2_{t-1})/M2_{t-1}$], and the lagged rate of wholesale price inflation $GPW = (PW_t - PW_{t-1})/PW_{t-1}$, where PW is the Producer Price Index for all commodities. The OLS estimates of this equation, using data for the period January 1960 through August 1995, are as follows (*t* statistics in parentheses):

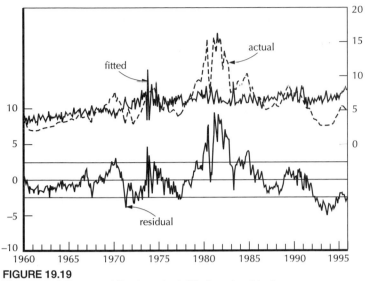

FIGURE 19.19
Three-month Treasury bill rate: actual, fitted, and residuals.

$$R3_t = 1.2141 + .0484IP_t + 140.33GM2_t + 104.59GPW_{t-1} \quad (19.20)$$
$$(2.20) \quad (8.79) \quad (3.89) \quad (6.00)$$

$$R^2 = .216 \quad s = 2.481 \quad F = 39.02 \quad DW = 0.18$$

Figure 19.19 shows the actual and fitted series, together with the regression residuals. Note that the residuals appear to have a high degree of autocorrelation; this is not surprising given the very low Durbin-Watson statistic. (Indeed, we found in Example 8.3 that we could significantly improve the forecasting performance of this regression equation by accounting for first-order serial correlation.) Also note that the model fits the data reasonably well during the 1960s and 1970s but performs poorly during the early 1980s and 1990s.

Let us now examine the residuals from this regression. Figure 19.20 shows the sample autocorrelation function for the residuals, which decline steadily toward zero, indicative of a stationary series. Figure 19.21 shows the sample autocorrelation function for the residuals after they have been first-differenced; now all the autocorrelations are close to zero. We will work with the undifferenced residuals.

After some experimenting, we fit the following ARIMA(8, 0, 2) model to the series of residuals, which we denote by u_t:

$$(1 - .9089B + .623B^2 - .4769B^3 + .0854B^4 - .2488B^5 + .1780B^6$$
$$- .0494B^7 - .1410B^8)u_t = -.1411 + (1 - .1981B + .6076B^2)\eta_t \quad (19.21)$$

$$R^2 = .846 \quad \chi^2(10, 36) = 32.22$$

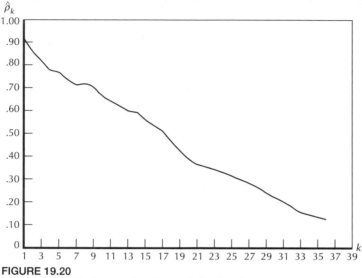

$\hat{\rho}_k$

FIGURE 19.20
Regression residuals: sample autocorrelation function.

With $36 - 10 = 26$ degrees of freedom, the chi-square statistic is insignificant at the 90 percent level, so that we can accept the hypothesis that the residuals of this ARIMA model are white noise.

We now have an ARIMA specification for the residuals which seems to fit well. However, rather than use this ARIMA model together with the regression model as they stand, we combine the two and reestimate all the parameters

FIGURE 19.21
First differences of regression residuals: sample autocorrelation function.

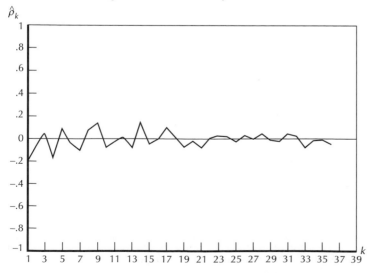

$\hat{\rho}_k$

simultaneously. In other words, we estimate the parameters of the following model:

$$R3_t = a_0 + a_1 IP_t + a_2 GM2_t + a_3 GPW_{t-1} + \phi^{-1}(B)\theta(B)\eta_t \quad (19.22)$$

where $\phi(B) = 1 - \phi_1 B - \phi_2 B^2 - \cdots - \phi_8 B^8$ and $\theta(B) = 1 - \theta_1 B - \theta_2 B^2$. The results of this estimation are as follows:

$$R3_t = -29.565 + .1927 IP_t - 40.29 GM2_t + 6.788 GPW_{t-1}$$
$$ (-0.42) \qquad (5.05) \qquad (-4.50) \qquad (2.89)$$

$$+\{(1 - .8395B + .4988B^2)/(1 - 2.090B + 2.021B^2 - 1.296B^3$$

$$+ .6119B^4 - .4395B^5 + .5198B^6 - .4934B^7 + .1670B^8)\}\eta_t \quad (19.23)$$

$$R^2 = .9729 \qquad s = 0.467 \qquad F = 1142.2 \qquad DW = 2.01$$

Note that the R^2 is now much higher and that the DW is very close to 2. The sample autocorrelations for the residuals of this equation (not shown here) are all very close to zero, so that the residuals appear to be white noise.

Figure 19.22 shows the fitted and actual interest rate series as well as the residuals. Unlike the simple regression model we started with, the fit of this equation is excellent throughout the sample period, and the residuals exhibit no autocorrelation.[7]

FIGURE 19.22
Combined regression–time-series model: actual, fitted, and residuals.

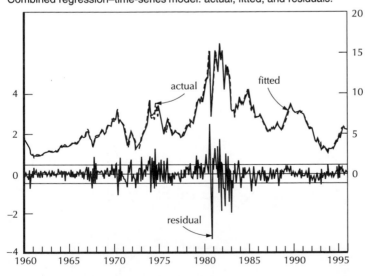

---

[7] The residuals do, however, exhibit conditional autoregressive heteroscedasticity. One could correct for this by including an ARCH or GARCH specification for the errors, as was discussed in Chapter 10. We have chosen not to do so to keep this example simple.

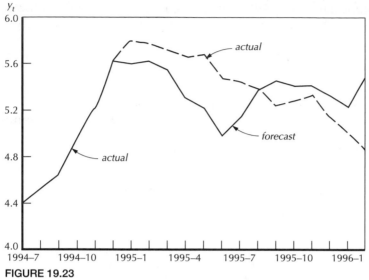

FIGURE 19.23
Combined regression–time-series model: 14-month forecast.

Figure 19.23 shows a forecast of the interest rate for the 14-month period January 1995 through February 1996. (Note that the first 8 months of this forecast include the sample period used in the estimation, while the remaining 6 months do not.) The forecasted values of the interest rate generally are close to the actual values. Finally, Fig. 19.24 shows an out-of-sample 6-month fore-

FIGURE 19.24
Combined regression–time-series model: 6-month forecast.

cast for the period September 1995 through February 1996. Note that the forecasted series tracks the actual series until the last 2 months, when it diverges significantly.

EXERCISE

19.1 The data for nonfarm inventory investment are reproduced in Table 19.1.

(a) Try to develop an ARIMA model that improves on the forecasting performance of the one presented in Section 19.2.

(b) Develop your own combined regression–time-series model of inventory investment. Can you improve on the forecasting performance of the pure ARIMA model?

TABLE 19.1
REAL NONFARM INVENTORY INVESTMENT

Obs.					Obs.				
1960	34.60	6.90	10.80	−17.10	1978	48.30	42.80	30.30	44.20
1961	−10.20	2.30	18.10	14.50	1979	28.80	34.40	7.20	6.60
1962	26.30	17.00	19.70	9.30	1980	13.20	6.80	−27.90	1.90
1963	17.00	14.90	21.20	12.70	1981	37.40	−0.20	35.90	18.30
1964	19.60	19.30	18.70	20.30	1982	−29.00	−9.60	−4.90	−47.90
1965	38.20	26.00	25.60	21.10	1983	−29.70	5.30	35.90	36.90
1966	41.40	43.60	39.70	53.90	1984	83.50	72.50	72.60	47.80
1967	39.90	15.00	30.80	32.50	1985	20.70	23.50	16.10	32.90
1968	15.40	27.70	23.00	25.60	1986	50.50	27.60	−12.70	−15.60
1969	29.70	24.30	33.90	21.40	1987	36.30	27.40	7.70	65.60
1970	0.40	11.60	19.80	1.20	1988	16.80	17.70	25.50	38.80
1971	25.50	18.70	18.80	9.10	1989	36.20	37.80	30.40	29.60
1972	14.40	27.40	35.80	24.00	1990	10.90	39.20	6.70	−25.90
1973	47.00	29.20	22.20	55.60	1991	−15.00	−23.40	13.60	19.90
1974	35.00	27.70	11.00	53.70	1992	−7.80	1.50	6.80	7.20
1975	−39.50	−32.80	−0.70	−1.10	1993	26.00	26.70	30.90	22.10
1976	31.10	42.50	29.90	25.00	1994	29.80	54.10	50.10	53.30
1977	28.40	30.30	47.50	20.70	1995	58.10	33.80	38.30	23.60

Source: Citibase, Series GVUQ.

STATISTICAL TABLES

TABLE 1
STANDARDIZED NORMAL DISTRIBUTION

z	.00	.01	.02	.03	.04	.05	.06	.07	.08	.09
.0	.5000	.4960	.4920	.4880	.4840	.4801	.4761	.4721	.4681	.4641
.1	.4602	.4562	.4522	.4483	.4443	.4404	.4364	.4325	.4686	.4247
.2	.4207	.4168	.4129	.4090	.4052	.4013	.3974	.3936	.3897	.3859
.3	.3821	.3873	.3745	.3707	.3669	.3632	.3594	.3557	.3520	.3483
.4	.3446	.3409	.3372	.3336	.3300	.3264	.3228	.3192	.3156	.3121
.5	.3085	.3050	.3015	.2981	.2946	.2912	.2877	.2843	.2810	.2776
.6	.2743	.2709	.2676	.2643	.2611	.2578	.2546	.2514	.2483	.2451
.7	.2420	.2389	.2358	.2327	.2296	.2266	.2236	.2206	.2217	.2148
.8	.2119	.2090	.2061	.2033	.2005	.1977	.1949	.1922	.1894	.1867
.9	.1841	.1814	.1788	.1762	.1736	.1711	.1685	.1660	.1635	.1611
1.0	.1587	.1562	.1539	.1515	.1492	.1469	.1446	.1423	.1401	.1379
1.1	.1357	.1335	.1314	.1292	.1271	.1251	.1230	.1210	.1190	.1170
1.2	.1151	.1131	.1112	.1093	.1075	.1056	.1038	.1020	.1003	.0985
1.3	.0968	.0951	.0934	.0918	.0901	.0885	.0869	.0853	.0838	.0823
1.4	.0808	.0793	.0778	.0764	.0749	.0735	.0721	.0708	.0694	.0681
1.5	.0668	.0655	.0643	.0630	.0618	.0606	.0594	.0582	.0571	.0559
1.6	.0548	.0537	.0526	.0516	.0505	.0495	.0485	.0475	.0465	.0455
1.7	.0446	.0436	.0427	.0418	.0409	.0401	.0392	.0384	.0375	.0367
1.8	.0359	.0351	.0344	.0366	.0329	.0322	.0314	.0307	.0301	.0294
1.9	.0287	.0281	.0274	.0268	.0262	.0256	.0250	.0244	.0239	.0233
2.0	.0228	.0222	.0217	.0212	.0207	.0202	.0197	.0192	.0188	.0183
2.1	.0179	.0174	.0170	.0166	.0162	.0158	.0154	.0150	.0146	.0143
2.2	.0139	.0136	.0132	.0129	.0125	.0122	.0119	.0116	.0113	.0110
2.3	.0107	.0104	.0102	.0099	.0096	.0094	.0091	.0089	.0087	.0084
2.4	.0082	.0080	.0078	.0075	.0073	.0071	.0069	.0068	.0066	.0064
2.5	.0062	.0060	.0059	.0057	.0055	.0054	.0052	.0051	.0049	.0048
2.6	.0047	.0045	.0044	.0043	.0041	.0040	.0039	.0038	.0037	.0036
2.7	.0035	.0034	.0033	.0032	.0031	.0030	.0029	.0028	.0027	.0026
2.8	.0026	.0025	.0024	.0023	.0023	.0022	.0021	.0020	.0020	.0019
2.9	.0019	.0018	.0018	.0017	.0016	.0016	.0015	.0015	.0014	.0014
3.0	.0013	.0013	.0013	.0012	.0012	.0011	.0011	.0010	.0011	.0010

The table plots the cumulative probability $Z \geq z$.
Source: Produced from Edward J. Kane, *Economic Statistics and Econometrics: An Introduction to Quantitative Economics* (New York: Harper & Row, 1968).

TABLE 2
PERCENTILES OF THE χ^2 DISTRIBUTION

df	.5	1	2.5	5	10	Percent 90	95	97.5	99	99.5
1	.000039	.00016	.00098	.0039	.0158	2.71	3.84	5.02	6.63	7.88
2	.0100	.0201	.0506	.1026	.2107	4.61	5.99	7.38	9.21	10.60
3	.0717	.115	.216	.352	.584	6.25	7.81	9.35	11.34	12.84
4	.207	.297	.484	.711	1.064	7.78	9.49	11.14	13.28	14.86
5	.412	.554	.831	1.15	1.61	9.24	11.07	12.83	15.09	16.75
6	.676	.872	1.24	1.64	2.20	10.64	12.59	14.45	16.81	18.55
7	.989	1.24	1.69	2.17	2.83	12.02	14.07	16.01	18.48	20.28
8	1.34	1.65	2.18	2.73	3.49	13.36	15.51	17.53	20.09	21.96
9	1.73	2.09	2.70	3.33	4.17	14.68	16.92	19.02	21.67	23.59
10	2.16	2.56	3.25	3.94	4.87	15.99	18.31	20.48	23.21	25.19
11	2.60	3.05	3.82	4.57	5.58	17.28	19.68	21.92	24.73	26.76
12	3.07	3.57	4.40	5.23	6.30	18.55	21.03	23.34	26.22	28.30
13	3.57	4.11	5.01	5.89	7.04	19.81	22.36	24.74	27.69	29.82
14	4.07	4.66	5.63	6.57	7.79	21.06	23.68	26.12	29.14	31.32
15	4.60	5.23	6.26	7.26	8.55	22.31	25.00	27.49	30.58	32.80
16	5.14	5.81	6.91	7.96	9.31	23.54	26.30	28.85	32.00	34.27
18	6.26	7.01	8.23	9.39	10.86	25.99	28.87	31.53	34.81	37.16
20	7.43	8.26	9.59	10.85	12.44	28.41	31.41	34.17	37.57	40.00
24	9.89	10.86	12.40	13.85	15.66	33.20	36.42	39.36	42.98	45.56
30	13.79	14.95	16.79	18.49	20.60	40.26	43.77	47.98	50.89	53.67
40	20.71	22.16	24.43	26.51	29.05	51.81	55.76	59.34	63.69	66.77
60	35.53	37.48	40.48	43.19	46.46	74.40	79.08	83.30	88.38	91.95
120	83.85	86.92	91.58	95.70	100.62	140.23	146.57	152.21	158.95	163.64

Source: Reprinted with permission from W. J. Dixon and F. J. Massey Jr., *Introduction to Statistical Analysis,* 3d ed. (New York: McGraw-Hill, 1969).

TABLE 3
PERCENTILES OF THE t DISTRIBUTION

df	.80	.60	.40	.20	.10	.05	.02	.01
1	.325	727	1.376	3.078	6.314	12.700	31.821	63.657
2	.289	.617	1.061	1.886	2.920	4.303	6.965	9.925
3	.277	.584	.978	1.638	2.353	3.182	4.541	5.841
4	.271	.569	.941	1.533	2.132	2.776	3.747	4.604
5	.267	.559	.920	1.476	2.015	2.571	3.365	4.032
6	.265	.553	.906	1.440	1.943	2.447	3.143	3.707
7	.263	.549	.896	1.415	1.895	2.365	2.998	3.499
8	.262	.546	.889	1.397	1.860	2.306	2.896	3.355
9	.261	.543	.883	1.383	1.833	2.262	2.821	3.250
10	.260	.542	.879	1.372	1.812	2.228	2.764	3.169
11	.260	.540	.876	1.363	1.796	2.201	2.718	3.106
12	.259	.539	.873	1.356	1.782	2.179	2.681	3.055
13	.259	.538	.870	1.350	1.771	2.160	2.650	3.012
14	.258	.537	.868	1.345	1.761	2.145	2.624	2.977
15	.258	.536	.866	1.341	1.753	2.131	2.602	2.947
16	.258	.535	.865	1.337	1.746	2.120	2.583	2.921
17	.257	.534	.863	1.333	1.740	2.110	2.567	2.898
18	.257	.534	.862	1.330	1.734	2.101	2.552	2.878
19	.257	.533	.861	1.328	1.729	2.093	2.539	2.861
20	.257	.533	.860	1.325	1.725	2.086	2.528	2.845
21	.257	.532	.859	1.323	1.721	2.080	2.518	2.831
22	.256	.532	.858	1.321	1.717	2.074	2.508	2.819
23	.256	.532	.858	1.319	1.714	2.069	2.500	2.807
24	.256	.531	.857	1.318	1.711	2.064	2.492	2.797
25	.256	.531	.856	1.316	1.708	2.060	2.485	2.787
26	.256	.531	.856	1.315	1.706	2.056	2.479	2.779
27	.256	.531	.855	1.314	1.703	2.052	2.473	2.771
28	.256	.530	.855	1.313	1.701	2.048	2.467	2.763
29	.256	.530	.854	1.311	1.699	2.045	2.462	2.756
30	.256	.530	.854	1.310	1.697	2.042	2.457	2.750
40	.255	.529	.851	1.303	1.684	2.021	2.423	2.704
60	.254	.527	.848	1.296	1.671	2.000	2.390	2.660
120	.254	.526	.845	1.289	1.658	1.980	2.358	2.617
∞	.253	.524	.842	1.282	1.645	1.960	2.326	2.576

Note: Pr represents the probability that the t value will exceed each number in the table in absolute value. This is appropriate for two-tailed tests. For one-tailed tests simply divide each probability in half. For example, .325 in row 1, column 1 tells us that the probability of t being less than $-.325$ *or* greater than .325 is .8.

Source: Obtained from Table III of Fisher and Yates, *Statistical Tables for Biological, Agricultural and Medical Research,* with the permission of the authors and publishers (Edinburgh: Oliver & Boyd, Ltd.).

TABLE 4a
F DISTRIBUTION, 5 PERCENT SIGNIFICANCE

	Degrees of freedom for numerator								
	1	2	3	4	5	6	7	8	9
1	161	200	216	225	230	234	237	239	241
2	18.5	19.0	19.2	19.2	19.3	19.3	19.4	19.4	19.4
3	10.1	9.55	9.28	9.12	9.01	8.94	8.89	8.85	8.81
4	7.71	6.94	6.59	6.39	6.26	6.16	6.09	6.04	6.00
5	6.61	5.79	5.41	5.19	5.05	4.95	4.88	4.82	4.77
6	5.99	5.14	4.76	4.53	4.39	4.28	4.21	4.15	4.10
7	5.59	4.74	4.35	4.12	3.97	3.87	3.79	3.73	3.68
8	5.32	4.46	4.07	3.84	3.69	3.58	3.50	3.44	3.39
9	5.12	4.26	3.86	3.63	3.48	3.37	3.29	3.23	3.18
10	4.96	4.10	3.71	3.48	3.33	3.22	3.14	3.07	3.02
11	4.84	3.98	3.59	3.36	3.20	3.09	3.01	2.95	2.90
12	4.75	3.89	3.49	3.26	3.11	3.00	2.91	2.85	2.80
13	4.67	3.81	3.41	3.18	3.03	2.92	2.83	2.77	2.71
14	4.60	3.74	3.34	3.11	2.96	2.85	2.76	2.70	2.65
15	4.54	3.68	3.29	3.06	2.90	2.79	2.71	2.64	2.59
16	4.49	3.63	3.24	3.01	2.85	2.74	2.66	2.59	2.54
17	4.45	3.59	3.20	2.96	2.81	2.70	2.61	2.55	2.48
18	4.41	3.55	3.16	2.93	2.77	2.66	2.58	2.51	2.46
19	4.38	3.52	3.13	2.90	2.74	2.63	2.54	2.48	2.42
20	4.35	3.49	3.10	2.87	2.71	2.60	2.51	2.45	2.39
21	4.32	3.47	3.07	2.84	2.68	2.57	2.49	2.42	2.37
22	4.30	3.44	3.05	2.82	2.66	2.55	2.46	2.40	2.34
23	4.28	3.42	3.03	2.80	2.64	2.53	2.44	2.37	2.32
24	4.26	3.40	3.01	2.78	2.62	2.51	2.42	2.36	2.30
25	4.24	3.39	2.99	2.76	2.60	2.49	2.40	2.34	2.28
30	4.17	3.32	2.92	2.69	2.53	2.42	2.33	2.27	2.21
40	4.08	3.23	2.84	2.61	2.45	2.34	2.25	2.18	2.12
60	4.00	3.15	2.76	2.53	2.37	2.25	2.17	2.10	2.04
120	3.92	3.07	2.68	2.45	2.29	2.18	2.09	2.02	1.96
∞	3.84	3.00	2.60	2.37	2.21	2.10	2.01	1.94	1.88

Degrees of freedom for denominator (left axis label)

Source: Reproduced with the permission of the Biometrika Trustees from M. Merrington and C. M. Thompson, "Tables of Percentage Points of the Inverted Beta (F) Distribution," *Biometrika,* vol. 33, p. 73, 1943.

			Degrees of freedom for numerator						
10	12	15	20	24	30	40	60	120	∞
242	244	246	248	249	250	251	252	253	254
19.4	19.4	19.4	19.5	19.5	19.5	19.5	19.5	19.5	19.5
8.79	8.74	8.70	8.66	8.64	8.62	8.59	8.57	8.55	8.53
5.96	5.91	5.86	5.80	5.77	5.75	5.72	5.69	5.66	5.63
4.74	4.68	4.62	4.56	4.53	4.50	4.46	4.43	4.40	4.37
4.06	4.00	3.94	3.87	3.84	3.81	3.77	3.74	3.70	3.67
3.64	3.57	3.51	3.44	3.41	3.38	3.34	3.30	3.27	3.23
3.35	3.28	3.22	3.15	3.12	3.08	3.04	3.01	2.97	2.93
3.14	3.07	3.01	2.94	2.90	2.86	2.83	2.79	2.75	2.71
2.98	2.91	2.85	2.77	2.74	2.70	2.66	2.62	2.58	2.54
2.85	2.79	2.72	2.65	2.61	2.57	2.53	2.49	2.45	2.40
2.75	2.69	2.62	2.54	2.51	2.47	2.43	2.38	2.34	2.30
2.67	2.60	2.53	2.46	2.42	2.38	2.34	2.30	2.25	2.21
2.60	2.53	2.46	2.39	2.35	2.31	2.27	2.22	2.18	2.13
2.54	2.48	2.40	2.33	2.29	2.25	2.20	2.16	2.11	2.07
2.49	2.42	2.35	2.28	2.24	2.19	2.15	2.11	2.06	2.01
2.45	2.38	2.31	2.23	2.19	2.15	2.10	2.06	2.01	1.96
2.41	2.34	2.27	2.19	2.15	2.11	2.06	2.02	1.97	1.92
2.39	2.31	2.23	2.16	2.11	2.07	2.03	1.98	1.93	1.88
2.35	2.28	2.20	2.12	2.08	2.04	1.99	1.95	1.90	1.84
2.32	2.25	2.18	2.10	2.05	2.01	1.96	1.92	1.87	1.81
2.30	2.23	2.15	2.07	2.03	1.98	1.94	1.89	1.84	1.78
2.27	2.20	2.13	2.05	2.01	1.96	1.91	1.86	1.81	1.76
2.25	2.18	2.11	2.03	1.98	1.94	1.89	1.84	1.79	1.73
2.24	2.16	2.09	2.01	1.96	1.92	1.87	1.82	1.77	1.71
2.16	2.09	2.01	1.93	1.89	1.84	1.79	1.74	1.68	1.62
2.08	2.00	1.92	1.84	1.79	1.74	1.69	1.64	1.58	1.51
1.99	1.92	1.84	1.75	1.70	1.65	1.59	1.53	1.47	1.39
1.91	1.83	1.75	1.66	1.61	1.55	1.50	1.43	1.35	1.25
1.83	1.75	1.67	1.57	1.52	1.46	1.39	1.32	1.22	1.00

TABLE 4b
F DISTRIBUTION, 1 PERCENT SIGNIFICANCE

		Degrees of freedom for numerator							
	1	2	3	4	5	6	7	8	9
1	4,052	5,000	5,403	5,625	5,746	5,859	5,928	5,982	6,023
2	98.5	99.0	99.2	99.2	99.3	99.3	99.4	99.4	99.4
3	34.1	30.8	29.5	28.7	28.2	27.9	27.7	27.5	27.3
4	21.2	18.0	16.7	16.0	15.5	15.2	15.0	14.8	14.7
5	16.3	13.3	12.1	11.4	11.0	10.7	10.5	10.3	10.2
6	13.7	10.9	9.78	9.15	8.75	8.47	8.26	8.10	7.98
7	12.2	9.55	8.45	7.85	7.46	7.19	6.99	6.84	6.72
8	11.3	8.65	7.59	7.01	6.63	6.37	6.18	6.03	5.91
9	10.6	8.02	6.99	6.42	6.06	5.80	5.61	5.47	5.35
10	10.0	7.56	6.55	5.99	5.64	5.39	5.20	5.06	4.94
11	9.65	7.21	6.22	5.67	5.32	5.07	4.89	4.74	4.63
12	9.33	6.93	5.95	5.41	5.06	4.82	4.64	4.50	4.39
13	9.07	6.70	5.74	5.21	4.97	4.62	4.44	4.30	4.19
14	8.86	5.51	5.56	5.04	4.70	4.46	4.28	4.14	4.03
15	8.68	6.36	5.42	4.89	4.56	4.32	4.14	4.00	3.89
16	8.53	6.23	5.29	4.77	4.44	4.20	4.03	3.89	3.78
17	8.40	6.11	5.19	4.67	4.34	4.10	3.93	3.79	3.68
18	8.29	6.01	5.09	4.58	4.25	4.01	3.84	3.71	3.60
19	8.19	5.93	5.01	4.50	4.17	3.94	3.77	3.63	3.52
20	8.10	5.85	4.94	4.43	4.10	3.87	3.70	3.56	3.46
21	8.02	5.78	4.87	4.37	4.04	3.81	3.64	3.51	3.40
22	7.95	5.72	4.82	4.31	3.99	3.76	3.59	3.45	3.35
23	7.88	5.66	4.76	4.26	3.94	3.71	3.54	3.41	3.30
24	7.82	5.61	4.72	4.22	3.90	3.67	3.50	3.36	3.26
25	7.77	5.57	4.68	4.18	3.86	3.63	3.46	3.32	3.22
30	7.56	5.39	4.51	4.02	3.70	3.47	3.30	3.17	3.07
40	7.31	5.18	4.31	3.83	3.51	3.29	3.12	2.99	2.89
60	7.08	4.98	4.13	3.65	3.34	3.12	2.95	2.82	2.72
120	6.85	4.79	3.95	3.48	3.17	2.96	2.79	2.66	2.56
∞	6.63	4.61	3.78	3.32	3.02	2.80	2.64	2.51	2.41

Degrees of freedom for denominator

		Degrees of freedom for numerator							
10	**12**	**15**	**20**	**24**	**30**	**40**	**60**	**120**	**∞**
6,056	6,106	6,157	6,209	6,235	6,261	6,287	6,313	6,339	6,366
99.4	99.4	99.4	99.4	99.5	99.5	99.5	99.5	99.5	99.5
27.2	27.1	26.9	26.7	26.6	26.5	26.4	26.3	26.2	26.1
14.5	14.4	14.2	14.0	13.9	13.8	13.7	13.7	13.6	13.5
10.1	9.89	9.72	9.55	9.47	9.38	9.29	9.20	9.11	9.02
7.87	7.72	7.56	7.40	7.31	7.23	7.14	7.06	6.97	6.88
6.62	6.47	6.31	6.16	6.07	5.99	5.91	5.82	5.74	5.65
5.81	5.67	5.52	5.36	5.28	5.29	5.12	5.03	4.95	4.86
5.26	5.11	4.96	4.81	4.73	4.65	4.57	4.48	4.40	4.31
4.85	4.71	4.56	4.41	4.33	4.25	4.17	4.08	4.00	3.91
4.54	4.40	4.25	4.10	4.02	3.94	3.86	3.78	3.69	3.60
4.30	4.16	4.01	3.86	3.78	3.70	3.62	3.54	3.45	3.36
4.10	3.96	3.82	3.66	3.59	3.51	3.43	3.34	3.25	3.17
3.94	3.80	3.66	3.51	4.43	3.35	3.27	3.18	3.09	3.00
3.80	3.67	3.52	3.37	3.29	3.21	3.13	3.05	2.96	2.87
3.69	3.55	3.41	3.26	3.18	3.10	3.02	2.93	2.84	2.75
3.59	3.46	3.31	3.16	3.08	3.00	2.92	2.83	2.75	2.65
3.51	3.37	3.23	3.08	3.00	2.92	2.84	2.75	2.66	2.57
3.43	3.30	3.15	3.00	2.92	2.84	2.76	2.67	2.58	2.49
3.37	3.23	3.09	2.94	2.86	2.78	2.68	2.61	2.52	2.42
3.31	3.17	3.03	2.88	2.80	2.72	2.64	2.55	2.46	2.36
3.26	3.12	2.98	2.83	2.75	2.67	2.58	2.50	2.40	2.31
3.21	3.07	2.93	2.78	2.70	2.62	2.54	2.45	2.35	2.26
3.17	3.03	2.89	2.74	2.66	2.58	2.49	2.40	2.31	2.21
3.13	2.99	2.85	2.70	2.62	2.53	2.45	2.36	2.27	2.17
2.98	2.84	2.70	2.55	2.47	2.30	2.39	2.21	2.11	2.01
2.80	2.66	2.52	2.37	2.29	2.20	2.11	2.02	1.92	1.80
2.63	2.50	2.35	2.20	2.12	2.03	1.94	1.84	1.73	1.60
2.47	2.34	2.19	2.03	1.94	1.86	1.76	1.66	1.53	1.38
2.32	2.18	2.04	1.88	1.79	1.70	1.59	1.47	1.32	1.00

TABLE 5

FIVE PERCENT SIGNIFICANCE POINTS OF d_l AND d_u FOR DURBIN-WATSON TEST[†]

N	k = 1		k = 2		k = 3		k = 4		k = 5	
	d_l	d_u	d_l	d_u	d_l	d_u	d_l	d_u	d_l	d_u
15	1.08	1.36	.95	1.54	.82	1.75	.69	1.97	.56	2.21
16	1.10	1.37	.98	1.54	.86	1.73	.74	1.93	.62	2.15
17	1.13	1.38	1.02	1.54	.90	1.71	.78	1.90	.67	2.10
18	1.16	1.39	1.05	1.53	.93	1.69	.82	1.87	.71	2.06
19	1.18	1.40	1.08	1.53	.97	1.68	.86	1.85	.75	2.02
20	1.20	1.41	1.10	1.54	1.00	1.68	.90	1.83	.79	1.99
21	1.22	1.42	1.13	1.54	1.03	1.67	.93	1.81	.83	1.96
22	1.24	1.43	1.15	1.54	1.05	1.66	.96	1.80	.86	1.94
23	1.26	1.44	1.17	1.54	1.08	1.66	.99	1.79	.90	1.92
24	1.27	1.45	1.19	1.55	1.10	1.66	1.01	1.78	.93	1.90
25	1.29	1.45	1.21	1.55	1.12	1.66	1.04	1.77	.95	1.89
26	1.30	1.46	1.22	1.55	1.14	1.65	1.06	1.76	.98	1.88
27	1.32	1.47	1.24	1.56	1.16	1.65	1.08	1.76	1.01	1.86
28	1.33	1.48	1.26	1.56	1.18	1.65	1.10	1.75	1.03	1.85
29	1.34	1.48	1.27	1.56	1.20	1.65	1.12	1.74	1.05	1.84
30	1.35	1.49	1.28	1.57	1.21	1.65	1.14	1.74	1.07	1.83
31	1.36	1.50	1.30	1.57	1.23	1.65	1.16	1.74	1.09	1.83
32	1.37	1.50	1.31	1.57	1.24	1.65	1.18	1.73	1.11	1.82
33	1.38	1.51	1.32	1.58	1.26	1.65	1.19	1.73	1.13	1.81
34	1.39	1.51	1.33	1.58	1.27	1.65	1.21	1.73	1.15	1.81
35	1.40	1.52	1.34	1.53	1.28	1.65	1.22	1.73	1.16	1.80
36	1.41	1.52	1.35	1.59	1.29	1.65	1.24	1.73	1.18	1.80
37	1.42	1.53	1.36	1.59	1.31	1.66	1.25	1.72	1.19	1.80
38	1.43	1.54	1.37	1.59	1.32	1.66	1.26	1.72	1.21	1.79
39	1.43	1.54	1.38	1.60	1.33	1.66	1.27	1.72	1.22	1.79
40	1.44	1.54	1.39	1.60	1.34	1.66	1.29	1.72	1.23	1.79
45	1.48	1.57	1.43	1.62	1.38	1.67	1.34	1.72	1.29	1.78
50	1.50	1.59	1.46	1.63	1.42	1.67	1.38	1.72	1.34	1.77
55	1.53	1.60	1.49	1.64	1.45	1.68	1.41	1.72	1.38	1.77
60	1.55	1.62	1.51	1.65	1.48	1.69	1.44	1.73	1.41	1.77
65	1.57	1.63	1.54	1.66	1.50	1.70	1.47	1.73	1.44	1.77
70	1.58	1.64	1.55	1.67	1.52	1.70	1.49	1.74	1.46	1.77
75	1.60	1.65	1.57	1.68	1.54	1.71	1.51	1.74	1.49	1.77
80	1.61	1.66	1.59	1.69	1.56	1.72	1.53	1.74	1.51	1.77
85	1.62	1.67	1.60	1.70	1.57	1.72	1.55	1.75	1.52	1.77
90	1.63	1.68	1.61	1.70	1.59	1.73	1.57	1.75	1.54	1.78
95	1.64	1.69	1.62	1.71	1.60	1.73	1.58	1.75	1.56	1.78
100	1.65	1.69	1.63	1.72	1.61	1.74	1.59	1.76	1.57	1.78

[†] N = number of observations; k = number of explanatory variables (excluding the constant term).

Source: Reprinted with permission from J. Durbin and G. S. Watson, "Testing for Serial Correlation in Least Squares Regression," *Biometrika*, vol. 38, pp. 159–177, 1951.

SOLUTIONS TO SELECTED PROBLEMS

1.1 (*a*) The regression line is $Y = 1.17 + 1.72X$.

(*b*) The slope tells us that on average a $1 million increase in the quantity of money will lead to a $1.72 million increase in national income. Interpreted literally, the intercept tells us that if the money supply fell to zero, national income would be $1.17 million. However, since no observations were available for values of X near zero, we cannot rely on such an interpretation.

(*c*) We would set the money supply at $6.3 million.

1.3 (*a*) The slope will be reduced by a factor of 10, and the intercept will remain unchanged.

(*b*) To evaluate the effects of the transformation on the slope and intercept, substitute the equations describing the transformed variables into the least-squares estimators:

$$\hat{b}* = \frac{\Sigma(X_i^* - \overline{X}*)(Y_i^* - \overline{Y}*)}{\Sigma(X_i^* - \overline{X}*)^2} \qquad \hat{a}* = \overline{Y}* - \hat{b}*\overline{X}*$$

(You should check that $\overline{Y}* = c_1 + c_2\overline{Y}$ and $\overline{X}* = d_1 + d_2\overline{X}$.) After some elementary algebra, it follows that

$$\hat{b}* = \frac{c_2}{d_2}\hat{b} \qquad \hat{a}* = \left(c_1 - \frac{c_2 d_1}{d_2}\hat{b}\right) + c_2\hat{a}$$

1.4 The least-squares intercept and slope are both undefined. When all independent-variable observations are identical, Σx_i^2 equals zero. Since there is no change in the independent variable (in the sample), it is impossible to tell how the dependent variable would respond to a change in the independent variable.

1.7 (*a*) $\qquad\qquad\qquad\qquad \hat{\alpha} = 2.88 \qquad \hat{\beta} = -.0185$

(*b*) $\qquad\qquad\qquad\qquad \hat{\alpha} = 1.47 \qquad \hat{\beta} = .11$

2.1
$$\overline{RENT} = 318.16 \qquad \overline{NO} = 2.44 \qquad \overline{RPP} = 138.17$$

$$\frac{\overline{RENT}}{\overline{NO}} = 130.39 \neq \overline{RPP}$$

2.3 (*a*)
$$Z = \frac{\overset{\overline{X}}{\overline{RPP}} - 135.00}{(\sigma^2_{RPP}/N)^{1/2}} = .387$$

Since Prob ($|Z| > 1.96$) = .05 from the normal table, we fail to reject the null hypothesis.

$$t = (\overline{RPP} - 135.00)\frac{\sqrt{N}}{s} = .381$$

Since Prob ($|t| > 2.042$) = .05 from the *t* table, we again fail to reject the null hypothesis.

2.4 The correct statistic is

$$Z = \frac{\overline{X}^m - \overline{X}^f}{(\sigma^{2m}_{RPP}/N^m + \sigma^{2f}_{RPP}/N^f)^{1/2}} = -2.44$$

Using a normal table, we reject at the 5 percent level of significance.

2.6 The correct statistic is

$$V = \frac{(N - 1)s^2}{2,150} = 32.01$$

Using a chi-square table, we fail to reject the null hypothesis.

2.9 Prob ($X \geq 30$) = .2119.

2.12 $[(X - \mu)/\sigma]^2$ follows a chi-square distribution.

3.1 $s^2 = .14$ and $t_c = 2.3$. Therefore, the 95 percent confidence interval for the intercept is

$$1.17 \pm (2.3)(.484) = 1.17 \pm 1.11 = (.06, 2.28)$$

The 95 percent confidence interval for the slope is

$$1.72 \pm (2.3)(.126) = 1.72 \pm .29 = (1.43, 2.01)$$

Yes, you can reject the null hypothesis in both cases.

3.4 $R^2 = \hat{b}^2\Sigma x_i^2/\Sigma y_i^2$. If $R^2 = 1$, $\hat{b}^2 = \Sigma y_i^2/\Sigma x_i^2$. But, by construction, $\hat{b} = \Sigma x_i y_i/\Sigma x_i^2$. Therefore

$$\Sigma x_i^2 = \frac{(\Sigma x_i y_i)^2}{\Sigma y_i^2} \qquad \text{and} \qquad \hat{b} = \frac{\Sigma y_i^2}{\Sigma x_i y_i} = \frac{1}{\hat{B}}$$

3.8 $\Sigma x_i \hat{\varepsilon}_i = \Sigma x_i (y_i - \hat{\beta} x_i) = \Sigma x_i y_i - \hat{\beta} \Sigma x_i^2$. But $\hat{\beta} = \Sigma x_i y_i / \Sigma x_i^2$. Therefore, $\Sigma x_i \hat{\varepsilon}_i = \hat{\beta} \Sigma x_i^2 - \hat{\beta} \Sigma x_i^2 = 0$.

3.9 $y_i^* = a_2 y_i$ and $x_i^* = b_2 x_i$ (since $\overline{Y}^* = a_1 + a_2 \overline{Y}, \overline{X}^* = b_1 + b_2 \overline{X}$). Then from the transformed data

$$(R^*)^2 = \frac{\hat{\beta}^{*2} \Sigma x_i^{*2}}{\Sigma y_i^{*2}}$$

But from Exercise 1.3, $\hat{\beta}^{*2} = (a_2/b_2)^2 \hat{\beta}^2$. Substituting, we find that $(R^*)^2 = R^2$.

3.10 (a) B is the slope of the line passing through the points $(\overline{X}_1, \overline{Y}_1)$ and $(\overline{X}_2, \overline{Y}_2)$. Dividing the data into two groups is sufficient to fit a straight line, which yields an estimate of the slope.

   (b) B does not equal $\hat{\beta}$, but it is an unbiased estimator of β:

$$\overline{Y}_1 = \alpha + \beta \overline{X}_1 + \overline{\varepsilon}_1 \quad \text{and} \quad \overline{Y}_2 = \alpha + \beta \overline{X}_2 + \overline{\varepsilon}_2$$

Then

$$E(\overline{Y}_2 - \overline{Y}_1) = \beta(\overline{X}_2 - \overline{X}_1)$$

and

$$E(B) = \frac{E(\overline{Y}_2 - \overline{Y}_1)}{\overline{X}_2 - \overline{X}_1} = \beta$$

   (c) We know that Var $(B) \geq$ Var $(\hat{\beta})$ from the Gauss-Markov theorem, which states that $\hat{\beta}$ is the *best* linear unbiased estimator of β. (It is easy to show that B is a linear estimator.) In this particular case Var $(B) = .157\sigma^2$, while Var $(\hat{\beta}) = .115\sigma^2$.

4.1 (a) Let $Z_i = Y_i - X_{2i}$; then by substitution into Eqs. (4.3) to (4.5),

$$\hat{\beta}_2' = \hat{\beta}_2 - \frac{(\Sigma x_{2i}^2 \Sigma x_{3i}^2) - (\Sigma x_{2i} x_{3i})^2}{(\Sigma x_{2i}^2)(\Sigma x_{3i}^2) - (\Sigma x_{2i} x_{3i})^2} = \hat{\beta}_2 - 1$$

Likewise $\hat{\beta}_3' = \hat{\beta}_3$ and $\hat{\beta}_1' = \overline{Y} - \overline{X}_2 - \hat{\beta}_2 \overline{X}_2 + \overline{X}_2 - \hat{\beta}_3 \overline{X}_3 = \hat{\beta}_1$.

   (b) In model I

$$\hat{\varepsilon}_i = Y_i - \hat{\beta}_1 - \hat{\beta}_2 X_{2i} - \hat{\beta}_3 X_{3i}$$

In model II

$$\hat{\varepsilon}_i' = Y_i - X_{2i} - \hat{\beta}_1' - \hat{\beta}_2' X_{2i} - \hat{\beta}_3' X_{3i} = Y_i - X_{2i} - \hat{\beta}_1 - \hat{\beta}_2 X_{2i} - \hat{\beta}_3' X_{3i} = \hat{\varepsilon}_i$$

   (c) $R^2 = 1 - \Sigma \hat{\varepsilon}_i^2 / \Sigma (Y_i - \overline{Y})^2$ in model I, and $R'^2 = 1 - \Sigma \hat{\varepsilon}_i'^2 / \Sigma (Z_i - \overline{Z})^2$ in model II. Since the regression residuals are identical, the relationship between R^2 and R'^2 will depend directly on the relationship between the variance of Y and the variance of Z.

4.2 From the regression $X_{2i} = \alpha_1 + \alpha_2 X_{3i} + \varepsilon_i'$, the residuals $\hat{\varepsilon}_i' = X_{2i} - \hat{\alpha}_1 - \hat{\alpha}_2 X_{3i}$. Substituting into the regression $Y_i = \beta_1' + \beta_2' \hat{\varepsilon}_i + \beta_3' X_{3i} + \varepsilon_i^*$, we find that $Y_i =$

$(\beta_1 - \beta_2' \hat{\alpha}_1) + \beta_2' X_{2i} + (\beta_3' - \beta_2' \hat{\alpha}_2) X_{3i} + \varepsilon_i^*$. Comparing this with the original regression makes it clear that $\hat{\beta}_2' = \hat{\beta}_2$. ($\hat{\varepsilon}_i$ measures the portion of X_{2i} which is uncorrelated with X_{3i}.)

4.4 Each stadardized coefficient will equal the corresponding regression parameter, except for the intercept, which does not exist.

4.7 In the two-variable model,

$$\hat{\beta}^* = \hat{\beta} \frac{s_x}{s_y} = \frac{\Sigma x_i y_i}{\Sigma x_i^2} \left(\frac{\Sigma x_i^2}{\Sigma y_i^2} \right)^{1/2} = \frac{\Sigma x_i y_i}{(\Sigma x_i^2)^{1/2} (\Sigma y_i^2)^{1/2}} = r_{XY}$$

5.1
$$\beta_2 = \frac{\partial \log Y}{\partial \log X_2} = \frac{1/Y \, dY}{1/X_2 \, dX_2} = \frac{dY}{dX_2} \frac{X_2}{Y_2}$$

Thus, $\hat{\beta}_2$ provides an estimate of the elasticity of Y with respect to X_2. The analogous result holds for $\hat{\beta}_3$. These elasticities are constant because the least-squares slope estimates are constant.

5.2 (a) $t = 3.02$ (on the coefficient ROOM PER), so we reject the null hypothesis using a one-tailed test.
  (b) $t = -1.35$ (on the coefficient DIST), so we fail to reject using a one-tailed test.
  (c) $t = 1.21$, so we fail to reject. The corresponding F test leads to an identical result.

5.3 (a) $t = -.96$ (on the coefficient [(ROOM PER)(SEX)]), so we fail to reject.
  (b) We calculate $F = A/B$, where $A = (\text{ESS}_{\text{I}} - \text{ESS}_{\text{III}})/2$ and $B = \text{ESS}_{\text{III}}/26$, so that $F = 2.61$. Using an F distribution with $(2, 26)$ degrees of freedom, we fail to reject.

(c)
$$\bar{R}^2 = \begin{cases} .29 & \text{model I} \\ .28 & \text{model II} \\ .37 & \text{model III} \end{cases}$$

5.7 $\hat{\beta}_2^* = .20$, $\hat{\beta}_3^* = .48$, $\hat{\beta}_4^* = -.22$.

6.2 Yes, we might expect that the error terms associated with communities with high educational expenditures would have larger variances than the error terms associated with communities with low educational expenditures. To use the Goldfeld-Quandt test, order the observations by the median income in the community.

6.4 In cross-section studies there is usually no natural sequence to the data, and no reason to expect that errors associated with different observations will be correlated. However, serial correlation may be present if observations are geographically related as in a regional model of economic growth or a metropolitan model of local government behavior.

6.6 The test statistic is $\hat{\sigma}_{\text{male}}^2 / \hat{\sigma}_{\text{female}}^2 = 1.47$ which follows an F distribution with $(19, 7)$ degrees of freedom. At the 5 percent level we fail to reject the null hypothesis.

7.1 Measurement error in the dependent variable results in increased error variance, but as long as the measurement error is uncorrelated with the independent variable, parameter estimates will be unbiased and consistent. When an independent variable is measured with error, however, the measurement error will be correlated with the independent variable, causing parameter estimates to be biased and inconsistent.

7.2
$$\hat{\beta} = \frac{\Sigma y_i z_i}{\Sigma z_i^2} = \beta \frac{\Sigma x_i z_i}{\Sigma z_i^2} + \frac{\Sigma z_i \varepsilon_i}{\Sigma z_i^2}$$

If z is an instrument, the second term will approach zero as the sample size gets large, but the first term will approach β only when $\Sigma x_i z_i / \Sigma z_i^2$ approaches 1.

7.4
$$\hat{\beta}_2^* = \frac{\Sigma x_{2i} y_i}{\Sigma x_{2i}^2} = \beta_2 + \beta_3 \frac{\Sigma x_{2i}^3}{\Sigma x_{2i}^2}$$

Therefore, the specification bias is equal to $\beta_3 \Sigma x_{2i}^3 / \Sigma x_{2i}^2$. Thus, the slope coefficient will be biased upward when $\beta_3 \Sigma x_{2i}^3$ is positive and biased downward when $\beta_3 \Sigma x_{2i}^3$ is negative.

7.5
$$\hat{\beta}_3^* = \frac{(\Sigma x_{3i} y_i)(\Sigma x_{2i}^2) - \beta_2(\Sigma x_{2i} y_i)(\Sigma x_{2i} x_{3i})}{(\Sigma x_{2i}^2)(\Sigma x_{3i}^2) - (\Sigma x_{2i} x_{3i})^2}$$

Substituting for $y_i = \beta_2 x_{2i} + \varepsilon_i$ and taking expected values, we get

$$E(\hat{\beta}_3^*) = \frac{\beta_2(\Sigma x_{2i} x_{3i})(\Sigma x_{2i}^2) - (\Sigma x_{2i}^2)(\Sigma x_{2i} x_{3i})}{(\Sigma x_{2i}^2)(\Sigma x_{3i}^2) - (\Sigma x_{2i} x_{3i})^2} + \frac{E(\Sigma x_{3i}\varepsilon_i)(\Sigma x_{2i}^2) - E(\Sigma x_{2i}\varepsilon_i)(\Sigma x_{2i} x_{3i})}{(\Sigma x_{2i}^2)(\Sigma x_{3i}^2) - (\Sigma x_{2i} x_{3i})^2} = 0$$

9.3 Using time as an instrument, $\hat{X}_T = \hat{\alpha}_1 + \hat{\alpha}_2 T$ and $\hat{X}_t = X_t$, $t = 1, 2, \ldots, T - 1$, where $\hat{\alpha}_2 = \Sigma x_t t / \Sigma t^2$. The least-squares slope estimate is $\hat{\beta} = \Sigma \hat{x}_t y_t / \Sigma \hat{x}_t^2$. Now, substituting $y_t = \beta \hat{x}_t + \beta(x_t - \hat{x}_t) + \varepsilon_t$, we get

$$\hat{\beta} = \beta + \frac{\beta \Sigma \hat{x}_t (x_t - \hat{x}_t)}{\Sigma \hat{x}_t^2} + \frac{\Sigma \hat{x}_t \varepsilon_t}{\Sigma \hat{x}_t^2}$$

$$\text{plim } \hat{\beta} = \beta + \beta \text{ plim } \frac{\hat{x}_T (x_T - \hat{x}_T)}{\Sigma \hat{x}_t^2} + \text{plim } \frac{\Sigma \hat{x}_t \varepsilon_t}{\Sigma \hat{x}_t^2} = \beta$$

if time is a proper instrument. However, if the error term is serially correlated, time t and the error will be correlated and the consistency of $\hat{\beta}$ will disappear.

9.4 The appropriate test statistic is

$$F_{N-1, NT-N-1} = \frac{(ESS_1 - ESS_2)/(N - 1)}{(ESS_2)/(NT - N - 1)}$$

where ESS_1 is the residual sum of squares using ordinary least squares and ESS_2 is the residual sum of squares using cross-section dummies.

9.7 Using a second-degree polynomial specification, we assume that

$$w_i = C_0 + C_1 i + C_2 i^2 \qquad i = 0, 1, 2, 3$$

Substituting into the original specification and combining terms,

$$Y_t = \alpha + \beta C_0(X_t + X_{t-1} + X_{t-2} + X_{t-3}) + \beta C_1(X_{t-1} + 2X_{t-2} + 3X_{t-3})$$
$$+ \beta C_2(X_{t-1} + 4X_{t-2} + 9X_{t-3}) + \varepsilon_t$$

which can be estimated using ordinary least squares if there are no endpoint restrictions. If the tail and the head are set equal to zero, then $W_{-1} = C_0 - C_1 + C_2 = 0$ and $W_4 = C_0 + 4C_1 + 16C_2 = 0$. Solving, we find that $C_1 = -3C_2$ and $C_0 = -4C_2$. Then we can rewrite the original equation to be estimated by eliminating C_0 and C_1

$$Y_t = \alpha - \beta C_2(4X_t + 6X_{t-1} + 6X_{t-2} + 4X_{t-3}) + \varepsilon_t$$

Using least squares we can estimate one of the lag weights, and by substitution we can determine the remaining two.

10.2
$$S = \sum_{t=1}^{T} (C_t - a_0 - a_1 \mathrm{YD}_t^{a_2})^2$$

The normal equations are

$$\sum_{t=1}^{T} (C_t - a_0 - a_1 \mathrm{YD}_t^{a_2}) = 0 \qquad \sum_{t=1}^{T} \mathrm{YD}_t^{a_2}(C_t - a_0 - a_1 \mathrm{YD}_t^{a_2}) = 0$$

$$\sum_{t=1}^{T} \mathrm{YD}_t^{a_2} \log \mathrm{YD}_t(C_t - a_0 - a_1 \mathrm{YD}_t^{a_2}) = 0$$

Solution of these equations for a_0, a_1, and a_2 would typically require a computer algorithm that iteratively linearizes the normal equations around values for the parameters.

11.1 There is a *unique* error variance associated with each observation on X_i and Y_i. It is impossible to obtain an estimate of each error variance from a single residual observation.

11.2 All coefficients will be doubled. This suggests that the estimated least-squares parameters are meaningful only relative to the magnitude of the other parameters and to the units of the dependent variable.

11.4 Assume that there exists an index Z_i, a linear function of the attributes of the ith community, which measures the probability that a community will default. Associated with each community is a normally distributed random variable Z_i^* which determines the cutoff point between default and nondefault. Then, the probit model will yield predicted probabilities that lie within the $(0, 1)$ interval, but it does necessitate a nonlinear estimation procedure.

11.6 The regression line is $\hat{Y} = \frac{1}{2} + \frac{3}{8}X$, $R^2 = .75$, and the number of correct classifications is five.

12.4 Ordinary least squares will yield biased and inconsistent estimates of the parameters in the first equation. Indirect least squares, instrumental variables, and two-stage least squares all yield biased but consistent parameter estimates (there are two possible estimates for each parameter in the indirect least-squares case). However, two-stage least-squares estimation is more efficient than either indirect least squares or instrumental variables. This regression of Y on Z_1 and Z_2 will not yield estimates of either parameter in the first equation.

12.6 Let G = number of predetermined variables in system
$\quad G_1$ = number of predetermined variables in equation being considered
$\quad H$ = number of endogenous variables in system
$\quad H_1$ = number of endogenous variables in equation being considered
The first form of the order condition is equivalent to

$$G - G_1 \geq H_1 - 1$$

The second form of the order condition is equivalent to

$$(G - G_1) + (H - H_1) \geq H - 1$$

Subtracting $H - H_1$ from both sides of the second condition yields the first.

12.8 There are four endogenous variables and three predetermined variables in the system. Thus, according to the order condition, a necessary condition for identifiability is that the number of excluded predetermined variables be three or more. According to this criterion the first equation is just identified, while the second and third equations are unidentified. The first equation can be estimated by using two-stage least squares.

13.1 The rms error is usually a better performance criterion when the variable of interest exhibits fluctuations and turning points; if the simulated series misses a turning point in the actual series, one would like to penalize heavily for the larger error that results. The mean absolute error might be preferred if the variable of interest exhibits a steady trend, in which case the concern is only how far above or below the actual trend line the simulated series is. Since we usually construct models to explain fluctuations in economic variables, the rms error is the standard statistic calculated in most computer simulation programs.

13.4 The underprediction of GNP is largely the result of the inability of the model to predict turning points in the interest rate, combined with a negative error in the estimated propensity to consume resulting in a general underprediction of consumption. In the historical simulation consumption is usually below the actual series. (Consumption and GNP are close to the actual series in 1970–1971 because of a positive error in simulated investment, resulting in turn from large negative errors in the simulated interest rate in 1969–1970.) Observe in the *ex post* forecast that the interest rate is overpredicted in 1972 so that investment is underpredicted in 1973. Consumption is underpredicted throughout the *ex post* forecast. The result is an underprediction of GNP.

14.2 (a) The fundamental dynamic equation for the model is given by

$$Y_t - (a_2 + b_2 a_2)Y_{t-1} + b_2 a_2 Y_{t-2} = a_1 + b_1 + G_t$$

so that the characteristic equation is

$$\lambda^2 - (a_2 + b_2 a_2)\lambda + b_2 a_2 = 0$$

The characteristic roots are therefore

$$\lambda_1, \lambda_2 = \frac{a_2 + b_2 a_2}{2} \pm \tfrac{1}{2}\sqrt{(a_2 + b_2 a_2)^2 - 4 b_2 a_2}$$

(b) The solution will oscillate if the characteristic roots are complex, i.e., if $4 b_2 a_2 > (a_2 + b_2 a_2)^2$. The solution will explode if the roots are greater than 1 in magnitude. The type of solution will depend on a_2 and b_2 as follows:

$$a_2 > \frac{4 b_2}{(1 + b_2)^2} \qquad b_2 < 1 \qquad \text{stable, nonoscillatory solution}$$

$$a_2 > \frac{4 b_2}{(1 + b_2)^2} \qquad b_2 > 1 \qquad \text{explosive, nonoscillatory solution}$$

$$\frac{1}{b_2} < a_2 < \frac{4 b_2}{(1 + b_2)^2} \qquad \text{explosive, oscillatory solution}$$

$$a_2 < \frac{1}{b_2} \qquad \text{stable, oscillatory solution (damped cycles)}$$

16.1 We know that the process is nonstationary since its mean and variance increase indefinitely. It is first-order homogeneous since

$$w_t = \Delta y_t = d + \varepsilon_t$$

This process has a constant mean d and a constant variance σ_ε^2 and is stationary.

17.1 The variance and covariances for the MA(3) process are

$$\gamma_0 = \sigma_\varepsilon^2(1 + \theta_1^2 + \theta_2^2 + \theta_3^2) \qquad \gamma_1 = \sigma_\varepsilon^2(-\theta_1 + \theta_2\theta_1 + \theta_3\theta_2)$$

$$\gamma_2 = \sigma_\varepsilon^2(-\theta_2 + \theta_3\theta_1) \qquad \gamma_3 = -\theta_3\sigma_\varepsilon^2 \qquad \gamma_k = 0, \qquad k > 3$$

17.2 Observe that y_t tends to be positively correlated with adjacent values; e.g., a positive value is more likely to be preceded and followed by a positive value than by a negative value. The correlation, however, does not extend more than one period out, so that the realization appears very "noisy." A realization of the process $y_t = 1 + \varepsilon_t - .8\varepsilon_{t-1}$ would show negative correlations between adjacent values, so that a positive value of y_t would be more likely to be followed by a negative value.

17.4 $\quad \rho_1 = \dfrac{\phi_1}{1 - \phi_2} - \dfrac{\theta_1(1 - \phi_1^2\phi_2 - \phi_1^2 - \phi_2)}{(1 - \phi_2)^2(1 - 2\phi_1\theta_1 + \theta_2^2) - 2\phi_1\phi_2\theta_1(1 - \phi_2)}$

$$\rho_2 = \phi_2 + \phi_1\rho_1 \qquad \rho_3 = \phi_1\rho_2 + \phi_2\rho_1$$

17.6 $\qquad\qquad\qquad y_t = \Sigma w_t \quad$ and so $\quad E(y_t) = \Sigma E(w_t)$

$$E(w_t) = \frac{1}{1 - .9} = 10$$

Then $\qquad\qquad\qquad\qquad\qquad E(y_t) = 10t$

18.1 (*a*) This misspecification will result in residuals that are autocorrelated. The diagnostic check described in Section 18.2 can be used, and the statistic Q is likely to be above the 90 percent point on the chi-square distribution.

(*b*) Let us assume that the parameters of the process are known with certainty. Write the true ARMA(1, 2) process as

$$\varepsilon_t = y_t - \phi_1 y_{t-1} + \theta_1\varepsilon_{t-1} + \theta_2\varepsilon_{t-2}$$

and write the ARMA(0, 2) model as

$$\tilde{\varepsilon}_t = y_t + \theta_1\varepsilon_{t-1} + \theta_2\varepsilon_{t-2}$$

The error term for the model is thus related to the error term for the true process by

$$\tilde{\varepsilon}_t = \varepsilon_t + \phi_1 y_{t-1}$$

The error term $\tilde{\varepsilon}_t$ will therefore be autocorrelated:

$$E(\tilde{\varepsilon}_t\tilde{\varepsilon}_{t-1}) = E[(\varepsilon_t + \phi_1 y_{t-1})(\varepsilon_{t-1} + \phi_1 y_{t-2})] = \phi_1\sigma_\varepsilon^2 + \phi_1^2\gamma_1$$

where γ_1 is the covariance (for displacement 1) of the true process ARMA(1, 2). Generally $\phi_1^2\gamma_1$ will be much smaller than $\phi_1\sigma_\varepsilon^2$, so that we can write

$$E(\tilde{\varepsilon}_t\tilde{\varepsilon}_{t-1}) \approx \phi_1\sigma_\varepsilon^2$$

Similarly $E(\tilde{\varepsilon}_t\tilde{\varepsilon}_{t-2}) \approx \phi_1^2\sigma_\varepsilon^2$, and so on. Thus the residual autocorrelations for the ARMA(0, 2) model will look like those for a *first-order autoregressive process*, and this would indicate that ARMA(1, 2) is a more correct specification.

18.6 Note that in making a forecast one period ahead, the only missing information is the value of the error term ε_t in the next period, i.e., the value of ε_{T+1} (the values of $w_T, w_{T-1}, \ldots, \varepsilon_T, \varepsilon_{T-1}, \ldots$ are all known, assuming that the parameters of the model are known). Therefore the forecast error variance for the one-period forecast should simply be the variance of ε_t.

18.7 The one-, two-, and three-period forecasts for the AR(2) process are

$$\hat{y}_T(1) = \phi_1 y_T + \phi_2 y_{T-1} + \delta$$

$$\hat{y}_T(2) = \phi_1 \hat{y}_T(1) + \phi_2 y_T + \delta = (\phi_1^2 + \phi_2) y_T + \phi_1 \phi_2 y_{T-1} + (1 + \phi_1)\delta$$

$$\hat{y}_T(3) = (\phi_1^3 + 2\phi_1 \phi_2) y_T + (\phi_1^2 \phi_2 + \phi_2^2) y_{T-1} + (1 + \phi_1 + \phi_1^2 + \phi_2)\delta$$

These forecasts have error variances:

$$E[e_T^2(1)] = \sigma_\varepsilon^2 \qquad E[e_T^2(2)] = (1 + \phi_1^2)\sigma_\varepsilon^2$$

$$E[e_T^2(3)] = [1 + \phi_1^4 + \phi_1^2(1 + 2\phi_2) + \phi_2^2]\sigma_\varepsilon^2$$

AUTHOR INDEX

SUBJECT INDEX